Texas
Environmental
Almanac

T E X A S
ENVIRONMENTAL
A L M A N A C
SECOND EDITION

TEXAS CENTER FOR POLICY STUDIES
AUSTIN, TEXAS

COMPILED BY MARY SANGER AND CYRUS REED

UNIVERSITY OF TEXAS PRESS
AUSTIN

Second edition, 2000

Requests for permission to reproduce material from this work should be sent to Permissions, University of Texas Press, Box 7819, Austin, TX 78713-7819.

∞ The paper used in this book meets the minimum requirements of ANSI/NISO Z39.48-1992 (R1997) (Permanence of Paper).

Library of Congress Cataloging-in-Publication Data
Sanger, Mary, 1944–
   Texas environmental almanac / Texas Center for Policy Studies,
Austin ; compiled by Mary Sanger and Cyrus Reed.—2nd ed.
      p. cm.
Rev. ed. of: Texas environmental almanac / compiled and written
by the Texas Center for Policy Studies. c1995.
Includes bibliographical references and index.
   ISBN 0-292-77749-3 (pbk. : alk. paper)
   I. Title. II. Reed, Cyrus, 1965– III. Texas Center for Policy Studies.
IV. Texas Center for Policy Studies. Texas environmental almanac.
1. Texas—Environmental conditions—Handbooks, manuals, etc.
2. Environmental policy—Texas—Handbooks, manuals, etc.
3. Environmental protection—Texas—Handbooks, manuals, etc.
   GE155.T4 S36 2000
      363.7'009764—dc21

99-006872

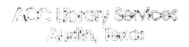

Contents

Introduction   vii

Chapter 1 Water Quantity   1

Focus: NAFTA and the Texas/Mexico Border Environment   35

Chapter 2 Water Quality   39

Focus: Environmental Justice   103

Chapter 3 Land   105

Focus: Mitigation   141

Chapter 4 Wildlife and Biodiversity   143

Focus: Texas "Takings" Legislation   167

Chapter 5 Air Quality   169

Focus: Pesticides   237

Focus: Comparative Risk   251

Chapter 6 Energy   253

Chapter 7 Municipal Waste   269

Focus: Getting Information   287

Chapter 8 Industrial Waste   291

Focus: The Right to Know   333

Appendix: County Environmental Indicators   337

Index   355

Introduction

We want to begin the *Texas Environmental Almanac* by telling you what it is not. It is not a prescription for change. It is not a definitive description of the environmental health of the state. It is an environmental road map of our state, drawn from a wide array of sources, including state and federal agencies, publications of nationally renowned environmental organizations, scientific articles, legislative bills and legal statutes, and books offering historical overviews and critiques of environmental issues. By studying this road map, we can begin to understand where we are in terms of our state's environmental health. We can begin to decide where we want to be in terms of the future environmental well-being of Texas.

This almanac was created to provide timely information on the state of the state's environment. This information can help citizens and their elected officials plan for the future and design future policy. While various state and federal agencies maintain ongoing documentation of key components of the state's environment, this documentation rarely reaches the public or elected officials in a format that is useful for public debate or for guiding public policy decisions. Before the first edition of *Texas Environmental Almanac* was published in 1995, environmental documentation by various state and federal agencies had never before been brought together under one cover to provide a comprehensive look at the Texas environment.

This second edition of the almanac is expanded in scope. It draws on the most recent data available to update and broaden the portrait provided in the first edition. It is our hope that the almanac will serve as a useful reference book for anyone studying the Texas environment, as well as for those engaged in public debates shaping environmental policy.

Environmental protection continues to be a major concern of most Texans, according to a 1996 survey conducted by the Rice University Department of Sociology. "The data clearly indicate that generalized concerns about environmental pollution have increased substantially in Texas during the past two years," said Rice University sociology professor Stephen Klineberg, director of the biannual Texas Environmental Survey. "The respondents in the latest survey were also consistently more likely than in 1994 to be concerned about air and water pollution, about the management of hazardous wastes and exposure to dangerous substances, both in their communities and in the state of Texas."[1]

A study released by the Institute for Southern Studies indicates that environmental protection and economic development are not necessarily as incompatible as conventional wisdom would have us believe. In fact, some elements of an environmental protection policy may enhance economic development. "States with stronger environmental standards tended to have higher growth in their gross state products, total employment, construction employment, and labor productivity than states that ranked lower environmentally," reported Dr. Stephen Meyer of the Massachusetts Institute of Technology, after tracking twenty years of economic performance by state.[2] In a report for the Economic Policy Institute, Dr. Eban Goodstein reports that "when the job creation aspects of pollution control policies are factored in, environmental protection has probably increased net employment in the U.S. economy by a small amount."[3]

In the long run, the economic health of a city, a region, or an entire state depends upon the integrity of the natural resources upon which that city, region, or state depends. Looking at some of the information in this almanac allows us to see how this plays out in our own state. We are, for instance, doing some things right. Since 1972, the amount of pollution discharged in wastewater by Texas municipal facilities has decreased by approximately 70 percent. While the population of Texas grew from 14 million in 1980 to 19 million in 1995, the amount of water Texas residents, industries, and agriculture consumed declined from 17.8 million acre-feet in 1980 to 16.8 million acre-feet by 1996. Texas industries have reduced their release of toxic compounds into the air by nearly 42 percent since 1987.

But the evidence suggests we could do a better job in many areas. Texas industries, for instance, inject more hazardous wastes and toxic chemicals underground than those of any other state in the nation. Texas industries release more toxic waste into the air, water, and land combined than any other state. Texas industries generate more hazardous waste than any other state. More than 30 percent of our river and stream miles do not comply with set water quality standards. More than half of Texas's population lives in areas that do not meet federal clean air standards for ozone. An estimated 27,000 acres of Gulf shoreline were lost to erosion between the mid-1800s and 1982. Gulf shoreline erosion continues at a pace of approximately 225 acres per year. Since European settlement, Texas has lost 63 percent of its original bottomland hardwood and forested wetlands. Texas has more cropland than any other state—28 million acres—and leads all other states in total wind and water erosion of cropland. Between 1982 and 1992, Texas also lost more high-quality farmland to urban development than any other state. In this century, Texas has seen a dramatic increase in the extinction of native species. Currently, Texas ranks sixth among the states for federally listed endangered and threatened species.

Environmental losses such as these, if not addressed, could have a seriously detrimental effect in years to come on the quality of life and the economic prosperity of thousands of Texans. By using information found in the almanac, we may be able to avert growing environmental problems before it is too late.

The almanac is divided into five sections. In these sections we consider the classic environmental elements once believed to characterize all material substance: earth (land), air, fire (energy), and water. To this we have added a new element: waste. Taken as a whole, these sections provide a comprehensive portrait of the state of the state's environment.

The Texas Center for Policy Studies (TCPS) has been responsible for writing and organizing the almanac. Mary Sanger directed the project. She and Cyrus Reed, both TCPS staff members, were the chief writers and researchers for the almanac. Mary Kelly, Alicia Isaac-Cura, Geoff Rips and intern Victoria Salinas, also from TCPS, provided research and editorial assistance. Ramon Alvarez of the Environmental Defense Fund and freelance writer Robert Bryce and Benjamin Isgur contributed to the section on energy. Susan Raleigh Kaderka provided editing assistance. Harrison Saunders, of Worldwise Design, designed the layout and graphics. The authors wish to thank Sherry Matthews of Sherry Matthews Advertising of Austin for helping to develop the original concept behind this publication.

The *Texas Environmental Almanac* depended upon the cooperation and collaboration of many state and federal agencies. These agencies provided access to technical reports and other data, as well as offering guidance and helpful comments.

Finally, this edition of the *Texas Environmental Almanac* would not have been possible without the generous support of the Houston Endowment, Inc. and the Rockwell Fund of Houston. It allowed us to build on the work of the first edition, which was supported by funding from the Meadows Foundation of Dallas. We are grateful for their support.

We also wish to thank the Hoblitzelle Foundation which provided funds to put the first edition on the Internet.

NOTES

1. Dr. Stephen Klineberg, "Texas Survey: Environmental Concerns Rise Dramatically," Rice University News Office, Press Release, March 5, 1997.

2. Stephen Meyer, quoted in "Gold & Green," by Bob Hall, *Southern Exposure*, October 12, 1994, 52 (Durham, N.C.: Institute for Southern Studies).

3. E. B. Goodstein, *Jobs and the Environment* (Washington, D.C.: Economic Policy Institute, 1994), 4.

Texas
Environmental
Almanac

CHAPTER 1

Water Quantity

"When the well's dry, we know the worth of water."
Benjamin Franklin

INTRODUCTION

For many regions of Texas, 1996 was a particularly severe drought year. Overall, conservation storage levels in Texas's largest 77 reservoirs dipped to about 23 million acre-feet in the summer of 1996—the lowest levels since the record drought of 1984 and a fall of nearly 8 million acre-feet in just a year.[1]

FYI ☞ *One acre-foot is equal to 325,851 gallons —an area about the size of a football field covered with one foot of water.* (Source: Texas Water Development Board, Texas Water Facts [1991], 4.)

The lack of rain and surface water also affected many of the state's main aquifers, such as the Bolson Deposits in El Paso and the Edwards Aquifer in San Antonio, as people turned increasingly to groundwater resources to water their rain-depleted lawns and crops.[2]

All told, nearly 350 public water systems reported

CONSERVATION STORAGE DATA FOR SELECTED MAJOR TEXAS RESERVOIRS

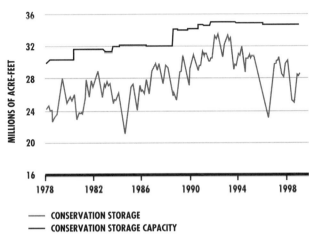

— CONSERVATION STORAGE
— CONSERVATION STORAGE CAPACITY

Note: Data based on elevation at 77 reservoirs that represent 98 percent of total conservation storage capacity in Texas reservoirs having a capacity of 5,000 acre-feet or more.
Source: Texas Water Development Board, "Reservoir Storage," Water Conditions (March 1999), 1.

TEXAS AGENCIES WITH MAJOR WATER RESOURCE RESPONSIBILITIES

TEXAS WATER DEVELOPMENT BOARD

Water quantity planning	Grants and loans for wastewater protection and surface water treatment and water supply facilities

TEXAS NATURAL RESOURCE CONSERVATION COMMISSION

Water use permitting	Water quality inventory and monitoring	Wastewater discharge permits	Water quality standards	Enforce Clean Water Act, Safe Drinking Water Act and Texas Water Code	Overall responsibility for water quality (other agencies share responsibility)

TEXAS DEPARTMENT OF AGRICULTURE
Responsibility for regulating agricultural chemicals

TEXAS GENERAL LAND OFFICE
Management of coastal areas
Oil spill clean-ups

TEXAS PARKS AND WILDLIFE DEPARTMENT
Review of water use and wastewater discharge permits to ensure protection of aquatic habitats, parks, and endangered species

TEXAS RAILROAD COMMISSION
Water quality aspects of oil and gas exploration and production
Water quality aspects of surface mining

TEXAS STATE SOIL AND WATER CONSERVATION BOARD AND LOCAL SOIL CONSERVATION DISTRICTS
Authority over many aspects of agricultural and silvicultural non-point source pollution

RIVER AUTHORITIES
Manage water supply reservoirs and act in conjunction with state and local governments to monitor and protect water quality

GROUNDWATER CONSERVATION DISTRICTS
Collect information on groundwater use and quality in district
Some limited authority to regulate pumping and protect water quality

LOCAL GOVERNMENTS
Limited authority to protect water quality through ordinances, enforcement such as sewer discharge ordinances

REGIONAL WATER PLANNING GROUPS
16 groups throughout state design regional water management plans with TWDB, TNRCC and TPWD oversight and supervision

drought-related shortages to state agencies, and 200 Texas towns and cities limited residential water by enacting drought ordinances or short-term emergency measures.[3] Industrial production facilities in some cases closed when streamflows were so low that the facilities could not legally discharge their wastewater because pollutants would be too concentrated. Agricultural losses approached approximately $5 billion as the result of damaged crops and cattle losses.[4] The effect on wildlife species—the plants, animals, and microorganisms dependent upon water and rivers, wetlands, bays, and estuaries—is more difficult to quantify. Still, to many state residents and leaders the lesson was clear—with a booming population and economy, better water planning and management are necessary to ensure future growth—and to protect water levels in the rivers, reservoirs, and bays for aquatic life and recreational uses.

The following year brought above-normal precipitation throughout the state, and most reservoirs, people, and businesses rebounded.[5] In 1997 the Texas legislature—in part reacting to the drought—

passed Senate Bill 1, more popularly known as the "Water Bill," which, among other features, changes the way the state conducts water planning, water-availability modeling, financing, and drought management. SB 1 shifts the emphasis from water development to better management of existing water resources through conservation, drought management, reallocation, and reuse of treated wastewater. This is being accomplished at the regional level through regional citizen planning groups.

Management of water resources in Texas is, however, a daunting task. Consider just a few factors:

■ Geographical variations cause large disparities in available water supplies, from water shortages in arid West Texas to abundant supplies in the eastern portion of the state.

■ A growing population and industrial base will continue to increase pressure on existing supplies and generate demand for development of additional water delivery facilities, such as reservoirs.

■ Reliance on groundwater is facing serious limita-

SKETCH OF SOME ELEMENTS OF EARTH'S HYDROLOGICAL CYCLE

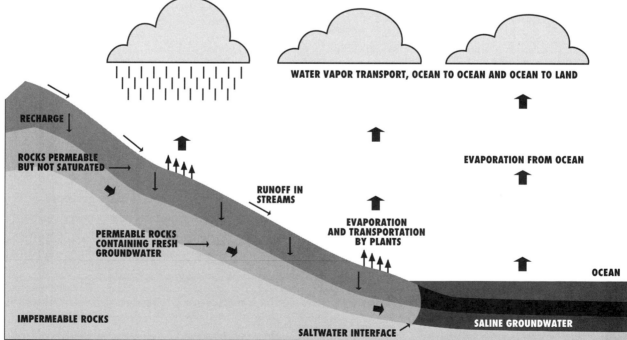

Source: Wendy Gordon, A Citizen's Handbook on Groundwater Protection (San Francisco: Natural Resources Defense Council, 1984), 5.

THE HYDROLOGICAL CYCLE

All water, whether captured from a stream, collected as rain, or mined from below the surface, is recirculated to the atmosphere. This never-ending exchange of water from earth to atmosphere, accomplished through precipitation and evaporation, is known as the hydrological cycle.

Water quality may be affected in several ways as water moves through the phases of the hydrological cycle. For example, as water percolates into the ground it may gather contaminants from the soil that affect the quality of groundwater. Rainwater may collect impurities from the air, and runoff from rainfall may gather impurities from the land surface, both of which can affect the surface water quality in lakes and rivers.

The overall quantity of water moving through the cycle also may change. Water used in industrial processes, for example, may become so contaminated that it cannot be treated and returned to the cycle as wastewater, but instead must be kept on site in impoundments. Such water would therefore be permanently removed from the hydrological cycle. Thus, in the cycle, groundwater, surface water, and human activities are all interrelated.

RIVER AND COASTAL BASINS OF TEXAS

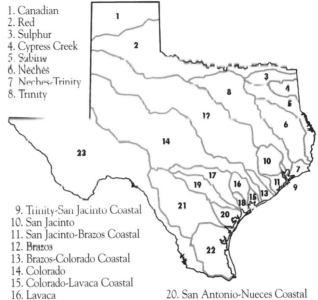

1. Canadian
2. Red
3. Sulphur
4. Cypress Creek
5. Sabine
6. Neches
7. Neches-Trinity
8. Trinity

9. Trinity-San Jacinto Coastal
10. San Jacinto
11. San Jacinto-Brazos Coastal
12. Brazos
13. Brazos-Colorado Coastal
14. Colorado
15. Colorado-Lavaca Coastal
16. Lavaca
17. Lavaca-Guadalupe Coastal
18. Guadalupe
19. San Antonio

20. San Antonio-Nueces Coastal
21. Nueces
22. Nueces-Rio Grande Coastal
23. Rio Grande

Source: Texas Natural Resources Information Service.

tions in many areas of the state because of overpumping and water quality problems.

■ The Texas institutional structure for managing water quantity and protecting water quality is divided among several state and local government agencies. These agencies are charged with implementing a convoluted set of statutes and court decisions, even though all water forms part of the same hydrological cycle (see box: The Hydrological Cycle).

HOW MUCH WATER IS IN TEXAS?

Texas receives about 366 million acre-feet of rain in an average year. Levels of precipitation and runoff vary greatly across the state. In the eastern portion, precipitation averages 56 inches per year; in West

Texas, annual rainfall is only about 8 inches.[6] This rainfall feeds 191,228 miles of streams and rivers contained in 15 major river basins and 8 coastal basins, 6,700 inland reservoirs that comprise over 3 million square acres—about 6,690 square miles—nearly a million square miles of bays, almost 8 million acres of wetlands, and vast underground storage areas known as aquifers.[7] About 11,250 streams and rivers, flowing 80,000 miles through Texas landscapes, are named; the rest are—officially at least—nameless.[8]

Texas has only one natural lake—Caddo Lake in East Texas. The other 6,700 lakes are reservoirs that have been constructed by humans.[9] About 97 percent of the surface water consumed by Texas is drawn from 191 reservoirs that each hold more than 5,000 acre-feet of water.[10] Texas's major reservoirs contain approximately 11 million acre-feet of dependable-yield surface water, although they have a capacity to hold 34.5 million acre-feet. At present, the state uses only about 65 percent of this dependable yield.

Texas also has an estimated 3 to 4 billion acre-feet

SURFACE WATER SUPPLY

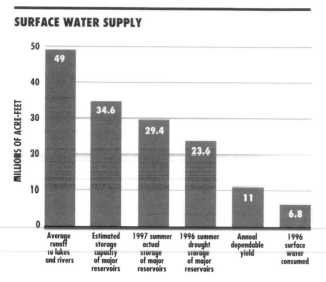

Source: Texas Water Development Board, Water for Texas 1997 (June 1997); and Texas Water Development Board, "Summary Historical Water Use 1996" (1998).

GROUNDWATER SUPPLY

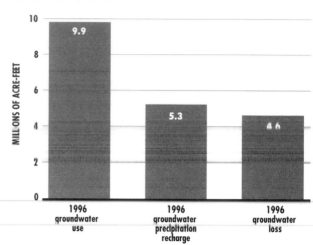

Source: Texas Water Development Board, "Summary Historical Water Use 1996" (1998).

of groundwater stored in 9 major aquifers and 20 minor aquifers, underground natural rock formations that hold groundwater. However, only about 10 percent of this groundwater is recoverable through the use of traditional technology.[11]

Each year, about 5.3 million acre-feet of annual rainfall recharges the state's aquifers. In 1996 the 9.94 million acre-feet of water pumped from underground exceeded natural recharge—the downward replenishing flow of rainfall through the soil to the aquifer.[12]

WHO USES THE WATER?

Texans pump, move, convey, consume, and discharge water for all kinds of uses. In 1996 the municipal,

1996 WATER USE IN TEXAS (In millions of acre-feet)

CATEGORY OF USE	TOTAL	GROUND-WATER USE	SURFACE WATER USE	% OF TOTAL
Irrigation	10.63	7.88	2.75	63.3%
Municipal	3.58	1.44	2.14	21.3%
Manufacturing	1.50	0.25	1.24	8.9%
Power	0.44	0.06	0.38	2.6%
Mining	0.25	0.15	0.10	1.5%
Livestock	0.37	0.16	0.21	2.2%
Total	16.78	9.94	6.83	100%

Source: Texas Water Development Board, "Summary Historical Water Use 1996" (1998).

industrial, and agricultural demands for water totaled about 16.8 million acre-feet statewide, a 6 percent increase from 1990 (15.8 million acre-feet). Groundwater use equaled about 59 percent of the total, with surface water use making up the other 41 percent.[13] Water use in Texas can be divided into three major categories: irrigation (66 percent), municipal (21 percent), and industrial (including manufacturing, mining, and power generation).[14]

HISTORY OF WATER OWNERSHIP: EIGHTEENTH- AND NINETEENTH-CENTURY WATER LAW

The history of the state's water regulation began with the Spanish settlers in Texas. Spanish water law required specific authorization to use surface water. The Spanish (and later Mexican) type of water law evolved into the "prior appropriation" doctrine and is not related to the ownership of land. Under the appropriation doctrine, surface water "rights" are separate and apart from the rights of land ownership, much like oil and mineral rights are today.[15] However, in the 1800s Anglo-American settlers in Texas introduced English common law to govern the use of water. This water law establishes the right-of-use based on ownership of land. The owner of land adjacent to a river had the right to

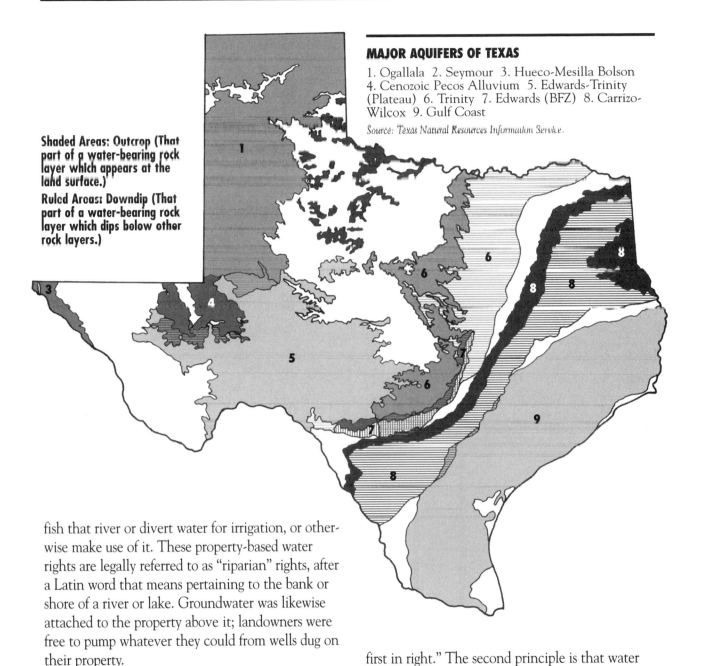

MAJOR AQUIFERS OF TEXAS

1. Ogallala 2. Seymour 3. Hueco-Mesilla Bolson
4. Cenozoic Pecos Alluvium 5. Edwards-Trinity
(Plateau) 6. Trinity 7. Edwards (BFZ) 8. Carrizo-
Wilcox 9. Gulf Coast

Source: Texas Natural Resources Information Service.

Shaded Areas: Outcrop (That part of a water-bearing rock layer which appears at the land surface.)

Ruled Areas: Downdip (That part of a water-bearing rock layer which dips below other rock layers.)

fish that river or divert water for irrigation, or otherwise make use of it. These property-based water rights are legally referred to as "riparian" rights, after a Latin word that means pertaining to the bank or shore of a river or lake. Groundwater was likewise attached to the property above it; landowners were free to pump whatever they could from wells dug on their property.

THE STATE BEGINS TO MANAGE SURFACE WATER USE

With the Texas Irrigation Act of 1889, all streams "within the arid areas of the state" not already claimed by a landowner were declared the property of the state and therefore subject to state regulation. In essence, Texas formally adopted the principle of "prior appropriation." The foundation of the prior appropriation doctrine is the recognition and protection of senior claims to water use, or "first in time,

first in right." The second principle is that water shall be put to a "beneficial" use.[16] Under this system, those wishing to divert water from a streambed could be granted a right to a similar amount in the future provided the water was used in a fashion the state deemed reasonable and beneficial.[17]

In 1913, and again in 1917, the legislature extended the state's jurisdiction to regulate surface water use through amendments to the 1889 act. By 1917 the state had jurisdiction over all surface water. However, the courts upheld water rights claimed by individuals for property they owned prior to the

1889 and 1913 laws, leaving the state with two sometimes overlapping systems for allocating surface water rights.[18]

The flaw inherent in such a dual system, the appropriation and riparian doctrines, became apparent in the 1950s when a severe drought in the Lower Rio Grande Valley drastically reduced the volume of water in the Rio Grande. As a result of the drought, the amount of water appropriated under surface water rights exceeded the river's supply.

REGULATION OF SURFACE WATER RIGHTS TODAY

The drought of 1996 was not the first time that a drought caused the state to change the way it manages water. In 1967, following a historic drought, the Texas legislature passed a law known as the "Water Rights Adjudication Act." This act consolidated all surface water rights into a unified system by transforming previously held Spanish and Mexican grants, riparian water rights, and claims into "certificates of adjudication." The act required all riparian and unrecorded users of water to file claims with the Texas Water Commission (now the Texas Natural Resource Conservation Commission, or TNRCC) to be based upon actual use during the years 1963–1967. The Water Commission then evaluated all water right claims, including any claim filed prior to the act. Approval of any water right by the commission also required court approval. All rights approved by the courts are called "Certificates of Adjudication." After 1969, anyone wishing to obtain a new water right must seek a permit from the state. Today, only water claims in the upper Rio Grande near El Paso remain unadjudicated.[19]

Thus, today, surface water rights are issued to irrigators, cities, industries, and individuals with the following terms and conditions:
(1) a maximum amount of water (in acre-feet) that may be used each year,
(2) a maximum diversion rate,
(3) a diversion point(s),
(4) a purpose of use (e.g., municipal, irrigation, mining),
(5) a place of use, and

SURFACE WATER RIGHTS HOLDERS IN TEXAS AS OF JULY, 1998

TYPE	TOTAL NO.	SIZE*	MORE THAN 10,000 ACRE-FT	SIZE*
Municipal	451	9.24	106	8.77
Industrial	338	14.81	90	14.51
Irrigation	4,670	5.92	62	4.61
Mining	163	0.18	3	0.10
Hydroelectric	26	12.60	23	12.60
Other	977	0.15	3	0.06
Total	6,740	42.90	287	41.3

The 42.90 total million acre-feet of authorized use includes impoundments and authorized but unbuilt reservoirs, as well as non-consumptive uses. Total non-consumptive uses total 21.93 million acre-feet. The industrial use includes cooling uses of which some is brackish waters of the estuaries.
*Millions of acre-feet.

Source: Texas Natural Resource Conservation Commission, Water Rights Data Base.

(6) other additional restrictions, including:
  (a) streamflow restrictions in some cases to protect:
    - existing water rights holders,
    - water quality,
    - aquatic fish and wildlife habitat,
    - inflows for bays and estuaries,
    - recreational uses,
  (b) habitat mitigation measures, and
  (c) water conservation measures.

To change any of the terms or conditions of the right requires authorization from the TNRCC. In its administration of water rights, the TNRCC, by law, must balance requests for new rights or for amendments against statutory responsibilities to also protect water quality, in-stream uses, and freshwater inflows to bays and estuaries.

Currently there are about 6,740 water rights held by some 6,200 water rights holders.[20] However, a small number of these water rights—287—have access to most of the water.[21] Irrigation rights make up the greatest percentage of the number of rights, but most of these irrigation rights are for 100 acre-feet or less.[22] Irrigators in Texas rely principally on groundwater.

RIVERS WITH LITTLE OR NO WATER AVAILABLE FOR APPROPRIATION

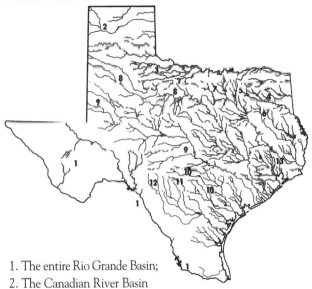

1. The entire Rio Grande Basin;
2. The Canadian River Basin upstream of Lake Meredith;
3. The Red River Basin upstream of Lake Kemp and Lake Arrowhead;
4. The Cypress River Basin upstream of Lake O' the Pines;
5. The Sabine River Basin upstream of Lake Tawakoni and Lake Fork;
6. The Neches River Basin upstream of Lake Palestine;
7. The Trinity River Basin upstream of the Dallas/Fort Worth area reservoirs;
8. The Brazos River Basin upstream from Possum Kingdom Lake;
9. The Colorado River Basin;
10. The Guadalupe River Basin upstream from Canyon and Coleto Creek Reservoirs;
11. The San Antonio River Basin upstream from Medina Lake;
12. The Nueces River Basin upstream of the Zavala/Dimmit counties water rights; and
13. The San Jacinto River Basin upstream from Lake Houston.

Source: Texas Natural Resource Conservation Commission, State of Texas Water Quality Inventory, 12th Edition (TNRCC, 1995), 82.

Surface water rights can be sold, amended, leased, or transferred. In Texas, over 90 percent of surface water has already been adjudicated, and some rivers, like the Rio Grande, are actually overappropriated. This means that if all holders used all their water rights—particularly during dry periods—there would be no flow in the river.[23] To encourage conservation, the TNRCC in April 1993 modified its rules to allow water rights holders to retain for future use the rights to water conserved through water use

efficiency. Prior to this rule change, permit holders were in a "use it or lose it" position, which discouraged conservation.[24]

DIRECT AND INDIRECT REUSE OF WATER RIGHTS

The passage of SB 1, which took effect on September 1, 1997, reconfirmed that existing water rights holders who take water out of a reservoir or stream can use and reuse up to 100 percent of the water prior to its discharge to the stream, providing there is no return-flow requirement in the permitted water right itself.[25] For example, a municipality can reuse wastewater for a variety of domestic and municipal uses—irrigation of golf courses and parks—without needing an additional water rights permit. This type of reuse is known as direct reuse.

Once water is used and is discharged to a streambed, however, it becomes property of the state. Any water rights holders who wish to divert their water for reuse after it has been discharged must obtain authorization from the TNRCC through a "bed and banks" permit. Under SB 1, this type of indirect reuse might require that some surplus water be returned to the river or stream to protect senior downstream water users and environmental needs. In addition, SB 1 allows the TNRCC to condition new or amended water rights to provide for return flows, potentially limiting the direct reuse of wastewater as well.[26]

GROUNDWATER AND PROPERTY RIGHTS

In contrast to surface water regulations, Texas law allows property owners an absolute "right of capture" to the groundwater under their property. Any property owner may pump as much water as needed, generally without incurring any responsibility even if other property owners are affected.

The law makes an exception to this right of capture: when groundwater flows in a well-defined channel and thus constitutes an underground river, it becomes state property, just as if it were surface water.[27] No underground water source has been legally designated as an underground river in Texas, although the Texas Water Commission in 1992 declared the Edwards Aquifer an underground stream. A state district court later overturned the decision.

Because the state is charged with protecting groundwater quality, however, some controls have been established. In critical areas of groundwater depletion such as the Ogallala Aquifer in the High Plains and the Edwards Aquifer in the San Antonio area, either the legislature or the TNRCC has established local management authorities, which can manage groundwater withdrawals through a permitting system. The Harris-Galveston Coastal Subsidence District, the Fort Bend Subsidence District and the Edwards Aquifer Authority are underground water districts that regulate groundwater withdrawal.[28] SB 1 expanded this ability, stating that the Texas Water Development Board (TWDB) and the TNRCC will evaluate areas outside of existing groundwater districts and may name areas experiencing water quantity or quality problems part of a "priority groundwater management area." If so, local voters could approve formation of an underground conservation district. If they failed to approve a district, the TNRCC could ask the legislature to do so.

While SB 1 moves groundwater districts toward further management of groundwater resources, it does not alter the rule of capture. Critics have long argued that this rule, even with some controls, leads to overpumping of the state's natural resources and does not properly protect the water rights of others using both surface and groundwater. However, both the Texas Supreme Court, most recently in a 1999 case, and the Texas legislature have continued to treat groundwater as a basic property right.[29]

WATER USE PLANNING IN TEXAS
A variety of water districts and authorities as well as several state agencies have been involved in water use planning in Texas. At the state government level, Texas has moved from three agencies in 1957, to a single agency in the late 1970s, to a current structure of two state agencies, the TNRCC and TWDB.[30]

The TWDB is charged with developing a state water plan to ensure that "sufficient water will be

EVOLUTION OF 3 TEXAS STATE WATER AGENCIES

1913 TEXAS BOARD OF WATER ENGINEERS	1953 TEXAS WATER POLLUTION ADVISORY COUNCIL
1962 TEXAS WATER COMMISSION	1961 TEXAS WATER POLLUTION CONTROL BOARD
1965 TEXAS WATER RIGHTS COMMISSION	1967 TEXAS WATER QUALITY BOARD
1977 TEXAS DEPARTMENT OF WATER RESOURCES	1977 TEXAS DEPARTMENT OF WATER RESOURCES
1985 TEXAS WATER COMMISSION	1957 TEXAS WATER DEVELOPMENT BOARD
1993 TEXAS NATURAL RESOURCE CONSERVATION COMMISSION	1977 TEXAS DEPARTMENT OF WATER RESOURCES
	1985 TEXAS WATER DEVELOPMENT BOARD

Source: Ernest Smerdon, et al., State Water Policies: A Study of Six States (New York: Praeger, 1988).

available at a reasonable cost to further the economic development of the entire state."[31] "The first plan was developed in 1967. This plan, which is usually updated every two years, estimates the supply and demand for water for the next generation. The TWDB then administers state and federal funds to build water supply and wastewater treatment facilities in accordance with those demands.

The TWDB, the TNRCC, and the Texas Parks and Wildlife Department (TPWD) came together to jointly produce "a consensus-based update"—the 1997 Texas Water Plan. The plan uses supply and demand projections that have been agreed on by all three agencies.

The TNRCC issues water rights permits and wastewater discharge permits and attempts to balance economic and environmental needs by considering the effects of consumptive water use on various in-stream and estuarine habitats. The TNRCC also oversees drinking water quality under the Safe Drinking Water Act. In addition, the TNRCC measures the water quality of all state rivers, streams, reservoirs, and bays to determine if they meet their designated uses, such as drinking water, water for aquatic life, or fishing. Under the federal Clean Water Act, the TNRCC reports this information through the Texas Water Quality Inventory, which is produced every two years.[32]

The TPWD participates in the water rights permit process by automatically reviewing water

PAST AND PROJECTED WATER DEMAND PER SECTOR

	1974	1980	1990	1995	2000	2010	2020	2030	2040	2050
Population	12.29	14.23	16.99	18.72	20.23	23.49	27.28	30.67	33.84	36.67
Total Water Use	17.34	17.82	15.73	16.60	16.59	16.87	17.14	17.49	17.90	18.35
Manufacturing	1.60	1.52	1.56	1.51	1.79	1.97	2.09	2.19	2.39	2.60
Municipal	1.93	2.01	3.20	3.32	4.09	4.48	4.88	5.34	5.78	6.21
Irrigation	13.08	12.71	10.12	10.78	9.61	9.29	8.94	8.65	8.36	8.09

Sources: Texas Water Development Board, "Summary Historical Water Use 1996" (1998); and Texas Water Development Board, Water for Texas 1997 (June 1997), 3-2 and 3-3.

rights permits and recommending whatever changes in permits it deems necessary to protect aquatic habitat and wildlife in state parks or wetlands, endangered and threatened species, the aquatic ecosystems of streams, or the estuaries. If the agency's concerns are not met, it may request that the TNRCC hold a public hearing on the water rights application. TPWD, jointly with the TNRCC and the TWDB, has initiated a series of studies for more accurate quantification of the amount of water needed to preserve aquatic life in the bays and estuaries.

With legislative approval of SB 1 in 1997, water planning in Texas shifted from the state to the regional level. The TWDB has divided the state into 16 regional planning areas, each of which is required to submit a regional plan by September 1, 2000. Both the TNRCC and the TPWD will be involved in the review process. Once approved, these regional plans will form the basis for the next state water plan, due no later than September 1, 2001, which must be updated within five years.

TRENDS IN WATER USE

Between 1930 and 1980, statewide water use increased more than fivefold, from 3 million to about 18 million acre-feet per year. Over the same period, the population more than doubled, growing from 5.8 million to 14.2 million.[33] Between 1980 and 1990, however, statewide water use actually declined, largely because the number of irrigated acres declined. With the exception of irrigation for agriculture, which is expected to continue declining, all of the major use categories—municipal and industrial—are likely to increase, according to the 1997 Water for Texas plan.[34]

USE OF GROUNDWATER IN TEXAS, 1996

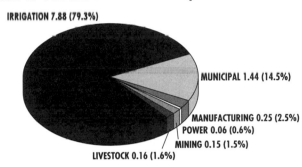

Total use: 9.94 million acre-feet

Source: Texas Water Development Board, "Summary Historical Water Use 1996" (1998).

USE OF SURFACE WATER IN TEXAS, 1996

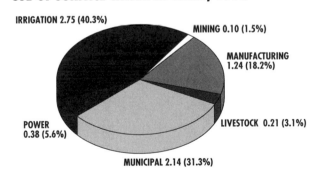

Total use: 6.83 million acre-feet

Source: Texas Water Development Board, "Summary Historical Water Use 1996" (1998).

Of the 16.8 million acre-feet of water Texas consumed in 1996, groundwater supplied 9.9 million acre-feet, or about 59 percent, and surface water provided the rest.[35] Almost 95 percent of the groundwater came from 9 major aquifers; the remaining 5 percent was drawn from 20 minor aquifers.[36]

The consumption pattern for water pumped from

TEXAS IRRIGATION DEVELOPMENT, 1889–1994

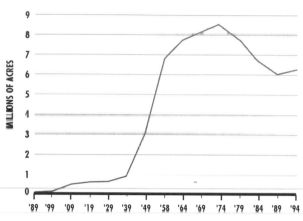

Data from Agricultural Census		Data from Irrigation Surveys	
1889	18,419	1958	6,723,614
1899	49,652	1964	7,706,881
1909	451,130	1969	8,206,249
1919	586,120	1974	8,618,054
1929	594,287	1979	7,817,681
1939	894,638	1984	6,752,625
1949	3,131,534	1989	6,077,604
		1994	6,313,222

Source: Texas Water Development Board, Surveys of Irrigation in Texas *(January 1996), 2.*

PERCENTAGE OF TOTAL MUNICIPAL USE SUPPLIED BY GROUNDWATER IN MAJOR URBAN COUNTIES, 1990 AND 1995

	1990	1995
El Paso (El Paso, San Elizario, Anthony, Socorro)	79%	63%
Ector (Odessa, Penwell)	41%	36%
Midland (Midland, Greenwood, Spraberry)	41%	18%
Potter (Amarillo, Ady)	49%	49%
Lubbock (Lubbock, Shallowater)	28%	39%
Tarrant (Fort Worth, Arlington)	7%	6%
Dallas (Dallas, Irving)	2%	1%
Travis (Austin, Manor, Lakeway)	7%	8%
Bexar (San Antoni, Kirby)	100%	100%
Harris (Houston, Pasadena, Waller)	71%	64%
Galveston (Galveston, Texas City)	20%	14%
Jefferson (Beaumont, Port Arthur)	24%	24%
Cameron (Brownsville, Harlingen, San Benito, Port Isabel)	4%	3%

Note: Percentages represent all municipal use within county boundaries, not within city limits.

Source: Texas Water Development Board, "Summary Historical Water Use 1995" (1997).

the ground is different from the pattern for water taken from rivers and reservoirs. Irrigation used about 80 percent of groundwater, while municipalities and their residents used less than 15 percent in 1996.[37] In contrast, that same year municipalities consumed 31 percent of all surface water, while irrigators utilized 40 percent.[38]

The share of water demands met by groundwater and surface water has changed over time. Groundwater use has dropped from 70 percent of all water used in 1974 to 59 percent in 1996. Reliance on groundwater should continue to decline for two reasons. First, the decline of agricultural acreage overall has reduced the number of irrigated acres in the state, and the acres dropped were almost all irrigated by groundwater. For example, total irrigated acreage has declined from 8.6 million in 1974 to 6.1 million in 1989. Since then, there has been only

THE MINING OF AQUIFERS

The term mining, when used in connection with an aquifer, refers to the practice of pumping more water from the aquifer than will be replaced through the natural recharge process. In some areas of Texas, mining of major aquifers has caused subsidence of the land. In other areas, mining has affected water quality by allowing the saline water that lies deep in most aquifers to encroach on the layers of fresh water nearer the surface. The aquifers most affected by mining include the Ogallala Aquifer in the High Plains; the Carrizo-Wilcox Aquifer in the Cypress Creek river basin; the Trinity Aquifer in Dallas and Tarrant counties; and the Gulf Coast Aquifer in the Houston-Galveston region and the Baytown, Freeport, and San Jacinto River Basin areas. Finally, mining of the Hueco-Mesilla Bolson near El Paso has changed groundwater flow and reduced the quality of the water as saline water from adjacent saline-bearing sands encroaches upon higher-quality groundwater.[39]

WATER PUMPED FROM TEXAS' MAJOR AQUIFERS, AND GROUNDWATER AVAILABILITY, 1990–1995

	PUMPED 1990 (ACRE-FEET)	PUMPED 1995 (ACRE-FEET)	EFFECTIVE ANNUAL RECHARGE RATE	PROJECTED SAFE ANNUAL AVAILABILITY, 1990–1999
Ogallala	5.55 million	6.22 million	0.30 million	3.81 million
Edwards (Balcones)	0.53 million	0.47 million	0.11 million	0.44 million
Edwards-Trinity (Plateau)	0.19 million	0.25 million	0.78 million	0.78 million
Carrizo-Wilcox	0.45 million	0.49 million	0.64 million	0.85 million
Trinity	0.19 million	0.19 million	0.10 million	0.11 million
Gulf Coast	1.23 million	1.15 million	1.23 million	1.23 million
Bolson and Alluvium Deposits (Hueco-Mesilla Bolson, Cenozoic, Seymour)	0.32 million	0.39 million	0.43 million	0.97 million
Total	8.56 million	9.15 million	3.92 million	8.19 million

Recharge Rate is the amount of precipitation and infiltration of surface water which adds to the level of the aquifer each year. Safe annual availability refers to both the annual recharge and additional waters stored in the aquifer which can be pumped without unduly creating either water quality problems or land subsidence. Thus, aquifers which have no storage can only provide the annual recharge rate. Note that annual recharge is an estimated average; actual recharge depends upon annual precipitation.

Source: Texas Water Development Board, "1995 Estimated Ground Water Pumpage Summary by Major Aquifer Units" (1997), and Texas Department of Water Resources, Groundwater Availability in Texas: Estimates and Projections through 2030 (July 1987), Table 1.

a slight increase in the number of acres irrigated and total water used. Second, many of the large metropolitan areas are converting to surface water or mixing groundwater with surface water.[40] For example, Houston is gradually switching from groundwater sources because of subsidence problems—the ground is actually sinking as water is pumped out (see box: The Mining of Aquifers). El Paso and Midland are switching to surface water because of the increasingly elevated salinity—and declining quality—of groundwater resources. Though this trend is expected to continue, groundwater will still supply most of the water for large, arid areas of the state.[41]

IRRIGATION USE

Irrigation of agricultural lands accounted for 65 percent of the water used in Texas in 1995. Five crops in Texas made up more than 80 percent of the irrigated land in 1994: cotton (33 percent), wheat (16 percent), corn (16 percent), grain sorghum (9 percent), and pasture and other feed (8 percent).[42]

From 1980 to 1990, annual water use for irrigation declined from 12.7 million acre-feet to 10.2 million acre-feet—a decline of nearly 20 percent. While irrigation water use was stable between 1990 and 1995, the general decline is expected to continue over the next 50 years, with projected agricultural use in 2050

of 8.1 million acre-feet. This projection assumes the most likely adoption of water efficient technology and no reduction in Federal Farm Program payments, which help keep agricultural lands in business.[43]

DISTRIBUTION OF IRRIGATED ACREAGE BY COUNTIES, 1994

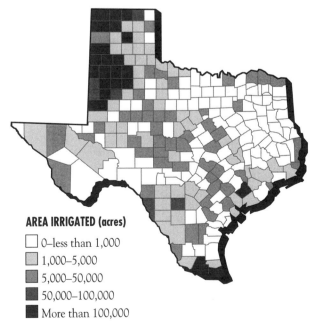

AREA IRRIGATED (acres)

- ☐ 0–less than 1,000
- 1,000–5,000
- 5,000–50,000
- 50,000–100,000
- More than 100,000

Source: Texas Water Development Board, Surveys of Irrigation in Texas (January 1996), 6.

MAJOR TEXAS CROPS: IRRIGATED LAND USE vs. WATER USED FOR IRRIGATION PURPOSES, 1994

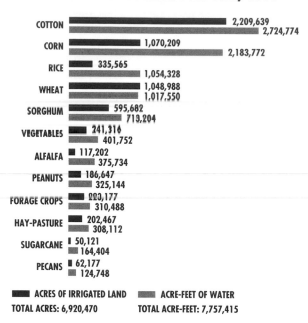

COTTON 2,209,639 / 2,724,774
CORN 1,070,209 / 2,183,772
RICE 335,565 / 1,054,328
WHEAT 1,048,988 / 1,017,550
SORGHUM 595,682 / 719,204
VEGETABLES 241,316 / 401,752
ALFALFA 117,202 / 375,734
PEANUTS 186,647 / 325,144
FORAGE CROPS 223,177 / 310,488
HAY-PASTURE 202,467 / 308,112
SUGARCANE 50,121 / 164,404
PECANS 62,177 / 124,748

■ ACRES OF IRRIGATED LAND   ▨ ACRE-FEET OF WATER
TOTAL ACRES: 6,920,470   TOTAL ACRE-FEET: 7,757,415

Source: Texas Water Development Board, "Crop Acres and Water Loss— 1994" (1996).

However, the 1996 Farm Bill cut some farming subsidies, which may impact the use of water for irrigation in Texas.

There are two reasons for both the present and the expected future decline: the number of irrigated acres in production dropped 30 percent between 1975 and 1990, and farmers are practicing better water conservation techniques. Irrigation surveys, however, show a slight increase in irrigated land between 1990 and 1994. The amount of water used per acre has remained relatively stable, in part because of increases in high-water-use crops like corn, pecans, and sugarcane.[44]

MUNICIPAL USE

Municipal water use is the fastest growing category of water use in Texas. Municipal water use includes water for households and businesses, restaurants and public offices, sanitation and landscaping, and, of course, fire protection. Generally, the largest cities in the state use the most water, with Houston and Dallas consuming 14.5 percent and 13.7 percent of

1990 AND 1995 PER CAPITA WATER USE BY MAJOR MUNICIPALITIES (GALLONS PER DAY)

	1990	1995
Abilene	216	159
Amarillo	234	223
Brownsville	191	184
Dallas	237	230
El Paso	183	179
Fort Worth	210	189
Irving	188	196
Laredo	254	190
Lubbock	176	189
Mesquite	152	165
Plano	210	220
Waco	198	172
State Average	**167**	**158**
Arlington	101	162
Austin	180	157
Beaumont	158	159
Corpus Christi	186	140
Garland	159	151
Houston	157	126
Pasadena	129	117
San Antonio	159	149

Note: Includes both residential and commercial water use. Industrial use and sales to other utilities are excluded.

Source: Texas Water Development Board, "1995 Per Capita Water Use for Texas Cities" (1997).

all municipal water. However, even accounting for a city's overall size, per capita use varies widely across the state. In 1995 the average Dallas resident used 230 gallons per day, while the average Houstonian only used 126 gallons per day.[45] The difference between the two? More rain in Houston to feed residents' and business owners' lawns and a more aggressive conservation program. Statewide, average per capita municipal use was about 100 gallons per day in the 1950s and rose to a high of 182 gallons in 1978. Since that time, per capita use in the state has begun to decline, leveling off to an estimated 158 gallons per capita per day in 1995, before rising to 167 in 1996 during the drought.[46]

FYI ☞ *A partnership between the City of Houston's Water Conservation Branch and the Housing Authority of the City of Houston to install low-water-use fixtures, promote water conservation*

WHAT IS THE TRUE PRICE OF WATER?

Water is relatively cheap in Texas. Some agricultural users pay virtually nothing for their water, except a small distribution fee to the irrigation district and taxes on their land. Texas city users pay varying prices depending upon where they live. These differing prices to some extent reflect cost of service. However, water in cities is controlled by utilities, and different cities set different prices according to their conservation goals.

In recent years, the idea that utilities should set a market-clearing price has come into favor among policymakers. Whether for irrigation, industry, or residential use, water prices do not often reflect their true prices. Policymakers argue that if the true price were reflected, people, industries, and irrigators would use water more efficiently, just as people began to use gasoline more efficiently when

WATER AND WASTEWATER RATES IN MAJOR TEXAS CITIES, 10,000 GALLONS

TEXAS CITY	WATER	WASTEWATER	COMBINED
Dallas	$17.00	$30.00	$47.00
Houston	$29.00	$32.00	$61.00
Tyler	$21.00	$16.00	$37.00
Corpus Christi	$19.00	$24.00	$43.00
El Paso	$12.00	$12.50	$24.50
Austin	$25.36	$37.64	$63.00

Source: Texas Natural Resource Conservation Commission, Natural Outlook (Summer 1997), 8; and City of Austin Utilities, City of Austin Utility Rates and Fees Schedules (December 31, 1998).

the prices rose in the late 1970s. According to the market-clearing price theory, when water is a scarce commodity, as in a drought, prices will rise and consumption will fall.[47]

---

education, and repair leaks reduced water consumption by more than 72 percent in a low-income family housing complex. (Source: Texas Water Resources Institute, "Houston Partnership Nets 72 Percent Water Cut," Water Savers 3, no. 3.)

Since 1986 the state has helped promote water conservation by requiring that recipients of federal and state water and wastewater loans over $500,000 implement a water conservation program. In addition, the TNRCC has recently instituted rules that require the adoption of water conservation measures as a condition of receiving any type of permit to use state water.[48]

Finally, SB 1, passed by the legislature in 1997, requires all major water users—water utilities, municipalities, and water supply corporations—to adopt both a drought management plan and a water conservation plan.

INDUSTRIAL WATER USE
Water use within the industrial sectors in Texas is projected to climb over the next 30 years, as it has in the recent past. Between 1986 and 1990, for

example, water use for manufacturing rose 15 percent, from about 1.4 million acre-feet to 1.6 million acre-feet. This increase was due primarily to the resurgence of the petrochemical industry.[49] In 1995

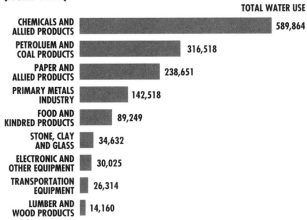

WATER USE BY MAJOR INDUSTRIES IN TEXAS, 1995 (ACRE-FEET)

	TOTAL WATER USE
CHEMICALS AND ALLIED PRODUCTS	589,864
PETROLUEM AND COAL PRODUCTS	316,518
PAPER AND ALLIED PRODUCTS	238,651
PRIMARY METALS INDUSTRY	142,518
FOOD AND KINDRED PRODUCTS	89,249
STONE, CLAY AND GLASS	34,632
ELECTRONIC AND OTHER EQUIPMENT	30,025
TRANSPORTATION EQUIPMENT	26,314
LUMBER AND WOOD PRODUCTS	14,160

Totals include only freshwater use by industrial sectors. In addition, industries used 1,148,014 acre-feet of saline water, and 20,848 acre-feet of treated wastewater in 1995.

Source: Texas Water Development Board, "Water Use by Major Industries 1995" (1997).

RESIDENTIAL USE

A significant portion of municipal water use is lost in transmission and distribution. A recent study by the TWDB found that Texas water utilities cannot account for 10 to 20 percent of the water they treat and distribute.[50] Most of this loss is due to leaky distribution systems.

About a quarter of all municipal water used is for the maintenance of lawns and gardens during the spring and summer.[51]

In the typical home, about 50 percent of all water is used in the bathroom for the shower, toilet, and sink. In schools and public buildings, toilet flushing is the predominant water use.[52] In 1991 the Texas legislature passed a law requiring that, beginning in 1992, all new fixtures sold must include water conserving plumbing devices such as 1.6-gallons-per-flush toilets and 2.75-gallons-per-minute shower heads.[53] The TWDB estimates that if all homes and public buildings used these new, water-efficient toilets, which use 1.6 gallons of water per flush instead of the more conventional 3.5 to 8 gallons, Texas would save about 200 million gallons of water each day. This translates into 459,000 acre-feet per year by 2010.[54] This could reduce the need to build additional water and wastewater treatment plants by 15 percent, saving some $3.5 billion dollars over the next 50 years.[55] The TWDB also estimates that the average family

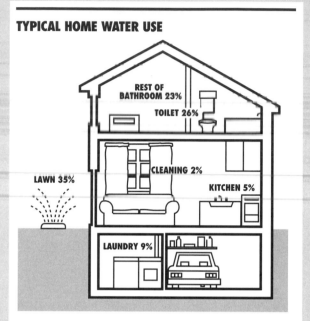

TYPICAL HOME WATER USE

REST OF BATHROOM 23%
TOILET 26%
CLEANING 2%
LAWN 35%
KITCHEN 5%
LAUNDRY 9%

Source: Texas Water Development Board, A Homeowner's Guide to Water Use and Water Conservation (1990), front cover.

of four could save $627 annually by installing water-efficient toilet, shower, and sink fixtures.[56]

FYI ☞ By 2040 the total amount of water saved by using new, water-efficient toilets could reach 800 million gallons per day, enough to fill the Astrodome once every thirteen hours.[57]

industrial water use fell slightly to 1.5 million acre-feet.[58] Five industrial sectors accounted for over 90 percent of that amount.[59] In fact, just 20 companies accounted for more than half the water used in manufacturing in 1990.[60]

The use of water conservation practices has increased within Texas's industrial sector since the early 1980s. Using saline water or treated wastewater in cooling processes and substituting electric heat for steam or hot water are two such examples.[61] Industries that use a large amount of process water, such as the paper and pulp and the semiconductor industries, have enormous potential to reduce their water use.[62]

WATER AND ENVIRONMENTAL USE

Perhaps the single biggest policy issue related to the use of water is the question of the appropriate amount of fresh water needed to maintain the state's bays and estuaries located along 367 linear miles of gulf coastline. An estuary occurs where a river meets the sea and fresh- and saltwater mix. The estuary and its adjacent wetlands—coastal vegetative areas with inundated or saturated soils—serve as important spawning grounds for many species of marine life. The state's 2.6 million acres of coastal habitat, which include 1.5 million acres of open bays, 1.1 million acres of wetlands, and about 250,000 acres of

TEXAS'S MAJOR AND MINOR ESTUARIES

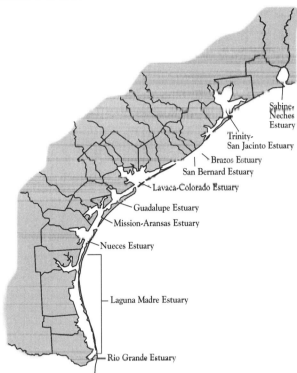

Sabine-Neches Estuary

Trinity-San Jacinto Estuary

Brazos Estuary

San Bernard Estuary

Lavaca-Colorado Estuary

Guadalupe Estuary

Mission-Aransas Estuary

Nueces Estuary

Laguna Madre Estuary

Rio Grande Estuary

Source: Texas Water Development Board, Water for Texas 1990 *(1990), 1-11.*

submerged aquatic vegetation, are also home to a variety of native and migratory birds. These estuaries and their adjacent wetlands depend greatly upon the inflow of fresh water from rivers and streams, including associated sediments and nutrients. As river water winds its way down to the gulf and is used and reused for industry, irrigation, and municipalities, both its quality and quantity are altered, affecting bays and estuaries.

Estuaries, bays, and related aquatic habitats contribute significantly to the state's economy. They are used for navigation and provide a base for recreational and commercial fishing and boating, contributing around $2.9 billion annually to the state economy.[63] In addition, preserving these wetlands and estuarine systems helps ensure water quality, since they act as a natural filtering system for many pollutants.

The TPWD, in conjunction with the TWDB and the TNRCC, has developed estimates of the quantities of fresh water needed to protect San Antonio Bay and the Guadalupe Estuary, while the Lower Colorado River Authority, with oversight by the state agencies, has developed a working model of inflow needs for Matagorda Bay and the Lavaca-Colorado Estuary. Finally, TPWD and the two other agencies are scheduled to complete work on the Galveston Bay and Trinity-San Jacinto Estuary and the Sabine Lake and Sabine-Neches Estuary in 1999.[64]

The three agencies will use these "beneficial inflows" to determine how much flow must be allowed to pass through any new reservoirs or direct diversion located within 200 miles of the bay or estuary, as well as how much flow is required to be set aside in new and amended water rights permits.[65] Since 1986 the state has required new reservoirs that are within 200 miles of the coast to dedicate at least 5 percent of their firm yield for in-stream needs of aquatic habitat and the inflow needs of the bays and estuaries. Proposals to construct reservoirs or dam rivers require both a state and a federal permit. The federal permit process also requires applicants to consider effects upon stream-flow and habitat.

In addition to the bays and estuaries, Texas's 191,000 miles of rivers and streams provide habitat for 150 native and 247 total species of fishes, as well as a variety of aquatic flora and fauna. In addition, riparian areas, playa lakes, and hardwood-bottom-lands wetland ecosystems also depend upon natural flow conditions of rivers and streams. Diminished flows cause losses in habitat diversity, reduce stream productivity, and degrade water quality. Estimating the amount of fresh water needed for in-stream habitat viability is also problematic. There is considerable controversy, for example, about whether the federal government's in-stream flow methodology, which was developed using cold, mountainous Western rivers as models, can be applied to Texas's slow, meandering, warm water streams.[66]

FYI 🔊 *Only Missouri, Alabama, Georgia, Tennessee, Kentucky, and Arkansas—all connected to the immense drainage basin of the Mississippi River—*

have more native freshwater fishes than Texas. (Source: Texas Water Development Board, Water for Texas 1997, *3-17.)*

For the 1997 Texas Water Plan, the three main agencies came up with an environmental planning methodology to consider in-stream needs when evaluating the possibility of a new reservoir or the diversion of water from new or amended water rights. The methodology is based on the concept of establishing target flows, while allowing diversion for human use when target flows are exceeded. The methodology also establishes provisions to protect flows for all users during drought conditions, though the agencies are moving away from a "minimum streamflow concept" toward a more flexible watershed planning effort.

Since 1985 all new surface water use permits and all amendments to existing use permits may contain provisions to reserve water for public purposes. Water rights holders are required to limit their diversion of water from rivers and streams when streamflows are below a certain level. Before 1985, however, no such diversion was explicitly required. Thus, water rights for rivers like the Rio Grande have been fully appropriated without any water having been reserved for environmental and public purposes.[67]

Under SB 1 the TNRCC is required to produce water availability models for six river basins by the end of 1999 and for all major river basins by the end of 2001. In addition, the TNRCC must use these models to estimate water availability during a drought, the amount of effluent available for reuse, and the amount of water available if unused water rights cancellation procedures were instituted. Finally, SB 1 establishes a Texas Water Trust, where unused water rights can be deposited by interested individuals for the purpose of maintaining environmental flow in rivers and into the bays.

PROJECTING FUTURE DEMAND FOR WATER

The current Texas state water plan was published in 1997. A comparison of state water plans over the years illustrates how substantially projections can vary. The TWDB's projected demands for the year

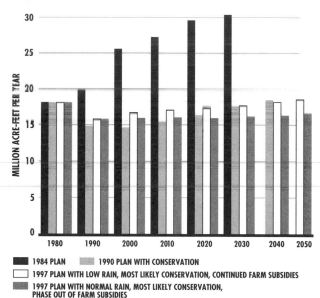

COMPARISON OF TOTAL PROJECTED STATEWIDE DEMANDS OF THE 1984, 1990, AND 1997 WATER PLANS

■ **1984 PLAN**   ▨ **1990 PLAN WITH CONSERVATION**
□ **1997 PLAN WITH LOW RAIN, MOST LIKELY CONSERVATION, CONTINUED FARM SUBSIDIES**
▦ **1997 PLAN WITH NORMAL RAIN, MOST LIKELY CONSERVATION, PHASE OUT OF FARM SUBSIDIES**

Source: Texas Water Development Board, "Water Use Projections for State and Counties in Texas" (1998); TWDB, Water for Texas 1997 *(June 1997) and TWDB,* Water for Texas *(December 1990), 3-3.*

2000 are about 9 million acre-feet higher in the 1984 water plan than they are in the 1997 plan.[68] In fact, total water use between 1996 and 2000 would have to increase by nearly 9 million acre-feet to meet 1984 projections.

The 1997 plan assumes that population will reach 36.7 million by 2050 and that municipal water use—assuming below normal rainfall—will increase nearly twofold, from 3.2 million to 6.2 million by 2050.[69]

There are considerable uncertainties in these demand projections. Two fundamental differences between demand projections in the previous water plans and the 1997 plan are: (1) the water conservation effects vary from city to city; and (2) the conservation effects are more aggressive (greater) than in previous plans. Assuming below-average rainfall, continued federal farm subsidies, some conservation, and the most likely population growth scenario, these projections in the 1997 plan show total demands increasing only from 15.8 to 18.35 million acre-feet over the 60-year period.[70] An alternative

WHAT ABOUT CAPTURING RAIN?

More than 4,000 years ago, residents of the Negev Desert would capture the occasional rain and divert it to holding tanks for later use. On the island of Gibraltar, rainwater is the only source of water, and Gibraltar has one of the largest rainwater collection systems in the world.[71] Today in Texas, rainwater harvesting is being seen as a way to augment traditional water supplies for individual homes, ranches, businesses, and farms, and even for entire cities.

The concept is simple: catch the rain before it hits the ground. A rainwater collection system might be as simple as a bucket below a gutter, or it might be an extensive as several tanks connected to pipes and pumps to service entire subdivisions.

Rainwater is one of the purest sources of water available.[72] Not only is the water softer—less mineralized and therefore requiring less detergents and soaps for cleaning—it has also most likely been less adversely affected by human activity.

For more information on rainwater harvesting, copies of *Texas Guide to Rainwater Harvesting* or a companion videotape, *Rainwater Harvesting for Texas* (in both English and Spanish) can be obtained from the TWDB (Attn: Patsy Walters, PO Box 13231, Austin, TX 78711-3231). The American Rainwater Catchment Systems Association, headquartered in Austin, also is a good source for information (contact the association at PO Box 685283, Austin, TX 78768-5283).

RAINWATER HARVESTING SYSTEM MAIN COMPONENTS

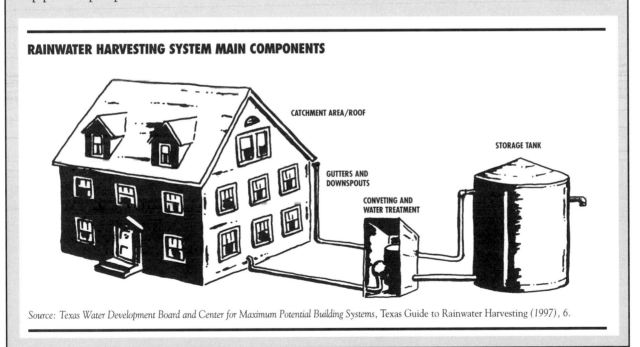

Source: Texas Water Development Board and Center for Maximum Potential Building Systems, Texas Guide to Rainwater Harvesting (1997), 6.

scenario, which assumes normal rainfall and the elimination of federal farm subsidies, lowers this total by almost 2 million acre-feet. The most likely scenario assumes that aggressive water conservation and efficiency plans will account for annual savings of 1.5 million acre-feet by 2020 and 2.6 million acre-feet by 2050.[73]

ESTIMATING THE FUTURE SUPPLY OF WATER

Can Texas meet all of the demands for water? Water supply projections for 2050 take into account the continued use of existing surface and groundwaters, the use of return flows and reuse of treated wastewater, more efficient reallocation of reservoir storage, freeing up water through the buying and selling of

PROJECTED STATEWIDE WATER SUPPLY AND WATER DEMAND IN 2050

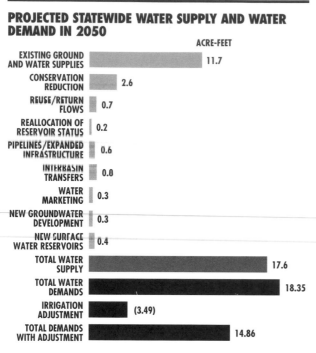

ACRE-FEET

EXISTING GROUND AND WATER SUPPLIES	11.7
CONSERVATION REDUCTION	2.6
REUSE/RETURN FLOWS	0.7
REALLOCATION OF RESERVOIR STATUS	0.2
PIPELINES/EXPANDED INFRASTRUCTURE	0.6
INTERBASIN TRANSFERS	0.8
WATER MARKETING	0.3
NEW GROUNDWATER DEVELOPMENT	0.3
NEW SURFACE WATER RESERVOIRS	0.4
TOTAL WATER SUPPLY	17.6
TOTAL WATER DEMANDS	18.35
IRRIGATION ADJUSTMENT	(3.49)
TOTAL DEMANDS WITH ADJUSTMENT	14.86

Source: Texas Water Development Board, Water for Texas 1997 *(June 1997), 3-26 and 3-93.*

water rights ("water marketing"), new surface water supplies generated by new conveyance systems to move water from one area to another, and new reservoirs. The TWDB projects that in 2050 Texas supplies will meet expected municipal and industrial demands, so long as tough conservation measures reduce water use by an expected 2.6 million acre-feet per year. However, by 2050 the water supply will not be able to meet all irrigation demands. TWDB projections assume that irrigation demands will not be met because groundwater resources will be depleted or will be of lower quality and quantity. Some farming will no longer be affordable because of the replacement costs of these depleted resources. In fact, the TWDB assumes that there will be an irrigation "adjustment" in Texas of nearly 3.5 million acre-feet.[74]

An assumption made in the TWDB's 1997 water plan is that the sustainable yield from existing ground- and surface water in 2050 is about 12 million acre-feet per year, a reduction of 5 million acre-feet as groundwater is further depleted in quality and quantity. In fact, there is considerable debate about how much water is actually available. The Texas Committee on Natural Resources, for example, argues that the figure is closer to 25 million acre-feet in nondrought years when run-of-the-river flows are considered along with what is available in the reservoirs themselves.[75]

WHAT ABOUT YOUR LAWN?

Since lawns and gardens—whether for home, office, or business—are the primary drinkers of municipal water during summer months in Texas, many cities and utilities as well as individual homeowners are turning toward "water smart" landscaping, also known as *xeriscaping*. Xeriscaping —the word was coined from combining the Greek word *xeros*, meaning dry, and *landscape*—uses drought-tolerant, adaptive, and native landscape plants, utilizes water in a less intensive way, and generally requires less maintenance and fertilizers. Most of the major municipal utilities in Texas have developed xeriscape programs. For example, the City of Austin offers residential water customers a rebate of up to $150 for installing drought-tolerant ground covers in areas that receive at least six hours of direct daily sunlight.[76]

More information about xeriscaping can be obtained by calling the TWDB at (512) 463-7955. This agency has published *A Directory of Water Savings Plants and Trees for Texas*, as well as two pamphlets, *Saving Water Outside the Home* and *Lawn Watering Guide*. The Texas Agricultural Extension Service also has published two guides, *Landscape Water Conservation—Xeriscape* and *Landscape Development for Coastal Areas*. Call the Extension Service at (409) 845-6573. Finally, the Arizona Water Resources Research Center has developed a multimedia CD-ROM, *Desert Landscaping: Plants for a Water-Scarce Environment*, available for $25. Call the center at (520) 792-9591.

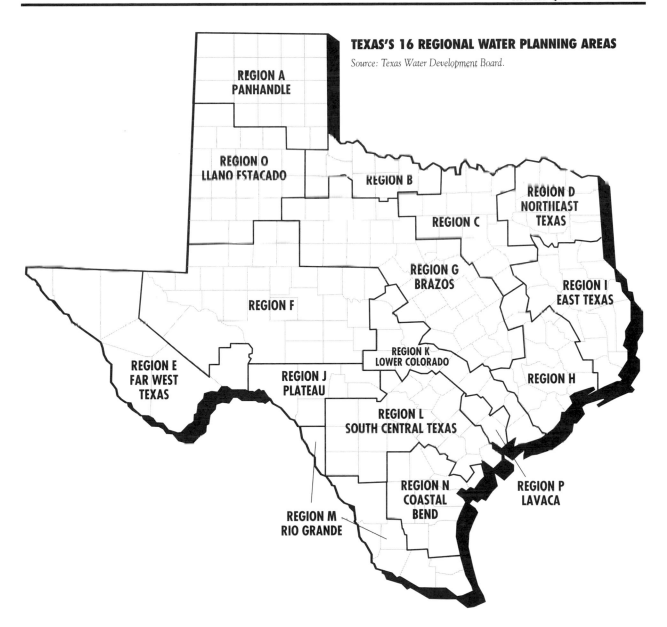

TEXAS'S 16 REGIONAL WATER PLANNING AREAS
Source: Texas Water Development Board.

REGION A
PANHANDLE

REGION O
LLANO ESTACADO

REGION B

REGION D
NORTHEAST
TEXAS

REGION C

REGION G
BRAZOS

REGION I
EAST TEXAS

REGION F

REGION K
LOWER COLORADO

REGION E
FAR WEST
TEXAS

REGION J
PLATEAU

REGION H

REGION L
SOUTH CENTRAL TEXAS

REGION N
COASTAL
BEND

REGION P
LAVACA

REGION M
RIO GRANDE

REGIONAL DEMAND AND SUPPLY ISSUES[77]

Most water supply and demand projections show that Texas has enough water in the state as a whole, but each region in the state has different water resources, has differing needs, and faces different problems. This section looks at the 16 regional water planning areas designated by the TWDB and highlights the expected demands and water resource challenges in each of them. Under the new water bill (SB 1), each of these planning areas must produce a 50-year water plan by September 1, 2000.

FYI 🖝 *The longest river in Texas? The Rio Grande, which begins in Colorado and covers 1,896 miles, second only to the Missouri-Mississippi.*

The second longest? The Red River, which forms the border between Texas and Oklahoma and Texas and Arkansas.

The shortest river? The Comal, which is only two and a half miles long.

What's the biggest aquifer? The Ogallala, which covers four states and in 1974 had more than 281.7 million acre-feet of recoverable groundwater. By 2031, this total will have been reduced to 76.1 million acre-feet in Texas.

REGIONAL WATER PLANNING AREA A (PANHANDLE): WATER SUPPLY AND DEMAND DISTRIBUTION, 1995–2050

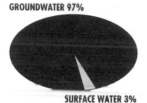

WATER SUPPLY, 1995

GROUNDWATER 97%

SURFACE WATER 3%

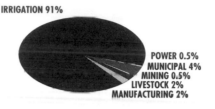

WATER DEMAND, 1995

IRRIGATION 91%

POWER 0.5%
MUNICIPAL 4%
MINING 0.5%
LIVESTOCK 2%
MANUFACTURING 2%

WATER DEMAND, 2050

IRRIGATION 87%

MINING 1%
MUNICIPAL 6%
POWER 0.5%
LIVESTOCK 3%
MANUFACTURING 3%

Counties in region: Armstrong, Carson, Dallam, Gray, Hansford, Hartley, Hemphill, Hutchinson, Lipscomb, Moore, Ochiltree, Oldham, Potter, Randall, Roberts, Sherman, Wheeler

Major cities:	Amarillo
Population, 1995:	324,885
Population, 2050:	498,281

Total water use, 1995:	1,889,207 Acre-Feet
Total water use, 2050:	1,741,605 Acre-Feet
Primary rivers:	Canadian, Red
Major aquifers:	Ogallala
Annual precipitation:	16–24 inches
Net evaporation:	48–56 inches

SUPPLY AND DEMAND ISSUES BY REGION

Water Region Planning Area A (Upper Panhandle)

■ Amarillo's population is projected to increase by more than 50 percent between 1995 and 2050.

■ The region depends almost exclusively on the Ogallala Aquifer. In 1995, 97 percent of the total water used was drawn from the Ogallala. The aquifer, however, is a rapidly depleting resource.

■ Surface water availability from the Canadian and Red rivers is limited. Salinity and silting problems in

Lake Meredith have limited the use of this reservoir—which provides some of Amarillo's municipal supply—by more than 70 percent from its original permitted level.

■ Groundwater has high fluoride, arsenic, and nitrate levels and has also been contaminated by abandoned oil fields.

Water Region Planning Area B (Rolling Plains Region)

■ Low population growth and a decrease in irrigation needs should allow the region to meet

REGIONAL WATER PLANNING AREA B: WATER SUPPLY AND DEMAND DISTRIBUTION, 1995–2050

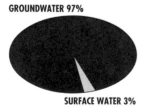

WATER SUPPLY, 1995

GROUNDWATER 97%

SURFACE WATER 3%

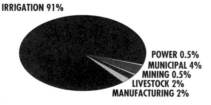

WATER DEMAND, 1995

IRRIGATION 91%

POWER 0.5%
MUNICIPAL 4%
MINING 0.5%
LIVESTOCK 2%
MANUFACTURING 2%

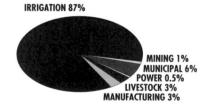

WATER DEMAND, 2050

IRRIGATION 87%

MINING 1%
MUNICIPAL 6%
POWER 0.5%
LIVESTOCK 3%
MANUFACTURING 3%

Counties in region: Archer, Baylor, Childress, Clay, Collingsworth, Cottle, Donley, Foard, Hall, Hardeman, King, Montague, Wichita, Wilbarger

Major cities:	Wichita Falls
Population, 1995:	212,471
Population, 2050:	220,730

Total water use, 1995:	150,098 Acre-Feet
Total water use, 2050:	171,595 Acre-Feet
Primary rivers:	Red
Major aquifers:	Seymour, Nacotoch
Annual precipitation:	20–36 inches
Net evaporation:	36–52 inches

REGIONAL WATER PLANNING AREA C: WATER SUPPLY AND DEMAND DISTRIBUTION, 1995–2050

WATER SUPPLY, 1995

GROUNDWATER 8%

SURFACE WATER 92%

WATER DEMAND, 1995

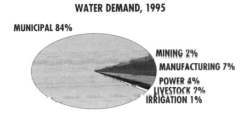

MUNICIPAL 84%

MINING 2%
MANUFACTURING 7%
POWER 4%
LIVESTOCK 2%
IRRIGATION 1%

WATER DEMAND, 2050

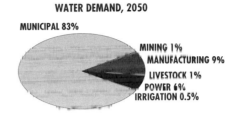

MUNICIPAL 83%

MINING 1%
MANUFACTURING 9%
LIVESTOCK 1%
POWER 6%
IRRIGATION 0.5%

Counties in region: Collin, Cooke, Dallas, Denton, Ellis, Fannin, Freestone, Grayson, Henderson (Trinity River Basin only), Jack, Kaufman, Navarro, Parker, Rockwall, Tarrant, Wise

Major cities:	Dallas, Fort Worth
Population, 1995:	4,501,387
Population, 2050:	8,843,253

Total water use, 1995:	1,065,810 Acre-Feet
Total water use, 2050:	1,936,556 Acre-Feet
Primary rivers:	Trinity, Red
Major aquifers:	Trinity
Annual precipitation:	28–44 inches
Net evaporation:	24–44 inches

growing demands in industrial water use, including both manufacturing and the generation of electrical power.

■ Natural salt pollution in the Middle Red River Basin prevents the full utilization of this surface water in this region for municipal uses, while sedimentation has also reduced the amount of water the reservoirs in the area can hold.

■ High nitrate concentrations in portions of the Seymour Aquifer—from both natural phenomena and from pollution by feedlots, septic tanks, cesspools, and agriculture—preclude the aquifer's use for drinking water without expensive treatment.

■ Wichita Falls's two reservoirs—Kickapoo and Arrowhead—have an available yearly supply of 45,600 acre-feet, about 39,000 acre-feet less than the permitted total.

Water Planning Region C
(North-Central Texas Region)

■ Population in the 17-county area will nearly double between 1995 and 2050, reaching almost 9 million and nearly doubling municipal water demand.

■ Groundwater levels and quality have been lowered over the Trinity Aquifer due to prolonged usage.

■ Urban pressures have impacted surface water

quality, leading to low dissolved oxygen content, suspended solids, fecal coliform, and phosphates in the Upper Trinity River Basin.

■ The Texas Department of Health has issued aquatic closures and restricted fishing due to high pesticide and PCB concentrations in fish in several reservoirs.

■ The region has imported, and will continue to import, water from the neighboring river basins to the east.

■ The TWDB projects that new water supply reservoirs may be required in the region for the three major water providers—Dallas Water Utilities, North Texas Municipal Water District, and Tarrant Regional Water District.

Regional Water Planning Area D
(Northeast Texas)

■ There will be little population growth over the 55-year planning period in this area, but manufacturing water demand will increase.

■ Shallow groundwater often has high concentrations of iron and is acidic, making it unusable for most municipal and manufacturing purposes. The construction of deeper wells or expensive treatment would be necessary for groundwater use in this area.

REGIONAL WATER PLANNING AREA D (NORTHEAST TEXAS): WATER SUPPLY AND DEMAND DISTRIBUTION, 1995–2050

WATER SUPPLY, 1995

GROUNDWATER 12%

SURFACE WATER 88%

WATER DEMAND, 1995

MANUFACTURING 57%

LIVESTOCK 6%

POWER 9%

IRRIGATION 3%

MINING 2%

MUNICIPAL 22%

WATER DEMAND, 2050

MANUFACTURING 61%

LIVESTOCK 4%

POWER 14%

IRRIGATION 2%

MINING 4%

MUNICIPAL 16%

Counties in region: Bowie, Camp, Cass, Delta, Franklin, Gregg, Harrison, Hopkins, Hunt, Lamar, Marion, Rains, Red River, Smith (Sabine River Basin only), Titus, Upshur, Van Zandt, Wood

Major cities: Longview, Marshall, Texarkana
Population, 1995:   657,254
Population, 2050:   784,058

Total water use, 1995:   448,274 Acre-Feet
Total water use, 2050:   687,789 Acre-Feet
Primary rivers: Sabine, Cypress, Sulphur, Red
Major aquifers: Carrizo-Wilcox
Annual precipitation: 40–52 inches
Net evaporation: 16–32 inches

■ Excess water in Lake Cooper is being sold outside the region to the Upper Trinity Regional Water District, while water in Lake Fork and Lake Tawakoni is contracted to the Dallas Water Utilities.

Regional Water Planning Area E (Upper Rio Grande and Far West Texas)

■ Population will double between 1995 and 2050, and municipal water use will increase from 22 to 44 percent of the total water demands, as irrigation water use declines.

■ The major aquifers in the area—the Hueco Basin and the Mesilla-Bolson—are shared by Texas, New Mexico, and Mexico and provide most municipal and industrial water needs. Groundwater has suffered in quality and has become more saline.

■ El Paso is continuing to shift from groundwater to surface water. One proposal—a pipeline from New Mexico to bring Rio Grande water more directly to the city—is controversial because of its potential effects on the riparian habitat of the Rio Grande and on the aquifers, which rely on natural recharge from the river.

REGIONAL WATER PLANNING AREA E (FAR WEST TEXAS): WATER SUPPLY AND DEMAND DISTRIBUTION, 1995–2050

WATER SUPPLY, 1995

GROUNDWATER 40%

SURFACE WATER 60%

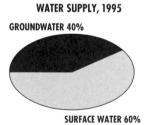

WATER DEMAND, 1995

IRRIGATION 75%

POWER 0.5%

MUNICIPAL 22%

MINING 0.5%
MANUFACTURING 2%
LIVESTOCK 1%

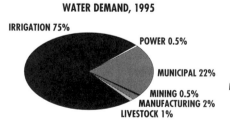

WATER DEMAND, 2050

IRRIGATION 50%

LIVESTOCK 1%
MANUFACTURING 3%

MINING 1%
POWER 1%

MUNICIPAL 44%

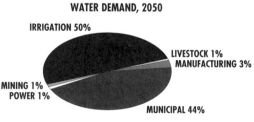

Counties in region: Brewster, Culberson, El Paso, Hudspeth, Jeff Davis, Presidio, Terrell

Major cities: El Paso
Population, 1995:   688,547
Population, 2050:   1,585,685
Total water use, 1995:   636,753 Acre-Feet

Total water use, 2050:   600,894 Acre-Feet
Primary rivers: Rio Grande
Major aquifers: Hueco Mesilla-Bolson, Cenozoic
                          Pecos Alluvium (Terrell County)
Annual precipitation: 8–20 inches
Net evaporation: 52–68+ inches

REGIONAL WATER PLANNING AREA F: WATER SUPPLY AND DEMAND DISTRIBUTION, 1995–2050

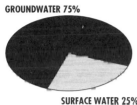

WATER SUPPLY, 1995

GROUNDWATER 75%

SURFACE WATER 25%

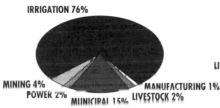

WATER DEMAND, 1995

IRRIGATION 76%

MINING 4%
POWER 2%
MANUFACTURING 1%
MUNICIPAL 15%   LIVESTOCK 2%

WATER DEMAND, 2050

IRRIGATION 56%

LIVESTOCK 4%
POWER 2%
MANUFACTURING 2%
MINING 4%
MUNICIPAL 32%

Counties in region: Andrews, Borden, Brown, Coke, Coleman, Concho, Crane, Crockett, Ector, Glasscock, Howard, Irion, Kimble, Loving, Martin, Mason, McCulloch, Menard, Midland, Mitchell, Pecos, Reagan, Reeves, Runnels, Schleicher, Scurry, Sterling, Sutton, Tom Green, Upton, Ward, Winkler

Major cities:	San Angelo, Midland, Odessa
Population, 1995:	588,964
Population, 2050:	884,707

Total water use, 1995:	810,962 Acre-Feet
Total water use, 2050:	556,164 Acre-Feet
Primary rivers:	Colorado, Rio Grande
Major aquifers:	Edwards-Trinity Plateau, Cenozoic Pecos Alluvium, Ogallala
Annual precipitation:	8–28 inches
Net evaporation:	36–68 inches

■ Water quality and quantity of the Rio Grande in Big Bend National Park has been severely degraded because of upstream use of both the Rio Grande and the Pecos River.

■ The Pecos River is naturally salty because of intrusions from a brine artesian aquifer in New Mexico.

■ Hundreds of small, unincorporated communities along the Mexico-Texas border lack adequate water supply and wastewater treatment, although the problem is slowly being addressed with state and federal funds.

■ Testing by the Environmental Protection Agency (EPA) and the TNRCC along the Rio Grande has revealed high levels of toxics and other contaminants.[78] Untreated wastewater flows from Ciudad Juárez have an adverse effect on river water quality by raising nutrients and fecal coliform bacteria in the river.

Regional Water Planning Area F
(Upper Colorado and West Texas Region)
■ Population growth will be moderate.

■ Irrigation use as a category is projected to decline from 76 percent to 56 percent of total water use by 2050.

■ The major cities in the region—Odessa, Midland, and San Angelo—receive their water from reservoirs built on the Colorado River. High levels of dissolved minerals and nutrients necessitate expensive treatment and degrade the quality of the water.

■ Petroleum industry activities in Loving, Ward, and Winkler counties and irrigation practices in Pecos, Reeves, and Ward counties have degraded the water quality of the Cenozoic Pecos Alluvium Aquifer.

■ Depletion of the Ogallala Aquifer in the north part of the planning area is of significant concern, especially for agriculture.

Regional Water Planning Area G
(Middle Brazos Region)
■ Population is expected to double between 1995 and 2050. Water demand will increase for the municipal, manufacturing, mining, and power water use categories during this time, while livestock and irrigation water use will decline.

■ Declining water quality in the Trinity Aquifer will necessitate conversion to surface water by some cities.

■ Runoff from local dairy farms has led to elevated fecal coliform bacteria levels in the north Bosque River, while runoff from confined animal feeding

REGIONAL WATER PLANNING AREA G (BRAZOS): WATER SUPPLY AND DEMAND DISTRIBUTION, 1995–2050

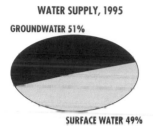

WATER SUPPLY, 1995

GROUNDWATER 51%

SURFACE WATER 49%

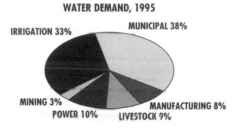

WATER DEMAND, 1995

IRRIGATION 33%
MUNICIPAL 38%
MINING 3%
POWER 10%
LIVESTOCK 9%
MANUFACTURING 8%

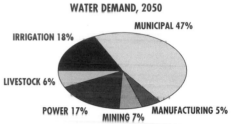

WATER DEMAND, 2050

IRRIGATION 18%
MUNICIPAL 47%
LIVESTOCK 6%
POWER 17%
MINING 7%
MANUFACTURING 5%

Counties in region: Bell, Bosque, Brazos, Burleson, Callahan, Comanche, Coryell, Eastland, Erath, Falls, Fisher, Grimes, Hamilton, Haskell, Hill, Hood, Johnson, Jones, Kent, Knox, Lampasas, Lee, Limestone, McLennan, Milam, Nolan, Palo Pinto, Robertson, Shackelford, Somervell, Stephens, Stonewall, Taylor, Throckmorton, Washington, Williamson (Brazos River Basin only), Young

Major cities: Abilene, Bryan, Temple/Killeen, Waco

Population, 1995:   1,484,456

Population, 2050:	2,807,003
Total water use, 1995:	648,909 Acre-Feet
Total water use, 2050:	971,677 Acre-Feet
Primary rivers:	Brazos
Major aquifers:	Seymour, Trinity, Carrizo-Wilcox
Annual precipitation:	20–44 inches
Net evaporation:	24–56 inches

operations is becoming a concern in the Leon River watershed.

■ Localized water quality problems in the middle Brazos River Basin are common. In some cases, such as in Lake Waco and along the Paluxy River, dissolved metals have been identified as a concern.

■ Natural salt pollution in the Upper Brazos River Basin in the western part of the planning area precludes use of this water or requires expensive treatment for municipal use.

Regional Water Planning Area H (Houston Region)

■ Population in this planning area will double from 1995 to 2050. Municipal and manufacturing water use will increase, while rice-farming water use will decline.

REGIONAL WATER PLANNING AREA H: WATER SUPPLY AND DEMAND DISTRIBUTION, 1995–2050

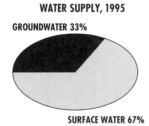

WATER SUPPLY, 1995

GROUNDWATER 33%

SURFACE WATER 67%

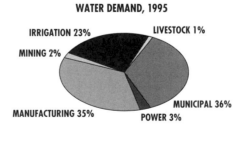

WATER DEMAND, 1995

IRRIGATION 23%
LIVESTOCK 1%
MINING 2%
MANUFACTURING 35%
POWER 3%
MUNICIPAL 36%

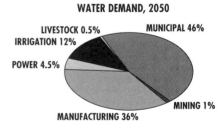

WATER DEMAND, 2050

LIVESTOCK 0.5%
MUNICIPAL 46%
IRRIGATION 12%
POWER 4.5%
MINING 1%
MANUFACTURING 36%

Counties in region: Austin, Brazoria, Chambers, Fort Bend, Galveston, Harris, Leon, Liberty, Montgomery, Polk (Trinity River Basin Only), San Jacinto, Trinity (Trinity River Basin Only), Walker, Waller

Major cities: Houston, Galveston, Brazoria, Texas City

Population, 1995:   4,311,839

Population, 2050:   8,627,029

Total water use, 1995:	1,808,301 Acre-Feet
Total water use, 2050:	2,918,953 Acre-Feet
Primary rivers:	San Jacinto, Trinity, Brazos, Neches-Trinity, Trinity-San Jacinto, San Jacinto-Brazos
Major aquifers:	Gulf Coast, Carrizo-Wilcox
Annual precipitation:	40–60 inches
Net evaporation:	16–28 inches

REGIONAL WATER PLANNING AREA I (EAST TEXAS): WATER SUPPLY AND DEMAND DISTRIBUTION, 1995–2050

WATER SUPPLY, 1995

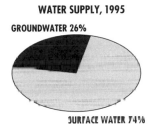

GROUNDWATER 26%

SURFACE WATER 74%

WATER DEMAND, 1995

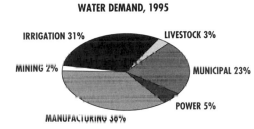

IRRIGATION 31%   LIVESTOCK 3%

MINING 2%   MUNICIPAL 23%

MANUFACTURING 36%   POWER 5%

WATER DEMAND, 2050

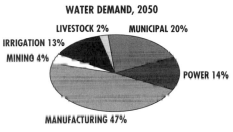

LIVESTOCK 2%   MUNICIPAL 20%

IRRIGATION 13%

MINING 4%   POWER 14%

MANUFACTURING 47%

Counties in region: Anderson, Angelina, Cherokee, Hardin, Henderson (Neches River Basin Only), Houston, Jasper, Jefferson, Nacogdoches, Newton, Orange, Panola, Polk (Neches River Basin Only), Rusk, Sabine, San Augustine, Shelby, Smith (Neches River Basin Only), Trinity (Neches River Basin Only), Tyler

Major cities: Beaumont, Port Arthur, Orange, Tyler
Population, 1995:   992,970
Population, 2050:   1,337,125

Total water use, 1995:   714,636 Acre-Feet
Total water use, 2050:   898,028 Acre-Feet
Primary rivers: Neches, Sabine, Trinity, Neches-Trinity
Major aquifers: Gulf Coast, Carrizo-Wilcox
Annual precipitation: 40–60 inches
Net evaporation: <16–32 inches

■ Additional freshwater inflows will be required from the Trinity and San Jacinto rivers to manage and protect environmental water needs in the Galveston Bay system (Trinity-San Jacinto Estuary).

■ Groundwater use will decline because of regulations imposed by the Harris-Galveston Coastal Subsidence District regarding limitation of groundwater withdrawal. Groundwater use must be limited to 20 percent of total water use by 2020. Additional surface water resources will be needed to make up for this loss, possibly including the importing of water from the Sabine River Basin.

■ Overpumping of the Gulf Coast Aquifer has lowered this aquifer's levels by 200 to 300 feet. This has led to subsidence of up to 9 feet and saltwater intrusion of poor-quality water into the aquifer.

■ Numerous municipal and industrial wastewater treatment plants, as well as urban runoff in the Houston area, have increased organic and nutrient loading and fecal coliform bacteria in all major tributaries of Lake Houston. Downstream, the Houston Ship Channel and Buffalo Bayou are heavily industrialized and water quality has been impacted by petrochemical spills and wastewater discharges.

■ A fish-consumption advisory by the Texas

Department of Health has been issued for the tidally affected portions of the lower Brazos River because of the potential for dioxin contamination.

Regional Water Planning Area I (East Texas)

■ Population growth will be moderate.

■ Manufacturing and electric utility plants are expected to more than double their share of total water use.

■ Groundwater in the northern portion of the planning area can be acidic and have high concentrations of iron.

■ Overpumping of the Gulf Coast Aquifer has led to subsidence and saltwater intrusion.

■ A saltwater barrier to prevent bay water from impacting the fresh river water on the lower Neches River may be needed to ensure a safe supply of surface water for Beaumont and Port Arthur.

■ Several smaller cities will need to upgrade their water treatment plants to comply with the amendments of the Safe Drinking Water Act.

■ Wastewater from paper manufacturing plants has impacted the quality of the water in Sam Rayburn Reservoir, while high mercury levels in fish in Sam

REGIONAL WATER PLANNING AREA J (PLATEAU): WATER SUPPLY AND DEMAND DISTRIBUTION, 1995–2050

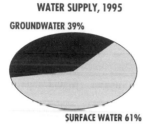

WATER SUPPLY, 1995

GROUNDWATER 39%

SURFACE WATER 61%

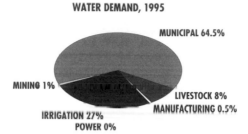

WATER DEMAND, 1995

MUNICIPAL 64.5%

MINING 1%

LIVESTOCK 8%

MANUFACTURING 0.5%

IRRIGATION 27%

POWER 0%

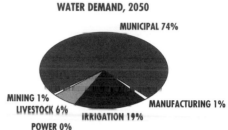

WATER DEMAND, 2050

MUNICIPAL 74%

MINING 1%

LIVESTOCK 6%

MANUFACTURING 1%

IRRIGATION 19%

POWER 0%

Counties in region: Bandera, Edwards, Kerr, Kinney, Real, Val Verde

Major cities: Del Rio, Kerrville

Population, 1995:   105,102

Population, 2050:   178,176

Total water use, 1995: 36,037 Acre-Feet

Total water use, 2050: 49,564 Acre-Feet

Primary rivers: Rio Grande, Nueces, San Antonio, Guadalupe

Major aquifers: Edwards-Trinity, Trinity, Edwards (BFZ)

Annual precipitation: 16–32 inches

Net evaporation: 40–56 inches

Rayburn and B. A. Steinhagen reservoirs has led the Texas Department of Health to issue fish-consumption advisories.

Regional Water Planning Area J (Central West Texas)

■ This sparsely populated planning area will witness a 70 percent population growth between 1995 and 2050, and municipal water use will rise from 64.5 to 74 percent of total water demand.

■ Rapid population growth and out-migration from Austin and San Antonio have led to concerns in Kerr and Bandera counties over groundwater quality and quantity in both the Trinity and Edwards Plateau aquifers.

Regional Water Planning Area K (Lower Colorado River Basin)

■ Rapid population growth in Austin and outlying areas will more than double present population

REGIONAL WATER PLANNING AREA K (LOWER COLORADO): WATER SUPPLY AND DEMAND DISTRIBUTION, 1995–2050

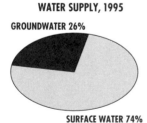

WATER SUPPLY, 1995

GROUNDWATER 26%

SURFACE WATER 74%

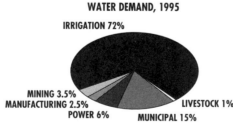

WATER DEMAND, 1995

IRRIGATION 72%

MINING 3.5%

MANUFACTURING 2.5%

POWER 6%

MUNICIPAL 15%

LIVESTOCK 1%

WATER DEMAND, 2050

IRRIGATION 47%

MANUFACTURING 2.5%

MINING 3%

LIVESTOCK 1.5%

POWER 9%

MUNICIPAL 37.5%

Counties in region: Bastrop, Blanco, Burnet, Colorado, Fayette, Gillespie, Hays (Colorado River Basin Only), Llano, Matagorda, Mills, San Saba, Travis, Wharton, Williamson (Colorado River Basin Only)

Major cities: Austin

Population, 1995:   931,031

Population, 2050:   2,073,653

Total water use, 1995: 1,099,005 Acre-Feet

Total water use, 2050:   1,076,898 Acre-Feet

Primary rivers: Colorado, Colorado-Lavaca, Lavaca-Brazos

Major aquifers: Trinity, Edwards (BFZ), Carrizo-Wilcox, Gulf Coast

Annual precipitation: 24–48 inches

Net evaporation: 20–44 inches

REGIONAL WATER PLANNING AREA L (SOUTH CENTRAL TEXAS): WATER SUPPLY AND DEMAND DISTRIBUTION, 1995–2050

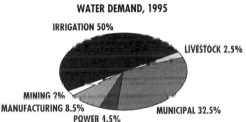

WATER SUPPLY, 1995

GROUNDWATER 76%

SURFACE WATER 24%

WATER DEMAND, 1995

IRRIGATION 50%

LIVESTOCK 2.5%

MINING 2%
MANUFACTURING 8.5%
POWER 1.5%

MUNICIPAL 32.5%

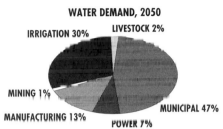

WATER DEMAND, 2050

IRRIGATION 30%   LIVESTOCK 2%

MINING 1%

MANUFACTURING 13%

MUNICIPAL 47%

POWER 7%

Counties in region: Atascosa, Bexar, Caldwell, Calhoun, Comal, DeWitt, Dimmit, Frio, Goliad, Gonzales, Guadalupe, Hays (Guadalupe River Basin Only), Karnes, Kendall, La Salle, Medina, Refugio, Uvalde, Victoria, Wilson, Zavala

Major cities:	San Antonio, Victoria
Population, 1995:	1,867,503
Population, 2050:	4,347,355
Total water use, 1995:	1,015,345

Total water use, 2050:	1,599,733
Primary rivers:	Guadalupe, San Antonio, Nueces, Lavaca-Guadalupe, San Antonio-Nueces
Major aquifers:	Edwards (BFZ), Trinity, Carrizo-Wilcox, Gulf Coast
Annual precipitation:	20–44 inches
Net evaporation:	28–56 inches

between 1995 and 2050. Total water use, however, is not projected to increase due to declines in irrigation water use.

■ Out-migration from Austin and San Antonio to counties like Llano, Blanco, and Gillespie has put a sudden demand on limited groundwater resources from the Trinity Aquifer.

■ Population and development over the recharge zone of the Edwards Aquifer in the Austin area have impacted water quality in aquifer-fed streams like Barton Springs.

■ Oil-field activity and natural salt deposits have affected water quality in the Middle Colorado River Basin, while urban runoff is believed to have contaminated fish with chlordane in Town Lake in the City of Austin.

■ In the Lower Colorado River Basin, high nutrient levels, low dissolved oxygen content, and possible concerns over dissolved metals have impacted water quality.

■ Bay and estuary flow needs and in-stream flow needs below Lake Travis will require careful management of releases from the lakes in the Austin region.

Regional Water Planning Area L (San Antonio Region)

■ Population in the region will more than double between 1995 and 2050, and new water supply resources will be needed.

■ The Edwards Aquifer—the sole source of water for San Antonio's more than one million residents—also provides stream inflow to the Leona, San Pedro, San Antonio, Hueco, Comal, and San Marcos springs north of San Antonio (as well as Barton Springs in the Austin area). Continued pumping of the aquifer affects these streams' water availability and ecosystems, curtailing the recreational opportunities they afford. Recent droughts and a lawsuit brought by the Sierra Club, a national environmental group, have forced restrictions on water use during the dry summer months to protect spring flows and endangered species.

■ The Edwards Aquifer Authority has developed a management plan that will force many cities, irrigators, and industries to change their water use practices.

■ San Antonio will need to augment its reliance on the Edwards Aquifer with surface water, especially during the summer months.

REGIONAL WATER PLANNING AREA M (RIO GRANDE): WATER SUPPLY AND DEMAND DISTRIBUTION, 1995–2050

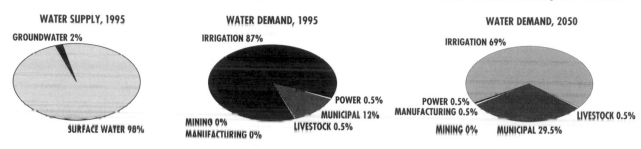

WATER SUPPLY, 1995
GROUNDWATER 2%
SURFACE WATER 98%

WATER DEMAND, 1995
IRRIGATION 87%
POWER 0.5%
MUNICIPAL 12%
LIVESTOCK 0.5%
MINING 0%
MANUFACTURING 0%

WATER DEMAND, 2050
IRRIGATION 69%
POWER 0.5%
MANUFACTURING 0.5%
LIVESTOCK 0.5%
MINING 0%
MUNICIPAL 29.5%

Counties in region: Cameron, Hidalgo, Jim Hogg, Maverick, Starr, Webb, Willacy, Zapata

Major cities:	Laredo, Brownsville, Harlingen, McAllen
Population, 1995:	1,074,900
Population, 2050:	2,965,263
Total water use, 1995:	1,622,910 Acre-Feet

Total water use, 2050:	1,665,731 Acre-Feet
Primary rivers:	Rio Grande, Nueces-Rio Grande
Major aquifers:	Gulf Coast, Carrizo-Wilcox
Annual precipitation:	20–28 inches
Net evaporation:	40–64 inches

■ Pumping from the Carrizo-Wilcox Aquifer in the Winter Gardens area has lowered water levels by more than 100 feet in some places, causing encroachment of poor-quality water into the aquifer.

■ San Marcos and New Braunfels will need to continue to convert from Edwards Aquifer groundwater to surface water from Lake Canyon.

■ Pumping from the Gulf Coast Aquifer in the eastern portion of the planning area could lead to saltwater intrusion and decreased quality in the future. Victoria will have to improve its water treatment facilities to meet amendments of the Safe Drinking Water Act.

■ The bays and estuaries along the coast depend on maintaining sufficient flows from the San Antonio and Guadalupe rivers.

Regional Water Planning Area M (Lower Rio Grande Valley)

■ This area entered its sixth consecutive year of severe drought conditions in 1999.

■ Population will increase 175 percent between 1995 and 2050. Water demands will need to be met by converting irrigation water use to municipal water use.

■ Surface water rights are totally appropriated, and, during drought periods, demands cannot be met.

■ Groundwater from the southern portion of the Gulf Coast Aquifer is too saline for drinking water purposes in the Lower Rio Grande Valley without expensive desalinization plants.

■ Many unincorporated subdivisions lacking proper water supply and wastewater treatment facilities exist within the region, predominantly in Cameron and Hidalgo counties. As infrastructure needs are met for these residents, water demand will increase.

■ Laredo, McAllen, Edinburg, and Brownsville will need to locate additional water supplies or purchase agricultural water rights. Brownsville is also considering supplementing its surface water with saline groundwater from wells and is also studying the construction of a controversial channel dam to capture Rio Grande floodwater.

■ Sufficient in-stream flows in the Rio Grande and Nueces must be maintained to ensure flows into the bays and estuaries of the Gulf of Mexico and the Laguna Madre, a unique ecosystem for thousands of colonial nesting and migratory birds and aquatic life.

■ The Rio Grande's water quality suffers from high fecal coliform bacteria, low dissolved oxygen, and high nutrient levels in most of the planning area. In addition, dissolved metals and pesticides also have been identified in the water, sediment, and fish tissue along the Rio Grande.

REGIONAL WATER PLANNING AREA N (COASTAL BEND): WATER SUPPLY AND DEMAND DISTRIBUTION, 1995–2050

WATER SUPPLY, 1995

GROUNDWATER 25.5%

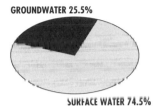

SURFACE WATER 74.5%

WATER DEMAND, 1995

MUNICIPAL 49%

POWER 2%

LIVESTOCK 3%
IRRIGATION 5%
MINING 9.5%
MANUFACTURING 29.5%

WATER DEMAND, 2050

MUNICIPAL 54%

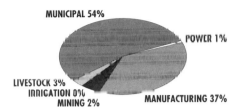

POWER 1%

LIVESTOCK 3%
IRRIGATION 0%
MINING 2%
MANUFACTURING 37%

Counties in region: Bailey, Briscoe, Castro, Cochran, Crosby, Dawson, Deaf Smith, Dickens, Floyd, Gaines, Garza, Hale, Hockley, Lamb, Lubbock, Lynn, Motley, Parmer, Swisher, Terry, Yoakum

Major cities: Corpus Christi
Population, 1995: 524,603
Population, 2050: 918,571

Total water use, 1995: 175,968 Acre-Feet
Total water use, 2050: 299,596 Acre-Feet
Primary rivers: Nueces, Nueces-Rio Grande, San Antonio-Nueces
Major aquifers: Gulf Coast, Carrizo-Wilcox
Annual precipitation: 24–36 inches
Net evaporation: 40–52 inches

Regional Water Planning Area N (South Texas Gulf Coast)

■ Population is expected to grow by 75 percent between 1995 and 2050. Water demand will increase by a similar amount because of municipal and manufacturing demands.

■ The region has insufficient surface water supplies to meet expected demands.

■ Several of the smaller cities in the region will require expensive upgrades of their drinking water systems to meet Safe Drinking Water Act requirements.

■ Corpus Christi will not be able to meet its demands from Lake Corpus and Choke Canyon. The TWDB recommends the construction of conveyance facilities from Lake Texana on the Lavaca River by 2010, and from Garwood Irrigation District in the Colorado Basin by 2040.

REGIONAL WATER PLANNING AREA O (LLANO ESTANCADO): WATER SUPPLY AND DEMAND DISTRIBUTION, 1995–2050

WATER SUPPLY, 1995

GROUNDWATER 98.5%

SURFACE WATER 1.5%

WATER DEMAND, 1995

IRRIGATION 95.5%

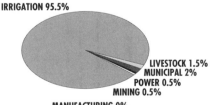

LIVESTOCK 1.5%
MUNICIPAL 2%
POWER 0.5%
MINING 0.5%
MANUFACTURING 0%

WATER DEMAND, 2050

IRRIGATION 93.5%

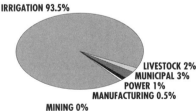

LIVESTOCK 2%
MUNICIPAL 3%
POWER 1%
MANUFACTURING 0.5%
MINING 0%

Counties in region: Bailey, Briscoe, Castro, Cochran, Crosby, Dawson, Deaf Smith, Dickens, Floyd, Gaines, Garza, Hale, Hockley, Lamb, Lubbock, Lynn, Motley, Parmer, Swisher, Terry, Yoakum

Major cities: Lubbock
Population, 1995: 450,111
Population, 2050: 586,156

Total water use, 1995: 4,395,423 Acre-Feet
Total water use, 2050: 3,161,490 Acre-Feet
Primary rivers: Red, Brazos, Colorado
Major aquifers: Ogallala, Seymour
Annual precipitation: 16–24 inches
Net evaporation: 52–64 inches

REGIONAL WATER PLANNING AREA P (LAVACA): WATER SUPPLY AND DEMAND DISTRIBUTION, 1995–2050

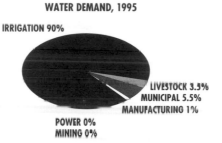

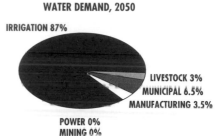

WATER SUPPLY, 1995
GROUNDWATER 90%
SURFACE WATER 10%

WATER DEMAND, 1995
IRRIGATION 90%
LIVESTOCK 3.5%
MUNICIPAL 5.5%
MANUFACTURING 1%
POWER 0%
MINING 0%

WATER DEMAND, 2050
IRRIGATION 87%
LIVESTOCK 3%
MUNICIPAL 6.5%
MANUFACTURING 3.5%
POWER 0%
MINING 0%

Counties in region:	Jackson, Lavaca, Part of Wharton	Total water use, 2050:	92,710 Acre-Feet
Major cities:	None	Primary rivers:	Lavaca
Population, 1995:	34,178	Major aquifers:	Gulf Coast
Population, 2050:	40,733	Annual precipitation:	36–44 inches
Total water use, 1995:	85,734 Acre-Feet	Net evaporation:	28–32 inches

Regional Water Planning Area O (Southern High Plains Region)

■ Population growth in this region will be moderate.

■ This planning area uses more water than any other but will reduce water use by more than a million acre-feet by 2050 because of decreasing groundwater supplies and reduced irrigation demands.

■ The Ogallala Aquifer is a dwindling supply and in the future will not be able to meet irrigation demands at the present level.

■ Groundwater contamination from past oil-field practices, particularly the disposal of oil-field brines into unlined surface pits, has led to high dissolved-solid concentrations.

■ Lubbock relies on nearby groundwater wells and surface water from Lake Meredith on the Canadian River for its municipal and manufacturing demands. Lubbock may need to find additional surface water.

Regional Water Planning Area P (Lavaca River Basin)

■ Saltwater intrusion in the Gulf Coast Aquifer may affect groundwater quality as pumping continues to meet irrigation and municipal needs.

■ Elevated levels of fecal coliform bacteria and nutrients in the lower reaches of the Lavaca River affect water quality and the bays and estuaries.

■ Lake Texana, the only reservoir in the planning area, is slated to provide water to Corpus Christi through a major conveyance system.

■ Flows from the Lavaca River and releases from Lake Texana must be sufficient to maintain inflow needs of Lavaca Bay and associated estuaries.

PAYING FOR THE COST OF FUTURE WATER DEMANDS

Texas currently spends about $1 billion a year on new water treatment, sewage, and drainage facilities.[79] Between 1995 and 2050, the TWDB estimates Texas will need $65 billion in funds for wastewater treatment and water systems, reservoirs, conveyance, pipelines, and flood control. About 50 percent of the total cost needed for water utilities—$32.5 billion—is associated with meeting the provisions of the 1996 amendments to the Federal Safe Drinking Water Act (see Water Quality chapter, Drinking Water section).[80] Only 7.2 percent of the total estimated costs are due to the TWDB's estimated need for new water supply and conveyance systems.

The effort to ensure an adequate supply to meet future demand can involve varying water development strategies. These strategies can be divided roughly into two categories: supply-side alternatives, which rely on increasing the water supply, and

ESTIMATED CAPITAL COSTS OF MAJOR WATER-RELATED PROJECTS IN TEXAS, 1996–2050

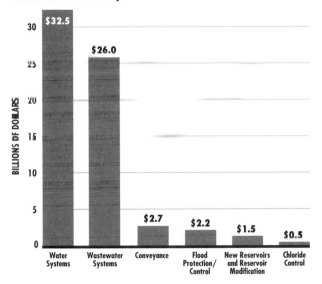

Source: Texas Water Development Board, Water for Texas 1997 (June 1997), Table 3-3.

demand-side alternatives, which focus on reducing demand. Supply-side alternatives include new reservoirs, expanded water re-use, and interbasin transfers. Demand-side strategies include drought management, water transfers from one category of use to another—such as irrigation to municipal— and conservation.

In the past, new reservoirs and other water supply projects were built to meet expected water needs. In 1913 Texas had only 8 major reservoirs, with a capacity of about 359,000 acre-feet, the largest of which was Lake Medina. By 1930 that figure had risen to 32, with more than a million acre-feet of capacity. The damming of rivers and creation of new reservoirs continued, and by 1980 there were 168 reservoirs. Today, there are 191 major reservoirs, covering nearly 1.7 million acres.[81] The construction of reservoirs in Texas has replaced over 600,000 acres of forested wetlands with deep-water aquatic systems.

Past state water plans favored supply-side solutions. The 1969 Texas Water Plan advocated importing water from the Mississippi River to Northeast Texas and moving the water through a series of canals and aqueducts to the Rio Grande Valley and West Texas.

Texas voters rejected a constitutional amendment to provide initial funding for the project, which would have required 67 dams. A similar plan to import water and build 27 new reservoirs also was voted down in 1974.[82] In 1981, Texas Speaker of the House Billy Clayton proposed a Water Trust Fund, which would have set aside one-half of the state's budget surplus for future water projects. "Proposition Four" was defeated by voters. The 1984 water plan also called for the construction of 44 new reservoirs, although the TWDB sought no bonding authority from the legislature for these water projects.

While the TWDB continues to recommend construction of new reservoirs to meet long-term water needs, other supply and demand options also are being considered. The 1997 water plan calls for conservation methods to reduce demand by 2.6 million acre-feet, about 15 percent of total demand; expanding existing local supplies by the use of pipelines, reuse, and return flows; water marketing; and development of eight new surface water reservoirs.[83] The construction of the reservoirs would cause the loss of an additional 52,667 acres of wetlands.[84] In addition to the reservoirs, the plan also includes two projects to divert return flows into off-channel reservoirs, three projects to reallocate currently permitted reservoirs, and 26 major conveyance projects, including 12 that would move water from one river basin to another.

The proposal to build more reservoirs is controversial. Opponents claim it is both environmentally destructive and not the most efficient way to meet demand. They argue, for example, that the construction of reservoirs harms wildlife habitat and destroys wetlands.[85] Reservoir construction also penalizes downstream users because run-of-the-river flows are reduced, impacting water use. Also, wastewater discharges must meet more stringent permit standards when there is less water in the rivers to dilute the discharge. While reservoir proponents recognize the need to mitigate environmental damage, they believe that some reservoirs are needed to meet the demands of a growing population. Both sides agree, however, that other water development strategies are needed, given the scarcity of resources and the increasing regulations to protect the environment. In essence, water resource planners are calling for a shift from water development of new supplies to water management of existing supplies.

ALTERNATIVE WATER DEVELOPMENT STRATEGIES

What are the alternatives to traditional supply-side water development projects like reservoirs and conveyance systems?[86]

Demand-based Strategies

■ *Water conservation.* Conserving water by consuming less, wasting less, or reusing some water helps reduce current costs, preserves future supplies, and postpones or eliminates the need for expensive new developments. A modest conservation program that reduces municipal water demand by 15 percent would save $25 billion over the next 50 years.[87] SB 1 requires all major water rights holders to adopt water conservation plans.

■ *Waste prevention.* By state law, when water is not applied to a specific beneficial use as specified in water rights permits, it is a violation of the right to use the water. Waste is not a beneficial use. Ensuring that faulty sprinkler heads, broken or leaky pipes, or the overapplication of irrigation water does not result in waste could be a part of the state's permitting process or, alternatively, could be encouraged through various incentives.

■ *Cancellation of water rights.* Water rights that are not being used, or not being used in a "beneficial" way, can be cancelled by the state and set aside for environmental use or for future demand. For example, a city that had set aside large amounts of water based upon future growth might have that right cancelled based upon its "wasteful" non-use of water. It is difficult to estimate how much water is available through the cancellation of water rights, since it has never been done in Texas. SB 1 requires the TNRCC to look at water availability as a result of cancellation of underused water rights. Inevitably, cancellation would likely be a time-consuming and costly process.

■ *Water transactions and banking.* Water rights can be traded, sold, or leased in Texas, though the state imposes limits on the free transfer and marketing of these rights. In 1993 the legislature charged the TWDB with creating a "Water Bank" to facilitate the transfer of water between water rights holders. Water rights holders may "deposit" water rights into the bank. The TWDB can then help negotiate prices between the purchaser and the depositor; maintain a clearinghouse of depositors and those needing supplies; encourage water rights holders to implement water conservation practices by depositing the conserved water in the bank; and sell, buy, and hold water rights itself. The 1997 Water Bill expanded the concept of water marketing by increasing the amount of a water right that could be deposited in the water bank from 50 to 100 percent. Any unused water right deposited is not subject to cancellation. SB 1 also established a separate Texas Water Trust where unused water rights could be dedicated to maintaining in-stream flow for wildlife and habitat (see Water and Environmental Use section, above).

Nontraditional Supply Strategies

■ *Conjunctive use of groundwater and surface water.* One conjunctive use alternative involves injecting excess surface water into an aquifer for storage and subsequently withdrawing it during times of insufficient surface flows. The City of El Paso is currently injecting up to 10,000 acre-feet of highly treated effluent per year into the Hueco-Mesilla Bolson Aquifer for use in times of drought. The recharging of water prevents loss through evaporation and also avoids the environmental impacts associated with the construction of surface reservoirs. However, in some situations, it may not be desirable because it reduces wastewater return flows to rivers or streams.

■ *Interbasin transfer.* Water rights may be transferred from one river basin to another to help areas with high demand meet their supply needs, providing certain conditions ensuring no detriment to the river basin of origin occurs.

■ **Desalination.** Desalination is the treatment of seawater or brackish groundwater by desalting the water and making it into fresh water. In 1992 there were 89 desalting plants in Texas, mainly for industrial use.[88] Desalting of salt water is one recommended solution to meet the needs of coastal cities like Corpus Christi, while cities in the Lower Rio Grande Valley are considering desalting saline groundwater for industrial and municipal uses. However, desalting water is very expensive.

■ **Weather modification.** The modern science of weather modification—also known as cloud seeding or precipitation enhancement—began in 1946 when scientists working at the General Electric Laboratory in upstate New York discovered that silver iodide could be used—possibly—to augment natural rainfall by helping spur crystal formation in clouds. In Texas in the 1970s, dozens of experiments were held in the High Plains, Corpus Christi, Edwards Aquifer, and West Central Texas areas to see if damage from hail could be reduced and rain increased.[89] The Colorado River Municipal Water District has for years used weather modification to attempt to increase water supplies and to increase rainfall on cotton farms. Proponents of cloud seeding believe that it has increased rainfall and lake levels in West Texas. Opponents, however, believe that cloud seeding is, at best, an unmeasurable science that simply shifts rainfall from one local area to another and, at worst, is akin to ancient rain dances. The 1997 Water Bill recognizes cloud seeding as a fundable water management strategy for irrigators and cities.

NOTES

1. Texas Water Development Board (TWDB), "Conservation Storage Data for Selected Major Texas Reservoirs," *Water Conditions*, September 1997. The Amistad and Falcon reservoirs along the U.S.-Mexico border were particularly hard hit by the drought, measuring in at 42 percent and 11 percent of total storage capacity, respectively, in August 1996. In 1999, the Rio Grande was entering its sixth consecutive year of drought conditions.

2. TWDB, "Ground Water Levels in Observation Wells," *Water Conditions*, August 1996.

3. Texas Natural Resource Conservation Commission (TNRCC), *Learning from the Drought* (February 1997), 1.

4. TWDB, "The Drought in Perspective, 1996–1998," *Water Conditions*, March 1999, 1.

5. TWDB, "Conservation Storage Data for Selected Major Texas Reservoirs." However, drought conditions returned in 1998 for most areas.

6. TWDB, *Texas Water Facts* (1991), 3.

7. Texas Water Commission (TWC), *State of Texas Water Quality Inventory*, 11th ed. (1992), 8.

8. TNRCC, *The State of Texas Water Quality Inventory—1996*, 13th ed. (1996), Waters of the State Table.

9. Texas Comptroller of Public Accounts (TCPA), *Forces of Change: Shaping the Future of Texas*, vol. 2, pt. 1 (November 1993), 413.

10. TWDB, *Water for Texas 1990: Today and Tomorrow* (1990), 1-4.

11. TWDB, *Water for Texas 1990*, I-4.

12. TWC, Groundwater Protection Committee, *Texas Groundwater Protection Strategy* (January 1989), 10.

13. TWDB, "County Summary Historical Water Use" (1998).

14. It is important to differentiate between water withdrawals and water consumed. For example, the thermo-electric power generation sector withdraws about 40 to 45 percent of all water in Texas, but consumes only between 2 and 3 percent, since most is returned as streamflow. World Resources Institute, *The 1994 Information Please Environmental Almanac* (Boston, Mass: Houghton Mifflin, 1994), p. 272.

15. Ronald Kaiser, *Handbook of Texas Water Law: Problems and Needs* (College Station: Texas A&M University, 1987), 18–19.

16. TWC, *Reallocating Surface Waters in Texas: Facilitating the Development of Water Markets While Protecting the Public Interest* (1992), 2.

17. TCPA, *Forces of Change*, vol. 2, pt. 1, 414.

18. TCPA, *Forces of Change*, vol. 2, pt. 1, 415.

19. The TNRCC has been attempting to hold public hearings to adjudicate the Upper Rio Grande water rights, but a lawsuit by the Bureau of Reclamation over ownership of the water rights in the reservoirs in New Mexico has held up the adjudication process.

20. While there are 6,198 individual water rights, there are many with multiple purposes of use, giving a total of 6,740 water rights. TNRCC, "Water Rights Database," electronic file sent to author, July 1998, Austin.

21. TNRCC, "Water Rights Database."

22. TNRCC "Water Rights Database."

23. TWDB, *Water for Texas 1990*, 1-8.

24. Mike Personett, TWDB, "Evolution of State Water Conservation Policy in Texas" (Paper presented at Conserve 93, Las Vegas, December 1993), 5.

25. TWDB, *Water for Texas Today and Tomorrow* (June 1997), 2-29.

26. TWDB, *Water for Texas 1997*, 2-29.

27. William Goldfarb, *Water Law* (Stoneham, Mass: Butterworth, 1984).

28. TCPA, "Watershed Legislation: Texas Enacts First Statewide Water Management Plan," *Fiscal Notes*, September 1997, 8.

29. *Houston & TC Railway v. East* 98 Tex 146, 81 SW 279 (1904). This 1904 court case established that groundwater was equivalent to a property right. In 1999, in a case brought against Ozarka Spring Water Co., the Supreme Court of Texas again upheld the right of capture which allowed the water bottle company to continue to pump groundwater even though it drained local landowners' wells. "Cattle raisers welcome Supreme Court rule of capture decision," *The Big Bend Sentinel* (May 13, 1999), 9.

30. Ernest Smerdon, et. al., *State Water Policies: A Study of Six States* (New York: Praeger, 1988).

31. TWDB, *Water for Texas 1990*, 1-1.

32. See TNRCC, *The State of Texas Water Quality Inventory—1996*, 13th ed.

33. Personett , TWDB, "Evolution of State Water Conservation Policy in Texas," 1.

34. TWDB, *Water For Texas 1997*, 3-3.

35. TWDB, "County Summary Historical Water Use."

36. TWDB, Planning Division, "1995 Groundwater Pumpage Summary by Major Aquifers" (1997).

37. TWDB, "County Summary Historical Water Use."

38. TWDB, "County Summary Historical Water Use."

39. TWDB, *Water for Texas 1997*, 3-3.

40. Personett, TWDB, "Evolution of State Water Conservation Policy in Texas."

41. Personett, TWDB, "Evolution of State Water Conservation Policy in Texas."

42. TWDB, *Surveys of Irrigation in Texas* (January 1996), 6.

43. TWDB, *1996 Consensus Texas Water Plan: Water Use Projections for Irrigation for State and Counties* (1997),

44. For example, between 1974 and 1994, cotton irrigated acres increased from 707,955 to 1,070,209 acres, pecans from 16,588 to 62,177 acres, and sugarcane from 36,748 to 50,121 acres. From TWDB, *Surveys of Irrigation in Texas*, 53.

45. For planning purposes and projecting water demand, the "dry" year use average—whenever in the past 10 years the most water was used, usually in the driest year—is used, not whatever the latest year's average is. For example, while Houston's average gallons per capita per day (GPCD) in 1993 was 159, for water supply purposes the dry year figure of 189 GPCD—which occurred during 1986—is used as a base, and then adjusted for conservation.

46. TWDB, "County Summary Historical Water Use."

47. Personett, TWDB. "Evolution of State Water Conservation Policy in Texas," 9.

48. Robert A. Collinge, "Let Market-Clearing Prices Prevent Urban Water Crisis." Paper presented at Headwater to Economic Growth: Market Solutions to Water Allocation in Texas, Federal Reserve Bank of Dallas, San Antonio, August 22, 1997. Collinge suggests two methods to introduce market-clearing prices to public utilities. One is through the distribution of an equal number of discount coupons that water customers can apply to their bills up to a certain amount of water. A customer who needs to use more water would simply "purchase" additional coupons. The utility would set the maximum number of coupons each month depending on water supply. Another method would set a baseline usage for each type of user, and then reward water frugal customers with rebates and charge water wasters with fees. The fees and rebates would cancel one another out.

49. TWDB, *Water for Texas 1992: Today and Tomorrow* (1992), 10-11.

50. TWDB, *Water for Texas, 1990*, 2-8.

51. TWDB, *Water for Texas 1990*, 2-8.

52. TWDB, *Water For Texas 1990*, 2-9.

53. Ric Jensen, "Indoor Water Conservation: Toilets, Shower Heads, Washing Machines and Faucets Can All Use Less Water," *Texas Water Resources* (College Station) 17, no. 4 (winter 1992), 1.

54. TWDB, Population and Water Use Web page (http://www.twdb.state.tx.us/www/twdb/popwuse.html), June 1997.

55. Jensen, "Indoor Water Conservation," 1.

56. Jensen, "Indoor Water Conservation," 1.

57. TWDB, *A Homeowner's Guide to Water Use and Water Conservation*, 3.

58. TWDB, "County Summary Historical Water Use."

59. TWDB, "Summary Manufacturing Water Use 1995" (1997).

60. TWDB, *Texas Water Facts*, 9.

61. TWDB, "Summary Manufacturing Water Use 1995."

62. Pequod Associates, Inc., *Texas Industrial Water Usage Survey* (Pequod Associates, Austin, August 1993). This special survey conducted for the TWDB found that semiconductors had reduced their water use by 33 percent over the past few years.

63. *1994–1995 Texas Almanac* (Dallas: Dallas Morning News, 1993), 118.

64. TPWD, "Environmental Target Flows," Web page (http://www.tpwd.state.tx.us/conserve/sb2/enviro/enviro.htm), April 1999.

65. TWDB, *Water for Texas 1997*, 2-24.

66. Kevin Mayes, TPWD, phone interview with author, August 1994, Austin.

67. Mike Personett, TWDB, "Evolution of State Water Conservation Policy in Texas" (Las Vegas: Paper presented at Conserve 93, December 1993), 5.

68. TWDB, *Water for Texas 1997*, 3-3, and *Water for Texas 1990*, 3-3.

69. TWDB, *Water For Texas 1997*, 3-3.

70. TWDB, "Projections of Population and Water Use" (1997).

71. Jan Gersten, "Rainwater Harvesting: A New Water Source," *Water Savers* 3, no. 2.

72. TWDB and Center for Maximum Potential Building Systems, *Texas Guide to Rainwater Harvesting*, 2d ed. (Austin: TWDB, 1997), 2.

73. TWDB, *Water For Texas 1997*, 3-4.

74. TWDB, *Water for Texas 1997*, 3-93.

75. Janice Bezanson, Texas Committee on Natural Resources, interview by author, April 1994, Austin.

76. "Water Thrifty Landscapes: Low Maintenance, Attractive and Easy on the Environment," *Water Savers* 3, no. 3.

77. Information for this section is from TWDB, *Water for Texas 1997*; TWDB, "County Summary Historical Water Use"; TNRCC, *The State of Texas Water Quality Inventory—1996*, 13th ed.

78. TNRCC, *Water Quality Assessment of the Rio Grande* (1996), Appendix B.

79. TWDB, *Texas Water Facts*, 12.

80. TWDB, *Water for Texas 1997*, 3-33.

81. *1994–1995 Texas Almanac*, 84.

82. TCPA, *Forces of Change 2*, no. 1: 415.

83. TWDB, *Water for Texas 1997*, 3-26–3-29.

84. TWDB, *Water for Texas 1997*, 3-20.

85. All proposed reservoirs must undergo a federal permitting process to protect wetlands and environmental habitats.

86. This section is based on information from various sources, including: TWDB, *Texas Water Facts*; TWDB, *Water for Texas, 1992*; and Mark Jordan, Director, Water Policy Division, TNRCC, October, 1993, "Alternative Water Development Strategies," TNRCC internal memo.

87. TWDB, *Texas Water Facts*, 13.

88. TWDB, *Desalination in Texas: A Status Report* (1992).

89. Ric Jensen, "Does Weather Modification Really Work?" *Texas Water Resources* (College Station) 20, no. 2 (summer 1995).

NAFTA and the Texas/ Mexico Border Environment

The North American Free Trade Agreement (NAFTA) was signed in December 1992 and approved by the U.S. Congress in the fall of 1993.[1] The agreement, which strengthens trade relationships between the United States, Mexico, and Canada, was the culmination of more than three years of sometimes difficult negotiations between the three countries. Part of the public debate surrounding NAFTA centered on the environment, especially the implications of increased U.S.-Mexico economic integration for the border environment and public health. In an attempt to address these concerns, NAFTA was accompanied by environmental "side agreements." These agreements set up new binational and trinational agencies to deal with some of the environmental issues. One agreement created the trinational Commission for Environmental Cooperation (CEC), based in Montreal. The other—an agreement between the United States and Mexico—created the Border Environment Cooperation Commission (BECC) and the North American Development Bank (NADBank). In addition, both the U.S. Environmental Protection Agency (EPA) and the Texas Natural Resource Conservation Commission (TNRCC) have strengthened their border-related operations.

BORDER ISSUES:
AN HISTORICAL OVERVIEW
In 1965 Mexico initiated the Border Industrialization Program, widely known now as the maquiladora program. Under this program, foreign companies (primarily from the United States and Asia) can construct factories in Mexico and import parts and materials to those factories duty-free. Final products from the factories can then be exported back out of Mexico, with a duty paid only on the "value-added" during manufacturing or assembly.

Some maquiladoras were established during the 1970s, but the number of plants greatly increased after the 1982 devaluation of the Mexican currency,

the peso. By 1991 there were almost 700 maquiladoras located in the Mexican border cities along the Rio Grande.

While the maquiladora program achieved its purpose of providing jobs for Mexican workers, it also attracted a growing population to the border. As a developing country, Mexico was not fully equipped to cope with the environmental or public and worker health implications of the rapid industrial development at its northern border—an area far-removed from the center of regulatory authority in Mexico City.

The effects of the maquiladora industry on the border drew increased attention during the NAFTA debate. Attention was focused on several issues,[2] including:

■ The lack of wastewater treatment and drinking-water systems for Mexican border cities and for unincorporated subdivision, or colonia, developments on the Texas side of the border (see *Water Quality* chapter for a discussion of Texas colonia issues);

■ Problems in tracking and accounting for hazardous waste generated at maquiladora plants;

■ Concerns about industrial air and water pollution associated with maquiladora plants and other border industry; and

■ Concerns about whether worker health protections were being adequately implemented, especially in assembly plants with high solvent usage.

RECENT DEVELOPMENTS
Population and Maquiladoras Continue Increasing
Both the population and maquiladora employment along the Texas-Mexico border continue increasing at a rapid pace. The 1994 devaluation of the peso resulted in wage rates below a dollar an hour in many border cities, which resulted in lower labor costs for the industry. There have been increases in employment and the number of maquiladora plants since then.

POPULATION INCREASES IN TEXAS-MEXICO BORDER AREA

TEXAS COUNTY	1995 EST.	1990–1995 % CHANGE	1980–1990 % CHANGE
Brewster	9318	7.34	14.63
Cameron	300,385	15.48	24.03
El Paso	661,864	11.88	23.28
Hidalgo	476,235	24.17	35.42
Hudspeth	3,282	12.59	6.85
Jeff Davis	2,105	8.17	18.15
Kinney	3,291	5.51	36.86
Maverick	43,572	19.78	15.86
Presidio	7,291	9.85	27.93
Starr	48,068	18.63	48.60
Terrell	1,314	-6.81	-11.60
Val Verde	42,962	10.95	7.83
Webb	171,574	28.77	34.24
Willacy	19,344	9.26	1.20
Zapata	10,388	8.17	18.15

Source: Md. Nazrul Hoque & Steve H. Murdock, Texas Population Growth at Mid-Decade (College Station, Texas A&M Department of Rural Sociology, 1996), Appendix Table 1.

MEXICO BORDER CITY	1995 EST.	1990–95 % CHANGE	1980–1990 % CHANGE
Cd. Juarez	1,101,000	18.8	50
Cd. Acuna	81,600	43.7	35.2
Piedras Negras	116,000	18.1	22.3
Nuevo Laredo	275,000	25.0	8.4
Reynosa	337,000	19.1	32.9
Matamoros	363,000	19.8	26.8

Source: Environmental Protection Agency, US-Mexico Border XXI Program: Framework Document (Washington, D.C., October 1997), VI.1, VII.1, VIII.1.

The CEC

The three new institutions set up by the NAFTA environmental side agreements are all fully operational. The CEC, headed by the environmental ministers of the United States, Mexico, and Canada, had a $9.94 million annual budget for FY 1997, including a $1.6 million fund for small grants to nongovernmental organizations in North America.[3] Most of the CEC's projects, directed and implemented by the secretariat of the CEC, assess various North American environmental issues; develop better cooperation on various issues among the three countries; and develop consensus plans addressing particular discrete problems, such as reducing the use

INCREASE IN MAQUILADORAS IN MEXICO-TEXAS BORDER CITIES (1991–1999)

CITY	# PLANTS (1991)	EMPLOYEES (1991)	# PLANTS (1999)	EMPLOYEES (1999)
Cd. Juárez	250	116,989	254	216,435
Cd. Acuña	44	14,261	53	27,067
Piedras Negras	43	7,182	45	11,966
Nuevo Laredo	60	16,862	54	21,156
Reynosa	73	27,858	103	55,268
Matamoros	91	36,210	117	56,225
TOTAL	561	219,362	626	388,117

Note: Number of plants and employees are as reported in January 1991 and January 1999.

Sources: Instituto Nacional de Estadística, Geografía e Informatica (INEGI), Federal Government of Mexico, Estadísticas de la Industria Maquiladora de Exportación (Aguascalientes, Mexico, 1999).

of various hazardous chemicals or preserving certain migratory species habitats.

The most relevant CEC-initiated project for the Texas-Mexico border is the attempt to reach an agreement on transboundary environmental impact assessment procedures. The NAFTA environmental side agreement stated that the CEC should develop such procedures within three years (or by 1996). As of early 1999, the three countries were still negotiating the details of the procedures, although the CEC secretariat did produce a series of recommendations.[4]

Updates on the CEC work and links to useful North American environmental Web sites can be found at its Web page: http://www.cec.org.

The BECC and NADBank

The BECC and NADBank developed more slowly than the CEC, due primarily to a delay in appointing members of the binational governing board of directors for the BECC. Once operational, the BECC developed comprehensive criteria for entities seeking certification for water supply, wastewater treatment, or municipal solid-waste infrastructure projects.[5] BECC certification is a necessary precursor to eligibility for financing from NADBank. The criteria emphasize technical and financial viability, public participation, and sustainable development.

As of mid-1999, the BECC had certified 27 border

NEW NAFTA-RELATED INSTITUTIONS FOR ENVIRONMENTAL ISSUES

**BORDER ENVIRONMENT
COOPERATION COMMISSION (BECC)**

BOARD OF DIRECTORS ⟷ **PUBLIC ADVISORY COMMITTEE**
5 members from U.S. and   9 members from each country
5 from Mexico

BECC
General Manager and Staff

BECC certifies Border projects to
NADBank for funding decision

**NORTH AMERICAN DEVELOPMENT
BANK (NADBank)**

BOARD OF DIRECTORS ⟶ **STAFF**
3 government officials from
U.S. and 3 from Mexico

**NORTH AMERICAN COMMISSION FOR
ENVIRONMENTAL COOPERATION**

**JOINT PUBLIC
ADVISORY COMMITTEE** ⟶ **COUNCIL**
5 citizens from each country   Environment Ministers of U.S.,
Canada and Mexico

SECRETARIAT
Legal and technical staff

---

infrastructure projects—including eight on the Texas border and four along Mexico's border with Texas.[6] The most significant project is the proposed construction of two new sewage treatment plants for Ciudad Juárez. While these plants will initially provide only primary treatment—as opposed to the secondary treatment plants that are more common in most U.S. cities—even basic treatment for the estimated 60 millions of gallons per day of sewage generated by Juárez homes and businesses should benefit water quality in the Upper Rio Grande.[7]

Of the 27 projects certified by the BECC, six had been approved by NADBank for loans as of October 1998.[8] In addition, NADBank is now managing $170 million of EPA grant money for water and wastewater projects, as well as the $450 million paid-in capital and $2.55 billion in "callable" capital it has available for loans. In fact, nine projects had received grants through the EPA funds as of October 1998.[9] In early 1998, NADBank announced that the Juárez project would receive $11 million in EPA grants—almost one-third of the total project cost. The remainder of the project will be funded through a combination of grants from the Mexican federal government, a possible NADBank loan to the local government, and some funds from the private firm with the contract to construct the plants.[10] The availability of the grant funds is likely to make many more projects financially viable than if the bank

were, as originally conceived, limited to loans, credit guarantees, or credit enhancements.

Both the BECC and NADBank established grant programs that provide assistance to local governments needing help in developing the technical aspects of proposed projects or needing to upgrade or modernize their water and wastewater utility operations.[11]

FYI *Current information on the status of BECC and NADBank projects can be found on the institutions' respective Web sites: http://www.cocef.org and http://www.nadbank.org.*

Border Activities of the EPA and the TNRCC
Since 1991 both the EPA and the TNRCC have increased their level of effort with respect to border problems. Following up on the 1992 Border Plan, the EPA and the Mexican federal environmental agency, SEMARNAP, issued an updated plan to guide the efforts of the U.S. and Mexican federal governments on border environmental issues over the next few years. Known as Border XXI, the plan includes an inventory of existing and planned projects in the areas of water quality, air quality, waste management, public health, protection of natural resources, and enforcement and other binational cooperation.[12] In 1997 the EPA's total budget for border-related activities was about $25 million, exclusive of infrastructure grant funds.

FYI ☞ *Detailed information on EPA and other federal activity agencies can be found in the project compendium, available at http://www.epa.gov/ usmexicoborder. Also, university research projects supported with EPA grant money and carried out through the Southwest Center for Environmental Research and Policy can be found at http://www.civil. utah.edu/scerp/project_index.*

The TNRCC Border Affairs Office was established in 1993, and through this office the agency has also increased its border-related activities and has strengthened its relationships with state-level environmental agencies in the four states of northeastern Mexico that border Texas.[13] TNRCC activities with neighboring states have included some limited joint air quality monitoring; training of inspectors; training in wastewater operations; and exchange of information on pollution prevention techniques, with a particular focus on the type of processes most often used in maquiladora plants.

NOTES

1. This focus piece provides only a brief overview of the institutional developments regarding border environmental issues, as well as some data on trends in population and maquiladora growth. More detail on border water, air, and land issues are found in the respective chapters.

2. EPA, *Integrated Environmental Protection Plan for the Mexican-U.S. Border Area (1992-1994)* (Washington, D.C., February 1992), chapter 3 (hereinafter cited as 1992 Border Plan).

3. Commission for Environmental Cooperation, *1996 Annual Report* (Montreal, Canada), 62–68.

4. The experts' recommendations can be found at http://www.cec.org/english/resources/publications.

5. The criteria were revised in 1996. The currently applicable criteria can be found in BECC, *Project Certification Criteria,* (Cd. Juárez, Mexico, Nov. 9, 1996).

6. Border Environment Cooperative Commission, "BECC Board Certifies Heber, California, Wastewater Project," (March 31, 1999 Press Release).

7. International Boundary and Water Commission, et al., *Binational Study Regarding the Presence of Toxic Substances in the Rio Grande/Rio Bravo and Its Tributaries along the Boundary Portion between the United States and Mexico* (1994).

8. NADBank, "Status of Bank Projects," *NADBANK News,* Vol 11, no. 23 (October 23, 1998).

9. NADBank, *1996 Annual Report* (San Antonio, 1997), 9, 18–20.

10. NADBank, "NADBank Recommends $37 Million in Funding for Water and Wastewater Facilities," (January 22, 1998 Press Release).

11. NADBank, *1996 Annual Report*, 16–17; BECC, *Current Status Report,* (Cd. Juárez, Mexico, December 1997).

12. EPA, *US-Mexico Border XXI Program: Framework Document,* (Washington, D.C., October 1996), and *US-Mexico Border XXI Program: 1996 Implementation Plans,* (Washington, D.C., October 1996).

13. For detailed information on TNRCC border-related activities see http://www.tnrcc.state.tx.us/exec/ba/ba1.html.

CHAPTER 2

Water Quality

"Man is a complex animal; he makes deserts bloom and lakes die."
Gil Stern

INTRODUCTION

The competing demands made on water have affected not only its supply and future availability, but also its quality. In some watersheds, diversion and damming of rivers have reduced streamflow, which has concentrated pollutants in a smaller volume of water and thereby degraded overall surface water quality. Some Texas rivers are kept from drying up entirely only by the return flow of wastewater, which, even when optimally treated, is of lower quality than the river's original water.

Underground water quality has likewise suffered the effects of high demand. Continual mining of aquifers has lowered the quality of groundwater by drawing salt water that lies deep in most aquifers into the upper layers from which water for human consumption is drawn.

Mitigating the effects of high demand on the

LAND USE EFFECTS ON THE HYDROLOGICAL CYCLE

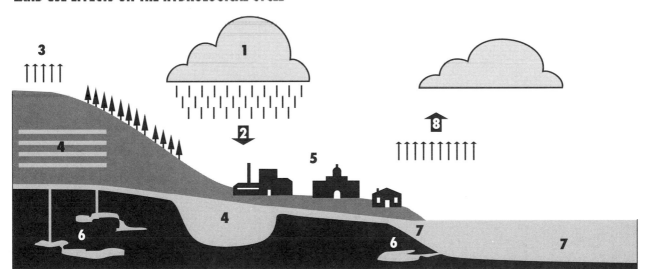

1. Water vapor mixes with gas and dust clouds.
2. Vapor condenses to form rain or snow.
3. Evaporation increases the concentration of minerals in water left on earth.
4. Water quality of lakes changes due to physical, chemical, and biological processes. The quality of surface water is modified by contact with soil and air. Irrigation increases the concentration of salts in the water. Surface water quality is further modified by chemical reaction among salts, sediments, and biological materials in the water.
5. Cities and factories add chemical and organic pollutants to the water.
6. Groundwater is modified chemically and physically by minerals and gases dissolved from rocks. There is also mixing along the salt and fresh water (groundwater) interface.
7. Salt water from the ocean mixes with fresh water from rivers (surface water). Water quality in the ocean is also altered by physical, chemical, and biological processes.
8. Dust and spray are picked up by air movement from land and/or water surfaces and introduced into the atmosphere.

Source: H.A. Swanson and H.L. Baldwin, A Primer on Water Quality (Washington, D.C.: U.S. Geological Survey, 1965).

quality of both surface water and groundwater will require a long-term commitment to conservation and limits on development. Representing a more acute risk to water quality, though, is contamination that results from such human activities as industry, agriculture, and urban life. Water moves in a continuous hydrological cycle from earth to atmosphere and back. This means that all bodies of water—rivers, lakes, oceans, and aquifers—are essentially connected to each other, making it possible for many sources of contamination to enter and move through the system.

In Texas, human activity has affected water quality in all 15 river basins, in the eight coastal basins where rivers drain into the Gulf of Mexico, and in all major aquifers, including some that are sources of drinking water. This chapter examines four aspects of water quality:
- surface water quality,
- groundwater quality,
- drinking water quality, and
- water quality in coastal areas.

HISTORY OF FEDERAL LEGISLATION
For more than 100 years, the federal government has been passing laws to provide funding and oversight for the development of dams, reservoirs, and canals. Not until the 1940s and 1950s, however, did Congress begin to address water pollution legislatively. And initial efforts in this area, like the Federal Water Pollution Control Act of 1948, did not address pollution prevention plans or the development of water quality standards. Instead they focused on funding water treatment plants, identifying polluted bodies of water, and locating the polluters for legal action. Unfortunately, the strategy of determining which polluter caused which pollution was expensive and often unsuccessful.[1]

Comprehensive legislation to protect water quality did not occur until the 1960s. Rachel Carson's 1962 bestseller *Silent Spring*, bolstered by articles and scientific reports detailing pollution problems, provided the impetus for the nation's first water quality legislation.[2] During the early 1960s, the National Wildlife Federation, the Izaak Walton League, and the National Audubon Society campaigned for strong federal water quality bills.

One result was the 1965 Water Quality Act, which established the Water Pollution Control Administration within the Department of the Interior. With the creation of this new federal agency, water quality was for the first time treated as an environmental concern, apart from the more traditional public health concern. The 1965 law was soon followed by the 1966 Clean Water Act, which provided construction grants for wastewater treatment facilities.

The Wild and Scenic Rivers Act of 1968, administered by the Department of the Interior, attempted to preserve waters with outstanding scenic, recreational, or habitat value by placing them on a Secretary of Interior-approved list. To a limited degree, the law protects these listed "wild and scenic rivers" from water projects and from additional discharges. It prohibits the development of public or private hydroelectric power plants on these rivers and restrains certain other types of development. In Texas, only the Rio Grande has been designated as a wild and scenic river, and this designation has not protected the river from degradation. In fact, in 1993, American Rivers, a nonprofit watchdog organization, named the Rio Grande the most endangered river in the United States.[3]

The Clean Water Act of 1972 forms the basis today for water quality protection for surface water in streams, rivers, and lakes as well as for groundwater. It was enacted as a series of amendments to the Federal Water Pollution Control Act of 1948, a law spurred by public concern over epidemics of disease caused by waterborne bacteria. The 1972 Act was prompted by the worsening state of U.S. rivers and by several high-profile oil spills, including the Santa Barbara channel spill, in which 250 million gallons of crude oil escaped to damage miles of California coastline.[4]

The Clean Water Act set water quality standards for major rivers and lakes and required discharge permits for both public and private facilities. The act was strengthened in 1977 in an effort to address the most visible causes of water pollution. It explicitly prohibited the discharge into waterways of

MONITORING WATER QUALITY

In 1992, and again in 1994, the river authorities for all 15 inland rivers and 8 coastal basins where the rivers flow into the Gulf of Mexico identified the lack of monitoring of surface water as the single biggest pollution issue facing their river basins.[5] In 1996 under the administration of the Texas Natural Resource Conservation Commission (TNRCC) and as required by the federal Clean Water Act, the state conducted approximately 1,700 samples at 446 fixed monitoring stations.[6] While the number of samples has been stable since 1991, the number of stations has declined by nearly 25 percent since 1994.[7] Most sites are sampled quarterly. However, these sites included only about one in three miles of continually flowing, or "perennial," streams and rivers. Thus, almost nothing is known about the quality of 25,000 out of 40,000 miles of the state's permanent rivers and streams. Also unexamined is the water quality in some 145,000 miles of "intermittent" streams, which flow only during periods of high rainfall.

In 1996 the TNRCC monitored water quality in only 43 of an estimated 6,700 lakes and reservoirs.[8] Though these reservoirs represent more than 50 percent of the total acres stored in the state's lakes and reservoirs, the sampling protocol nevertheless leaves almost 6,600 smaller bodies of water virtually unmonitored, including 160 reservoirs with over 5,000 acre-feet of water.[9] Presently the TNRCC does not have a wetlands monitoring program, although bays and estuaries with wetland characteristics are monitored.[10]

Most of the water quality sampling is concentrated on monitoring physiochemical parameters, such as dissolved oxygen content, pH, streamflow, temperature, fecal coliform levels, total dissolved solids, sulfate, and chloride. Much less is known about toxics. In 1996, 92 of the fixed stations monitored water and 106 stations monitored sediments for heavy metals, while 25 stations monitored water and 67 stations monitored sediment for organics, including pesticides.[11] Finally, 49 stations also

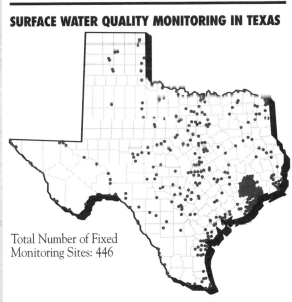

SURFACE WATER QUALITY MONITORING IN TEXAS

Total Number of Fixed Monitoring Sites: 446

Source: Texas Natural Resource Conservation Commission, The State of Texas Water Quality Inventory — 1996, 13th ed. (1996), 28.

monitored fish and macrobenthos to assess biological health. In addition, under a joint program with the EPA, 31 sites are monitored for sediment and water ambient toxicity, to assess the effects on organisms.

Even less information is available on the quality of groundwater. In 1990 the Texas Water Development Board (TWDB) began a program to monitor the state's aquifers every six years. In 1996 the TNRCC began analyzing groundwater monitoring data—mainly from the TWDB—on certain aquifers. Nevertheless, the monitoring does not include many human contaminants like pesticides or volatile organic compounds (VOCs). Limited monitoring for these substances is done around certain potential contamination sources, such as hazardous waste sites and uranium mines. Otherwise, periodic studies of water wells by the TWDB, the Texas Department of Agriculture, and some local groundwater conservation districts are the only source of information on groundwater quality.

hazardous substances, including industrial waste, sewage, accidental spills, toxics, and other point sources. (The term point sources refers to sources of pollution that discharge directly from a discrete location, or point, into a water body. Non-point-source pollution refers to pollution that cannot be identified as coming from one discrete location.) The act also further protected wetlands by requiring the U.S. Army Corps of Engineers to issue permits, known as Section 404 permits, for all dredging and filling projects.

Between 1972, when the first Clean Water Act was passed, and 1990, about $260 billion in private and public funds was spent on wastewater treatment facilities. Another $20 billion, most of it from the public sector, was spent to comply with federal requirements on drinking water quality.[12]

The 1987 amendments to the Water Quality Act were the first concerted effort by the federal government to address pollution from non-point sources, including agricultural fields and feedlots, urban streets, and runoff channeled through municipal storm-water systems. The law required states to develop a non-point-source management plan. However, states are not required to go beyond voluntary programs. The 1987 act also created and funded several special programs, including one to deal with toxic hot spots and one to protect estuaries of national importance.

In 1994 and 1995, the U.S. Congress debated making major changes in the scope of the Clean Water Act, giving industries and cities much greater flexibility in meeting clean water standards. However, national and state environmental groups voiced opposition and these changes were defeated.

Early in the twentieth century, contamination of the water supply and outbreaks of disease led to questions about how we purify our water and how we protect our drinking water supplies. The Public Health Service Act of 1912 set guidelines for allowable levels of contaminants related to communicable diseases like typhoid. The federal Safe Drinking Water Act of 1974 created national drinking water standards to limit a range of substances that can adversely affect human health. These maximum-

contaminant levels set by the Environmental Protection Agency (EPA) are based on the health effects of a single contaminant. They do not consider the cumulative impact of a combination of contaminants on human health, because little is known about possible synergistic effects.[13]

The 1986 amendments to the Safe Drinking Water Act accelerated the EPA's schedule for bringing contaminants under regulation and expanded the number of contaminants covered. It also banned all future use of lead pipes and lead solder in public drinking water systems, increased fines and enforcement, and mandated greater protection of drinking water obtained from groundwater through the establishment of a well-head protection program.[14]

In 1993 the largest outbreak of waterborne disease in modern U.S. history occurred in Milwaukee, Wisconsin, when the pathogen cryptosporidium infiltrated the water supply system following heavy rains. Over 4,000 people were hospitalized with the gastrointestinal disease cryptosporidiosis, and more than 50 deaths were attributed to the outbreak.[15]

In 1996 Congress passed additional amendments to the Safe Drinking Water Act. These amendments provide an increased emphasis on protecting local sources of drinking water by requiring a source water assessment program to identify potential contaminants of all major water sources. In addition, the amendments require that consumers receive more information about the quality of the water they drink and what is being done to protect it. Beginning in 1999, systems have to prepare and distribute annual "consumer confidence" reports about drinking water sources, quality, and violations. Finally, the water act provides over $9.6 billion over six years for improving drinking water infrastructure through state revolving fund programs.

Though these laws have enhanced the safety of the public water supply, they have been a major expense for public water systems, especially systems serving smaller populations. The EPA estimated that it would cost $24 billion per year for 200,000 systems across the country to monitor the regulated contaminants. Monitoring for 30 to 35 as-yet-unregulated contaminants in anticipation of future regulations would cost these public water systems an additional $89 billion.[16]

Other federal environmental laws related to water quality include:

■ National Environmental Policy Act of 1969 Required an Environmental Impact Statement for federally funded projects.

■ Endangered Species Act of 1973 and 1988— Protects animal and plant species that the U.S. Fish and Wildlife Service has designated as threatened or endangered.

■ Coastal Zone Act Reauthorization Amendments of 1990—Focused efforts on reducing polluted runoff in 29 coastal states.

■ Resource Conservation and Recovery Act of 1976 and Superfund Authorization and Renewal Act of 1984—Regulated management of solid wastes and underground storage tanks.

■ Comprehensive Environmental Response, Compensation, and Liability Act of 1980—Created a $1.6 billion Superfund to clean up abandoned hazardous waste sites and required major industries to report annual releases of toxic wastes onto the air, water, or land.

■ Federal Insecticide, Fungicide and Rodenticide Act of 1972—Required registration and regulation of pesticides and other agricultural chemicals.

STATE LEGISLATIVE ACTION

Along with Congress, the Texas legislature has recognized the need to protect water quality. In 1991 the legislature adopted a policy of "no net loss" of state-owned wetlands and authorized a state wetlands conservation management plan. Also in 1991 the legislature adopted the Clean Rivers Act, which directed the river authorities to conduct a regional assessment of water quality for each major river basin, with the TNRCC overseeing the effort.

The Clean River Act supports the TNRCC's overall efforts to move water pollution management to a river basin or "watershed" approach. For example, instead of looking individually at each permit relating to water discharge and water rights, the TNRCC has rewritten its rules to require that all permit renewals pertaining to a given river basin be considered in the same year. In this way, the TNRCC can take a river-basin-by-river-basin approach and better ensure that water quantity and quality are being maintained in the whole watershed.[17]

In 1997 the legislature amended the Clean Rivers Act by limiting funding to the monitoring and assessment of water quality to support site-specific water quality standards and wastewater discharge permitting. This water quality data must be considered in developing water quality standards.

The legislature has also taken steps to protect groundwater. In 1989 the legislature created the Texas Groundwater Protection Committee as an interagency committee to coordinate all state agency actions for the protection of groundwater quality. In 1991 the state created a $10-million oil-field cleanup fund to plug abandoned oil wells and pits. To protect endangered species and the sustainability of the Edwards Aquifer in San Antonio, the legislature in 1993 created the Edwards Aquifer Authority, which in turn has enacted a management plan and established a permit system for groundwater withdrawals to ensure adequate spring flows at the Comal and San Marcos springs. The law gives the Edwards Aquifer Authority the power to set limits on pumping.

In 1997 the legislature passed SB 1, commonly referred to as the "Water Bill." While the intent behind the bill is to ensure sufficient water quantity through a regional planning effort, drought management, conservation plans, and emergency authorizations of water transfers during droughts, the legislation also deals with water quality. Groundwater district management plans and regional water plans must address water quality. In addition, the bill authorizes the TWDB to administer the Federal Safe Drinking Water Revolving Fund to provide low-interest loans to small communities for drinking water and wastewater treatment.[18]

SURFACE WATER: RIVERS, RESERVOIRS, AND BAYS

SURFACE WATER REGULATION TODAY

Texas has approximately 191,228 miles of streams and rivers, of which 40,194 miles (21 percent) are considered perennial; nearly 6.5 million acres of inland wetlands and 1.7 million acres of coastal wetlands; more than three million acres of reservoirs and 1,990.7 square miles of bays; and 3,879 square miles of open gulf water along its 624 miles of coast. All of these waters are afforded at least minimal amounts of protection by the state and federal governments.[19]

There are three different types of water quality standards set by state and federal regulations:

(1) stream standards, also referred to as surface water quality standards;

(2) effluent standards (set for wastewaters); and

(3) drinking water standards, which also cover groundwater used as a public water supply.

Today, the TNRCC is the primary agency responsible for water quality management in Texas, although it shares the responsibility with other state agencies. Under the Clean Water Act and Chapter 26 of the Texas Water Code, the TNRCC has the sole authority to develop and amend surface water quality standards for the state that are implemented via agency permitting programs.

Water quality is protected by regulating certain activities; primarily, the discharge of wastewaters from cities and industrial operations is prohibited unless a permit is received from the state. (In late 1998, the state was awarded full delegation of the permitting program from the EPA. Previously, applicants had to obtain permits from both the TNRCC and the EPA.) These wastewater permits regulate the quality of wastewater that is discharged into a stream, river, lake, or bay.

There are three types of wastewater permits issued by the TNRCC:

(1) municipal,

(2) industrial, and

(3) confined animal feeding operations (CAFOs) such as feedlots, dairies, and poultry operations.

Permits may be either to discharge wastewaters into a stream, river, lake, or bay or "no-discharge" permits. No-discharge permits relate to the disposal of wastewater by irrigation or evaporation. For example, all CAFOs of a certain size must obtain no-discharge permits. Permits normally expire after five years, at which time they must be renewed. The TNRCC is attempting to renew, amend, and issue new permits on a watershed basis as part of its watershed management strategy. Eventually all permits within a watershed will be on the same schedule and come up for renewal at the same time.

The Railroad Commission of Texas issues wastewater discharge permits related to oil and gas activities.

TEXAS SURFACE WATER QUALITY STANDARDS

Under the Clean Water Act, Texas must define how water bodies will be used and must develop and enforce a comprehensive set of water quality standards. There are two components to surface water quality standards: (1) designated uses and (2) chemical, physical, and biological criteria to protect those uses.

The uses that may be established for a water body are:

(1) protection of aquatic life and habitat so that the water is fishable;

(2) use for recreation such as swimming;

(3) use as a drinking water supply;

(4) use for navigation; and

(5) use for industrial water supply.

A water body may be assigned more than one of these uses.

To each water body, upper and lower limits for common water quality criteria are established. Some of these criteria, or standards, are:

(1) dissolved oxygen,

(2) temperature,

(3) pH,

(4) total dissolved solids,

(5) fecal coliform bacteria, and

(6) toxic limits.

Not all waters in Texas are protected by site-specific criteria. For example, in Texas, only 14,348 of 40,194 perennial river miles (36 percent) and 1.54 million of 3.0 million acres of reservoirs (51 percent) have been classified for a particular use. All 1,991 square miles of bays and 3,879 square miles of ocean waters have been classified with site-specific criteria.[20]

Unclassified waters are those smaller water bodies for which site-specific study analyses have not been performed in order to set site-specific standards. Unclassified waters are protected by general aquatic life standards, which apply to all surface waters in the state.

The EPA is required to review state water quality standards to ensure that they meet the Clean Water Act goals of "fishable and swimmable quality waters."[21] States are required to evaluate and, if necessary, revise their water quality standards every three years. While most bodies of water are designated a use to meet these broad goals of swimming (contact recreation) or fishing (high or exceptional aquatic life), the Houston Ship Channel and Buffalo Bayou are so polluted that they are designated for navigation purposes only.

When the TNRCC or the EPA considers applica-tions for wastewater discharge permits, these water quality standards are used to develop limits on the amount and type of contaminants that will be allowed in the discharge.

Texas must regularly monitor the water bodies to determine whether they meet the standards, and through 1996 a water quality inventory was produced once every two years. However, in 1997 the TNRCC divided the state into five basin planning groups. In 1998 the agency conducted a water quality assessment in two of the five basin planning groups. Beginning in 2000, the TNRCC will conduct water quality assessments in one basin group annually, following a rotating cycle of five years.[22]

The water quality inventory is also the basis of the Clean Water Act 303 (d) list, which identifies all "impaired" water bodies that do not meet their designated uses. Finally, the state is required to implement "watershed action plans" to restore those impaired water bodies identified in the 303 (d) list. The basis for the watershed action plans is the development of total maximum daily loads (TMDLs) for all pollutants that prevent the attainment of water quality standards. A TMDL is an estimate, made through a detailed site-specific study process, of the maximum amount of a certain kind of

USES OF RIVERS, RESERVOIRS, ESTUARIES, AND OCEANS UNDER THE TEXAS WATER QUALITY STANDARDS

DESIGNATED USE	PERENNIAL RIVERS AND STREAMS (MILES)	RESERVOIRS (ACRES)	BAYS (SQUARE MILES)	OCEAN (SQUARE MILES)
Total Unclassified*	25,846	1,528,661	0.0	0
Total Classified	14,348	1,536,939	1,990.7	3,879
Contact Recreation	14,291	1,536,415	1,987.0	3,879
Noncontact Recreation	57	524	3.7	0
Public Water Supply	8,881	1,501,437	0.0	0
Aquatic Life Support	14,315	1,536,939	1,990.7	3,879
Exceptional	636	50,104	1,325.5	3,879
High	12,914	1,486,311	664.5	0
Intermediate	502	0	0.7	0
Limited	111	524	0.0	0
Fish Consumption	14,348	1,536,939	1,990.7	0
Oyster Waters	0	0	1,970.8	0

*Presumed Use for Unclassified Waters: High Quality Aquatic Life

Note: Applicants for discharge permits have the opportunity to show that the particular stream into which they want to discharge does not have existing high quality aquatic habitat.

Source: Texas Natural Resource Conservation Commission, The State of Texas Water Quality Inventory—1996, 13th ed. (1996), 23, 156, 165.

pollution a body of water can receive and still meet water quality standards. A TMDL for an individual water body or stream segment may lead to stricter discharge standards or even enforcement actions against a source of pollution. The process of developing TMDLs for all impaired water bodies will take approximately a decade.[23]

ANTIDEGRADATION POLICY

Under the Clean Water Act, each state must develop a statewide antidegradation policy for protecting water quality while allowing the discharge of wastewater into water bodies.[24] In Texas, this antidegradation policy is developed as part of the state's surface water quality standards. All applications for wastewater permits before the TNRCC or the Railroad Commission of Texas must be evaluated with respect to this policy.

The antidegradation policy consists of three parts (or tiers). The first tier provides a minimum level of protection to all waters by prohibiting any activity that could affect the existing use (for example, swimming, fishing) of the water, although its overall quality may be affected. A second tier is applied to those water bodies which have a "high" quality of water and prohibits any degradation of these waters, even if they can still meet their designated use. Thus, the TNRCC could deny a wastewater discharge permit on the grounds that it would degrade a high-quality water. However, if such an activity—and the resulting degradation—is demonstrated to be economically and socially justified, the permit can be granted.

The third and most restrictive tier of the antidegradation policy allows states to designate Outstanding National Resource Waters, or ONRWs. These water bodies receive the highest level of protection under state water quality standards. Unlike the provisions for high-quality waters, no activity that would degrade such waters would be allowed, even if they were economically or socially needed by the region. Thus, additional wastewater discharge permits or construction requiring stormwater permits would probably not be allowed in an ONRW watershed.

In 1994 the TNRCC proposed designating Christmas Bay, South Bay near Port Isabel, Caddo Lake, stream segments in Guadalupe Mountains National Park, and Barton Creek and Barton Springs in Austin as the state's first ONRWs. However, the TNRCC, after receiving opposition from many regulated sources of pollution and from political representatives, later chose not to request ONRW designation for these five water bodies. In contrast, there are approximately 70 ONRWs designated in Arkansas, 40 in Louisiana, and 120 in Oklahoma.[25]

SURFACE WATER POLLUTION: HAVE WE ACHIEVED SWIMMABLE AND FISHABLE WATERS IN TEXAS?

Pollution has to some degree impacted all of Texas's 15 inland river basins and 8 coastal basins, several of its reservoirs, and all of its estuaries, coastal wetlands, and bays.[26] According to the TNRCC's 1996 Water Quality Inventory, only 69 percent of the number of river miles with specific state standards fully supported the uses for which they were designated by the state.[27] In general, overall river and stream water quality remained remarkably

USE SUPPORT SUMMARY FOR CLASSIFIED STREAMS AND RIVERS

USE	TOTAL MILES	MEET USE	PARTLY MEET USE	DON'T MEET USE	CAN'T MEET USE	NOT ASSESSED
All Uses	14,348	9,743.5	1,313	3,119.5	0	172
Aquatic Life Support	14,315	12,892	491	780	33	152
Contact Recreation	14,291	10,264	1,266.5	2,628.5	20	152
Noncontact Recreation	57	45	12	0	0	0
Public Water Supply	8,838	8,838	0	0	0	0
Fish Consumption	14,348	14,056.7	63	228.3	0	0

Source: Texas Natural Resource Conservation Commission, The State of Texas Water Quality Inventory—1996, 13th ed. (1996), 156.

USE SUPPORT SUMMARY FOR CLASSIFIED RESERVOIRS

USE	TOTAL ACRES	MEET USE	PARTLY MEET USE	DON'T MEET USE
All Uses	1,536,939	1,195,703.5	266.993.5	74,242
Aquatic Life Support	1,536,939	1,397,763.5	73,834.5	65,342
Contact Recreation	1,536,415	1,486,650	12,240	37,525
Noncontact Recreation	524	0	524	0
Public Water Supply	1,501,437	1,501,437	0	0
Fish Consumption	1,536,939	1,199,839	336,600	500

Source: Texas Natural Resource Conservation Commission, The State of Texas Water Quality Inventory 1996, 13th ed. (1996), 165.

similar between 1994 and 1996.[28] Of the 4,431 miles of rivers and streams that did not fully meet their designated use in 1996, 3,855 miles did not meet safe swimming ("contact recreation") conditions, 1,304 miles did not meet standards for aquatic life, and 12 miles could not fully support boating and noncontact recreation uses.

Between 1994 and 1996, overall use support in reservoirs declined from 98 to 78 percent, indicating a substantial decline in reservoir water quality. The decline in overall use support was caused by higher levels of dissolved oxygen, higher levels of metals and organic substances, and elevated fecal coliform bacteria densities. Finally, the issuance of consumption advisories and aquatic life closures by the Texas Department of Health increased the number of reservoirs determined to yield fish that could not be safely consumed. Some 336,600 acres of reservoirs were covered by fish-consumption advisories, while 500 acres of reservoirs were also determined to yield

fish unsafe for consumption and were subject to aquatic life closures.[29]

While all reservoirs used as public water supplies did fully support this use, some reservoirs did not meet secondary drinking water standards for chloride, sulfate, and total dissolved solids, requiring expensive treatment processes to support this use. In all, 11 of the 99 classified reservoirs had elevated levels of one or more of these three secondary drinking water standards.[30]

Assessments of 44 classified bay segments indicated that approximately 65 percent fully supported their use, 30 percent partially supported their use, and six percent did not support their use at all. Aquatic life support was met in 94 percent of the square miles of the bays, with only the Corpus Christi Inner Harbor (due to elevated copper levels) not completely meeting the criteria. High fecal coliform bacteria levels did not support safe swimming in three bays and caused 776.2 square miles of bays and ocean waters to not fully support oyster fishing.

USE SUPPORT SUMMARY FOR CLASSIFIED BAYS

USE	TOTAL MILES	MEET USE	PARTLY MEET USE	DON'T MEET USE
All Uses	1,990.7	1,287.1	592.4	111.2
Aquatic Life Support	1,990.7	1,863.9	126.1	0.7
Contact Recreation	1,987.0	1975	5.7	6.3
Noncontact Recreation	3.7	3.7	0	0
Fish Consumption	1,990.7	1,953.6	0.0	37.1
Shellfishing	1,990.7	1,194.6	701.3	74.9

Source: Texas Natural Resource Conservation Commission, The State of Texas Water Quality Inventory—1996, 13th ed. (1996), 184.

CAUSES OF POLLUTION IN SURFACE WATER

Overall, in Texas, 79 segments have been impacted by high fecal coliform levels in water or shellfish, while low dissolved oxygen has impacted 33 segments. Other causes of impairment include high metal content (33 segments), high organics in fish and shellfish (36), and elevated concentrations of dissolved solids (17).[31]

However, each type of water body is impacted by different types of impairment. Major contributors to nonsupport of uses in bays included elevated fecal

CAUSES OF IMPAIRMENT OF SURFACE WATER SEGMENTS NOT MEETING DESIGNATED USES

CONTAMINANT	USE IMPAIRED	SEGMENTS AFFECTED
Fecal coliform	Contact recreation	59 segments
Fecal coliform and other bacteria, viruses	Shellfish consumption	20 segments
Organics	Aquatic life Fish/shellfish consumption	36 segments
Low dissolved oxygen	Aquatic life	33 segments
Metals	Aquatic life Fish/shellfish consumption	33 segments
Dissolved solids	Aquatic life (16), public water (1)	17 segments
High temperature	Aquatic life	1 segment
pH imbalance	Aquatic life	1 segment
Totals		**144 segments**

Note: Totals do not add because some segments are affected by more than one contaminant and have more than one use impaired; 56 segments are counted in several categories because they have multiple impairments.

Source: Texas Natural Resource Conservation Commission, "Texas' Future: Clean Rivers Run Through It," National Outlook (Spring 1998), 13.

coliform bacteria and low dissolved oxygen contents. In the streams and rivers, the most frequently violated water quality standards were those for pathogens (high levels of fecal coliform bacteria), low dissolved oxygen, and, in some areas, toxics such as metals and pesticides. Excess plant nutrients (nitrogen and phosphorus) also were identified as a problem in some waters of the state. In reservoirs, impairment of use was related to elevated levels of metals and high levels of pathogens and pesticides.[32]

According to the 1996 Water Quality Inventory and data drawn from the state's limited monitoring of toxics, 521.5 miles of streams and rivers, 22,240 acres of reservoir, and 0.7 miles of bays and estuaries have toxicity levels so high they do not meet their use for aquatic life.[33] In addition, the TNRCC has identified 21 segments of concern for toxic substances in ambient water, as well as 18 segments where at least two tests evidenced in-stream toxic effects from water or sediment. Ambient water toxicity is due to metals such as cadmium, zinc, lead, silver, and aluminum, while diazinon, an organic pesticide,

CAUSES THAT CONTRIBUTE TO USE IMPAIRMENT IN CLASSIFIED STREAMS, RIVERS, RESERVOIRS, AND BAYS

Impaired Streams and Rivers (% of Total Miles)

CAUSES	MAJOR SOURCE	MINOR SOURCE
Fecal coliform	17%	28%
Heavy metals	2%	5%
Low dissolved oxygen	2%	4%
Nutrients	1%	2%
Organics	1%	2%
Pesticides	1%	2%
pH	0%	1%

Total affected by cause: 31% (4,433 miles)

Impaired Reservoirs (% of Total Acres)

CAUSES	MAJOR SOURCE	MINOR SOURCE
Metals	15%	23%
Low dissolved oxygen	3%	6%
Fecal coliform	1%	4%
Pesticides	1%	2%
Nutrients	1%	0%
Thermal modification	0%	1%

Total affected: 22% (341,176 acres)

Impaired Bays and Estuaries (% of Total Square Miles)

CAUSES	MAJOR SOURCE	MINOR SOURCE
Fecal coliform	3%	34%
Depressed oxygen	0%	6%
Metals	1%	0%
Priority organics	1%	0%

Total affected: 35% (703.6 square miles)

Note: Totals do not add since more than one minor source can affect the same water body. In addition, major sources could not be identified for all water bodies.

Source: Texas Natural Resource Conservation Commission, The State of Texas Water Quality Inventory—1996, 13th ed. (1996), 157, 166, 185.

has exceeded both acute and chronic screening levels in two water segments.[34] Finally, eight segments have been identified as being of concern for toxic substances in fish tissue.

SOURCES OF POTENTIAL SURFACE WATER POLLUTION

The sources of water pollution typically fall into one of two categories: point-source pollution and non-point-source pollution. The term point-source pollution refers to pollutants discharged from one discrete location or point, such as an industry or municipal

SUMMARY OF WATERBODIES AFFECTED BY TOXICS

WATER BODY/ UNITS	TOTAL SIZE	TOTAL SIZE MONITORED FOR TOXICS	TOTAL SIZE IMPAIRED BY TOXICS
Streams and rivers/miles	14,348	6,872	521.5
Reservoirs/acres	1,536,939	563,655	22,240
Bays/square miles	1,990.7	1,389.2	0.7
Gulf of Mexico	3,879	3,879	0

Note: Includes only those water bodies which do not meet their aquatic life use because of the presence of toxics.

Source: Texas Natural Resource Conservation Commission, The State of Texas Water Quality Inventory—1996, 13th ed. (1996), 216.

wastewater treatment plant. Pollutants discharged in this way might include, for example, fecal coliform bacteria and nutrients from sewage, heavy metals, or synthetic organic contaminants. The term non-point-source pollution refers to pollutants that cannot be identified as coming from one discrete location or point. Examples are oil and grease that enter the water with runoff from urban streets, nitrogen from fertilizers and pesticides, and animal wastes that wash into surface waters from agricultural lands.

Natural and unknown causes of pollutants also can impact water quality and may be related to human activities. For example, highway or housing construction may help precipitate the runoff of natural pollution sources, such as sediment.

In 1996 different sources of pollution had differing effects on reservoirs, rivers, and bays. While the major sources of pollution in reservoirs and bays were non-point sources, the major source of pollution in streams and rivers was wastewater discharges from cities.

POINT-SOURCE DISCHARGES

Since the passage of the 1972 Clean Water Act, most water pollution control efforts have focused on point-source pollution. Point-source pollution generally comes from the millions of gallons of wastewater discharged from the pipes of industrial facilities and municipal sewage treatment plants into rivers, streams, lakes, and the ocean. Sources of wastewater may include domestic wastewater inflow and infiltra-

SOURCES THAT CONTRIBUTE TO USE IMPAIRMENTS IN CLASSIFIED STREAMS, RIVERS, RESERVOIRS, AND BAYS

Impaired Streams and Rivers (% of Total Miles affected by major or minor source) SOURCES	% OF MILES	Impaired Reservoirs (% of Total Acres affected by major or minor source) SOURCES	% OF SQUARE ACRES	Impaired Bays and Estuaries (% of Total Square Miles affected by major or minor source) SOURCES	% OF MILES
Domestic wastewater	16%	Unknown	16%	Agriculture	17%
Unknown	9%	Atmospheric deposition	8%	Urban runoff	11%
Agriculture	8%	Natural	4%	Septic tanks	5%
Urban runoff	6%	Domestic wastewater	4%	Natural	5%
Septic tanks	3%	Industrial	2%	Domestic wastewater	4%
Industrial	3%	Agriculture	2%	Industrial wastewater	2%
Natural	3%	Septic tank	2%	Marinas	1%
Impoundments	2%	Urban runoff	1%	Unknown	1%
Hazardous waste	1%	Impoundment	1%	Total square miles affected by sources: 35% (703.6 square miles)	
Recreational	1%	Hydromodification	1%	Total square miles of bays: 100% (1990.7 square miles)	
Flow modifications	1%	Land disposal	1%		
Total miles affected by sources: 31% (4,433 miles)		Total square acres affected by sources: 22% (341,176 Square Acres)			
Total miles of rivers and streams: 100% (14,196 miles)		Total square acres of reservoirs: 100% (1,536,939 Square Acres)			

Note: Totals do not add since more than one source can affect the same water body.

Source: Texas Natural Resource Conservation Commission, The State of Texas Water Quality Inventory—1996, 13th ed. (1996), 158, 167, 186.

tion—where storm water and groundwater get into the wastewater collection system—commercial operations such as restaurants, food processing facilities such as canneries, agricultural operations, and industrial facilities.[35]

Wastewater is considered a potential source of pollution because it may—especially if it is untreated or only partially treated—contain organic and inorganic materials that can be hazardous to both humans and other life forms. In many streams, treated wastewater may actually be cleaner than what is already contained in the stream; however, treated, untreated, or partially treated wastewater may also contain small amounts of radiation or toxics that increase the temperature of waters, affecting aquatic wildlife and habitat. Finally, discharged wastewater, especially if it is untreated or partially treated, may lower the amount of dissolved oxygen in the receiving stream (oxygen is required by microorganisms that consume the organic material).

FYI ☞ *Different organic materials in wastewaters require different amounts of oxygen—commonly known as biochemical oxygen demand (BOD)—in order to break down and stabilize the material. The greater the BOD, the greater the oxygen-depleting effect of the wastewater upon the receiving stream. The BOD of typical untreated domestic wastewater varies from 100 to 300 milligrams per liter. Chicken blood from a food processing plant, on the other hand, might require from 1,000 to 4,000 milligrams per liter of BOD to treat.[36]*

Since the 1977 Clean Water Act, all municipal and industrial dischargers have been required to obtain from the EPA a National Pollutant Discharge Elimination System, or NPDES, permit. Despite its name, the NPDES permit does not eliminate pollution; it instead is designed to control pollution by setting limits on the quality of the discharged wastewater. In 1998 the EPA awarded the NPDES program to the TNRCC. Previously, most industrial and municipal discharges had to obtain both a state and a federal wastewater permit. Under the NPDES program, the state establishes basic effluent limits for all facilities to protect surface water quality standards.

STATE DISCHARGE PERMITS

As of January 1996, 2,343 municipal wastewater treatment facilities, both publicly and privately owned, were operating with state wastewater discharge permits. Most of these—1,922—involved direct discharge into state waters. In addition to these domestic treatment facilities, there were 996 industrial facilities with active state permits.[37]

FYI ☞ *The combined authorized municipal and industrial discharge of wastewater—about 61.5 billion gallons per day—is enough to fill Texas Stadium, home of the Dallas Cowboys, 79 times over with wastewater every day.[38]*

About 17 percent of both industrial and domestic wastewater permits are no-discharge permits, which means that wastewater is stored, evaporated, or used for irrigation instead of being discharged into a river or stream. Finally, in 1996 there were 602 permits for agricultural activities, primarily CAFOs—feedlots, poultry and dairy operations—that were required to obtain no-discharge permits from the TNRCC, meaning that the animal wastes cannot be discharged directly into state waters.[39]

While most permits are based on site-specific water quality standards and reviews, some discharge limitations have been issued by rule pertaining to a specific class of wastewater treatment facility. In 1997 the Texas legislature amended Section 26 of the Water Code, allowing the TNRCC to issue "general permits" by rule for specific classes of users, providing that discharges of wastewater did not exceed 500,000 gallons in any 24-hour period and that the discharge would not cause significant adverse effects to water quality.[40] In 1999, legislation eliminated the 500,000 gallon limit, allowing the TNRCC to issue general permits for a wide variety of discharges.

FYI ☞ *Wastewater is mostly water (99.9 percent). Various kinds of solids make up only 0.1 percent of sewage. Solids include organic and inorganic materials from feces, urine, washing, laundering, and, in some cases, from food processing, agricultural, and industrial operations. It is this tiny amount of solids that can contaminate receiving waters. (Source: Texas Engineering and Extension Service, Texas A&M University System, Basic Wastewater Operation [College Station, 1994], 5-1.)*

DOMESTIC AND INDUSTRIAL WASTEWATER DISCHARGE PERMITS AND TOTAL DAILY DISCHARGE FLOW BY RIVER BASIN, 1994

RIVER BASIN	NO. OF PERMITS	DAILY FLOW MILLIONS OF GALLONS/DAY
Canadian River Basin	47	31
Red River Basin	111	236
Sulphur River Basin	46	28
Cypress River Basin	68	340
Sabine River Basin	166	1,647
Neches River Basin	225	1,341
Neches-Trinity River Basin	89	214
Trinity River Basin	435	3,997
Trinity-San Jacinto River Basin	60	402
San Jacinto River Basin	1,027	1,961
San Jacinto-Brazos Coastal Basin	229	784
Brazos River Basin	424	2,751
Brazos-Colorado	51	24
Colorado River Basin	286	3,505
Colorado-Lavaca	33	6
Lavaca River Basin	13	5
Lavaca-Guadalupe River Basin	25	23
Guadalupe	65	1,407
San Antonio River Basin	67	1,106
San Antonio-Nueces	37	264
Nueces River Basin	35	20
Nueces-Rio Grande Coastal Basin	191	1,024
Rio Grande River Basin	57	129
Total	**3,787**	**21,245**

Source: Texas Natural Resource Conservation Commission, Texas Water Quality: A Summary of River Basin Assessments (1994).

FYI 👉 *Wastewater flows from domestic sources average about 100 gallons per day for each person served. During dry weather, however, highest flows are about twice the average flow, while minimum flows are only about half the average flow.* (Source: Texas Engineering and Extension Service, Texas A&M University System, Basic Wastewater Operation [College Station, 1994], 4-3.)

Since 1972 the amount of pollution discharged in wastewater by domestic facilities has decreased about 70 percent in Texas. At the same time the amount of waste requiring treatment has increased by 85 percent.[41] This improvement is due mainly to better technology and to requirements that wastewater in Texas be cleaned up to stricter standards. About 67

NUMBER OF STATE WASTEWATER PERMITS FROM 1980 TO 1996

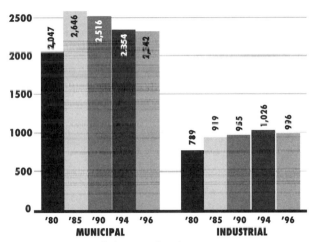

Note: Does not include agricultural permits.

Source: Texas Natural Resource Conservation Commission, Wastewater Permit Database.

percent of domestic waste produced by municipal facilities receives advanced treatment.[42]

Most discharges in Texas are concentrated near major population centers like Dallas and Houston. The state processes about 200 new or revised industrial permits and about 500 new or revised municipal permits each year.[43] Since 1980, combined industrial and municipal permits have increased from 2,907 to 3,309. While the number of industrial permits has risen due to increased economic activity, the number of permitted municipal facilities has actually declined in recent years as some city systems have regionalized their wastewater treatment.

TOXICS IN TEXAS WASTEWATER DISCHARGES

Toxics are poisonous compounds that have been identified as being harmful to human health and the environment. Discharges of toxic water pollutants into the surface waters of the state are a mounting public concern. Some toxics are soluble in water and pose a threat to human health if the water is used for drinking or swimming. Other toxics are not soluble in water but may become attached to sediment and be consumed by aquatic life forms, thereby entering into the food chain. This process, known as bioaccumulation, puts humans at risk if the toxics become concentrated in higher life forms like fish.

Not until 1988 did limits on toxics became a major part of the water quality standards. The state water quality standards of 1991 addressed only 61 specific toxic compounds out of thousands of potential compounds. The 1995 water quality standards raised this number by setting numerical criteria for 39 toxic pollutants for aquatic life and 65 toxic pollutants for drinking water and human consumption of fish.[44] In addition, for larger dischargers, the TNRCC requires biomonitoring—also known as whole effluent testing—in which the ambient toxicity of the effluent is tested on aquatic species. Still, despite specific numerical criteria and ambient toxicity testing, many chemicals could be directly discharged into Texas's surface waters without any discharge permit limits.

Finally, some industries route their toxic discharges through publicly owned treatment works (POTWs), which are often not designed to remove toxic chemicals and metals. Most cities, large or small, require that the industrial facilities that release toxics through POTWs pretreat their wastewater to limit toxins. In addition, under federal law, 21 categories of industries must pretreat their wastes to "best available technology" before discharging wastes to a public wastewater treatment plant.[45] However, neither industrial nor municipal pretreatment programs are universally applied or enforced.[46]

One of the best sources of information for the amount of toxics entering Texas waters is the Toxics Release Inventory (TRI). Under the federal Superfund Authorization and Renewal Act, manufacturing companies with 10 or more employees that use or manufacture more than 25,000 pounds per year of any of more than 650 toxic chemicals or chemical compounds must file an annual report with the state.[47]

Until the 1997 reporting year, the TRI program required only manufacturing facilities to report, leaving out other industries, including utilities, that produce toxics. Also, there are more than 650 toxic compounds, and the TRI does not track the releases of the additional chemicals.[48]

Texas manufacturers reported releases of 20.8 mil-

PRETREATMENT OF INDUSTRIAL WASTE DISCHARGES

Source: Texas Extension Educational Service, Texas A & M University System, Basic Wastewater Operations (College Station: Texas Engineering Extention Service, 1994), 4-10.

lion pounds of toxic chemicals directly into surface water in 1997. More than 67 percent of this total was due to releases of nitrates and other compounds from BASF Corporation in Brazoria County. Texas ranked third only to Louisiana and Pennsylvania in total releases to surface waters in 1997.[49] In 1993 Texas facilities released only 553,642 pounds of toxics into Texas streams and rivers.[50] However, the two years are not directly comparable because in 1993 only 332 chemicals were required to be reported. In fact, if only the releases of the chemicals that were required to be reported in both 1993 and 1997 are reported, total releases only increased by 400,000 pounds.

In 1997, over 46.8 million pounds of toxic chemicals were transferred to public sewage plants.[51] More than 70 percent of the amount of chemicals transferred were produced by three companies in Pasadena —Air Products, Hoescht-Celanese Chemical Co. and Simpson Pasadena Paper Company—in the Houston-Bay Port region. About 87 percent of all toxics transferred to public sewers in 1997 were in Harris County.

The most common chemicals reported being released to surface water and public treatment plants were nitrate compounds, methanol, ammonia, ethylene glycol, and nitric acid.[52]

TOP 10 FACILITIES RANKED BY TOTAL WATER RELEASES, 1995–1997

RANK	FACILITY	CITY	COUNTY	1995	TOTAL RELEASES IN LBS 1996	1997
1	BASF Corp.	Freeport	Brazoria	17,011,408	14,008,559	14,011,739
2	Bayer Corp. (Formerly Miles, Inc.)	Baytown	Chambers	3,013,160	2,209,865	3,139,790
3	Rohm & Haas Texas Inc.	Deer Park	Harris	441,371	373,771	539,634
4	Dow Chemical Company	Freeport	Brazoria	727,074	301,705	260,506
5	Du Pont	La Porte	Harris	512,564	180,731	201,548
6	Exxon Baytown Refinery	Baytown	Harris	298,039	196,265	194,746
7	Citgo Refining Company	Corpus Christi	Nueces	--------	273,784	188,055
8	Shell Oil Company	Deer Prark	Harris	195,758	163,844	184,009
9	Inland Eastex	Evadale	Jasper	165,255	158,155	164,355
10	Amoco Oil Company	Texas City	Galveston	161,032	153,517	156,119
	Cumulative Total				90.68%	

Source: Texas Natural Resource Conservation Commission, Toxics Release Inventory Program, Office of Pollution Prevention and Recycling; and Environmental Protection Agency, 1997 Toxics Release Inventory Database, 1999.

COMPLIANCE AND ENFORCEMENT

Facilities that discharge wastewater directly into surface waters are required to submit to the state monthly effluent reports that show whether or not they meet their permit limits. Between 1990 and 1995, approximately 750 industrial facilities and 2,000 municipalities were required to submit monthly effluent reports.[53]

In addition to these effluent reports, large municipalities and industries whose permits contain numerical limits on toxics are required to perform total toxicity testing, or biomonitoring, to determine whether their effluent is adversely affecting aquatic life. If biomonitoring reports—and two retests— show the effluent to be lethal to certain species, municipalities and industries must perform what's known as a TRE, or toxicity reduction evaluation, to identify which toxics are affecting the species and adopt a plan to reduce the toxicity of their effluent.

Where self-reports or inspections show violations,

TOP 10 FACILITIES RANKED BY TOTAL TRANSFERS TO PUBLICLY OWNED TREATMENT WORKS, 1995–1997

RANK	FACILITY	CITY	COUNTY	1997	TOTAL TRANSFERS IN LBS 1996	1995
1	Air Products, Inc.	Pasadena	Harris	17,230,385	18,574,290	18,908,920
2	Hoechst-Celanese Chemical Co.	Pasadena	Harris	8,813,459	441,580	2,831,250
3	Simpson Pasadena Paper Company	Pasadena	Harris	7,432,100	4,998,000	8,909,500
4	Union Carbide Corp.	Texas City	Galveston	3,316,767	4,134,177	2,480,966
5	Arco Chemical Company	Pasadena	Harris	2,046,912	2,241,995	1,644,400
6	Occidental Chemicals Plant	Pasadena	Harris	895,168	872,338	1,010,060
7	Rohm & Haas Bayport	La Porte	Harris	843,310	864,819	744,572
8	Lyondell-Citgo Refining	Houston	Harris	686,654	670,793	507,538
9	Motorola Inc.	Austin	Travis	557,120	297,000	323,100
10	Akzo Nobel Chemicals Inc.	Pasadena	Harris	433,613	366,064	287,821
	Cumulative Total				90.10%	

Source: Texas Natural Resource Conservation Commission, Toxics Release Inventory Program, Office of Pollution Prevention and Recycling; and Environmental Protection Agency, 1997 Toxics Release Inventory Database, 1999.

RELEASES OF TOXIC CHEMICALS INTO TEXAS WATERS AND SEWERS BY TOP COUNTIES IN 1996 AND 1997

COUNTY	TOXIC WATER RELEASES (LBS.)		TOXIC TRANSFERS TO MUNICIPAL SEWERS	
	1996	1997	1996	1997
Brazoria	14,424,271	14,377,778	0	0
Chambers	2,209,865	3,140,054	0	250
Harris	1,256,763	1,473,170	29,934,038	40,670,248
Nueces	370,939	427,517	8,600	25,000
Galveston	167,443	209,785	1,157,053	3,365,873
Jefferson	150,315	344,725	0	250
Tarrant	690	2,396	88,836	90,298
Moore	0	0	197,438	327,116
Dallas	998	566	530,594	319,077
Travis	79	64	694,902	1,227,085

Source: Texas Natural Resource Conservation Commission, Toxics Release Inventory Program, Office of Pollution Prevention and Recycling, 1998 and Environmental Protection Agency, 1997 Toxics Release Inventory Database, 1999.

the TNRCC may begin enforcement action against a permittee. A municipal or industrial discharger must be noncompliant for four months for enforcement actions to be undertaken automatically. Besides these self-reporting requirements, permittees are subject to compliance inspections by the approximately 65 wastewater inspectors employed by the TNRCC.[54] These inspectors conduct annual inspections on a selected number of facilities. Due to cuts in funding for inspections, the number of facilities inspected has decreased substantially, from 100 percent of facilities in 1990 to approximately 30 percent in 1995, even as the number of violations or deficiencies has increased from 20 percent to nearly 60 percent of all systems.[55]

FYI *According to EPA data for January 1995 through March 1996, 22 percent of all major municipal and industrial wastewater treatment facilities were in significant noncompliance for clean water permits, making Texas first in the nation for the number of major facilities in significant noncompliance.*
(Source: Clean Water Network, A Prescription for Clean Water: How to Meet the Goals of the Clean Water Act [Washington, D.C., October 1997], 20.)

Between 1986 and 1997, the TNRCC issued 694 enforcement orders with penalties due totaling over $7.4 million for municipal and industrial wastewater discharge and water quality violations. In addition,

the agency ordered violators to initiate supplemental environmental projects worth another $1.3 million between 1992 and 1997.[56]

Finally, the self-reporting data are utilized by the TNRCC to determine if daily maximum flow is 75 percent or more of the permitted daily maximum flow for more than three consecutive months. If so, dischargers must begin engineering and financial planning to construct additional facilities. If daily flows equal 90 percent or more of the maximum

NUMBER OF ANNUAL COMPLIANCE INSPECTION AND PERMIT COMPLIANCE OF WASTEWATER PLANTS IN TEXAS, 1990 TO 1995

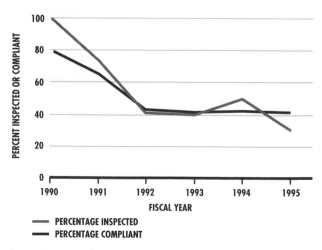

Source: Texas Natural Resource Conservation Commission, The State of Texas Water Quality Inventory—1996, 13th ed. (1996), 297.

permitted daily flow, the plant operators must authorize the construction of additional facilities. Between 1988 and 1996, some 880 facilities were required to take corrective action, either by reducing flows or expanding facilities.[57]

UNTREATED WASTEWATER

While the treatment and discharge of most wastewater in Texas is managed through the permit system, some effluent is discharged into surface waters without treatment. In 1996 the TWDB estimated that 380,000 Texans lived in 1,500 unincorporated subdivisions within 100 miles of the Texas-Mexico border that lacked either proper potable water or wastewater treatment service.[58] The majority of "colonias," as they are known, are concentrated in Hidalgo, Cameron, and El Paso counties. Most of these Texans use improperly operated septic tanks, cesspools, outhouses, privies, or no treatment at all before discharging their wastewater directly into surface water or into the ground. This practice affects the quality of both groundwater and surface water.

In recent years, state and federal funds have been spent to bring many of these colonias into regional wastewater and water systems. As of June 1998, 17 projects costing more than $67.5 million helped

over 36,000 colonia residents receive potable water or wastewater treatment. In addition, another 100,000 colonia residents will benefit from projects costing about $220 million that are either under construction or in the design phase. Finally, according to the TWDB, if all the projects currently completed, under construction, or in the planning stages are actually completed, over 285,000 colonia residents will receive water or centralized wastewater treatment service.[59]

The Rio Grande, the river that forms part of the border between Texas and Mexico, serves as both the major source of drinking water and the principle recipient of wastewater for the region. Water quality for many segments of the Rio Grande has been severely degraded over the years, in part because of the discharging of untreated or partially treated wastewater by Mexican cities. Together, the Mexican border cities of Juárez, Ojinaga, Acuña, Piedras Negras, Reynosa, and Matamoros discharge an estimated 151 million gallons of wastewater into the Rio Grande and Gulf of Mexico per day. About

NUMBER OF BORDER RESIDENTS WITHOUT ADEQUATE WASTEWATER TREATMENT FACILITIES BY COUNTY

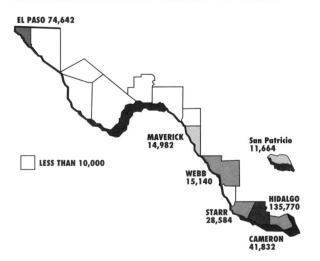

EL PASO 74,642

MAVERICK 14,982

San Patricio 11,664

☐ LESS THAN 10,000

WEBB 15,140

HIDALGO 135,770

STARR 28,584

CAMERON 41,832

Source: Texas Water Development Board, Water and Wastewater Needs of Texas Colonias: 1996 Update (1997).

UNTREATED OR PARTIALLY TREATED WASTEWATER DISCHARGED ALONG THE TEXAS-MEXICO BORDER FROM MEXICAN CITIES*

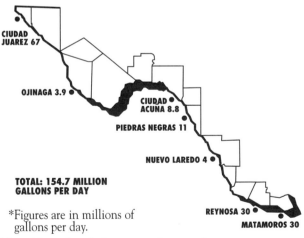

CIUDAD JUAREZ 67

OJINAGA 3.9 ●

CIUDAD ● ACUNA 8.8

PIEDRAS NEGRAS 11

NUEVO LAREDO 4 ●

TOTAL: 154.7 MILLION GALLONS PER DAY

REYNOSA 30 ●

MATAMOROS 30

*Figures are in millions of gallons per day.

Note: Nuevo Laredo has operated a secondary treatment wastewater plant since 1996. However, an estimated 4.3 of more than 21 million gallons a day is still going into the river without passing through the treatment plant. In 1998, Ciudad Juárez began construction of a primary treatment plant.

Source: U.S. Army Corps of Engineers, International Boundary and Water Commission Sanitary Issues (Fort Worth: U.S. Army Corps of Engineers, September 1992). Additional Source: John M. Bernal, Office of the Commissioner, International Boundary and Water Commission, United States Section, letter to Mary Kelly, Texas Center for Policy Studies, September 19,1997.

HOW IS WASTEWATER PROCESSED?

Wastewater can undergo several levels of treatment, each of which makes the water progressively cleaner. The first level, called primary treatment, removes solids, usually by mechanical means. During secondary treatment, water is aerated and microorganisms are used to remove remaining small particles. Tertiary treatment removes nitrates and phosphates, and the water is then chlorinated.

Due to the high construction and operating costs of conventional systems, as shown in the diagram, many smaller communities have begun looking into so-called innovative and alternative wastewater treatment plants.[60] Alternative collection systems often use smaller-diameter pipes that follow the topography of the land to reduce excavation costs and take advantage of gravity flows. Innovative treatment systems may also utilize natural processes to reduce effluent contaminants to acceptable levels. These processes include using the wastewater to irrigate land, which uses the soil's biological activity to treat the wastewater. Or, the system may rely on specially constructed wetlands, which physically filter the water and break down contaminants through biological and microbial activity. Communities such as Beaumont and Johnson City have utilized constructed wetlands for secondary and tertiary treatment.

88 million gallons per day is untreated. The remaining 63 million gallons receives only primary treatment, which means that solids and sludge have been removed but no chlorination or other chemical or biological treatment of the wastewater has occurred.[61]

In 1996 the U.S. and Mexican governments funded the construction of a joint wastewater treatment facility for Nuevo Laredo; however, the plant does not cover all of the city's residents, and some untreated wastewater still flows from the city. In 1997 the BECC certified a pair of wastewater treatment plants for Ciudad Juárez, which is being constructed with $31.1 million in grant and loan dollars from the United States and Mexico packaged through NADBank (see focus piece on NAFTA and the Texas-Mexico Border Environment).[62]

Not surprisingly, significant portions of the Rio Grande do not meet standards for aquatic life and contact recreation uses, in large part because of the large amount of discharged untreated wastewater.

A TYPICAL WASTEWATER TREATMENT PLANT

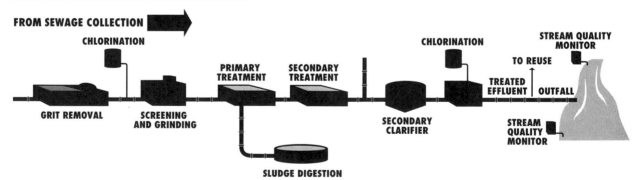

Primary Treatment: Separates large suspended solids from water through sedimentation. Solids thickened into sludge. Sludge sent to sludge treatment and disposal.

Secondary Treatment (Aeration Basin): Uses aeration and microbial bacteria to rid remaining solid particles.

Secondary Clarifier: Remaining solids are settled out.

Final Step: Chlorination. Some plants also require dechlorination before final release into stream.

Tertiary Treatment: Removal of phosphates and nitrates. Required for some facilities.

Source: Texas Extension Educational Service, Texas A & M University System, Basic Wastewater Operations (College Station: Texas Engineering Extension Service, 1994), 3-5.

AN EXAMPLE OF AN ALTERNATIVE SECONDARY TREATMENT WASTEWATER PLANT: CONSTRUCTED WETLAND

CELL 1   3

CELL 2   8

(1) Wastewater enters the constructed wetland where it is distributed evenly across the width of the first cell by a series of plastic valves or PVC tees. (2) The first cell contains gravel. A waterproof liner is used on the sides and bottom of the first cell to conserve water and provide more effective treatment. (3) Cattails and bulrushes are usually planted in the first cell. The roots of these marsh plants form a dense mat among the gravel. Here chemical, biological, and physical processes take place which purify the water. (4) Water from the first cell passes into the second cell through a perforated pipe embedded in large

stone. (5) The water level within each cell is regulated by swivel standpipes in concrete tanks at the end of each cell. (6) Wastewater is distributed evenly across the second cell through another perforated pipe. (7) Cell 2 has a layer of gravel covered with topsoil and then mulch. (8) This cell is planted with a variety of ornamental wetland plants such as iris, elephant ear, and arrowhead. (9) The water in Cell 2 eventually seeps into the soil below or passes into another perforated pipe where (10) it is released into a drainfield similar to those used with conventional septic tanks.

Source: Tennessee Valley Authority, General Design, Construction and Operation Guidelines: Constructed Wetlands Wastewater Treatment Systems for Small Users Including Individual Residences.

NON-POINT-SOURCE POLLUTION

Apart from point-source discharges, toxics and other pollutants can enter surface water through urban and agricultural runoff, seepage from landfills and hazardous waste facilities, spills on land or water, and seepage from underground injection sites. Toxics can also be caused by acid rain, which occurs when airborne contaminants are absorbed by clouds and return to earth in the rain. The impact of non-point-source pollution on water quality is significant: the EPA now estimates that non-point-source pollution accounts for 65 percent of pollution in rivers, 76 percent in lakes, and 45 percent in estuaries in the United States.[63]

The 1987 amendments to the Water Quality Act were the first comprehensive attempt by the federal government to control non-point-source pollution from urban streets and sewers as well as from agricultural activities. The law requires states to conduct an assessment of waters contaminated by non-point-source pollution and to devise best management pollution-abatement plans to help clean up these waters. The law also provides the states funding

for up to 60 percent of the cost of implementing these plans. From 1989 to 1995, Texas received about $14 million in federal funds for a variety of abatement programs.[64]

In addition to this federal money, the state has supported some pilot projects to control non-point-source pollution through fees established as part of the Clean Rivers Program. Finally, some local governments have adopted their own non-point-source pollution abatement programs using either federal or local dollars.

According to the TNRCC, of the 142 segments that do not meet their designated uses, 62 have been identified as not meeting their use because of non-point-source pollution, while 42 segments have been identified as being affected by both point and non-point-source, and only 37 segments are impaired solely because of point or natural sources.[67]

Despite these documented effects on Texas rivers, lakes, and streams, pollution abatement and management plans have not been implemented in most areas in Texas. Part of the difficulty lies in identifying the sources of pollution that affect water quality.

EXAMPLES OF NON-POINT-SOURCE POLLUTION CONTROL PROGRAMS IN TEXAS

Federally Funded Projects
(1) The federal government has funded a demonstration project in the Lower Rio Grande Valley to manage nutrient application to agricultural lands and to use an integrated pest management program in certain agricultural activities. These techniques are being tested for their effectiveness in limiting nutrient and pesticide loadings into the nearby Arroyo Colorado.

(2) The federal government has also funded a Dairy Outreach Program to help dairy operations in Erath County limit discharge and runoff of animal wastes. This project is jointly managed with the State Soil Conservation Board and TNRCC.

State-Funded Project
Through the Clean Rivers Program, the TNRCC developed a comprehensive water quality assessment of the Bosque River-Lake Waco watershed. Under this study, the Institute of Applied Environmental Research at Tarleton State University and the Brazos River Authority have implemented a water quality sampling program to characterize pollution loadings from watersheds dominated by dairy farms, urban storm-water runoff, loadings from septic tanks, and wastewater treatment plant discharges.[65]

Local Pollution Abatement Program
Under state regulations, municipalities have the authority to adopt ordinances designed to protect water quality.

The City of Austin has adopted an ordinance designed to prevent development from affecting stream water quality in the sensitive Barton Springs watershed. The controversial ordinance, which was passed by voters in 1992, limits impervious cover—the percentage of land covered by pavement or buildings—in any new development along the watershed of Austin's streams and creeks. Impervious cover cannot exceed 15 percent in the recharge zone of Barton Springs and 25 percent in the Barton Springs-Edwards Aquifer contributing zone, which feeds into Barton Springs.[66]

In San Antonio, where the Edwards Aquifer is currently the sole source of water, a water quality ordinance expands zoning authority within city limits. The water quality ordinance also places limits on impervious cover in areas of the city's extraterritorial jurisdiction that are located above the aquifer.

One of the major purposes of the state's 1991 Clean Rivers Act—which requires river authorities to assess the water quality of their river basins—is to establish better data regarding non-point-source causes and impacts.

AGRICULTURAL NON-POINT-SOURCE POLLUTION
Agricultural activity accounts for most of the reported cases of non-point-source pollution in Texas.[68] The irrigation of crops, the application of fertilizers to pasture or range land, and the use of feedlots all generate such non-point-source pollutants as plant nutrients, pesticides, sediment, and animal wastes.

RIVERS, STREAMS, RESERVOIRS OR BAYS IDENTIFIED AS HAVING BEEN IMPACTED BY NON-POINT-SOURCE POLLUTION

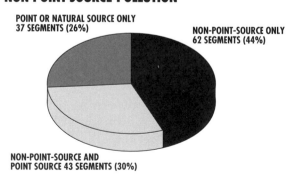

POINT OR NATURAL SOURCE ONLY
37 SEGMENTS (26%)

NON-POINT-SOURCE ONLY
62 SEGMENTS (44%)

NON-POINT-SOURCE AND
POINT SOURCE 43 SEGMENTS (30%)

Source: Texas Natural Resource Conservation Commission, Clean Water for Texas: Solving Water Quality Problems (1997), Table 1.

CAFOs

Major contributors of non-point-source pollution are CAFOs (confined animal feeding operations), facilities that house animals used for the production of eggs, milk, and meat. CAFOs generate a variety of potential pollutants. Animal wastes contain pathogens, chlorides and potassium salts, and high levels of nitrogen. CAFOs may degrade state waters by increasing nutrient loads and fecal coliform in many rivers. This type of contamination ultimately lowers dissolved oxygen levels, which threatens the viability of aquatic habitats and consequently the use of the river for fishing, swimming, or drinking.

State regulations now prohibit these facilities from discharging wastewater or animal waste directly into streams and rivers. Operators must also not allow the waste to run off the site, where it could contaminate surface water or groundwater. Currently, every large CAFO must obtain a no-discharge permit from the state, which requires that the facility control runoff except when there is excessive rain. Most large cattle operations are located in the Panhandle, while dairy-farm operations are concentrated in Erath County, near Stephenville.

NUMBER OF PERMITTED CONFINED ANIMAL FEEDING OPERATIONS BY COUNTY

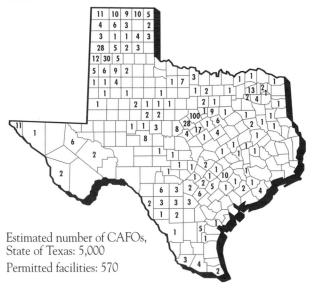

Estimated number of CAFOs, State of Texas: 5,000
Permitted facilities: 570

Source: Texas Natural Resource Conservation Commission, Agriculture and Rural Assistance Division, 1998.

SCHEMATIC OF A TWO-STAGE LAGOON DAIRY OPERATION

Note: Waste from dairy cows is collected in primary lagoon, where most solids settle to bottom. Wastewater is then sent to a secondary lagoon for further treatment. Finally, after further settling of solids, wastewater is used to irrigate crops. Contamination may occur from improper irrigation techniques, from heavy rains which cause lagoons to overflow or from leaching of wastewater below the ground.

Source: Texas Agricultural Extension Service, Texas A & M University, College Station, Texas.

Even the smaller non-permitted CAFOs, are expected to comply with the no-discharge policy. The state can initiate an enforcement action on these facilities if they discharge into the state's waters.

In 1993 the Texas legislature transferred much of the responsibility for regulating non-permitted, smaller CAFOs from the TNRCC to the Texas State Soil and Water Conservation Board. The move was designed to change the state's oversight of these operations from a traditional regulatory role to a technical assistance role. The Soil and Water Conservation Board, with assistance from the TNRCC, is attempting to help agriculture adopt better runoff control practices, mainly through waste management plans, allowing the facilities to come into compliance voluntarily. Currently, the Dairy Outreach Program is implemented in both North-Central Texas, in a five-county area, and in East Texas, in a three-county area.[69]

FYI *An average open feedlot receives about 300 tons of manure containing 24,000 pounds of nitrogen per acre per year. By contrast, animals on typical open rangeland deposit about 1/10 of a ton of manure containing eight pounds of nitrogen per acre per year.[70]*

Other Agricultural Non-Point-Source Pollution
Apart from CAFOs, agricultural lands may contribute other sources of non-point-source pollution.

Runoff from croplands may dump fertilizers and pesticides into surface waters. Runoff from rangeland often contains eroded soil, which causes sedimentation of rivers and streams. Such runoff may also contain high concentrations of nitrogen and phosphorus from animal waste and fertilizers. In Texas, from 1968 to 1990, 470 out of nearly 55,000 samples of surface water tested for nitrates exceeded the recommended drinking water standard of 10 milligrams per liter. Though this overall rate of violations is low—less than 1 percent—the problem samples were concentrated in a handful of counties, indicating a potentially serious regional problem with nitrate contamination.[71]

Surface water in Texas has not been extensively monitored for pesticides. However, arsenic, which is used in some pesticides, has been identified in several counties as a surface water concern. About five percent of total samples taken by the state between 1968 and 1990 exceeded the drinking water standard of 50 micrograms per liter for arsenic. Since arsenic occurs naturally and is also an industrial pollutant, it is difficult to pinpoint the source of arsenic in surface water. Most of the samples that exceeded standards were collected in counties with high industrial activity as well as agricultural production.[72]

Enforcement and Compliance of Agricultural Surface Water Pollution

In part because of the voluntary compliance agreement with the State Soil and Water Conservation Board, the TNRCC does not issue as many orders for agricultural water quality violations as it does for industrial and domestic water quality violations. Still, between FY 1992 and 1997, the TNRCC issued 45 administrative orders and assessed penalties of $360,542, although more than $130,000 of this total was deferred under agreements with the agricultural operators.[73] Most of these enforcement cases were related to unauthorized discharge of wastewater from CAFOs.[74]

URBAN NON-POINT-SOURCE POLLUTION

Water that enters streams and rivers from urban areas is often routed through a storm-water drainage system that collects rainwater. These systems are usually separate from wastewater treatment systems. Typically, rainfall picks up contaminants like oil and grease from roads, herbicides and pesticides from lawns and gardens, and household chemicals improperly disposed of by residents.

Under the NPDES permit, large cities and construction companies are required to treat storm water

WHO MUST PERMIT STORM WATER?

Municipal and industrial wastewater permits may include requirements to regulate the discharge of storm-water runoff based upon site-specific circumstances. In 1991, for example, 439 of 966 state discharge permits regulated storm-water discharges from industry.[75]

Until the federal government delegated to Texas responsibility for the NPDES program in 1998 to the TNRCC, storm-water permits were issued by the EPA. The 1987 amendments to the Clean Water Act required that storm-water discharges be permitted in two phases. Phase 1 requires all pre-1987 dischargers as well as industries, construction projects covering more than five acres, and cities over 100,000 population with a separate storm-water sewer system to obtain an NPDES permit.

There are 19 cities in Texas, as well as unincorporated portions of Harris County, that must obtain storm-water discharge permits. However, as of December 1996, only Corpus Christi had received a final storm-water permit, while San Antonio had been issued a draft permit.[76] The EPA issued final regulations for Phase II, which covers municipalities with less than 100,000 population, as well as commercial, retail, and institutional facilities. However, some municipalities will have up to six years to apply for a permit, and only those Phase II dischargers considered to be significant sources of pollution to water quality will be required to seek a full-blown permit. Supplemental Phase II rules are being developed to offer flexibility in the permitting process.

and develop management techniques to address these pollution sources (see box: Who Must Permit Storm Water?).

Construction, Pollution, and Impervious Cover

Construction, especially that associated with highway building, can also be a major source of sediment and other non-point-source pollution. The Texas Department of Transportation requires contractors to meet standards for mitigation of construction runoff during roadwork, but many environmentalists consider these standards inadequate. They argue that construction and development inevitably increase impervious cover, which prevents rain from being absorbed into the ground and thereby increases runoff that can contaminate streams and rivers.

Previously, under Section 26.177 of the Texas Water Code, all Texas cities with a population above 5,000 had to submit a pollution abatement plan to the TNRCC. These abatement plans must address both storm-sewer discharges and urban runoff.[77] However, in 1997 the legislature loosened this requirement to apply only to cities with populations greater than 10,000 and only to those cities where either TNRCC

MAP SHOWING WHERE CLASSIFIED STREAMS, RESERVOIRS, AND BAY SEGMENTS WERE IMPAIRED IN TEXAS IN 1999

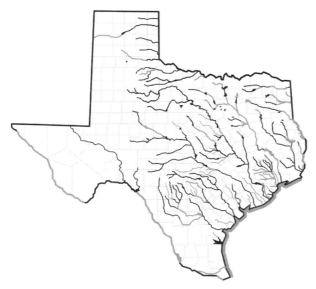

Source: Texas Natural Resource Conservation Commission, State of Texas 1999 Clean Water Act Section 303(d) List (April 9, 1999).

or Clean Rivers Program assessments had demonstrated pollution impacts from nonpermitted sources.[78]

FYI *The EPA estimates that each American household generates twenty pounds of home-chemical waste each year, much of which is improperly disposed of and ends up in rivers, lakes, and aquifers. In an effort to control this non-point-source pollution, many communities have set up home-chemical waste programs to encourage proper disposal of household chemicals. In Texas, such programs are voluntary.*

WHERE POLLUTION OCCURS IN TEXAS

Under Section 303 (d) of the Clean Water Act, the State of Texas must identify which stream, reservoir, and bay segments have been impaired by pollution and do not meet their designated water uses—such as aquatic life or contact recreation. The TNRCC has identified problems in 144 of the 368 classified water segments in Texas that do not support, or only partially support, their designated use.[79] In 1998 the TNRCC conducted its latest assessment of water quality in reservoirs.[80]

RIVER AUTHORITIES LOOK AT WATER QUALITY

Under a 1991 state law, local river authorities and coastal basin authorities are required to assess their river basins every two years, identifying major water quality issues. In 1992 all river authorities identified lack of monitoring, and the resulting limited water quality data, as the major water quality issue.[81] The 1992, 1994, and 1996 assessments demonstrated that elevated levels of nutrients and fecal coliform bacteria continued to be the most common water quality problems affecting state waters, while in West Texas, salinity (total dissolved solids) is one of the largest concerns.[82]

Water quality standards for fecal coliform bacteria are designed to prevent human illness, since they are an indicator of other pathogens that cause infectious diseases like hepatitis and cholera. In the 1996 assessment, high fecal coliform levels were identified as a concern in all 30 coastal and river basins. (While there are only 23 river and coastal basins, several

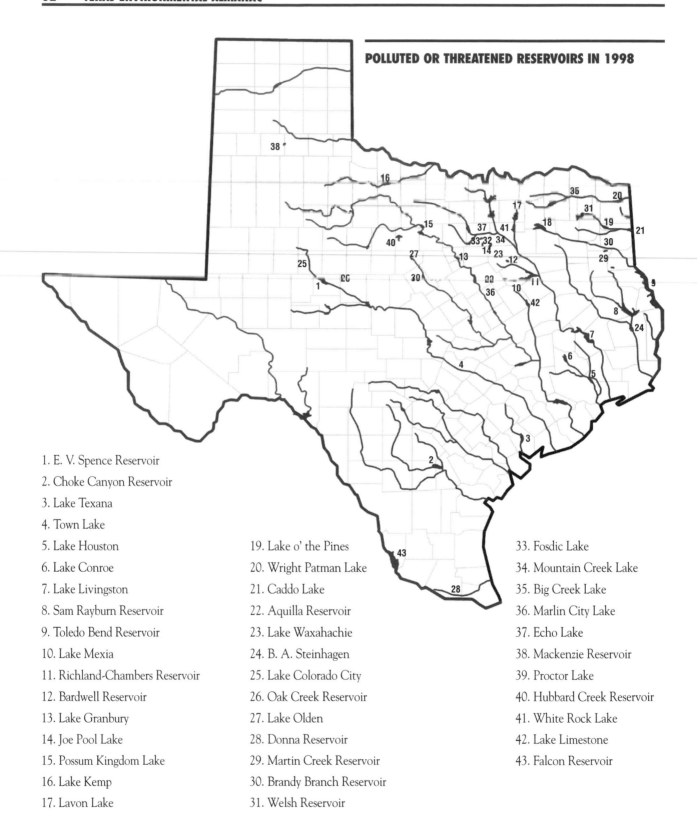

POLLUTED OR THREATENED RESERVOIRS IN 1998

1. E. V. Spence Reservoir
2. Choke Canyon Reservoir
3. Lake Texana
4. Town Lake
5. Lake Houston
6. Lake Conroe
7. Lake Livingston
8. Sam Rayburn Reservoir
9. Toledo Bend Reservoir
10. Lake Mexia
11. Richland-Chambers Reservoir
12. Bardwell Reservoir
13. Lake Granbury
14. Joe Pool Lake
15. Possum Kingdom Lake
16. Lake Kemp
17. Lavon Lake
18. Lake Tawakoni

19. Lake o' the Pines
20. Wright Patman Lake
21. Caddo Lake
22. Aquilla Reservoir
23. Lake Waxahachie
24. B. A. Steinhagen
25. Lake Colorado City
26. Oak Creek Reservoir
27. Lake Olden
28. Donna Reservoir
29. Martin Creek Reservoir
30. Brandy Branch Reservoir
31. Welsh Reservoir
32. Lake Como

33. Fosdic Lake
34. Mountain Creek Lake
35. Big Creek Lake
36. Marlin City Lake
37. Echo Lake
38. Mackenzie Reservoir
39. Proctor Lake
40. Hubbard Creek Reservoir
41. White Rock Lake
42. Lake Limestone
43. Falcon Reservoir

Reservoirs with threatened drinking water supplies where secondary drinking water criteria are exceeded

E.V. Spence Reservoir	Chloride, sulfate, total dissolved solids	Possum Kingdom Lake	Total dissolved solids
		Lake Olden	Total dissolved solids
Oak Creek Reservoir	Sulfate	Lake Colorado City	Total dissolved solids
Donna Reservoir	Sulfate	Oak Creek Reservoir	Total dissolved solids
Lake Granbury	Total dissolved solids		

Reservoirs not meeting contact recreation designated use

Sam Rayburn Reservoir	Fecal coliform bacteria	Choke Canyon	Fecal coliform bacteria

Reservoirs designated for but not fully supporting human health criteria

Lake Houston	Mercury	Lake Conroe	Mercury

Reservoirs not fully supporting aquatic life use

Lavon Lake	High pH (basic)	Mackenzie Reservoir	Total dissolved solids
Caddo Lake	Elevated water temperature, low pH (acidic), elevated zinc, mercury levels	Joe Pool Lake	Total dissolved solids, sulfates
		Proctor Lake	Total dissolved solids, chlorides
Wright Patman Lake	Low dissolved oxygen (sluggish flows and point and non-point-source nutrient build-up)	Hubbard Creek Reservoir	Sulfate
		White Rock Lake	Total dissolved solids
		Lake Limestone	Sulfate
Sam Rayburn Reservoir	Low dissolved oxygen (in Angelina River Arm due to naturally depressed levels and discharge from Paper Mill Creek)	E.V Spence Reservoir	Total dissolved solids, sulfates
		Falcon Reservoir	Total dissolved solids, chlorides
Lake Livingston	Low dissolved oxygen (nutrient build-up from wastewater discharge and urban run-off)		
Lake Mexia	Low dissolved oxygen (nutrient build-up in upper portion of reservoir)		
Lake Texana	Low dissolved oxygen (in headwater region of reservoir)		
Lake o' the Pines	Elevated zinc levels		

Reservoirs with fish consumption advisories or bans

Caddo Lake	Mercury	Brandy Branch Reservoir	Selenium (cooling water from coal power plant)
Toledo Bend Reservoir	Mercury		
B.A. Steinhagen Reservoir	Mercury	Welsh Reservoir	Selenium (cooling water from coal power plant)
Sam Rayburn Reservoir	Mercury		
Austin Town Lake	High chlordane (non-point-source pollution, urban run-off)	Lake Como	Chlordane, PCBs, dieldrin, DDE
		Fosdic Lake	Chlordane, PCBs, dieldrin, DDE
Donna Reservoir	PCBs (source unknown)	Echo Lake	PCBs
Martin Creek Reservoir	Selenium (cooling water from coal power plant)	Mountain Creek Lake	PCBs, chlordane, heptachlor epoxide, dieldrin, DDE, DDD, DDT

Reservoirs with threatened public water supply use

Big Creek Lake	Elevated atrazine levels	Richland-Chambers Reservoir	Elevated atrazine levels
Lake Tawakoni	Elevated atrazine levels		
Bardwell Reservoir	Elevated atrazine levels	Joe Pool Lake	Elevated atrazine levels
Lake Waxahachie	Elevated atrazine levels	Marlin City Lake	Elevated atrazine levels
Lavon Lake	Elevated atrazine levels	Aquilla Reservoir	Elevated atrazine, alachlor levels

Source: Texas Natural Resource Conservation Commission, 1998 State of Texas Reservoir Water Quality Assessment (December 1998).

WATER QUALITY ISSUES IDENTIFIED BY RIVER AUTHORITIES

ISSUE	NUMBER OF RIVER BASINS REPORTING ISSUE	% OF TOTAL
Lack of Monitoring	23	100%
High Fecal Coliform Levels	20	87%
Toxic Materials	18	78%
Depressed Dissolved Oxygen Levels	14	61%
Metals	14	61%
Excess Chlorides	12	52%
Pesticides	10	43%
Phosphorous	8	35%
Non-Point-Source Pollution	6	26%
Excessive Vegetation	6	26%
Shellfish Harvesting Closures/ Fishing Advisories	4	17%
Septic Tanks	4	17%
Oil and Gas Degradation	4	17%
Loss or Degradation of Habitat	3	13%
Salt Water Contamination	3	13%
Nitrogen	2	9%
Excess Total Suspended Solids	2	9%
Fish Kills	2	9%

Source: Texas Water Commission, Summary Report: Regional Assessments of Water Quality Pursuant to the Texas Clean Rivers Act (December 1992), 12.

CLASSIFIED SEGMENTS WITH ELEVATED FECAL COLIFORM BACTERIA LEVELS, INCLUDING THOSE WHERE IT ISN'T SAFE TO SWIM

Source: Texas Natural Resource Conservation Commission, State of Texas 1999 Clean Water Act, Section 303(d) List (April 9, 1999).

river basins, including the Red, Sabine, Neches, Brazos, and Colorado, were divided in the analysis into upper and lower basins.)

Other river authorities identified toxics as a major concern. Specific toxic materials identified by river authorities, based on limited monitoring data, include pesticides like Aldrin, and PCBs, which are also banned for new uses. However, very limited monitoring data were available for these substances, and most problems pinpointed by the river basin assessments include high levels of nickel, zinc, cadmium, lead, mercury, and other metals, which probably are from industrial sources.

Over 86 percent of the 108 fish kills reported in the past four years are believed to be due to four causes—depletion of levels of dissolved oxygen, toxics, wastewater bypasses, and unknown causes. Toxics were the cause of 23 of the kills.[83] In two water bodies, the Rio Grande downstream of Laredo-Nuevo Laredo and the Alligator Bayou in the Neches-Trinity coastal river basin, unusually high numbers of fish abnormalities may indicate the presence of toxic pollutants.[84]

In 19 of the 30 river and coastal basins, low oxygen levels were identified as a major water quality concern.[85] This condition, also referred to as high biological oxygen demand (BOD), is considered one of the most obvious indicators of degraded water quality because it directly impacts aquatic life.

Twenty-six of the river basin areas identified high levels of nutrients—usually phosphorus, nitrogen, ammonia, and nitrates—as a water quality concern or possible concern. Wastewater discharges, improperly functioning wastewater systems, septic tanks, agricultural runoff, and other kinds of non-point-source pollution were identified as probable sources of these nutrient loadings. Excess nutrients in water can cause growth in aquatic vegetation, which reduces dissolved oxygen in rivers and streams, affecting fish and other aquatic species.

Degradation of habitat is a major water quality concern. Development, erosion, and the dredging and filling of coastal areas have destroyed some

CLASSIFIED SEGMENTS WITH HIGH METAL OR PESTICIDE TOXICITY CONCERNS IN AMBIENT WATER QUALITY, 1996

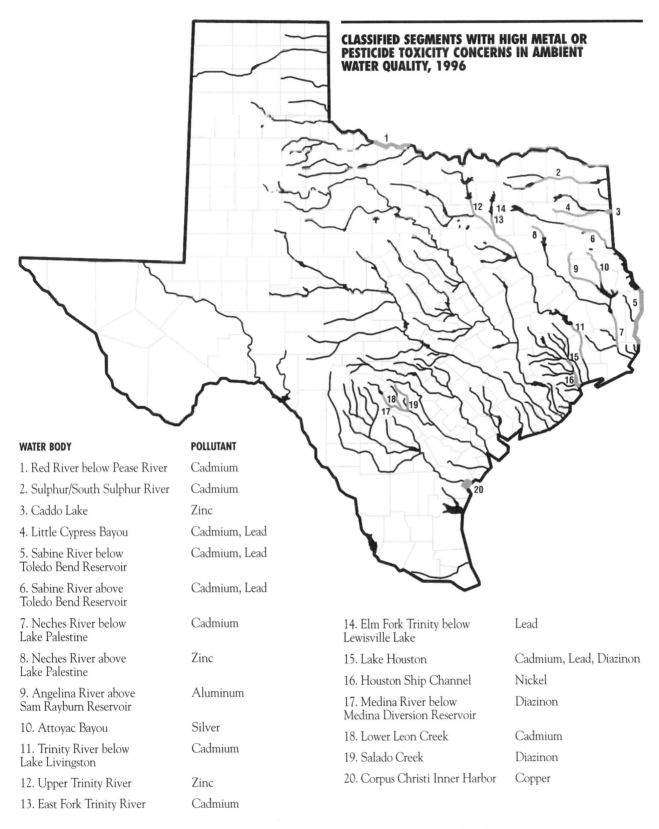

WATER BODY	POLLUTANT
1. Red River below Pease River	Cadmium
2. Sulphur/South Sulphur River	Cadmium
3. Caddo Lake	Zinc
4. Little Cypress Bayou	Cadmium, Lead
5. Sabine River below Toledo Bend Reservoir	Cadmium, Lead
6. Sabine River above Toledo Bend Reservoir	Cadmium, Lead
7. Neches River below Lake Palestine	Cadmium
8. Neches River above Lake Palestine	Zinc
9. Angelina River above Sam Rayburn Reservoir	Aluminum
10. Attoyac Bayou	Silver
11. Trinity River below Lake Livingston	Cadmium
12. Upper Trinity River	Zinc
13. East Fork Trinity River	Cadmium
14. Elm Fork Trinity below Lewisville Lake	Lead
15. Lake Houston	Cadmium, Lead, Diazinon
16. Houston Ship Channel	Nickel
17. Medina River below Medina Diversion Reservoir	Diazinon
18. Lower Leon Creek	Cadmium
19. Salado Creek	Diazinon
20. Corpus Christi Inner Harbor	Copper

Source: Texas Natural Resource Conservation Commission, The State of Texas Water Quality Inventory—1996, 13th ed. (1996).

TOXICS ON THE BORDER

Because of concern over toxic contamination from industrial and agricultural sources in the Rio Grande, which forms the border between Texas and Mexico, the U.S. and Mexican main federal environmental agencies, as well as the TNRCC, the Texas Parks and Wildlife Department (TPWD), and the Texas Department of Health, have conducted a series of toxic studies along the Rio Grande and its tributaries. The first phase of the study, conducted in 1992 and 1993 and released to the public in 1994, found a disturbing trend of high levels of toxics in water, sediment, and fish in several of the mainstem monitoring sites and in almost all the tributaries. The study monitored 19 mainstem sites and 26 tributary sites. At least one toxic substance was found in water, sediment, or fish tissue that exceeded at least one screening criterion at each of the sites.[86] The 30 chemicals that exceeded screening levels included some of significant concern, such as PCBs, cyanide, mercury, lead, and residual chlorine.

In 1995 Mexican and U.S. agencies conducted Phase II of the study, sampling 27 sites on the mainstem and 19 on tributaries in low-flow conditions.[87] The report confirms the Phase I findings: for significant reaches of the Rio Grande, such as downstream of El Paso-Ciudad Juárez, Laredo-Nuevo Laredo, and Ojinaga-Presidio and in the Amistad Reservoir, there is a high potential for toxic contamination.[88]

SEGMENTS WITH A HIGH AND MODERATE POTENTIAL FOR TOXIC CHEMICAL IMPACTS ALONG THE RIO GRANDE, PHASE I OF RIO GRANDE TOXIC SUBSTANCES STUDY

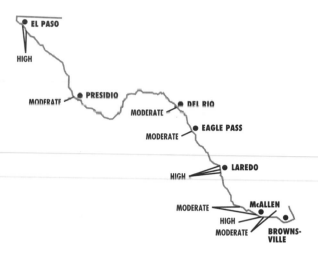

Source: Texas Natural Resource Conservation Commission, 1996 Regional Assessment of Water Quality in the Rio Grande Basin (1996), Appendix B.

RIVER SEGMENTS WITH CONCERN FOR DEPRESSED DISSOLVED OXYGEN LEVELS AND/OR HIGH NUTRIENT LEVELS

Source: Texas Natural Resource Conservation Commission, Summary Report: Regional Assessments of Water Quality Pursuant to the Texas Clean Rivers Act (December 1996).

animal habitat in rivers and streams. The Sabine River Authority conducted ambient toxicity and rapid bioassessment studies to determine impacts of toxic pollution and non-point-source pollution on biological health. The tests revealed several areas of concern or biological impairment throughout the basin.[93]

In addition to water quality problems identified by river authorities, excessive levels of toxics such as metals and pesticides in edible fish tissue has led the Texas Department of Health (TDH) to issue

LIST OF FISH CONSUMPTION ADVISORIES AND CLOSURES

WATER BODY	DATE ISSUED	SIZE	POLLUTANTS	SOURCE
Restricted or No-Consumption Advisories				
Gulf of Mexico	1997	3,879 square miles	Mercury (King Mackerel Species)	Unknown
Caddo Lake	1995	26,800 acres	Mercury	Unknown
Big Cypress Creek		63 miles		
Toledo Bend Reservoir		181,600 acres		
B.A. Steinhagen Reservoir		13,700 acres		
Sam Rayburn Reservoir		114,409 acres		
Welsh Reservoir	1992	1,365 acres	Selenium	Power plant
Brandy Branch Res.		1,240 acres		
Martin Creek Res.		5,020 acres		
Houston Ship Channel/ San Jacinto River	1990	12 miles	Dioxin	Paper mill
Houston Ship Channel		6 miles		
Houston Ship Channel/Buffalo Bayou		14 miles		
Upper Galveston Bay		22 square miles		
Tabbs Bay		3.6 square miles		
San Jacinto Bay		2.1 square miles		
Black Duck Bay		0.6 square miles		
Scott Bay		1.7 square miles		
Barbours Cut		0.2 square miles		
Burnett Bay		2.7 square miles		
Clear Creek Tidal	1993	8 miles	Volatile Organic Compounds	
Clear Creek Above Tidal		30 miles	Chlordane	Hazardous waste site
Town Lake, Austin	1987	500 acres	Chlordane	Urban runoff
Arroyo Colorado above Tidal, Llano Grande and Main Floodway	1993	63 miles	Chlordane, Toxaphene, DDT	Agricultural and urban runoff
Aquatic Life Closures				
Lake Como	1995	15 acres	Chlordane, PCBs, Dieldrin, DDE	Urban runoff
Fosdic Lake		6 acres	Dieldrin, DDE Chlordane, PCBs	Urban runoff
Echo Lake	1995	17 acres	PCBs	Urban runoff
Mountain Creek Lake	1996	2,710 acres	PCBs , Chlordane, Heptachlor Epoxide, Dieldrin, DDE, DDD, DDT	Unknown
Upper Trinity River	1990	19 miles	Chlordane	Urban runoff
West Fork Trinity River		22 miles		
Clear Fork Trinity River		1 mile		
Lower West Fork Trinity River		27 miles		
Donna Reservoir and Irrigation System	1994	333 acres	PCBs	Unknown
Upper Lavaca Bay	1988	54.8 sq miles	Mercury	Spill
Cox Bay		2.9 sq miles		

Source: Texas Department of Health, Seafood Safety Division, Fish Advisories & Bans, 1997 (1998).

FISHING FOR MERCURY AND PCBS?

Like most states, Texas has no comprehensive fish-monitoring program. The state does test fish tissue for contaminants when a report of a chemical spill or some other information leads state health officials to believe human health may be threatened. Testing fish is expensive; a detailed tissue sampling of one fish might cost $500, and a full scan, which examines the liver and reproductive organs to pinpoint sources of dangerous contaminants, might exceed $1,000 per sample.[89]

The Texas Department of Health's Seafood Safety Division is charged with surveillance of miles of oyster-harvesting areas along the Gulf Coast and has the authority to close bays and estuaries. This program is funded in part by a $1-per-sack fee paid by oyster fishermen.

No comparable revenue source is available for testing inland fish, although there is evidence that such monitoring is warranted. In 1993 the EPA conducted a study on the types of environmental problems to which Texas families living along the border are exposed. As part of the study, the EPA tested a carp caught by a Brownsville family from the Donna Reservoir. The tests of the fish's tissue revealed PCB levels of 400 parts per million, or 200 times the recommended limit for human consumption.[90] When further tests of Donna Reservoir fish identified eight more fish contaminated by PCBs, the Texas Department of Health issued a fish-consumption advisory for the reservoir and its connecting canals. Ten more PCB-contaminated fish caught from an irrigation canal between the reservoir and the Rio Grande were found in January 1994. Following this study, the department banned any taking or consumption of fish in the area.[91]

PCBs have been banned in the United States since the late 1970s because they cause liver disorders and developmental delays in infants. (The only exception to the ban is for use in electrical transformers.) To date, officials have been unable to identify the source of the PCBs found in the Donna area.

While startling, the problems at Donna with PCBs are not unique. Over the past ten years, TNRCC officials have also identified nine segments around the state where elevated concentrations of PCBs in whole fish tissue are a concern.[92] In 1996, following similar findings of high concentrations of PCBs in fish tissue, the Texas Department of Health issued aquatic-life closures of both Echo Lake and Mountain Creek Lake in the Trinity River Basin in the Fort Worth area.

"aquatic life closures" or total bans on consumption of fish and shellfish in two bays—Cox Bay and the upper portion of the Lavaca Bay, due to elevated mercury levels—five reservoirs or irrigation systems, and four river segments of the Trinity River (see Coastal Resources section for details on bays and estuaries). The TDH has issued fish-consumption advisories for 23 other water bodies.[94]

Fishing in areas closed to fishing is a violation of state law. Most recently, in 1996, following the discovery of fish contaminated with high levels of PCBs, the TDH declared Mountain Lake Creek closed to fishing and fish consumption because of high levels of PCBs. In addition, in 1995 the department issued consumption advisories for five reservoirs in Northeast Texas because of elevated mercury levels (see box: Fishing for Mercury and PCBs?).

GROUNDWATER: AQUIFERS

BACKGROUND

Like surface water, groundwater is vulnerable to contamination from a variety of sources. In Texas, all nine major aquifers and 20 minor aquifers have experienced some form of contamination. These contamination problems stem partly from land-based development and industry and partly from over-pumping, which causes infiltration of saline waters.

Despite these problems, state laws do not protect groundwater to the same extent as surface water. There are, for example, no groundwater quality standards to parallel those for surface water. The state does have standards in place for groundwater utilized for drinking water.

Clean groundwater is needed for more than

drinking purposes. Agriculture depends heavily on groundwater for irrigation; in 1995 some 80 percent of all groundwater pumped was used for crop irrigation.[95] Poor or contaminated groundwater could jeopardize crops and threaten the health of livestock.

Clean groundwater is also essential to clean surface water. Groundwater is connected to surface water in the hydrological cycle, and some aquifers actually feed area springs and rivers. For example, the Edwards Aquifer is the major source for Central Texas rivers through the Comal and San Marcos springs. Poor quality water—or a lack of water—harms the springs.

Sometimes contamination occurs naturally. Saline water from deeper aquifers may reach aquifers that provide water for humans. Some groundwater may

TYPICAL ROUTES OF GROUNDWATER CONTAMINATION

Source: Adapted from Environmental Protection Agency, Office of Water Supply and Solid Waste Management Programs, Waste Disposal Practices and Their Effects on Groundwater (Washington, D.C.: U.S. Government Printing Office, 1977).

have naturally high background levels of nitrates, metals, iron, sulfate, or chloride, all of which can give water an odd odor, color, or taste.

Groundwater contamination has become a major public policy concern in recent decades. Human activity on virtually any piece of land in the state has the potential to affect groundwater quality, since 76 percent of the state's surface area of 267,277 square miles lies above major and minor aquifers. A variety of potential threats to groundwater are the result of human activities.

SOURCES OF GROUNDWATER POLLUTION

It is difficult to ascertain how much groundwater contamination has resulted from human activities. Under a 1991 state law, the legislature created the Texas Groundwater Protection Committee, which is formed by nine state agencies. As part of its duties, the committee tracks instances of groundwater contamination. The committee, utilizing data from all state agencies, reported 7,459 instances of groundwater contamination between 1989 and 1997 that had yet to be cleaned up.[96] These figures

represent only the cases reported and confirmed. In addition to these instances of groundwater contamination, action was completed on a total of 2,637 cases of groundwater contamination between 1989 and 1997.[97]

Monitoring of groundwater quality is divided among different state, federal, and local entities. In 1996 the TNRCC began a water quality assessment program for aquifers as part of the Water Quality Inventory conducted by the TNRCC under the Clean Water Act.[98] In 1996 one major aquifer (the Trinity) one minor aquifer (the Dockum, in the High Plains) and two local aquifers (the Rio Grande Alluvium and Laredo formations) were analyzed. Since 1990 the TWDB has begun a groundwater monitoring program that attempts to cover all the major and minor aquifers within six years. In a typical year, the TWDB conducts samples in 800 to 1,000 different sites, while other entities—such as groundwater conservation districts, the U.S. Geological Survey, and the TNRCC—conduct about 900 samples per year.[99] In addition, three state agencies—the TNRCC, the Railroad Commission, and the TDH—require monitoring at more than

MAJOR SOURCES OF GROUNDWATER CONTAMINATION THAT HAVE NOT BEEN CLEANED UP, 1989–1997

ACTIVITY	1989–1997 CASES	TYPES OF CONTAMINANTS
Underground and above-ground storage tanks	6,338	Gasoline, diesel, waste oil, kerosene, hydraulic fluid
Industries and land disposal facilities, including hazardous waste facilities and unauthorized wastewater discharges	563	Trichloroethylene, arsenic, PCBs, VOCs, solvents, creosote, chromium, lead, heavy metals, phenols, chlorides, pesticides, sulfates, cadmium
Permitted and illegal municipal landfills	26	Total dissolved solids, chlorides, trichloroethylene, vinyl chloride
Federal and state supefund hazardous waste sites	92	Arsenic, lead, chromium, benzene toluene, xylenes, PCBs, VOCs, pesticides, trichloroethylene
Voluntary clean-up abandoned hazardous waste sites	267	Arsenic, lead, chromium, benzene toluene, xylenes, PCBs, VOCs, pesticides, trichloroethylene
Septic tanks, CAFOs, Class V wells, sludge disposal, wastewater treatment facilities	21	Nitrates, chlorides, salt water, copper, selenium, iron, ammonia
Public drinking water systems	24	Benzene, trichloroethylene, carbon tetrachloride, chromium
Emergency spills and leaks	11	Benzene, toluene, xylenes, hydrocarbons, vinyl chloride
Agricultural chemicals and pesticides	26	Arsenic, prometon, Atrazine, dicamba, metolachlor, propazine, bromacil, DDT dieldrin, DDE, cyanize
Oil and gas waste injection wells, underground and surface storage of oil and gas and oil and gas waste	77	Sodium chloride, chlorides, refined oil, crude oil, hydrochloric acid, total dissolved solids
Miscellaneous and unknown (reported by local groundwater districts)	18	Lead, mercury, hydrocarbons, sediment

Source: *Texas Groundwater Protection Committee*, Joint Groundwater Monitoring and Contamination Report, 1997 (1998), *Tables 1–3.*

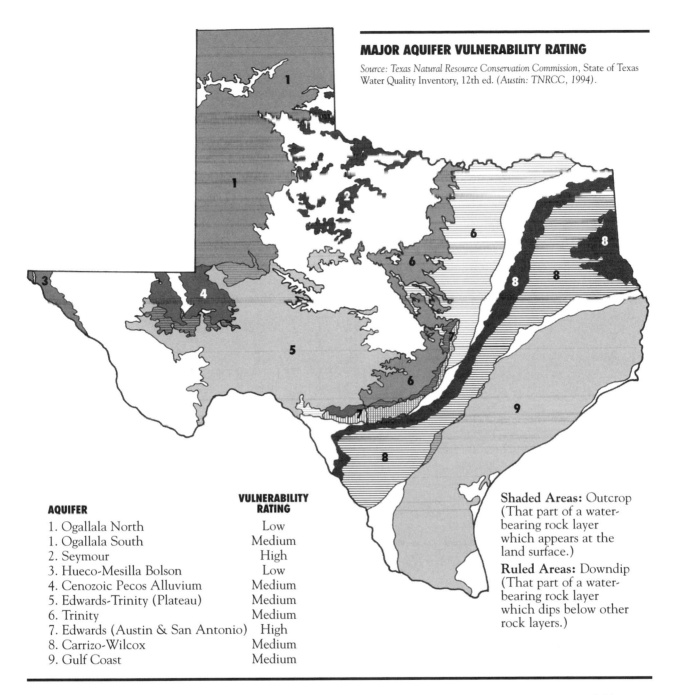

MAJOR AQUIFER VULNERABILITY RATING

Source: Texas Natural Resource Conservation Commission, State of Texas Water Quality Inventory, 12th ed. (Austin: TNRCC, 1994).

AQUIFER	VULNERABILITY RATING
1. Ogallala North	Low
1. Ogallala South	Medium
2. Seymour	High
3. Hueco-Mesilla Bolson	Low
4. Cenozoic Pecos Alluvium	Medium
5. Edwards-Trinity (Plateau)	Medium
6. Trinity	Medium
7. Edwards (Austin & San Antonio)	High
8. Carrizo-Wilcox	Medium
9. Gulf Coast	Medium

Shaded Areas: Outcrop (That part of a water-bearing rock layer which appears at the land surface.)

Ruled Areas: Downdip (That part of a water-bearing rock layer which dips below other rock layers.)

8,400 industrial, agricultural, and municipal facilities statewide for permit and operational requirements. Most of this monitoring is self-reported. However, the majority of this groundwater quality monitoring data provides very little information about anthropogenic (i.e., human-made) sources of constituents such as heavy metals, petroleum products, or pesticides.

Finally, the TNRCC has ranked the aquifers'
vulnerability to contamination using a model known as the DRASTIC index. This index looks at both hydrological and geological components of the aquifers to gauge the potential for groundwater pollution.

UNDERGROUND STORAGE TANKS

From 1989 through 1996, the source of groundwater contamination in 86 percent of cases reported to the TNRCC were underground or above-ground storage tanks. Usually these were petroleum storage tanks used by gas stations. To date, 2,720 of the 9,058 documented cases (about 30 percent) have been successfully cleaned up.[100]

There are some 158,000 underground and 21,000 above-ground storage tanks registered with the TNRCC.[101] Most contain petroleum products like diesel fuel, waste oil, and gasoline and are found at gas stations. A smaller number store regulated hazardous substances. In addition to contamination of groundwater, another 13,500 underground storage tanks have contaminated soils but not groundwater.[102] Contamination from petroleum storage tanks has affected not only groundwater quality but also real estate values in some areas, as prospective buyers have considered cleanup costs and pollution liability.[103]

In 1989 the Texas legislature created a fee-supported reimbursement fund that enabled the state to assume most of the cleanup costs of the leaking petroleum storage tanks. Any owner of a petroleum storage tank can make a claim to the fund, although an initial deduction of approximately 15 percent of the cleanup costs is not eligible for reimbursement.[104] When the party responsible for contamination is unwilling or unable to pay or cannot be located, the fund can be used to pay for clean up. From 1990 to 1993, almost $200 million from this fund was spent on petroleum-storage-tank cleanup, but fee revenue was not sufficient to pay for all necessary cleanups.[105] In 1995 the legislature doubled the fee charged to petroleum cargo tankers at bulk stations, which is collected by the Office of the Comptroller. The fee—charged according to the size of the cargo truck—averages about one cent per gallon. In FY 1996, $71 million was spent, while in FY 1997, $52 million was spent from the fund on cleanup.[106]

HAZARDOUS AND MUNICIPAL SOLID-WASTE DISPOSAL

Abandoned hazardous waste sites are regulated through the federal Superfund program, which designates abandoned hazardous waste sites for cleanup by placing them on a National Priorities List. States may also designate hazardous waste sites on a state

Superfund list. As of early 1998, Texas had 32 federally designated Superfund sites on the National Priorities List and 47 sites proposed or listed on the state Superfund registry (see *Industrial Waste* chapter for more detail). All of these sites are subject to groundwater monitoring by the TNRCC. There is evidence that at least 26 National Priorities List sites and 22 state Superfund sites in Texas have led to groundwater contamination with such constituents as arsenic, lead, chromium, and PCBs.[107]

In addition to these Superfund sites, 40 additional abandoned hazardous waste sites that have not been selected for either the federal or state lists have contaminated groundwater. Under the state's new Voluntary Cleanup Program, created by legislative action in 1995, sites are also investigated to see if groundwater impacts have occurred. By the end of 1997, a total of 267 of these sites had been identified as having contaminated groundwater.[108] Between 1989 and 1997, industrial hazardous-waste disposal facilities were responsible for 563 cases of groundwater contamination that have not yet been cleaned up.[109] Municipal solid-waste facilities have been linked with another 26 cases of contamination. These sources of groundwater contamination are more fully discussed in the *Industrial Waste* and *Municipal Waste* chapters.

MINING ACTIVITIES

Another potential threat to groundwater is mining activities. While there is currently no strip mining of uranium in Texas, four sites are being restored following uranium strip-mining activity. This activity requires groundwater monitoring under Texas Railroad Commission guidelines. In addition, four tailings and waste sites—where the uranium was milled and extracted from the ore—in Karnes and Live Oak counties are being closed and covered to prevent further contamination of subsurface aquifers or radioactive waste emissions. The reclaimed sites have resulted in groundwater contamination, including one confirmed case at the Chevron Resources facility in 1996.[110]

Coal mining also has been common in Texas, the largest coal consumer in the nation (see *Energy* and

Air Quality chapters for more information). As of early 1997, there were 11 companies mining 25 different sites, while two other sites had closed and were being cleaned up. While the Railroad Commission requires that companies monitor groundwater quarterly for some basic parameters, such as fluoride, nitrates, and magnesium, companies are required to monitor for trace metals, such as lead, arsenic, mercury, and selenium, only once per year. There have been no confirmed cases of groundwater contamination from coal- or uranium-mining activities under Railroad Commission jurisdiction. However, the major groundwater impact has been the drawdown of localized aquifers. Once the mined areas and localized aquifers are resaturated through precipitation, adjacent aquifers and streamflows could be impacted by the mining activities.[111]

INJECTION WELLS

Injection wells, where pressurized liquid wastes or other fluids are injected into aquifers, are a major method of disposal for industrial and hazardous wastes. Injection wells are also used to help recover oil, gas, and minerals. Uranium and sulfur are often mined by injecting hot water into formations to loosen up these materials.

The Railroad Commission of Texas has jurisdic-

WHAT DO WE INJECT UNDERGROUND IN TEXAS?

TYPE OF UNDERGROUND INJECTION	SOURCE
Industrial and hazardous waste	Manufacturing industry
Oil and gas waste	Oil and gas exploration, development, production
Superheated water	Brine mining, sulfur and sodium, sulfate mining, uranium mining
Sewage disposal	Municipalities, individuals
Agricultural drainage	Agriculture, particularly citrus production

Source: Texas Department of Water Resources, Underground Injection Wells in Texas (1984).

tion over injection wells used to inject oil and gas wastes. Most wastes consist of salt water, which is recovered along with natural gas during drilling. The Railroad Commission can also issue permits for wells to be used for secondary recovery or to store hydrocarbons. In December 1997 the Railroad Commission reported 8,201 saltwater disposal wells, 26,251 active secondary-recovery wells, and some 539 active hydrocarbon and gas storage wells.[112] Two confirmed cases of groundwater contamination resulting from injection wells have been documented in the past few years.[113]

Injection wells have been involved in a number of controversial lawsuits and permit battles, as well as

CONTAMINATION POTENTIAL OF MISCELLANEOUS INJECTION WELLS

WELL TYPE	CONTAMINATION POTENTIAL	POTENTIAL CONTAMINANTS
Agricultural Drainage	High	Pesticides, fertilizers, pathogens, metals via soil sediments, salts.
Storm Water Drainage	Moderate	Heavy metals (Cu, Pb, Zn), organics, coliform bacteria, contaminants from streets, pesticides.
Industrial Drainage	High-Moderate	Organic solvents, acids, pesticides and various other storm drainage wells.
Heat Pump/Air Conditioning Return Flow	Low	Potable Waters (90° to 110° F) may contain scale or corrosion inhibitors.
Sewage Disposal (septic tanks)	High-Low	Suspended solids, nitrates, chlorides, sulfates, sodium, calcium, fecal coliform.
Mine Backfill	Moderate	Acidic waters.
Automobile Service Station	High	Heavy metals, solvents, cleaners, used oil and fluids, detergents, organic compounds.
Artificial Recharge	High-Low	Variable, sediments, pesticides, fertilizers. Water is generally of good quality.
Abandoned Water	Moderate	Potentially any fluid, saline waters, hazardous chemicals, fertilizers, sewage, sediments.
Others	Unknown	Variable.

Source: Texas Department of Water Resources, Underground Injection Wells in Texas (1984).

high-profile groundwater contamination cases, usually resulting from improper handling of the waste at the surface prior to injection (see *Industrial Waste* chapter). According to the TNRCC, there have been no confirmed cases of groundwater contamination from the injection of hazardous and other industrial wastes in the past five years. However, in the case of injection wells used for mining, the movement of mining fluids into groundwater is not considered a case of groundwater contamination so long as the facility cleans up the water and ensures that it does not spread past the mining area. All groundwater contamination resulting from these activities has been cleaned up.

Currently, 58 hazardous waste injection wells are permitted and are in service, while 39 nonhazardous wells are permitted and in service.[114] Most are located in the coastal area and dispose of wastes associated with the petrochemical industry. Presently only three commercial facilities are accepting hazardous waste from other facilities.

FYI ☞ *It is estimated that from 1961 through 1981, more than 60 billion gallons of industrial wastes were disposed of in underground injection wells in Texas.* (Source: Texas Department of Water Resources, Underground Injection Operations in Texas, 3-11.)

Another class of injection wells are those used for uranium or sulfur mining or for the recovery of brine (subsurface salt deposits). While sulfur mines are regulated by the TNRCC, uranium mines are regulated by the Texas Department of Health, and brine mining by the Railroad Commission. These wells can contribute to the contamination of groundwater by increasing its salinity or by moving naturally occurring radioactive material.

Most of the 80 brine-mining facilities operating in Texas are located in the High Plains and Trans-Pecos regions. Thirty-four uranium mining sites, three sodium-sulfate mining sites, and six sulfur mining sites have been permitted in South-Central Texas, near San Antonio. All of the uranium mines and 71 of the 80 brine mines are required to sample and monitor groundwater quarterly because of potential contamination.[115] All of the sodium-sulfate

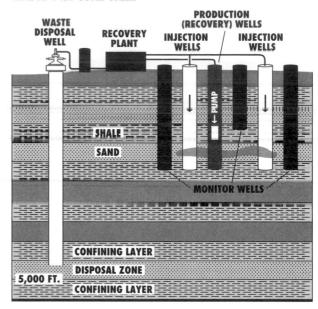

EXAMPLE OF A URANIUM MINE AND INDUSTRIAL WASTE DISPOSAL WELL

Source: Prepared by Texas Natural Resource Conservation Commission.

and sulfur mines are either closed or in the process of being closed, while only three uranium mines are presently in operation. Uranium mines take background levels before mining begins, and mine operators are expected to return any affected groundwater to background or pre-mining levels.[116] In general, injection wells used in mining are not as deep as those used for injection of wastes. They are thus more likely to impact near-surface water used for drinking, which is the reason they are monitored.

Another type of well is used to inject urban or agricultural runoff into underground formations. The Lower Rio Grande Valley is the major area of Texas where agricultural drainage wells are used. These wells help eliminate excess water from agricultural production. Because this part of the state is flat and has clay soils and high water tables, surface drainage is limited. Agricultural drainage wells collect near-surface waters and drain them into subsurface formations. They dispose of waters containing nitrates, dissolved solids, and pesticides, all of which have a high potential for contamination of groundwater.

These wells are used mainly in citrus production, which has been rapidly declining in the Valley.[117]

Some 108 wells have been located in the Lower Rio Grande Valley counties of Hidalgo and Starr and in south-central Runnels County. Other agricultural drainage wells are located in Oldham County, where they could impact the Ogallala Aquifer.[118]

WATER, OIL, AND GAS WELLS

Groundwater may also be affected by the thousands of wells in Texas drilled for water or for oil and gas exploration. When improperly drilled or cased, or when the casing has corroded, old oil, gas, and water wells serve as conduits for contamination of the aquifers below. Improperly completed and abandoned water wells may allow direct access from the surface to groundwater for contaminants such as pesticides, or they may facilitate the comingling of groundwater from one aquifer to another. Additionally, they can be a safety hazard to humans and livestock.

According to TWDB estimates, more than 800,000 water wells have been drilled this century in Texas. The TWDB estimates that about 20,000 new wells are drilled each year, most of which are not properly inventoried.[119] Currently, the TWDB maintains a groundwater database that contains information on 114,300 wells, about 64,000 of which have some water quantity or quality data. All new wells must meet specific casing and construction standards, and abandoned wells must be plugged. This plugging activity is overseen by the Water Well Drillers Team, which in 1997 was transferred from the TNRCC to the Texas Department of Licensing and Regulation.[120] About 150 wells per month are plugged by individual landowners and reported to the Water Well Drillers Team.[121]

In addition to water wells, an estimated 1.5 million holes have been drilled in this century for oil- and gas-related activities[122] Currently, 281,981 oil wells and 73,151 gas wells across the state are registered with the Railroad Commission, and about 124,000 of these are not currently producing.[123] Commission records indicate that 522,713 wells have been plugged, and 22,968 abandoned wells remain inactive and in violation of the commission's plugging rule.[124]

Abandoned oil wells are channels for the upward movement of brine—salt water often found in

oil-bearing zones—and they are paths to contamination by oil and gas, drilling fluids, and other contaminants. Salt water from abandoned oil wells has already polluted the upper portions of the Colorado River.[125] These wells must be plugged to prevent the contamination of aquifers by salt water and oil wastes.

To address the large number of unplugged wells, the Texas legislature in 1984 created an Abandoned Well Plugging Fund, which had spent $54 million and had helped plug approximately 12,588 wells through FY 1997.[126]

OTHER OIL AND GAS INDUSTRY IMPACTS

The EPA estimates that about one million tons of hazardous waste is produced each year in American oil fields.[127] The disposal of these wastes has the potential to affect groundwater. Until 1969, when the Railroad Commission adopted its no pit rule—also known as Statewide Rule 8—oil companies typically disposed of salt water and chemicals in open pits, creeks, and roads. The chemicals used during the oil-well drilling process and disposed of in these pits include such highly toxic elements as barium, arsenic, and cadmium.

Today, the storage and disposal of major oil and gas wastes requires a permit or authorization. Statewide Rule 8 identifies three types of oil-field pits: prohibited pits, authorized pits, and pits authorized through permit. Authorized activities include land farming, where toxic materials are mixed with soils; burial; road-spreading; commercial hauling, treatment, and disposal; and the use of pits such as reserve pits, fresh mining water pits, and others. Other pits such as saltwater disposal pits, brine pits, drilling-fluid storage and disposal pits, and gas-plant evaporation and retention pits, require a permit from the Railroad Commission.[128] There are currently 40 land-farming facilities permitted for disposal of oil and gas waste and 4,857 pits permitted for storage or disposal of such wastes or the retention of brine.[129] However, only 58 sites regulated by Statewide Rule 8 require groundwater monitoring.[130]

The Railroad Commission reported 77 cases of groundwater contamination from oil and gas

COUNTIES WITH CONFIRMED GROUNDWATER CONTAMINATION FROM OIL AND GAS ACTIVITIES, 1997

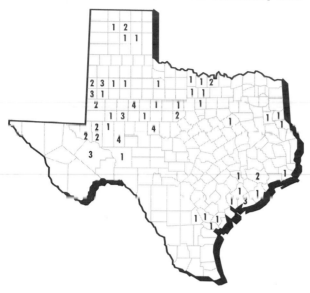

Source: Texas Natural Resource Conservation Commission, Joint Groundwater Monitoring and Contamination Report, 1997 (June 1998), Figure 12.

AREAS OF POTENTIAL OR KNOWN GROUNDWATER POLLUTION RESULTING FROM AGRICULTURAL ACTIVITIES

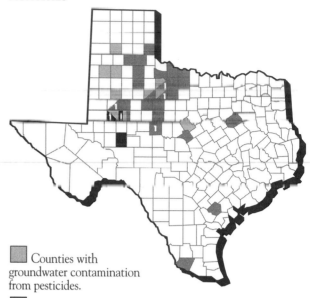

Counties with groundwater contamination from pesticides.

Counties with nitrate levels exceeding EPA recommended drinking water standard of 44 mg/L in more than 20 percent of samples. 1) More than 60 percent.

Counties with arsenic concentrations exceeding the recommended EPA drinking water standard of 0.05 mg/L in more than 20 percent of samples. 1) more than 50 percent.

Source: Texas State Soil and Water Conservation Board, A Comprehensive Study of Texas Watersheds and Their Impact on Water Quality and Water Quantity (Temple: Texas State Soil and Conservation Board, January 1991), 131-137; and Texas Natural Resource Conservation Commission, Joint Groundwater Monitoring and Contamination Report, 1997 (1998), Table 1.

activities in 49 different counties, including 30 new cases between 1996 and 1997. These cases included facilities covered under Rule 8, injection waste facilities, and brine mining.[131]

AGRICULTURE

Agricultural and forestry activities, just as they have contaminated surface water, have also degraded groundwater quality in Texas. Unauthorized discharges and runoff from CAFOs have been responsible for nitrate contamination of shallow groundwater. (However, excess nitrate in groundwater can be caused by other sources, such as poorly designed or old septic tanks.) However, only one contamination case, from a large CAFO between Tom Green and Runnels counties just outside of San Angelo, has led to enforcement action by the TNRCC.[132] The primary causes of agriculture-related groundwater contamination are runoff from CAFOs, pastures, and barnyards; excessive nitrogen fertilization of cropland; and land-clearing and other agricultural practices that change soil composition, altering its ability to filter out pollutants. The contamination of groundwater from pesticides and

fertilizers is of greatest concern in the High Plains, the southern rice belt, and the Rio Grande Valley, while contamination from CAFO runoff is of concern in the Panhandle, North-Central, and East-Central portions of the state.[133]

Agricultural chemicals such as pesticides and herbicides also are a major concern for groundwater protection. From 1987 to 1990, the Texas Department of Agriculture, which regulates pesticide use, surveyed water wells for pesticide residues in 11 counties and discovered 75 cases of pesticide-contaminated groundwater. The pesticides found included arsenic, dicamba, atrazine, and prometon. None of these high levels, however, was determined to be in violation of state agricultural regulations. In 1996 the department transferred the cases to the TNRCC for further analysis. The TNRCC was able to confirm contamination in 6 of the cases and plans to resample an additional 18 sites as funds allow. In addition to these data, the TNRCC since 1991 has kept an interagency pesticide database, which compiles the results of sporadic groundwater monitoring for pesticides statewide. An additional 19 cases of pesticide contamination of groundwater were listed in this database.[134]

Other risks to groundwater from agricultural activities include contamination by nitrates and arsenic. High nitrate levels are sometimes caused by infiltration from fertilizers and animal wastes. Some 23 confirmed cases of elevated arsenic groundwater in Howard and Martin counties near the city of Knott have been attributed to point sources such as cotton gins, gin waste, gin trash, and hull pits, among other sources.[135] These high levels of arsenic were mainly found in wells pumping from the Ogallala Aquifer, which is the major source of drinking and irrigation water for the Panhandle and High Plains region of Texas.

DRINKING WATER

FEDERAL DRINKING WATER LAW
The federal Safe Drinking Water Act, enacted in 1974 and amended in 1986, 1991, and 1996 is designed to ensure safe drinking water by establishing drinking water standards for treated potable water and by creating special protection for sources of drinking water.

FYI *An adult drinks about 2 liters of water a day.* (Source: Richard Denison and John Ruston, eds., Recycling and Incineration: Evaluating the Choices [Washington, D.C.: Island Press for the Environmental Defense Fund, 1990], 222.)

As part of the 1996 amendments, Congress, for the first time, funded the drinking water program by providing over $9.6 billion over the next six years to states for improving drinking water infrastructure through the creation of state revolving funds, similar to the funding for wastewater treatment plants. In Texas, the TWDB is charged with overseeing the fund, which will provide low-interest loans to municipalities, utilities, irrigation districts, and other entities providing water for drinking. In FY 1997, Congress appropriated $740 million for direct and guaranteed loans, and Texas received a total of $71 million under the program. None of the funds can be dispersed without public participation in all aspects of the planning and implementation of the program.[136]

TYPES OF WATER SYSTEMS
The law classifies public water systems into two major categories. Those serving permanent populations like cities and towns are called "community systems." Those serving facilities like hotels, restaurants, youth camps, highway rest stops, and travel-trailer campgrounds are called "noncommunity systems." These noncommunity systems are further divided into those serving a transient population, such as restaurants and campgrounds, and those serving a nontransient population, such as hotels and schools. In Texas there are about 4,600 community systems and 2,600 noncommunity systems.[137]

Under the federal Safe Drinking Water Act, the level of regulation depends on the type of system. Transient noncommunity systems are required only to monitor and treat for nitrate, nitrites, and fecal coliform. Both community systems and nontransient noncommunity systems must monitor and treat water to standards set by the federal government and enforced by the states. Communities with less than 15 connections or 25 people are not considered to be "public water systems" and are therefore not regulated.

THE STATE PROGRAM
Under changes made in the 1986 Safe Drinking Water Act amendments, the EPA required all public

MAXIMUM CONTAMINANT LEVELS AND HEALTH EFFECTS OF CONTAMINANTS MONITORED IN PUBLIC DRINKING WATER SUPPLIES

CONTAMINANT	MAXIMUM LEVELS ([MG/L] UNLESS OTHERWISE NOTED)	HEALTH EFFECTS	SOURCES
ORGANIC CHEMICALS			
Acrylamide	0.05% dosed at 1 mg/L	Nervous system or blood problems; cancer risk	Added to water in some systems during wastewater treatment
Alachlor	0.002	Eye, liver, kidney or spleen problems; cancer risk	Runoff from herbicide used on row crops
Atrazine	0.003	Cardiovascular system problems; reproductive difficulties; under special review as cancer risk	Runoff from herbicide used on row crops
Benzene	0.005	Cancer risk; anemia; decrease in blood platelets	Fuel (leaking tanks and landfills), solvents used in manufacture of industrial chemicals, pharmaceuticals, pesticides, paints, and plastics
Benzo(a)pyrene	0.0002	Reproductive difficulties; cancer risk	Leaching from linings of water storage tanks and distribution lines
Carbofuran	0.04	Problems with blood or nervous system; reproductive difficulties	Leaching of soil fumigant used on rice and alfalfa
Carbon tetrachloride	0.005	Cancer risk; liver problems	Common in cleaning agents, industrial waste from manufacture of coolants and other chemicals
Chlordane	0.002	Liver and nervous system problems; cancer risk	Residue of banned termiticide
Chlorobenzene	0.1	Liver or kidney problems	Discharges from chemical and agricultural chemical factories
2,4-D	0.07	Liver and kidney effects; adrenal gland problems	Runoff of herbicide used to control broad-leaf weeds in agriculture, used on forests, range, pastures, and aquatic environments
Dalapon	0.2	Minor kidney changes	Runoff from herbicide used to control right-of-way
1,2-Dibromo-3-chloropropane (DBCP)	0.0002	Reproductive difficulties; cancer risk	Runoff/leaching from soil fumigant used on soybeans, cotton, pineapples, and orchards
o-Dichlorobenzene	0.6	Liver, kidney, circulatory system problems	Discharge from industrial chemical factories
p-Dichlorobenzene	0.075	Anemia; liver, kidney and spleen damage; blood changes	Used in insecticides, moth balls, air deodorizers, discharge from factories
1,2-Dichloroethane	0.005	Cancer risk	Discharge from industrial chemcial factories
1,1-Dichloroethylene cis-1,2-Dichloroethylene	0.007	Liver/kidney effects	Discharge from industrial chemical factories (Used in manufacture of plastics, dyes, perfumes, paints, SOCs)
trans-1,2-Dichloro-ethylene	0.1	Liver problems	Discharge from industrial chemical factories
Dichloromethane	0.005	Liver problems; cancer risk	Discharge from pharmaceutical and chemical factories
1,2-Dichloropropane	0.005	Cancer risk	Discharge from industrial chemical factories
D(2-ethylhexyl)adipate	0.4	General toxic effects or reproductive difficulties	Leaching from PVC plumbing systems; discharge from chemical factories
Di(2-ethylhexyl) phthalate	0.006	Reproductive difficulties; liver problems; cancer risk	Discharge from rubber and chemical factories

Continued on next page

MAXIMUM CONTAMINANT LEVELS AND HEALTH EFFECTS OF CONTAMINANTS MONITORED IN PUBLIC DRINKING WATER SUPPLIES (Continued)

CONTAMINANT	MAXIMUM LEVELS ([MG/L] UNLESS OTHERWISE NOTED)	HEALTH EFFECTS	SOURCES
ORGANIC CHEMICALS (Continued)			
Dinoseb	0.007	Reproductive difficulties	Runoff from herbicide used on soybeans and vegetables
Dioxin	0.00000003	Reproductive difficulties; cancer risk	Emissions from waste incineration and other combustion; discharge from chemical and paper factories
Diquat	0.02	Cataracts	Runoff from herbicide use
Endothall	0.1	Stomach and intestinal problems	Runoff from herbicide use
Endrin	0.002	Nervous system/kidney effects	Residue of banned insecticide used on cotton, small grains, orchards
Epichlorohydrin	0.01% dosed at 20 mg/L	Stomach problems; reproductive difficulties; cancer risk	Discharge from industrial chemical factories; added to water during treatment process
Ethylbenzene	0.7	Liver or kidney problems	Discharge from petroleum refineries
Ethelyne dibromide	0.00005	Stomach problems; reproductive difficulties; cancer risk	Discharge from petroleum refineries
Glyphosate	0.7	Kidney problems; reproductive difficulties	Runoff from herbicide use
Heptachlor	0.0004	Liver damage; cancer risk	Residue of banned termiticide
Heptachlor epoxide	0.0002	Liver damage; cancer risk	Breakdown of heptachlor
Hexachlorobenzene	0.001	Liver/kidney problems; cancer risk; reproductive difficulties	Discharge from metal refineries and agricultural chemical factories
Hexachlorocyclo- pentadiene	0.05	Kidney or stomach problems	Discharge from chemical factories
Lindane	0.0002	Nervous system/liver and kidney effects	Insecticide used on gardens, foliage applications, wood protection, cattle
Methoxychlor	0.04	Nervous system/kidney effects reproductive difficulties	Runoff from insecticide used on fruit trees, vegetables, alfalfa, livestock
Oxamyl (Vydate)	0.2	Nervous system effects	Runoff/leaching from insecticide used on apples, potatoes, and tomatoes
Polychlorinated Biphenyls (PCB)	0.0005	Developmental effects in fetuses; skin changes; cancer risk; nervous system difficulties; immune deficiencies, thymus gland problems	Electrical transformers, lubricants (banned), runoff from abandoned hazardous waste sites
Pentachlorophenol	0.001	Liver and kidney problems; cancer risk	Discharge from wood preserving factories
Picloram	0.5	Liver problems	Herbicide runoff
Simazine	0.004	Problems with blood	Herbicide runoff
Styrene	0.1	Liver, kidney and circulatory problems	Discharge from rubber and plastic factories; leaching from landfills, abandoned waste sites
Tetrachloroethylene	0.005	Liver problems; cancer risk	Leaching from PVC pipes; discharge from factories and dry cleaners.
Toluene	1	Nervous system, kidney and liver problems	Discharge from petroleum factories
2,4,5-TP (Silvex)	0.05	Liver/kidney effects	Residue of banned herbicide

Continued on next page

MAXIMUM CONTAMINANT LEVELS AND HEALTH EFFECTS OF CONTAMINANTS MONITORED IN PUBLIC DRINKING WATER SUPPLIES (Continued)

CONTAMINANT	MAXIMUM LEVELS ([MG/L] UNLESS OTHERWISE NOTED)	HEALTH EFFECTS	SOURCES
ORGANIC CHEMICALS (Continued)			
Total Trihalomethanes (TTHM) (Chloroform, Bromoform, Bromodichloromethane, Dibromochloromethane)	0.1	Cancer risk; liver, kidney and central nervous system problems	Primarily formed as byproduct when surface water containing organic matter is treated with chlorine
Toxaphene	0.003	Cancer risk; liver, kidney and thyroid problems	Insecticide used on cotton, corn, grain, cattle
1,2,4-Trichlorobenzene	0.07	Changes in adrenal glands	Discharge from textile finishing factory
1,1,1-Trichloroethane	0.2	Nervous system effects; liver and circulatory problems	Used in manufacture of food wrappings, synthetic fibers; discharge from metal degreasing sites and other factories
1,1,2-Trichloroethane	0.005	Liver, kidney or immune system problems	Discharge from industrial chemical factories
Trichloroethylene (TCE)	0.005	Cancer risk; liver problems	Waste from disposal of dry cleaning materials and discharge from pesticide, paints, waxes, varnishes, paint stripper, and metal degreaser factories and petroleum refineries
Vinyl Chloride	0.002	Cancer risk	Leaching from polyvinylchloride (PVC) pipes; discharge from plastic factories
Xylenes (total)	10	Nervous system damage	Discharge from petroleum refineries; discharge from chemical factories

MICROBIOLOGICAL/SURFACE WATER TREATMENT RULE

CONTAMINANT	MAXIMUM LEVELS ([MG/L] UNLESS OTHERWISE NOTED)	HEALTH EFFECTS	SOURCES
Total Coliforms (Coliform Bacteria, Fecal Coliform Streptococcal and other bacteria)	Presence. If more than 40 samples in month, then 5% cannot be positive. If less than 40 samples then not more than one can be coliform-positive.	Not necessarily disease-producing themselves, but coliforms can be indicators of organisms that cause assorted gastroenteric infections, dysentary, hepatitis, typhoid fever, cholera and others; also interfere with disinfection process	Human and animal fecal matter
Turbidity	Turbidity cannot go above 5 nephololometic turbidity units (NTUs); systems that filter cannot go higher than 1 NTU in 95% of daily samples	Interferes with disinfection process	Erosion, runoff, discharges
Giardia lamblia	99.9% killed/inactivated	Giardiasis, gastrointestinal disease	Human and animal fecal matter
Legionella	No limit at present, but goal of zero	Legionnaire's disease, also known as pneumonia	Found naturally in water; multiplies in heating systems
Heterotrophic plate count	500 bacterial colonies/milliliter	No health effects, but indicator of effectiveness of treatment	Natural, various sources
Viruses (enteric)	99.99% killed/inactivated	Gastroenteric disease	Human and animal fecal matter

Continued on next page

MAXIMUM CONTAMINANT LEVELS AND HEALTH EFFECTS OF CONTAMINANTS MONITORED IN PUBLIC DRINKING WATER SUPPLIES (Continued)

CONTAMINANT	MAXIMUM LEVELS ([MG/L] UNLESS OTHERWISE NOTED)	HEALTH EFFECTS	SOURCES
INORGANIC CHEMICALS			
Antimony	0.006	Increase in blood cholestoral; decrease in blood glucose	Discharge from petroleum refineries; fire retardants; ceramics, solder, electronics
Arsenic	0.05	Dermal and nervous system toxicity effects	Geological, pesticide residues, industrial waste and smelter operations
Asbestos	7 million fibers per liter	Increased risk of developing benign intestinal polyps	Decay of asbestos cement in water mains; erosion of natural deposits
Barium	2.0	Increase in blood pressure	Discharge of drilling wastes; discharge from metal refineries; erosion of natural deposits
Beryllium	0.004	Intestinal lesions	Discharge from metal refineries and coal-burning factories; discharge from electrical, aerospace, and defense industries
Cadmium	0.005	Kidney effects	Corrosion of galvanized pipes; erosion of natural deposits; discharge from metal refineries; runoff from waste batteries and paints
Chromium	0.1	Allergic dermatitis	Discharge from steel and pulp mills; erosion of natural deposits
Copper	1.3	Short term: gastrointestinal distress Long term: Liver or kidney damage	Corrosion of household plumbing systems; erosion of natural deposits; leaching from wood preservatives
Cyanide	0.2	Nerve damage or thyroid problems	Discharge from steel/metal factories; discharge from plastic and fertilizer factories
Flouride	4.0	Skeletal damage; mottled teeth in children	Geological; additive to drinking water, toothpaste, foods processed with flouridated water
Lead	0.015	Central and peripheral nervous system damage; kidney effects; delays in infant and children's physical/mental development	Leaches from lead pipe and lead-based solder pipe joints; erosion of natural deposits
Mercury	0.002	Central nervous system disorders; kidney effects	Manufacture of paint, paper, vinyl chloride; runoff from refineries/power plants/factories; runoff from landfills, cropland (fungicides)
Nitrate (measured as nitrogen)	10.0	Methomoglobinemia ("baby-blue syndrome")	Runoff from fertilizer, sewage, feedlots, septic tanks, erosion of natural, geologic deposits
Nitrite (measured as nitrogen)	1.0	Methomoglobinemia ("baby-blue syndrome")	Runoff from fertilizer, sewage, feedlots, septic tanks, erosion of natural, geologic deposits
Selenium	0.05	Gastrointestinal effects, numbness in fingers/toes, hair/fingernail loss	Discharge/runoff from mining; discharge from refineries; erosion of natural deposits
Thallium	0.002	Hair loss; changes in blood; kidney, intestinal or liver problems.	Leaching from ore-processing sites; discharge from electronics, glass and pharmaceutical companies
RADIONUCLIDES			
Gross alpha particle activity	15 picocuries/ Liter	Cancer risk	Radioactive waste, decay of uranium deposits
Gross beta/photo particle activity	4 millirems per year	Cancer risk	Radioactive waste, decay of uranium deposits
Radium 226 & 228	5 picocuries/ Liter	Bone cancer risk	Radioactive waste, decay of uranium deposits

Continued on next page

MAXIMUM CONTAMINANT LEVELS AND HEALTH EFFECTS OF CONTAMINANTS MONITORED IN PUBLIC DRINKING WATER SUPPLIES (*Continued*)

CONTAMINANT	MAXIMUM LEVELS ([MG/L] UNLESS OTHERWISE NOTED)	HEALTH EFFECTS
SECONDARY DRINKING WATER STANDARDS		
pH	6.5–8.5	Water should not be too acidic or too basic
Chloride	250	Taste and corrosion of pipes
Color	15 color units	Aesthetic
Copper	1.0	Taste and straining of porcelain
Corrosivity	Non-corrosive	Aesthetic and health related (corrosive water can leach pipe materials, such as lead, into the drinking water)
Flouride	2.0	Dental flourosis (a brownish discoloration of the teeth)
Foaming agents	0.5	Aesthetic
Iron	0.3	Taste
Manganese	0.05	Taste
Silver	0.10	Taste
Aluminum	0.05 to 0.2	Taste
Zinc	5.0	Taste
Odor	3 threshold odor number	Aesthetic
Sulfate	250	Taste and laxative effects
Total Dissolved Solids	500	Taste and possible relation between low hardness and cardiovascular disease; also an indicator of corrosivity (related to lead levels in water); can damage plumbing and limit effectiveness of soaps and detergents

Source: League of Women Voters Education Fund, Safety on Tap: A Citizen's Drinking Water Handbook (*Washington: League of Women Voters, 1987*), 12-13.; *and U.S. Environmental Protection Agency, Office of Ground Water and Drinking Water, Current Drinking Water Standards (1999)*.

water systems to monitor for 16 inorganic and 54 organic contaminants for which maximum contaminant levels have been established. The EPA currently has such levels in place for 81 contaminants, including total coliform, lead, and copper. In addition, the EPA requires monitoring of other organic chemicals for which levels have not yet established.

In Texas the EPA has delegated authority for regulating drinking water to the state government. Currently, the state requires water systems to test for 126 chemicals, of which 73 have maximum contaminant levels. In addition, the state requires public water suppliers to test for bacteria and viruses and for secondary contaminants such as iron, manganese, and chloride that do not affect human health but lead to odor or taste problems.

Currently, the EPA has also begun a rule-making process to establish a standard for *Cryptosporidium*, a pathogen that can sometimes pass through disinfec-

tion and water treatment filtration to affect human health. In 1993 an outbreak of cryptosporidiosis— a disease caused by the pathogen—in Milwaukee, Wisconsin, led to 400,000 affected residents, including 4,000 hospitalizations and at least 50 deaths.[138]

ORGANIC TESTING

Beginning in 1993, public water systems were required to begin testing their treated water for the presence of organic compounds. Between then and the end of 1995, samples for organic chemical analysis were taken for all 5,000 community and all nontransient noncommunity (such as schools and prisons) public water supply systems in Texas. By the end of 1998, all 5,000 systems were tested again for organic compounds as part of the three-year cycle.[139]

All pesticide samples were analyzed by TNRCC field inspectors and taken at the entry point—where the treated waters enter the distribution system. In

HOW FREQUENTLY MUST PUBLIC WATER SYSTEMS MONITOR?

CONTAMINANT	MINIMUM MONITORING FREQUENCY	APPLICABLE SYSTEMS
Bacteria	Monthly or quarterly, depending on system size and type	CNT
Protozoa and Viruses	Continuous monitoring for turbidity, monthly for total coliforms, as indicators	CNT
Volatile Organics (e.g. benzene)	Groundwater systems, annually for two consecutive years; surface water sytems, annually.	CN
Synthetic Organics (pesticides)	Larger systems, twice in three years; smaller systems, once in three years	CN
Inorganic/Metals and nitrites	Groundwater systems, once every three years; surface water systems, annually	CN for most CNT for nitrates
Lead and Copper	Annually	CN
Radionuclides	Once every four years	C

C=Community; N= Non-Transient, Non-Community; T=Transient, Non-Community.

Source. Environmental Protection Agency, Water on Tap: A Consumer's Guide to the Nation's Drinking Water (Washington, D.C., 1997).

the future, these samples will be conducted by the Texas Rural Water Association under a contract with the TNRCC. Under TNRCC regulations, if a pesticide is detected at any level, a confirmation sample is taken. If confirmed, then public water systems are required to conduct quarterly samples (every three months) until the water tests reliably and consistently below the maximum contamination level. While groundwater supply systems must monitor only for a minimum of two quarters to determine whether there is a problem, surface water systems must conduct samples for a minimum of one year.[140]

RESULTS OF TESTING IN TEXAS

Despite the passage and implementation of the Safe Drinking Water Act, drinking water in the United States and Texas is not always completely safe to drink. For example, in 1994, more than 45 million people in the United States were served by community drinking water systems that violated health-based requirements at least once.[141] In Texas, violations are less common than nationally. According to EPA drinking water standards, Texas had 598 systems in violation, about six percent of all systems, affecting 1,658,406 people, or eight percent of the population, between 1994 and 1996.[142] In 1997 only four percent of the population in Texas was served by public drinking water systems that did not meet health-based standards.[143]

FYI *Texas ranked ninth in the nation for the number of people affected by drinking water violations between 1994 and 1996.* (Source: Clean Water Network, A Prescription for Clean Water: How to Meet the Goals of the Clean Water Act [Washington, D.C., October 1997].)

Between 1995 and 1997, 186 drinking water systems yielded samples that exceeded at least one of the primary organic and inorganic maximum containment levels.[144] Nearly all of the violations were related to inorganics such as nitrates, arsenic,

U.S. AND TEXAS POPULATION SERVED BY COMMUNITY DRINKING WATER SYSTEMS VIOLATING HEALTH-BASED REQUIREMENTS

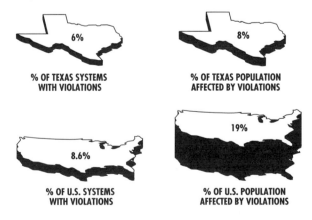

% OF TEXAS SYSTEMS WITH VIOLATIONS — 6%

% OF TEXAS POPULATION AFFECTED BY VIOLATIONS — 8%

% OF U.S. SYSTEMS WITH VIOLATIONS — 8.6%

% OF U.S. POPULATION AFFECTED BY VIOLATIONS — 19%

Source: Clean Water Network, A Prescription for Clean Water: How to Meet the Goals of the Clean Water Act (Washington, D.C.: Clean Water Network, 1997).

VIOLATIONS OF THE ORGANIC AND INORGANIC MCLS BY CONTAMINANT IN TEXAS, 1995–1997

CONTAMINANT	NUMBER OF VIOLATIONS
Nitrate Nitrogen	72
Flouride	44
Combined Radium	21
Gross Alpha	16
Arsenic	4
Selenium	7
Asbestos	3
Barium	1
Benzene	1
Trichloroethylene	3
Trihalomethanes	12
1,1 -Dichloroethylene	2
Total	**186**

Source: Texas Natural Resource Conservation Commission, Water Utilities Division, 1998.

COUNTIES WITH NUMBER OF PUBLIC WATER SUPPLY SYSTEMS VIOLATING MCL STANDARDS BY COUNTY, 1995–1997

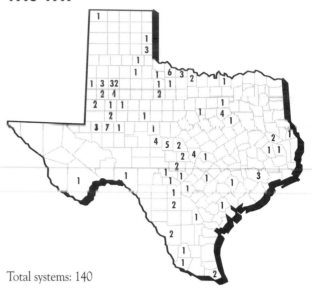

Total systems: 140

Source: Texas Natural Resource Conservation Commission, Water Utilities Division, 1998.

fluoride, and selenium. In addition to these violations, there were 229 violations of total coliform standards in 1996 and 1997.

Since 1993 the federal government has required public drinking water systems to monitor for pesticides and other synthetic organics. Between 1993 and 1997, nine water systems serving half a million people had a least one sample exceeding the maximum containment level for atrazine, a herbicide.[145] However, in order for a system to be considered in violation of the level requirements, the average of the four quarterly samples must be over the level. By 1998, only one system—the Aquilla Water Supply District—was in violation of the standard.

Two drinking water contaminants pose the most acute threat to human health: nitrates and bacteria. Nitrates in concentrations above the national standard threaten the health of infants. Nitrates can react with the blood's hemoglobin, interfering with its ability to carry oxygen and resulting in the sometimes fatal "blue baby" syndrome. Bacteria in contaminated water can cause diseases such as typhoid, cholera, infectious hepatitis, and dysentery.[146] These disease-causing bacteria are signaled by high levels of coliform bacteria, itself a relatively benign bacteria. Fecal coliform bacteria are commonly found

PUBLIC WATER SYSTEMS WHERE PESTICIDES HAVE EXCEEDED THE MAXIMUM CONTAMINANT LEVEL FOR ONE OR MORE SAMPLES, 1995–1997

SYSTEM	CONTAMINANT	YEAR OF EXCEEDENCE
City of Midlothian	Atrazine	1997
Sagemeadow Municipal Utility	Atrazine	1997
Aquilla Water Supply District (Gets water from City of Houston)	Atrazine, Alachlor	1997
City of Dawson	Atrazine	1997
Friona Municipal Water System	Atrazine	1997
City of Ft. Worth	Atrazine	1997
Combined Water Supply Corporation (Lake Tawakoni)	Atrazine	1997
City of Robinson	Atrazine	1996
City of Marlin	Atrazine	1995

Source: Texas Natural Resource Conservation Commission, Water Utilities Division, Organic Substances Database, 1997.

in human and animal waste and may indicate sewage contamination and the presence of disease-causing organisms.

Lead in drinking water is another major concern. Lead usually enters the drinking supply from old lead pipes in homes, from brass fixtures, or from lead-based solder in copper pipes.[147] Lead is now banned in the installation or repair of public water systems and household plumbing. There were 68 exceedences of lead standards in 36 public water systems throughout the state in 1996 and 1997.[148] These systems must conduct anticorrosion and other tests to determine what is affecting their systems and correct the problem. Fortunately, these systems represented less than three percent of all systems tested in the state.[149]

Finally, a newly emerging concern is what happens with the disinfectant (like chlorine) once it leaves the water treatment plant. While chlorine helps eliminate any remaining pathogens, it also leads to the formation of dangerous particles called trihalomethanes, or THM. THMs were regulated beginning in 1980 for systems serving populations over 10,000, and today most systems have switched from free chlorine to other disinfectants, thus reducing the formation of THMs. Only a few drinking water systems in Texas—located primarily in the Lower Rio Grande Valley—have exceeded THM standards in recent years.[150] The EPA is currently expanding regulations for these by-products, which could bring some systems in Texas out of compliance.[151]

COUNTIES WITH NUMBER OF PUBLIC WATER SUPPLY SYSTEMS EXCEEDING FECAL COLIFORM STANDARDS IN 1996 AND 1997

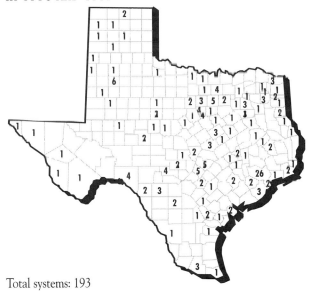

Total systems: 193

Source: Texas Natural Resource Conservation Commission, Water Utilities Division, 1998.

GETTING YOUR WATER FROM IRRIGATORS

In parts of Texas, some residents obtain their water supply through irrigation canals and irrigation districts, which are often ill-equipped to supply drinking water. In the past, however, these irrigation districts have been exempt from meeting the health-based requirements of the Safe Drinking Water Act, even if they were serving more than 25 residents or 15 connections.

Under the 1996 amendments, however, as long as they are serving at least 25 people, irrigation districts that are providing water to residents for domestic uses—such as bathing, brushing teeth, or drinking—or have knowledge or should have knowledge that residents are using the water for this purpose, must meet the same requirements as any community public water system, including

monitoring. Individuals, on the other hand, who are taking water from irrigation canals for domestic use without the irrigator's knowledge are not protected under the amendments. Irrigation districts are eligible under the act for federal and state funding for water treatment systems.[152]

In Texas, residents in counties such as El Paso, Willacy, Cameron, and Hidalgo where thousands of residents lack potable water have often relied upon irrigation canals and districts for their water. In addition, property owners around lakes who take water from the lake for indoor use could also be covered by the amendment. The TNRCC is currently awaiting final guidance from the EPA on how to proceed to identify these systems.[153]

COUNTIES IN TEXAS WITH NUMBER OF PUBLIC WATER SYSTEMS EXCEEDING LEAD LIMIT OF 15 PARTS PER BILLIONS IN DRINKING WATER DURING 1996 AND 1997

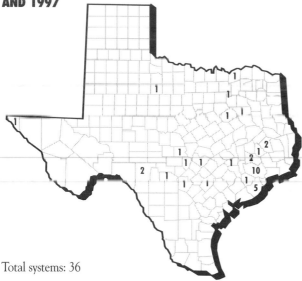

Total systems: 36

Source: Texas Natural Resource Conservation Commission, Water Utilities Division, 1998.

ENFORCEMENT OF DRINKING WATER STANDARDS IN TEXAS

The TNRCC ensures compliance with federal and state drinking water standards through self-reported monitoring, conducting compliance and complaint inspections, issuing notices of violation, and seeking administrative orders and penalties when violations are not corrected. If administrative orders and penalties issued by the TNRCC do not achieve compliance, then the agency may pursue compliance through the Texas Attorney General's Office.

In FY 1996, the public water supply division conducted 4,098 compliance inspections, issued 270 notices of violations, and issued 59 administrative orders with penalties worth $56,073, while the Attorney General's Office issued 11 judicial orders worth $894,330. In FY 1997, the agency conducted 4,258 inspections, issued 3,184 notices of violation, and issued 87 administrative orders with penalties due of $275,682. The Attorney General's Office issued four judicial orders with penalties totaling $13,000.[154]

THE RIGHT TO KNOW WHAT'S IN YOUR WATER

The 1996 amendments to the Safe Drinking Water Act require that the public receive better and more timely information about the quality of the water they drink and what is being done to improve it. These "right-to-know" provisions will lead to fundamental changes in the way drinking water systems must inform their customers. For example, water

---

HOW DOES WATER COME INTO YOUR HOME?

Water is delivered from a groundwater or surface water source to a treatment plant, where it is first aerated to allow volatile gases to escape. Next, small particles are clumped together through the use of coagulating agents and allowed to settle out of the water. Particles that do not settle out through coagulation slowly filter out to the bottom of a mazelike settling tank in a process known as sedimentation. The material at the bottom, called sludge, often creates a disposal problem, since it may contain some toxic elements (see *Municipal Waste* chapter). Next, water flows through long horizontal tanks with filters made of gravel, sand, or granulated activated carbon and is collected at the bottom of these filters. Filtration removes additional particles and bacteria. Finally, chlorination or other disinfectants kill any remaining microbes.

Source: Raymond Gabler and the Editors of Consumer Reports, Is Your Water Safe to Drink? (Mount Vernon, NY: Consumers Union, 1989), 330–333.

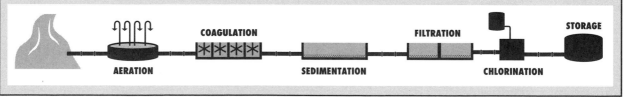

systems now must inform their customers within 24 hours of exceeding EPA standards that "have the potential to have serious adverse effects on human health as a result of short-term exposure." This announcement must be made through local media and include information about whether customers should seek an alternative source, what the possible health effects are, and what is being done to correct the problem. Customers must also be notified of other violations of less-immediate concern through water bills, annual reports, or separate mailings.[155]

In addition, starting in 1999, all community water systems will have to mail annual "consumer confidence reports" to their customers. The reports will identify contaminants found in the water and discuss violations and health effects, as well as potential sources of pollution. Finally, the EPA is replacing its present database on drinking water quality—which is incomplete and difficult to access—with a new national database accessible via the Internet.[156]

SOURCE WATER ASSESSMENT PROGRAM
Under the 1996 amendments to the Safe Drinking Water Act, all states are required to develop a Source Water Assessment Program in which sources of regulated contaminants that could impact public water supply sources are identified. This assessment program will lead to a publicly accessible database of information on each water source and its actual and potential impacts of contamination sources. Currently, the TNRCC is implementing the program and the EPA is adopting rules. However, the first analysis from this assessment will not be due for several years.

PROTECTIONS FOR UNDERGROUND DRINKING WATER
The federal Safe Drinking Water Act contains a number of safeguards to protect groundwater used for drinking water. First, the act's Sole Source Aquifer provision gives special protection to aquifers designated as the sole source of drinking water in the area. Any construction or development project that could impact that sole source aquifer cannot receive federal assistance. In Texas the Edwards Aquifer, which supplies San Antonio with drinking water, has been designated as a sole source aquifer. Interestingly, the Edwards Aquifer is the only major supply of water in Texas that requires no advanced

BOTTLED WATER ANYONE?

Concerns about drinking water quality have led to a surge in the number of U.S. and Texas residents buying bottled water at the local supermarket or gas station. In 1996, for example, U.S. residents drank three billion gallons of bottled water— about 11 gallons per person—and spent more than $4 billion.[157]

Is the water actually safer to drink? The answer really depends. While bottled water often undergoes more extensive treatment—such as extra filtration or reverse osmosis—or comes from pristine springs where treatment is not needed—often it is no different than the water people drink out of their taps. In fact, 35 percent of all bottled water sold in the United States is just municipal water run through a filter.[158] Recent Food and Drug Administration (FDA) regulations have strength-

ened truth-in-advertising for bottled water. For example, spring water must mean that the water comes from a spring coming from the ground. However, other terms, such as mountain fresh or glacier pure, are marketing terms, not a reference to where the water originates. FDA regulations on water quality are equivalent to EPA drinking water standards, meaning there is no guarantee the bottled water is any cleaner, providing that local water supplies meet EPA standards.[159]

Because of the success of bottled-water companies, some cities such as Houston are producing their own bottled water for sale. Thus, what Houstonians drink for less than a penny could be purchased for $1.29 or so a quart at supermarkets throughout the United States.

treatment. The water is merely pumped out of the aquifer, chlorinated, and drunk by over one million San Antonio residents.

The act's second major safeguard for groundwater is its Wellhead Protection Program. This program seeks to protect from human-made contamination the wells used for municipal water supplies, as well as the land surrounding those wells. To participate in the program a city must conduct a field inventory to identify all potential sources of contaminants for the public water supply and must adopt an ordinance that requires generators of contaminants to use best-management practices to reduce the risk of contamination. It may also require limits on certain agricultural or industrial activities, to prevent contamination from occurring. Since the program's inception in Texas, 171 local governments have delineated 856 wellhead protection areas encompassing 1,550 public water supply wells. Fifteen

UNREGULATED DRINKING WATER

About 1.1 million Texans rely on private wells for their drinking water.[160] Under the Safe Drinking Water Act, water supply systems for communities with less than 15 connections or 25 people are not regulated, meaning they do not have to meet federal and state monitoring and treatment standards. Those served by private wells must test waters themselves to determine if it is safe to drink, particularly to ascertain high levels of coliform bacteria and nitrates. There are a number of government-run laboratories—mainly county health departments—around the state that can help citizens test their water.

Texas cities, through 1995, had adopted wellhead protection ordinances to plug abandoned wells and limit the potential for contamination.[161]

COASTAL RESOURCES

BACKGROUND

Coastal waters—estuaries, wetlands, and bays—are critical to the economy and ecology of Texas. Almost three-fourths of the fish harvested in the Gulf of Mexico are species that depend on estuaries and wetlands for mating and spawning.[162] The estuaries—where fresh water from rivers and streams mixes with salt water from the ocean—are home to more than 80 species of animals and plants.[163] Species that either live in or depend upon the estuaries include shrimp, oysters, crabs, blue crabs, and finfish.

Thirty-two of Texas's 44 segments of estuarine waters as well as the Gulf of Mexico as a whole are classified as oyster waters. (For estuaries, a segment is usually a seven-mile stretch of coastline.) These oyster waters cover about 5,850 square miles.[164] About 30,000 commercial fishermen each year catch almost 100 million pounds of coastal fish and shellfish worth an estimated $200 million.[165] The total economic contribution to the state's economy from commercial fishermen and the nearly 850,000 sport fishing enthusiasts is an estimated $2.9 billion per year.[166] These habitats also attract 30,000 to 40,000

TEXAS'S COASTAL RESOURCES

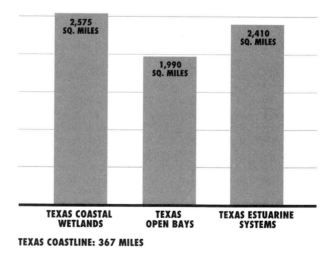

TEXAS COASTAL WETLANDS: 2,575 SQ. MILES
TEXAS OPEN BAYS: 1,990 SQ. MILES
TEXAS ESTUARINE SYSTEMS: 2,410 SQ. MILES

TEXAS COASTLINE: 367 MILES

Source: Texas General Land Office, EnviroNomics (Winter 1993).

SHELLFISH HARVESTING WATERS NOT MEETING OYSTER WATERS USE DUE TO FECAL COLIFORM CONTAMINATION, 1996

BAY	TOTAL AREA (SQ. MI.)	AREA NOT MEETING USE	% OF AREA
1. Sabine Pass	2.1	0.5	24
2. Sabine Lake	68.7	17.2	25
3. Upper Galveston Bay	108.2	0	0
4. Trinity Bay	130.1	0	0
5. East Bay	52.1	0	0
6. West Bay	69.3	0	0
7. Chocolate Bay	7.6	0	0
8. Bastrop Bay/ Oyster Lake	3.9	0	0
9. Christmas Bay	8.9	0	0
10. Drum Bay	1.7	0	0
11. Lower Galveston Bay	139.6	0	0
12. East Matagorda Bay	59.1	0	0
13. Cedar Lakes	6.9	1.7	24
14. Matagorda Bay/ Powderhorn Lake	261.7	13.1	5
15. Tres Palacios Bay/ Turtle Bay	14.7	3.7	25
16. Lavaca Bay/ Chocolate Bay	54.8	2.5	5
17. Cox Bay	2.9	0	0
18. Keller Bay	7.5	0	0
19. Carancahua Bay	19.0	1.9	10
20. Espiritu Santo Bay	60.8	0	0
21. San Antonio Bay/ Haynes Bay/ Guadalupe Bay	119.5	11.9	10
22. Mesquite Bay/Carlos Bay/ Ayers Bay	12.6	0	0
23. Aransas Bay	87.8	0	0
24. Copano Bay/Port Bay/ Mission Bay	65.2	0	0
25. St. Charles Bay	13.1	0	0

Shellfish harvesting waters not meeting oyster waters use due to high fecal coliform contamination

BAY	TOTAL AREA (SQ. MI.)	AREA NOT MEETING USE	% OF AREA
26. Corpus Christi Bay	123.1	12.3	10
27. Nueces Bay	28.9	2.9	10
28. Redfish Bay	28.8	0	0
29. Oso Bay	7.2	7.2	100
30. Laguna Madre	347.4	0	0
31. Baffin Bay/Alazan Bay	49.8	0	0
32. South Bay	7.8	0	0
33. Gulf of Mexico	3,879	388	10
Totals	**5,849.3**	**479.3**	**8.0**

Source: Texas Natural Resource Conservation Commission, The State of Texas Water Quality Inventory — 1996, 13th ed. (1996), 225-226.

coastal waterfowl hunters, photographers, swimmers, campers, bird-watchers, boaters, and sightseers, generating an additional $3 billion per year.[167]

One of the most important water resources is the Gulf Intracoastal Waterway, a human-made channel that parallels the coastline from Brownsville to St. Marks, Florida, where it meets up with other inland waterway transportation canals that extend all the way to Maine. The Gulf Intracoastal Waterway is thus an integral part of this transportation network for moving commodities and also serves as an important habitat resource for birds and aquatic life.[168] In 1994 more than 78 million short tons, worth approximately $22 billion, were moved on the Gulf Intracoastal Waterway, which is maintained by the Army Corps of Engineers.

As more people move into the coastal area, fragile habitat is being lost. More than one-third of the state's population—and about 70 percent of its industrial base, commerce, and jobs—now is located within 100 miles of the coast.[169] Twenty percent of the state's population lives in the four counties surrounding Galveston Bay—Galveston, Chambers, Brazoria, and Harris. The Texas General Land Office (GLO) estimates that by the year 2000 more than 5.3 million people will live in the coastal areas.[170]

More than half the nation's chemical and petroleum production is located along the Texas coast.[171] Along with population growth will come increased development and demands for water and wastewater facilities, and potential threats of pollution to estuaries, wetlands, and bays.

STATE EFFORTS TO PROTECT COASTAL WATERS

The GLO has primary responsibility for managing the habitats and waters of the Texas coastal region. In 1987 the GLO and the TPWD agreed to set up a series of coastal preserves to help protect the estuaries. In 1988 the South Bay and Welder Flats preserves were established, followed in 1991 by the Christmas Bay preserve and the Brazoria National Wildlife Refuge.

In 1991 the Texas legislature directed the GLO to head up a new Coastal Coordination Council, which has since developed a Coastal Zone Management Plan with other state agencies. The plan, which became effective in 1995, sets policies, standards, and regulations affecting private and public property in all counties contiguous to the Texas coastline. It can impact such activities as development permits, dredge-and-fill operations, siting of oil and gas waste-disposal pits, agricultural activities, and highway construction.

BAYS AND ESTUARIES

Estuaries and bays are threatened by a variety of pollution sources and are among Texas's most endangered waters. About 36 percent of open bays do not fully meet their designated uses under the state's

RISKS TO BAYS AND ESTUARIES

■ **Dams and reservoirs.** These structures stem the regular flow of rivers feeding the estuaries.

■ **Upstream water use.** Diversion of water from rivers decreases estuary inflow. New surface water use permits sometimes require that a portion of fresh water be set aside to protect the inflow needs of estuaries. But fresh surface water is not always available because surface water rights in most rivers in Texas have already been fully allocated. Instead, estuaries must often rely on return flows from wastewater treatment plants.

■ **Floods.** Land development increases the amount of impervious cover, which in turn increases the rate of surface water runoff that eventually reaches the estuaries. The wetlands surrounding estuaries act as natural filtering systems for pollutants, and these systems' filtering abilities can be overwhelmed when large volumes of water, some of it contaminated with non-point-source pollution, rush in after periods of heavy rainfall.

■ **Drought.** In periods of little rainfall, municipalities, agriculture, and industry all use more water.

■ **Toxic pollution.** Toxic contaminants like metals and pesticides can settle into estuaries and bays and

remain there for years. Dredging can stir them back into the water and into the aquatic-life food chain.

■ **Nutrients.** Municipal and industrial wastewater discharges, leaky sewers, and runoff from cities, suburbs, and farms can all increase the loading of nutrients (nitrogen and phosphorus) to the estuaries. While some level of nutrients is needed for plant life, too much can lead to an overabundance of algae and eventually to loss of dissolved oxygen, which reduces animal life and ultimately damages the overall health of the estuary.

■ **Oil spills and marine pollution.** Thousands of oil spills along the coast and offshore, as well as illegal dumping of trash, impact coastal waters.

■ **Untreated sewage.** The Army Corps of Engineers estimates that 1.2 million gallons per day of partially treated sewage flows into the Rio Grande from the city of Reynosa, only about 60 miles from the Gulf of Mexico.[172] The city of Matamoros discharges an estimated 2.5 million gallons a day of completely untreated wastewater into a canal that flows into the Gulf of Mexico, about 23 miles south of the international border.[173] Prevailing southeast winds drive it up toward the Texas coast.

water quality standards.[174] These uses include swimming, shellfish harvesting, aquatic life, and recreational fishing. One segment—the Corpus Christi Inner Harbor—did not meet its aquatic life use due to elevated levels of copper.[175]

Most of these water quality problems are related to

WHAT DOES IT MEAN WHEN THE TIDE IS RED OR BROWN?

In September 1996 and again in September 1997, residents of Texas's coasts witnessed an increasing problem: discolored, red patches of ocean waters and thousands and even millions of dead fish washed up on the shores. Red tides are produced when microscopic toxic algae increase in number and "bloom," causing the telltale discoloration of the oceans. The type of red tide that has affected Texas's fish and shellfish is caused by an organism called *Gymnodinium breve*, which produces a toxic affecting the central nervous system of fish.[176]

Another form of microscopic algae produces brown tide, which is not toxic to fish but does block out sunlight, killing underwater plants and ultimately the fish themselves, which depend upon this vegetation. Brown tide has plagued the Corpus Christi area for several years by killing eelgrass and other vegetation, ultimately destroying the fish habitat.[177]

Still a third type of dangerous microscopic organism called *pfiesteria* was discovered in 1991 and has killed millions of fish in North Carolina. *Pfiesteria* usually remain in a cystlike condition in the sediment of bays and estuaries, but when fish swim by, the organisms strike, using whiplike tails, or flagella. Their increasing numbers have been tied to development along the North Carolina coast, which has led to an influx of pollutants rich in nutrients like nitrogen and phosphorus. The growth in gigantic hog farms, leading to untreated hog feces and urine contaminating rivers, bays, and estuaries has also been linked to the increasing cases of *pfiesteria*.[178] This organism, however, has never been confirmed as occurring in Texas.

These so-called harmful algal blooms (HABs) can also affect humans who either handle or eat affected fish and shellfish. For example, consumption of shellfish contaminated by *Gymnodinium*

breve can lead to neurotoxic shellfish poisoning with symptoms such as tingling skin, nausea, vomiting, and some loss of muscle control.[179] The consumption of finfish, crabs, and shrimp contaminated with red tide cells, however, does not appear to lead to these kinds of problems. Airborne toxins created by red tide can cause nose, throat, and eye irritations.[180] The eating or handling of fish contaminated by *pfiesteria* can cause open sores, nausea, memory loss, fatigue, dizziness and disorientation, and even near incapacitation.[181]

In September 1996, millions of fish in the Corpus Christi and Aransas bays washed up on shore. Following extensive water and shellfish testing, the Texas Health Department issued an aquatic closure for oyster, clam, and mussel beds in both areas. The closure lasted until January 1997.

In September 1997, red tide struck again—this time farther south near South Padre Island, Padre Island National Seashore, and Mustang Island. In November and December, fish began dying from red tide farther north in Oso and Corpus Christi bays and the Upper Laguna Madre. The high counts of red tide cells led to the closings of Corpus Christi and Aransas bays once again.[182]

Unfortunately, there is little information on exactly why red tide increases generally from August to February. While some posit climactic and hydrological conditions, others believe that increased nutrients and pollution from the shore may be a factor.

The TPWD provides information about where red tide has been spotted or confirmed (call 1-800-792-1112). To report a fish kill, call the TPWD Kills and Spills Team (512-912-7055). Finally, the Texas Department of Health provides information about aquatic life closures or consumption advisories due to red tide (call 1-800-685-0361).

high levels of fecal coliform bacteria in Texas's shell-fish harvesting areas. In 1996, of the 32 segments that have been designated to support oyster fishing, 12 had fecal coliform contamination levels above the water quality standards that determine nonsupport of the use. This contamination did not impact the entire segments, but only portions.[183] In addition, parts of Lavaca and Cox bays are closed to finfish and blue crab harvesting because of a 1988 mercury spill, while the Texas Department of Health has issued a restricted consumption advisory for catfish and blue crabs from parts of Black Duck, Burnett, San Jacinto, Scott, Tabbs, and Upper Galveston bays and Barbours Cut because of dioxin contamination from paper mills.[184]

THE NATIONAL ESTUARY PROGRAM

In Texas both Galveston Bay and Corpus Christi Bay have been designated as national estuaries, making them eligible for federal and state funds to develop comprehensive management plans under the National Estuary Program. The designation of the 560-square-mile Galveston Bay Estuarine System is particularly significant, since more than 60 percent of the wastewater produced in Texas flows into Galveston Bay.[185]

As part of the program run by the TNRCC, a five-year assessment study of Galveston Bay preceded the development of a management plan that addresses water quality, habitat, wildlife, and human health aspects of the estuary. The Galveston Bay Plan was submitted by the Galveston Bay National Estuary Program in 1994 and approved by the EPA in 1995.[186] In 1995 the TNRCC commissioners established the Galveston Bay Council, a 41-member council that advises the TNRCC and the GLO.

The cost to the state for implementing the recommendations in the Galveston Bay Plan was estimated to be $1.5 million per year in 1996 and 1997. However, the 1995 legislature cut the appropriation in half, with annual funding set at $750,000. The Galveston Bay Plan identified 17 problems that needed to be addressed.

The Corpus Christi Bay National Estuary Program was established in 1992 and began with a four-year effort to identify the problems in the 600-square-mile estuarine "Coastal Bend" system and develop a management plan, known as the Coastal Bend Bays Plan. Some of the initial activities include a wetlands restoration project, an analysis of agricultural point-source runoff to Baffin Bay, and an urban non-point-source pollution reduction project for small municipalities.[187] Perhaps the major problem facing the estuaries is the lack of freshwater flow, causing pollutants to concentrate in the estuaries. The lack of fresh water is due both to low rainfall and to the increasing demand for water in a growing Corpus Christi.[188] Another problem facing the area, as well as other areas in Texas, is red tide, a condition caused by a tiny organism that can kill fish and shellfish almost instantly and is also harmful to humans (see box: What Does It Mean When the Tide Is Red or Brown?).

The Corpus Christi National Estuary Program study area includes Aransas and Corpus Christi bays and the Upper Laguna Madre, and is bounded on the east by a series of barrier islands, including Padre Island. In February 1998 the program began taking comments on the draft Coastal Bend Bays Plan and in August 1998 submitted the plan to the EPA.[189]

WETLANDS

Wetlands can be located either near the coast (coastal wetlands) or farther inland (interior wetlands). Though less than five percent of the state's total area is wetlands, and an even smaller percentage is coastal wetlands, Texas has been identified as one of 19 states with significant coastal wetlands.

Wetlands are defined in state law as areas that are inundated or saturated by surface or groundwater at a frequency and duration sufficient to support, and that under normal circumstances do support, a prevalence of vegetation typically adapted for life in saturated soil conditions. Coastal wetlands include salt, intermediate, brackish, and fresh marshes, tidal inlands, and forested scrub.

Coastal wetlands act as a natural filter for various natural and human-made contaminants, protecting the overall estuarine system. Coastal wetlands also help control excessive runoff to the bays and erosion of lands, protecting people and property from storms, floods, and erosions by serving as a buffer between land and water. The wetlands also provide important nutrients for the bay ecosystem, as well as essential habitat for many species of waterfowl, reptiles, mammals, fish, and other wildlife.

In addition to these benefits in habitat, water quality, flood control, and erosion control, coastal wetlands provide direct benefits to the Texas economy through commercial and sport fishing, hunting, nature tourism, and bird-watching. Shrimp, oysters, blue crab, black drum, and southern flounder either depend directly on habitat provided by wetlands for spawning and nursery grounds or receive important nutrients and food from fish and wildlife that depend on these wetlands. Finally, property values of developments near open spaces such as wetlands increase, resulting in higher tax revenues for local governments and schools.[190]

In 1991 wetlands were recognized for the first time as "waters of the state" under Texas Water Quality Standards and are now afforded better water quality protection. Unfortunately, the TNRCC has no permanent wetlands monitoring program, although some wetlands monitoring does occur as part of regular monitoring of bays and estuaries.[191] Also in 1991, the legislature adopted a policy of no-net-loss of state-owned wetlands for the state of Texas. This policy has led the TPWD to develop a wetlands management plan, which other state agencies are directed to uphold to protect wetlands from destruction (see *Wildlife and Biodiversity* chapter for details).

AMOUNT OF WETLANDS AND WETLANDS LOSS

In the United States as a whole, an estimated 156,000 acres of wetlands—both coastal and interior —are lost each year.[192] This includes both wetlands lost as a result of draining and filling projects requiring Army Corps of Engineers Section 404 permits and estimated loss from other sources not requiring such permits. In fact, about 80 percent of lost wetlands in the United States are not reported to the Corps of Engineers.[193]

Despite the continued loss of wetlands, overall,

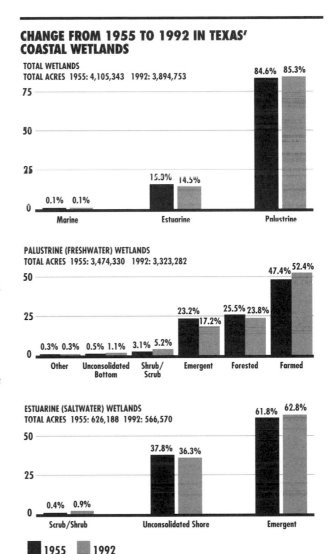

CHANGE FROM 1955 TO 1992 IN TEXAS' COASTAL WETLANDS

TOTAL WETLANDS
TOTAL ACRES 1955: 4,105,343 1992: 3,894,753

PALUSTRINE (FRESHWATER) WETLANDS
TOTAL ACRES 1955: 3,474,330 1992: 3,323,282

ESTUARINE (SALTWATER) WETLANDS
TOTAL ACRES 1955: 626,188 1992: 566,570

■ 1955 ▨ 1992

Source: D.W. Moulton, T.E. Dahl, and D.M. Dahl, Texas Coastal Wetlands: Status and Trends, mid-1950 to early 1990s (Albuquerque, New Mexico: Fish and Wildlife Service, U.S. Department of the Interior, 1997), 11.

net loss of wetlands in the United States has been reduced in recent years. The biggest reason for the decline is the reduction in the amount of wetlands utilized for agriculture. Areas such as the Northern and Southern Plains actually experienced a net gain of wetlands between 1982 and 1992, according to National Resources Inventory, a program under the Natural Resources Conservation Service (NRCS) of the U.S. Department of Agriculture (USDA).[194] In addition, both volunteer mitigation programs like the North American Waterfowl Management Plan

CAUSES OF COASTAL WETLAND LOSS

Direct Causes

- Drainage for crop production, timber production, and mosquito control.
- Dredging and stream channelization for navigation channels, flood protection, coastal housing development, and reservoir maintenance.
- Filling by dredged material and other solid waste disposal, roads and highways, and urban development.
- Construction of dikes, dams, levees, and seawalls for flood control, water supply, irrigation, and storm protection.
- Discharge of materials into waters and wetlands.
- Mining of wetlands soils for peat, coal, sand, gravel, phosphate, and other materials.

Indirect Causes

- Subsidence due to extraction of groundater, oil and gas, sulfur, and other materials.
- Hydrological alterations by canals, spoil banks, roads, and groundwater withdrawals.
- Sediment diversion by dams, deep channels, and other structures.

Natural Causes

- Subsidence (including natural rise of sea level)
- Droughts
- Hurricanes
- Erosion
- Muskrat, nutria, grasscarp, and goose "eat outs"

Source: Tom Calnan, Comprehensive Strategies for Protecting Coastal Wetlands (Austin: Texas General Land Office, 1994).

and the Partners for Wildlife Program, run by the U.S. Fish and Wildlife Service, as well as mitigation requirements under the Army Corps of Engineers Section 404 program, have actually offset losses in some years.

FYI ☞ *Even a net gain of 50,000 acres a year would require more than 40 years of sustained effort to replace only one percent of the nation's original wetland acreage.* (Source: David Smith, "Comparing Apples to Oranges," National Wetlands Newsletter 19, no. 4 [July-August 1997]: 13.)

Estimates of the amount of coastal wetlands loss in Texas vary by source. Using a study area of approximately 20,000 square miles along the coast and aerial photographs, scientists from the U.S. Fish and Wildlife Service—in cooperation with other federal and state agencies—estimated that 4.1 million acres

CHANGES IN SEA GRASSES OF THE LAGUNA MADRE, 1965–1988

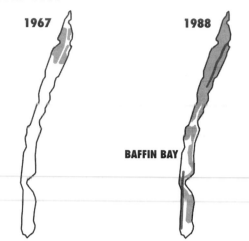

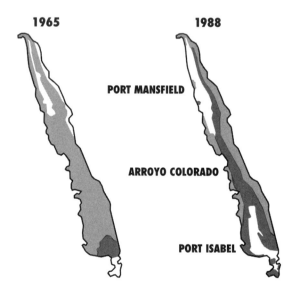

▨ Shoalgrass

▨ Clovergrass, turtlegrass, and manatee grass
South Bay was not sampled in 1965. 1965 Seagrass data were not available for all portions of Upper Laguna Madre.

Source: Compiled by Doug Houston, Texas General Land Office, Resource Management/Coastal Division. Adapted from M. L. Quammen and C. P. Onuf, "Laguna Madre: Seagrass Changes Continue Decades After Salinity Reduction," Estuaries (June 16, 1993), 304.

of coastal wetlands existed in the mid-1950s. By 1992, the U.S. Fish and Wildlife Service estimated that Texas had 3.9 million square acres of coastal wetlands, including 3.3 million acres of freshwater wetlands and 567,000 acres of saltwater wetlands.[195]

ESTIMATED LOSS OF WETLAND BY SOURCE IN GALVESTON BAY

CAUSE	TYPE OF WETLAND AFFECTED	NET LOSS, 1950–90 (ACRES)
Subsidence and sea level rises (aquifer overpumping)	Estuarine bay marshes	24,600
Conversion to urban and agricultural use	Freshwater marshes	35,600
Dredge and fill activities	Estuarine bay marshes	7,070
Modifications of shoreline (flood control, salt water barriers, cooling ponds)	Estuarine bay marshes	6,300

Source: Galveston Bay National Estuary Program, Galveston Bay Environmental Characterization Report *(Houston: Galveston Bay National Estuary Program, 1993), 218.*

The study does not define the quality of wetlands, but simply the number of acres they cover. Thus, while the total amount of coastal wetlands has declined by only 210,590 acres, or 5,700 acres a year, in the past forty years, the type and quality of wetlands has changed dramatically. For example, about 52 percent of the coastal freshwater wetlands were used for farmlands—mainly rice farming—in 1992, compared to 47 percent in 1955. Saltwater intrusion caused by canals, land subsidence (sinking), and drainage ditches has severely damaged some of the remaining wetlands.[196]

Several efforts are underway to digitize the National Wetlands Inventory Program's maps and aerial photographs to better map and monitor changes in the state's wetlands. The TPWD plans to classify the entire Texas coastal zone and determine wetlands change in five-year periods.[197]

THREATS TO WETLANDS

Like estuaries, wetlands are subject to a variety of threats.

Subsidence of land along the coast and the loss of coastline caused by soil erosion and a rising sea level have contributed to the loss of coastal wetlands. Each year, 225 acres of gulf shoreline wash into the sea. An estimated 21,000 acres of shoreline were lost between the mid-1800s and 1982.[198] In some areas of Texas, overpumping of groundwater has led to subsidence of the land. This impact alone has led to the

HOW ARE 404 PERMITS APPROVED?

(1) An individual wishing to discharge dredge or fill material applies to the Army Corps of Engineers for a Section 404 permit.

(2) The Corps of Engineers publishes a public notice that it has received a Section 404 application.

(3) The TNRCC and the Corps of Engineers review the application under Section 401 of the Federal Clean Water Act.

(4) A public hearing is held if any party requests one during the 30-day public notice period.

(5) The TNRCC completes review of the request for Section 404 certification. The state may:
    (a) deny the certification,
    (b) grant the certification,
    (c) grant the certification only if certain conditions are met, or
    (d) waive certification of the 401 permit.

(6) If the state waives certification or certifies the Section 404 application, a Section 404 permit may be granted by the Corps of Engineers. However, the Corps of Engineers may also choose to deny the permit, based on its own review. Both the Corps of Engineers and the TNRCC must approve of the permit in order for filling and dredging activities to begin.

loss of about 24,600 acres of marshes since the 1950s in the four-county Galveston Bay area.[199] The U.S. Fish and Wildlife Service reports a loss of 20,000 acres of coastal marshes to open bays from land subsidence due to extraction of oil, gas, and water.[200]

Another significant cause of coastal wetlands loss is conversion of wetlands for urban or agricultural development. Wetlands are sometimes drained and turned into rangeland or cropland or fitted for urban use, in part to keep up with population growth. They are sometimes impacted by dredging and filling operations, conducted mainly to widen canals such as the Gulf Intracoastal Waterway for navigation purposes, because dredged soil is often deposited in the wetlands' open water sites. Construction of roads and levees can also alter the original tidal hydrological characteristics.

One dramatic example of wetlands destruction resulting from land-use changes has been the loss of shoal grass in the Lower Laguna Madre. Over the past twenty years, there has been a 60 percent reduction in shoal grass beds in this water body. Studies attribute the loss of sea grasses to suspension of fine-particle sediment caused by the dredging of the Gulf Intracoastal Waterway.[201]

WETLANDS PROTECTION

With the Clean Water Act of 1977 the federal government initiated the first truly comprehensive wetlands protection program. Section 404 of the Clean Water Act requires the Army Corps of Engineers to issue a permit for any dredging or filling of waters of the United States. In 1986 this provision was expanded to include wetlands and water serving as habitat for migratory birds or endangered species. Normal farming, forestry, and ranching activities are exempt from permit requirements.

Though the Corps of Engineers actually issues the Section 404 permits, applicants must also obtain certification from the state that a permit will not violate state water quality standards under Section 401 of the Clean Water Act. Of the 1,519 permits issued in 1993 by the Corps of Engineers, 733, or almost half, were for projects in the 18 counties along the Texas coast.[202] Usually, a permit requires some form of mitigation to require that other wetlands be restored to make up for destroyed wetlands (see focus piece on *Mitigation*).

THE GULF OF MEXICO

The Gulf of Mexico is a recreational and economic resource for Texas, for other states that share its shoreline, and for Mexico. Hazardous and industrial waste spills, illegal and legal dumping of garbage, and offshore drilling by oil and gas refineries have all led to widespread pollution of both the gulf and Texas beaches. Pollution is also likely responsible for a 3,000-square-mile "dead zone " off the Texas-Louisiana coast, where no aquatic life lives or spawns.

According to the TNRCC's Water Quality Inventory, only 388 square miles of the 3,491 square miles of the water along the gulf shoreline in Texas's jurisdiction did not meet their designated water quality parameters in 1996. This was due to elevated fecal coliform in close proximity to Sabine Pass, Point Bolivar, and San Luis Pass, causing these areas not to meet their oyster waters designation. Local marinas and housing developments are believed to be the cause of the pollution.[203]

OCEAN SPILLS

More than 102,000 vessels cart some 250 million tons of cargo to Texas's largest ports each year, about 45 percent of which is petroleum- and oil-related.[204]

Spills and dumping from these ships during transit are among the chief causes of both marine and beach debris. Offshore oil rigs and other petroleum-industry activities result in the discharging of chemicals and oil into Texas coastal waters, further degrading their quality.

About a quarter of the nation's refining capacity and almost 65 percent of its petrochemical capacity are located along 367 miles of Texas shoreline. In 1989 more than 115,000 tanker and barge transports carried some 1.6 billion barrels of crude oil, fuels, and other petroleum products across Texas gulf waters.[205]

In the summer of 1990, the Norwegian tanker *Mega Borg* exploded, discharging 4.6 million gallons of crude oil into the gulf. A collision between a tanker and a tank-barge in August 1990 caused some 700,000 gallons of oil to spill into Galveston Bay, blocking the Houston Ship Channel for days.[206]

In response to these spills, the Texas legislature in 1991 passed the Oil Spill Prevention and Response Act. The act put the GLO in charge of oil spills and established a clean-up fund, generated by a two-cent-per-barrel fee on all crude oil being loaded

OIL SPILLS IN COASTAL WATERS 1996–1997

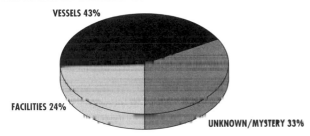

VESSELS 43%

FACILITIES 24%

UNKNOWN/MYSTERY 33%

TOTAL NUMBER OF SPILLS: 2,681

Source: Greg Pollock, Oil Spill and Clean-Up Division, Texas General Land Office, 1998.

or unloaded in Texas ports, to clean up "mystery spills" for which no responsible party can be identified. In late 1997 the Coastal Protection Fund had a positive balance of $17.1 million to help clean up these spills.[207]

Between FY 1996 and 1997, there were more than 2,400 responses by the GLO to individual oil spills in coastal waters, about a third of which were classified as mystery or unknown spills. In those same years, more than $1 million from the Coastal Protection Fund was spent for state-funded cleanups of these and other spills.[208] The majority of these funds were used to respond to a single spill in March 1996, when more than 5,000 gallons of fuel oil were sprayed out into the Gulf of Mexico from a barge in Galveston Bay.[209]

The State of Texas holds title to four million acres of submerged land off the coast, which can be leased for oil and gas activity. In 1993, 11 rigs were operating in state waters offshore, two were operating in inshore waters, and another 227 on state land.[210] Oil and gas production on federal waters is managed by the U.S. Department of the Interior. The central and western gulf off the coasts of Texas and Louisiana has one of the highest rates of oil and gas production in the world.

OCEAN DUMPING

Improperly disposed waste in gulf waters is a major threat to marine mammals, birds, and other aquatic life. Waste materials thrown off of ships that transport wastes often entangle, maim, and kill these aquatic

creatures. Fish and marine mammals often eat synthetic materials, which then enters the food chain. Finally, this debris accumulates on the Texas coast, affecting both tourism and estuarine habitats (see *Land* chapter for a further discussion of beach debris).

To address this beach debris problem, the Gulf of Mexico has been established as a special area under the international MARPOL treaty, which regulates marine pollution around the world. Under the treaty, the dumping of solid wastes by any boat from any nation is prohibited in a special area. Thus, only food that has been reduced to particles can be dumped legally in the Gulf of Mexico.

NOTES

1. The first water pollution legislation—the Federal Water Pollution Control Act of 1948—required states to locate these polluters, and billions of dollars of public money was spent, with little result. See Andrew Dzurick, *Water Resources Planning* (Savage, Md.: Rowman and Littlefield, 1990), 56.
2. Dzurick, *Water Resources Planning*, 56.
3. American Rivers, *North America's Most Endangered and Threatened Rivers of 1993* (Washington, D.C., 1993), Executive Summary.
4. Joseph Petulla, *American Environmental History* (Columbus, Ohio: Merill Publishing, 1988), 413.
5. TNRCC, *Texas Water Quality: A Summary of River Basin Assessments* (December 1996), 15–16.
6. TNRCC, *The State of Texas Water Quality Inventory*, 13th ed. (December 1996), 27. (Hereinafter cited as *Water Quality Inventory—1996.*)
7. TNRCC, *Water Quality Inventory—1996*, 27.
8. TNRCC, *Water Quality Inventory—1996*, 30.
9. TNRCC, *Water Quality Inventory—1996*, 30.
10. TNRCC, *Water Quality Inventory—1996*, 205.
11. TNRCC, *Water Quality Inventory—1996*, 35.
12. EPA, *Environmental Investments: The Costs of a Clean Environment* (Washington, D.C., November 1990), as reported in U.S. General Accounting Office (GAO), *Environmental Infrastructure: Effects of Limits on Certain Tax-Exempt Bonds* (Washington, D.C., October 1993), 18–20.
13. Raymond Gabler and the Editors of Consumer Reports Books, *Is Your Water Safe To Drink?* (Mt. Vernon, N.Y.: Consumers Union, 1988), 21.
14. EPA, *Is Your Drinking Water Safe?* (Washington, D.C., September 1991), 4.
15. EPA, *Water on Tap: A Consumer's Guide to the Nation's Drinking Water* (Washington, D.C., 1997), 3.
16. EPA, *Safe Drinking Water Act: Phase II Fact Sheet* (Washington, D.C., January 1991), 2.
17. Laura Koesters, Director, Office of Water Resources Management, TNRCC, interview by author, February, 1994, Austin.
18. TNRCC, *Legislation of Interest to TNRCC: 75th Legislature* (August 1997), 31.

19. TNRCC, *The State of Texas Water Quality Inventory, 12th ed.* (1995), 14. (Hereinafter cited as *Water Quality Inventory—1994.*)

20. TNRCC, *Water Quality Inventory—1994*, 14.

21. Clean Water Act of 1972.

22. TNRCC, *1998 State of Texas Water Quality Inventory for Planning Basin Groups B and C* (1998), 1.

23. TNRCC, "Texas' Future: Clean Rivers Run through It," *National Outlook*, (Spring 1998), 11.

24. See EPA, *Water Quality Standards Handbook* (Washington, D.C., 1993). Texas Antidegradation Policy is contained in 30 Texas Administrative Code 307.5.

25. EPA, Region VI, information provided to author, July 1994.

26. Texas' coastal resources are discussed later in this chapter.

27. TNRCC, *Water Quality Inventory—1994*, 127.

28. For example, in 1994, 66 percent of the classified rivers and streams supported their use, 15 percent only partially supported their use, and 19 percent did not support their use.

29. TNRCC, *Water Quality Inventory—1996*, 165.

30. TNRCC, *Water Quality Inventory—1996*, 168.

31. TNRCC, "Texas' Future: Clean Rivers Run through It," 11.

32. TNRCC, *Water Quality Inventory—1994*, 129–132.

33. TNRCC, *Water Quality Inventory—1996*, 216.

34. TNRCC, *Water Quality Inventory—1996*, 217. The two segments are Salado Creek and the Medina River below Medina Diversion Dam.

35. Texas Engineering and Extension Service, Texas A&M University System, *Basic Wastewater Operation* (College Station, 1994), 4-2.

36. Texas Engineering and Extension Service, *Basic Wastewater Operation*, 4-5.

37. TNRCC, *Texas Water Quality: A Summary of River Basin Assessments* (1994), 3.

38. There are 0.133 cubic feet in a gallon of water; Texas Stadium is 792 feet long, 633 feet wide, and 208 feet tall, or approximately 104.2 million cubic feet; about 8.2 billion cubic feet of wastewater is discharged every day.

39. Texas Groundwater Protection Committee, *Joint Groundwater Monitoring and Contamination Report—1996* (Austin: TNRCC, 1997), 41.

40. TNRCC, *Legislation of Interest to TNRCC: 75th Legislature* (August 1997), 31.

41. TNRCC, "The New Texas Environment: The State of Our Land, Air, and Water in 1994," *The Texas Environment* (spring 1994), 9.

42. TNRCC, "The New Texas Environment: The State of Our Land, Air, and Water in 1994," 9.

43. For example, in FY 1995 the Industrial Permits Team of the TNRCC processed 171 applications, while the Municipal Permits Team processed 486 applications. TNRCC, *Water Quality Inventory—1996*, 304.

44. TNRCC, *Water Quality Inventory—1996*, 289.

45. Texas Engineering and Extension Service, *Basic Wastewater Operation*, 4-10.

46. Vickie Reat, Toxicity Evaluation Team Leader, TNRCC, interview by author, February 1994, Austin.

47. EPA, *Toxics Release Inventory: Public Data Release* (Washington, D.C., April 1994), 14–16.

48. It is important to note that the TRI data under-represents the problem of toxic chemical releases because only large manufacturers and processors are required to report to the state. Agricultural operations, gas stations, vehicles, incinerators, hazardous landfills, and other producers of toxics are not required to submit information. In addition, enforcement is lax and many facilities do not report , and many toxics recognized as known or probable carcinogens are not included in the list of some 650 toxic chemicals. (Texas Citizens Action, *Poisons in Our Neighborhoods: Toxic Pollution in Texas*, September 1992, 4–5).

49. EPA, *1997 Toxics Release Inventory: Public Data Release* (Washington, D.C., April 1999), Table 2-4.

50. TNRCC, Toxics Release Inventory Program, Office of Pollution Prevention and Recycling, TNRCC, information provided by electronic file transfer, July 1998.

51. EPA, *1997 Toxics Release Inventory*, Table 2-4.

52. TNRCC, file transfer, July 1998.

53. TNRCC, *Water Quality Inventory—1996*, 298.

54. TNRCC, *Water Quality Inventory—1994*, 256.

55. TNRCC, *Water Quality Inventory—1996*, 297.

56. TNRCC, *Water Quality Inventory—1996*, 302; TNRCC, *Final Annual Enforcement Report, Fiscal Year 1997* (December 17, 1997), Tables 6 and 7.

57. TNRCC, *Water Quality Inventory—1996*, 298.

58. TWDB, *Water and Wastewater Needs of Colonias in Texas: 1996 Update* (1997), 3.

59. Ralph Haurwitz, "Scant Relief from Filth, Disease for the Poorest of Texans," *Austin American-Statesman*, July 12, 1998, A9.

60. For a good discussion of alternative systems used in Texas see Michael Barret and Joseph Malina, *Wastewater Treatment Systems for Small Communities: A Guide for Local Government Officials* (Center for Research in Water Resources, University of Texas at Austin, September 1991).

61. U.S. Army Corps of Engineers, *International Boundary and Water Commission Sanitation Issues* (Fort Worth, September 1992).

62. North American Development Board, *Annual Public Session, 1998* (San Antonio, January 22, 1998), Project Reviews.

63. World Resources Institute, *The 1992 Information Please Environmental Almanac* (Boston: Houghton Mifflin, 1992), 90.

64. TNRCC, *Water Quality Inventory—1996*, 330.

65. TNRCC, *Texas Water Quality: A Summary of River Basin Assessments* (December 1996), 5.

66. The ordinance in Austin known as the Save Our Springs (SOS) ordinance was passed by voters in 1992. There is, however, considerable opposition to the ordinance. Opponents predicted that the ordinance would curtail economic development by burdening businesses wanting to develop within the watershed and recharge zones. These opponents argued that limits on development should be linked to technical pollution-control equipment and to the actual pollution caused by development, not to the amount of impervious cover. The SOS ordinance is being and has been challenged in a number of court cases throughout the Austin area.

67. TNRCC, *Clean Water for Texas: Solving Water Quality Problems* (September 1997), Table 1.

68. Texas Water Commission, *1990 Update to the Non-point Source Water Pollution Management Report for the State of Texas*, Tables B-1–B-5; TNRCC, *Water Quality Inventory—1994*, 261–265.

69. TNRCC, *Water Quality Inventory—1996*, 304.

70. John M. Sweeten, Charles Baird, and Leah Manning, *Animal Waste Management, Agricultural and Silviculture Non-Point Source Pollution Management*, # L-5043 (Temple: Texas State Soil and Water Conservation Board and Texas Agricultural Extension Service, 1991), 1.

71. Texas State Soil and Water Conservation Board, *A Comprehensive Study of Texas Watersheds and Their Impacts on Water Quality and Water Quantity* (Temple, Texas, 1991), 149.

72. Texas State Soil and Water Conservation Board, A Comprehensive Study of Texas Watersheds and Their Impacts on Water Quality and Water Quantity, 150.

73. Information for 1992–1995, TNRCC, Water Quality Inventory—1996, 304. Information for 1996 and 1997, TNRCC, Final Annual Enforcement Report Fiscal Year 1997 (December 17, 1997), Tables 6 and 7.

74. Claudia Chaffin, Water Section, Enforcement Division, TNRCC, phone interview by author, January 20, 1998, Austin.

75. Stephen Ligon, Texas Water Commission, "Water Quality Permitting: Stormwater," Paper presented at the Environmental Trade Fair, Austin, April 7, 1993.

76. TNRCC, Water Quality Inventory—1996, 331.

77. Arthur Tally, Watershed Management Division, TNRCC, interview by author, February 1994, Austin.

78. TNRCC, Legislation of Interest to TNRCC: 75th Legislature, 30. HB 1190 was passed by the 75th Legislature and is referred to as the Water Quality in Watersheds Bill.

79. TNRCC, "Texas' Future: Clean Rivers Run through It," 11.

80. TNRCC, 1998 State of Texas Reservoir Water Quality Assessment (December 1998).

81. Texas Water Commission, Summary Report: Regional Assessments of Water Quality Pursuant to the Texas Clean Rivers Act (December 1992), 12.

82. TNRCC, Texas Water Quality: A Summary of River Basin Assessments, 15.

83. TNRCC, Water Quality Inventory—1996, 227.

84. TNRCC, Water Quality Inventory—1994, 181.

85. TNRCC, Texas Water Quality: A Summary of River Basin Assessments, 19–111.

86. TNRCC, 1996 Regional Assessment of Water Quality in the River Grande Basin (October 1996), 40.

87. TNRCC, draft copy of vol. 2 of Phase II of Binational Rio Grande Toxic Substances Study (May 1997), 7.

88. TNRCC, draft copy of vol. 2 of Phase II of Binational Rio Grande Toxic Substances Study, 9.

89. Richard Thompson, Texas Department of Health, interview by author, February 1994, Austin.

90. EPA, Lower Rio Grande Valley: Environmental Monitoring Study (Washington, D.C., June 1994), 20.

91. Richard Thompson, Texas Department of Health, interview by author, February 1994.

92. TNRCC, Water Quality Inventory—1994, 173. Segments where whole fish tissue has shown levels of concern for PCBs include the Sabine River above Toledo Bend Reservoir; the Trinity River below Lake Livingston; Lake Livingston; the West Fork of the Trinity River below Lake Worth; the Concho River; the Upper San Antonio River; the Arroyo Colorado above Tidal; the Houston Ship Channel; and the Corpus Christi Inner Harbor.

93. TNRCC, Texas Water Quality: A Summary of River Basin Assessments, section on Sabine River.

94. TNRCC, Water Quality Inventory—1996, 217.

95. TWDB, County Historical Water Use in Texas (1998).

96. Texas Ground Water Protection Committee, Joint Groundwater Monitoring and Contamination Report—1997 (Austin: TNRCC, June 1998), 7.

97. Texas Ground Water Protection Committee, Joint Groundwater Monitoring and Contamination Report—1997, 7.

98. TNRCC, Water Quality Inventory—1996, 258.

99. Texas Ground Water Protection Committee, Joint Groundwater Monitoring and Contamination Report—1996, 5.

100. Texas Groundwater Protection Committee, Joint Groundwater Monitoring and Contamination Report—1997, 43.

101. Texas Groundwater Protection Committee, Joint Groundwater Monitoring and Contamination Report—1997, 42.

102. TNRCC, Petroleum Storage Tank Division, "Number of Leaking Petroleum Storage Tanks," information provided to author, January 1998.

103. Tom Lewis, Petroleum Storage Tank Division, TNRCC, interview by author, February 1994, Austin.

104. Dan Neal, Reimbursements Section, Petroleum Storage Tank Division, TNRCC, phone interview with author, January 21, 1998. According to Neal, the TNRCC will cover most costs of cleanup, although the agency will fund the required clean-up only to appropriate health-based levels. If an owner wishes to clean up to higher-quality levels, however, for liability or other reasons, that cost cannot be reimbursed. In addition, there is an insurance deductible that the TNRCC will not cover, which has worked out to about 15 percent of clean-up costs.

105. Tom Lewis, Petroleum Storage Tank Division, TNRCC, interview by author, February 1994, Austin.

106. Dan Neal, Reimbursements Section, Petroleum Storage Tank Division, TNRCC, phone interview by author, January 21, 1998.

107. Texas Groundwater Protection Committee, Joint Groundwater Monitoring and Contamination Report—1997, 45.

108. Texas Groundwater Protection Committee, Joint Groundwater Monitoring and Contamination Report—1997, 45.

109. Texas Groundwater Protection Committee, Joint Groundwater Monitoring and Contamination Report—1997, 39, 45.

110. Texas Groundwater Protection Committee, Joint Groundwater Monitoring and Contamination Report—1996, Table I.

111. Texas Groundwater Protection Committee, Joint Groundwater Monitoring and Contamination Report—1996, 76.

112. Richard Ginn, Oil and Gas Division, Railroad Commission of Texas (RCC), letter to author, January 30, 1998, Austin.

113. Ginn, letter to author, January 30, 1998.

114. Underground Injection Control Program, TNRCC, information provided to author, October 1997. This total includes only wells that have been permitted and actually are in service. Other wells have been permitted but were never constructed or used.

115. Ginn, letter to author, January 30, 1998.

116. Texas Groundwater Protection Committee, Joint Groundwater Monitoring and Contamination Report—1966, 50.

117. For example, over the 1970s, Hidalgo County shifted 20 square miles of rural citrus lands to urban use. Charles Ellard and J. Michael Patrick, "Changing Land Use Patterns in the Lower Rio Grande Valley: A Case Study of Cameron and Hidalgo Counties," Journal of Borderland Studies 3, no. 2: 57.

118. Texas Water Commission, Groundwater Quality of Texas: An Overview of Natural and Man-Affected Conditions, Report 89-01 (March 1989), 161–165.

119. Texas Water Commission, Ground-Water Quality of Texas, 113.

120. TNRCC, Legislation of Interest to TNRCC: 75th Legislature, 34.

121. Steve Wiley, Water Well Drillers Board, TNRCC, interview by author, March, 1994, Austin.

122. TWDB, Water for Texas 1990, 1-9.

123. Ginn, letter to author, January 30, 1998.

124. Ginn, letter to author, January 30, 1998.

125. Robert Bryce, "More Precious than Oil," Texas Monthly, February 1991, 108.

126. Ginn, letter to author, January 30, 1998.

127. Robert Bryce, "More Precious than Oil," 109.

128. State Bar of Texas Environmental Law Journal 25 (1994): 65–66.

129. Ginn, letter to author, January 30, 1998.

130. Ginn, letter to author, January 30, 1998.

131. Texas Groundwater Protection Committee, *Joint Groundwater Monitoring and Contamination Report—1997*, 55.

132. The case against the CAFO, San Angelo Feedyards, was referred to the TNRCC Enforcement Division in 1995. Despite some progress made by the facility in operating its facility, groundwater contamination from high nitrates continues to be a problem, and as of 1998 the TNRCC was still pursuing an enforcement strategy. Claudia Chaffin, Water Section, Enforcement Division, TNRCC, phone interview by author, January 20, 1997.

133. TNRCC, *Water Quality Inventory—1996*, 255.

134. Texas Groundwater Protection Committee, *Joint Groundwater Monitoring and Contamination Report—1996*, 64.

135. Texas Groundwater Protection Committee, *Joint Groundwater Monitoring and Contamination Report—1996*, 65.

136. EPA, *Water on Tap*, 1.

137. Texas Ground Water Protection Committee, *Texas Ground Water Protection Strategy* (Austin: Texas Water Commission, January 1988), 49.

138. EPA, "How Safe Is my Drinking Water?," in *Water on Tap*, 3.

139. Texas Groundwater Protection Committee, *Joint Groundwater Monitoring and Contamination Report—1997*, 49.

140. TNRCC, Water Utilities Division, *Draft Summary of Public Drinking Water Synthetic Organic Chemical (Pesticide) Sampling* (December 1997).

141. EPA, *Safe Drinking Water Information System*, 1994.

142. Clean Water Network, Texas Waters section in *A Prescription for Clean Water: How to Meet the Goals of the Clean Water Act* (Washington, D.C., October 1997).

143. TNRCC, *Final Annual Enforcement Report: Fiscal Year 1997* (December 17, 1997), 5.

144. Water Utilities Division, TNRCC, electronic information provided to author, March 1998.

145. Water Utilities Division, TNRCC, electronic information provided to author, December 1997.

146. EPA, *Is Your Drinking Water Safe?* 6.

147. World Resources Institute, *The 1994 Information Please Environmental Almanac* (Boston: Houghton Mifflin, 1993), 69.

148. Tony Bennet, Water Utilities Division, TNRCC, interview by author, March 1994, Austin.

149. TNRCC, *The Texas Environment* (Spring 1994), 10.

150. Water Utilities Division, TNRCC, electronic file provided to author, March 1998, Austin.

151. TNRCC, *Water Quality Inventory—1996*, 109.

152. Robert Perciaspe, EPA, "Memorandum on Safe Drinking Water Act Amendment to Public Water System Definition," December 6, 1996.

153. Doug Halcomb, Water Utilities Division, TNRCC, phone interview by author, January 1998.

154. TNRCC, *Final Annual Enforcement Report: Fiscal Year 1997*, Tables 1-12.

155. EPA, "How Will I Know if My Drinking Water Remains Safe in the Future?" *Water on Tap*, 1.

156. Gabler et al., *Is Your Water Safe To Drink?* 330–333.

157. Sam Howe Verhovek, "A Few Cities See a Profit in Bottling L'Eau de Tap," *New York Times*, August 6, 1997, A10.

158. Verhovek, "A Few Cities See a Profit in Bottling l'Eau de Tap," A10.

159. EPA, "What Can I Do If There Is a Problem with My Drinking Water?" In *Water on Tap*, 1.

160. Texas Ground Water Protection Committee, *Ground Water Protection Strategy* (Austin: Texas Water Commission , January 1988), 57.

161. TNRCC. *Water Quality Inventory—1994*; Texas Water

Commission, internal memo, "Wellhead Protection Program," (1992), 1.

162. National Oceanic and Atmospheric Administration, *Estuaries of the United States: Vital Statistics of a Natural Resource Base* (Dockville, Md.: Strategic Assessment Branch, Ocean Assessments Division, National Oceanic and Atmospheric Administration, 1990).

163. Randy Lee Loftus, "Texas Beaches Draw Big Pollution and Big Profits," *Dallas Morning News*, November 24, 1991, 13.

164. TNRCC, *Water Quality Inventory—1996*, 224.

165. Texas General Land Office (GLO), *Texas Coastal Wetlands: A Handbook for Local Governments* (1997), 5.

166. *1994-1995 Texas Almanac* (Dallas: Dallas Morning News, 1993), 118.

167. GLO, *EnviroNomics 2*, no. 3 (winter 1993): 1.

168. Texas Department of Transportation, *The Gulf Intracoastal Waterway in Texas* (1996), I-7.

169. GLO, *Texas Coastal Management Program* (1995), II-51.

170. GLO, *Texas Coastal Management Program* (1995), II-51.

171. D. W. Moulton, T. E. Dahl, and D. M. Dall, *Texas Coastal Wetlands; State and Trends, Mid-1950s to Early 1990s* (Albuquerque: U.S. Department of the Interior, Fish and Wildlife Service, 1997), 6.

172. U.S. Army Corps of Engineers, *International Boundary and Water Commission Sanitation Issues*, 14

173. U.S. Army Corps of Engineers, *International Boundary and Water Commission Sanitation Issues*, 14.

174. TNRCC, *Water Quality Inventory—1996*, 184.

175. TNRCC, *Water Quality Inventory—1996*, 183. In addition, 126.1 miles of bays did not partially support aquatic life use due to other contaminants.

176. Corpus Christi Bay National Estuary Program, "Red Tide—Unwelcome Visitor to the Coastal Bend," *Around the Bend: News of the Coastal Bend's Bays and Estuaries 3*, no. 3 (Summer 1997), 4.

177. Michael Satchell, "The Cell from Hell," *U.S. News and World Report*, July 28, 1997, 26.

178. Satchell, "The Cell from Hell," 28.

179. Corpus Christi Bay National Estuary Program, "Red Tide—Unwelcome Visitor to the Coastal Bend," 4.

180. "Red Tide Frequently Asked Questions," Texas Parks and Wildlife Department (TPWD) Web page (http://www.tpwd.state.tx.us).

181. Satchell, "The Cell from Hell," 26.

182. TPWD Web page (http://www.tpwd.state.tx.us). The Web page has a link to an update on the occurrence of red tide from TPWD biologists working along the shore.

183. TNRCC, *Water Quality Inventory—1996*, 225–226.

184. TNRCC, *Water Quality Inventory—1996*, 219–221.

185. Galveston National Estuary Program, *Characterization of Non-Point Sources and Loadings to Galveston Bay* (Houston, March 1992), 53; *The Galveston Bay Plan: The Comprehensive Conservation and Management Plan for the Galveston Bay Estuary* (Houston, 1994), xiii.

186. TNRCC, *Water Quality Inventory—1996*, 188.

187. TNRCC, *Water Quality Inventory—1996*, 196.

188. EPA, *National Estuary Program: Bringing Our Estuaries New Life*, Web page (http://www.epa.gov/nep), 1997.

189. Coastal Bend Bays and Estuaries Program, *Coastal Bend Bays Plan* (TNRCC, August 1998).

190. GLO, *Texas Coastal Wetlands*, 9.

191. TNRCC, *Water Quality Inventory—1996*, 205.

192. Jonathan Tolman, "How We Achieved No Net Loss," *National Wetlands Newsletter 19*, no. 4 (July–August 1997), 1. Tolman cites figures based on the USDA's *National Resources Inventory*, which surveyed wetlands from 1982 to 1992. Tolman further states that by

1995, total losses had been reduced to 141,000 acres per year.

193. Tolman, "How We Achieved No Net Loss," 19.

194. Tolman, "How We Achieved No Net Loss," 20.

195. Moulton et al., *Texas Coastal Wetlands: State and Trends*, 5.

196. Texas Comptroller of Public Accounts, *Forces of Change*, vol. 2 (November 1993), 421.

197. TNRCC, *Water Quality Inventory—1996*.

198. GLO, *Texas Coastal Management Program*, II-2.

199. Galveston Bay National Estuary Program, *The State of the Bay: A Characterization of the Galveston Bay Ecosystem*, GBNEP 11 (Austin, 1994), 232.

200. Moulton et al., *Texas Coastal Wetlands: State and Trends*, 13.

201. Millicent Quammen and Christopher Onuf, "Laguna Madre: Seagrass Change Continue Decades after Salinity Reduction," *Estuaries* 16: 302–310.

202. U.S. Army Corps of Engineers, Fort Worth Office, "404 Permits in 1993," information provided to author, 1994.

203. TNRCC, *Water Quality Inventory—1996*, 197.

204. GLO, *EnviroNomics 2*, no. 3 (winter 1993): 4–5.

205. GLO, *EnviroNomics 2*, no. 3 (winter 1993): 3.

206. GLO, *EnviroNomics 2*, no. 3 (winter 1993): 3.

207. GLO, Oil Spill Prevention and Response, information provided to author, November 6, 1997.

208. Greg Pollock, Oil Spill Prevention and Response, GLO, phone interview by author, January 27, 1998.

209. Pollock, Oil Spill Prevention and Response, GLO, phone interview by author, January 27, 1998.

210. *Oil and Gas Journal*, July 23, 1993.

Environmental Justice

Citizen groups and environmental organizations have for years challenged state and federal governmental agencies to respond to the environmental and public-health hazards disproportionately affecting low-income communities and communities of color.

An increasing body of research has confirmed claims by environmental justice leaders that toxic pollution does indeed disproportionately affect low-income communities and communities of color. A 1994 analysis of 64 empirical studies on environmental impacts on communities reported that racial disparities were found more frequently than income disparities. The examination also shows that racial disparities were found for a whole range of environmental hazards, including air pollution, pesticide exposure, and the proximity to noxious facilities.[1]

Moreover, according to an analysis of the EPA's enforcement of Superfund laws by the *National Law Journal*, glaring procedural inequities exist. The *Journal* report stated: "There is a racial divide in the way the U.S. government cleans up toxic waste sites and punishes polluters. White communities see faster action, better results and stiffer penalties than communities where blacks, Hispanics and other minorities live. This unequal protection occurs whether the community is wealthy or poor."[2]

In response to solid evidence and public demand, in February 1994, President Clinton signed the executive order entitled "Federal Actions to Address Environmental Justice in Minority Populations and Low-Income Populations." This order required all federal agencies to develop an environmental justice strategy that identifies and addresses the adverse human health or environmental effects of their programs, policies, and activities on minority populations and low-income populations.[3] In response to that order, the EPA in 1998 adopted a guidance policy that uses the pollution-permitting process as one means of addressing the issue. The EPA policy maintains that even if a pollution permit passes all the legal tests, the permit might be illegal under the civil rights law, more specifically Title VI of the Civil

Rights Act of 1964, if it causes a disproportionate pollution burden on a minority community or neighborhood. Therefore, permit reviews might include an examination of community demographics and the cumulative impacts of neighboring industries.[4] (The TNRCC has not adopted the EPA's guidance policy.)

Several events have given rise to the movement for environmental equity in Texas. Starting in the 1980s at least a half-dozen citizen-based groups in Texas's communities of color organized around environmental and public health issues. In West Dallas a Latino and African American community began fighting the effects of lead contamination from a smelting plant located in their neighborhood. African American residents of the Carver Terrace neighborhood in Texarkana discovered that their homes were built on an abandoned creosote plant and their yards were filled with contaminated soil, resulting in human health problems. Latino community groups in Rosenberg, Austin, El Paso, and San Antonio have been battling authorities about the toxic dangers in their midst. For example, Rosenberg's Concerned Citizens for Community Development opposed the expansion of a landfill in their low-income Mexican American neighborhood; in Austin, Latinos and blacks fought for the removal of gasoline storage tanks in the heart of their neighborhoods; and in El Paso residents are fighting to stop the truck transportation of toxic chemicals through their neighborhoods. Residents of East San Antonio, already home to a Superfund site, fought the siting of a die-cast facility. The plant would release into the air hydrogen fluoride, hydrogen chloride, and other pollutants within 1,000 feet of homes. In response to these types of issues and activities, regional and statewide networks, such as the Southwest Network for Environmental and Economic Justice and the Texas Network for Environmental and Economic Justice, have brought together grassroots organizations of people of color to address these issues at the state, regional, and national levels.

Responding to citizen complaints, Texas environmental regulatory agencies took action in 1993. The heads of the state's two environmental regulatory agencies at that time (the Texas Water Commission and the Texas Air Commission) jointly appointed an Environmental Equity and Justice Task Force. The first of its kind in the nation, the task force was created to provide guidance to the soon-to-be-created TNRCC. One of the recommendations that was accepted by the commissioners of the new agency was the establishment of an Environmental Equity Office within the TNRCC. In addition, the task force recommended the development of a database with demographic information to help the agency in comprehensive environmental planning, encouraging local governments to develop master plans that include environmental and public-health provisions, and encouraging regulatory agencies to develop information that meets the diverse language needs of communities of color.

For some Texas legislators, the TNRCC's commitment to environmental equity has been neither sufficiently proactive nor resolute. During the 1997 legislative session, a bill was introduced to establish a state policy to prevent the disproportionate siting of solid waste facilities in low-income, minority communities and to minimize the adverse and cumulative impacts of such facilities where they are located. This bill, supported by Republicans and Democrats, was passed solidly by the House of Representatives, but because of the parliamentary maneuvering of a state senator, the bill was not reported out of committee and sent to the full Senate for a vote. The bill would have (1) established state policy to prevent the disproportionate siting of solid waste facilities in vulnerable communities, (2) implemented state policy by adding provisions to the state's strategic solid waste plan, (3) given the TNRCC Office of Pollution Prevention responsibility for coordinating the agency's environmental justice activities, (4) included an evaluation of the agency's progress toward achieving state policy in existing reports to the governor and the legislature, (5) allowed evidence of cumulative or multiple risks in administrative proceedings of the TNRCC, (6) directed the

TNRCC to implement policies to protect the public from cumulative risks, and (7) required public meetings and notice in the county where the new solid waste facility is proposed.

At the local level, officials have taken steps to address the issue of environmental equity. In response to residents' outcries and organizing efforts, the Travis County Attorney successfully negotiated the removal of twelve gasoline storage tanks from an East Austin neighborhood. In addition, the City of Austin, at the requests of neighborhood residents, established a year-long moratorium on all zoning requests while the city conducted a land-use analysis of a predominantly low-income African American and Mexican American neighborhood. The study concluded that a very large amount of zoning in that neighborhood allowed industry. As a result of the study, the city established recommended guidelines for zoning and required that all new industrial or commercial services applying for zoning notify residents and appear before the City Planning Commission. The city has also rolled back some zoning to prevent further degradation of the residential quality of the neighborhood.

NOTES

1. Benjamin A. Goldman, *Not Just Prosperity: Achieving Sustainability and Environmental Justice* (Washington, D.C.: National Wildlife Federation Corporate Conservation Council, February 1994), 7–9.

2. Marianne Lavelle, Marcia Coyle, and Claudia MacLachlan, "Unequal Protection: The Racial Divide in Environmental Law," *National Law Journal*, September 21, 1994, S1.

3. Executive Order 12898, "Federal Actions to Address Environmental Justice in Minority Populations and Low-Income Populations." Signed by President Bill Clinton on February 11, 1994.

4. For example, on September 10, 1997, the EPA disallowed the State of Louisiana's approval of a license for a Shintech polyvinyl chloride (PVC) plastics plant in Convent, Louisiana, a primarily African American community with a large concentration of industrial plants. The application is still pending both the EPA decision and a separate Title VI lawsuit brought on behalf of the local community. See Jim Motavalli, "Toxic Targets: Polluters That Dump on Communities of Color Are Finally Being Brought to Justice," *E: The Environmental Magazine* 9, no. 4 (July–August 1998): 28–41.

CHAPTER 3

Land

"As civilization advances, land suffers."
John Graves, *Goodbye to a River.*

THE ORIGIN OF PUBLIC LAND IN THE UNITED STATES

By the mid-1800s, the depletion of the United States' natural resources by a growing and westward-moving European population had drawn sporadic cries of alarm from the citizenry. The documented decline of bird and other wildlife species forced the creation of state and federal hunting regulations. There was a dramatic loss of forests to farmland in the Midwest with accompanying soil erosion, and the redwoods in California were being rapidly cleared by the timber industry. In response to the human activity that was changing the landscape of America, and in particular to the devastation of forestland, early conservationists began a battle to put certain lands under the public domain.

A number of ideas and principles influenced these nineteenth-century conservationists. Some were motivated by spiritual belief in the holiness of nature. Others regarded private ownership of land as inherently unjust and felt that at least portions of the countryside should belong to the public. Others were concerned with preventing development and deforestation of watersheds. The author and founder of the Sierra Club, John Muir, who helped lead the fight for Congressional action to protect Yosemite Valley, was a foremost preservationist (see box: Conservation/Preservation) whose views were motivated by a strong belief in the holiness of the wilderness. He and other like-minded people pressed Congress to grant Yosemite Valley to the State of California in 1864. Yosemite thus became the first tract of wilderness set aside by Congress.

The first park to be created by Congress, however, was Yellowstone Park in 1872. Because no state existed in that region at that time, Yellowstone Park was put directly under federal protection. Advocates for the creation of Yellowstone Park believed that the public had a right to enjoy its beauty and "curiosities" and that private interests should not be allowed to control it.[1] It was to be another twenty years before another national park was established.[2]

The prevailing attitude of the nineteenth century was that natural resources were commodities to be used for trade, for human consumption, and for fuel. This utilitarian perspective on nature made nineteenth-century Congressional leaders reluctant to establish national parkland. According to conservation historian John Petulla, it was the railroad companies, who thought bringing train travelers through scenic territory would increase their profits, who were the most influential lobbyists for the national park movement.[3] Even so, the U. S. Congress of the nineteenth century would not establish a national park unless it was demonstrated that the area could not be exploited for commercial purposes.

A fundamental schism began to appear in the conservation movement in the mid-1800s. Historian Roderick Nash explains, ". . . initially, anxiety over the rapid depletion of raw materials, particularly forests, was broad enough to embrace many points of view. The exploiters of the natural resources were the enemy and this view united all. But two distinct ideas began to divide them: conservation as the wise use or planned development of resources as advocated by Gifford Pinochet, and the preservationists' view that rejected all utilitarian use of the resources and advocated that nature remain undisturbed by man."[4] These two views have marked the environmental movement throughout the twentieth century.

When Theodore Roosevelt became president in 1901, half of America's timberland had been cut. Aware of the great importance of wilderness to his own life, Roosevelt disregarded the views of Congress and business interests by establishing national parks, forests, and refuges. He believed that the public's right to enjoy and explore the wilderness should take precedence over the rights of private interests to exploit it for financial gain. So angry was Congress over Roosevelt's conservation initiatives that, in 1904, it passed legislation that stripped Roosevelt of his authority to establish national parkland. But before the legislation passed, Roosevelt put an additional 16 million acres into national forests. By the time Roosevelt left office in 1909, he had single-handedly put 32 million acres of land under federal protection.

The perseverance of the conservation movement led to the establishment of the U.S. Park Service in 1916. Today, there are 374 federal parks, monuments,

CONSERVATION/PRESERVATION: WHAT'S THE DIFFERENCE?

One of the central controversies of the twentieth-century environmental movement has been between those who want to preserve "wilderness" and those who support managed use of the material resources. The latter is sometimes referred to as the management of resources on a sustainable yield basis. "Conservation: The maintenance of environmental quality and resources or a particular balance among the species present in a given area. The resources may be physical (e.g. fossil fuels), biological (e.g. tropical forests), or cultural (e.g. ancient monuments). In modern scientific usage conservation implies sound biosphere management within given social and economic constraints, producing goods and services for humans without depleting natural ecosystem diversity, and acknowledging the naturally dynamic character of biological systems. This contrasts with the preservationist approach which, it is argued, protects species or landscapes without reference to natural change in living systems or to human requirements."

(Source: Michael Allaby, The Concise Oxford Dictionary of Ecology [Oxford: Oxford University Press, 1994], 92.)

PUBLICLY OWNED OR MANAGED LAND

AGENCY	ACREAGE
U.S. Forest Service	
National Forests	637,000 acres
National Grasslands	118,000 acres
National Park Service	1,231,988 acres
U.S. Fish and Wildlife Service	256,227 acres
U.S. Defense Department	
U.S. military bases	517,000 acres
Corp of Engineers	235,895 acres (parkland acreage)

State owns mineral rights on 7.5 million acres and the Veterans Land Board holds liens on 1.5 million acres.

Texas Permanent University Fund	2.1 million acres
Special Texas School Fund	2.6 million acres
State Parks (Natural) Historical and Recreational Areas)	625,232 acres
State Wildlife Management Areas	452,930 acres
State Forest	7,500 acres
State Highway Rights-of-Way	2.9 million acres (a percentage of this is dedicated to parkland)
State Owned Submerged Land	4 million acres (wet beaches)
Texas River Authorities	4,743 acres (parkland)
Municipal/County Owned Parkland	227,590 acres (parkland)

Source: Information obtained from Texas Parks and Wildlife Department, Texas Outdoor Recreational Plan, 1995, 43–44; Texas Comptroller for Public Accounts, and the Texas General Land Office. Texas ranks 43rd in the nation in the amount of federally owned land.

and historical sites in the United States visited by 275 million people annually. The nineteenth-century debate regarding the use of public land—for private interests or public—has led to today's national parks and other public lands serving at least three simultaneous, often conflicting functions: they have been set aside as recreational spaces for people, as undisturbed habitat for wildlife, and as resources for livestock grazing, oil and gas drilling, and timber

STATE SPENDING BLUEPRINT FOR 1998-1999

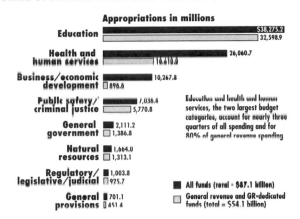

Appropriations in millions

	All funds	General revenue and GR-dedicated funds
Education	$38,275.2	32,598.9
Health and human services	26,060.7	10,619.8
Business/economic development	10,267.8	896.6
Public safety/criminal justice	7,038.4	5,770.8
General government	2,111.2	1,386.8
Natural resources	1,664.0	1,313.1
Regulatory/legislative/judicial	1,003.8	925.7
General provisions	701.1	451.4

Education and health and human services, the two largest budget categories, account for nearly three quarters of all spending and for 80% of general revenue spending

■ All funds (total = $87.1 billion)
☐ General revenue and GR-dedicated funds (total = $54.1 billion)

According to the Comptroller, the environmental spending figures are based on the budgets of the Texas Department of Agriculture, the Animal Health Commission, the General Land Office, the Low Level Radioactive Authority, the Texas Natural Resource Conservation Commission, Texas Parks and Wildlife, River Compact Commission, Soil Water Conservation Board, Water Development Board, and the Railroad Commission of Texas.

Source: Texas Comptroller for Public Accounts, Fiscal Notes (September 1997), 3.

harvesting. To this day, resource planners are trying to balance those different interests.

PUBLIC LANDS IN TEXAS

Nineteenth-century political leaders in Texas sold off state lands as rapidly as possible to pay off debt remaining from the War of Independence and to encourage settlement and economic development. By the turn of the century, most of the state's 266,807 square miles were privately owned.[5] In 1997 approximately 25 million acres of the state's approximate 176 million acres (includes submerged coastal lands) was owned or managed by a public entity.[6]

Significant Public Land Legislation in Texas

■ In 1923 the Texas legislature appropriated money for a state forester.

■ In 1923 the Texas Legislature created the Texas State Parks Board to accept donated parkland.

■ In 1926 federal legislation established the Texas Forest Service, located at Texas Agricultural and Mechanical College (now Texas A&M University).

SPENDING ON THE AVERAGE TEXAN

Although no two Texans receive the same type or level of government services, state government will spend slightly more than $2,275 on average for every man, woman and child in Texas in each of the next two fiscal years. (1998 & 1999)

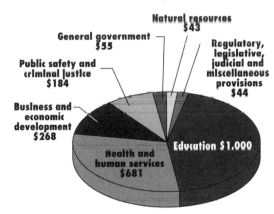

Annual spending per Texan Total: $2,275

- Natural resources $43
- General government $55
- Regulatory, legislative, judicial and miscellaneous provisions $44
- Public safety and criminal justice $184
- Business and economic development $268
- Education $1,000
- Health and human services $681

Source: Texas Comptroller for Public Accounts, Fiscal Notes (September 1997), 3.

■ In 1930 the Texas State Parks Board received its first appropriations to acquire parkland. Those first purchases of Texas parkland included Palo Duro Canyon, Longhorn Cavern, and Big Bend State Park (now Big Bend National Park).

NATIONAL AND STATE PUBLIC AREAS IN TEXAS

Source: Texas Parks and Wildlife Department.

■ In 1933 the Texas legislature authorized the federal government to purchase land to create national forests in Texas.

■ In 1963 the State Parks Board and the Game and Fish Commission were merged to form the Texas Parks and Wildlife Department (TPWD).

Defining Public Lands[7]

Submerged coastal lands: in Texas, the wet beach is state-owned submerged land protected for the public by the Texas General Land Office (GLO). There are four million acres of state-owned submerged lands.

State parks: large areas of outstanding natural or scenic land. Allowable uses are designated by the TPWD and may include camping, hiking, picnicking, and hunting. There are 587,939 acres in the state park system (includes state natural areas and historical areas).

State recreational areas: areas of natural or scenic character, selectively developed to provide recreational opportunities.

State natural areas: areas established for the protection and stewardship of outstanding features of statewide significance. These areas may be used in sustainable manner for scientific research, education, esthetic enjoyment, and such other appropriate public use as sound biological management permits. There are 301,687 acres of natural areas.

State historical areas: areas established for the preservation and interpretation of prehistoric and historic resources of statewide or national significance. Historic areas shall provide for recreation or other public uses that are not detrimental to the long-term preservation of the cultural and natural resources. These historical areas encompass 8, 906 acres.

State wildlife management areas: areas primarily devoted to preservation of the state's wildlife resources. Wildlife areas are acquired, however, for multiple uses, including demonstration areas for wildlife management, public hunting and fishing, and other outdoor recreational activities. There are 452,930 acres of wildlife areas.

State and national forests: national and state forests are set aside for multiple uses, including timber harvesting, mining, cattle-raising, wildlife habitat, and public recreation. There are 633, 308 acres of federal forests and 7,500 acres of state forests.

National wilderness areas: lands designated for special protection by Congress. They must meet certain minimum size requirements and can be used for multiple purposes.

National wildlife refuges: areas intended for protection of wildlife and their habitat. They are usually open to the public for bird watching, and wildlife viewing. There are fourteen national wildlife refuges located in Texas.

National grasslands: there are approximately 118,000 acres of national grasslands in Texas. These grasslands have been set aside for multiple purposes, including recreational opportunities, forage for grazing, and oil and gas production.

State Land Management and Funding

The TPWD, governed by a nine-member board appointed by the governor, is the lead agency

---

WHO PAYS THE BILLS—ESTIMATED FY98 REVENUE

Texas Parks and Wildlife's appropriations as approved by the 75th Legislature are $144.3 million for FY98 and $143.9 million for FY99. These amounts do not include a bond appropriation of approximately $60 million or various riders which allow appropriation of revenues.

All agency revenues, with the exception of the rider appropriation for revenue bonds and debt service, are generated by users of agency services and products. Over 50% of annual revenues come specifically from hunting and fishing license sales, park entrance and use fees, and boat registration and titling fees.

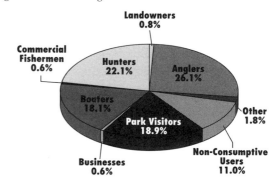

Source: TPW CFO Division.

COMPARISON OF STATE PARK ACREAGE 1990

STATE	TOTAL PARK ACREAGE	PERCENT OF TOTAL U.S. PARK ACREAGE	PARK ACREAGE PER 100 RESIDENTS	RANK	PARK ACREAGE AS A PERCENT OF STATE LAND AREA	RANK
Alabama	48,985	0.4%	1.21	42	0.2%	41
Alaska	3,237,032	29.3	588.51	1	0.9	13
Arizona	39,478	0.4	1.08	44	0.1	49
Arkansas	47,509	0.4	2.02	36	0.1	43
California	1,287,047	11.6	4.32	19	1.3	7
Colorado	230,400	2.1	6.99	9	0.4	24
Connecticut	170,252	1.5	5.18	13	5.3	2
Delaware	11,898	0.1	1.79	39	0.9	12
Florida	418,930	3.8	3.24	22	1.1	9
Georgia	61,734	0.6	0.95	46	0.2	38
Hawaii	24,861	0.2	2.24	34	0.6	17
Idaho	46,808	0.4	4.65	15	0.1	45
Illinois	400,806	3.6	3.51	21	1.1	10
Indiana	56,767	0.5	1.02	45	0.3	29
Iowa	82,500	0.8	2.97	26	0.2	31
Kansas	30,219	0.3	1.22	41	0.1	47
Kentucky	41,842	0.4	1.14	43	0.2	39
Louisiana	38,003	0.3	0.90	48	0.1	44
Maine	70,303	0.6	5.73	12	0.3	26
Maryland	221,905	2.0	4.64	16	3.3	4
Massachusetts	268,728	2.4	4.47	18	5.1	3
Michigan	262,454	2.4	2.82	27	0.7	16
Minnesota	200,000	1.8	4.57	17	0.4	23
Mississippi	22,795	0.2	0.89	49	0.1	46
Missouri	109,186	1.0	2.13	35	0.2	30
Montana	51,208	0.5	6.41	11	0.1	48
Nebraska	148,666	1.3	9.42	7	0.3	27
Nevada	141,610	1.3	11.78	5	0.2	34
New Hampshire	32,967	0.3	2.97	25	0.6	18
New Jersey	300,815	2.7	3.89	20	6.0	1
New Mexico	118,951	1.1	7.85	8	0.2	40
New York	258,400	2.3	1.44	40	0.8	14
North Carolina	128,698	1.2	1.94	37	0.4	22
North Dakota	17,186	0.2	2.69	29	0.0	50
Ohio	207,682	1.9	1.91	38	0.8	15
Oklahoma	95,552	0.9	3.04	24	0.2	32
Oregon	89,935	0.8	3.16	23	0.1	42
Pennsylvania	276,322	2.5	2.33	32	1.0	11
Rhode Island	9,223	0.1	0.92	47	1.2	8
South Carolina	79,308	0.7	2.27	33	0.4	21
South Dakota	92,421	0.8	13.28	4	0.2	37
Tennessee	133,044	1.2	2.73	28	0.5	20
Texas	433,366	3.9	2.55	30	0.3	28
Utah	115,533	1.0	6.71	10	0.2	33
Vermont	170,483	1.5	30.29	2	2.8	5
Virginia	51,878	0.5	0.84	50	0.2	35

Continued on next page

COMPARISON OF STATE PARK ACREAGE 1990 (Continued)

STATE	TOTAL PARK ACREAGE	PERCENT OF TOTAL U.S. PARK ACREAGE	PARK ACREAGE PER 100 RESIDENTS	RANK	PARK ACREAGE AS A PERCENT OF STATE LAND AREA	RANK
Washington	231,498	2.1	4.76	14	0.5	19
West Virginia	206,250	1.9	11.50	6	1.3	6
Wisconsin	120,055	1.1	2.45	31	0.3	25
Wyoming	119,429	1.1	26.33	3	0.2	36
Total	11,060,922	100.0%	4.46 (Average)		0.5% (Average)	

Note: Includes state parks, natural areas, historical areas, water use areas, environmental education areas, and miscellaneous areas.

Source: Texas Comptroller of Public Accounts, Forces of Change, Volume 2, Part 1 (1994), 399. From National Association of State Park Directors, Annual Information Exchange, April, 1990.

responsible for the management of state parks, natural areas, and wildlife management areas, as well as for the protection of fish and wildlife species and their habitats. The GLO, established in 1837, is responsible for leasing state land, including Gulf Coast beaches, bays, and other submerged lands. These are leased primarily for oil and gas production. The GLO also manages programs to protect coastal natural resources. The Texas land commissioner is a statewide elected official.

PERCENTAGE OF THE STATE LAND AREA IN PARKS

Across the United States, about one-half of one percent of the average state's land area is dedicated to state parks. Texas is about one-half the national average.

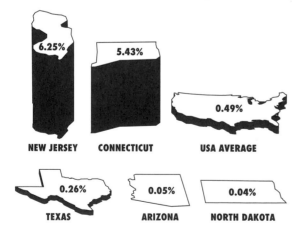

Note: The discrepancy between the percentages in this graph and the "State Park Acreage" table is due to the varying definitions of state parks.

Source: Texas Parks and Wildlife Department, National Agenda: A Strategic Plan for Texas Parks and Wildlife (June, 1994), 15.

PARKLAND IN TEXAS

With 0.2 percent of Texas's state budget spent for parks, a 1991–1992 state-by-state guide ranked Texas 37th in the nation for the percentage of its state budget used for park maintenance, acquisition, and development.[8] According to Texas Parks and Wildlife Department, Texas ranks 48th in per capita spending on state parkland acquisition and development.[9] According to the Texas Outdoor Recreation Plan, in 1995 Texas had statewide 4,051,936 acres of parkland accounting for 2.4 percent of the total area of the state.[10] (The Texas Outdoor Recreation Plan's figures include federal, state, local, and commercial parkland, while the State Park Directors' include only state-owned parkland.)

Fifty-six percent (2,281,384 acres) of the state's total outdoor recreation lands is provided by the

PARKLAND IN TEXAS BY ADMINISTRATION

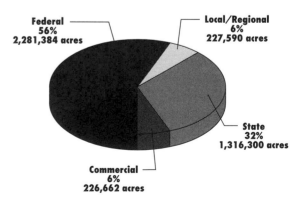

Source: TPWD, 1995 Texas Outdoor Recreation Plan, (1997), 44.

PARTICIPATION IN OUTDOOR RECREATION ACTIVITIES BY TEXAS RESIDENTS, AGES 16 YEARS AND OLDER, IN 1994

RANK	ACTIVITY	PERCENTAGE OF POPULATION PARTICIPATING	MILLIONS OF PARTICIPANTS	RANK	ACTIVITY	PERCENTAGE OF POPULATION PARTICIPATING	MILLIONS OF PARTICIPANTS
1	Walking	65	8.9	19	View Nature in a Water-Based Surrounding	24	3.3
2	Visit the Beach	61	8.4	20	Attend Outdoor Concerts, Plays	21	2.7
3	Family Gathering	60	8.2	21	Visit Prehistoric/ Archaeological Sites	19	2.6
4	Sightseeing	55	7.5				
5	Visit Outdoor Nature Museums or Zoo	47	6.4	22	Hiking	18	2.5
6	Picnicking	45	6.2	23	Off-road Riding	17	2.3
6	Pool Swimming	45	6.2	24	Volleyball	14	1.9
8	Visit Historic Sites	44	6.0	25	Fish Viewing or Photographing	13	1.8
9	Swimming in Non-pool	37	5.1	25	Golf	13	1.8
10	Visit Visitors Centers	35	4.8	25	Softball	13	1.8
10	Yard Games/Horseshoes, Croquet	35	4.8	28	Basketball	12	1.6
12	Camping	30	4.1	28	Hunting	12	1.6
12	Viewing/Photographing Other Wildlife	30	4.1	28	Saltwater Fishing	12	1.6
14	Freshwater Fishing	28	3.8	31	Tennis	11	1.5
14	Boating	28	3.8	32	Baseball	8	1.1
16	Running/Jogging	27	3.7	32	Football	8	1.1
17	Watching or Photographing Birds	25	3.4	32	Horseback Riding	8	1.1
17	Bicycling	25	3.4	35	Soccer	6	0.8

Adapted by Eley and DeLoney, Statewide Planning and Research, TPWD 1996 from Cordell, Distefano, and Lewis 1995 and Texas State Data Center 1995.

Note: To calculate millions of participants, Texas State Data Center population figures for population aged 16 years and older, 13,691,083, was used (74.5 percent of total 1994 population which was 18,378,185). Millions of participants = (percent of population participating) X 13,691,083.

Source: Texas Parks & Wildlife Dept, 1995 Texas Outdoor Recreation Plan (1997), 58.

federal government. This includes land managed by the U.S. Fish and Wildlife Service, the U.S. Forest Service, the National Park Service, and the U.S. Army Corps of Engineers. The state provides 32 percent of the recreational land in the state.[11] The remainder is provided by local governments, river authorities, and private sources.

OUTDOOR RECREATION

According to the TPWD's Outdoor Recreation Plan, wildlife viewing gained the largest number of participants in the ten years from 1985 to 1994, increasing from 2.2 million to 4.1 million.[12]

In a 1993 statewide citizen survey of 2,688 Texans, conducted by Texas A&M, respondents stated that the most-needed facilities for local communities were bike trails, walking and jogging trails, and nature trails. The need for trails was rated substantially higher than for other community-based recreational facilities.[13]

Many factors influence recreational planning issues: land prices, urbanization, source and availability of funds, tourism, and population make-up. From 1980 to 1994, Texas's population grew 29 percent. Most of this growth occurred in metropolitan areas. By the year 2030, demographers expect Texas's population will be about 33 million. This population growth will put more pressure on state and national parks and other natural resources in the state. It will increase pressure on local governments to provide for recreational open space at a time when land in

OUTDOOR RECREATIONAL ACTIVITIES MOST IMPORTANT TO THE CITIZENS OF TEXAS

RANK	ACTIVITY	PERCENT OF TOTAL FREQUENCY
1	Camping	12.0
2	Fishing	11.5
3	Swimming	6.9
4	Hiking	5.3
5	Baseball	4.7
6	Softball	4.3
7	Walking	3.6
7	Golf	3.6
9	Boating	3.0
10	Bicycling	2.9
11	Picnicking	2.7
11	Volleyball	2.7
13	Hunting	2.4
14	Football	2.3
15	Tennis	2.2
16	Basketball	1.6
17	Water Skiing	1.5
18	Soccer	1.3
19	Sightseeing	1.2
20	Jogging/Running	0.9

Adapted by DeLoney, Statewide Planning and Research, TPWD 1996 from Love, McGregor, and Crompton 1993.

Note: Percentages = Frequency by activity/Total frequencies all activities

Source: TPWD, 1995 Texas Outdoor Recreation Plan (1997), 56.

urban areas will be getting both more expensive and harder to find.

Given the concentration of Texans in metropolitan areas, the TPWD recognizes a need for recreational parks closer to urban centers. State park officials are also concerned that as more generations of Texans grow up in, and live exclusively in, urban environments they will have less concern for natural resources and natural settings.

Another demographic change that resource professionals expect to affect the Texas park system is the increase in African American and Mexican American populations, which are expected to make up half of the state's population by 2030. For the past twenty years, minorities have been less likely than Anglos to participate in TPWD programs and to use its services. TPWD surveys show that 83 percent of

visitors to state parks were Anglo, 13 percent were Hispanic, 4 percent were African American, and 7 percent were marked down as other.[14] If this trend continues, support for public land acquisition could decline. As TPWD Director Andrew Samson has stated, "Our minority populations are the key to Texas's future. Without minorities' interest in natural and cultural resources and involvement in outdoor recreation, it is uncertain what the future will hold for Texas's parks and wildlife."[15]

PARKLAND ACQUISITION

In Texas, decisions about parkland acquisitions are made by the governing board of the TPWD. Acquisitions are recommended by the department's director and staff and then approved by the board. Purchases are funded with legislative appropriations.

During the past few years, TPWD's priority has been to improve and add to existing parkland rather than establishing new parks. The department's Strategic Plan: 1997–2001 states that "more pressing than our desire to acquire more state parkland, or develop new facilities, is our commitment to repair and improve existing facilities."[16]

At the federal level, parkland acquisitions are authorized by Congress and carried out by the National Park Service, an agency of the U.S. Department of the Interior. Each national park has its own legislation, which defines, among other things, the boundaries of the park. However, some national parks in Texas, such as the LBJ Park, the Big Thicket, and the Fort Davis National Historic Site may accept land donations and thus extend their boundaries without legislative approval. As of August 1997, there was no Congressional legislation designating additional acquisitions in Texas by the National Park Service. The following is a list of public lands in Texas under the supervision of the National Park Service as of August 1997.[17]

The U.S. Fish and Wildlife Service, an agency of the Interior Department, acquires wildlife habitat and refuges, which can also provide recreational opportunities for the public. These acquisitions are in response to Congressional action (see *Wildlife and Biodiversity* chapter for further discussion of

NATIONAL PARKS IN TEXAS

NAME	ACRES
Alibates Flint Quarries National Monument, Fritch, Texas	1.371
Amistad National Recreation Area	58,500
Big Bend National Park	801,163
Big Thicket National Preserve	96,678
Chamizal National Memorial, El Paso	55
Fort Davis National Historic Site	460
Guadalupe Mountains National Park	86,416
Lake Meredith National Recreation Area, Amarillo	44,978
San Antonio Missions	819
LBJ National Historic Park	1,157
Padre Island National Seashore	130,434
Palo Alto Battlefield Historic Site	357
Rio Grande Wild & Scenic River (segment)	9,600 acres 191.2 miles

acquisitions). The U.S. Forest Service, an agency of the U.S. Department of Agriculture (USDA), acquires national forestland, which also provides recreational opportunities. These acquisitions also are made at the direction of Congress. The National Forest Service does not anticipate acquiring new forestland in Texas in the near future.[18]

URBAN PARKLAND AND OPEN SPACE

Since at least the mid-nineteenth century in Western Europe, urban parks have played a significant role in the cultural life of communities. Well-known urban parks include Hyde Park and Kensington Gardens in London, the Bois de Boulogne in Paris, the Retiro Park in Madrid, and the plazas of the cities and towns in Mexico and in Central and South America.[19] The first landscaped public park in the United States, New York City's Central Park (modeled after the urban parks of Paris and London) was designed in 1857 by Frederick Law Olmsted, who believed that urban parks were essential to the life of communities, in part because they allowed urban residents to experience nature.

Olmsted's philosophy regarding urban parkland has special relevance today. Charles Jordan, a leading

African American parks proponent and one-time director of parks in both Portland, Oregon, and Austin, Texas, has suggested that neighborhood parks are the key to fostering a sense of stewardship for nature in our children. Jordan warns that without this sense of stewardship, future generations will have no inclination to protect nature: "What people don't understand, they will not value. And what they will not value, they will not protect. And what they will not protect, they will lose."[20] Motivated by a similar concern, the Lila Wallace Reader's Digest Fund in 1996 committed $16 million to an urban parks initiative to increase the number and quality of parks in American cities, including Texas communities.

In Texas, counties, cities, and other local entities provide 222,837 acres of parkland at the local level, or approximately 5 percent of the state's total parkland. Of these 222,837 acres, cities provide 71 percent and counties provide 18 percent of the park space. Commercially owned recreational sites (guest ranches, etc.) total 226,662 acres, or approximately 6 percent of the state's parkland.[21] Cities are dependent primarily upon local bonds for funding and receive less than 16 percent of all federal funding for parks.

Of the 35 U.S. cities that responded to a study conducted by the World Resources Institute in 1993, Dallas ranked fourth highest in percentage of land area devoted to parkland. With 42.2 percent of its area in parkland, Honolulu had the highest percentage, while Washington, D.C., had 29.3 percent, New Bedford had 20.0 percent, and Dallas had 19.4 percent.[22] Portland, Oregon, had 12.8 percent of its land area in parks, Austin had 8.8 percent, Seattle had 8.5 percent, Houston had 5.2 percent, Fort Worth had 4.8 percent, San Antonio had 2.9 percent, and Galveston had 0.8 percent.

Numerous studies have documented the quality-of-life benefits of open space and parks to a community. But parks may also benefit homeowners. A study in Boulder, Colorado, concluded that a property's proximity to community greenbelts had a significant impact on the price of the property, and that all things being equal, property values decrease by $4,200 for every 1,000 feet one moves away from a greenbelt. Other studies have shown similar results.[23]

"WISE USE" MOVEMENT

Since 1988 a loose coalition of organizations, known as the "wise use" coalition, has been lobbying for changes in public land policies. For example, the coalition wants to increase and expand logging in publicly owned old-growth forests and livestock grazing on public lands. The coalition also wants to open national parks, such as Yellowstone, to mining and oil drilling. Barring the federal government from acquiring any additional private land for parks or wildlife habitat has also been advocated by the wise use coalition. Though the wise use movement originated in the northwestern United States (88 percent of federal lands are in 11 Western states), some of its sentiments were expressed in the 1994 Texas Republican Party platform: "The Party understands that government ownership of land is an ideal of socialism. We affirm our belief in the fundamental constitutional concept of a person's right to own property without government interference. We decry the vast acquisition of Texas land by conservancy groups and government agencies. We call on our State Legislature to reclaim lands under federal control and return them to the people of Texas." *(Source: Texas Republican Party, 1994 State Republican Party Platform, 5–6.)* Today's wise use coalition has appropriated a

nineteenth-century term but not the underlying conservation philosophy. According to historian Douglas McCleery, the idea of "conservation as wise use" of natural resources began with conservation leader Gifford Pinochet in the late nineteenth century. The original wise use movement was a product of the progressive era and included the concept of multiple use—public land can be used simultaneously for recreation, for timber, for mining, and for wildlife habitat. The multiple-use and wise use concepts advocated by Pinochet reflected the view that nature's resources should be scientifically managed so as "to protect the basic productivity of the land and its ability to serve future generations." Today's wise use movement advocates not only selling off federal lands, but no more buying of land by the federal government. This modern-day cause also might be more concerned with short-term private gain over Pinochet's advocacy of long-term productivity of nature's resources. On the other hand, there are also natural resource leaders who advocate that some lands be set aside as undisturbed ecosystems with no use made of their resources.

(Source: For Pinochet's views see Douglas McCleery, American Forests: A History of Resiliency and Recovery *[Washington D.C.: USDA, Forest Service, FS-540,1992].)*

Of particular interest to Texans is a 1994 survey that sought to determine which features buyers most want in a community. The survey responses from people who had purchased a home in a planned community and people who were looking to buy homes in a planned community in Texas, Georgia, Florida, and California showed that open space was a very high priority. The survey found that golf courses, popular with developers, were a highly desirable feature for less than half of those surveyed: 39.5 percent of the home buyers surveyed said that a golf course within the community was "very or extremely important," while 60.5 percent preferred open space, wilderness areas, and gardens with walking paths.[24] These findings

may be good news for the developers and members of planned communities, for the cost of maintaining open space is less than the cost of maintaining a golf course.

FYI *In 1994 dollars (1983 estimates adjusted for inflation), Texans spent $14.9 billion on recreation trips related to 20 outdoor activities. (Source: TPWD, 1995* Texas Outdoor Recreation Plan *[1997], 19.)*

PUBLIC AND PRIVATE CONSERVATION ACTIVITIES

The conservation and preservation of land for public enjoyment and wildlife habitat have depended not only on the actions of state and federal governments, but also on the activities of private not-for-profit organizations operating in the public interest.

The Nature Conservancy of Texas, a not-for-profit organization that helps preserve significant natural areas, has been working in Texas since 1966. The Conservancy identifies acreage that needs to be protected and then preserves the land through gift, lease, trade, or purchase. The organization also works with private landowners who want to manage land for conservation purposes. In 1997 the Nature Conservancy of Texas had 28,000 members and had acquired more than 350,000 acres of land.[25]

Also active in Texas is the Trust for Public Land, a national not-for-profit organization that helps communities acquire land for parks, community gardens, recreational areas, trails, and greenways. Since 1979 the Trust has helped protect 13,781 acres in Texas, including Barton Creek Wilderness Park and Colorado River Park in Austin, Great Trinity Forest in Dallas, a community park in Arlington, and part of Katy Prairie in Katy. The Trust is also instrumental in helping communities develop urban trails and urban parks in low-income neighborhoods.[26]

TEXAS ECOLOGICAL REGIONS

Texas is a large land area covering approximately 267,000 square miles . It is located at a geographic crossroads where many of the major regions of the United States come together: the coastal prairies, the southeastern pinewoods, the central hardwoods, the Great Plains, the southwestern deserts, and the southern extension of the Rocky Mountains. This accounts for the tremendous climatic and geographic diversity of the state. Texas has 10 climatic regions, 14 soil regions, and 11 distinct ecological regions. These ecological regions of the state represent differences in soils, topography, geology, rainfall, and plant and animal communities.[27] There are, however, several ways of classifying the natural environment, such as by river basin, hydrologic sub-basins, or vegetation systems.

The following descriptions draw heavily on a number of books and resource materials.

(1) Piney Woods. Located in eastern Texas, covering over 15 million acres, this is gently rolling to hilly forested land. The soils of the region are characterized as deep loamy or sandy soils. Prior to European settlement, this area of Texas supported longleaf pine, shortleaf pine, loblolly pine, and oak-hickory forests. Today the region is composed of fragmented pine and pine-hardwood forests with some cropland and pastureland. The majority of national forests and other forestland located in Texas are found in this region, as is Texas's only natural lake, Caddo Lake. Dogwoods and red and white oaks are plentiful throughout the area. Though rapidly diminishing, the bottomland hardwood forests of oak-hickory, elm, sweetgum, sugarberry, and ash—the most diverse and richest wildlife habitats left in Texas—are located in the pincy woods. The cndangered red-cockaded woodpecker's habitat is in the pine forest. Rare plants found in the region include the southern lady's slipper orchid, golden glade cress, white bladderpod, and Texas trailing phlox. Rare plant communities include longleaf pine savannas and beech-magnolia forest. Swamps, bogs, and man-made lakes extend through the region, which has the state's highest rainfall, with annual precipitation of 32 to 56 inches. Lumber and cattle production are major industries in the area. Four national forests are located in the piney woods.

(2) Oak Woods and Prairies. This area is divided into two parts, with one section to the east of the Blackland Prairie and the other to the west. Portions of the area to the west were called Cross-Timbers by early European settlers because they once had post oak forests crossing strips of prairie grassland. The region is approximately 19,000 square miles of gently rolling to hilly landscape. The bottomland soils range from sandy loam to clay, while the prairies have sandy loam or sands. Flora include post oaks, oak-hickory forest, plateau live oak, and tallgrass and mid-grass prairies. Most of the flora and fauna have ranges that extend northward into the Great Plains or eastward into the forests. This area attracted early European settlers because the open grasslands and surrounding forest areas were ideal for settlement. Native American tribes also were attracted by this unique combination of prairie and forestland. Today, most of those grasslands have been altered. Large concentrations of migrating

geese and ducks winter in this region and can be observed in places like Hagerman National Wildlife Refuge on Lake Texoma. Cattle ranching is a major agricultural industry in parts of the region. The endangered Houston toad occurs in the eastern post-oak savanna ecoregion.

(3) Blackland Prairie. The Blackland Prairie region is gently rolling and level land covering 23,500 square miles. It is named for the rich, deep, fertile black soils that once supported the original tallgrass prairie communities and, due to land-use change, today support crop production and cattle ranching. Prior to the seventeenth century, this area in East-Central Texas had 12 million acres of tallgrass prairie; now there are less than 5,000 acres. It is the grassland communities themselves—the big bluestem, little bluestem, switchgrass, and sideoats and associated herbaceous flora that make these prairies unique. Agriculture and development have threatened the remaining grassland communities with extirpation from Texas. In portions of the region, farmland is threatened with extinction by urban sprawl and development.

(4) Gulf Coast Prairies and Marshes. This nearly level plain area of 13 million acres borders the Gulf of Mexico from the Sabine River to Corpus Christi Bay. Prior to European settlement and twentieth-century development, this landscape included woodlands of sugarberry, pecan, elms, and live oaks, and open prairies with native grasses. The soils of the area range from acidic sands to sandy loams, with clays occurring in the river bottoms. The flora include tallgrass and mid-grass prairies, cordgrass marshes, mesquite, and acacia. The region includes the barrier islands that protect the coastline from high winds and high ocean waves. The marshes along the bays and estuaries are important habitat for estuarine and marine species including finfish and shellfish. Rare and near-extinct plants and animals include the slender rush-pea, Attwater's prairie chicken, and the ocelot.

(5) Coastal Sand Plains. The region occupies approximately 2.5 million acres. The vegetation of this area can be described as grasslands with coastal oak motts, mesquite granjeno, and salt marshes. It is home to the King Ranch and other large cattle ranches. In the nineteenth century wild horses roamed the area, and consequently it has been known as the Wild Horse Prairie.

(6) South Texas Brush Country. This area encompasses approximately 18 million acres. It was once covered with open grasslands and a scattering of trees. The original grasslands have become shrubland due to overgrazing. Today the area is characterized by thorny shrubs (such as mesquite, acacia, and prickly pear) and patches of palms and subtropical woodlands. The area is home to many wild and rare species of plants and animals, including the ocelot and jaguarundi. The aplomado falcon was dependent upon these grasslands, and the loss has caused the falcon's demise. Urban development and agricultural use threaten the existing wildlife habitat. The natural resources of this region, the Gulf Coast Prairies, and the Coastal Sand Plains region contribute to the local economy of this area, where bird watching and game hunting have become a source of revenue for the region.

(7) Edwards Plateau. The plateau is approximately 1,500 to 3,000 feet above sea level and encompasses approximately 19.8 million acres. Rivers, streams, and springs flow through the region. Two major aquifers underlie the area: the Edwards and the Trinity. It is dominated by limestone terrain but includes a wide variety of soil types, topography, and ecological conditions. Plateau live oak savanna and other oak woodlands and limestone glades occur throughout this region. It is home to one of the world's most diverse collections of aquifer fauna and endangered and rare species. Some of these plants and animals are found nowhere else on earth. The golden-cheeked warbler nests only in the Ashe juniper (aka cedar) of the area. The springs and rivers of the region are home to the endangered San Marcos salamander, and the endangered fountain darter. The rare plants of the region include the basin bellflowers and Texas snowbells. Ranching is the primary agricultural industry, but the natural beauty and opportunities

for wildlife viewing and hunting have created a growing tourist industry in the region as well. The Balcones Escarpment—marked by a sharp topographic relief along the Balcones Fault Zone—borders the southeastern edge of the region and marks the transition zone between the plateau and the plains country on the south and east. The Balcones Escarpment runs from Del Rio to San Antonio and then northeast through Austin.

(8) Llano Uplift. This area is known as the central mineral region and is characterized by large granite domes like Enchanted Rock in Gillespie County. The Llano Uplift is a unique geological formation — a granite mass that runs 70 miles across and is approximately 1,000 feet above sea level. The area encompasses approximately 3.2 million acres and is surrounded by the Edwards Plateau. The vegetation consists of oak-hickory, oak juniper, mesquite, and grasslands. Ranching is the dominant agricultural industry, and tourism is emerging as an important economic activity for the region.

(9) Rolling Plains. The rolling plains in North-Central Texas cover approximately 28 million acres. This area, along with the High Plains, is the southern end of the Great Plains of the central United States. Four Texas rivers run through the Rolling Plains: the Canadian, the Colorado, the Concho, and the Red. The soils are soft prairie sands and clays, and flora include juniper woodlands and prairie mid-grasses. The Cap Rock Escarpment — a cliff that runs north-south — separates the High Plains and the Rolling Plains. Crop and livestock production are the major agricultural industries of this region.

(10) High Plains. The High Plains region was called the Llano Estacado, or Staked Plains, by the early Spaniards. (The precise meaning of this designation is not certain.) This region occupies approximately 20 million acres. Like the Rolling Plains, the High Plains is the southern extension of the Great Plains of the central United States. The High Plains region has also been cited as the outwash sediments from the Rocky Mountains. The region was once home to herds of buffalo, pronghorn antelope, gray wolves, grizzly bear,

and elk. It is now home to the sandhill crane, the kit fox, and the lesser prairie chicken, as well as prairie dogs and coyotes. The flora include blue gama and buffalo grass. Cottonwoods and willows are found along the rivers and tributaries. Mesquite, sandsage, and Harvard shin oak also occur in this region. Each fall thousands of wintering waterfowl stop over to rest and feed at the playa lakes (shallow lakes) that dot the region. The Ogallala Aquifer underlies the High Plains and the central United States. Cotton farming and cattle ranching are the major agricultural industries.

(11) Trans-Pecos. The Trans-Pecos region is the northern portion of the Chihuahua desert. Regarded as the most complex region of the state, it includes plateaus, desert valleys, and wooded mountains where many rare species are found. The only true mountain ranges in Texas are in the Trans-Pecos: the Guadalupe, Franklin, Chisos, and Davis ranges. Each mountain range has its own type of plants and animals. The flora of the region include desert scrub, such as the creosote bush, desert grasslands, pinyon-oak juniper woodlands, yuccas, and agaves. The American peregrine falcon nests in this region. The Rio Grande creates the region's southern border, separating Texas from Mexico. Big Bend National Park is in the southern edge of the area in Brewster County, the largest county in Texas.

TEXAS GULF COAST: BEACHES, DUNES, AND BARRIERS

The Texas Gulf Coast, stretching for 367 miles from Orange County to Cameron County, is one of the most ecologically diverse and active regions of the state. Environmental resources include marshes, coastal prairies, bays, estuaries, the world's longest barrier island, tidal flats, irrigated agriculture, and semiarid rangeland. The region provides feeding, breeding, and nesting habitats for a wide variety of water birds, fish, and wildlife.

The 18 counties adjacent to the Gulf of Mexico are also home to approximately 4.5 million people, and the population is expected to increase by 1.2 million people by the year 2005.[28] In 1995 Texas ranked fourth nationally in coastal residential construction; third

ECOLOGICAL REGIONS OF TEXAS

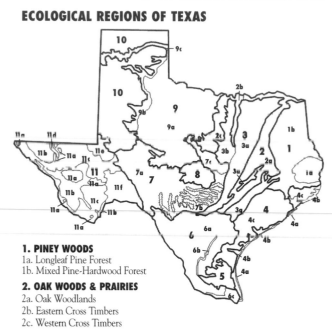

1. PINEY WOODS
1a. Longleaf Pine Forest
1b. Mixed Pine-Hardwood Forest

2. OAK WOODS & PRAIRIES
2a. Oak Woodlands
2b. Eastern Cross Timbers
2c. Western Cross Timbers

3. BLACKLAND PRAIRIES
3a. Blackland Prairie
3b. Grand Prairie

**4. GULF COAST PRAIRIES
& MARSHES**
4a. Dunes/Barrier
4b. Estuarine Zone
4c. Upland Prairies & Woods

5. COASTAL SAND PLAINS

**6. SOUTH TEXAS
BRUSH COUNTRY**
6a. Brush Country
6b. Bordas Escarpment
6c. Subtropical Zone

7. EDWARDS PLATEAU
7a. Live Oak-Mesquite Savanna
7b. Balcones Canyonlands

7c. Lampasas Cut Plain

8. LLANO UPLIFT
Mesquite Savanna, Oak &
Oak-Hickory Woodlands

9. ROLLING PLAINS
9a. Mesquite Plains
9b. Escarpment Breaks
9c. Canadian Breaks

10. HIGH PLAINS

11. TRANS PECOS
11a. Mountain Ranges
11b. Desert Grassland
11c. Desert Scrub
11d. Salt Basin
11e. Sand Hills
11f. Stockton Plateau

*Source: Texas Parks and Wildlife Department. Texas Outdoor Recreation Plan,
1995 (1997), 38.*

nationally in coastal retail, office, and industrial building construction; and fifth nationally in coastal hotel and recreational building construction.[29]

The region provides feeding, breeding, and nesting habitats for a wide variety of water birds, marine life, and wildlife.

The Texas coastal region is famed for its documented bird species, including wintering shorebirds, migratory waterfowl, songbirds, and raptors. More than 75,000 people visit Aransas National Wildlife Refuge each year, and the Laguna Atascosa National Wildlife Refuge hosts 48,000 birders each year. In 1996 the TPWD and the Texas Department of Transportation developed a 500-mile marked trail featuring directions and tips on best times to spot certain birds. Counties along the Coastal Birding Trail also hold special birding events, particularly in the winter and spring of each year. According to the GLO in 1993 coastal tourism generated about $5.4 billion and accounted for 25 percent of the state's travel industry. Most coastal travel occurs in Harris, Nueces, Cameron, and Galveston counties. The Coastal Bend area, which includes Nueces, Aransas, Kleberg, and San Patricio counties, welcomes more than 9 million visitors each year, bringing $400 million to the local economies.[30] The Texas coast also appeals to approximately 850,000 saltwater sport fishers annually; their direct expenditures in 1996 amounted to $887 million and supported approximately 24,802 jobs.[31] The coastal region's economic activity also naturally includes commercial fishing, which in 1996 had a total economic impact coastwide at the wholesale commercial level of approximately $550 million.[32] The increase of population, business activity, and tourism along the Texas coast has placed increased pressures on the natural resources of the area.

FYI *The Coastal Birding Trail information packet is available from the TPWD in Austin.*

Data compiled by the World Resources Institute in 1995 show that roughly half of the world's coasts, including their fertile ecosystems and aquatic life, are threatened significantly by development-related activities.[33] According to the institute "The majority of the world's known marine species reside within near shore zones or depend on coastal habitats for part of their life cycles. And most of the world's marine fish catch is taken from coastal zones."[34] The threats to coastal systems include habitat destruction, sewage and industrial pollution, and the introduction of exotic species. The not-for-profit Washington, D.C.-based Coast Alliance reports that areas around Galveston Bay and the Lower Laguna Madre led all other coastal regions in the United States in the amount of fertilizer applied to agricultural lands.[35] Pesticides, fertilizers, and eroded soil can all be potentially harmful to marine systems. Runoff from urban areas also threatens fish, wildlife, and water quality.

COASTAL DEFINITIONS

Barrier islands: the 280 rocky, sandy islands and beaches, dunes, and wetlands along the Atlantic and Gulf coasts. They protect inland coastal areas from sea level rise, erosion, and storms.

Beach: an accumulation of sand and gravel found at the landward margin of a sea or lake. The upper and lower limits approximate the water levels at highest and lowest tides.

Coastal barriers: beaches, dunes, wetlands, and barrier islands that protect waterfront communities from storms, erosion, waves, and wind. Coastal barriers also support wetlands, which provide critical habitat for a wide variety of wildlife.

Coastal erosion: the wearing away of land or the removal of beach or dune sediments by wave action, tidal currents, wave currents, or drainage.

Dune: a landform produced by the action of wind on uncompacted sediment, normally sand. Dunes can also be man-made, of vegetation and sand.

Public beach (Texas only): "Any beach area, whether publicly or privately owned from the line of mean low tide to the line of vegetation bordering on the Gulf of Mexico to which the public has acquired the right of use or easement to or over the area by dedication, presumption, or has retained a right by virtue of continuous right in the public since time immemorial. . . ."

(Source: GLO, Texas Coastal Management Program. Public Document [March 1994].) Generally, a beach is where the water meets the land.

Estuary: a coastal area where fresh water from rivers and streams comes together with the salt water from the ocean. Many bays, sounds, and lagoons along coasts are estuaries.

Tide: the periodic rise and fall of the earth's oceans, caused by the relative gravitational attraction of the sun, moon, and earth. Variations in tides are caused by: (a) changes in the relative positions of the sun, moon and earth; (b) uneven distribution of water on the earth's surface; and (c) variation in the seabed topography.

(Sources: Michael Allaby, The Concise Oxford Dictionary of Ecology [Oxford: Oxford University Press, 1994]); Coast Alliance, Using Common Sense To Protect the Coasts: The Need To Expand the Coastal Barrier Resource System [Washington, D.C.: Coast Alliance, 1990].)

Recognition that our nation's coastal resources are being affected by vigorous economic and population activity has spurred national and state legislation for the past twenty-five years. Federal action began in 1972 when Congress passed the Federal Coastal Zone Management Act in response to reports on coastal pollution and erosion. (See *Water Quality* chapter for discussion of state and national legislation regarding pollution of coastal waters.) With this act, the federal government established a program to encourage coastal states and territories to develop land-use plans, called "coastal management plans" that would protect coastal resources, including wetlands, dunes, and barrier islands, and would maintain public access to beaches. According to conservationist Wallace Kaufman and marine geologist Orrin Pilkey, "the federal government, through its constitutional power to regulate commerce and activities affecting navigable waters, had great but unused authority over most of coastal America."[36] However, rather than exercise that federal authority, Congress chose to delegate responsibility to the states by encouraging them to establish coastal plans.[37] Even so, not all states were quick to respond to the federal appeal. It took Texas twenty-five years to develop a State Coastal Management Plan. Texas's first attempt to develop a coastal plan failed in the late 1970s when the governor declined to submit its program to the federal government for approval. The effort to develop a state coastal plan was revived in the mid-1980s when coastal residents, local governments, and some businesses expressed renewed interest in the program. In 1989 the legislature designated the GLO as the lead agency to coordinate and develop a long-range management plan for the Texas coast. After many public hearings and draft plans, the National Oceanic and Atmospheric Administration approved Texas's Coastal Management Plan in January 1997.

Much of the debate in Texas concerning the Coastal Management Plan was focused on three issues: the potential delay of permits for regulated industrial and commercial entities, the wetlands permitting process, and the dredging policies of the Army Corps of Engineers, specifically the disposition of dredging materials. The Texas plan established uniform coastal policies that address beach access, coastal erosion, dredging, protection of dunes, energy facility siting, wetlands management, and other topics. With the plan's approval, Texas receives some $2.5 million annually for coastal projects. Under the plan, local coastal governments and not-for-profit organizations endorsed by local governments can apply for grants through the GLO. As with other natural resources in the public domain, the Texas coast is being used for multiple purposes. Whether it can continue to provide for industrial, business, and human needs as well as the needs of aquatic life is unknown, particularly as the industrial and population pressures on the coast increase.

COASTAL RESOURCE LEGISLATION
Significant Federal Coastal Legislation
■ The Rivers and Harbors Act of 1899 requires a permit from the Army Corps of Engineers for structures, such as piers and docks, in waters of the United States.
■ The Coastal Zone Management Act of 1972 established federal guidelines to preserve, protect, develop, and restore the resources of the nation's coastal zone. The plans must address beach access, wetland protection, erosion controls, ocean pollution, and siting of pipelines. As incentives to coastal states and territories to develop coastal management plans, the act allows states to receive federal grants under the program once coastal management plans are approved.
■ The Clean Water Act of 1972 (and subsequent amendments) regulates discharges into U.S. waters and established a wetlands protection program.

■ The Coastal Barrier Resources Act of 1982 directed the Secretary of the Interior to establish the Coastal Barrier Resource System nationwide and to limit federal spending in designated coastal-barrier resource areas. (Coastal barriers are beaches, dunes, wetlands, and barrier islands.) For example, in order to protect these environmentally fragile areas, the law prohibits undeveloped lands in the barrier system from receiving federal flood insurance for new development. (See *Water Quality* chapter for other Federal coastal legislation, particularly legislation regarding pollution of coastal waters and dredging in coastal areas.)

Significant State Coastal Legislation
■ The Open Beaches Act of 1959, amended in 1991, guarantees the public's right of free and unrestricted access to the "public beach." It requires the commissioner of the GLO to develop rules protecting the public's right to use and enjoy Texas beaches.
■ The Coastal Coordination Act of 1977, amended in 1989, 1991, 1995, and 1997, directed the GLO to coordinate with other state agencies on the development of a long-term plan for the management of activities affecting coastal resources. The act also created the Coastal Coordination Council and established the larger framework for the Texas Coastal Management Plan.
■ The Dune Protection Act of 1973, amended in 1991, requires coastal counties to establish a program to protect dunes within their jurisdiction. The act directed the GLO to establish minimum requirements.[38]

BEACH OWNERSHIP AND BEACH ACCESS
In the United States, the ownership of coastal beaches varies from state to state, and each coastal state's response to the question of ownership has been developed through legislation and court cases. The dispute over beach ownership and access is complicated by, among other factors, the categorization of beaches: the wet sand or tidelands, the dry sand beach from mean high water to the vegetation line, and the uplands that lie landward of the dunes. However, due to the law's reliance on the public

trust doctrine of English common law, it is generally recognized that the public owns the tidelands, though some coastal states have allowed private ownership to the low-tide line.[39] For example, 90 percent of Maine's coastline is privately owned, while about 90 percent of Oregon's coast is public.[40] States like Maine have allowed private ownership all the way to the low-tide line.

In Texas, the wet beach is state-owned submerged land held in trust for the public by the GLO, but the dry beach can be privately held land subject to public easement. The public has retained this easement — the right to use and enjoy the dry beach — by virtue of a tradition dating back to European settlement, when the beach was actually used as a road. In the nineteenth century, for instance, a stagecoach line traveled the beaches of Galveston Island. Today Texas beaches quite literally continue to be used as roads; not only are vehicles allowed to drive on many coastal beaches, but some local coastal governments maintain the beach surface for that purpose. Since 1959, with the enactment of the Texas Open Beaches Act, the legislature has guaranteed the public's right of access and use of Texas beaches that are accessible by public road or public ferry.

Of the 367 miles of Texas coastal beaches, 293 miles are open for public use. Of these, 173 miles are considered accessible to the public. In this context, "accessible" is defined by state law as "accessible by driving along the shore or by walking no more than one mile from a point that can be reached by a two-wheel-drive vehicle."[41] Under rules developed by the GLO, local governments have the option of limiting vehicular traffic on beaches as long as adequate off-beach parking is developed. Local governments also have primary responsibility for developing and maintaining public entrances to beaches. To ensure a minimum of public entrances, the GLO, at the direction of the state legislature, created beach access rules. All coastal communities were required to develop access plans based on these rules by August 1993 for approval by the GLO. Resource planners are aware that increased beach access may also increase the public use of beaches, which in turn might increase the amount of beach trash and

also threaten dunes, coastal vegetation, and other coastal resources.

GULF AND BAY SHORELINE LOSS

Shoreline erosion is an issue of economic and environmental concern on the Texas coast. Erosion, caused by both natural and human actions, results in the loss of beaches, coastal highways, residential and commercial structures, and wildlife habitat.

Several factors can determine the amount of erosion that takes place on a given beach: wave energy might remove more sediment from the beach than is "supplied by longshore currents"; human-made structures, such as jetties, and coastal dredging can affect the amount of beach sediment; and droughts and other climatic occurrences might determine the amount of sediment brought to the beaches by rivers.[42] The economic and environmental costs of erosion have prompted action at local, state, and federal levels. To slow down erosion, some states have required set-back rules, which prohibit construction of buildings and homes so many feet onto the beach, and some communities have prevented "hard structures" like jetties.

It has been estimated that more than 27,000 acres of gulf shoreline were lost to erosion from the mid-1800s to 1982.[43] Erosion rates vary up and down the Texas coast from an average of 24 feet per year at Sargent Bay to 7 feet per year at South Padre Island.[44] According to the University of Texas Bureau of Economic Geology, where there has been human modification (residential and commercial development, jetties, dredging) along the Texas Gulf Coast, the rate of shoreline erosion has accelerated.[45]

The causes of bayfront erosion are different from the causes of gulf shore erosion. Within the bay system, which is considered more complex than the gulf shore system, erosion is caused primarily by human actions, particularly the subsurface withdrawal of groundwater and oil and gas. Texas bay shores are eroding at rates that vary from 1 to 10 feet a year.[46]

According to the GLO, an effective response to the problem of coastal erosion is thwarted by the lack of economical sand sources for replacement sediment and by poor coordination among federal, state, and local agencies.[47] The GLO does not point to the lack of controls over residential or commercial development, though other coastal experts do. State guidelines for responding to coastal erosion for the most part recommend "soft" remedies, such as establishing shoreline vegetation, providing beach nourishment, and rebuilding dunes, rather than erecting permanent structures. Hard structures such as seawalls and bulkheads erected by property owners can accelerate erosion and damage neighboring properties. In Galveston Bay, where shoreline loss has been about 2.2 feet per year, specific grasses are being planted at various sites, and wave barriers made of used parachute material are being used to protect the new plantings.[48]

FYI ☞ *For more detailed information on erosion response activities, see the GLO's 1996 Texas Coastwide Erosion Response Plan: A Report to the 75th Legislature and Dune Protection and Improvement Manual for the Texas Gulf Coast.*

DUNE LOSS AND DUNE PROTECTION

Coastal dunes are an invaluable resource. Dunes protect beaches from erosion and therefore also protect commercial and residential property and wildlife habitat. By acting as natural barriers, dunes also protect inland areas from storms, high waves, and wind. Dunes also hold sand that can replenish eroded beaches. Dunes are damaged and destroyed primarily by residential and commercial development and recreational activity. Because there have been no comprehensive baseline studies, the exact extent of dune loss over time on the Texas coast is not known.

With the enactment of the Texas Dune Protection Act, coastal counties are required to establish a dune protection line and to control activity seaward of the line. The line may lie up to 1,000 feet landward of the mean high tide. The Dune Protection Act does not apply to "any dune area not accessible by public road or common carrier ferry facility."[49] In other words, the act protects only dunes on public beaches. Before any activity other than livestock grazing and oil and gas production can occur seaward of the protection line, a permit is required from the county or municipal

government.[50] For the protection of dunes, the state's Coastal Management Plan encourages the development of beach traffic lanes, off-beach parking, dune walkovers, and dune revegetation and restoration.

BEACH DEBRIS

Unfortunately, recreational users of Texas beaches encounter literally hundreds of thousands of pounds of trash. This trash is generated by both beachgoers and by ships that have dumped garbage at sea that has washed upon the beaches. Over the years, the amount of offshore garbage found on Texas beaches has decreased, while beachgoer litter has increased.

The cleanup and maintenance of Texas beaches is the responsibility of coastal local governments. It is the responsibility of the county governments to maintain the public beaches located inside the county but outside the boundaries of any incorporated city. Approximately $5.5 million annually is used by coastal local governments for beach cleanup activities. Nueces County, Port Aransas, Galveston Island, and South Padre spend most of this amount.[51] Revenue sources for cleanup activities include the hotel occupancy tax, the local sales tax , and, in some communities, car-parking fees. The amount of revenue available for these activities, therefore, varies from community to community.

1996 INTERNATIONAL COASTAL CLEANUP TEXAS'S PERCENT COMPOSITION OF DEBRIS

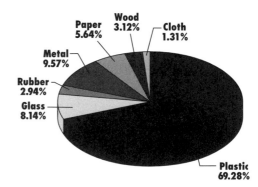

The "Plastic" and "Foamed Plastic" categories are combined. The chart includes all debris reported, minus cigarette butts, which are so numerous their inclusion would distort data interpretation.

Source: Texas General Land Office, Adopt-a-Beach Program (1997).

BARRIER ISLANDS

Barrier Islands are rocky, sandy islands and beaches, dunes, and wetlands located along the Atlantic and gulf coasts. There are 280 barrier islands along the U.S. coastline. Texas has 17 barrier islands that total 191,762 acres. Texas also has the longest and broadest barrier islands: Mustang and Padre islands joined together create a 130-mile beach.[52] These beaches and the wildlife resources of these islands attract thousands of tourists and millions of tourist dollars to coastal communities every year. In addition, the islands play an important role in protecting mainland communities from storms, high tides, and erosion. Barrier islands also provide critical habitat for songbirds, shorebirds, turtles, and other wildlife, and they contribute to the production of fish and shellfish. But, over the years, heavy commercial and residential development on barrier islands has threatened these resources and diminished their protective role.

WHAT GOES AROUND, COMES AROUND: OCEAN TRASH

The international Marine Pollution Treaty regulates marine pollution around the world. The treaty contains five "annexes" (sections), each of which regulates a different type of pollution. Annex V prohibits the dumping of plastics in the world's oceans. The International Maritime Organization has designated the Wider Caribbean Region (which includes the Gulf of Mexico) as a "special area," where dumping from ships except for food scraps is prohibited. Eighteen countries have agreed to the designation, including the United States and Mexico. This "special area" designation was to go into effect in April 1993; however, enforcement of the "special area" rules cannot begin until there are adequate garbage-reception facilities at each port. Ports in the United States do have adequate garbage facilities, but most ports in the Caribbean countries do not.[53]

FYI ☞ *The Texas Adopt-a-Beach program recruits volunteers twice a year to help clean up and remove trash from Texas beaches. From 1986 to 1998, more than 217,000 volunteers removed more than 4,171*

tons of trash along approximately 150 miles of beaches. For more information, contact the Texas Adopt-a-Beach Program at the GLO (1700 North Congress Avenue, Austin, TX 78701).

TEXAS RIVERS AND PUBLIC ACCESS

Texas has 191,228 miles of streams and rivers, and 11,247 rivers and streams have been given names by the TPWD.

Texas law, relying on the public trust doctrine of English common law, has long recognized the public's right to use navigable streams for canoeing, swimming, and fishing. They are considered "highways of the state." Under Texas law dating from 1837, a river is considered navigable (and therefore open to public use) as long as its bed averages at least 30 feet wide from its mouth up.[54] Erecting fences and other barriers across navigable rivers is forbidden. Hundreds of streams in Texas meet this navigability test. Unlike regulation of the coastal beaches, however, no state agency has day-to-day responsibility for protecting or securing the public's right of access to rivers. Moreover, no state agency has undertaken the task of identifying all these navigable streams. Limited budgets and the need for field investigations have made state agencies reluctant to respond to public inquiries about the navigability of streams.

Public access is limited even for the major rivers known to be navigable, such as the Brazos, Trinity, Colorado, and Guadalupe. Under state law, the right of access to lakes, streams, and rivers rests with the owners of the land that borders the surface water, and the majority of this "riparian" land is in private hands. Therefore, the public depends on public parks, boat ramps, or highway rights-of-way to gain access to rivers. A citizen survey conducted in 1987 showed that Texans wanted more public accesses.[55] Also, a 1990 TPWD survey of citizens and recreation professionals showed that 67 percent of the respondents wanted more public recreation areas along rivers and streams.[56]

THE MOVEMENT FOR NATIONAL FORESTS IN THE UNITED STATES

In the United States, the public interest in the

protection of forests and concern over wasteful forest practices date back to at least the mid-1800s. Nineteenth-century conservationists loudly protested the destruction of the giant redwoods in California, and there was a general public outcry over the denuding of lands and resulting soil erosion around the Great Lakes. In the nineteenth century, European settlers moving west clear-cut forests aggressively, using the timber for fuel, housing, and boats and the cleared land for farming. The conservationists of the time, however, feared that the wholesale destruction of old-growth forests would result in destruction of biological diversity, changes in climate, erosion of soil, and damage to wildlife and to water flow. These are today's concerns as well.

FOREST LEGISLATION
Significant Federal Forest Legislation

■ In 1875 the Division of Forestry under the USDA was created to report to Congress on forest production and consumption.

■ In 1891, spurred by the misuse and rapid loss of U.S. forestlands, President Benjamin Harrison created six forest reserves, totaling 3 million acres, and nine timber reserves totaling 13 million acres.

■ In 1897, despite the opposition of some conservationists, Congress gave the Secretary of the Interior the authority to allow timber harvesting and mining within national forests. This law paved the way for the multiple-use policy — lands managed for a variety of uses, including recreation, timber, and mineral production, and wildlife habitat — that still guides the use of our national forests, grasslands, and parkland. The multiple-use policy was advanced by conservationist Gifford Pinochet, the first director of the U.S. Forest Service, who believed the forest could withstand some cutting of trees and still be preserved.

■ In 1911 the Weeks Law was passed to allow for the establishment of a federal financial program to help states develop wildfire control initiatives.

■ In 1916 the National Park Service Organic Act set up the national park system to provide public recreational areas and to conserve ecologically sensitive acreage.

DEFINITIONS RELATING TO FORESTLANDS

Clear-cutting: the felling of all trees in a designated area in one operation.

Deforestation: conversion of forest to other uses, such as cropland or urban development.

Forest: a plant formation that is composed of trees, the crowns of which touch, so forming a continuous canopy; or, the trees that make up a forest area.

Old-growth or virgin forests: forests that have developed over a long time without "catastrophic disturbance." Old-growth forests can have trees that are from 300 to 1,000 years old. These forests are considered more complex in species composition and in function than young forests. In the United States, old-growth forests are nearly all destroyed, except for those in national parks and wilderness areas.

Temperate deciduous forest: deciduous summer forests are dominated by broad-leaved hardwoods. Most of the temperate forests are found in parts of North Africa, the Russian Federation, Europe, Australia, Canada, and the United States.

Tropical rain forests: tropical rain forests are forests of the permanently wet tropics. The trees are evergreen, at least 30 meters tall, rich in thick-stemmed lianes (woody, free-hanging, climbing plants) and in woody as well as herbaceous epiphytes (a plant that uses another plant, typically a tree, for its support but not for food, such as bromeliads or orchids). Tropical forests are found in Central America, Mexico, South America, Africa, and Southeast Asia.

(*Major sources: Michael Allaby.* The Concise Oxford Dictionary of Ecology [*Oxford: Oxford University Press, 1994*]; *Stephen Whitney.* Western Forests: National Audubon Society Nature Guide [*New York: Alfred A. Knopf, 1997*].)

■ In 1926 federal legislation established the Texas Forest Service, located at Texas Agricultural and Mechanical College (now Texas A&M University).
■ In 1956 the Federal Soil Bank program was established to provide landowners assistance with erosion-control activities.
■ In 1960 the Multiple Use Act required the National Forest Service to manage the national forests for recreation, wildlife habitat, livestock grazing, timber supplies, and watershed protection.
■ In 1964 after acrimonious debates, Congress passed the Wilderness Act, requiring that some national forestland be preserved in its natural state and prohibiting timber sales and other resource uses, such as mining, on those lands.
■ In 1973 Congress created the Federal Forest Incentive Program to provide cost-share incentives to landowners for reforestation activities that would increase wood production on privately owned forestland.
■ In 1990 the Farm Bill established the Stewardship Incentive Program, a cost-share program to help private landowners protect wetlands and wildlife habitat, enhance recreational opportunities, and otherwise improve the management of privately held forestland.

Significant State Forest Legislation
■ In 1923 the Texas legislature appropriated money for a state forester and created a state department of forestry at the Agricultural and Mechanical College of Texas (now Texas A&M University).
■ In 1933 the Texas legislature authorized the federal government to purchase land to create national forests in Texas.
■ In 1997 the Texas legislature enacted legislation allowing non-agriculturally productive open land converted to timber production to continue to be appraised as open land for fifteen years. The purpose of the law is to provide an incentive to plant open lands with trees to help meet timber supply needs.

FORESTLAND IN TEXAS
According to Texas foresters, in the early 1800s most of East Texas, from the Red River to the Gulf

coastal plain, was covered with yellow pine, hickory, elm, sweetgum, oaks, and bottomland hardwoods. By the late 1800s, the forests in the northeastern United States had been ravaged, and lumber companies, looking for new supplies of timber, moved to the South and to Texas, specifically to the Beaumont-Orange area. They found in Texas not only a supply of raw timber but also a growing population in need of lumber to build cities. This combination of factors resulted in the harvesting of most of Texas's old-growth forests by 1915. According to Roger Lord, former staff forester for the Texas Forest Service, this depletion of forests led to the creation of the state department of forestry in 1923.

By 1930 the timber industry and wildfires had taken their toll: thousands of acres of virgin forests had been logged over, timber supplies were depleted, and the Texas lumber industry was finished.[57]

In the 1940s and 1950s, the introduction of fire-management practices and new technology that allowed the use of southern pine pulpwood as newsprint, combined to create a new market for Texas timber.[58] In the 1980s, the state experienced yet another resurgence in demand for Texas timber, resulting in part from federal restrictions on timber harvesting in the national forests of the Northwest. These federal restrictions, which were passed to protect the habitat of the northern spotted owl and other endangered wildlife, affected 75 percent of the nation's timber supply and caused lumber companies to search out new unregulated supplies on private lands. In recent years, both the Texas Forest Service and the timber industry have become concerned that, over the long term, demand for timber will outpace the growth of trees.

In fact, in 1997, overharvesting of pine and hardwoods for wood products resulted in Texas's importing 10 percent of its raw wood material.[59]

At the same time, forest experts and biologists are concerned that increased demand for wood products will turn the natural forests of East and East-Central Texas into rows of man-made pine plantation monocultures, altering the ecosystem of the entire region. In fact, biologists are concerned with the rapid replacement of natural forests with industrial,

OWNERSHIP OF TEXAS FORESTS

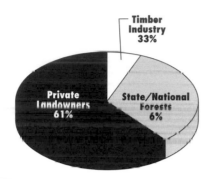

About 33% of Texas's forests are owned by the timber industry, 6% are in national/state forests, and the remainder are owned by private landowners. There are approximately 2.4 million acres of artificially regenerated forests (75% on timber industry land).

Source: Texas Forest Service, 1998.

monoculture plantations throughout the southeastern United States as well as in Southeast Asia, Mexico, and Central and South America. Natural forests, unlike man-made tree plantations, are biologically diverse and therefore have a great deal of wildlife value. On the other hand, monoculture tree farms offer very little habitat or forage opportunities for wildlife. This lack of biological diversity also makes tree plantations much more susceptible to pests and disease, which in turn requires the need to use pesticides.[60] The Forest Stewardship Council and the International Tropical Timber Organization are leading efforts to establish sustainable management practices for industrial forests.

In 1975 East Texas had about 550,000 acres of pine plantation, in 1986 it had 1.2 million acres, and in 1992 it had 4.2 million acres.[61] (In 1997 Texas ranked fifth in the nation, with 3,726 private tree farms.) However, even as concerns regarding monoculture plantations are being voiced, state and federal cost-share incentives are encouraging private landowners to help increase wood fiber supplies by developing pine tree plantations. For example, state legislation HB 1723 passed in 1997 allows open land that is converted to timber production to continue to be appraised as open land for the next fifteen years. In addition, since 1973, the Forestry

Incentives Program, created by Congress, provides cost-share incentives to private landowners to grow pine trees in designated counties, as does USDA's Agricultural Conservation Program. In addition to these programs, the Texas Reforestation Foundation, a privately funded program, provides the same type of cost-share incentives to private landowners in designated Texas counties.

The continued global consumption of paper and wood products is, of course, driving the development of tree plantations. World Watch Institute reports that the "United States, with approximately 4.7 percent of the world's population, consumes over 31 percent of the world's paper and paperboard. The United States, Japan, and Western Europe combined represent less than 20 percent of the world's population and account for nearly 70 percent of its paper consumption."[62] The World Institute claims that this appetite for paper can be curbed and that, in fact, industrial countries could radically reduce their consumption of paper without radically altering

FORESTLAND—1992

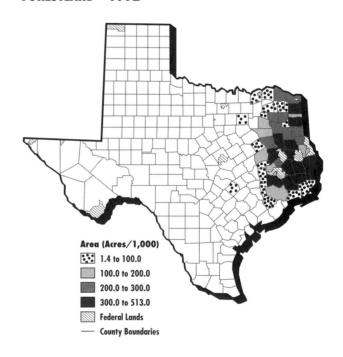

Area (Acres/1,000)
- 1.4 to 100.0
- 100.0 to 200.0
- 200.0 to 300.0
- 300.0 to 513.0
- Federal Lands
- County Boundaries

Source: USDA, Natural Resources Conservation Service, Resource Issues (Temple: USDA NRCS, 1997), N.P.

their quality of life. The use of recycled paper and nonwood fiber such as kenaf, hemp, and wheat straw could play a more important role in paper production than they do today.

FYI *"In the 1990s, the value of nonindustrial landowner Texas timber has gone from $250 million to $500 million in 1992 to the 1997 value of $700 million."* (Source: John Piland, "Texas Timber," Texas Business, April 1997, 47.)

NATIONAL FORESTS IN TEXAS

Of the 733 million acres of forests in the United States, 191 million acres are managed by the U.S. Forest Service. National forests in Texas represent a small percentage of the total amount of forestland in the state: of the approximately 12 million acres of timberland, 633,308 acres are in national forests. National forests are designated by and funded by Congress. However, the U.S. Forest Service, without Congressional approval, is able to engage in land exchanges with private landowners, and according to the Forest Service's office in Texas this has resulted in a small net annual increase of national forest acreage in the state.[63]

Much of the national forests in Texas were originally privately owned lands that were abandoned by the lumber industry during the economic decline of the 1930s. These abandoned forestlands were put up for sale, but at the time there were neither commercial nor private interests willing to buy the lands, and the USDA acquired them for national forests. (Further discussion of forestland is found in the section on agricultural land.)

As a result of the multiple-use management policy, national forests in Texas and elsewhere can be used for timber production, grazing, and oil and gas production, as well as for recreational uses. It is estimated by the U.S. Forest Service that 521,000 out of 633,308 acres of national forests in Texas are suitable for timber production on a sustained-yield basis (reforestation after cutting).[64] Timber from national forests is used for such items as lumber, plywood, poles, furniture, pulp, and paper.

In 1996 the U.S. Treasury received approximately $16 million from timber sales from the national

forests in Texas. A quarter of the timber sale revenues are returned to the states, which means that in 1996, 12 Texas counties where national forest are located shared approximately $4,337,310 in revenues.[65]

CLEAR-CUTTING IN NATIONAL FORESTS

There continues today to be a concern about forest management practices on both federally held and private and industrial lands. To many recreational users of national forests and to conservationists, the U.S. Forest Service has been more interested in timber sales than in managing the forestland for wildlife habitat and human recreation.

Some Texas environmental organizations have been concerned over the Forest Service practice of clear-cutting—the felling of all trees in a designated area in one operation. This practice converts the native mixed forests to single-species, even-age timber crops and has a number of negative consequences.[66] Clear-cutting often results in: (1) the elimination of the native forest ecosystem, causing vastly reduced habitat for wildlife; (2) increased erosion, with attendant stream silting and nutrient loss from the soil; (3) impairment of recreational values because of loss of wildlife viewing and other experiences associated with forests; and (4) susceptibility of the forest to insect damage, diseases, acid rain, and blown-down trees.[67]

An alternative to clear-cutting is a process called selection management. Under selection management, individual trees are marked and cut, creating small clearings that allow for regeneration through natural reseeding from remaining trees. Authorities believe that shifting from even-age management to selection management would yield enormous benefits to wildlife and to the productivity of forestland.

FYI *The term sustainability refers to economic development that takes full account of the environmental consequences of economic activity and is based on the use of resources that can be replaced or renewed and therefore are not depleted.* (Source: Michael Allaby, The Concise Oxford Dictionary of Ecology [Oxford: Oxford University Press, 1994], 376.)

NATIONAL GRASSLANDS IN TEXAS

Millions of acres of farmland in Texas, New Mexico, Colorado, and Montana were abandoned during the drought of the 1930s. Some of this acreage was acquired and designated for restoration by the federal government in 1933 and became a part of the Dust Bowl Land Unit Projects under the National Industrial Recovery Act.[68] In 1960, under the Multiple-Use Sustained Yield Act, approximately 4 million acres were designated as national grasslands to be managed, like national forests, by the U.S. Forest Service. Texas has 118,000 acres of national grasslands. Prior to European settlement, more than 20 million acres of tallgrass communities covered the Texas Blackland Prairie, the Fort Worth Prairie, the Fayette Prairie, and the Coastal Prairie. The national grasslands, like our national forests, are used for multiple purposes, including wildlife habitat, cattle grazing, and recreation. The Forest Service has no plans to purchase additional lands or otherwise acquire new grasslands in Texas.[69]

GRASSLANDS IN TEXAS

Source: Henry Chappell, "Discovering the Grasslands," Texas Parks and Wildlife, No.3 (TPWD, March 1997), 34.

AGRICULTURE

When Congress established the USDA in 1862, it also established land grant universities in every state to help agriculture and rural communities. By that time, soil depletion was a recognized problem and pests like the boll weevil were destroying cotton plantations. There was also a concern that farmers needed to engage in some uniform agricultural practices that would enhance food and fiber production and protect the environment, particularly practices that would reduce soil erosion. Since that time, the federal government's involvement with agriculture has greatly expanded and includes overseeing many regulatory programs and the expenditure

NUMBER OF FARMS AND RANCHES IN TEXAS

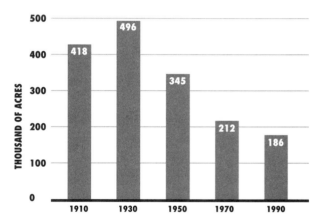

Throughout the years, the definitions used by the different Censuses of Agriculture have directly affected the number of farms and ranches. From 1910 through 1924, a farm was any place of 3 or more acres on which there were agricultural operations. Any place less than 3 acres had to have a value of production of $250 or more. Places less than 3 acres having less than $250 in value of production were counted as farms, provided they required the continuous services of at least one person. From 1925 through 1949, a farm was any place having 3 or more acres or any place having $250 or greater value of production. From 1950 through 1954, a farm was (1) any place of 3 or more acres with a value of farm products of $150 or more, or (2) any place less than 3 acres with a value of sales of $250 or more. From 1955 through 1974, a farm was (1) any place of 10 or more acres that had annual sales of $50 or more, or (2) any place with less than 10 acres that had annual sales of $250 or more. From 1975 to the present, a farm is defined as a place that sells or normally would sell $1,000 or more of agricultural products annually.

Source: USDA Agricultural Statistic Service (Austin, 1997), 126.

of millions of dollars to support production agriculture.

But, according to a report issued in 1995 by the Delta Land and Community Corporation, neither U.S. farmers nor the environment is doing well. Delta Land and Community points out that "Farms are increasingly unprofitable yet agricultural production is higher than at any time in the country's history. Food processing companies expect an 18% to 20% return on their investment, while farmers get 2-3% if they are lucky."[70] While farmers are known for establishing some of the country's first environmental organizations (county soil and water conservation organizations) and are seen as foremost stewards of the land, agriculture is now seen as the cause of major environmental problems. These problems include soil erosion, pesticide, and nutrient runoff into streams, bays, and estuaries; diminished groundwater supplies due to extensive irrigation; and alteration and destruction of wildlife habitat. In addition, the use of agricultural pesticides may pose threats to wildlife and human health.

Despite its popular image, Texas is an urban state. Urban residents became a majority as early as 1950, and in 1992, 82 percent of the population lived on 6 percent of the land.[71] Still agriculture remains important to the state's economy. In 1998 gross cash receipts for agricultural crops and livestock totaled

NUMBER OF FARMS AND RANCHES IN TEXAS

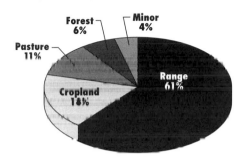

Only 5 percent of the total surface area in Texas is developed. Federal land makes up 2 percent, and water is 2 percent. The rest of Texas, 91 percent, is rural.

Source: USDA Natural Resources Conservation Service, Resource Issues *(Temple: USDA NRCS, 1997), N.P.*

$13.3 billion. This figure represents approximately 2.1 percent of the state's total $649 billion gross state product (the value of all goods and services produced in the state.).[72] The figure for cash receipts, however, does not reflect agriculture's full contribution to the economy. Farmers and ranchers usually do not pay themselves a wage. Moreover, the sale of some agricultural equipment, such as tractors, and agricultural inputs, such as seed, are considered retail trade and are therefore not represented as an agricultural good. Likewise, food processing and kindred products,

DEFINITIONS RELATING TO AGRICULTURAL LANDS

Pastureland: land used primarily for the production of adapted, introduced, or native species in a pure stand, a grass mixture, or a grass-legume mixture.

Rangeland: land on which the vegetation is predominantly grasses, grasslike plants, forbs, or shrubs suitable for grazing and browsing.

Prime farmland: land having the best combination of physical and chemical characteristics for producing food, feed, forage, fiber, and oil-seed crops. Prime farmland is land on which crops can be produced for the least cost and with the least damage to the resource base. It has an adequate and dependable supply of moisture from precip-

itation and irrigation, a favorable climate and growing season, and soils that have not been excessively eroded.

Forestland: land at least 10 percent stocked by forest trees that will be at least 13 feet tall at maturity. The minimum area for classification of forestland is one acre, and the acre must be at least 100 feet wide.

Minor land: includes farmsteads, ranch headquarters, commercial feedlots, nurseries, and land in the USDA's Conservation Reserve Program.

(Source: NRCS, Texas Summary Report 1992 National Resources Inventory *[Washington, D.C., 1992].)*

TRENDS IN TEXAS LAND

In 1982, Texas was made up of

Rangeland	95.5 million acres
Cropland	33.3 million acres
Pastureland	17.1 million acres
Forestland	9.3 million acres
Urban land	6.8 million acres
Federal land	3.0 million acres
Miscellaneous/ Minor Land	2.2 million acres

In 1992, Texas was made up of

Rangeland	94.2 million acres
Cropland	28.3 million acres
Pastureland	16.7 million acres
Forestland	10.0 million acres (U.S. Forest Service estimates there is 12 million acres)
Urban land	8.2 million acres
Federal land	3.2 million acres
Miscellaneous/ Minor Land	6.4 million acres

The trend from 1982 to 1992 was:
Rural land decreased by 2 million acres.
Developed land increased by 1.4 million.
Water areas increased by almost 275 thousand acres.
Federal land increased by 223,000 acres.

Sources: USDA NRCS. Resource Issues (Temple: USDA NCRS, 1997), 129.

which were $5.7 billion in gross cash receipts in 1996, are considered part of the manufacturing sector, not the agricultural sector.

The state led the country in the value of farm real estate, valued at approximately $71 billion in 1996.[73]

Yet the role of agriculture in the state's economy has declined. According to the State Comptroller's Office, "During the 1920s, two-thirds of the total value of goods produced in the state came from farming, oil and natural gas production, and petroleum-related manufacturing. By 1993 those sectors accounted for less than half of all goods produced and, more significantly, just 14 percent of all goods and services produced in Texas. By 2005, it is estimated that these natural resources will make up only one-third of all Texas-produced goods, and only 8 percent of the total economy.[74]

HIGHEST PASTURELAND—1992

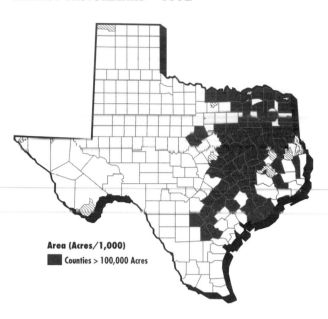

Area (Acres/1,000)
■ Counties > 100,000 Acres

Source: USDA, NCRS, Resource Issues (Temple: USDA NCRS, 1997), N.P.

During the past fifty years the number of Texans employed in agriculture also has declined. In 1940 approximately 23 percent of Texans were producers on farms and ranches and 17 percent were employed in agricultural processing and distribution. In 1995, two percent were producers on farms and ranches and 20 percent were involved with agricultural marketing or services.[75] Moreover, from 1982 to 1992, rural land in Texas had decreased from 157 million acres to 155 million acres. Developed land increased by 1.4 million acres in this same time period.

FYI ☞ *Only five percent of the total surface area in Texas is developed. Federal land makes up two percent, and water is two percent. The remaining 91 percent of the land area is considered rural.*

AGRICULTURE AND THE ENVIRONMENT

The quality of rural land is critical for more than just the production of food and fiber. Rural land provides wildlife habitat and affects the quality and quantity of the state's water supply. Agriculture, however, takes a fairly significant toll on the environment. It is one of the chief causes of habitat destruction and alteration, which results in a loss of

HIGHEST CROPLAND AREAS—1992

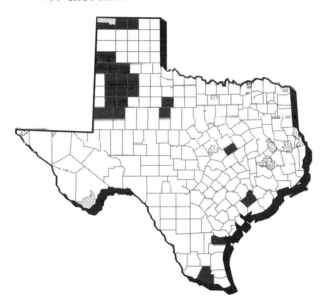

Source: USDA, NCRS, Resource Issues (Temple: USDA NCRS, 1997), N.P.

HIGHEST RANGELAND AREAS—1992

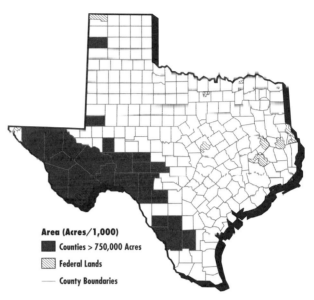

Area (Acres/1,000)
- ■ Counties > 750,000 Acres
- ▨ Federal Lands
- — County Boundaries

Source: USDA, NCRS, Resource Issues (Temple: USDA NCRS, 1997), N.P.

biological diversity. Pesticides and nutrients in runoff from agricultural lands have major environmental effects as well. Nationally, agriculture is the largest cause of non-point-source pollution of surface water. It is a significant cause of surface water pollution in Texas as well. In addition, both pesticides and fertilizers have been found in groundwater in Texas. (The issue of pesticides and their use is examined in a separate focus piece.) Finally, since the 1930s, soil erosion has continued to be a significant problem in parts of the state.

CONDITION OF AGRICULTURAL AND RURAL LAND IN TEXAS

In 1997 the USDA's state office of Natural Resources Conservation Service listed these problems:[76]

Twenty-four percent of the rangeland in Texas is considered in poor condition. (This land might not be considered highly productive for beef cattle but it might be productive for other classes of livestock and very good for certain wildlife.)

Sixty-eight percent of cropland in Texas could benefit from some form of conservation treatment to preserve the soil's productivity and prevent erosion.

Thirty-seven percent of pasture land needs better grazing management.

Seventy-two percent of the forestland could benefit from conservation treatment to preserve productivity.

Nationally agriculture is the largest non-point-source of surface water pollution and is a significant cause of surface water pollution in Texas. Both agricultural pesticides and fertilizers have been found in groundwater in Texas. Moreover, soil erosion since the 1930s has been a significant problem in the state. (See *Water Quality* chapter for discussion of non-point-source pollution; see also *Pesticides* focus piece.)

FYI ☞ *"A nation that destroys its soils, destroys itself."* – President Franklin D. Roosevelt, from a letter sent to governors on February 26, 1937.

SOIL EROSION

Though there has been much effort over the past sixty years to address the issue, cropland erosion in Texas continues to be a major environmental and economic problem. Concern for soil erosion in the United States dates back to Presidents Washington and Jefferson. The tobacco plantations in Virginia in the eighteenth century were managed in a way that caused tremendous soil erosion, and one impetus for westward expansion by the European settlers was the need for "fresh" land. The problem of soil erosion was first addressed at the federal level in the 1930s under the presidency of Franklin Roosevelt. The drought and dust storms of the 1930s, particularly in Texas, Oklahoma, Colorado, and Kansas, resulted in tremendous crop and farm losses and left thousands of farmers unemployed. This brought presidential and congressional attention to the issue.

Though some progress has been made to arrest cropland erosion since that time, human mismanagement, economic forces, and climatic changes have allowed the problem to continue. Some of the soil-erosion correctives recommended in the 1930s included crop rotation, contour plowing, and reserving marginal lands (not good cropland) as pastureland. These practices were credited with arresting soil erosion for a time. But in the 1970s an increase in the worldwide demand for farm commodities led the U.S. government to create new crop-subsidy incentives to encourage farmers to plant "fencerow to fencerow." Many farmers, eager to increase production, put marginal lands into production and discontinued the practice of crop rotation. To combat the nutrient depletion of overused soils, farmers had to increase their use of chemical fertilizers. By the mid-1980s, federal action was again needed to address the problem of soil erosion. This action was taken in the 1985 Farm Bill.

FYI ☞ *Soil is the material that is formed from rocks and decaying plants and animals; it makes up the outermost layer of the earth. There are at least 70,000 kinds of soil in the United States. Topsoil is considered the most productive soil layer. According to the USDA, it takes 500 years to form one inch of topsoil.* (Source: USDA, Soil Conservation Service, Fact Sheet [April 1993].)

SIGNIFICANT SOIL CONSERVATION LEGISLATION

■ In 1935 the Civilian Conservation Corps was established to put unemployed men, including farmers, to work reseeding and planting trees and building erosion dams. The Civilian Conservation Corps also built state park facilities, including many in Texas.

■ In 1935 the Soil Conservation Service was established within the USDA to provide technical assistance to farmers.

■ In 1939 the Texas Soil Conservation Law passed and enabled landowners to establish local soil and water conservation districts as special subdivisions of state government. Each district has a governing board that is responsible for managing conservation functions within the prescribed area. Texas established, in 1939, the Texas Soil and Water Conservation Board to coordinate the activities of 213 conservation districts.

■ In 1977 Congress established the Soil and Water Resources Conservation Act

■ In 1985 the federal Farm Bill (the Food Security Act of 1985) established the Conservation Reserve Program to provide financial incentives to farmers who take highly erodible cropland and other environmentally fragile land out of production.

■ In 1996 Congress reauthorized the Farm Bill (the Federal Agriculture Improvement and Reform Act), which refunded and restructured the Conservation Reserve Program.

THE CONSEQUENCES OF SOIL EROSION

A total of 2.1 billion tons of U.S. cropland soil was lost to wind and water erosion in 1992.[77] Large-scale loss from erosion results in at least two major environmental problems. First, cropland becomes less productive because the soil left after erosion loses its fertility and is unable to supply plants with necessary nutrients. The soil's ability to retain water also is greatly diminished. These changes, in turn, result in higher production costs, including costs for the increased use of petrochemical-based fertilizer. Second, eroded soil causes sedimentation in waterways, which threatens aquatic life and hinders water flow. The erosion of soil by water also carries polluting agricultural chemicals into rivers, streams, lakes, and reservoirs. Though it is difficult to assess the costs of soil erosion, the USDA has estimated that the offsite costs (to society at-large) in the United States are between $2 billion and $8 billion annually, and the direct on-site farm cost is estimated at $1 billion to $18 billion per year.[78]

TYPES OF SOIL EROSION

Soil erosion is caused by wind and water.

Wind erosion: the soil is detached, transported, and deposited by wind.

Sheet erosion: the removal of a fairly uniform layer of soil from the land surface by the action of rainfall and surface runoff.

Rill erosion: the formation of numerous small waste channels, which are only a few inches deep.

Gully erosion: an advanced state of rill erosion in which water accumulates in channels and washes away soil to depths ranging from 1 or 2 feet to as much as 75 to 100 feet.

Streambed erosion: the widening of streams due to water flow and soil loss.

(Sources: Nancy Blanpied, editor, Farm Policy: The Politics of Soil, Surpluses, and Subsidies *[Washington, D.C.: Congressional Quarterly, Inc., 1984],28, NRCS, Texas Summary Report 1992 National Resources Inventory [Washington, D.C., 1997].)*

HIGHLY ERODIBLE CROPLANDS IN TEXAS

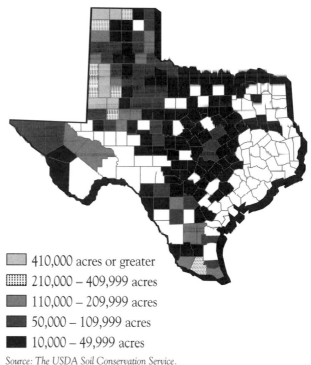

410,000 acres or greater

210,000 – 409,999 acres

110,000 – 209,999 acres

50,000 – 109,999 acres

10,000 – 49,999 acres

Source: The USDA Soil Conservation Service.

Soil erosion levels vary among types of soil. Some erosion is caused by nature and is therefore inevitable, but erosion is also the result of human actions. The amount of soil erosion that most cropland can tolerate without reducing production is termed by the USDA the "T" factor. In Texas, the "T" factor for most cropland is about five tons of soil per acre per year. That is, cropland can lose five tons per acre per year for an indefinite period of time without sacrificing productivity. The objective of conservation practices is to bring erosion levels down to or below this "T" factor.

Of the 28.3 million acres of cropland in Texas, the National Resources Conservation Service estimated that over 36 percent was highly erodible and that 68 percent could benefit from some form of conservation treatment.[79] With an average of approximately 326 million tons of cropland soil lost annually (approximately 13 tons per acre), in 1992 Texas led the nation in the number of tons of eroded cropland soil.[80] Water erosion is the primary concern for the central and eastern parts of Texas. Wind erosion is the primary concern in far west Texas and the Plains region. Both wind and water erosion are concerns in the Rolling Plains and in the southern parts of the state.

FYI 👉 *With 36.8 million acres of prime farmland, Texas has more prime farmland than any other state (see definition of prime farmland, which includes lands in addition to cropland).* (Source: NRCS, *National Resources Inventory,* Graphic Highlights of Natural Resource Trends in the U.S. between 1982 and 1992 *[Washington, D.C., April 1995].)*

CROPLAND EROSION AND SURFACE WATER

The erosion of cropland has impact on more than agricultural production. According to a 1989 study conducted by the National Academy of Sciences, 350 to 400 million acres of agricultural land are estimated to contribute to more than 50 percent of the suspended sediments deposited in surface waters in the United States.[81]

The deposit of sediments in rivers and streams (and their eventual migration into reservoirs, lakes, and estuaries) is a natural, ongoing process, but when accelerated by poor land management, it can cause problems.

The increased murkiness in the water caused by sediment loading decreases light for submerged aquatic vegetation. As a result, both aquatic vegetation and aquatic species that depend on it for breeding and food can decrease. (The relationship between sediment and nutrient runoff from agricultural lands and their effects on estuaries is discussed in the *Water Quality* chapter.) Sediment loading can also fill reservoirs, reducing the amount of available water. It can clog navigable waterways, reduce recreational use of waters, and increase operating costs of water treatment facilities. Still, some sediment deposits can be beneficial. For example, the replenishment of coastal beaches is dependent upon sediment deposits from rivers. In 1989 the USDA estimated that putting 30 to 40 million acres of highly erodible cropland out of production nationally would reduce sediment delivery into surface waters by as much as 200 million tons per year.[82]

Sediments from rivers are continuously deposited in Texas reservoirs, affecting their storage capacity. But the rate and amount of deposition cannot be easily evaluated. The Texas Water Development Board (TWDB), in cooperation with other state and federal agencies, has established a hydrographic survey program to monitor reservoir storage capacity.

The following federal and state agencies have major responsibility for the well-being of the soil:

The Farm Service Agency is the state-level administrative arm of the USDA. It distributes federal funds to producers to assist them in implementing what the USDA regards as the best management practices, including terracing, ponds, wells, irrigation, and agriculture waste facilities. It also administers the Conservation Reserve Program.

The USDA's Natural Resources Conservation Service in Temple, Texas, is responsible for all soil and water conservation programs, the Wetlands Reserve Program, and other programs related to natural resource conservation.

The Texas State Soil and Water Conservation Board in Temple is a state agency with a five-member board elected by delegations from the 213 Soil Conservation Districts. The board coordinates the activities of the Soil and Water Conservation Districts, develops a statewide conservation plan, and is the lead agency for designing site-specific programs to abate non-point-source pollution resulting from agriculture and silviculture.

Texas A&M Research, Education and Extension Service provides a link between agricultural producers and agricultural research. Through county offices, it provides educational programs and materials to producers, farmworkers, and homeowners on a range of subjects, including the proper use of agricultural chemicals, new developments in agricultural technology, and the implementation of effective conservation practices.

SOIL EROSION ABATEMENT PROGRAMS

One of the best treatments for soil erosion and its consequences is to take highly erodible land out of production. To speed this practice along, the 1985 Farm Bill's Conservation Reserve Program (CRP) was formulated to provide financial incentives to farmers who voluntarily take highly erodible cropland and other environmentally sensitive land (e.g., wetlands, wildlife habitat) out of production for ten to fifteen years. "Out of production" means no haying, grazing, or harvesting of the land. The major objectives of the CRP are to decrease erosion, improve water quality, and preserve wildlife habitat.

At the introduction of the program in 1985, the CRP provided farmers with the opportunity to enter into a ten- to fifteen-year contract to take land out of production and in turn to receive an average of $40 per acre per year rental fee and a one-time, fifty-fifty cost share payment to plant a permanent soil-conserving cover. The CRP imposes a 25 percent cap per county on the amount of land eligible for the program. On average, cropland retired under the CRP was eroding at 13 tons per acre per year (the "T" factor for Texas is soil loss greater than 5 tons per acre per year). After the land was taken out of production and grass coverage was established, the average per-acre rate of erosion was reduced to 2 tons per year. Since its inception, the CRP program has been credited with saving nationally 694 million tons of soil per year. It has been estimated that, from 1985 to 1993, the CRP was responsible for reducing erosion nationally by 22 percent.

Experts also point out that there are additional environmental benefits to the CRP, including improvements in air and water quality and an increase in wildlife habitat for game and nongame birds, mammals, and reptiles. These benefits have become apparent in parts of Texas. Soil conservation specialists in Terry and Lubbock counties reported a noticeable reduction in wind erosion and change in air quality as well as increase in wildlife after cropland was enrolled in the CRP. In 1994 the Environmental Working Group stated that the CRP had saved Texas 144.8 million tons of soil. [83]

As the CRP program was beginning to phase out in 1995, criticism began to be voiced. Some critics believed the program was a form of "welfare" for retired farmers because the average age of participating landowners was sixty-four years.[84] Others complained that too much good farmland had been allowed into the program. Meanwhile, residents of the Texas Panhandle, where 20 percent of the farmland went out of production, complained that agriculture-related services, such as cotton gins and seed, pesticide, and equipment dealers were forced out of business. There has also been criticism about the high cost of the program. The direct costs of setting aside 36. 5 million acres nationally is estimated to be $19.2 billion over the life of the CRP contracts. But CRP advocates point out that if farmers who are currently enrolled in the CRP were growing rice, cotton, grains, and other crops eligible for income supports, the deficiency payments would be equal to, if not more than, the CRP costs.[85] As the Congress considered the reauthorization of the 1996 Farm Bill and the CRP, proponents of the CRP suggested that the environmental benefits of the CRP at between $6 billion and $13 billion[86] Proponents of the CRP also suggested that much of the acreage taken out of production would revert to row crops and therefore continue the cycle of crop erosion. Texas Tech University's Department of Agricultural Economics predicted that economic considerations would force farmers to return 64 percent of the land in the

55 counties of the Plains to crop production unless the CRP was extended in 1996.[87]

In the 1996 Farm Bill, the USDA and Congress made some significant changes to the CRP to address some of the above-mentioned criticism. Those changes included the addition of environmental criteria in recognition that agriculture is a major cause of wildlife habitat destruction and alteration, and of non-point-source pollution.

Under the 1996 Farm Bill's CRP, land must meet a new minimum erosion standard. The land must meet one of the following criteria: (1) have an erosion index of eight or higher; (2) be considered a cropped wetland; (3) be devoted to any of number of highly beneficial environmental practices (wildlife habitat, wetland); (4) be subject to scour erosion; (5) be located in a national or state CRP conservation priority area; or (6) be cropland associated with or surrounding non-cropped wetlands. At the encouragement of a wide range of interested parties, the 1996 CRP also incorporated an Environmental Benefit Index (EBI) designed to rank and prioritize CRP applications. The more EBI points received, the better an applicant's chances of being accepted into the program. Some of the EBI factors related to the environment are: (1) proposed planting of a mixture of different native plant species, including legumes, or forbs that will improve wildlife habitat and increase plant diversity; (2) location of offered acreage in the range of a threatened, endangered, or candidate species (one being considered for listing as endangered or threatened) and use of a ground cover that benefits one of these species; and (3) the establishment of permanent wildlife habitat corridors or wildlife habitat.[88]

THE CRP IN TEXAS

From 1986 to 1996, Texas producers received approximately $164 million in rental fees and approximately $100 million in cost sharing in return for taking 3.9 million acres out of production and converting that acreage to grass, legumes, and trees. Texas has had more land in the program than any other state from 1986 until 1996. (Due to the large amount of cropland in Texas, of course, the state has

SOIL CONSERVATION PRACTICES

- Conservation tillage: no till, ridge till, or mulch till (leaving crop residue on top of the soil).
- Taking land out of production.
- Terracing and contour planting to prevent water run-off and soil erosion.
- Planting of high-residue-producing crops.

more acres eligible to be in the CRP.) More than 80 percent of the CRP acreage in Texas, as well as 60 percent of the participating farmers, are in the High Plains and Rolling Plains regions. In 1997 only North Dakota had more acreage enrolled in the CRP than Texas.[89]

The other major erosion-abatement measure created by the 1985 Food Security Act is the Conservation Compliance Provision. This provision required farmers who had highly erodible land and who wanted to retain eligibility for government program benefits, such as deficiency payments, to implement a conservation plan and have it approved by the USDA's Natural Resources Conservation Service by December 31, 1994. Conservation tillage is one good example of mature conservation practices. According to the Conservation Technology Information Center, a not-for-profit organization that provides research on soil conservation, 22.4 percent (4,482,961 acres) of Texas cropland is in conservation tillage.[90] Critics of conservation tillage claim that it increases the use of weed-killing herbicides. Though herbicides might be heavily used during the transition period from conventional tillage to conservation tillage, their use is thereafter phased out.[91] Experts suggest that continued research is needed to better understand the effects of conservation tillage and which crops respond best to the practice.

SUSTAINABLE AGRICULTURE

To address some of the environmental problems associated with agricultural production, agriculture specialists, farmers, and ranchers have been promoting and engaging in practices that lead to sustainable agriculture: a system that protects the environment and increases the vitality of family farms. The underlying goals of sustainability are agricultural productivity and profitability, and environmental quality.[92]

The National Research Council defines sustainable agriculture or alternative agriculture as an approach to agriculture that "deliberately integrates and takes advantage of naturally occurring beneficial interactions."[93] It is not a singular approach to production agriculture, but rather a range of practices, including integrated pest management (see focus piece on *Pesticides* for definition), organic farming, crop rotations, and tillage and planting practices that reduce soil erosion.

A seminal study of conventional and alternative farming practices conducted by the National Research Council in 1989 concluded that (1) farmers who successfully adopt alternative farming systems generally derive significant sustained economic and environmental benefits; (2) broader adoption of successful alternative systems would result in greater economic benefits to farmers and in environmental gains for the nation; (3) federal policies, such as pesticide regulation, water regulation, and agricultural commodity programs, work against the adoption of alternative agricultural practices; (4) a "systems approach" to research is essential to the success and adoption of alternative agricultural practices; and (5) farmers need information and technical assistance to develop the skills to implement alternative agricultural practices.[94] A study conducted in 1995 by Delta Land and Community of Southern agricultural institutions and farmers, concluded that "the lack of marketing alternatives is the key constraint to a more sustainable agricultural systems in the Southern United States."[95] The study also concluded that substantial research will be needed to support sustainable agriculture, but, in turn, sustainable agriculture will help create a profitable rural economy and a healthy environment.

SUBURBAN/URBAN SPRAWL AND THREATS TO FARMLAND

According to the American Farmland Trust, the United States is losing as much topsoil to urban sprawl as it is saving through programs like the Conservation Reserve Program. According to the

Trust, from 1982 to 1992 Texas lost approximately 489,000 acres of prime farmland to suburbs—more than any other state during that period. Two regions in the state were most affected: the Texas Blackland Prairie and the Lower Rio Grande Plain. The Texas Blackland Prairie includes the metropolitan regions of Austin-San Marcos, Waco, Dallas-Fort Worth, and two of the fastest developing counties in the country, Williamson and Collin. The Blackland Prairie is known for its productive soils; they include fertile cropland, pastureland, and rangeland. The Lower Rio Grande Plain, a 2,550-square-mile region, includes the rapidly growing counties of Starr, Hidalgo, and Cameron. According to the Farmland Trust, 85 percent of the development in these counties is on prime farmland that once produced the ruby-red grapefruit, the 1015 sweet onion, and many varieties of oranges, vegetables, and cotton[96] The American Farmland Trust warns that the loss of prime farmland to other uses over the next fifty years could lead the nation to be a net food importer. Loss of prime farmland to urban development can also negatively affect wildlife habitat and aquifer-recharge areas.

Across the country a similar trend is evident. Cities have expanded geographically and have exploded into the adjacent countryside at much greater growth rates than their population increases. For example, architect and city planner Robert Geddes points out that from 1970 to 1990, the population of Cleveland declined by 8 percent, but the city expanded geographically by 33 percent. At the same time, Chicago grew by 4 percent while its urbanized land increased by 46 percent.[97] Demographers predict that there will be a long-term dispersal of the U.S. population into smaller, less densely settled cities and towns. In other words, the pressures to develop on farmland and wilderness areas will continue. This trend is evident in Texas; in 1982, 6.8 million acres, or 4 percent of the state's total surface area, was urban; by 1992 urban acreage had increased 1.4 million acres to 8.2 million acres, or 5 percent of total surface area.[98] Harris County represents another dramatic example of urban expansion. In 1982 urban areas within the county covered 516,000 acres; by 1992, it had expanded 17 percent to cover

approximately 606,000 acres. From 1982 to 1992, Bexar County added 43,000 acres of urban land, Dallas County added 56,000 acres, and Tarrant County added 83,000 acres.

Moreover, an examination of 1994 population data by the Texas Data Center's population expert Steve Murdock concluded that "Texas nonmetropolitan counties, particularly those adjacent to metropolitan counties, continued to show rates of net in-migration, reversing the patterns of net out-migration which occurred during the latter part of the 1980s. Nonmetropolitan counties showed net migration rates that exceeded those for central city areas but were less than those for suburban areas."[99] The Texas State Data Center's figures show that Texas's population will almost double to 33 million by 2030. The majority of this population growth will occur along the I-35 corridor and to the east of it. The Lower Rio Grande Valley is expected to receive the largest increase in population (the result of births, in-migration, and immigration)—a 173 percent increase from 1995 to 2030.[100] This population growth will result in more threats by development to productive agricultural lands, wildlife habitat, and open space.

FARMLAND PROTECTION EFFORTS

Efforts at the federal, state, and local levels are being made to preserve agricultural land threatened by urban sprawl and development. Many communities want to protect agricultural land and timberland not just for its productivity, but also for its environmental, cultural, and scenic benefits.

At the federal level, the 1996 Farm Bill (the Federal Agriculture Improvement and Reform Act) reallocated $2 million for 1997 and $18 million for 1998 to support state and local governments' efforts to protect farmland from development. In 1996, 17 states used these federal dollars to protect farmland through the purchase of agricultural easements. Since Texas is not among the states that has enacted a farmland protection program, it is not eligible for these federal funds. An agricultural easement is a voluntary, legally recorded agreement between a landowner and a not-for-profit conservation organization or land trust. The legal agreement ensures land will be available for agriculture or other open-space uses. The easement limits or prohibits any development or practice that would damage the agricultural or open-space value of the land. The landowner holds title to the land and controls access to the land. Land that has a conservation easement can be bought, sold, and inherited, but the conservation easement is fixed to the land. There are federal, state, and local tax benefits to be derived from the formation of an easement. (See *Wildlife and Biodiversity* chapter for further discussion of conservation easements.) In yet another effort to protect agricultural land, in 1998 a bill was introduced in Congress that would eliminate estate taxes on farm- and ranchland.

Local governments can take actions to preserve farmland. For instance, in Texas the City of Cedar Park in Williamson County passed a land-use ordinance to preserve the rural character of the area and protect existing family ranches. The city council designated approximately 1,700 acres as a "rural/ agricultural district." This special zoning designation allows among other items: (1) hunting, (2) a minimum of 35 acres per home, and (3) ranches and dairy farms, but no commercial feedlots. Another example of local action is the Michigan township of Peninsula, where residents voted to increase their property taxes in order to preserve surrounding farmlands under pressure from development. The voters approved a program called Purchase and Development Rights. Under this program, the township paid selected farmers not to subdivide or sell their land to developers. Here's how it works: If a farm's agricultural value is $2,000 an acre and a developer is willing to pay the landowner $3,500 an acre, the $1,500 per acre difference is considered the "development rights." The township will use program funds to contract to buy the "development rights" and will pay the farmer $1,500 per acre in installment payments over a fifteen-year period.[101] Cities and counties around the country have used similar methods to maintain the economic productivity of agricultural lands and to retain the environmental, scenic, and cultural benefits of those lands. States like California have enacted legislation that supports agriculture by providing property tax relief to landowners who want to continue farming but who live in areas where property taxes are increasing due to real estate speculation and development.

NOTES

1. Roderick Nash, *Wilderness and the American Mind* (New Haven: Yale University Press, 1982), 108.

2. In an effort to the protect one of the state's critical watersheds (denuded forested mountains change the flow of water which can lead to floods and droughts because the eroded soil cannot hold water), New York State designated a large area of the Adirondacks Mountains as a state park some thirteen years after Yellowstone.

3. Joseph Petulla, *American Environmental History*, 2d ed. (Columbus, Ohio: Merrill Publishing, 1988), 239.

4. Roderick Nash, *Wilderness and the American Mind*, 129. According to Gifford Pinochet's grandson, "when he [Gifford Pinochet] spoke of '"wise use"' he meant producing the greatest good for the largest number of people for the longest time. His broad definition of 'good' included watershed protection, recreation, wildlife habitat, as well as timber production, mining, and grazing." According to the grandson, Pinochet would not have agreed with today's national forest and public land policies that favor commodity production over recreation, soil conservation, and genetic diversity. Gifford Pinochet III, "What Is Wise Use?" *Yes: A Journal of Positive Futures* (fall 1997), 36.

5. Texas Parks and Wildlife Department (TPWD), *Texas Parks and Wildlife Conservation Chronicle* (1990), 1. This figures includes 4,790 square miles of inland water area.

6. The Texas General Land Office (GLO) shows that Texas has 3,9997,000 acres of submerged coastal lands, bringing the state's total acreage to 176,190,269.

7. TPWD, Proposed Preamble to the Public Lands Classification System, November 3, 1994. In 1993 the state legislature directed the TPWD to establish a classification system for state parks, wildlife management areas, natural areas, and historical areas.

8. Bob Hall and Mary Lee Kerr, *1991–1992 Green Index: State by State Guide to the Nation's Environmental Health* (Washington, D.C.: Island Press, 1991), 110.

9. Texas Parks and Wildlife Department, *Texas Outdoors, A Report to the Texas Parks and Wildlife Department* (October 1998).

10. TPWD, *1995 Texas Outdoor Recreation Plan* (March 1997), 43.

11. TPWD, *1995 Texas Outdoor Recreation Plan*, 43.

12. TPWD, Consumer Research Division, *1995 Texas Outdoor Recreation Plan : Assessment and Policy Plan* (March 1997), 1.

13. Lisa Love, Brian McGregor, and John L. Crompton, *Recreation in Texas: The 1993 Citizen Survey* (College Station: Texas A&M University, Department of Recreation and Tourism Science, October 1993).

14. TPWD, *Natural Agenda: A Strategic Plan for 1997–2001* (September 1996), 19.

15. TPWD, *Natural Agenda: A Strategic Plan for 1997–2001*, 14.

16. TPWD, *Natural Agenda*, 14.

17. David Barna, National Park Service, Washington, D.C., phone interview with authors, August 1997.

18. Dennis Robertson, USDA, Forest Service, Lufkin, Texas, phone interview with authors, September 1997.

19. The authors do not have information on the historical development of parks in Asia or Africa.

20. Charles Jordan, speech delivered at Urban Park Institute meeting, March 1996, in Austin. Sponsored by Project for Public Spaces, New York.

21. TPWD, *1995 Texas Outdoor Recreation Plan*, 45.

22. World Resources Institute, *The 1994 Information Please Environmental Almanac* (New York: Houghton Mifflin, 1994), 200. (The Texas legislature in 1997 appointed an interim joint committee—the Appropriations and the Recreation and Resources committees—chaired by Representative Edward Kuempel, to study the status of the park system of Texas. The interim study should be completed by the year 2000.)

23. American Lives, Inc., "Community Features Home Buyers Pay For," in *1994 Shopper and Homeowner Study* (San Francisco, March 1995), 2.

24. American Lives, Inc., "Community Features Home Buyers Pay For," 2.

25. Niki McDaniel, public relations director of Nature Conservancy of Texas, phone interview with authors, May 6, 1997.

26. Ted Siff, director, Trust for Public Lands Texas Field Office, letter to authors, December 2, 1997.

27. Some resource planners prefer to rely on vegetation regions to describe the physical differences within the state. According to TPWD, the largest vegetation designations are 10 ecological regions. These 10 ecological regions are, in turn, subdivided into a total of 53 cover types, including 47 plant associations of 2 or 3 characteristic genera or species. Also according to TPWD, "The confusion as to why there are 11 ecoregions (or natural regions) as opposed to 10 vegetative types of regions is a result of a 1978 study and publication of the LBJ School of Public Affairs, in which eleven natural regions were identified." The TPWD recognizes these 11 ecoregion descriptions. The authors wish to thank Jason Singhurst of TPWD for his assistance with the descriptions of the regions.

28. GLO, *Texas Coastal Wetlands: Handbook for Local Governments* (n.d.), ix.

29. Coast Alliance, *State of the Coasts: A State by State Analysis of the Vital Link between Healthy Coasts and a Healthy Economy* (Washington, D.C., 1995), 36.

30. GLO, *Texas Coastal Wetlands: A Handbook for Local Governments* (December 1996), 11. According to this document, in 1993 coastal tourism in Texas provided 103,600 jobs.

31. American Sportfishing Association, *The 1996 Economic Impact of Sport Fishing in Texas* (Alexandria, Va., 1997), 6. This report concludes that the economic impacts of freshwater fishing in Texas in 1996 was $1,916,488,984 and supported 53,401 jobs.

32. Lance Robinson, TPWD, phone interview with authors, January 14, 1997.

33. World Resources Institute, *A WRI Indicator Brief: Coastlines at Risk: An Index of Potential Development-Related Threats to Coastal Ecosystems* (Washington, D.C., 1995),1.

34. World Resources Institute, *A WRI Indicator Brief*, 1.

35. World Resources Institute, *A WRI Indicator Brief*, 1.

36. Wallace Kaufman and Orrin Pilkey, Jr., *The Beaches Are Moving: Drowning of America's Shoreline* (Durham: Duke University Press, 1983), 246.

37. Kaufman and Pilkey, Jr., *The Beaches Are Moving*, 246.

38. The authors wish to thank Peter Ravella, attorney, GLO, for his assistance with the history and interpretation of the Coastal Management Act.

39. Under English common law, the king held title to the tidelands, but the title was held in public trust. English common law in turn relied on Roman law, which declared that the sea and its shore are "res communes," things of common use by all citizens. Kaufman and Pilkey, *The Beaches Are Moving*, 231.

40. Beth Milleman, *And Two If By Sea: Fighting the Attack on America's Coasts* (Washington, D.C.: Coast Alliance, Inc., 1986), 2–8.

41. GLO, *Texas Coastal Management Plan* (993), IX-1.

42. GLO, *Texas Coastal Management Program: Public Document* (March 1994), IX-1.

43. GLO, *Coastal Management Plan: Public Comment Document* (December 1993), II-44.

44. GLO, *Coastal Management Plan: Public Comment Document*, II-44.

45. Bob Morton, Bureau of Economic Geology, phone interview with authors, October 7,1997. For a description and maps of shoreline changes, see Bureau of Economic Geology, 1993 Open-File Report 93-1 and other related documents prepared by Morton.

46. GLO, *Texas Coastwide Erosion Response Plan: A Report to the 75th Legislature* (August 1996), 9.

47. GLO, *Texas Coastwide Erosion Response Plan*, 31.

48. GLO, *Dune Protection and Improvement Manual for the Texas Gulf Coast* (1991), 7–13.

49. Vernon's Texas Statutes and Codes Annotated, Natural Resources Code Sec. 63.001–63.181. See section 63.052 for exemptions.

50. Natural Resources Code Sec. 63.001–63.181. See section 63.052 for exemptions.

51. John Hamilton, GLO, phone interview with authors, July 1997.

52. Kaufman and Pilkey, *The Beaches Are Moving*, 100.

53. GLO, information provided to authors, summer 1997.

54. Joe Riddell, assistant attorney general, Natural Resource Division, Texas Attorney General's Office, information provided to authors, summer 1997. The authors wish to thank Mr. Riddell for his assistance with this subject.

55. TPWD, *Recreational Issues in Texas: A Citizen Survey, The Technical Report* (1987), 9.

56. TPWD, *Texas Outdoor Recreation Plan of 1990* (1990).

57. William H. McWilliams and Roger C. Lord, *Forest Resources of East Texas, Resource Bulletin SO-136* (Washington, D.C.: USDA Forest Service, July 1988), 1–5.

58. McWilliams and Lord, *Forest Resources of East Texas*, 1-5.

59. Kelly Bell, Jr., *Forests and the Texas Economy: Growing toward the 21st Century* (College Station: Texas Forest Service, n.d.).

60. Forests experts predict that 70 percent of the native pine forests in the southern United States will be converted to industrial monoculture pine forests by 2020. Ashley T. Mattoon, "Paper Forests," *World Watch*, March–April 1998, 23.

61. McWilliams and Lord, *Forest Resources of East Texas*, 136; USDA Forest Service, Forest Statistics for East Texas Counties, 1992, Resource Bulletin SO 173 (December 1992).

62. Mattoon, "Paper Forests," 27.

63. Dennis Robertson, USDA, Forest Service, Lufkin, Texas, phone interview with authors, August 27, 1997.

64. U.S. Forest Service, National Forests and Grasslands in Texas: A Congressional Briefing (Lufkin, 1993), 8.

65. U.S. Forest Service, National Forests and Grasslands in Texas: Fingertip Facts (Lufkin, June 20, 1997).

66. See Edward C. Fritz, *The Sterile Forest: The Case against Clearcutting* (Austin: Eakin Press, 1989). Few Texans have been more influential in the efforts to preserve the natural resources and forests of East Texas than Edward ("Ned") Fritz. In 1966 he founded the Texas Committee on Natural Resources, an advocacy group that has for over thirty years worked to ensure that Texas's forest-lands are maintained for wildlife habitat, rather than just timber production. As primary organizer of the Big Thicket Coordinating Committee, Fritz also is credited with persuading Congress to establish the Big Thicket National Preserve.

67. The authors wish to thank Janice Dezanson, issues coordi-nator, Texas Committee on Natural Resources, for her assistance with this segment on forest practices.

68. Henry Chappell, "Discovering the Grasslands," *Texas Parks and Wildlife Magazine* 55, no. 3 (March 1997): 27–34.

69. Dennis Robertson, USDA Forest Service, Lufkin, Texas, letter to authors, September 5, 1997.

70. Delta Land and Community, Inc., *Southern Futures: Opportunities for Sustainable Agricultural Systems* (Almyra, Ark., 1995), 1.

71. TCPA, *The Challenging Face of Texas: Texas through the Year 2026: Economic Growth, Cultural Diversity*. A Report of the Comptroller's Forces of Change Project (August 1992), 21.

72. Gary Preuss, Texas Comptroller's Office, phone interview with authors, May 1999. Total cash receipts for crops and livestock is about twice the gross state product in agriculture. Cash receipts represent total expenditures and GSP represents a value-added quantity.

73. USDA, Natural Resource Conservation Service (NRCS), *Resource Issues* (Temple, Texas, 1997), n.p.

74. TCPA, *Forces of Change: Shaping the Future of Texas* (March 1994), 98–99.

75. USDA, Soil Conservation Service, and NRCS, *Texas Summary Report 1992 National Resources Inventory* (Washington, D.C., 1992).

76. USDA NRCS, *Resource Issues* (Temple, Texas, 1997), n.p.

77. NRCS, *National Resources Inventory, Graphic Highlights of Natural Resource Trends in the U.S. between 1982 and 1992* (Washington, D.C., April 1995), n.p.

78. Nancy Blanpied, ed., *Farm Policy: The Politics of Soil, Surpluses and Subsidies* (Washington, D.C.: Congressional Quarterly, Inc., 1984), 28.

79. NRCS, *Resource Issues* (Temple, Texas, 1997), n.p.

80. USDA, NRCS, *National Resources Inventory, 1982-1992,* (Washington D.C., April 1995), n.p.

81. National Resource Council, *Alternative Agriculture* (Washington, D.C.: National Academy Press, 1989), 115–116.

82. National Resource Council, *Alternative Agriculture*, 115–116.

83. Jean Pagel, "Farm Programs All Played Out?" *Houston Chronicle*, December 4,1994, 1.

84. Susan Warren, "As Soil Conservation Program Expires, Farms Are Bracing for the Consequences," *Wall Street Journal*, September 21, 1994, T4.

85. Farmers growing wheat, cotton, rice, soybeans, sugar, and other crops are eligible to collect deficiency payments. Deficiency payments are based on the difference between the target price and the market price, whichever difference is less. The target price is set by Congress and the USDA and is based on the national average cost of producing a crop. Farmers are eligible to receive a deficiency payment if the market price fails to reach the target price.

86. Soil and Water Conservation Society, *Future Use of Conservation Reserve Program Acres, Policy Position* (Ankemy, Iowa, November 6, 1993).

87. R. T. Erwin and P. N. Johnson, *Economic Evaluation of the Conservation Reserve Program* (Lubbock: Texas Tech University, Department of Agricultural Economics, December 1992), ix.

88. USDA, NRCS, *Fact Sheet: Conservation Reserve Program, Sign-up 16* (Washington, D.C., October 1997).

89. Sam Orange, Farm Service Agency, letter to authors, June 1997.

90. Conservation Technology Information Center, 1220 Potter Drive, West Lafayette, Indiana, phone interview with authors, April 28, 1994.

91. Norman Kempf, USDA, phone interview with authors, April 1994.

92. Jim Worstell, *Opportunities for Sustainable Agricultural Systems* (Almyra, Ark.: Delta Land and Community, September 1995), 1.

93. National Research Council, *Alternative Agriculture*, 3–25.

94. National Research Council, *Alternative Agriculture*, 3–25.

95. Delta Land and Community, Inc., *Southern Futures.*

96. American Farmland Trust, *Farming on the Edge* (Dekalb, Ill.: American Farmland Trust Center for Agriculture in the Environment, Northern Illinois University, March 1997), 10-11. According to the Texas Comptroller's office, Cameron County farmers and ranchers in 1993 earned approximately $116.4 million from field crops and livestock, and crop receipts for Hidalgo County totaled $287.1 million. TCPA, Gaining Ground: A Regional Outlook: Lower Rio Grande, 1995 (1995), 16, 20.

97. Robert Geddes,"The Sprawling American City and the Search for Alternatives: Metropolis Unbound," *The American Prospect*, November-December 1997, 40.

98. USDA, NRCS, *Resource Issues* (Temple, Texas, 1997), n.p.

99. Steve H. Murdock, *Research Brief: Substate Estimates for 1994 Show Strong Growth Continuing in Texas* (College Station: Department of Rural Sociology, Texas A&M University), 1.

100. Texas A &M University System, *Environment and Natural Resources: Trends and Implications,* a publication prepared for the Texas Agricultural and Natural Resources Summit on Environmental and Natural Resource Policy for the 21st Century, held in Kerrville, Texas, November 14–15, 1996 (College Station: Texas A&M University, November 1996), 4.

101. Ron Swoboda," Stopping the Urban Steamroller," *Texas Farmer Stockman*, March 1995.

Mitigation

Mitigation is the attempt to offset potential adverse effects of human activity on the environment. The development of mitigation measures has become an integral part of the regulatory process and of conservation planning efforts. The National Environmental Policy Act of 1969 requires that mitigation measures be included in environmental impact statements, which are detailed studies of the environmental effects of major actions undertaken, funded, or permitted by the federal government. Texas also has established state mitigation policies. For example, the TPWD and the GLO require mitigation for adverse impacts on wetlands.[1] There is also a statutory requirement for mitigation for fish and wildlife habitat lost to large reservoir-development projects.[2] The GLO has an informal policy requiring at least a three-to-one compensation ratio for unavoidable adverse impacts to natural resources on state-owned submerged land.[3] Many state natural resource regulations, moreover, must meet minimum federal standards, which often include mitigation requirements. For example, regulations governing highway construction require revegetation of lands damaged by road development.

Most federal or state legislation requiring mitigation measures does not prescribe the specific mitigation activity that must take place, and mitigation can take many forms. Unfortunately, enforcement of mitigation commitments is sometimes sporadic.[4] For instance, rarely does anyone monitor to see if a developer or an agency has kept its promise to replace a natural wetland with a man-made one. The National Environmental Policy Act regulations define mitigation as follows:[5] (1) Avoiding adverse impacts can be achieved by not taking an action. For example, the Texas State Department of Transportation rerouted a section of State Highway 71 to avoid destroying large old oak trees. (2) Minimizing impacts can be accomplished by limiting the degree of action. For example, the state has built several Austin freeways without frontage roads because

WETLAND BANKERS

In Texas and elsewhere across the country, not-for-profit and for-profit entities are creating and restoring wetlands and selling those wetlands as credits to developers. These credits are used by developers whose projects have destroyed natural wetlands where state and federal regulations require that they mitigate that loss. Texas has six wetlands banks.

they cross aquifer recharge areas. This approach is intended to help limit development near the freeway in order to help protect water quality in the aquifer. (3) Rectification can be accomplished by repairing, rehabilitating, or restoring the affected environment. For example, coal companies operating in some parts of the state are required to design reclamation projects, including revegetation of mined areas. (4) Reducing or eliminating impacts over time can be done through preservation and maintenance activities. (5) Compensating for an impact can consist of replacing or providing substitute resources or environments.

In most mitigation agreements, more of a resource or habitat must be provided than was originally present. Ratios greater than 1:1 are required in part to compensate for unrealized losses and the inability of technology to completely restore the natural environment. For example, if a developer wants to build a planned community in Houston that will destroy 100 acres of wetlands, the developer can propose to create 400 acres of wetlands in a nearby site.

Except for the avoidance option, most mitigation efforts under the National Environmental Policy Act assume that some loss of natural resources is permissible. Options two, three, and four above assume a level of human expertise in designing natural environments or funding that in some situations can be unrealistic. Option five suffers from the same risk. Replacement activities, such as creating a wetland, assume that human-made environments are equal to natural ones and can serve the same valuable functions. There is still much dispute among scientists about whether this is actually the case. No one really knows how to mimic natural systems. This is particularly true with respect to complex systems such as wetlands. A five-year study conducted in Oregon to see how restored and created wetlands measured up to natural ones found that the initial designs were inadequate, that the designs outlined in the permit were not adhered to, and that overall the wetland projects were "fundamentally different" from the wetlands they were supposed to replace.[6] On the other hand, compensation may indeed be a viable option for mitigation activities that involve less-complex ecosystem decisions.

NOTES

1. Texas Parks and Wildlife Code, Section 14.002.
2. Texas Water Code, Section 11.152.
3. Texas General Land Office, *Texas Coastal Management Program: Public Comment Document* (March 1994), IX-21-22.
4. John E. Bonine and Thomas O. McGarity, *The Law of Environmental Protection* (St. Paul, Minn.: West Publishing Co., 1984), 203. For example, in Texas, the Army Corps of Engineers does not monitor its mitigation agreements.
5. 40 CFR 1508.20
6. Leslie Roberts, "Wetlands Trading Is a Loser's Game, Say Ecologists," *Science*, June 25, 1993, 2.

CHAPTER 4

Wildlife and Biodiversity

"The possibility of a healthy relationship between people and the rest of the natural world has been steadily pulled apart."

The Land Report

Judging by the attention that U.S. environmental protection laws are being given today, it would seem that the country's focus on wildlife protection has just begun. In fact, confronted with diminished wildlife species due to increasing populations and extensive hunting, the United States began protecting wildlife and their habitats legislatively in the nineteenth century. By 1870 game animals were rapidly disappearing, elk were almost extinct throughout the country, and buffalo were all but gone.[1] Conditions had become so bad that in 1886 the U.S. Cavalry was called into Yellowstone Park to protect wildlife from poachers. At the same time that protective legislation was being enacted at the national level, game laws to protect the productivity of birds and animals were being adopted at the state level. For the most part, the past and present laws and regulations governing wildlife treat animals, birds, and fish as harvestable resources, much like trees: they limit the amount of wildlife an individual can take at one time in order to protect and maintain the species' reproduction process.

FYI ☞ *Worldwide, several species per hour are facing extinction because of human activity.*

As several recognized scientists noted in a 1997 *Atlantic Monthly* article, "we are entering the first episode of mass extinction in 65 million years—the first ever since human beings came into existence." [2]

Scientists estimate that there could be 14 million to 100 million different species in the world, of which only 1.7 million have been scientifically classified. Of the 1.7 million species, the United Nations Environment Programme's Assessment of Biodiversity reported that between five percent and 20 percent of some groups of animals and plant species are threatened with extinction.[3] As of April 1998, 1,135 endangered plant and animal species that occur in the United States were listed under the Endangered Species Act by the U.S. Fish and Wildlife Service. In a 1997 report, the Nature Conservancy stated that approximately one-third of U.S. plant and animal species are at risk of extinction. Of special concern are the animals that depend on freshwater ecosystems, including mussels, crayfish, fish, and amphibians—and flowering plants.[4]

In 1998 a twenty-year worldwide analysis of the condition of vascular plants painted a grim picture. According to this first global assessment of plants, 34,000 plant species, or one out of every eight plant species worldwide, are at risk of extinction.[5] In the United States, 29 percent of the nation's 16,000 plant species are at risk of extinction. Scientists find this to be alarming news, for plants are the organisms on which all animal life depends. Plants are critical to nature's functioning and to humankind. The loss of plant species can result in the loss of biological diversity, which can in turn cause great changes in the way natural ecosystems function.

The scientists who participated in this worldwide assessment also concluded that agriculture, logging, development, and the invasion of non-native species that crowd out indigenous plants cause the extinction of plant species. In other words, human activity is the cause of plant extinction as well as the extinction of animals.

Still, for some the question remains: Why do we care if the salamander or jaguar or any number of mammals, nonvertebrates, or plant species become extinct? What difference does it make if bottomland forests or coastal dunes or playa lakes are destroyed? Putting aside moral and esthetic reasons, most scientists agree humankind benefits tremendously from the biodiversity of the natural world. From this biodiversity, humanity receives all the tools and products it needs to support life and to flourish. The natural world, on its own, without human interference, has always been able to perform "critical life-support services" that allow civilization to flourish: the purification of air and water; the mitigation of droughts and floods; the generation and preservation of soils and renewal of their fertility; the detoxification and decomposition of wastes; the pollination of crops and natural vegetation; control of the vast majority of potential agricultural pests; and partial control of climate.[6] All of these environmental benefits depend on the intricate and complex interaction and interdependency of species on the planet. Scientists do not know which species we can do without or what losses might result from the extinction of any one species. With that in mind, some scientists conclude that humanity cannot afford the extinction of any species.

SIGNIFICANT FEDERAL WILDLIFE AND HABITAT LEGISLATION

■ In 1900 the Lacy Act authorized activities to protect, preserve, and restore game and other wild birds.
■ In 1903 the Pelican Island National Refuge off the coast of Florida was established as the first federally protected habitat.[7] President Theodore Roosevelt created the Refuge after learning that hunters were killing the birds and selling their feathers to hat makers for use on ladies' hats.
■ In 1916 the National Park Service Organic Act set up the national parks system to provide public recreational areas and to conserve ecologically sensitive acreage.[8]
■ In 1918 the Migratory Bird Treaty prohibited the hunting of all migratory and insect-eating birds except as specifically allowed under federal regulations.
■ In 1937 the Pittman-Robertson Act imposed excise taxes on hunting equipment, such as rifles, shotguns, and ammunition, to support state wildlife conservation programs.
■ In 1958 the Fish and Wildlife Coordination Act

was established to determine how proposed water-resource development projects might adversely affect wildlife.
■ In 1969 the National Environmental Policy Act (NEPA) imposed environmental responsibilities on all agencies of the federal government. With the enactment of NEPA, every federal agency was required to consider the environmental consequences of its actions. One of the most important sections of the act requires an environmental impact statement for federal agency activities or federally funded activities.
■ In 1972 the Marine Mammal Protection Act banned the killing and importing of whales and most other marine mammals.
■ In 1973 the Endangered Species Act was enacted to "provide a means whereby the ecosystems upon which endangered and threatened species depend may be conserved, and to provide a program for the conservation of these species."[9] The Fish and Wildlife Service is responsible for the protection of most threatened and endangered species. The Department of Commerce's National Marine Fisheries Service is responsible for marine mammals and anadromous fish (fish that spend part of their life in fresh water and part in salt water).
■ The 1985 Farm Bill's Swampbuster provisions penalized farmers for wetland conversion to cropland or grazing land.
■ Both the 1990 Farm Bill and 1996 Farm Bill included the Conservation Reserve Program that provides financial assistance to farm and ranch owners for the improvement of wildlife habitat for game and nongame birds, mammals, and reptiles.

In addition to federal laws, the United States is party to a number of international agreements to conserve and protect wildlife, including among others migratory bird treaties with Canada and Mexico; a migratory bird treaty with Japan; the Convention on Nature Protection and Wildlife Preservation in the Western Hemisphere; the International Convention for Northwest Atlantic Fisheries; and the Convention of International Trade in Endangered Species of Wild Fauna and Flora.

ENDANGERED SPECIES ACT

Many authorities believe the most far-reaching legislation protecting wildlife and habitat in the United States has been the federal Endangered Species Act of 1973. Though more than twenty-five years old, this legislation remains controversial. The act establishes not only a process to protect species, but also a process to "conserve the ecosystems upon which threatened and endangered species depend."[10]

In enacting the Endangered Species Act, Congress addressed the question of why we should spend dollars to save nonhuman species. The preamble of the act states that "species of fish, wildlife and plants are of aesthetic, ecological, educational historical, recreational, and scientific value to the Nation and its people."[11] Some people also point out that plant and animal species have important cultural and spiritual significance to humans. Proponents of the act have argued that all living things are part of a biosphere in which each living creature plays a vital role: the loss of one can be detrimental to the whole. In terms of scientific value, scientists point out that the smallest creature—even a slug—can benefit mankind by yielding scientific knowledge, even cures for diseases. By way of illustration, they point to the fungus that produced penicillin, the bark of the yew tree that offers a treatment for some forms of cancer, and an Asian viper's venom that is used in a stroke-prevention medicine. Chemicals from sea sponges and some marine organisms might block arthritis inflammation and fight cancer. Plants and small creatures also benefit agriculture: farmers use insects, plants, and other animals as alternatives to synthetic chemicals for pest and predator control. Aside from these utilitarian and anthropomorphic reasons to preserve earth's species, many believe that every creature has intrinsic value and a right to live no matter what its relationship to humankind or its economic value. Harvard University professor, author, and scientist E. O. Wilson has expressed it this way: "Every kind of organism has reached this moment in time by threading one needle after another, throwing up brilliant artifices to survive and reproduce against nearly impossible odds."[12]

FYI *In the United States about 10 percent of the major medical drugs used today still have as the primary active ingredient a compound extracted from plants, and more than 25 percent of our common medicines contain at least some compounds obtained from plants. (Source: Beryl Brintall Simpson and Molly Conner Orogzaly, Economic Botany. Plants in Our World, 3d edition [New York: McGraw Hill, 1995], 376.)*

The key elements of the Endangered Species Act include:

■ The U.S. Fish and Wildlife Service is required to devise a process for listing endangered or threatened species. An endangered species is one that is threatened with extinction throughout all or a significant portion of its range. A threatened species is one that is on the verge of being endangered. The agency is also required to list the status of the candidate species, a species that is likely to become threatened in the near future.[13] Any person has the right to petition the Fish and Wildlife Service to list a species for the endangered or threatened list. The determination for listing is based on scientific evidence.

■ The Fish and Wildlife Service must develop and implement a recovery plan for listed endangered and threatened species. Recovery plans describe what is needed for a species to recover to the point that it no longer needs to be listed as endangered or threatened. In the United States, fewer than 60 percent of listed species have recovery plans.[14] Species with recovery plans have a better chance of survival than those without.

■ The Fish and Wildlife Service must identify critical habitat of the species. Critical habitat is considered to be any ecosystem that, if altered or destroyed, would lead to species extinction or would hinder the recovery of a species.

■ The Endangered Species Act also sets out requirements that prohibit "the taking, possession, transportation, or sale of any species designated as threatened or endangered without a permit." "Take" under the Endangered Species Act includes killing, capturing, harming, and harassing. Harm includes modifying habitat to the point that the species' breeding, feeding, or sheltering is impaired. There is an exception to the prohibition against "take" in which the service may allow a project to go forth if the "taking" is "incidental" to the project and not the purpose of the project (see discussion below).

■ Under the Endangered Species Act, any federal agency whose actions (building a road, dam, etc.) might affect an endangered species or its habitat requires approval from the Fish and Wildlife Service. The federal agency must first review its own actions to see if those actions might affect any endangered species or its habitat. For projects occurring in Texas, the acting federal agency can consult with the Texas Parks and Wildlife Department (TPWD) to determine whether its proposed actions might affect endangered species or its habitat.

■ Nonfederal actions require approval of the Fish and Wildlife Service where there is a "take" of endangered and threatened species, providing such "taking" is incidental to and not the purpose of the activity. For example, a private landowner who wants to clear land to build a home where land serves as habitat for endangered or threatened species must obtain a 10(a) permit—an incidental taking permit—from the Fish and Wildlife Service.[15] The agency cannot issue an incidental taking permit unless the applicant prepares and submits a Habitat Conservation Plan that spells out the actions to be taken to minimize and mitigate the project's impact on the species, outlines available alternatives to the proposed project, and explains why the alternatives will not be used. Further, an incidental taking permit cannot be issued if the activities prevent a species' survival or recovery. As of April 1999, nationwide there were 252 incidental taking permits with conservation plans and 200 awaiting action. Of the 200 plans in development, the land involved ranges from 10,000 to 500,000 acres.[16]

FYI ☞ *Though the Section 10(a) permitting process—the incidental taking permit—has been available since 1982, the first permit was not issued in Texas until 1992, which gave rise to criticism that the Fish and Wildlife Service was not implementing the most important element of the Endangered Species Act. From 1992 to 1997, the Fish and Wildlife*

Service has not denied any request for incidental-taking permits in Texas, though all the permits have required some form of mitigation activities, including Habitat Conservation Plans.[17]

FYI ☞ *Relying on English common law, the federal Endangered Species Act has treated plant species as different from wildlife. Plants are considered to be a part of the real estate on which they grow, and thus they are legally treated as a part of private property. Animals, however, are part of the public trust and are not owned by the property holder. Therefore, under the Endangered Species Act, the prohibition against a "take" (harming, destroying) of endangered or threatened plant species on private land does not apply. On federal lands, however, it is illegal to destroy, damage, or remove federally listed endangered or threatened plants.*

ENDANGERED SPECIES ACT'S CRITICAL HABITAT DESIGNATION

In addition to listing species as endangered or threatened, the Secretary of Interior can also designate "critical habitats," the habitats necessary to support endangered species. "Critical habitat consists of those areas of land, water, and air space that an endangered or threatened species needs to survive and recover. Under the Endangered Species Act, critical habitat may be one or more large geographic areas, or just a small area depending on the needs and distribution of the species."[18] The Fish and Wildlife Service must take the following steps before designating a critical habitat: (1) the areas of importance to the species must be identified by wildlife biologists; (2) the economic and other impacts of designating an area as a critical habitat are examined; (3) a list of proposed areas is prepared and published in the Federal Register, and comments are requested; (4) after the public review period, any necessary changes are made; and (5) the critical habitat is then officially designated.

Designating a critical habitat has two consequences. Federal agencies must consult with the Fish and Wildlife Service if any of their activities, such as building a reservoir or highway, could affect the critical habitat. Because the Endangered Species Act

TOP 12 CAUSES OF SPECIES LOSS (1992)
(for 660 U.S. endangered and threatened species)

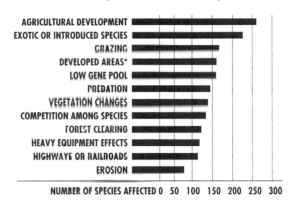

*Note: Developed areas include rural, residential, and industrial areas.

Source: World Resources Institute, The 1994 Information Please Environmental Almanac (New York: Houghton Mifflin Co. 1994), 350. As of April 1999, there were 703 species of plants and 478 species of animals on the federal endangered and threatened list. Another 35 species of plants and 35 species of animals were proposed for listing.

WHERE ARE OUR AT-RISK SPECIES (1992)?
(Habitats supporting 660 U.S. endangered and threatened species)

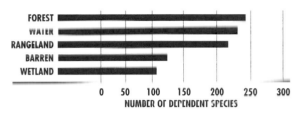

Note: Numbers add to more than 660 species since individual species often rely on more than one habitat to survive. Forest includes deciduous, evergreen, and mixed forests. Rangeland includes herbaceous, mixed, and shrub or brushlands. Barren includes beaches and sand regions other than beaches, dry salt flats, exposed rock, mines/quarries/pits, mixed barren lands, and transition lands. Water includes bays and estuaries, lakes, reservoirs, streams, and canals and other undesignated water ecosystems. Wetland includes forested, nonforested, and non-designated wetlands.

Source: World Resources Institute, The 1994 Information Please Environmental Almanac (New York: Houghton Mifflin Co. 1994), 351.

prevents any federal action that adversely affects critical habitat, the activity planned might have to be altered. The same holds true for any activity or project that requires a federal permit or involves federal funding. The second consequence is to make people aware that the area is important to the survival of an endangered species.

As of April 1999, nationwide 120 species have designated critical habitats and 9 species have proposed critical habitats. The Fish and Wildlife Service has designated critical habitats in Texas for the San Marcos salamander, the San Marcos gambusia (a fish that is probably extinct), the fountain darter, and Texas wild rice, all found in springs in Hays County; the Houston toad, found in parts of Bastrop County; and the Leon Springs pup fish, found in Leon Springs in Pecos County.

For activity occurring on private land that is part of a designated critical habitat, the federal government gets involved only in two instances: (1) if the landowner is planning a project that requires a federal permit or uses federal funds, or (2) if a private landowner's proposed activity might "harm" or "take" endangered or threatened species, in which case the property owner would need to obtain a permit from

the Fish and Wildlife Service.[19]

The Endangered Species Act has received its share of criticism over the years. Environmentalists claim that high-profile species (what some call the "charismatic megafauna" or those with a high "cuddly factor"), such as the bald eagle and grizzly bear, receive disproportionate funding for recovery while plants and invertebrates are allowed to disappear. Meanwhile, others worry that the population of a species may decline substantially while the species waits to be listed as endangered. For example, the golden-cheeked warbler was identified as endangered in 1976 but was not listed until 1990, and during that waiting period, it declined in numbers. Others note that the Endangered Species Act has been more successful in recovery of species on public lands than on private lands.[20] In the United States, 51 percent of endangered and threatened species are found on private lands. For this reason, conservationists and property owners alike are encouraging more financial incentives for private landowners to preserve the habitat of endangered and threatened species.

A fundamental criticism of the Endangered Species Act by conservationists is that it is a crisis-based approach to species protection, designed to save species already on the verge of extinction, rather than fostering a strategy that protects whole ecosystems and thereby prevents species from decreasing to the point where they are endangered. According to these critics, habitat or ecosystem management would constitute a preventive approach to species protection.[21] The act also does not protect species that are declining but unlisted. Moreover, conservationists argue that the lack of dollars is preventing the Fish and Wildlife Service from effectively carrying out the mandates of the act.[22]

Private landowners, who in Texas own approximately 97 percent of the land, argue that the Endangered Species Act has burdened them with

DEFINITIONS RELATING TO ENDANGERED SPECIES

Species: a group of organisms that resemble one another and includes subspecies of fish or wildlife or plants, and any distinct population segment of any species of vertebrate, fish, or wildlife that interbreeds when mature.

Endangered species: those species threatened with extinction throughout all, or a significant portion, of their range. Species can be listed as endangered or threatened for a number of reasons, including disease or predation. Natural or human factors affecting chances for survival: over utilization for commercial, scientific, or recreational purposes, or current or threatened destruction of habitat or range.

Threatened species: species slated to become endangered in the future.

Candidate species: species that are being considered for listing as endangered or threatened, but for which not enough information has yet been collected to warrant listing.

Proposed species: species that have been proposed for listing as endangered or threatened but for which no final ruling by the Department of the Interior has been made.

Biodiversity: the variety of life forms that have developed on earth.

Biosphere: the part of the earth's environment in which living organisms are found and with which they interact to produce a steady-state system, effectively a whole-planet ecosystem.

Community: a group of interacting plants and animals inhabiting a particular area.

Critical habitat: the habitat necessary for an endangered or threatened species to survive and recover. a technical designation used by the Fish and Wildlife Service.

Ecology: the study of the inter-relationship among organisms and between organisms and between all aspects, living and nonliving, of their environment.

Ecosystem: a discrete unit that consists of living and nonliving parts, interacting to form a stable system.

Ecosystem management: a management process that rather than considering natural resources only as commodities (such as timber or fuel) for human use, focuses instead on the ecosystem processes of population (plants, animals) community (a grouping of different organisms living together), and biogeochemical interactions to maintain the condition and function of a site as a whole.

Extirpation: the complete extermination of all individuals of a group in a given area.

Habitat: the living place of a species or community characterized by its physical or biotic properties.

Take: as used in the Endangered Species Act, refers to the harming, hunting, capturing, or killing of endangered or threatened species. Harming includes altering the habitat to the point that it kills or injures endangered or threatened species through the impairment of its breeding, reproductive, and feeding behaviors.[23]

(Sources: Michael Allaby, The Concise Oxford Dictionary of Ecology [Oxford: Oxford University Press, 1994], 51, 187; Endangered Species Act of 1973, 16 US. C.A. SS 1531-1544; National Research Council, Science and the Endangered Species Act [Washington, D.C.: National Academy Press, 1995], 106.)

the major responsibility for protecting endangered species without providing any financial incentive or compensation. These landowners claim that the act lowers property values, and, because of a cumbersome permit process, hinders the owners' ability to sell their property. Some private landowners assert further that the act is an assault on the Fifth Amendment private property right.[24] Many farmers and ranchers who oppose the act argue that they have long been the best stewards of the land and can manage it in an ecologically sound manner without federal guidance or interference. The prevailing myth regarding the Endangered Species Act among landowners is that it prevents private enterprise on private land, such as cutting timber or selling hunting licenses (see discussion, above, of key elements of the Endangered Species Act).

Regardless of the criticism, and while recognizing the limitations of the Endangered Species Act, the National Research Council of the National Academy of Sciences concluded in a 1995 study that the act has "prevented the extinction of some species and slowed the declines of others."[25]

Of equal importance, in Texas and across the country, states, municipalities, conservation groups, and landowners are fashioning new approaches and economic incentives for wildlife and habitat protection that address the concerns of both conservationists and landowners and are mindful of the need for an ecosystem-based approach to managing natural resources. A discussion of these ideas will come later in this chapter.[26]

SIGNIFICANT WILDLIFE AND HABITAT PROTECTION LEGISLATION IN TEXAS

Texas has a legislative history of species and habitat protection. According to author Robin Doughty, overhunting led to a noticeable decline in deer, turkey, and fur-bearing animals in Texas by the 1830s and 1840s.[27] A decline in certain bird species also was documented at this time. In response, the Texas legislature enacted game laws. Game laws are still prevalent today and are used to prevent the demise of, or in some cases to control the proliferation of, specific species.

■ In 1860 the first game law in Texas designated closed season for the hunting of quail on Galveston Island. This law was aimed solely at protecting the quail of Galveston Island, which were being overhunted.[28]

■ In 1879 Governor Oran M. Roberts created the first state institution for the conservation of animals. The State Fish Commissioner was appointed to improve the conditions of freshwater fish species and marine organisms that were being heavily exploited as a food resource and were also being affected by water pollution.[29]

■ In 1903 under the Act to Preserve and Protect Wild Game, Wild Birds and Wild Fowl, the state established a five-year closed season for the hunting of antelope, mountain sheep, and pheasants, and ended commerce in wild animal meat, skins, and plumage.

■ In 1907 a law authorized the new Game, Fish and Oyster Commissioner to sell hunting licenses to finance enforcement of game laws. (In 1910, however, the Texas legislature appropriated the fund for other purposes and little enforcement took place.)

■ In 1925 a state law was passed to establish game preserves on privately held land.

■ In 1973 the Texas legislature enacted a state Endangered Species Act, which was amended in 1981, 1985, and 1987. The act gave the TPWD the authority to establish a list of fish, wildlife, and plants endangered or threatened with statewide extinction. Once listed, these species are afforded protection. The staff of the TPWD makes recommendations stating which species should be listed to the executive director and appointed commissioners of the TPWD. (All federally listed endangered species in Texas are automatically put on the state list.) The Texas legislature has not allowed invertebrates to be listed as endangered and threatened. The state Endangered Species Act does not require the TPWD to design a recovery program for species on the state list, but the agency does develop action plans for those species and does receive money to assist the Fish and Wildlife Service in designing and implementing recovery plans for federal endangered species found in Texas.

Unlike the federal Endangered Species Act, the

STATE AND FEDERAL THREATENED AND ENDANGERED SPECIES IN TEXAS, MARCH 1999

	E	T	LE	ESS	LT	TSS	PE	PT	C1	PD	D
Amphibians	3	10	3		1						
Birds	14	20	15	1	3			1	1		
Fish	9	21	9				1		2		
Mammals	12	20	12		2	1	1		2		
Reptiles	3	21	3		3	1			1		
Invertebrates	2		12					9	4		
Plants	23	5	23		4				7	1	1

Total State Listed: 163

Total Federal Listed: 93 (listed or by similarity of appearance) 5 (proposed listed)

E - State Endangered
T - State Threatened
LE - Federal Listed Endangered
ESS - Federal Endangered Subspecies Similarity

LT - Federal Listed Threatened
TSS - Federal Threatened Subspecies Similarity
PE - Federal Proposed Endangered
PT - Federal Proposed Threatened

C1 - Federal Warrants Listing
PD - Federal Proposed Delisting
D - Federal Delisted

Source: Texas Parks & Wildlife Department, Endangered Resource Division (April 1999).

state's Endangered Species Act makes no provision for the protection of wildlife species from indirect take (e.g., destruction of habitat or unfavorable management practices). The TPWD does have a Memorandum of Understanding with every state agency to conduct a thorough environmental review of state initiated and funded projects, such as highways, reservoirs, land acquisition, and building construction, to determine their potential impact on state endangered or threatened species.

■ In 1983 the Texas legislature established a Special Non-game and Endangered Species Fund to support nongame and endangered species research and management. The fund receives money from fines, the sale of posters, stamps, and decals, and from private donations. Also, the Fish and Wildlife Service shares with the state a portion of the money it receives from the federal excise tax on hunting equipment. The money is used to support nongame and endangered species research and management.

■ In 1991 the 72nd Legislature adopted a bill adding wildlife management to the list of "agricultural uses" that qualified otherwise taxable open land for special appraisal valuation for property tax purposes. Essentially farmers and ranchers who take land out of production and return it to a natural state for the purpose of wildlife management may be taxed according to the land's productivity value rather than its market value.

PUBLIC OPINION

A 1989 Texas A&M survey revealed that 93 percent of Texans believe that endangered species should be protected.[30] A Rice University poll conducted in 1994 showed that 56 percent of those surveyed were willing to spend more tax dollars to set aside and protect wilderness areas for endangered species, while 37 percent were against spending more tax dollars for those purposes. In this same survey, 61 percent of the respondents accepted the idea that "when humans change the natural environment, by

SIX STATES WITH THE MOST ENDANGERED SPECIES

STATE	NUMBER OF FEDERALLY LISTED ENDANGERED SPECIES
Hawaii	298
California	225
Florida	100
Alabama	90
Tennessee	88
Texas	73

The discrepancy between the number listed for Texas by FWS and TPWD is due to several factors: FWS does not associate marine species, such as whales and some turtles, with a specific state, and the FWS web site does not reflect the recent data on the range of certain species.

(Source: U.S. Fish and Wildlife Service Web Page [www.fws.gov]. June 1998].)

building dams or clearing forests, it often produces disastrous results." Moreover, 64 percent of those interviewed agreed with the following view: "Some restrictions on property rights are justified to protect important aspects of the environment, such as wetlands or endangered species."[31] A nationwide telephone poll conducted in May 1996 found that 63 percent of those Americans surveyed opted to protect the environment rather than develop the economy if an impasse between the two occurred. Fifty-eight percent of those surveyed agreed that

a portion of federal government spending should be shifted to environmental programs from other budget areas.[32]

FISH AND WILDLIFE CONDITIONS IN TEXAS

Known for its ecological diversity, Texas is home to 5,500 plant species, 425 of which occur only in Texas. Of the 1,245 vertebrate species (fish, amphibians, reptiles, birds, and mammals) in Texas, 126 are found nowhere else in the world. Texas has more

---

PARTIAL LIST OF SPECIES THAT NO LONGER OCCUR IN TEXAS

MAMMALS
Jaguar: common in Texas during the 1800s; last reported in South Texas in the early 1950s. Now found primarily in Central and South America.
Red wolf: last found in Texas and the United States in 1979; as a pure species in the wild, it is believed to be extinct.
Mexican wolf: believed to have been extirpated from the United States; a few may exist in Mexico.
Black-footed ferret: last seen in Texas in 1963; extinct in the wild in the United States since the mid-1980s.
Grizzly bear: disappeared from Texas about 1890.
Louisiana vole (similar to a mole): last reported seen in eastern Texas about 1900.
Bison: extirpated from Texas prior to 1900; some domesticated herds exist on private ranches.
Desert bighorn: extirpated from Texas by 1959 but is being reintroduced in the state.
Elk: extirpated from Texas prior to 1900; different subspecies have been reintroduced.

BIRDS
Sharp-tailed grouse: last noted in northwest corner of Panhandle in about 1906.
Passenger pigeon: last one reported in the United States died in 1914 and the last reported sighting in Texas was before that; the species is extinct worldwide.
Carolina parakeet: last report of one killed in Bowie County in about 1987.

Ivory-billed woodpecker: has been extinct in the United States since 1972; some might be found in Cuba.
Texas Henslow's sparrow: has been extinct in Texas and the United States since 1983.
Aplomado falcon: is being reintroduced in Texas but is listed as endangered in the United States.

FISHES
Amistad gambusia: last seen in Texas 1968.
San Marcos gambusia: last seen in Texas in 1982 and now considered extinct.
Phantom shiner: last seen in 1975 in the Rio Grande.
Bluntnose shiner: last seen in 1975.

PLANTS*
Boyton's oak
Nickel's cory cactus
Terlingua brickel bush
Old blue penny royal
Small fixed-wort
Grand Prairie evening rose
Young's snowbell
Short-fruited spikes edge
Rose meadow bush

*The plants listed have not been seen in twenty to thirty years and, therefore, are considered "historical" and possibly extinct.

(*Source: Information provided to authors by TPWD, November, 1997. This is not a complete list of all extirpated species.*)

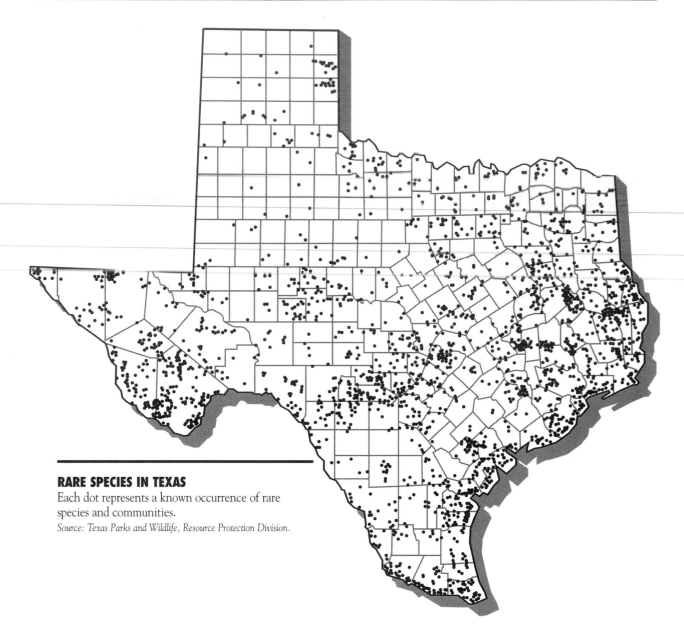

RARE SPECIES IN TEXAS

Each dot represents a known occurrence of rare species and communities.

Source: Texas Parks and Wildlife, Resource Protection Division.

bird species than any other state in the United States. Over 600 species and subspecies of birds regularly breed, migrate, winter, or nest in Texas. The total number of invertebrate species has not been identified, though some sources claim there are 25,000 to 30,000 insects found in Texas.[33]

As of March 1999, under the state's endangered species act, 163 species were listed as endangered or threatened. The number of Texas species included on the federal endangered list totaled 73 (see box on page 150).[34]

Extinction of animal species in Texas has increased dramatically since the turn of the century.

Prior to 1900, three species were known to have disappeared. Between 1901 and 1958, four species are known to have disappeared. From 1959 to the present, 10 species have disappeared. Of these 17 species, six are globally extinct.

The extinction rate of plant species in Texas is difficult to ascertain. The survival of plant species has become of public concern only recently, and inventories are limited. The Environmental Defense Fund's analysis of the Fish and Wildlife Service's 1994 report to Congress concluded that despite protection afforded plants and animals under the Endangered Species Act, federally listed endangered plants and animals in Texas continue to decline.[35] The Fish and Wildlife Service report shows that of 63 endangered plants and animals in Texas for which it had information, 39 percent (25 species) are declining and 24 percent (15 species) are stable or improving. The status of the remaining 37 percent (24 species) could not be determined due to lack of information.[36]

According to the Environmental Defense Fund's analysis of this 1994 report, endangered wildflowers and plants in Texas are faring worse than federally listed endangered animals.[37] Of the 27 endangered plant species found in Texas that the Fish and Wildlife Service studied, 67 percent (18 species) were declining, 8 percent (2 species) were improving, none were considered stable, and the status of 26 percent (7 species) was unknown due to lack of information.[38] Moreover, endangered plants in Texas are faring worse than endangered plants in the rest of the country; Texas endangered plants are declining at twice the national rate. On the other hand, endangered animals found in Texas are doing somewhat better than endangered plant species: 35 percent of the endangered animals in Texas were improving or stable as of 1994.

According to the American Fisheries Society's endangered species committee, Texas is one of the most inhospitable places in the United States for fish species. The state has lost six species of fish since 1900 and four since 1980.[39] In 1997, 25 fish species were on Texas's endangered and threatened list. Interestingly, concern over the decline in freshwater fish species in the mid 1800s helped create Texas's first conservation institution—the Office of Fish Commissioner. Because the Fish Commissioner had limited resources and authority, however, the office did little to improve conditions for fish species. Instead, the Fish Commissioner attempted to compensate for the decline in native species by introducing European carp to Texas.[40]

Though scientists understand the importance of habitat to the life of a species, many questions remain to be answered regarding what constitutes livable space for a species and how species are dependent upon one another for support. Scientists do agree that the destruction or alteration of habitat can threaten the existence of a species. Biologists also know that the loss of one species in an ecosystem can sometimes threaten the balance of the entire ecosystem and may cause its demise.[41]

There are 678 species identified as special to the state of Texas, based on global rarity or federal and state endangered and threatened listing status:[42]

Amphibians	20
Arachnids	5
Birds	56
Crustaceans	19
Fishes	39
Insects	44
Mammals	61
Mollusks	46
Natural Communities	94
Plants	257
Reptiles	37
TOTAL	**678**

In 1996 the TPWD had sufficient funds only to

SPECIES DESIGNATIONS

Flagship species: a species that represents a conservation effort, such as an elephant or giant panda.

Indicator species: a species whose population and health can serve as signals of the overall health and balance of its ecosystem.

Keystone species: an indicator species of pivotal importance to an ecosystem and its biodiversity. Loss of a keystone species changes the makeup of a biological community and could contribute to extinction of other species.

Umbrella species: species whose protection entails the protection of habitats and ecosystems that would confer protection on other (endangered) species.

(*Sources: World Resources Institute*, The 1994 Information Please Environmental Almanac [Boston: Houghton Mifflin, 1994], 348; *National Research Council*, Science and the Endangered Species Act [Washington, D.C.: National Academy Press, 1995], 171.)

study the status of 43 of 68 state-listed endangered and threatened species.[43] The agency's priority is to engage in activities that will help species recover before they are listed. The TPWD has developed regional recovery plans for two species that are not yet listed on the federal endangered and threatened list but are likely candidates: the swift fox and the lesser prairie chicken, both found in the Panhandle.

FYI ☞ *It is estimated that all wildlife viewing in Texas generates $1.4 billion of economic activity in Texas per year. In 1997 a study of three birding sites in South Texas found that birding activity brought in $90 million of revenue to the neighboring communities.* (Source: Ted Eubanks, Austin-based consultant, as reported in "Only California and Florida Draw More U.S. Tourists," Austin American-Statesman, February 27, 1997, D8.)

THE LOSS OF TEXAS WILDLIFE HABITAT

Today the overwhelming majority of losses of, and threats to, wildlife, plants, and natural communities are a direct result of habitat alteration, fragmentation, or destruction, caused by urbanization, development, timber production, reservoirs, and agriculture.[44] A TPWD report entitled *Endangered Resources: Annual Status Report* identified the following habitat losses in Texas:

". . . all but a fraction of the prairies of central and coastal Texas have been converted to farmland, and as a result the Attwater's Prairie Chicken is on the brink of extinction and Texas Prairie Dawn, a plant of the coastal prairies, is now rare . . .

. . . river bottom hardwood forests in Texas have been reduced from 16 to 6 million acres and longleaf pine forests have nearly all been cut-over. As a result of these changes, Texas Trailing Phlox and many other plants are rare, the Ivory-billed Woodpecker is gone from Texas, and the Red-cockaded Woodpecker is threatened with the same fate . . .

. . . the original grasslands of South Texas have been lost to brush invasion, the grassland-dependent Aplomado Falcon disappeared from Texas, the Slender Rush-Pea is endangered, and the South Texas Ambrosia has become rare . . .

. . . sub-tropical woodlands of the Rio Grande Valley have been converted to farmlands and citrus

plantations, resulting in near-extinction of the Ocelot in Texas and increasing rarity for many plants, such as the Texas Ayenia . . .

. . . ground water pumping in West Texas and dam construction throughout the state have modified springs and rivers so that species such as the Amistad Gambusia and Phantom Shiner are extinct, and many other species, such as the Puzzle Sunflower, are rare . . .

THE 21 MOST ENDANGERED ECOSYSTEMS OF THE UNITED STATES

South Florida landscape
Southern Appalachia spruce-fir forest
Longleaf pine forest and savanna (the southeastern U.S., including Texas)
Eastern grasslands and barrens
Northwestern grasslands and savannas
California native grasslands
Coastal communities in lower 48 states and Hawaii
Southwestern riparian forests
Southern California coastal
Hawaiian dry forest
Large streams and rivers in lower 48 states and Hawaii
Caves and karst (a region that is underlain by limestone) systems (caves and karst systems in Texas are included)
Tallgrass prairie
California riparian forests and wetlands
Florida scrub
Ancient Eastern deciduous forest
Ancient forest of Pacific Northwest
Ancient red and white pine forest, Great Lake states
Ancient ponderosa pine forest
Midwestern wetlands
Southern forested wetlands (this includes Texas's forested wetlands)

(Source: U.S. Public Interest Research Group (PIRG) and Sierra Club, Wildlife Need Wild Places: The State of Disappearing Species and Their Habitat [Washington D.C.,1997], 12.)

. . . urbanization and land clearing in Central Texas have destroyed and fragmented woodland habitat of the endangered Golden-cheeked Warbler, along with several rare plants. . . ."[45]

Spring systems also have been affected by water pollution and overutilization by cities and agricultural projects.

Another indication of ecological change is the documentation that marine and brackish fishes have invaded the lower Rio Grande basin as a result of high salinity, which in turn is forcing out freshwater fish.[46]

In Texas 133 million acres of wildlife habitat remain. This includes springs, bottomland hardwoods, coastal wetlands, South Texas brush lands, and Texas prairies. Ninety-seven percent of the land in Texas is privately held. Therefore, the continued existence of wildlife habitat is very much in the hands of the private sector.

WETLANDS: CRITICAL HABITATS

Wetlands ecosystems are second only to the rain forests in the number of wildlife and plant species that depend on them for feeding and habitat. Texas is one of four states, among the lower 48 states, with the greatest wetland acreage.

Wetlands are defined "as areas that are inundated or saturated by surface or ground water at a frequency and duration sufficient to support, and that under normal circumstances do support, a prevalence of vegetation typically adapted for life in saturated soil conditions."[47] Wetlands include marshes, swamps, bogs, playa lakes (shallow lakes), and can include floodplains, and mud flats.

Among their many valuable functions, wetlands filter pollutants that might otherwise flow into rivers, streams, or lakes. Wetlands are often referred to as the "kidneys of the landscape." Riparian wetlands also help prevent erosion of streambeds; their spongelike quality enables them to store heavy rains that could otherwise cause floods. They are the breeding, feeding, and nesting grounds for many endangered species, including plants, and for nonendangered wildlife and natural communities. Wetlands are also used for recreational activities, such as bird

WETLANDS LOSSES (1790 - 1980)

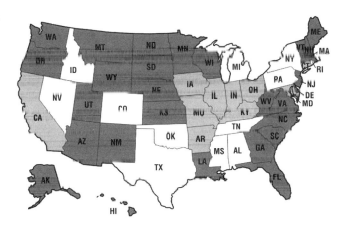

■ 70%
□ 50%
■ less than 50%

The lower 48 states support only an estimated 104 million acres, or 47% of the original wetland acreage.

Source: Texas Parks & Wildlife Department, Texas Wetlands Conservation Plan (1997), 32.

watching, canoeing, fishing, and hiking. Wetlands may be located in cities, on farmland, in forests, and along coastlines and include both saltwater and freshwater systems. The economic, environmental, and recreational value of wetlands is unmeasureable. The only continent on which wetlands do not exist is Antarctica.[48]

Recognizing the tremendous importance of wetlands, the federal government in 1985 established a national goal of "no overall net loss of wetlands." The Clean Water Act is the law that has had the greatest impact on wetlands. Section 404 of the Clean Water Act requires a permit from the Army Corps of Engineers for any dredging or filling into waters of the United States. This includes both terrestrial and coastal wetlands. The 1985 Farm Bill provided financial incentives to protect and restore wetlands on farmland and so too did the 1990 and 1996 farm bills. The farm bills provided financial payments to landowners who restore or protect wetlands on their property. According to the Fish and Wildlife Service, the programs of the 1985 Farm

ESTIMATES OF TEXAS WETLAND ACREAGE

WETLAND TYPE	SHAW AND FREDINE (1956)	DIENER (1975)	KIER et. al. (1977)	TPWD (1980)	GUTHERY et al. (1981)	McADAMS et al. (1982)	NRCS (1994)
Statewide				7,021,637			6,290,800[a]
Coastal Marshes	937,400	1,141,400[b]	472,320	611,760			
Coastal Potholes						89,000	
Bottomland Hardwood				5,973,000			
Swamp		106,880		95,342			
Playa Lakes					341,535		

a. Acreage does not include federal land
b. Acreage includes tidal flats as well as emergent marsh

Source: Texas Parks & Wildlife Department, Texas Wetlands Conservation Plan (1997), 32. S. P. Shaw and C. G. Fredine, Wetlands of the U.S.: Their Extent and Their Value to Waterfowl and Other Wildlife (Washington D.C.: USFS, 1956). R. A. Diener, Cooperative Gulf of Mexico Estuarine Inventory and Study Texas, NOAA Technical Report (Washington D.C., NMFS, 1975). R. S. Kier and L. F. Brun, Jr., Land Resources of Texas – A Map (Austin: University of Texas, Bureau of Economic Geology, 1997). Texas Parks & Wildlife Department, Statewide Vegetation Mapping. Unpublished data. 1980. F. S. Guthery, Playa Assessment Study. Unpublished report on file at Texas Tech University, Lubbock, Texas. M. S. McAdams, Proceedings, International Symposium on Tamaulipan Biotic Province, David Diskind, editor (Asutin: TPWD, 1982). Natural Resources Conservation Service, Texas Tables: 1992 National Resources Inventory (Temple: NRCS, 1992).

Bill restored 90,000 acres to the nation's wetlands between 1987 and 1990.[49]

It is estimated that since European settlement of the lower 48 states, the United States has lost more than half of its coastal and terrestrial wetlands. Today an estimated 104 million acres of wetlands exist. Though their disappearance continues, federal regulations, public awareness, and restoration programs have in the past two decades slowed down the rate of loss. A report issued in 1997 by the Fish and Wildlife Service estimated that between the 1950s and the 1970s the lower 48 states lost 458,000 acres of wetlands annually, and from the 1970s to the 1980s the annual loss rate was approximately 290,000 acres annually. Between 1985 and 1995, the lower states lost 1.2 million acres cumulatively, or 117,000 acres annually. During this period, half of these losses occurred among the forested wetlands in the Southeast, most of which were converted to pine forests (for lumber) or cropland. The Fish and Wildlife Service concluded that between 1985 and 1995, 79 percent of the total wetland losses were due to agriculture.[50] On the other hand, in challenging the study methodology of the Fish and Wildlife Service, the USDA attributes 58 percent of wetland loss during this period to urban development.[51] The Fish and Wildlife Service also reported a loss of 2.5 million acres of forested wetlands from 1985 to 1995, compared with 4.8 million acres in the previous ten years. In 1995 there were fewer than 50 million acres of freshwater, forested wetlands in the lower 48 states.

WETLAND SITES IN TEXAS

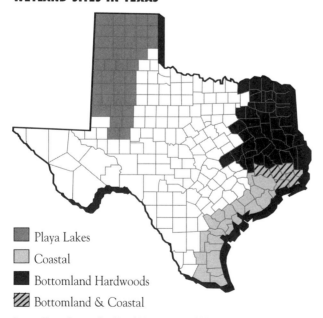

■ Playa Lakes
▨ Coastal
■ Bottomland Hardwoods
▨ Bottomland & Coastal

Source: Texas Comptroller, Fiscal Notes, May, 1993.

STATUS OF WETLANDS IN TEXAS

Texas has lost one-half of its coastal wetlands and 60 percent of its terrestrial wetlands in the past 200 years. There is no state law to protect wetlands. In the coastal management legislation of 1991, Texas legislators did incorporate a no-net-loss of wetlands policy for state-owned land, but the majority of wetlands are on private lands. Wetlands comprise less than 5 percent of the state's total land area.

Four state agencies have significant roles in wetlands protection: the TPWD, the Texas Natural Resource Conservation Commission (TNRCC), the Texas Water Development Board (TWDB), and the General Land Office (GLO). Among federal agencies, the Army Corps of Engineers, the Fish and Wildlife Service, the Farm Service Agency, and USDA's Natural Resources Conservation Service share responsibility for wetlands protection and enhancement.

In 1994 the TPWD initiated the development of a state wetlands conservation plan that focuses on nonregulatory, voluntary approaches to wetland conservation.[52] According to the agency, conserving wetlands will depend on acquisition, cooperative agreements, education, and technical assistance. The TPWD and the GLO were also directed by the

---

WETLAND TYPES: TECHNICAL TERMS

Lacustrine system: a type of wetland traditionally called by such names as lakes, playas, and reservoirs.

Palustrine: a term used to classify a group of vegetated wetlands such as marshes and swamps. Palustrine wetlands are typically dominated by trees, shrubs, and water grasses.

Riverine: a term used to describe a type of nonvegetated wetland that is contained within a channel, which may be natural or human-made. Riverine wetlands include rivers, streams, and creeks.

(*Source: National Resource Conservation Service*, Texas Summary Report: 1992 National Resources Inventory [Temple, Tex.,1995], 53-56.)

Texas legislature to develop a wetlands protection plan for state-owned coastal wetlands.

There are two major types of wetlands: inland/terrestrial wetlands and coastal wetlands. Inland wetlands include bottomland hardwood forest, shrub swamps, marshes, and lakes in East Texas; springs, and riparian vegetation (pertaining to a river-bank) in Central Texas; and playa lakes (shallow lakes), saline lakes, and riparian habitats in West Texas; and individual ponds, pot holes, and "relic meanderings of the Rio Grande" in South Texas.[53] A discussion of coastal wetlands, including salt- and freshwater marshes, is found in the chapter on water quality.

Interior wetlands account for 80 percent of the total wetland acreage in Texas. In the past 250 years, Texas has lost 60 percent of its most valuable inland wetlands: the riparian communities.[54] Most of the inland wetlands are on privately held properties.

BOTTOMLAND FORESTED WETLANDS

Bottomland hardwood systems are the most diverse Texas ecosystems; they are also ranked as one of the most endangered ecosystems in the United States. Bottomland wetlands are plant communities that have been created as a result of the actions of creeks, rivers, and floodplains. The bottomland hardwood forest is a part of a system that starts at a river's headwaters and ends in an estuary at the ocean. Trees found in the bottomland hardwood forests include bald cypress, pecan, oaks, elm, cottonwood, and hackberry. These hardwoods, particularly old-growth hardwoods (50 to 100 years old), contribute to the biodiversity of the wetland system. They also provide food and shelter for wildlife.

At least 189 species of trees and shrubs, 42 woody vines, 75 grasses, and 802 herbaceous plants occur in Texas bottomlands. Bottomland systems also support 116 species of fish, 31 species of amphibians, 54 species of reptiles, 273 species of birds, and 45 species of mammals.[55] Seventy-four species of threatened and endangered animals depend directly on bottomland hardwood systems. Over 50 percent of all the neotropical songbirds that are not listed as endangered or threatened live, nest, or migrate through bottomland hardwood forests. Thirty-one water bird species (mallards and wood ducks), 11 species of fur bearers, and the eastern wild turkey, swamp rabbit, and gray squirrel all depend on bottomland hardwoods.[56]

These bottomland systems, apart from their habitat functions, play a vital role in maintaining water quality. By serving as depositories for sediments, wastes, and pollutants from runoff, bottomland forests enhance the water quality of the bays and estuaries that lie at the lower end of these riparian corridors. Some pollutants are transformed into less-harmful substances by microbiological agents in the floodplain.[57] Bottomlands also help contain floodwaters when rivers overflow.

FYI ☞ *Forested wetland systems support fish and wildlife populations that are an integral part of the state's $4.2 billion hunting and fishing industry.*

In the eighteenth century, the area we now call Texas had approximately 16 million acres of hardwood-bottomland riparian corridors. Today, the state has 5.9 million acres of bottomland hardwoods— a 63 percent loss. This acreage currently comprises three percent of the total land area of the state.[58] The majority of bottomland hardwood acres are found in East Texas; only about one million acres are scattered throughout the western portion of the state.

Both the Texas Forest Service and the TPWD recognize that there has been a steady decline in bottomland hardwood forests since the early eighteenth century.[59] TPWD studies show that losses of bottomland hardwoods are continuing in Texas at the rate of about 12 percent per decade.[60] Reservoirs, development, and agriculture all threaten bottomland hardwood systems, but the consumption of hardwood pulp (ground-up wood fiber) is responsible for the recent upward trend in exploitation of Texas' bottomland ecosystems. Industry analysts expect pulpwood consumption in the United States to increase dramatically in the coming decades, from 82 million tons in 1986 to 173 million tons by 2040, and pulpwood demand worldwide has further stimulated consumption of hardwoods. Much of the wood being chipped in the South today is bound for pulp mills in Japan and Korea. This demand is fueled by the consumption of high-quality computer paper, white cardboard shipping cartons, and other paper products, such as six-pack soda carriers, which require a higher hardwood fiber component.[61] In the United States, Texas ranks seventh in pulpwood consumption by manufacturing industries.[62]

Existing bottomland hardwoods are also threatened by proposed water reservoirs. The 1997 State Water Plan calls for the construction of eight new reservoirs resulting in the loss of 52, 667 acres of bottomland hardwood forests.

PLAYA LAKES

Texas playa lakes—shallow, circular basins—are the wintering wetland habitat for millions of waterfowl that migrate from as far north as Canada. There are approximately 20,000 playa lakes located in 37 counties of the Texas High Plains. The total area of playa basins has been estimated at 341,000 acres. Fifteen million birds annually migrate through these playas in the fall and spring on their way to and from wintering habitat on the Gulf Coast and farther south.[63] Ducks, geese, and sandhill cranes also use these playas as stopovers. The majority of these oases of wildlife habitat are located within cultivated, privately held farmland. Precipitation and irrigation runoff contribute to the development of these wetlands. But land-use practices, such as filling-in wetlands so it can be used for cropland and changes in irrigation methods intended to limit runoff, are reducing the capacity of playas to provide food and water for waterfowl. (Though not officially considered playas, feedlots in the Panhandle also are used as way stations for migrating birds.)

FYI ☞ *A detailed description of recommended wetland conservation activities is found in TPWD's 1997 Texas Wetlands Conservation Plan. For landowners, there is TPWD's Wetlands Assistance Guide for Landowners, which provides a listing of federal and state regulatory and nonregulatory programs and discusses cost-share and technical assistance programs for wetlands and other wildlife habitats. Contact: Texas Parks and Wildlife Department, 4200 Smith School Road, Austin, TX 78744 or 512-389-4328.*

For local governments, the GLO has prepared Texas Coastal Wetlands: A Handbook for Local Governments. *Contact: Texas General Land Office, 1700 Congress, Austin, TX 78701.*

WETLAND AND WILDLIFE HABITAT CONSERVATION PROGRAMS

There are a number of ongoing nonregulatory programs, public-private partnerships, and country-to-country cooperative arrangements aimed at preserving the rich wetlands and other vital wildlife habitats found in Texas. Since most wetlands are located on private land, the success of wetland restoration and preservation is dependent on voluntary landowner participation. The following is a sampling of wetland conservation initiatives. For more information, contact the TPWD in Austin.

Federal Nonregulatory Programs

■ The North American Waterfowl Management Plan was signed in 1986 by the Canadian and U.S. governments. Mexico also has signed an agreement to assist in this effort. The plan's goal is to preserve six million acres of wetlands and to increase North America's waterfowl population to more than 100 million birds by the year 2000. Partnerships of public and private organizations work toward the goal of wetland preservation by purchasing or leasing wetlands or using conservation easements. Farm owners are provided economic incentives to strengthen wildlife habitats. The playa lakes of Texas, New Mexico, Oklahoma, Kansas, and Colorado, and wetlands on the Gulf Coast stretching from Texas to Alabama are joint ventures targeted under this program.

■ The Wetlands Reserve Program established in the 1985 Farm Bill offered landowners payments for restoring and protecting wetlands on their property. The program, though altered, was reauthorized in the 1996 Farm Bill. Under the program, landowners voluntarily sell permanent easements or a thirty-year easement of wetland acreage to the USDA in return for a set land payment and financial assistance to the landowner for wetland restoration activities. The goal of the program is to restore 950,000 acres nationally by the year 2002. For landowners who

sell permanent easements, the land payment equals no more than the agricultural appraisal of the land, and the USDA pays for all the restoration cost. For landowners who sell a thirty-year easement, the USDA provides 75 percent of the restoration cost. In 1997 Texas had eight landowners in seven different counties participating in the program.[64]

■ The 1996 Farm Bill established a new program entitled the Wildlife Habitat Incentive Program. From 1996 through 2002, $50 million has been appropriated to assist landowners around the country with wildlife protection and conservation activities. The USDA's Natural Resources Conservation Service in Temple administers the program in Texas. The program targets wildlife-habitat restoration activities, including restoration of prairies, savannas, and riparian and aquatic habitats.

■ U.S. Fish and Wildlife Service, TPWD, USDA's Natural Resources Conservation Service, and Ducks Unlimited created the Texas Prairie Wetlands Project to provide technical assistance and financial incentives to farmers and ranchers interested in improving or restoring wetland habitats along the Gulf Coast. Through January 1994, 4,901 acres of wetland projects had been completed or were under construction for 30 landowners. Another 132 landowners controlling 1,231,023 acres had received on-site technical assistance.[65]

State Non-Regulatory Programs

■ Since 1976, TPWD biologists through the agency's Private Lands Enhancement Program have provided technical assistance and, in some cases, cost-share assistance, to private landowners who want to enhance, conserve, or develop wildlife habitat, including wetlands, brushlands, and prairies. During fiscal year 1997, TPWD expects to have 1,641 landowners working under a management plan or management recommendations on nearly eight million acres.

■ In 1996 the TPWD established the Landowner Incentive Program, the first program in the United States to provide landowners with grants up to $10,000 to help conserve state or federally listed threatened or endangered species as well as selected vertebrates, invertebrates, and plants. A $100,000 annual budget is dedicated to this program The first $10,000 grant was given to a Lubbock area farmer to help him restore prairie habitat and plant maize for the endangered lesser prairie chicken. The agency anticipates funding 10 to 12 grants a year.

■ Mitigation efforts also are helping to offset the destruction of valuable wetlands.

In addition to these programs, cities such as San Antonio, Corpus Christi, McAllen, and Austin are using their wastewater treatment facilities to provide habitat for birds. The outdoor treatment facilities use grasses and vegetation to filter and purify the wastewater and, in turn, birds are able to use the facilities as watering holes.

INCENTIVES AND DISINCENTIVES FOR WILDLIFE HABITAT PROTECTION

Many resource planners, environmentalists, and landowners are looking toward community planning and various financial and tax incentives for private landowners as a means to preserve habitat. With 97 percent of all land in Texas held privately, an incentives approach seems reasonable. The following are some activities that are being used by other states or being proposed by conservation groups:[66]

■ Local and state property taxes paid on lands providing habitat for endangered, threatened, and candidate species and for lands representing significant biodiversity would be offset by an annual federal income-tax credit. Participating landowners would develop a Habitat Management Plan in cooperation with the Fish and Wildlife Service.

■ Expenses assumed for improving or creating new habitat for endangered, threatened, and candidate species would be eligible for federal tax credit.

■ Lands managed to support endangered species would be deductible from taxable income.

■ The conversion of wildlife habitat to some other use would be subject to a federal tax penalty.

■ The use of federal subsidies and tax benefits for activities causing the loss or degradation of endangered species habitat would be prohibited.

In 1991, the Texas legislature enacted a bill that added wildlife management to the list of agricultural uses that qualified otherwise taxable open land for special appraisal valuation for property tax purposes. To qualify for this wildlife management use, land must be qualified for agricultural appraisal or open-space agricultural appraisal at the time the owner changes its use to wildlife management. Land qualified for timber appraisal is not eligible to qualify for wildlife management use.[67]

HABITAT CONSERVATION PLANS

Most resource scientists agree that wildlife species protection and species conservation generally require an ecosystem approach.

The Endangered Species Act provides for residential and commercial development within an area that has endangered or threatened species habitat whenever a Habitat Conservation Plan is submitted and accepted by the Fish and Wildlife Service. Under this conservation plan, landowners give up their right to develop certain acreage considered critical habitat to the survival of endangered or threatened species. In return, landowners can develop nondesignated acreage without any obligation to protect endangered or threatened species on the land covered by the plan. As of 1999 nationwide there were 252 Habitat Conservation Plan permits issued by the Fish and Wildlife Service, and 200 more were in various stages of development. Nationwide, the majority of the permits are in California. As of April 1999, there were 107 in Texas.[68]

The Environmental Defense Fund, in response to criticism of the Habitat Conservation Plan permit process, conceived of the "safe harbor" conservation agreements for endangered species on private land. The Fish and Wildlife Service adopted a national policy regarding the use of safe harbor agreements in 1997. Under a safe harbor agreement, a landowner is allowed to "freeze" his Endangered Species Act obligations if the landowner agrees to restore, enhance, or create habitat for that species. That is, the landowner can do anything he wants on the new habitat even if another endangered species moves in. His only obligation is to maintain the original habitat for the original endangered or threatened species. For example, if a landowner has habitat on which there are 40 golden-cheeked warblers and the landowner is willing to create habitat for another 100 warblers, and in the future he or she decides to develop the land, the landowner can do so without obtaining an incidental take from the Fish and Wildlife Service if the original habitat for the 40 golden-cheeked warblers is not disturbed or destroyed. Proponents of safe harbor agreements believe that more habitat will be restored or created using this process. In Texas, the safe harbor agreement is being used to restore 14,000 acres of privately held ranchland to benefit the endangered Attwater's prairie chicken. The safe harbor agreement is also being used to enhance ranchland in South Texas for the reintroduction of the aplomado falcon, and in East Texas to preserve habitat for the red-cockaded woodpecker.

The National Wildlife Federation has proposed that the Habitat Conservation Planning process of the Endangered Species Act be incorporated into a newly authorized Community-Based Recovery Planning Process. The process would support local communities, counties, or regions in developing an endangered and threatened species and habitat recovery plan that is proactive and involves the local community and landowners in planning and implementing the recovery.[69]

A "Cooperative Conservation Plan" proposed by some conservation groups would encourage rural agricultural landowners to form cooperative agreements with contiguous or nearly contiguous property owners to accomplish the same goals as the Endangered Species Act's Habitat Conservation Plan without having to participate in a federal conservation plan. The cooperative would operate as a wildlife management cooperative.

A "Habitat Transaction Method" has been proposed by some conservation groups. Its goal is the preservation of habitats sufficient to sustain species or populations addressed by a Habitat Conservation Plan. A process is established for measuring the conservation value of all the land in the area covered by the plan. Any landowner who agrees to conserve or restore habitat within the planning area receives credits based on the conservation value that the landowner adds to the reserve system. Landowners who receive credits for conservation actions may either use the credits to develop elsewhere within the planning area or sell the credits to any other landowner who needs credits to compensate for project impacts.[70]

CONSERVATION EASEMENTS

Conservation Easements are being used in Texas and across the country to protect agricultural land, wildlife habitat, and open space. According to the TPWD, "A conservation easement is a restriction a landowner voluntarily places on specified uses of his property to protect natural, productive, or cultural features. A conservation easement is recorded as a written legal agreement between the landowner and the "holder" of the easement, which may be either a nonprofit conservation organization, a land trust, or a government entity."[71] Under a conservation easement, the landowner retains the legal title to the property and determines the types of land uses to continue (ranching, farming, right to build a home, etc.) and also determines the type of land-use restrictions. For example, a farmer in Hunt County decided to use the conservation easement to protect native prairie remains for future generations. He donated a conservation easement to the Nature Conservancy of Texas. This particular easement allows the landowner to continue to produce hay and to make other uses of the property but restricts any uses of his property that would harm the resource the farmer wants to protect—the native prairie. The Nature Conservancy, in turn, holds the conservation easement and has the obligation to ensure that it is maintained according to the legal agreement.[72] A conservation easement may qualify the landowner for various tax benefits. A landowner whose property has a conservation easement can sell the land at any time or will it to family members (or others), but the conservation easement remains tied to the land and obligates future owners to its terms. For example, a South Texas rancher has donated a conservation easement of 475 acres of prime brush land in order to protect the habitat of the ocelot, which used to thrive in South Texas and now is on

UNITED STATES FISH AND WILDLIFE SERVICE ADDITIONS IN TEXAS

	FY 1998	REMAINING
Brazoria National Wildlife Refuge	0	3,312
San Bernard National Wildlife Refuge	0	3,279
Lower Rio Grande Valley National Wildlife Refuge, Playa del Rio & Coastal Corridor additions	13,033	53,079
Texas Chenier Plain (wetlands for migratory waterfowl along Texas coast)	0	37,510
Trinity River National Wildlife Refuge additions	51	45,360
Additions to Federal Wildlife Refuges in Texas additions to the 7,984 already acquired	0	
Attwater Prairie Chicken National Wildlife Refuge	0	22,016
Balcones Canyonland National wildlife Refuge additions	340	29,979
Austin's woods Units of Brazoria National wildlife Refuge	0	27,277

The term "Remaining" refers to those acres the USFWS plans to acquire if granted congressional appropriations to do so.

the federal endangered species list. (The rancher wants to make certain that his heirs continue to have the opportunity to see this beautiful creature roam wild on the ranch.[73])

Land trusts are legal entities often used to accept conservation easements, though not all land trusts accept conservation easements and most trusts have broader conservation purposes. A land trust is defined as a local, regional, or national nonprofit organization that protects land for its natural, recreational, scenic, historic, or productive value. Land trusts may purchase land or accept donated properties and easements for conservation purposes. Some land trusts only advise and assist landowners in meeting their conservation objectives and do not accept land donations or manage easements. Some land trusts work in specific geographic areas or concentrate on protecting different natural or cultural features (open space, historic sites, park land, farmland).[74] There are twenty land trusts in Texas protecting thousands of acres of farms, ranches, wetlands, wildlife habitat, and river corridors. In addition, the TPWD has spurred the development of a Texas Land Trust Council that will promote land trusts and create uniform standards for their operation and other activities that would be useful to their purposes.

FYI *The TPWD has published a very comprehensive resource entitled* Conservation Easements:

A Guide for Texas Landowners. *Contact the Texas Parks and Wildlife Department, 4200 Smith School Road, Austin, TX 78744.*

WILDLIFE HABITAT ACQUISITION BY TEXAS PARKS AND WILDLIFE

For fiscal years 1998 and 1999, the TPWD was appropriated $1,635,000 for habitat acquisition and $17,116,943 to increase and improve wildlife habitat for public hunting and nonconsumptive activities.[75] Among other activities, the money will be used to operate the TPWD's 52 wildlife management areas, to assist private landowners in developing wildlife management plans, and to conduct wildlife surveys.[76]

WILDLIFE HABITAT ACQUISITIONS BY THE FISH AND WILDLIFE SERVICE

The Fish and Wildlife Service is the principal federal agency responsible for protecting and managing the nation's fish and wildlife and their habitats. In 1997 the agency managed 18 wildlife refuges in Texas, totaling approximately 500,000 acres.

The majority of planned future acquisitions by the Fish and Wildlife Service are additions to existing wildlife sanctuaries, not new refuges.

FYI *In 1997, the TPWD owned or leased approximately 52 wildlife management areas totaling 750,000 acres. The funds used for acquisition and operation of state wildlife management areas is derived* *from an excise tax on hunting equipment and from hunting stamps. No general revenue is used.*

URBAN WILDLIFE HABITAT

Urban Texans need not be left out of habitat conservation activities; they can provide wildlife habitat in their own yards by selecting specific plants and providing other amenities, such as ponds, that might attract songbirds, butterflies, mockingbirds, hummingbirds, small mammals, and reptiles. There is a growing effort by state wildlife agencies, in fact, to increase wildlife habitat in urban and suburban areas rather than to rely solely on national or state wildlife preserves. Even apartment terraces can provide food, water, and shelter. In 1997, 6,000 Texans had their backyards and patios voluntarily certified by the TPWD Backyard Habitat program. Some private developers are specializing in building residential communities that provide for both humans and wildlife by preserving existing trees and shrubs and by planting native and adaptive (naturalizing) plants and grasses that wildlife use for food and shelter. The use of adaptive and native plants and grasses benefits more than wildlife; it can also save homeowners and commercial landowners watering and maintenance costs. Residential and commercial developers are also setting aside land adjacent to developments to be used as both recreational space for humans and habitat for wildlife. (The state of Pennsylvania has published a community planning workbook, *Growing Greener*, that examines ways to incorporate conservation design into subdivision developments.)

FYI *The TPWD has a full packet of information on establishing backyard wildlife habitats, including the book,* The Backyard Naturalist, *and five useful resources booklets:* Texas Natives Ornamental Trees, Hummingbirds and How To Attract them to Your Garden, Butterflies and How to Attract Them to Your Garden, Providing and Maintain Nesting Chimney Swifts, *and* Designing a Backyard Habitat. *Contact: TPWD, Nongame and Urban Program, 4200 Smith School Road, Austin, TX 78744. Check with the agency for the cost of the packet. In addition, a very useful and colorful book entitled* Landscaping with Texas Native Plants, *by*

Sally and Andy Wasowski, provides landscape plans and descriptions of yard plants that are native to each of the 10 vegetation regions of the state.

FYI *During early October of every year, millions of monarch butterflies travel from Canada and the northern United States through Central Texas and Del Rio on their way to Mexico's fir forests, where they remain for the winter.*

FYI *According to a study prepared by the U.S. Census Bureau and the Fish and Wildlife Service, 63 million Americans in 1996 engaged in wildlife viewing as a form of recreation, and almost 40 percent of the U.S. population enjoyed an activity related to fish and wildlife. (Source: U.S. Fish and Wildlife Service, 1996 National Survey of Fishing, Hunting, and Wildlife-Associated Recreation [Washington D.C., 1997].)*

NATURE TOURISM

Starting in the mid-nineteenth century, middle-class and wealthy Europeans began to travel to "wilderness" areas, such as the Alps, to explore nature. Many Europeans also came to the American West to observe and enjoy such scenic areas as Yellowstone and Yosemite. This desire to be in the midst of undisturbed land has continued. As a result, nature travel has become big business in this country as well as others.

Today, nature tourism is defined as "discretionary travel to natural areas that conserves environmental, social, and cultural values while generating an economic benefit to the local community."[77] The Fish and Wildlife Service reports that Americans spent $18 billion in 1991 on wildlife-related travel items. During that same year, outdoor participants in Texas spent $244 million on trip-related (hotel, gasoline, food expenses) nonconsumptive wildlife expenditures (wildlife and bird watching, backpacking, hiking, camping, biking, climbing, photography, and similar activities) as compared to $282 million on trip-related hunting expenditures and $791 million on trip-related fishing expenditures.[78] According to the TPWD, fishing, hunting and nongame wildlife activities in Texas generate $3.4 billion in retail expenditures annually. Fishing generates $1.5 billion;

hunting, $1 billion; and nonconsumptive activities, $0.9 billion annually.

Though hunting and fishing have been the leading activities of nature tourism in Texas, nonconsumptive activities like bird watching, backpacking, camping, and similar activities are showing the most significant rise. In 1993, recognizing the importance of nature travel to the Texas economy, then Governor Ann Richards formed the Governor's Task Force on Nature Tourism in Texas. The task force was co-chaired by the executive directors of the TPWD and the Texas Department of Commerce. It was charged with helping local communities and private land-owners develop passive (viewing, observing) wildlife programs that would conserve wildlife habitat and stimulate economic growth through environmentally based tourism, and that would preserve local, social, and cultural values. The task force gave impetus to the development of the private not-for-profit Texas Nature Tourism Association.

Though nature tourism holds promise for eco-nomic development for local communities, as well as ranchers and farmers, it also has the potential to damage the very environments and the local com-munities it is meant to benefit. Several books have been written on how to minimize the threats that nature tourists pose for natural areas and wildlife habitats. Two useful volumes are *Policies for Maxi-mizing Nature Tourism's Ecological and Economic Benefits*, by Kreg Lindberg (World Resources Institute), and *Nature Tourism: Managing for the Environment*, edited by Tensie Whelan (Island Press).

FYI *A resource book entitled* Nature Tourism in the Lone Star State: Economic Opportunities *is available from the TPWD, 4200 Smith School Road, Austin, TX 78744. Also available from TPWD is* The Great Texas Coastal Birding Trail *map and information guide.*

FYI *For more information on nature tourism, contact the Texas Nature Tourism Association in Austin (www.tourtexas.com) or the Texas Department of Economic Development in Austin (www.tdep.state.tx.us).*

NOTES

1. Alston Chase, *Playing God in Yellowstone: The Destruction of America's First National Park* (San Diego: Harcourt Brace, 1987), 15.

2. Paul Ehrlich, Gretchen C. Daily, Scott C. Daily, Norman Myers, and James Salzman, "No Middle Way on the Environment," *Atlantic Monthly*, December 1997.

3. World Resources Institute, *World Resources: A Guide to the Global Environment, 1996-97* (New York: Oxford University Press, 1996), 247.

4. Stephanie R. Flack and Bruce Stein, *1997 Species Report Card: The State of U.S. Plants and Animals* (Arlington, Va.: The Nature Conservancy, 1997), 12.

5. International Union for Conservation of Nature and Natural Resources, *1997 IUCN Red List of Threatened Plants*. The "Red List" can be obtained from Dr. John Kress, Chair, Department of Botany, National Museum of Natural History, Smithsonian Institution, Washington, D.C.

6. Paul Ehrlich, et al., "No Middle Way on the Environment."

7. Kathryn Kohn, ed., *Balancing on the Brink of Extinction* (Washington, D.C.: Island Press, for the Defenders of Wildlife, 1991), 10.

8. Reed Noss, "From Endangered Species to Biodiversity," in *Balancing on the Brink of Extinction*, ed. Kathryn Kohn (Washington D.C.: Island Press, 1991), 227-230.

9. Endangered Species Act of 1973 16 U.S. C.A.

10. Endangered Species Act of 1973.

11. Endangered Species Act of 1973, 1531 to 1544.

12 . E.O. Wilson, *Diversity of Life* (Cambridge: Harvard University Press, 1992), 345.

13. Candidate species are taxa that are being considered for listing as endangered or threatened, but have not been the subject of a proposal rule. Federal candidate species may receive discretionary protection.

14. United States Public Interest Research Group (PIRG) and Sierra Club, *Wildlife Need Wild Places: The State of Disappearing Species and Their Habitat* (Washington, D.C., September 1997), 22.

15. Though the species themselves can be protected by restricting uses of both private and public lands, there has been judicial dispute over whether Congress intended for the term "taking" to include destruction or alteration of habitat on which species depend. In the 1995 Supreme Court case Babbit vs. Sweet Home Chapter of Com-munities for Greater Oregon, the court concluded that the regulations developed under the Endangered Species Act included protection from habitat destruction, which is the major cause of species extinction on nonfederal lands.

16. U.S. PIRG and Sierra Club, *Wildlife Need Wild Places*, 23.

17. Sybil Vosler, U.S. Fish and Wildlife Service, Austin, phone interview with authors, January 5, 1998.

18. Endangered Species Act of 1973, 1532.

19. U.S. Department of the Interior, Fish and Wildlife Service, Ecological Services, *Critical Habitat* (Austin, n.d.).

20. According to an analysis of U.S. Fish and Wildlife data compiled in 1993, of the endangered and threatened species found entirely on federal land, approximately 18 percent are judged to be improving, and the ratio of declining species to improving species is approximately 1.5 to 1. On the other hand, of species found entirely on private property, only 3 percent are improving, and the ratio of declining species to improving species is 9 to 1. See Environmental Defense Fund, *Rebuilding the Ark: Towards a More Effective Endangered Species Act for Private Lands* (New York, 1996), 3.

21. For in-depth discussion of the scientific aspects of the Endangered Species Act and habitat and ecosystem issues see National Research Council, *Science and the Endangered Species Act* (Washington, D.C.: National Academy Press, 1995).

22. According to the Environmental Defense Fund, since 1976 the number of endangered species has increased more than five-fold, but the funding for the endangered species program of the Fish and Wildlife Service has increased only three fold. Environmental Defense Fund, *Rebuilding the Ark*, 6.

23. There is also what has come to be known as "takings" legislation, which is a type of legislation enacted primarily to thwart the intent of the Endangered Species Act. The term takings in this sense is used by those asserting that the government does not have the right under the Fifth Amendment of the Constitution (". . . nor shall private property be taken for public use without due compensation") to carry out actions that would lower property values without compensating landowners.

24. The Fifth Amendment of the United States Constitution guarantees that private property shall not "be taken for public use, without just compensation."

25. National Research Council, *Science and the Endangered Species Act*, 4.

26. Wendy Hudson, ed., *Building Economic Incentives into Endangered Species Act: A Special Report from the Defenders of Wildlife* (Washington, D.C.: Defenders of Wildlife, December, 1993). This report provides an extensive discussion of the limitations of the Endangered Species Act and offers additional ideas on approaching species and habitat protection.

27. Robin W. Doughty, *Wildlife and Man in Texas* (College Station: Texas A&M Press, 1983), 156.

28. Doughty, *Wildlife and Man in Texas*, 156.

29. Doughty, *Wildlife and Man in Texas*, 107.

30. Lee Ann Linam and Dr. Gary Graham, *Draft Report on Endangered Species for the Environmental Scorecard Project Land Environmental Issues* (Austin: TPWD, Resource Protection Division, 1989).

31. Stephen Klineberg, *Texas Environmental Survey—1994* (Houston: Rice University. Department of Sociology, 1995).

32. National Environmental Education and Training Foundation, *Report Card: Environmental Attitudes and Knowledge in America: The Fifth Annual Survey of Adult Americans* (Washington, D.C., 1996) The survey was prepared for the foundation by Roper Starch Worldwide. The survey was based on a nationally representative sample of 1,003 adult Americans age 18 and older.

33. David Bowles, TPWD, interview by authors, July 22, 1997.

34. Dorinda Scott, TPWD, information provided to authors, April, 1999; U.S. Fish and Wildlife Service, Web Page www.fws.gov/. April 1999.

35. Environmental Defense Fund, *The Disappearing Texans: Improving the Lives of Texas' Rarest Citizens* (Austin, May 1998).

36. U.S. Fish and Wildlife Service, 1994 Report to Congress. *Recovery Program, Endangered and Threatened Species* (Washington D.C., 1994).

37. Environmental Defense Fund, *Disappearing Texans*.

38. Environmental Defense Fund, *Disappearing Texans*.

39. "Race for Survival," *Dallas Morning News*, November 24, 1991.

40. Doughty, *Wildlife and Man in Texas*.

41. For further discussion of the scientific aspects of ecosystems, see National Research Council, *Science and the Endangered Species Act*.

42. TPWD, Resource Protection Division, "Texas Parks and Wildlife Department Texas Natural Heritage Program Special Species/Element List, May, 1993."

43. Patricia Morton, Coordinator for Education and Outreach, TPWD, Endangered Resources Branch, letter to authors, January 7, 1998.

44. TPWD, Resource Protection Division, *Endangered Resources Annual Status Report* (January 1991).

45. TPWD Resource Protection Division, *Endangered Species Conservation in Texas* (n.d.).

46. Salvador Contreras-B. M. Lourdes Lozano-V., "Water, Endangered Fishes, and Development Perspectives in Arid Lands of Mexico," *Conservation Biology* 8, no. 2 (June 1994).

47. This is the definition that has been in use since the 1970s for regulatory purposes by the U.S. Army Corps of Engineers and the EPA.

48. TPWD, *A Wetlands Assistance Guide for Landowners* (1995), 7.

49. TPWD, *Texas Wetlands Conservation Plan* (1997), 28.

50. U.S. Fish and Wildlife Service, *Status and Trends of Wetlands in the Coterminous United States: Projected Trends 1985 to 1995* (Washington, D.C., September 1997).

51. Teresa Ophein, "Wetland Losses Continue But Have Slowed," *National Wetlands Newsletter* no. 6 (November-December 1997) 7.

52. TPWD, *Texas Wetlands Conservation Plan*.

53. TPWD, *Wetlands Assistance: Guide for Landowners* (1995), 7-10.

54. Larry McKinney, Memorandum, "State Wetlands Conservation Plan" (Austin: TPWD, Resource Protection Division, October 7, 1993).

55. Carl D. Fentress, "Wildlife of Bottomlands: Species and Status," in *Bottomland Hardwoods in Texas: Proceedings of an Interagency Workshop on Status and Ecology, May 6-7, 1986*, ed. Craig A. McMahan and Roy G. Frye (Austin: TPWD, Wildlife Division, March 1987), 37.

56. Fentress, "Wildlife of Bottomlands," 37.

57. Roy Frye, "Texas Bottomland Hardwood Forests" Summary Sheet (Austin: TPWD, Resource Protection Division, March 11, 1993).

58. TPWD, *The Texas Wetlands Plan: Addendum to the 1985 Texas Outdoor Recreation Plan* (May 1988), 7.

59. Roger Lord and William H. McWilliams, *Forest Resources of East Texas*, Forest Service Resource Bulletin SO-136 (Lufkin: USDA, n.d.), 29.

60. McKinney, Memorandum, "Statewide Wetlands Conservation Plan."

61. McKinney, Memorandum, "Statewide Wetlands Conservation Plan."

62. *1994-1995 Texas Almanac* (Houston: Gulf Publishing Co., 1994), 100.

63. TPWD, *Texas Wetlands Plan*.

64. Gary Valentine, USDA Natural Resources Conservation Service, Temple, Tex., interview by authors, September 1997.

65. GLO, Coastal Management Division, *Texas Coastal Management Newsletter*, May-June 1994.

66. For a full discussion and description of these ideas see: Wendy Hudson, ed., *Building Economic Incentives into Endangered Species Act*.

67. Texas Comptroller of Public Accounts, *Texas Property Tax: Guidelines for Qualification of Agricultural Land in Wildlife Management Use* (1996).

68. Sybil Vasler, U.S. Fish and Wildlife Service, Austin, information provided to authors, April 16, 1999 (also available at http://www.fws.gov).

69. National Wildlife Federation, *Involving Communities in Conservation: A Policy Position Paper on the Endangered Species Act* (Washington, D.C.: n.d.), 10-21.

70. For a full discussion and description of these ideas see: Wendy Hudson, ed., *Building Economic Incentives into Endangered Species Act.* Also see National Wildlife Federation, *The National Wildlife Federation: Involving Communities in Conservation.*

71. TPWD, *Conservation Easements: A Guide for Texas Landowners* (1997), 2.

72. TPWD, *Conservation Easements*, 2.

73. TPWD, *Conservation Easements*, 11.

74. TPWD, *The Bare Bones of Starting a Land Trust* (n.d.).

75. General Appropriations Bill, HB 1, 75th Legislature, Regular Session, 1997, Parks and Wildlife Department, VI-32.

76. General Appropriations Bill, HB 1, 75th Legislature, Regular Session, 1997, TPWD, VI-29; Bob Cook, TPWD, interview by authors, November 13,1997.

77. Texas Audubon Society, *Facts about Texas' Birds, Wildlife and Habitat: A Texas Briefing Guide for Policy Makers* (Austin, 1997), 1.

78. U.S. Department of the Interior, Fish and Wildlife Service, and U.S. Department of Commerce, Bureau of Census, *1991 National Survey of Fishing, Hunting, and Wildlife-Associated Recreation* (Washington, D.C.: U.S. Government Printing Office, 1993), 3-9. Note: nonconsumptive activities include observing, photographing, and feeding wildlife.

Texas "Takings" Legislation

During the 74th Texas legislative session what has become known as the "Takings" bill was passed.[1] This bill subjects a huge range of government actions to legal challenges from private property owners. The law allows property owners to bring a variety of legal actions to halt or invalidate government actions claimed to cause a "taking," which is defined as 25 percent or greater reduction in property value. If the government wants to carry out actions that result in a "taking," as defined by the terms of this law, it will have to first pay compensation to landowners who challenge the action.

The term "takings" is derived from the Fifth Amendment of the U.S. Constitution, which in part reads, ". . . nor shall private property be taken for public use without due compensation."

This law does not apply only to environmental regulations—it reaches a broad range of government actions in every field. The Texas Farm Bureau and other agricultural and rural landowner organizations were the driving force behind the Texas "takings" bill. Supported by extractive industries, such as mining, timber, agriculture, oil, and gas, "takings" legislation has also been introduced at the national level and in many western states. In fact, much of the "takings" legislation being proposed or passed at the national and state level is an attempt to thwart the intent of the Endangered Species Act and other major environmental and conservation legislation. However, the Texas legislation does not affect the Endangered Species Act or other federal environmental laws.

The Texas "takings" legislation affects only the actions of state and local governmental entities, including institutions of higher education, school districts, municipal utility districts, river authorities, and counties. It has two main components: (1) allowing landowners to sue to stop or invalidate government action that results in a "taking," as defined by the legislation, and (2) requiring that "takings impact assessments" be performed by government entities before they take action, with an option for landowners to sue to stop the action if the governmental entity does not prepare the impact assessment.

NOTES

1. Senate Bill 14, passed by the Texas legislature May 1995.

CHAPTER 5

Air Quality

"Remember when atmospheric contaminants were romantically called stardust?"
Lane Olinghouse

Air pollution can be hazardous to human health. When people breathe dirty air, pollutants may come into direct contact with their lungs. Polluted air can burn eyes, irritate throats, and affect breathing. On days when air pollution is bad, both deaths and hospital admissions increase.[1] So consistent is the association between dirty air and health problems that some epidemiological studies blame air pollution for the premature deaths of more than 50,000 individuals every year from heart disease, lung cancer, pneumonia, asthma, stroke, and bronchitis, among other diseases.[2] Because of the evidence of a rise in air-pollution-related deaths, hospital admissions, and sick days, the U.S. Environmental Protection Agency (EPA) strengthened its standards for both ozone and particulate matter in 1997.[3] Possible health effects of air pollutants that are toxic to human health include cancer; birth defects; damage to the brain, nervous system or respiratory tract; and even, in rare instances, death.[4]

Air pollution also threatens plants, animals, and the natural environment. Common air pollutants can also damage property, dirtying buildings and corroding monuments and statues. And the haze produced by air pollution reduces visibility, affecting a number of activities, including airplane transportation, astronomical investigations by observatories, and tourism at national parks such as the Grand Canyon and Big Bend National Park.

FYI *The average adult is assumed to breathe about 13,000 liters, or 13 cubic meters, of air per day. Children breathe more air per pound of body weight than adults.* (Source: EPA, Health and Environmental Effects of Ground-Level Ozone Fact Sheet [July 17, 1997].)

The first efforts to deal legislatively with visible air pollution occurred in the late nineteenth century and were directed at smoke emissions from steam boilers. Cincinnati and Chicago passed smoke regulations in 1881, and Ohio passed a law to limit these emissions in 1897. Not until the 1940s, however, were new technological designs being phased into factories to reduce black smoke and save fuel.[5] Much less effort was directed at controlling the grime and pollutants generated by oil and gas refineries, utilities, coal-burning locomotives, and automobiles.

By the 1960s new concerns were being raised about urban "smog." Smog is a haze made up of thousands of different compounds. Ozone is its best-known constituent. In fact, excessive ground-level ozone is the most pervasive air pollution problem in the United States, creating both health and environmental effects. (See box: What Is Air Pollution?)

Smog and other air pollutants are particularly damaging when "trapped" at ground level. This may happen in areas that have experienced a temperature inversion, a meteorological phenomenon in which a warm layer of air lies under a cooler, denser layer. A temperature inversion creates a kind of atmospheric blanket that can prevent pollutants generated on the ground from escaping into the upper atmosphere. When a temperature inversion lingers in an area and winds are calm, air pollutants become concentrated. The results can be deadly; in 1948, a temperature inversion over the Pennsylvania town of Donora resulted in the deaths of 20 people and hospitalized hundreds when sulfur, ozone, and air particulates were trapped at ground level.[6]

In the wake of the Donora incident, Congress passed a series of bills to study and research the problem of air pollution. It was not until the 1960 presidential campaign, however, that political leaders began calling for a coordinated, national approach to the problem of ground-level air pollution.

EVENTS IN THE QUEST FOR CLEANER AIR

The following mark significant air pollution events and important steps taken to prevent their recurrence:

■ **In 1948** air pollution trapped by a temperature inversion in Donora, Pennsylvania, resulted in over 6,000 sick residents and 20 deaths.

■ **In 1952** a five-day temperature inversion in London, in December, trapped smoke from open fireplaces and industrial emissions and resulted in the premature deaths of 4,000 people, many of whom had preexisting heart and lung conditions.[7]

■ **In 1963** the federal Clean Air Act provided funds to support state and local air-pollution agencies to initiate interstate air-pollution research and to enforce interstate pollution laws. The act is administered by the Public Health Service of the U.S. Department of Health, Education and Welfare.

WHAT IS AIR POLLUTION?

Air pollution has many different aspects. Whether the pollution is likely to cause environmental or health effects depends on the concentration of pollutants and the amount of time an individual is exposed to them.

Smog is an often-visible haze made up of thousands of constituents, the most abundant, but not necessarily the most toxic, of which is ozone. Ozone—made up of three oxygen atoms—is produced when volatile organic compounds (VOCs) and nitrogen oxides released from natural and human sources combine in the presence of sunlight. Ozone at elevated levels can create breathing problems, particularly in the young, the old, and persons with existing health problems. Exposure to excess ozone reduces lung function by increasing sensitivity to asthma and aging lungs. It may irritate eyes, cause nasal congestion, and reduce resistance to colds and other infections. Ozone at elevated levels is toxic to other living organisms as well; it damages plants and trees by affecting the stability of cell walls.

Particulate matter, which is made up of ash, smoke soot, dust, fibers, and liquid droplets, can be produced by the burning of wood, diesel, and other fuels; agricultural activities, mining, and industrial processes; and traffic on unpaved roads. Particulate matter produces a haze that can cause visibility problems. It also dirties and damages buildings and clothes. Smaller particulates can be inhaled deeply and, with elevated concentrations over an extended period of time, can cause lung damage and bronchitis. Recent studies have linked exposure to these smallest particles to a greater risk of premature death.[8]

Nitrogen oxides result from the burning of fossil fuels, such as coal, natural gas, gasoline, and oil. At present, automobiles are the main source of nitrogen oxide emissions in urban areas. Nitrogen oxides, at elevated concentrations, can damage the respiratory system. They can also be a key ingredient in the formation of both ozone and acid rain.

Sulfur dioxide is released when sulfur-containing fuels, such as coal and oil, are burned. Common sources of sulfur dioxide emissions are electric utilities and certain industrial processes, such as copper smelting. Sulfur dioxide at elevated concentrations can cause respiratory problems and also affects plant and crop production. It also can be a contributing component of acid rain.

Toxic chemicals, which include VOCs such as benzene, toluene and 1,1,1 trichloroethane, when inhaled in elevated concentrations over time, can cause birth defects, cancer, and various other health problems. Sources of toxic emission include industrial processes, such as refineries

Continued on next page

■ **In 1965** the Texas Air Control Board was created under the Texas Clean Air Act to protect Texas air quality by setting standards, criteria levels, and emission limits.

■ **In 1966** a temperature inversion trapped urban air pollution for three days in New York City. Epidemiologists attributed the premature deaths of 168 people to the episode.

■ **In 1970** amendments to the federal Clean Air Act reduced the allowable level of sulfur dioxide from utility smokestacks, phased out lead from gasoline, and required auto makers to cut emissions by 90 percent by 1975. (Congress later, after industry opposition, gave the automobile industry until 1978 to meet auto air pollution standards.) The 1970 act also gave the newly created EPA the power to establish national ambient air quality standards (NAAQs). Standards were authorized for particulate matter, carbon monoxide, sulfur oxides, ozone, and nitrogen dioxide. States were required to develop and implement plans to reduce air pollution to levels below these national standards by 1975.

■ **In 1971** amendments to the Texas Clean Air Act authorized the Texas Air Control Board (the predecessor to the Texas Natural Resource Conservation Commission) to issue air quality permits, which began the following year. Sources of air pollution constructed before 1971, however, are "grandfathered" under the Texas Clean Air Act and do not need to obtain state air quality permits.

WHAT IS AIR POLLUTION? (Continued)

and chemical manufacturers, and small businesses, such as print shops and dry cleaners. VOCs also contribute directly to the formation of ozone, another air pollutant.

Carbon monoxide (CO) is formed when fuel does not burn completely. Cars and trucks are the main contributors. Carbon monoxide interferes with the blood's ability to transport oxygen to cells and tissues. Exposure to elevated levels of carbon monoxide can cause drowsiness, headaches, and sometimes death. Carbon monoxide is particularly hazardous to those who have heart disease or pre-existing lung conditions.

Acid rain forms when the sulfur dioxide, nitrogen oxides, and carbon dioxide emitted from fossil-fuel-burning industrial plants and other combustion processes combine with rain, fog, or snow in the atmosphere. Over time, with conducive geologic conditions, acid rain can increase the acidities of lakes, streams, and soils, disturbing or destroying local environments. Wind can carry pollutants far away from where they originated, creating problems in other states or countries.

Lead is a heavy metal that persists in the environment for decades. The former use of leaded gasoline, which is no longer commercially available in most of the United States, the manufacture of lead-based paint, and lead-acid battery reclamation operations are sources of lead in the air. Emissions from metal smelters are another source. Exposure to lead at high levels and over time can cause brain and other nervous system damage, particularly in children. Excess exposure to lead can also harm wildlife and is known to cause cancer in animals.

Carbon dioxide, a compound naturally found in the atmosphere, is produced by humans and animals and utilized by plants in the photosynthesis process. Carbon dioxide is also produced, however, by electric utilities, cars, petroleum refineries, the burning of wood, and many other sources. The elevated presence of carbon dioxide, as well as other gases such as methane and nitrous oxide, is believed to influence global climate change by preventing heat from escaping out of the atmosphere in a phenomenon known as global warming. The implications of global warming over the long term are serious, including catastrophic floods and droughts.

(*Source:* EPA, The Clean Air Act Amendments: A Guide for Small Businesses [September 1992].)

■ **In 1972** Texas submitted to the EPA the first state implementation plan prepared by the Texas Air Control Board, detailing measures for meeting national ambient air quality standards.

■ **In 1973** the Arab oil embargo drove Congress to pass the Energy Supply and Environmental Coordination Act of 1973. To ease pressure on the oil supply, the act required power plants to switch their fuel sources from oil and natural gas to more-polluting coals. It also temporarily suspended emission limits on power plants and other stationary sources such as refineries.

■ **In 1977** amendments to the federal Clean Air Act required some companies to install new pollution control equipment or face stiff penalties.

■ **In 1979** the EPA relaxed the national ambient air quality standards for ozone, raising the permissible one-hour level from 0.08 to 0.12 parts per million.

■ **In 1979** Texas submitted a revised state implementation plan prepared by the Texas Air Control Board for achieving the national ambient air quality standards by December 1982.

■ **In 1983** the EPA decided to allow states additional time to submit state implementation plan revisions, where needed, and to negotiate the control strategy and rule provisions required to demonstrate attainment of the national ambient air quality standards.

■ **In 1984** an industrial accident in Bhopal, India, at a Union Carbide plant spewed methyl isocyanate gas into the local area, killing more than 2,500 people and hospitalizing tens of thousands.[10]

■ **In 1985** an accident at a Union Carbide plant in Institute, West Virginia, sent a poisonous plume of aldicarb oxime over the town, sending 135 people to the hospital. Only a new chemical batching process, instituted at the West Virginia plant after the Bhopal accident, prevented the release of the more toxic methyl isocyanate.[11]

■ **In 1985** amendments to the Texas Clean Air Act authorized the Texas Air Control Board to levy administrative penalties for violations of state and national air quality regulations and to require the

Texas Air Control Board to review operating permits at 15-year intervals. Texas submitted a revised state implementation plan for Dallas, Tarrant, and El Paso counties designed to achieve the ozone standard within those areas by the end of 1987.

■ **In 1986** the Emergency Planning and Community Right-to-Know Act required companies to report to the EPA both regular and accidental releases to the air, water, or land of more than 300 toxic chemicals. The act also required manufacturing companies to develop emergency response plans to use in the event of accidents.

■ **In 1987** Texas submitted a substantially revised state implementation plan prepared by the Texas Air Control Board to satisfy EPA requirements for demonstrating attainment of the ozone standard by the end of 1991.

■ **In 1990** the federal Clean Air Act amendments, the most far-reaching air pollution prevention legislation ever passed, addressed airborne toxics, acid rain, and the depletion of the ozone layer, and toughened regulations on vehicles, utilities, and other sources of smog-producing emissions.

■ **In 1993** the Texas Air Control Board, the Texas Water Commission, and other agencies merged to form the Texas Natural Resource Conservation Commission (TNRCC).

■ **In 1994** the TNRCC and local officials adopted a state implementation plan to meet federal standards for ozone in four "nonattainment" Texas metropolitan areas: El Paso, Dallas-Fort Worth, Houston-Galveston-Brazoria, and Beaumont-Port Arthur. TNRCC and El Paso officials adopted a state implementation plan for carbon monoxide and particulate matter.

■ **In 1997** the EPA, following a public comment period, adopted new standards for ozone and particulate matter and proposed new regional haze standards for wilderness and protected areas.

■ **In 1999** the EPA rejected a partial state implementation plan for Dallas-Fort Worth and threatened withholding highway funds if a stricter plan was not submitted within eighteen months.

THE 1990 FEDERAL CLEAN AIR ACT

With the passage of the 1990 federal Clean Air Act, Congress toughened national efforts to control air pollution. The 1990 act addresses some new areas in the field of air pollution control. For the first time, Congress took measures to reduce airborne toxics, acid rain, and the depletion of the ozone layer. It strengthened efforts to reduce urban air pollution, in part by imposing new restrictions on mobile sources (cars), and it adopted new market-based approaches to pollution control.

Criteria pollutants. The 1970 and 1977 federal Clean Air Acts required that local metropolitan areas be evaluated by state agencies and the EPA to determine whether they met air-quality standards for five pollutants: ozone, carbon monoxide, total suspended particulate matter, sulfur dioxide, and nitrogen dioxide. By the time the 1990 federal Clean Air Act was passed, lead had been added as a criteria pollutant (in 1978) and particulate matter less than 10 microns in diameter, known as PM10, had replaced total suspended particulates (in 1987). (See Particulate Matter section of this chapter for a discussion of PM10.)

The 1990 Clean Air Act also requires the EPA to periodically review its standards based upon the latest health-based information. In July 1997 the EPA adopted two new standards, adding a new standard for PM2.5, particulate matter less than 2.5 microns, as well as a more stringent 8-hour ozone standard.

Ninety-six metropolitan areas in the United States did not meet the standards for ozone as of April 1993.[12] By September 1998, 38 metropolitan areas still did not meet the 1-hour standard.[13] All but 10 of these cities are required to meet the 1-hour ozone standard by 1999 at the latest, unless they can get special approval from the EPA, and all but Los Angeles—the most heavily polluted city—must comply by 2007 (Los Angeles has until 2010). Further, the 55 most polluted cities had to reduce VOC emissions by 15 percent by 1996 and then continue to reduce either VOCs or nitrogen oxides to a level that will reduce ozone to the federal standard. Similarly, if an area does not meet federal standards for other criteria pollutants, a plan must be developed and implemented to reduce emissions of those pollutants.

Airborne toxics. The 1990 federal Clean Air Act added new protections against toxic air emissions by requiring the EPA to identify industries that release toxic chemicals and requiring major sources of these chemicals to install "maximum achievable control technology" by the year 2003. Sources other than major sources would be required to install less costly forms of control. Currently, 189 air pollutants have been identified by Congress and the EPA as toxic, and 174 industry classifications that release toxic compounds and could thus be subject to regulations also have been identified. Compounds may be added or deleted from the list through a petition process. Despite these improvements, there is still debate about whether the new control technology levels will be stringent enough to protect those living near industries that emit hazardous air pollutants.[14]

Acid rain. Emissions of sulfur dioxide—one of the gases that produces acid rain—are subject to stronger controls and monitoring. Under the 1990 Clean Air Act, power plants are limited to 8.9 million tons per year of sulfur dioxide emissions by the year 2010, down from 19 million tons per year emitted in 1980. This reduction is being accomplished in two phases. In Phase 1, which began in 1995, the 263 "dirtiest" units (at power plants with the most emissions)—most of which are located in the Midwest—had to meet an emissions cap for sulfur dioxide. These units reduced sulfur dioxide emission from 9.4 to 4.8 million tons between 1980 and 1997.[15] In Phase 2, in 2000, the remaining power plants, including those in Texas, must also reduce sulfur dioxide emissions. In addition, both Phase I (beginning in 1996) and Phase II (beginning in 2000) sources must cut nitrogen oxide emissions by some two million tons by 2010.

Atmospheric ozone. Ozone can be helpful or harmful to humans and the environment, depending on where it is. High above the earth in the stratosphere, an ozone layer protects life on earth from harmful ultraviolet radiation from the sun. At ground level, though, ozone is a harmful constituent of smog. The

1990 federal Clean Air Act phased out the production of certain chemicals such as methyl chloroform and freon that may deplete the stratospheric ozone layer and regulated the disposal of other possible ozone-depleting substances.[16]

Mobile sources. The 1990 federal Clean Air Act amendments imposed reductions in the amount of hydrocarbons and nitrogen oxides present in tailpipe exhaust beginning with 1994 vehicles and required that these standards be maintained for 100,000 miles. The act also required the sale of only "reformulated" gasoline, which contains less volatility and toxic components and higher oxygen content, in cities with the highest levels of ground-level ozone pollution. The act also mandates the sale of gasoline with a higher oxygen content in those cities that exceed standards for carbon monoxide. In cities where ozone pollution exceeds standards, the federal act requires consumers to have their car or vehicle tailpipe emissions tested. Vehicles that do not meet the emission standards they were built to meet are to be repaired.

The act encourages the development and sale of low-emission vehicles powered by alternative fuels, such as hydrogen gas, ethanol, liquefied petroleum gas, and natural gas or even electricity. It requires manufacturers to begin producing such cars for sale—starting with the manufacture of 500,000 of these clean-fuel cars for sale in Southern California in 2003.[17] The act also requires private and government owners of large fleets of cars to purchase certain clean-fuel vehicles for their fleets in those cities with the most severe ozone problems.

MARKET INCENTIVES IN TEXAS

Texas is actively developing a variety of market-based mechanisms to reduce air pollution, including ozone precursors, nitrogen oxide, and emissions from cars. These mechanisms can be divided into four basic levels of market-based incentive programs: emissions reduction credits; reasonably available control technology (RACT) emissions credits; mobile emissions reduction credits (MERC); and a proposed new type of emissions credit known as the discrete emissions reduction credit (DERC).

Emission reductions credit banking program. Under the federal Clean Air Act, any major new source of emissions in those areas that do not meet ozone standards — Houston-Galveston-Brazoria, Dallas-Fort Worth, El Paso and Beaumont-Port Arthur — must be more than offset by the reduced emissions from existing sources. For example, in order for a new industry that emits 50 tons per year of either nitrogen oxide or VOCs to locate in the El Paso area, there must be a corresponding reduction of 60 tons per year of those pollutants within El Paso.

"Emission reduction credits" are seen as a flexible alternative that allows growth to occur while reducing overall pollution as required by the Clean Air Act. Under Texas's Emission Reductions Banking Rule, adopted in 1993, sources of VOC and nitrogen oxide emissions receive emission reduction credits if they reduce emissions below the level required by law, either through a permanent reduction in emissions or by closing an emission source. These reduction credits are certified by the TNRCC and recorded or "deposited" in the Emissions Reductions Bank. A company can then sell its credits to companies within the same nonattainment area that need offsets for new permits or expansion of existing facilities. In all, by early 1999, 35 companies had engaged in 52 transfers of emission credits, totaling 2,500 tons of VOCs and 11,400 tons of nitrogen oxides.[18]

Reasonably available control technology (RACT) emissions credit. Under the Clean Air Act, existing major sources of VOC and nitrogen oxide emissions in nonattainment areas are expected to meet certain emission standards for these pollutants. Under rules developed by the TNRCC, rather than meet these standards, a

Continued on next page

USING THE MARKET TO CONTROL POLLUTION.

The 1990 Clean Air Act significantly changed the government's approach to controlling air pollution, embracing for the first time a market-based strategy designed to give utility companies incentives to comply.

Here's how the system works. Under Title IV of the Clean Air Act, each of the 110 electric utilities with the most sulfur dioxide emissions is granted a set number of pollution "allowances" based on its historical fuel use. An allowance is equivalent to one ton of sulfur dioxide emissions. Each utility may emit sulfur dioxide up to the limit—the "cap"—imposed by its allowances. However, if a utility emits less than its allotted amount, by being more efficient, by using a lower-sulfur fuel, or by using a renewable energy source like solar or hydroelectric power, it may sell its unused allowances to another utility as "pollution credits." Conversely, if a utility cannot stay within the limits imposed by its allowances, it can buy pollution credits from a less-polluting utility. The system has two major advantages: it rewards companies that pollute less and yet it is flexible enough to accommodate companies that cannot meet the standard of pollution control.

The traditional "command and control" approach usually employed in environmental legislation—where standards are set and enforced equally for all regulated entities—would have required two different companies to reduce emissions in the same way. The market system, on the other hand, permits company A to reduce emissions to meet the requirements for both emitters and then sell some of these

---

MARKET INCENTIVES IN TEXAS (Continued)

source could instead buy emission credits from other industries reducing emissions. For example, a single industrial plant with multiple production units could trade across those units to achieve allowable emission levels even if some individual units did not comply. Or, two different facilities could trade among themselves. In all cases, a company could not use emission credits to increase pollution, only to meet the RACT emission levels.

Mobile emission reduction credits. Under rules adopted by the TNRCC, a private or public fleet of vehicles that needs to comply with Clean Air Act requirements for low-emission vehicle (LEV) standards may earn mobile emission reduction credits (MERCs) or program compliance credits (PCCs) by acquiring LEVs earlier than required, by acquiring more than required, or by acquiring fleet vehicles that are certified to meet an emission standard more stringent than the LEV, including the zero-emission vehicle standard. These credits can be banked, traded, or transferred to other fleet operators unable to comply with fleet regulations within the ozone nonattainment area. In addition, under rules being developed for the state's accelerated vehicle retirement program,

high-emitting vehicles may be retired earlier by fleet operators, with the reduction credits being sold to other fleet operators or even to stationary sources trying to meet RACT rules.

Discrete emission reduction credit (DERC) program. Under rules adopted by the TNRCC in late 1997, an "open" market in reduction credits would be created in Texas, using DERCs. Unlike regular emission reduction credits, which are based upon permanent reductions certified by the TNRCC before being traded or banked, a source would measure an actual reduction and trade it to another company, which would then seek regulatory approval from TNRCC to comply with permit levels or new regulations based on the reduction. While this "open" market approach might spur more trading among companies, it might not help communities reduce actual emissions, because DERCs are not permanent reductions. In fact, it could even lead to an increase in emissions as a company produces a DERC one year but not the next. For this and other reasons, DERCs are quite controversial.

(Source: Office of Air Quality, TNRCC, Austin)

allowances to Company B at a lower price than would be needed for B to reduce pollutants. Both companies stay in business and overall pollution is reduced.

There are potential flaws in this "free trade" system. For example, the allowance program assumes that reductions in sulfur dioxide emissions will be of equal benefit to human health and the environment regardless of where they are made. This is not always true; some areas of the country are more prone to acid rain than others. Emission reductions in an area where such emissions do not contribute to an acid rain problem will do little to help regions that are subject to such problems. The Adirondack Council, the local governing structure of the famous state park in upstate New York, has protested the fact that New England utilities will be allowed to sell pollution credits to midwestern utilities, whose pollution is the source of acid rain already damaging northeastern forests, lakes, and rivers. Thus, even if utilities in the Northeast significantly reduce emissions, the area environment will not improve if midwestern utilities do not also reduce emissions.[19] Because of these problems, the EPA has recently proposed new, stricter regulations on major utilities in the Midwest and Northeast for nitrogen oxide emissions beginning in 2000 (nitrogen oxides, along with sulfur dioxide, contribute to acid rain formation).[20]

Texas has embraced several of these new market-based approaches in its effort to reduce pollution (see box: Market Incentives in Texas).

How these efforts will ultimately improve air quality is still unknown. The EPA says that 113 million Americans now live in 130 metropolitan areas that are nonattainment areas for at least one of the six main air pollutants targeted by the federal Clean Air Act.[21] In addition, there are possible global problems—such as ozone depletion and global warming—that may defy strictly national solutions and require international agreements, such as the December 1997 Kyoto Agreement, to reduce global greenhouse gas emissions. Other "air" issues, such as indoor air pollution, are not addressed by the federal Clean Air Act at all.

Moreover, none of the changes mandated by the law come cheaply. Industries large and small have felt the effects of the federal Clean Air Act and regulations adopted pursuant to the act. Because the act greatly expands the scope of government regulation, the government's cost of monitoring and enforcing air-quality law also has increased.

These anticipated economic impacts were a primary component in the debate over the 1990 Clean Air Amendments and in the recent debate over the strengthening of the ozone and particulate matter standard. Still, the federal Clean Air Act and new federal and state regulations are creating new markets for alternative fuels, pollution control equipment, and new services, thus creating new jobs. And supporters believe that the economic value of the act's public-health benefits—measured in fewer sick days, hospitalizations, and deaths—more than offset initial economic costs.[22]

FYI *A 1997 EPA study concluded that programs mandated by the federal Clean Air Act created between $6 and $50 trillion in savings and benefits due to avoidance of premature deaths and illnesses, while costing only $523 billion over the same 20-year period.* (Source: EPA, The Benefits and Costs of the Clean Air Act, 1970 to 1990 [October 1997]).

With 19 million cars on its roads; 437 electric utility generators using gas, oil, coal, and other sources of fuel; 60 percent of the nation's petrochemical production; 25 percent of the nation's refining capacity; and a population of approximately 19 million people, Texas must grapple with the full range of clean air issues. Nearly 45 percent of the state's population currently lives in metropolitan areas that do not meet federal standards for clean air.[23]

This chapter discusses air quality in Texas, outlining the problems and summarizing the efforts to deal with them. It is divided into six sections:

- **National Ambient Air Quality Standards**
- **Clean Air Act Compliance in Texas**
- **Other Air Quality Issues**
- **Mobile Sources**
- **Major Stationary Sources**
- **Small Businesses and Minor Stationary Sources**

NATIONAL AMBIENT AIR QUALITY STANDARDS (NAAQS)

POLLUTANT	AVERAGING PERIOD	PRIMARY NAAQS**	NOTES
Ozone*	1-Hour	0.125 ppm	1
	8-Hour	0.085 ppm	2
Carbon	1-Hour	35.50 ppm	3
Monoxide	8-Hour	9.50 ppm	3
Sulfur	Annual	0.035 ppm	4
Dioxide	24-Hour	0.145 ppm	3
Nitrogen	Annual	0.054 ppm	4
Dioxide			
Respirable	24-Hour	155.00 μg/m³	5
Particulate Matter	Annual	51.00 μg/m³	6
(PM10)			
Fine Particulate	24-Hour	65 μg/m³	7
Matter (PM2.5)	Annual	15.00 μg/m³	6
Lead	Quarter	1.55 μg/m³	4

ppm = parts per million
μg/m³ = micrograms per cubic meter

1. Not to be at or above this level more than 3 days over 3 years. The 1-hour ozone standard is being phased out.
2. Average of yearly fourth highest 8-hour ozone level over 3 years not be at or above this level.
3. Not to be at or above this level more than once per calendar year.
4. Not to be at or above this level.
5. Three-year average of the 99th percentile of concentrations not to be at or above this level.
6. Three-year average not to be at or above this level.
7. Three-year average of the 98th percentile of concentrations not to be at or above this level.
*The 1-hour standard applies only to communities that did not meet the one-hour standard when the 8-hour standard was adopted in July, 1997.
**Primary NAAQS levels reported here represent the concentrations required to exceed the standard. For example, standard for 24-hour respirable particulate matter is actually 150 μg/m³ but an exceedence is measured at 155 uμg/m³ due to rounding conventions.

NATIONAL AMBIENT AIR QUALITY STANDARDS

The 1990 federal Clean Air Act sets forth air-quality standards for six pollutants: ozone (O_3), carbon monoxide (CO), sulfur dioxide (SO_2), nitrogen dioxide (NO_2), respirable particulate matter (PM10), and lead (Pb). The EPA has determined an allowable ambient limit for each of these pollutants. This limit is intended to protect the public from exposure to dangerous levels of pollution. These national standards are known as the national ambient air quality standards.

COMPARISON OF OLD AND NEW NATIONAL AMBIENT AIR QUALITY STANDARDS FOR OZONE AND PARTICULATE MATTER

POLLUTANT	AVERAGING PERIOD	OLD PRIMARY STANDARD	NEW PRIMARY STANDARD	NOTES
Ozone	1-Hour	0.125 ppm	None	1
	8 Hour	None	0.085	2
Particulate	24-Hour	155 μg/m³	155 μg/m³	3
Matter 10	Annual	50 μg/m³	50 μg/m³	4
Particulate	24-Hour	None	65 μg/m³	5
Matter 2.5	Annual	None	15 μg/m³	6

ppm = parts per million
μg/m³ = micrograms per cubic meter

1. Not to be exceeded more than 3 days over 3 years.
2. Three-year average of annual fourth-highest ozone reading not to be at or exceed this level.
3. Old standard not to be exceeded more than 3 days over 3 years; new standard exceeded when 3-year average of the 99th percentile of concentrations is at or above 155 μg/m³.
4. Old annual standard not to be exceeded; 3-year average of annual PM10 concentrations not to exceed new annual standard.
5. Three-year average of the 98th percentile of concentrations of 24-hour PM2.5 not to exceed 65 μg/m³.
6. Three-year average of annual PM2.5 concentrations not to exceed 15 μg/m³.

Source: Environmental Protection Agency, 1997.

One set of standards, called primary standards, is designed to protect human health. Another set, called secondary standards, is designed to protect the environment and limit property damage. Any area of a city that exceeds a standard a specified number of times causes the entire metropolitan area to be in violation, also known as being in "nonattainment."

In 1997 the EPA, following a scientific assessment and public comment period that elicited more than 50,000 comments, adopted a new standard for "fine" respirable particulate matter up to 2.5 microns (PM2.5), while relaxing the previous PM10 standard, and replaced the 1-hour ozone standard with a slightly more stringent 8-hour ozone standard. (See box: Why Did the EPA Adopt New Standards?) However, in May 1999 the U.S. Court of Appeals for the District of Columbia Circuit ruled that the air standards revisions were unconstitutional because EPA did not precisely define their criteria for revising the standards. This decision is being appealed.[24] Providing the standards are not revoked, the new ozone standards will impact many communities

WHY DID THE EPA ADOPT NEW STANDARDS?

The decision to adopt new national ambient air quality standards for "fine" particulate matter and ozone did not come easily. Under the 1990 federal Clean Air Act, the EPA is expected to revisit its standards once every five years to make sure they are adequately protecting the public's health. Since 1987, when the PM10 standard was adopted, an impressive body of evidence had developed through studies which indicated that people's health was affected by PM10 even at concentration levels well below the standards. Furthermore, these scientific studies found that fine particles of 2.5 microns or less penetrate deeper into lungs and are therefore more likely to contribute to adverse health effects. These health effects include:

■ premature death and increased hospital admissions and emergency room visits;

■ increased respiratory symptoms and disease;

■ decreased lung function; and

■ alterations in lung tissue and structure and in respiratory-tract defense mechanisms.

Similarly, the ozone standard was last revised in 1979, and, since the late 1980s, thousands of studies have been published on the health and ecological effects of ozone. These studies suggest that present standards do not protect health and the environment, in part because the 1-hour standard protects the public against peak highs but not against sustained exposure to high ozone levels. The congressionally mandated Clean Air

Scientific Advisory Committee concluded that the studies and issues provided an adequate basis for revision of the primary and secondary standards for both particulate matter and ozone.

In November 1996 the EPA published its proposal to revise ozone standards, setting a proposed 8-hour ozone standard of .085 parts per million, based upon taking the third highest 8-hour ozone concentration each year and then averaging these over a three-year period. In December 1996 the EPA announced a new proposed PM2.5 daily standard of 15 micrograms per cubic meter ($\mu g/m^3$) and a 24-hour PM2.5 standard of 50 $\mu g/m^3$. More than 50,000 comments were received from industries, environmental groups, local government officials, congressional representatives, and the public. Finally, on July 17, 1997, the EPA adopted the new standards, although it raised the proposed PM2.5 24-hour standard from 50 to 65 ug/m^3 and changed the 8-hour ozone exceedence level from the third to the fourth highest 8-hour ozone concentration each year. These two changes weakened the standards initially proposed in December 1996, but the new standards still drew heated opposition from some industry sectors.

(*Source: Information from EPA*, Regulatory Impact Analysis of New Ozone and Particulate Matter Air Quality Standards *[July 17, 1997]*; EPA, Summary of EPA's Strategy for Implementing New Ozone and Particulate Matter Air Quality Standards Fact Sheet, *July 17, 1997.*)

throughout Texas and the United States and are expected to cause some metropolitan areas in Texas to fall out of compliance. (See section on Clean Air Compliance). Nevertheless, the 1-hour standard will continue to apply to nonattainment areas, and a determination of which areas do not meet the 8-hour standard will not be announced until 2000.

Since the EPA began regulating the criteria pollutants in 1970, emissions and accompanying ambient levels have declined overall. Between 1988 and

1997, the most dramatic decline in both ambient air concentrations (67 percent) and emissions (44 percent) between 1986 and 1995 was lead. This dramatic reduction is due largely to the phase-out of leaded gasoline, which began in the 1970s and continued in the 1980s. Other criteria pollutants have witnessed a much more modest decline due largely to a continued reliance on combustion of fossil fuels for transportation and power. Today, the most abundant single pollutant is carbon monoxide, accounting for about 50 percent of total emissions by weight.

At monitoring stations around the state, the four gaseous criteria pollutants (nitrogen dioxide, sulfur dioxide, carbon monoxide, and ozone) are monitored continuously, with 1-hour averages measured each hour, every day. PM10 and lead are measured at least once every six days for a 24-hour averaging period, although some sites in Texas are monitored more frequently. The TNRCC, local governmental agencies, and some private organizations monitor for criteria pollutants (see box: Air Quality Monitoring).

OZONE

In the upper atmosphere, ozone (O_3), an oxygen molecule with three, rather than two, oxygen atoms, forms a layer that filters out ultraviolet radiation from the sun. Concern about the thinning of the atmospheric ozone layer has led to bans on the use of certain chemicals, such as chlorinated fluorocarbons, that may destroy ozone.

Though atmospheric ozone helps sustain life, ozone formed near the ground may adversely affect plants, animals, and humans. Ozone is produced when reactive hydrocarbons known as volatile organic compounds (VOCs) combine with nitrogen oxides and oxygen in the presence of sunlight. Ozone problems are most common in the hot summer months because the warm air and sunlight speed ozone formation.

VOCs are emitted from a wide variety of sources, including: automobiles and other vehicles (referred

WHAT IS OZONE?

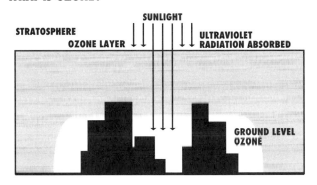

Ozone is formed in a photochemical reaction process. Other pollutants act on oxygen at the earth's surface on warm days and in the presence of ultraviolet radiation to produce ground level ozone.

Source: Texas Air Control Board, Air Quality in Texas: Twenty Years of Environmental Protection *(1992), 8.*

to as "mobile sources" in the federal Clean Air Act); refineries and chemical manufacturing plants ("major stationary sources"); paint shops and dry cleaners ("minor" or "area sources"); recreational boats, ships, barges, lawn and garden equipment, aircraft, and locomotives ("off-road mobile sources"); and even plants and trees ("biogenics") (see box: Do Trees Pollute?). Nitrogen oxide comes from some of the same sources—automobiles, boats, trains and planes, and refineries—as well as from service stations, home heating and cooling units, wastewater treatment plants, power plants, and forest fires. The TNRCC has estimated both the amount and the

UP AND DOWN OZONE TRENDS, NUMBER OF DAYS EXCEEDING OZONE STANDARD, 1985–1999.

	1985	1986	1987	1988	1989	1990	1991	1992	1993	1994	1995	1996	1997	1998	1999
Dallas/Fort Worth	18	11	11	9	4	7	7	4	4	9	15	4	12	5	10
Tyler/Longview	1	0	0	0	0	2	0	1	1	0	4	0	1	5	4
El Paso	10	11	12	6	10	4	5	5	4	6	4	4	3	2	1
Beaumont/ Port Arthur	0	8	3	7	9	5	9	5	0	2	8	0	3	4	3
Houston/Brazoria/ Galveston	58	48	54	59	37	52	37	28	28	30	56	28	50	38	37
San Antonio	0	1	1	1	0	0	0	0	0	0	0	2	0	2	0
Austin	2	0	0	0	0	0	0	0	0	0	0	0	0	0	0
Corpus Christi	0	0	2	0	0	1	0	0	1	1	1	0	0	0	0

Note: Totals include only state and local governmental ozone monitoring sites, not private networks. 1999 through Oct. 18.

Source: Texas Natural Resource Conservation Commission, Data Management and Analysis Division, 1999.

AIR QUALITY MONITORING: HOW DOES IT WORK?

If you can't always see it, taste it, or maybe even smell it, how do you know air pollution is there? Texas's extensive air monitoring network strives to answer that question by measuring concentrations of both criteria and toxic ambient air pollutants. The TNRCC, six local governmental entities, four private organizations, and even the federal government operate over 130 permanent monitoring sites located across the state.[25] Most of these stations monitor criteria pollutants like ozone, sulfur dioxide, and particulate matter, although many also monitor toxics, such as VOCs.

Two types of pollutants—ozone and respirable particulate matter—get more attention than any others. In 1995 the TNRCC, local governments, and private networks monitored ozone seven days a week, 24 hours a day at 51 sites in Texas.[26] Particulate matter was monitored at 55 sites in Texas during 1995, with most sites taking 24-hour averages every sixth day. In addition to these sites in Texas, sites in Ciudad Juárez, Mexico, and Doña Ana County, New Mexico, also measured ozone and particulate matter.

Continued on next page

GOVERNMENT-OPERATED ACTIVE MONITORING SITES IN TEXAS WHICH MEASURE TOXICS AND CRITERIA POLLUTANTS, 1997

REGION/CITY	TOXICS (VOCs & Hydrogen Flouride)	CRITERIA POLLUTANTS (One or more)	VISIBILITY
1. Pantex*	6	5	
2. Lubbock	0	1	
3. Frisco, Collin	0	5	
4. Midlothian	1	3	
5. Fort Worth	1	4	
6. Dallas	1	14	
7. Denton	0	2	
8. Garland	1	0	
9. Grapevine	1	0	
10. Longview	0	1	
11. Tyler	0	1	
12. Winona	1	0	
13. El Paso	4	13	
14. Big Bend	0	1	1**
15. Guadalupe Mts.	0	0	1**
16. Odessa	1	0	
17. Beaumont	1	1	
18. Port Arthur	2	1	
19. Groves	1	0	
20. Port Neches	1	0	
21. Orange	1	1	
22. Austin	1	2	
23. Clute	1	1	
24. Galveston	1	1	
25. Texas City	1	3	
26. Aldine	1	1	
27. Channelview	1	0	
28. Houston	3	11	
29. Deer Park	1	1	
30. Pasadena	0	1	

Area (Acres/1,000)
- ■ Counties > 750,000 Acres
- ▨ Federal Lands
- — County Boundaries

REGION/CITY	TOXICS (VOCs & Hydrogen Flouride)	CRITERIA POLLUTANTS (One or more)	VISIBILITY
31. San Antonio	1	4	
32. Corpus Christi	3	3	
33. Victoria	0	1	
34. Brownsville	1	2	
35. Edinburg	1	1	
36. Mission	1	1	
37. Laredo	1	1	
TOTALS	**41**	**87**	**2**

*Operated by TNRCC under contract with Federal Government
**IMPROVE site operated by National Park Service

In FY 1998 the TNRCC added the Lockheed Environmental Analysis and Display System, a continuous air monitoring system that allows the agency to immediately analyze and report the information from the monitors.[27]

In 1995 the TNRCC operated 23 monitoring sites in 15 counties that measured 69 VOCs as part of the Community Air Toxics Monitoring Network Sites.[28] While the TNRCC had plans to expand the network from 23 to a total of 50 sites, budget cuts have not allowed the agency to do so, although by 1997 a total of 35 sites were monitoring toxics.[29]

Limited ambient air toxics monitoring by the TNRCC has not identified these toxic emissions as a significant public health risk in any particular area (see section on toxics in "Other Air Quality Issues").[30] Air toxics selected for monitoring were those emitted in the largest quantities from multiple sources. Some monitoring methods, however, collect average samples of toxics, and thus higher peak concentrations would not be quantified, although the peak concentrations do influence the average itself.[31] In addition, most of the toxics monitoring sites measured 24-hour air samples every sixth day.[32]

The TNRCC, to complement its toxics monitoring system, has operated a mobile monitoring system since 1971 to help pinpoint local trouble spots. Recently, the TNRCC has expanded its use of mobile monitoring equipment, which includes a self-contained 40-foot mobile laboratory, 7 sampling vans (8 by 8 by 14 feet), and an air-toxics response trailer.[33] These vans have equipment for monitoring criteria air pollutants, 75 VOCs, polynuclear aromatic compounds, metals, and even take soil samples.[34] Examples of recent studies performed by the mobile monitoring system include two mobile laboratory trips in 1993 and 1994, to Brownsville to measure air toxics and to Corpus Christi to study refineries.[35]

Despite the presence of these monitors in the major metropolitan areas, federal requirements and citizen concern about the health effects of air pollution are generating a demand for more and better air-quality monitoring. For example, the TNRCC and the federal government will have to invest in dichotomous and regular PM2.5 samplers in all major metropolitan areas in Texas. Concerns along the U.S.-Mexico border have led to major investments in new monitoring sites in Mission and Edinburg, which sample for ozone, PM10, and VOCs and polyurethane foam, both of which measures toxics, while the Big Bend station run by the National Park Service has added capabilities to measure ozone as well as visibility. A contract with Baylor University also allows the agency to fly twin-engine airplanes with special equipment over Big Bend and other areas of the state to assess haze.[36]

sources of VOCs and nitrogen oxides released into the atmosphere in major Texas metropolitan areas.

The Houston-Galveston-Brazoria metropolitan area reports the highest number of days exceeding ozone standards in Texas. In general, the four metropolitan areas exceeding standards have shown a decline over the past fourteen years in the number of days exceeding national standards, although Houston has recently suffered an upsurge in the number of ozone exceedences. In fact, Houston had the highest 1-hour concentration—0.234 parts per million—reported in 1997 in the entire United States, beating out even Los Angeles, the perennial leader.[37] Other large Texas cities have met the ozone standards since the early 1980s. Still, in both 1993 and 1995, Corpus Christi exceeded the 1-hour ozone standard. San Antonio's ozone concentration exceeded the standard on two occasions in 1996 and once in 1998, while concentrations in Austin fell only slightly below the standard in both 1997 and 1998.

Whether or not ozone standards are exceeded is a

function of the amount of pollution emitted into the air, as well as temperatures, wind pattern, and the intensity of the sun. Thus, for example, there were significant increases in ozone days in 1995 in Dallas, Houston, and Northeast Texas due, in part, to hot, sunny weather during the summer months.

HEALTH AND ENVIRONMENTAL EFFECTS OF OZONE

High levels of ozone can have serious human health effects. Ozone reacts with lung tissue and can cause breathing problems, including an increased suscepti-bility to respiratory infection. Ozone may increase the risk of asthma. For unknown reasons, about 10 to 20 percent of the population, sometimes referred to as "responders," are especially sensitive to high ozone concentrations. This group, along with people with pre-existing respiratory diseases and people who exercise outdoors, are particularly at risk from high ozone levels.[38]

FYI ☞ *A 1988 study for the American Lung Association estimated that if ozone standards had been met throughout the United States in 1983, 49.9 million cases of adverse health symptoms and 1.9 million asthma attacks would have been eliminated. (Source: James Cannon,* The Health Costs of Air Pollution: A Survey of Studies Published 1984–1989 *[New York: American Lung Association, 1990], 43.)*

People with asthma, chronic bronchitis, and emphysema in Texas are at risk of adverse health effects if they are exposed to levels of ozone that have exceeded the national ambient air quality standards.[39]

High ground levels of ozone can also have nega-tive environmental effects. High levels are believed to affect vegetation, including urban ornamentals, crops, and forestry production, by damaging the cell walls of plants. In 1987 the East Texas Intensive Research Site was established near Nacogdoches to investigate how pollutants affect the development of one- to four-year-old shortleaf pines along coastal plains. The study subjected some trees to persistent exposure to ozone, and the trees showed loss of needles, stunted growth, and fewer stems.[40] Ozone also limits visibility in cities and national parks.

SULFUR DIOXIDE AND NITROGEN OXIDES—THE BUILDING BLOCKS OF ACID RAIN

Sulfur dioxide and nitrogen oxides are gases released when fossil fuels are burned. When constituents of these gases react with water in the atmosphere, sulfuric acid and nitric acids can form and fall as rain, commonly referred to as "acid" rain. In areas with little precipitation, the acids may become incorpo-rated into dust and smoke and fall to the ground as "dry" acid.[41] Acid rain can harm or kill fish by making lakes and rivers more acidic (by lowering the pH). It can also damage buildings, stone, and monuments, as well as crops and forests. Studies indicate that acid rain can also reduce crop yields both by damaging foliage and by causing minerals to leach from the soil.[42] While adverse affects have been reported in the Northeast, no major harmful effects of acid rain have been documented in Texas. This is attributed to two factors: (1) the strongly alkaline soils charac-teristic of much of the state; and (2) the absence of a snowpack melt common in more northern states. Nonetheless, there is evidence that rain at some sites —such as Big Bend National Park—has become more acidic.[43] One lake in Texas-Caddo Lake in Northeast

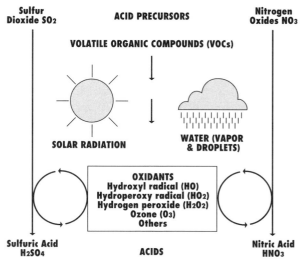

HOW ACID RAIN IS FORMED

A coupled chemical system: acid precursor gases are transformed into acids.

Source: National Acid Rain Precipitation Assessment Program, Annual Report 1984 to the President and Congress.

NITROGEN OXIDES AND VOLATILE ORGANIC COMPOUND EMISSIONS IN TEXAS'S MAJOR METROPOLITAN AREAS, TONS PER DAY

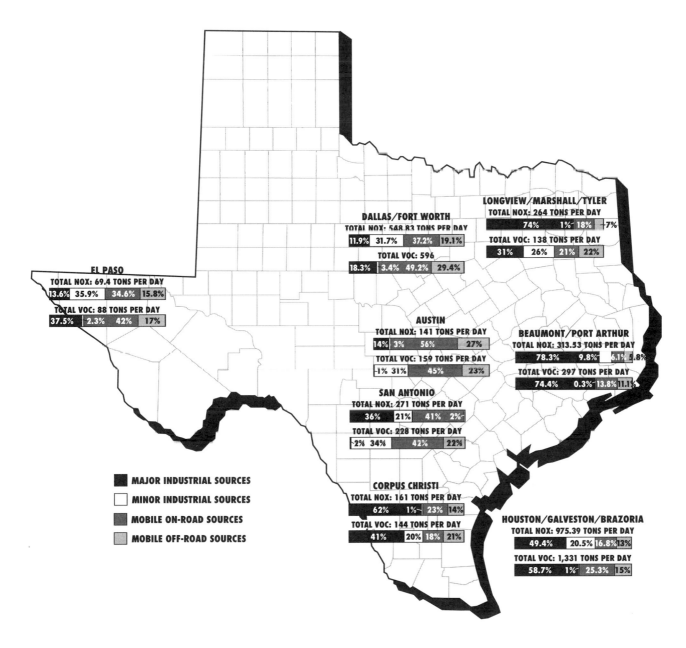

Note: El Paso represents a special case. The graphic shows only sources from within the El Paso County area, where an estimated 88 tons of NOx and 90 tons of VOCs are released into the atmosphere – a relatively low amount compared to Texas's other cities. However, El Paso shares the border with Ciudad Juárez, Mexico, which has a significant influence on air quality in Mexico. A special section later in this chapter – Sharing Air Along the U.S.-Mexico Border – will highlight some of these issues.
Stationary/Area Sources: Major industrial sources (petroleum storage and petrochemical facilities, major manufacturing plants, gasoline pipelines, power plants) and area minor industrial sources (gasoline stations, dry cleaners, oil and gas production, small coating and painting operations, small print shops, landfills, wastewater treatment facilities, consumer commercial solvent use).
Mobile Sources: Off-road (recreational boats, agricultural, construction, industrial equipment, lawn and garden equipment, airplanes) and on-road (highway vehicles, both gasoline and diesel).

Source: Texas Natural Resources Conservation Commission, Revisions to the State Implementation Plan for Ozone (1996).

COMPARISONS BY METROPOLITAN AREA, HIGHEST O₃ ONE-HOUR AVERAGES (PPM) 1996–1999

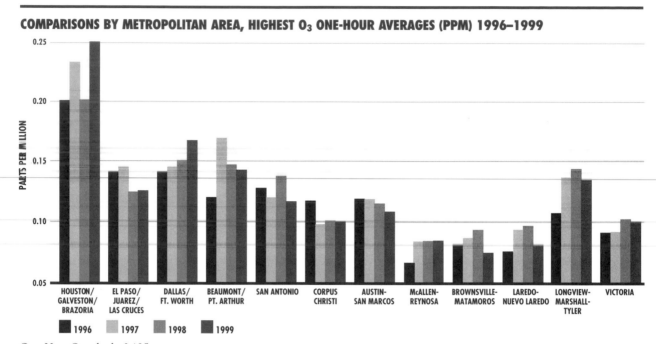

One-Hour Standard   0.125
Notes: All measurements from TNRCC and local monitors, except in Houston-Galveston-Brazoria, which includes data from Houston Regional Monitoring Network. Ozone data collection began in Laredo and McAllen in late 1996.

Source: Office of Air Quality, Texas Natural Resource Conservation Commission, 1999.

Texas—also has acidic water that does not meet water quality standards, and several other lakes in East Texas have high acidity levels. The reasons for this acidic water are not completely understood.[44]

Pinpointing the cause of acid rain is difficult, primarily because of multiple emission sources and complex meteorology. Rain can become acidic as a result of water reacting with nitrogen oxides and sulfur dioxide. But other factors, such as acidic waste runoff and naturally high acidic levels in lakes or streams, may also contribute to acidity. In 1991 the Texas Air Control Board (later the TNRCC) and the federal government through the National Atmospheric Deposition Program (NADP) began monitoring the acidity (pH) of rain. During 1996 the TNRCC and NADP monitored rain acidity at 13 sites. Samples taken at the most eastern monitors in the state— Longview and Forest Seed—had the lowest average pH values (the lower the pH the higher the acidity).[45]

Nitrogen oxide and sulfur dioxide air emissions have other harmful effects. As discussed in the previous section, nitrogen oxide emissions contribute to ground-level ozone formation. Moreover, at high

ACID RAIN SITES MONITORED IN 1995

SITE	AVE. pH	MAX. pH	MIN. pH	NO. OF SAMPLES
Longview	4.63	6.43	4.00	47
Austin	4.85	5.20	4.41	10
Forest Seed	4.78	6.02	3.90	44
Huntsville	4.85	5.48	4.11	13
Tyler	ISD	5.10	4.68	2
Attwater	4.81	6.29	3.97	45
LBJ	4.99	7.82	3.98	45
Beeville	5.01	6.39	4.07	45
Muleshoe	5.43	7.39	4.49	45
Sonora	4.98	6.59	4.25	50
Big Bend	5.58	6.84	5.02	45
Guadalupe	5.56	7.80	4.90	46
Y Experimental	5.07	6.56	4.54	42

Notes: ISD = Insufficient Data.

A pH of 7 is neutral. Higher numbers on the pH scale correspond to higher alkalinity, and lower numbers to increasing acidity. Unpolluted rainwater has a pH of 5.6, which is slightly acidic.

Source: Texas Natural Resource Conservation Commission, Air Monitoring Report 1995 *(April 1997), Table 9.*

ESTIMATES OF THE POPULATIONS-AT-RISK EXPOSED TO ADVERSE HEALTH CONSEQUENCES IN OZONE NON-ATTAINMENT AREAS IN TEXAS

| COUNTY | AGE-SPECIFIC POPULATIONS | | ADULT ASTHMA* | PEDIATRIC | |
	<13	65+		ASTHMA	COPD**
Brazoria	44,800	14,948	3,240	4,901	10,223
Chambers	4,582	1,903	344	512	1,104
Collin	60,752	13,769	4,407	6,768	13,524
Dallas	398,461	152,514	28,549	48,991	98,292
Denton	60,036	13,775	4,242	7,181	13,708
El Paso	148,885	48,267	11,106	14,416	31,634
Fort Bend	59,998	11,125	4,310	5,428	11,489
Galveston	47,515	22,771	3,450	5,712	12,046
Hardin	9,436	4,860	698	1,062	2,345
Harris	643,551	198,222	46,369	72,666	147,562
Jefferson	51,561	33,634	3,726	6,343	13,843
Liberty	12,022	6,192	887	1,356	2,980
Montgomery	42,414	15,693	3,116	4,647	9,904
Orange	17,981	8,740	1,325	2,091	4,527
Tarrant	257,220	97,424	18,289	30,784	62,214
Waller	4,694	2,562	342	631	1,284

*Pediatric asthma is calculated in the population less than 18 years of age.
**COPD includes chronic bronchitis and emphysema.

Source: *American Lung Association*, Breath in Danger II: Estimation of Populations-At-Risk of Adverse Health Consequences in Areas Not in Attainment With National Ambient Air Quality Standards of the Clean Air Act *(New York: American Lung Association, 1993), Table 3.*

levels, nitrogen oxides are known to cause lung damage and other respiratory illness, particularly in children and people suffering from asthma.[46] In Texas, however, nitrogen dioxide has never exceeded the national standard set in 1973.

High concentrations of sulfur dioxide in the air may cause difficulty in breathing and a choking sensation. Children, the elderly, asthma sufferers, and people with chronic lung and heart disease are particularly susceptible to the adverse effects of sulfur dioxide.

Studies for the EPA have documented that most asthmatics experience asthma attacks and other symptoms when exposed to high 5-minute concentrations of sulfur dioxide, such as those caused by highly concentrated plumes from large industrial sources. Such short-term concentrations, however, do not generally lead to violations of the annual or 24-hour standards. After first proposing to include a 5-minute sulfur dioxide standard to control peak

exposures, in 1996 the EPA decided not to adopt the 5-minute standard.[47]

Unlike nitrogen oxide—which is mainly the result of automobile and utility emissions—sulfur dioxide is emitted chiefly from industrial sources such as power plants using sulfur-containing fuel, metallic-

EXCEEDENCES OF 24-HOUR SO₂ STANDARD MEASURED BY TEXAS AIR CONTROL BOARD, 1975-1998

CITIES EXCEEDING STANDARD	HIGHEST VALUE RECORDED	# OF EXCEEDENCES
Beaumont/Port Arthur	.188 (1982)	1
El Paso	.147 (1982)	1
Beaumont/Port Arthur	.154 (1984)	1
Houston/Galveston/ Texas City	.173 (1985)	2
Beaumont/Port Arthur	.324 (1989)	2

Standard: .14 parts per million

Source: *Texas Natural Resource Conservation Commission, Data Management and Analysis Section, 1999.*

HIGH SO₂ 24-HOUR AVERAGES IN KEY METROPOLITAN AREAS, 1995

CITY	HIGHEST 24-HOUR SO2 LEVEL (PPM)
Houston/Galveston/Brazoria	0.073
El Paso/Juarez	0.050
Beaumont/Port Arthur	0.055
Corpus Christi	0.020
Dallas/Fort Worth	0.050
Brownsville	0.004
Standard:	0.145

Source: Texas Natural Resource Conservation Commission, Air Monitoring Report (Austin: TNRCC, April 1997).

ore smelting facilities, wood and paper industrial processors, and oil and gas refineries.

Sulfur dioxide levels in Texas vary across the state. The Houston-Galveston-Brazoria area, the Beaumont-Port Arthur area, and the El Paso metropolitan area have shown the highest levels of sulfur dioxide measured in the state, although not exceeding or approaching the federal ambient air quality standards for sulfur dioxide.[48] Tests conducted between 1985 and 1989 by the Houston Regional Monitoring Network, a private organization, showed sulfur dioxide levels in excess of national standards occurred 13 times in the industrial district of the Houston Ship Channel.[49] Cooperative action between local industries, the TNRCC, and the EPA has resulted in voluntary reductions in sulfur dioxide emissions in the local area, and no violations have been recorded since 1990.

In Milam County, the presence of a coal-burning aluminum smelting plant, Sandow, owned and operated by Alcoa (the Aluminum Company of America) has resulted in high levels of sulfur dioxide pollution, forcing the TNRCC and county officials to implement a special state implementation plan there. The EPA has designated the area as "unclassified"—neither attainment nor nonattainment.[50]

CARBON MONOXIDE

A colorless, odorless gas, carbon monoxide results from the incomplete combustion of fossil fuels, most often in motor vehicles and power plants. Carbon monoxide can interfere with the blood's ability to carry

1995 CARBON MONOXIDE EMISSIONS BY MAJOR SOURCE CATEGORY IN MAJOR TEXAS CITIES

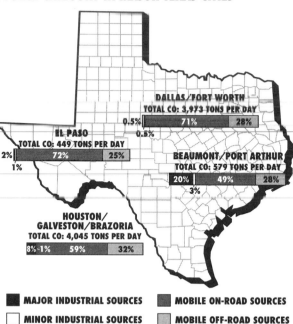

Note: El Paso totals do not include emissions from Ciudad Juárez, across the border in Mexico. A special section in this chapter discusses the shared airshed between the two neighboring cities.

Stationary/Area Sources: Major industrial sources (petroleum storage and petrochemical facilities, major manufacturing plants, gasoline pipelines, power plants) and area minor industrial sources (gasoline stations, dry cleaners, oil and gas production, small coating and painting operations, small print shops, landfills, wastewater treatment facilities, consumer commercial solvent use).

Mobile Sources: Off-road (recreational boats, agricultural, construction, industrial equipment, lawn and garden equipment, airplanes) and on-road (highway vehicles, both gasoline and diesel).

Source: Texas Natural Resource Conservation Commission, Revisions to the State Implementation Plan for Carbon Monoxide (CO) (September 1995).

oxygen to the heart, brain, and other tissues. People with heart disease and unborn or newborn children are especially susceptible to carbon monoxide poisoning.[51] Carbon monoxide has also been identified as a possible precursor to the formation of ozone.[52]

Sources of carbon monoxide vary by location. In Texas, only El Paso has consistently exceeded the 8-hour ambient air quality standard for carbon monoxide, although levels measured in recent years are lower than those measured ten years ago. In addition, Dallas exceeded standards twice in 1985,

EL PASO 8-HOUR CARBON MONOXIDE TREND, BY NUMBER OF EXCEEDENCES IN DAYS AND HIGHEST 8-HOUR LEVELS.

	HIGHEST LEVEL	EXCEEDENCES
1973	6.7	0
1974	11.7	1
1975	9.1	0
1976	13.5	6
1977	10.3	2
1978	11.0	2
1979	16.4	3
1980	12.1	7
1981	15.7	12
1982	14.2	8
1983	13.7	9
1984	15.4	9
1985	14.0	10
1986	15.2	12
1987	16.7	9
1988	12.1	6
1989	13.6	10
1990	15.2	8
1991	10.7	4
1992	10.5	3
1993	10.7	2
1994	9.8	1
1995	15.0	1
1996	10.5	2
1997	11.7	2
1998	8.5	0

Source: Environmental Protection Agency, AIRS Database, 1999.

ESTIMATES OF THE POPULATIONS-AT-RISK EXPOSED TO ADVERSE HEALTH CONSEQUENCES IN CARBON MONOXIDE NON-ATTAINMENT AREAS, 1992

AFFECTED AREA	PREGNANT WOMEN	CORONARY HEART DISEASE
El Paso County	11,793	19,181

Source: American Lung Association, Breath in Danger II: Estimations of Populations-At-Risk of Adverse Health Consequences in Areas Not in Attainment with National Ambient Air Quality Standards of the Clean Air Act (New York: American Lung Association, 1993), 22.

PARTICULATE MATTER

The category of air pollutants called "respirable particulate matter" includes liquids, hydrocarbons, soot, dusts, acids from aerosols, and smoke particles that are smaller than 10 microns in diameter. This 10-micron size limit has led to the abbreviation of respirable particulate matter as "PM10." The EPA has further divided these tiny particles—which make up about 55 percent of the total mass of suspended particles in air pollution—into "fine" particles of 2.5 microns or less and "coarse" particles of between 2.5 and 10 microns.

FYI *A particle of 2.5 microns is about 1/20th the width of a human hair, while a particle of 10 microns is about 1/5th the width of a human hair. (Source: EPA, Health and Environmental Effects of Particulate Matter Fact Sheet, July 17, 1997.)*

While the nose can filter out larger particulates, PM10 and especially PM2.5 particles can penetrate deep into the lungs. The farther a particle penetrates into the lungs and the higher the concentration, the more likely it is to cause wheezing, nose and throat irritation, bronchitis, and lung damage. Toxic chemicals attached to respirable particulate matter emissions can increase the potential for adverse health effects. Groups at high risk because of fine and coarse particles include children, the elderly, and people with pre-existing heart or respiratory conditions like asthma and emphysema. Beyond these health hazards, fine particles impair visibility throughout the United States and can discolor clothing and property.

In 1987 the EPA revised its air quality standards for PM10, allowing a maximum of 150 micrograms

while Houston exceeded standards nine times between 1974 and 1986.

El Paso is a special case because it shares a common airshed with Ciudad Juárez and is affected by that city's air pollution (see box: Achieving Clean Air Is a Binational Problem, in Federal Clean Air Act section). Unlike ozone, carbon monoxide levels usually rise with colder weather, when atmospheric conditions are more stable. According to the 1990 EPA database, El Paso ranked fifth in the nation for levels of 8-hour concentrations of carbon monoxide.[53] However, 1996 data place El Paso behind eight other U.S. cities.

NUMBER OF 24-HOUR EXCEEDENCES OF PARTICULATE MATTER PER LOCATION, 1986–1998

	EXCEEDENCES	# OF DAYS SAMPLED AT LOCATION OF EXCEEDENCE
1986		
El Paso-A	8	291
El Paso-B	1	164
Lubbock	1	150
1987		
El Paso	2	211
Houston	2	286
1988		
El Paso-A	12	311
El Paso-B	4	40
Lubbock	1	164
1989		
El Paso-A	7	328
El Paso-B	4	165
Lubbock	1	164
1990		
El Paso-A	4	328
El Paso-B	2	160
1991		
El Paso	1	336
1992		
El Paso	2	337
1993		
None		
1994		
El Paso	2	329
1995		
El Paso	6	178
Lubbock	2	168
1996		
El Paso	2	536
1997		
El Paso-A	1	244
El Paso-B	6	256
1998		
El Paso	8	200

Source: Texas Natural Resource Conservation Commission, Data Management and Analysis, 1997; and Environmental Protection Agency, AIRS Database, 1999.

HIGHEST PM10 DAILY AVERAGES IN MAJOR METROPOLITAN AREAS, 1995–1997

	1995	1996	1997
Austin	60	37	NA
Beaumont	57	42	NA
Brownsville	56	40	91
Corpus Christi	58	54	78
Dallas	85	92	77
Midlothian	83	107	126
El Paso	178	536	256
Fort Worth	62	67	58
Houston	95	71	137
Laredo	64	180	84
Lubbock	168	104	38
San Antonio	81	40	58
San Benito	49	41	58
Galveston/Texas City	94	73	116
Standard	155MG		

In 1997, under new PM10 standard, the 99th percentile of readings was used as the highest daily average.

Source: Texas Natural Resource Conservation Commission, Air Monitoring Report, 1996 (1998) and Environmental Protection Agency, National Air Quality and Emissions Trend Report, 1997 (Research Triangle Park, N.C., 1998), Table A-12.

per cubic meter in a 24-hour period, or 50 micrograms per cubic meter as an annual average. Previously, the EPA had no specific standard for PM10, instead relying on a standard for all particulate matter, including particulate matter larger than 10 microns. The EPA estimated that adherence to these new 1987 standards would save 3,600 lives, reduce lost work days by 190,000 days, and cut down on "reduced-activity" (days when people work less efficiently because of ill health) by 910,000 days.[54]

In 1997 the EPA created a new separate standard for PM2.5 because it determined that the PM10 standard did not provide adequate protection for human health.[55] It was the association between mortality due to cardiopulmonary diseases and particulate-matter air pollution that spurred the EPA to adopt a specific standard for PM 2.5.[56]

According to the EPA, the new PM2.5 standard and its eventual implementation will save 15,000 lives, reduce the risk of hospital admissions by thousands, reduce the risk of respiratory symptoms in children, and result in thousands fewer cases of child and adult asthma per year.[57] Based on these and other health and welfare benefits, the EPA estimated annual savings of between $19 and $104 billion in 2010, compared with annual pollution control costs of only $8.6 billion.[58]

In Texas, only El Paso County has repeatedly exceeded the 24-hour standard set in 1987 for PM10. Other areas—such as Lubbock—have occasionally

POPULATION IN TEXAS COUNTIES THAT WOULD BE CONSIDERED AT-RISK OF CALIFORNIA'S STANDARD (50 μg/m³) FOR RESPIRABLE PARTICULATE MATTER, 1992

COUNTY	PM10 VALUE	1991 TOTAL POPULATION	AGE SPECIFIC POPULATIONS < 13	65+	PEDIATRIC ASTHMA*	ADULT ASTHMA	COPD**
Cameron	62	268,837	61,054	27,211	4,828	8,023	14,460
Dallas	61	1,886,962	428,534	190,991	33,886	56,315	101,491
El Paso	150	611,000	138,961	61,933	10,988	18,261	32,911
Ellis	92	86,622	19,672	8,768	1,556	2,585	4,659
Galveston	64	222,894	50,620	22,560	4,003	6,652	11,988
Harris	102	2,905,051	659,744	294,038	52,168	86,700	156,250
Lubbock	58	224,538	50,993	22,727	4,032	6,701	12,077
Nueces	60	296,847	67,415	30,046	5,331	8,859	15,965
Tarrant	64	1,200,416	272,617	121,502	21,557	35,826	64,565
Webb	58	139,830	31,756	14,153	2,511	4,173	7,521
Totals		7,843,885	1,781,365	793,928	140,859	234,096	421,886

*Pediatric asthma is calculated in the population less than 18 years of age.
**COPD includes chronic bronchitis and emphysema.

Source: American Lung Association, The Perils of Particulates (New York: American Lung Association, 1994), 15.

exceeded the 24-hour standard.[59] In El Paso, particulate matter levels rise during winter months, due mainly to combustion of wood and other fuels for heating. These violations of the particulate standards exposed El Paso County's "at-risk" population to high PM10 concentrations in the 1990s. Other Texas "at-risk" populations that have been exposed to

PM10 levels that exceeded the tougher California PM10 standard of 50 micrograms per cubic meter (vs. the federal standard of 150 micrograms per cubic meter) include residents of Webb, Cameron, Dallas, Harris, and Galveston counties, among others.

Under the less rigorous 24-hour PM10 standard recently adopted by the EPA, Laredo and El Paso

DO TREES POLLUTE?

Do trees pollute? In the early 1980s, then-president Ronald Reagan and some noted scientists attracted attention when they confirmed that trees themselves are a possible source of some types of air pollution. Trees do contribute to the formation of ozone by releasing VOCs such as isoprene, monoterpene, and alpha-pinene.

Under Title 1 of the federal Clean Air Act, states are required to estimate how much trees and plants contribute to VOC production for those areas that exceed ozone standards. The sources of these VOCs, known collectively as "biogenics," include forests, crops, lawn grasses, and other vegetation. The more vegetation an area has, the more these biogenics will contribute to overall VOC levels. For example, biogenics are estimated to account for 22 percent of all

VOCs emitted in the woody Houston-Galveston area, but only 12 percent in the arid El Paso area. Nationally, the EPA estimates that biogenics and other natural sources actually produce more emissions of VOCs than do anthropogenic sources.[60] Of course, biogenic sources are natural sources of air pollution, and cutting down trees to reduce pollution would be counterproductive: the air quality benefits of biogenics far outweigh the costs, since plants produce oxygen, filter the air, and prevent erosion. Biogenic sources are not figured into the calculation of how much an area must reduce VOC emissions.

(Sources: TNRCC, Revisions to the State Implementation Plan for the Control of Ozone Air Pollution [May 13, 1994]; EPA, Regulatory Impact Analysis of New Ozone and Particulate Matter NAAQS Standards [July 17, 1997].)

COMPARISONS OF HIGH 24-HOUR AND ANNUAL PARTICULATE MATTER STANDARDS IN MONITORS IN CIUDAD JUAREZ AND EL PASO, 1995

SITE NAME	24-HOUR HIGH	EXCEEDENCES	ANNUAL AVERAGE	EXCEEDENCE
Standard	155 ug/m3	51 ug/m3		
Tillman, El Paso 1995 Levels	144	0	35.9	No
Vilas, El Paso 1995Levels	143	0	46.8	No
Camizal, El Paso 1995 Levels	84	0	18.7	No
Socorro, El Paso 1995 Levels	178	6	38.1	No
Zenith Corporation, Ciudad Juarez 1995 Levels	1000	18	90.6	Yes
Advanced Transformer, Ciudad Juarez 1995Levels	294	74	118	Yes
Technical Institute, Ciudad Juarez 1995 Levels	156	6	46.7	No

Source: Texas Natural Resource Conservation Commission, Air Monitoring Report 1995 (April 1997).

would continue to face the most difficulty meeting the 24-hour standard, which is based on a three-year average of the 99th percentile. However, they would have met the standards based upon data between 1994 and 1996.

Six Texas communities—El Paso, Houston, Beaumont, San Antonio, Corpus Christi, and Dallas—have begun a special air sampling study of respirable particulate matter 2.5 microns or less in size. Samples are being collected every six days, and extra samples are being taken when TNRCC meteorologists forecast conditions conducive to fine particulate matter formation. The fine particulate monitoring project is being used to forecast whether high levels of particulate matter in excess of the new standard are expected. Preliminary data from 1997 show that Houston, Dallas, and Corpus Christi have the highest average daily levels.[61] The EPA estimates that levels from 1993 to 1995 demonstrate that, among Texas cities, only Houston and Corpus Christi

currently appear to face difficulty meeting the annual PM2.5 standard.[62]

El Paso is impacted by particulate matter drifting in from Ciudad Juárez. Common sources of this particulate matter include numerous unpaved roads and industrial combustion processes, such as the incineration of garbage, including tires, without adequate controls. In fact, PM10 monitors in Mexico have continually registered 24-hour levels exceeding standards just across the border from El Paso. Nonetheless, these levels are often not valid for comparison to U.S. standards because of the incompleteness of samples.[63] In addition, without adequate emissions inventories and ambient air quality monitoring in Ciudad Juárez designed to record air quality over time, it is difficult to determine if emissions are going down.

LEAD

Between 1970 and 1997, air emissions of lead in the United States were reduced from 320,000 to 4,000 tons per year, largely as a result of the country's phase-out of leaded gasoline.[64] In Texas, data from the state emissions database reported a total of only 30 tons of lead emitted into the air each year from industries and utilities.[65] Nevertheless, lead continues to pose a potential public health threat, in part because of its persistence in the environment. Lead poisoning can lead to retardation in cognitive development in children, reduce mental ability, and damage nerves and organs like livers and kidneys. It also may interfere with the creation of blood and raise

ESTIMATED POPULATION AT-RISK IN TEXAS COUNTIES WHICH EXCEEDED FEDERAL STANDARD (150 μg/m³) FOR RESPIRABLE PARTICULATE MATTER IN 1992

	PM10 VALUE	CHILDREN	OVER 65
El Paso	158	138,961	61,933

	PEDIATRIC ASTHMA	ADULT ASTHMA	CHRONIC BRONCHITIS AND EMPHYSEMA
El Paso	10,988	18,261	32,911

Source: American Lung Association, The Perils of Particulates (New York: American Lung Association, 1994), 15.

HIGHEST LEAD QUARTERLY AVERAGES, 1996-1997
(Ambient lead levels in μg/m³)

	1996	1997
Frisco	0.69	0.45
Dallas	0.17	0.09
Midlothian	0.27	0.26
El Paso	0.40	0.12
Houston	0.02	0.00

Lead National Standard: 1.5 ug/m³

Source: Texas Natural Resource Conservation Commission, Air Monitoring Report 1996 (1998) and Environmental Protection Agency, National Air Quality and Emissions Trends Report, 1997 (Research Triangle Park, NC: EPA, 1998).

HIGHEST LEAD QUARTERLY AVERAGES IN EL PASO, 1980-1997
(Ambient lead levels in μg/m³)

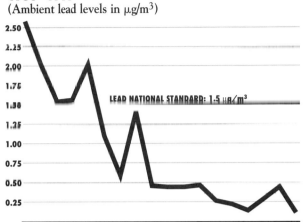

Source: Texas Natural Resource Conservation Commission, Office of Air Quality.

blood pressure, leading to cardiovascular disease.[66] Children and pregnant women are most at risk from exposure to high lead levels.[67] Because lead accumulates in the body organs, bones, and blood, even chronic exposure to small amounts can be harmful to both human and animal life. Besides leaded gasoline, sources of lead pollution in the air include metal smelters and the manufacture and reclamation of lead batteries.

In Texas, outdoor air pollution from lead is now limited to a handful of areas. In the Dallas-Fort Worth area, citizens were concerned about the number of lead smelters and battery plants in the area, but most of these facilities were shut down in the mid-1980s, and the lead standard has not been exceeded in Texas since 1990. Suspected health problems from exposure to high lead levels continue to concern Dallas-area residents. An area of approximately one-half mile next to a major battery plant in the city of Frisco, Collin County, previously exceeded national standards, in 1987, but has not done so since then.[68]

In the early and middle 1980s, air quality at several monitoring sites in the city of El Paso violated national standards for lead. However, the closing of a lead smelter plant in 1985 and the phase-out of leaded gasoline have brought ambient levels in El Paso to within the allowable limit since 1986.

FEDERAL CLEAN AIR ACT COMPLIANCE IN TEXAS
Under Title 1 of the 1990 federal Clean Air Act, any area that violates national ambient air quality

standards for any of the six criteria pollutants as few times as once per year and as often as four times over a three-year period is classified as a nonattainment area. Texas currently has four such areas, encompassing 17 counties. In addition, the Tyler-Longview-Marshall area has violated federal standards for ozone, but under a Flexible Attainment Region agreement with the EPA it is not considered a nonattainment area. Similarly, Corpus Christi has signed a Flexible Attainment Region agreement with the EPA to give the city more flexibility to comply with the standards. Finally, two counties in Texas—Harris and Milam—are considered "unclassified" because of localized problems with sulfur dioxide that require control strategies but do not cause the areas to be considered nonattainment.

Nonattainment areas for ozone, carbon monoxide, and PM10 are classified according to the severity of their air pollution. Each area is included in a state implementation plan (SIP) designed by the TNRCC to bring the area into compliance. Different areas may have different deadlines for complying with the plan, depending upon the severity of their air pollution problems. If a nonattainment area fails to comply with air pollution standards by the deadline, the EPA may extend the deadline but impose more stringent requirements to meet the standards.

Recently, for example, the EPA rejected Dallas-Fort Worth's bid for an extension to comply with the deadlines set for "moderate" ozone nonattainment areas, and instead reclassified the area as a "serious" ozone nonattainment area due to lack of progress on meeting the ozone standard.[69] The change forces Dallas-Fort Worth and the TNRCC to adopt more stringent control standards for cars, small commercial and business operations, and large industries.

The EPA, on the other hand, downgraded Beaumont-Port Arthur from a "serious" to a "moderate" nonattainment area for ozone.[70] The reclassification limits the types of controls the area is required to implement to reduce VOC emissions. The EPA is currently considering what additional steps Beaumont-Port Arthur must take to comply with the federal Clean Air Act.

The new 8-hour standard will force other cities in Texas into nonattainment status. Based on data from 1997 to 1999, there are six areas that do not meet the 8-hour standard. These include three of the four nonattainment areas for the 1-hour standard—all except El Paso—as well as Austin, San Antonio and the Longview-Marshall-Tyler metro-politan area. Nonetheless, attainment status for the 8-hour standard will not be announced until July 2000, and the pending lawsuit on the new 8-hour standard could affect the designation of these areas in Texas. Those areas currently classified as nonattainment for ozone will first have to meet the 1-hour standard before being assessed for the 8-hour standard.

If there is a failure to develop a proper state implementation plan or a failure to implement the plan, the EPA may develop a federal implementation plan for the area and may impose sanctions for noncompliance, including the loss of federal highway funds, bans or stiffer limits on further industrial expansion, and the loss of federal Air Pollution Control Program grant funds. In March 1999 the TNRCC submitted a preliminary federal implementation plan for Dallas-Fort Worth, which was rejected by the EPA in May 1999. The EPA threatened to impose sanctions by withholding highway funds if a more adequate plan was not submitted within eighteen months. It was the first time the EPA had ever threatened sanctions in Texas.[71]

By 1996 the four ozone nonattainment areas in Texas were supposed to reduce levels of VOCs by 15

AIR MONITORING: WHAT'S IN A NAME?

CAMS, SLAMS, PAMS, NAMS, Green Eggs and Ham? Air monitoring in Texas is tied to a dizzying number of acronyms that refer to the types and system of monitoring. Here's a brief guide.

Continuous Air Monitoring System (CAMS) refers to those monitoring sites which are continually monitoring for a variety of pollutants, including ozone. There are presently about 50 CAMS stations in Texas.

State and Local Air Monitoring System (SLAMS) simply means that a site is operated by either the TNRCC or a local governmental entity, such as the El Paso County Air Control District, to measure criteria and possibly toxic pollutants.

National Air Monitoring System (NAMS) indicates that the site has been recognized by, or is operated by, the EPA.

Photochemical Air Monitoring Sites (PAMS) refers only to sites located in areas that do not meet national standards for ozone and are installed to examine how the formation of ground-level ozone occurs. These sites monitor both ozone precursors (VOCs and nitrogen dioxide) as well as ozone itself and meteorological data (wind direction, speed, and temperature). PAMS help local governments and the TNRCC determine how and at what altitude ozone forms and therefore how best to prevent its formation. As of September 1997, there were six PAMS stations in El Paso and five in the Houston area, but, because of the new ozone standards, other communities are installing PAMS as well.[72]

Source: TNRCC, Information from Monitoring Operations Division, Office of Air Quality, Austin.

percent, net of growth, from 1990 levels. This net reduction requirement means that before any new sources of VOCs can be allowed to operate, reductions must be made in existing sources to offset the new emissions. Thus, the actual total reduction is significantly higher than 15 percent.

According to revisions to the state implementation plan produced by the TNRCC in 1997, all four nonattainment areas in Texas were able to reduce emissions by this amount through local and federal regulations. Even though these areas have been successful in reducing VOC emissions, as of mid-1998 the areas still continue to be out of compliance in meeting the ozone standard itself. Thus, the EPA issued a limited approval/disapproval for Texas's implementation plan to reduce VOC emissions by 15 percent. In essence, the EPA ruled that the emission reductions did not go far enough.[73]

In addition, the Dallas-Fort Worth—with its redesignation—and the Houston-Galveston nonattainment areas are required to reduce either VOCs or nitrogen oxides an average of 3 percent each year for three years, or until standards are met.[74] The TNRCC estimates that Houston-Galveston will meet this additional 9 percent reduction by 1999.

The decision of whether to target nitrogen oxide or VOC emission reductions is an important one, since they are emitted by different sources. Generally, refineries and electrical generation stations emit more nitrogen oxides than do other sources, while

NON-ATTAINMENT AREAS IN TEXAS

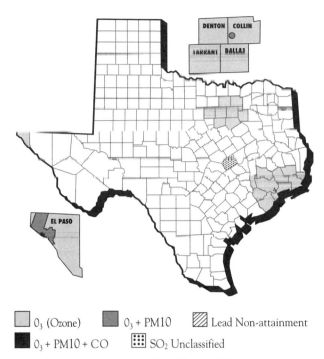

☐ O₃ (Ozone)   ■ O₃ + PM10   ▨ Lead Non-attainment
■ O₃ + PM10 + CO   ⊞ SO₂ Unclassified

Note: Suburban counties in the Dallas-Fort Worth area, while technically attainment counties, have agreed to participate in the State Implementation Plan for transportation control measures. These counties include Ellis, Johnson, Kaufman, Parker and Rockwall. Milam County and the Houston Ship Channel are unclassified because of high SO₂ Levels, although they are not considered nonattainment areas.

Source: Texas Natural Resource Conservation Commission, Revisions to State Implementation Plan (1996).

CATEGORIES OF NON-ATTAINMENT AREAS IN TEXAS AND COMPLIANCE DEADLINES

NON-ATTAINMENT OZONE AREA	EPA CLASSIFICATION	DEADLINE FOR COMPLIANCE
Dallas/Ft. Worth	Serious	November 1999
Beaumont/Port Arthur	Moderate	November 1996
El Paso	Serious	November 1999
Houston/Galveston/Brazoria	Severe II	November 2007
NON-ATTAINMENT CARBON MONOXIDE		
El Paso	Moderate	November 1995
NON-ATTAINMENT RESPIRABLE PARTICULATE MATTER		
El Paso	Moderate	November 1994

Note: The EPA is considering approving a Section 818 application from the City of El Paso, which states that due to pollution from Ciudad Juarez they are unable to meet compliance deadlines and will not be pushed into higher EPA classification. Nonetheless, they are still required to comply with the National Standards.

Source: Texas Natural Resource Conservation Commission, Office of Air Quality.

TEXAS STATUS UNDER PROPOSED FEDERAL 8-HOUR OZONE STANDARDS, 1997–1999

	1999	1998	1997
Houston-Galveston-Brazoria	0.124	0.117	0.124
Dallas-Fort Worth	0.106	0.102	0.113
Beaumont-Port Arthur	0.094	0.096	0.093
Longview-Marshall-Tyler	0.105	0.104	0.091
Austin	0.099	0.088	0.087
San Antonio	0.091	0.090	0.084
Standard	**0.085**	**0.085**	**0.085**
El Paso	0.071	0.092	0.075
Corpus Christi	0.085	0.082	0.077
Victoria	0.086	0.078	0.078
Brownsville-Edinburg	0.072	0.071	0.067
Laredo	0.067	0.067	0.063

Note: Based on fourth highest 8-hour day; concentrations in parts per million.

Source: Texas Natural Resource Conservation Commission, Office of Air Quality, 1999.

TNRCC PROPOSED 60-MILE AND 120-MILE OZONE CONTROL ZONES

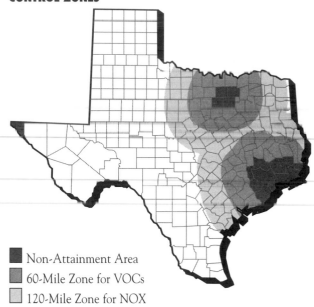

■ Non-Attainment Area
▨ 60-Mile Zone for VOCs
▢ 120-Mile Zone for NOX

Source: U.S. Census Bureau, 1990 TIGER Data.

VOCs are emitted by mobile sources, small sources, and industries. Between 1994 and 1997, Texas received approval for a nitrogen oxides waiver from the federal Clean Air Act, meaning that only VOCs have been targeted in the nonattainment areas for reduction.

However, based on the rising number of days exceeding standards, the TNRCC did not apply for a nitrogen oxides waiver in 1998. Instead, the TNRCC is proposing significant nitrogen oxides reductions in Houston, Dallas, and Beaumont and, even further, is proposing a regional ozone control strategy to include areas that currently meet the federal ozone standards but influence these cities through the transport of ozone. Under the proposed regional control strategy, a 60-mile line would be drawn around the nonattainment areas for control of VOCs, and a 120-mile line would be drawn around the nonattainment areas for control of nitrogen oxides.

The state implementation plan is also requiring consumers, small businesses, and major industries in nonattainment areas to alter their activities. For example, in nonattainment areas, the following programs, many of which are still undergoing refinement, are being required:[75]

■ Under the state's most recent plan to control ozone pollution, beginning in 1997 automobile owners in El Paso, Tarrant, Dallas, and Harris counties are required to have emissions from their vehicles tested either annually or every two years, depending on the type of test.[76] Vehicles that do not meet emission standards would have to be repaired at the owner's expense. Beaumont-Port Arthur is not required to test cars because of its smaller population.

■ Service stations are required to install equipment to control gasoline vapors at the pump and as fuel is being unloaded into storage tanks. Most stations had to comply by 1994; smaller stations built before 1992 and selling less than 10,000 gallons of gasoline per month are exempt.

■ Houston-Galveston and Dallas-Fort Worth area residents can use only reformulated gasoline, a cleaner-burning but more-expensive fuel.

■ El Paso residents have to use slightly more expensive oxygenated gasoline to reduce carbon monoxide emissions between October and March each year to help comply with carbon monoxide standards.

■ Specific industries will be required to install pollution control equipment beyond that required under current regulations.

OFFSET RATIOS FOR OZONE NON-ATTAINMENT AREAS

	CLASSIFICATION	OFFSET RATIO	% NET REDUCTION
Dallas/Fort Worth	Serious	1.20 to 1	20%
El Paso	Serious	1.20 to 1	20%
Beaumont/ Port Arthur	Moderate	1.15 to 1	15%
Houston/Galveston	Severe	1.30 to 1	30%

Source: Texas Natural Resource Conservation Commission, Revisions to the State Implementation Plan (1996) and Information from Office of Air Quality.

■ Small businesses like dry cleaners, paint shops, printers, and auto body shops will have to install pollution control equipment.

■ In El Paso, Dallas-Fort Worth, and Houston-Galveston, industrial wastewater systems are required to cover wastewater treatment areas and route the vapors through a control device.

■ All new or expanding major industries in a nonattainment area must apply for nonattainment source review permits, which are more stringent than attainment area permits, known as prevention of significant deterioration (PSD) permits.

■ All new or expanding major industries in non-attainment areas must first obtain corresponding reductions from other industrial facilities in the area before locating or expanding there. This offset ratio depends on the severity of ozone pollution in the nonattainment area.

NEAR NONATTAINMENT AREAS AND FLEXIBLE ATTAINMENT REGIONS

The TNRCC has designated five other metropolitan areas as "near nonattainment" areas: Austin, San Antonio, Corpus Christi, Victoria, and the Tyler-Longview-Marshall area. They are called near nonattainment because they have on occasion exceeded standards, because they were once non-attainment areas but have since come into compliance, or because of their potential for future non-attainment status. Tyler-Longview-Marshall exceeded the standard four times in 1995, five times in 1998 and three times in 1999—bringing it technically out of compliance with the 1-hour standard—while Corpus Christi exceeded the standard three times

FLEXIBLE ATTAINMENT REGIONS AND NEAR NON-ATTAINMENT AREAS IN TEXAS FOR OZONE

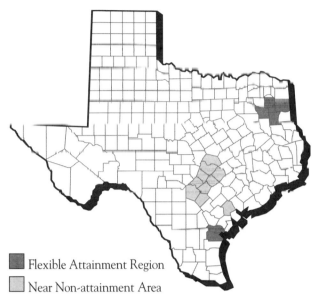

■ Flexible Attainment Region

□ Near Non-attainment Area

Source: Texas Natural Resource Conservation Commission, Texas Near Non-attainment Areas: Technical Background (Austin: TNRCC, 1994).

between 1993 and 1995. Similarly, San Antonio exceeded the standard twice in 1996 and twice in 1998. State and local officials are working on voluntary programs in these and other cities to reduce emissions of nitrogen oxides and VOCs.

In Corpus Christi and Tyler-Longview-Marshall, local officials reached formal agreements with the EPA and TNRCC in 1996 to participate in the Flexible Attainment Region (FAR) program for ozone. The cities have agreed to voluntary measures to reduce pollution, such as implementing vapor control from gasoline, improving their emissions inventory, and setting up local ozone-alert-day mechanisms. In exchange, the area will be given time to let its program work before sanctions from the EPA are imposed or a full state implementation plan and associated regulations are required. Under the flexible attainment agreements, both Corpus Christi and Northeast Texas have up to five years to let their programs work before additional requirements would apply.[77] Gregg County (Longview) will have to meet both the 1-hour and 8-hour standards.

Local business and political leaders have hailed such flexible, voluntary programs as an appropriate

ACHIEVING CLEAN AIR IS A BINATIONAL PROBLEM FOR EL PASO

El Paso is the only city in Texas in violation of national standards for both respirable particulate matter and carbon monoxide. The city is also designated as a "serious" nonattainment area for ozone. El Paso has been in compliance with national standards for nitrogen dioxide, sulfur dioxide, and, since 1986, lead.

El Paso and other cities along the Texas-Mexico border face unique pollution problems. Modeling studies designed by the TNRCC have shown that air pollution originating in Ciudad Juárez— which lies in a desert valley across the Rio Grande from El Paso—contributes as much or more to overall air pollution in El Paso than pollution originating on the U.S. side of the border.[78] In fact, pollution levels monitored in Ciudad Juárez are significantly higher than those in El Paso. These two cities, along with Sunland Park, New Mexico, share a common airshed in a valley characterized by the Rio Grande and surrounding mountain peaks. Temperature inversions in the area contribute to air pollution problems.

A 1990 joint study by the EPA, Texas Air Control Board, El Paso City/County Health Department, and Mexican authorities found that the highest concentrations of particulate matter occurred in urban Ciudad Juárez and in the mountain pass along the border.[79] The principle sources of carbon monoxide, particulate matter,

and ozone in the area include motor vehicles, industries located in the airshed, open burning of domestic and agricultural wastes, and the burning of common and hazardous wastes by brick kilns.

A problem specific to the area is the large number of vehicles waiting to enter or exit the United States from Mexico. The El Paso-Ciudad Juárez border crossing is one of the busiest crossings along the border. Each vehicle crossing the border, about 40 percent of which have Mexican license plates, must wait at least ten minutes at the border while its paperwork is processed. Vehicles at idle produce higher emissions. In addition, Mexican vehicles, because they are older and have less stringent maintenance and emission controls, tend to be higher emitters.

In 1995 and 1996 the TNRCC submitted a Section 818 Attainment Demonstration to the EPA to prove that pollution emanating from outside the United States prevents El Paso's compliance with national ambient air quality standards.[80] The "attainment demonstrations" are aimed at preventing the city from being bumped up from a serious to a severe ozone nonattainment area and from a moderate to a serious carbon monoxide and particulate matter nonattainment area.[81] It also keeps the city from suffering federal sanctions, including the loss of federal highway

Continued on next page

EXCEEDENCES OF MEXICAN CRITERIA POLLUTANT STANDARDS IN CIUDAD JUÁREZ, 1991–1995.

YEAR	OZONE EXCEEDENCES	HIGHEST LEVEL	CARBON MONOXIDE EXCEEDENCES	HIGHEST LEVEL	PARTICULATE MATTER EXCEEDENCES	HIGHEST LEVEL
1991	23	0.3081	23	13.85	15	18
1992	15	0.1322	1	11.45	14	314
1993	4	0.1543	2	11.35	13	251
1994	6	0.1459	0	8.88	20	341
1995	6	0.1171	8	14.67	7	242

Ozone 1-hour standard is 0.11 parts per million.

CO 8-hour standard is 11.00 parts per million.

PM-10 daily standard is 150mg/cubic meter.

Source: Oscar Ibáñez, Department of Ecology and Urban Development, Numicipality of Ciudad Juárez, 1996.

ACHIEVING CLEAN AIR IS A BINATIONAL PROBLEM FOR EL PASO (Continued)

EL PASO AND CIUDAD JUAREZ SHARE A COMMON AIRSHED

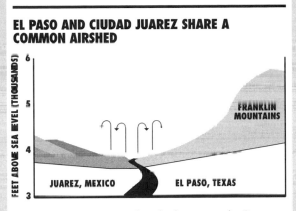

Inversions trap emissions from both cities in the Rio Grande river valley, causing pollution buildup.

Source: Texas Natural Resource Conservation Commission, Texas Near Non-attainment Areas: Technical Background (1994).

funds and construction grants even though the city continues to suffer poor air quality past compliance deadlines. In essence, El Paso is being given a break because of its inability to control pollution on the Mexican and New Mexican sides of the border. However, El Paso still has had to adopt and enforce stringent pollution control rules to comply with the federal Clean Air Act.

State and local officials, environmental groups, and business interests from the United States and Mexico have worked on setting up an International Air Quality Management District encompassing the two cities and surrounding areas. In 1996 the U.S. and Mexican governments agreed instead to the establishment of a Joint Advisory Committee on Air Quality Improvement, composed of local government, industry, and public representatives, which can make recommendations to a joint U.S.-Mexican Binational Air Quality Work Group led by the federal environmental authorities of both countries.[82] The advisory committee has made a number of recommendations and has adopted studies to help come up with creative solutions to the area's unique air pollution problems.

way to help regions come into compliance with the health-based standards of the Clean Air Act. Others have criticized the Flexible Attainment Region program for allowing cities to circumvent the health-based standards, if only for a time. For example, Northeast Texas violated the standard once in 1993 and four times in 1995, pushing it out of compliance, but the flexible program allowed it to adopt voluntary measures and did not impose growth-control mechanisms, such as offset emission requirements, on the area. In essence, Northeast Texas drivers, businesses, and industries got a regulatory break that residents in Houston, Dallas, El Paso, and Beaumont did not.

OTHER AIR QUALITY ISSUES

The criteria pollutants covered by the federal Clean Air Act are not the only air pollutants. Air toxics, greenhouse gases, ozone-depleting chemicals, and a wide variety of indoor air particulates also are of great concern. In addition, visibility impairment from air pollutants has become an increasing problem at wilderness areas and national parks.

Toxics

Air toxics is a term that describes a broad group of noncriteria pollutants, including National Emission Standards for Hazardous Air Pollutants (NESHAP) workplace pollutants, state-regulated pollutants, toxic compounds covered by the Toxics Release Inventory Program, and other toxic pollutants addressed by the federal Clean Air Act. While total emissions of these compounds are small compared to the criteria air pollutants — they are usually measured in pounds, not tons — their potential impact on human health can be great, especially for individuals living near a source of emissions. When air toxics are brought into the lungs through inhalation, some are readily absorbed into the bloodstream. Some air toxics can also irritate sensitive

POTENTIAL ADVERSE HUMAN HEALTH AND ENVIRONMENTAL EFFECTS OF THE TOP TRI CHEMICALS RELEASED TO THE AIR IN TEXAS IN 1997

	ACUTE TOXICITY	CARCINOGEN	HERITABLE GENETIC AND CHROMASOMAL MUTATION	CHRONIC TOXICITY	DEVELOPMENTAL TOXICITY
Ethylene				X	
Methanol	X				
Propylene					
N-Hexane					
Ammonia	X			X	
Toluene					X
Methyl Ethyl Ketone				X	X
Xylene				X	X
Styrene		X	X	X	X
Hydrochloric Acid	X			X	
Benzene	X	X		X	
Cyclohexane					
1,3-Butadiene		X		X	X
Glycol Ethers				X	
N-Butyl Alcohol					

	REPRODUCTIVE TOXICITY	ENVIRONMENTAL TOXICITY	OZONE DEPLETION	SMOG FORMATION	TOTAL LBS. RELEASED
Ethylene					16,101,199
Methanol					12,506,161
Propylene					9,670,831
N-Hexane					8,904,036
Ammonia		X			7,817,215
Toluene	X	X		X	5,550,241
Methyl Ethyl Ketone	X			X	4,574,445
Xylene	X	X			4,538,486
Styrene		X			3,259,878
Hydrochloric Acid					2,511,200
Benzene		X		X	2,439,940
Cyclohexane		X			2,145,656
1,3-Butadiene	X	X		X	1,480,344
Glycol Ethers		X			1,301,219
N-Butyl Alcohol					1,274,989

Note: N-Hexane was added as a reportable chemical in 1995 and is believed to affect the neurological system.

Source: Total pounds released from Environmental Protection Agency, 1997 Toxics Release Inventory Database, 1999; human health and environmental effects based on Clement Associates, Inc., Support Documentation for the SARA TITLE III, Sections 313/322 Toxicity Matrix (Fairfax, Virginia: Clement Associates, Inc., August, 1988, prepared for Environmental Protection Agency.

tissues in the eyes, throat, and nose. Some may cause cancer. Others may cause reproductive dysfunctions, birth defects, or nervous system disorders.

The 1986 Superfund Authorization and Renewal Act required businesses to report all releases into the air, water, or ground of more than 300 toxic chemicals and 20 toxic chemical compounds. These data are compiled into the Toxics Release Inventory Program. In the 1995 reporting year, the EPA added more than 300 chemicals to the list, and the number of chemicals and chemical compounds that must be reported now totals nearly 650.[83] In 1997 Texas industry again led the nation in air toxics releases, releasing more than 107 million pounds of toxics in all.[84]

1997 AIR EMISSIONS OF TOXICS IN MILLIONS OF POUNDS IN TEXAS, SELECTED STATES AND THE U.S.

	AIR EMISSIONS (in millions of pounds)
Texas	107.8
Tennessee	81.9
Louisiana	74.8
Ohio	66.8
Utah	65.6
Alabama	62.2
Indiana	57.0
North Carolina	52.1
Top Eight States	566.5
New Hampshire	2.2
North Dakota	1.9
Rhode Island	1.8
Nevada	1.7
Virgin Islands	1.4
Hawaii	0.4
Vermont	0.2
Guam	0.0
Bottom Eight	9.6
Total U.S.	**1,331.7**

Source: Environmental Protection Agency, 1997 Texas Release Inventory Public Data Release (Washington, D.C.: EPA, 1999), 2-18, 2-19

Industrial toxics emissions are just part of total toxic air emissions. In 1991 the Texas Air Control Board estimated that these releases accounted for only 18 percent of total toxic air emissions, while mobile sources—automobiles, motorcycles, pickups, vans, and trucks—accounted for 24 percent. On a statewide basis, "area sources"—dry cleaners, solvent and paint shops, and wastewater treatment plants, among others—emit up to three times the amount of toxics that major industries do statewide.[85] Still, the contribution of total air toxic emissions of each of these categories—industrial, mobile, and area sources—varies widely with location.

The EPA has had the authority to set standards for hazardous air pollutants since 1970. Because of sparse medical data, however, the EPA has faced numerous legal challenges in adopting regulatory measures. Up until 1993, the list of national hazardous air pollutant standards stood at seven and included the following chemicals: asbestos, beryllium, arsenic, mercury, benzene, vinyl chloride, and radionuclides.

Under the federal Clean Air Act, the EPA is required to designate control-technology standards for 174 types of facilities that emit 1 or more of the 188 listed hazardous air pollutants. While 39 standards were due by November 1994, by September 1998 the EPA had published final rules for only 29 standards, affecting 62 sources.[86] In some cases, the EPA has established the specific type of technology to be used to limit releases of pollutants; in others, industries will have flexibility in determining which type of technology they use to meet emission requirements.

For those compounds not classified as criteria pollutants or not having national hazardous air pollutant standards, air toxicologists and regulators at the TNRCC have conducted site-specific reviews of predicted or actual impacts for potential adverse effects. "Effects screening levels" (ambient air concentration guidelines, or ESLs) are used to gauge the potential of toxic air emissions associated with expansion of an existing facility or construction of a new facility to cause adverse health or welfare effects.[87]

Screening levels are set to protect against health effects, odor nuisance, effects on vegetation, or corrosive effects, and to protect the more sensitive members of the general public. If, during the permit review process, the TNRCC determines that proposed emissions may result in exposure of the general public outside of the facility to concentrations of air pollutants at levels above these screening levels, the commission may either deny the permit or require additional pollution control equipment as a permit provision.[88]

These health-based screening levels are controversial. Since each screening level is based on the effects of a single chemical, simultaneous exposure to several air pollutants that may similarly affect health may not be adequately addressed.[89] Another criticism is that the guidelines do not address specifically the potential accumulation in the environment, over time, of compounds like DDTs, PCBs, and metals. Although many toxics can degrade or be washed out of the environment in a short time, a few compounds are not readily degraded and may accumulate in the tissue of lower organisms, and eventually in fish, birds, and even mammals such as humans.

SOURCES OF AIR TOXICS, STATEWIDE AND IN MAJOR URBAN AREAS

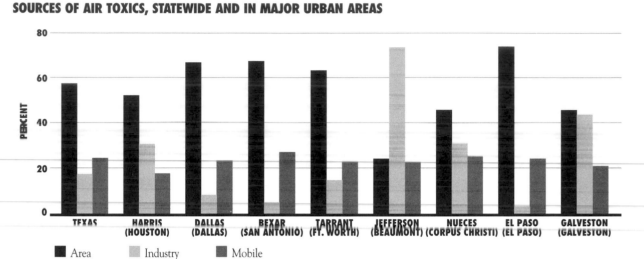

Source: *Joint Select Committee on Toxic Air Emissions and Greenhouse Effect,* Interim Report of the Joint Select Committee on Toxic Air Emissions and Greenhouse Effect *(June 199), 14.*

Some chemicals — including mercury, dioxins, and furans, among others — are placed in a special category and are referred to as "endocrine disruptors" because of their ability to affect the endocrine system, which secretes hormones into the body in humans and animals (see box: Endocrine Disruptors). Many of these bioaccumulate through the food chain. In reviewing the impacts of these chemicals, the TNRCC attempts to consider the potential for simultaneous exposure of toxics as well as the accumulation of toxics.[90]

While Texas keeps an extensive air toxic emission inventory — how many pounds of toxics are actually emitted in the air — there is much less data on levels of toxics in the ambient air. In 1992 the TNRCC established the Community Air Toxics Monitoring Program, composed of 15 monitoring sites.[91] By 1995 there were 23 monitoring sites located throughout the state, continuously measuring 69 VOCs in 15 counties. Since the toxics monitoring program began, benzene, a human carcinogen, has been the only compound consistently detected at levels above the effects screening levels. For example, in 1995 benzene concentrations exceeded the 24-hour screening level at 7 sites and the annual screening level at 8 sites.[92]

The TNRCC determined that the benzene

measurements that exceeded the 24-hour effects screening levels would not result in adverse acute health effects. While long-term exposure to benzene at levels significantly greater than the guidelines' annual levels may increase the lifetime risk of developing leukemia or affect the formation of blood, the TNRCC determined that measured levels of benzene have significantly decreased over the past ten years.[93] The commission did, however, note that it was important to prevent benzene levels from increasing and to take efforts to reduce potential public exposure.[94]

Benzene is a constituent of gasoline; it is released during refueling and is a component of car exhaust. Benzene is also released during industrial refining processes and from benzene storage tanks. In Texas the counties along the Gulf Coast have the greatest number of sources of benzene because of the large number of petrochemical companies and petroleum refineries. Air emissions of benzene, as well as other VOCs, like toluene and xylenes, from manufacturing facilities and ambient air concentrations near industrial sites decreased between 1989 and 1994.[95]

In addition, monitoring results showed that 1,3-butadiene exceeded its 24-hour effects screening level once in Port Arthur during 1995, while exceedences occurred in Port Neches, Odessa, and

ENDOCRINE DISRUPTORS

There is growing concern over a group of toxic chemicals that accumulate over time in the food chain and interfere with the endocrine system—the set of glands and the hormones they produce—and therefore impact reproduction, growth, and fetal development. Some of these chemicals may "mimic" natural hormones like estrogen and testosterone, upsetting normal reproductive and developmental processes. Others may block the effects of a hormone or stimulate the overproduction of hormones. Nonetheless, studies are still being conducted on these chemicals to determine if they indeed are endocrine disruptors and what long-term health effects they have.

The real-world effects of some of these chemicals is well documented if not well understood. The pesticide DDT—which especially affected the eagle and its ability to procreate—and the electric-transformer lubricant PCBs are the most famous of these chemicals and were banned in 1972 and 1979, respectively. Today, however, chemicals like dioxin and furans are considered by toxicologists to be even more dangerous. Dioxin is the common name for a family of 75 chemicals that are the unintended by-products of industrial processes involving chlorine. For example, in the paper pulp industry, dioxin forms when chlorine reacts with lignin, the "glue" that holds the wood of the trees together. Dioxin also forms in processes that burn chlorine with organic matter, such as occurs when cement kilns or incinerators burn hazardous wastes.[96] Furans are closely related compounds.

While dioxin and its possible harmful affects have been documented since the 1940s, not until the 1970s did dioxin become a national controversy. The controversy arose when Vietnam veterans who had been exposed to "Agent Orange," a herbicide contaminated with dioxin used to destroy rice fields during the war, began to experience a variety of health problems, including reproductive problems and cancer. Other well-known incidents involving dioxin include the evacuation of a New York town in 1978 because of the presence of dioxin in Love Canal, and the evacuation of Times Beach, Missouri, in 1983 after years of spraying of dioxin-laced waste oil to control dust had led to serious health problems.[97] In wildlife, evidence of dioxin's dangerous effects include the poisoning of fish and the deformation of birds; twisted beaks and reproductive inability occurred among fish-eating birds in the Great Lakes near pesticide and pulp- and paper-industry plants.[98]

Documented effects of dioxins and dioxinlike substances include:
- Cancer in wildlife and evidence of cancer in humans;
- Congenital anomalies;
- Weakening of the immune system;
- Liver defects;
- Reproductive and hormonal irregularities;
- Persistence in the environment; and
- Bioaccumulation.

Air emissions of dioxin are of particular concern because the dioxin particles bind to other particles such as incinerator ash and can then travel long distances, often covering more than 1,000 miles.[99] Eventually, they settle to the ground or are washed out by rain. Once in the soil, they can move rapidly through the food chain and are of particular concern when they accumulate in soil on dairy and beef farms, the main route of human exposure. Dioxin air emissions come from hazardous waste incinerators, municipal incinerators, medical incinerators, cement plants, wood and coal burning, forest fires, and copper smelting and refining, among other sources.[100] Water emissions of dioxin are mainly the result of wastewater discharges from the pulp and paper industry, while land emissions are the result of sludge from these plants and incinerator ash being deposited in quarries and landfills.

Continued on next page

ENDOCRINE DISRUPTORS (Continued)

ESTIMATES OF SOURCES OF DIOXIN EMISSIONS IN GRAMS OF TOXIC EQUIVALENT/YEAR, U.S.

EMISSIONS INTO MEDIA	SOURCE	EMISSIONS	% OF TOTAL
Air	Medical Waste Incineration	5,100	42%
	Municipal Waste Incineration	3,000	25%
	Cement Kilns	350	3%
	Industrial Wood Burning	360	3%
	Coal Burning	200	2%
	Secondary Copper Smelting	230	2%
	Iron Sintering	230	2%
	Transportation Vehicles	88	<1%
	Forest Fires	86	<1%
	Hazardous Waste Incineration	35	<1%
	Sewage Sludge Incineration	23	<1%
Total Air Emissions	9,800		81%
Water	Paper and Pulp Industry	110	<1%
Land/Landfill	Sludge and Incinerator Ash	2,100	18%
	Commercial Products	150	1%
Total Land/Landfills		2,250	19%
Total Emissions		**12,160**	**100%**

Source: Environmental Protection Agency, Estimating Exposure to Dioxin-Like Compounds, Vol. 2 (Washington, D.C.: June 1994). Estimates for emissions from coal burning and iron sintering are from the Center for the Biology of Natural Systems, as reported in Lois Marie Gibbs, Dying from Dioxin *(Boston: South End Press, 1995).*

In September 1994 the EPA released its second reassessment of dioxins and furans, their sources, and their human and environmental impacts. This reassessment has led to new air emission standards on municipal- and medical-waste incinerators, and to proposed new regulations on hazardous waste incinerators and cement plants, which burn hazardous wastes in part to reduce air emissions of dioxins. Similarly, the EPA, under the Hazardous Air Pollutant provisions of the Clean Air Act., is developing new regulations for the sources of mercury, which has a number of serious health impacts, including possible endocrine disruption.

In addition, the EPA has formed an Endocrine Disrupters Screening and Testing Advisory Committee (EDSTAC) to advise the agency on a strategy for testing new and existing chemicals for their potential to disrupt endocrine functions in humans and wildlife. The advisory committee held public meetings throughout the United States between 1996 and 1998. Under the 1996 Food Quality Protection Act and the Safe Drinking Water Act, the EPA must present a screening and testing program to Congress by August 1998 and implement the program by August 1999. The program determines which of the estimated 75,000 pesticides and chemicals currently approved need to be screened for endocrine disruption.

Texas City in 1994.[101] The Texas counties with the largest point-source emissions of 1,3-butadiene, like those for benzene, are located along the Gulf Coast.[102]

Another compound—1,2 dibromoethane— exceeded its effects screening levels at two sites in Houston and at sites in El Paso and Midlothian during the monitoring period running from October 1992 through September 1993.[103] During 1994 this

ANNUAL MEAN AND MAXIMUM BENZENE LEVELS AT SELECTED TOXICS MONITORING SITES, 1993–1995

SITE	ANNUAL MEAN ANNUAL EFFECTS 1 ppbv	MAXIMUM 24-HOUR SCREENING LEVELS 4 ppbv
HadenRd., Houston	1.72	10.83
	2.28	35.17
	2.70	63.63
El Paso	2.26	8.73
	2.34	11.27
	1.58	5.01
Odessa	1.51	4.78
	2.26	19.40
	0.72	2.24
Texas City	0.97	2.86
	1.21	4.16
	0.99	3.52
Channelview	1.16	3.11
	1.13	2.64
	1.05	3.01
Allendale, Houston	1.19	6.54
	1.24	4.03
	1.03	3.57
Clinton, Houston	1.29	2.40
	2.14	11.41
	1.49	3.64
Port Arthur	0.95	4.85
	1.37	5.38
	1.68	14.40
Groves, Jefferson County	2.17	7.81
	0.95	5.41
	1.08	6.46
Corpus Christi	1.17	5.01
	0.93	4.67
	1.06	5.70

Source: Texas Natural Resource Conservation Commission, Community Air Toxics Monitoring Network Report: January-December 1995 *(February 1997), Appendix A.*

compound exceeded the 24-hour screening levels on three occasions in Winona.[104] During 1995, the TNRCC decided not to monitor for this compound despite these past 24-hour exceedences.[105] Dibromoethane is released to the atmosphere primarily through its use as a pesticide and as a fuel additive for gasoline.[106] The manufacture of 1,2 dibromoethane has declined in recent years because its use as a fumigant has been banned and because the decline in lead content of gasoline has resulted in a decline in its use as a fuel additive. While 24-hour concen-

ANNUAL BENZENE POINT-SOURCE EMISSIONS IN TEXAS

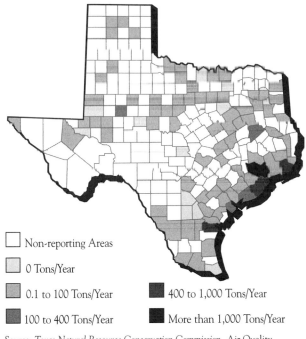

Non-reporting Areas

0 Tons/Year

0.1 to 100 Tons/Year

100 to 400 Tons/Year

400 to 1,000 Tons/Year

More than 1,000 Tons/Year

Source: Texas Natural Resource Conservation Commission, Air Quality Assessment Program: Community Air Toxics Monitoring Program Report, *October 1992–September 1993, (May 1994), 25*

trations did exceed the established effects screening level standards at these sites, the levels were not high enough to result in acute health effects according to TNRCC criteria.[107]

The TNRCC has also initiated special purpose studies at several sites around Texas. For example, after noticing high levels of arsenic in ambient air analyses in El Paso, the state initiated a special study in 1993 near the American Smelting and Refining Company (ASARCO). The Vilas Elementary School, about two miles southwest of the plant, was the site chosen for the study. The study showed that arsenic levels consistently exceeded both the annual and 24-hour screening levels. By comparing test results to levels measured when the ASARCO plant was shut down for a strike in 1980, the state concluded that the high arsenic levels were due to plant activity. During a permit hearing, the company agreed to reduce arsenic emissions by a factor of ten.[108]

Finally, the TNRCC also uses its mobile laboratory units to monitor air toxics. The mobile lab allows the

BENZENE, TOLUENE AND XYLENE AIR EMISSIONS IN THOUSANDS OF POUNDS AND AVERAGE ANNUAL CONCENTRATION IN PARTS PER BILLION BY VOLUME IN GULF COAST COUNTIES, 1989-1994

COUNTY	MEASURE	1989	1994	PERCENT
BENZENE				
Harris	Air Emissions	1,528	1,345	-12%
	Average Concentration	3.63	1.83	-50%
Chambers	Air Emissions	None Reported	N/A	
	Average Concentration	1.32	0.56	-58%
Jefferson	Air Emissions	933.9	657.4	-30%
	Average Concentration	2.02	0.89	-56%
Orange	Air Emissions	282.4	6.1	-98%
	Average Concentration	1.92	0.57	-70%
TOLUENE				
Harris	Air Emissions	3,107	1,872	-40%
	Average Concentration	5.02	2.31	-54%
Chambers	Air Emissions	449	147	-68%
	Average Concentration	1.91	0.73	-62%
Jefferson	Air Emissions	1,419	1,257	-11%
	Average Concentration	4.11	1.15	-72%
Orange	Air Emissions	12.4	9.6	-23%
	Average Concentration	5.97	0.70	-88%
TOTAL XYLENES				
Harris	Air Emissions	2,764	2.606	-6%
	Average Concentration	2.81	1.12	-60%
Chambers	Air Emissions	1.72	1.0	-42%
	Average Concentration	0.49	0.19	-61%
Jefferson	Air Emissions	684.7	372.2	-46%
	Average Concentration	2.21	0.35	-85%
Orange	Air Emissions	None Reported	94.0	N/A
	Average Concentration	2.09	0.32	-81%

Note: Ambient concentrations are from Houston Regional Monitoring sites and South East Texas Regional Planning Council Commission sites and do not include TNRCC sites. Emissions from Toxics Release Inventory.

Source: Texas Natural Resource Conservation Commission, Decrease in Ambient Air Concentrations of Benzene, Toluene, and Total Xylenes in Southeast Texas *(May1997).*

agency to do intensive, pollution-source-oriented monitoring trips downwind of industrial facilities, often in response to complaints by citizens (see Air Quality Monitoring section of this chapter).[109] Between January 1995 and August 1997, for example, the TNRCC conducted nearly 60 mobile monitoring studies throughout the state for a variety of toxic and criteria pollutant compounds. While most of the studies did not lead to evidence of major toxic problems or violations, tests conducted near chemical companies in August and October 1996 in the Beaumont-Port Arthur area and in February 1997 in Corpus Christi led to citations against six companies for violating sections of the Texas Clean Air Act.[110]

GREENHOUSE EFFECT

One reason the Earth is warm enough to support life is that carbon dioxide and other gases in the upper atmosphere act as a kind of transparent umbrella, allowing sunlight to pass through and then trapping the heat below. This intricate but natural process is known as the greenhouse effect.

With increased burning of coal, oil, and natural gas over the past century and with the destruction of much of the Earth's forest cover, the greenhouse effect may be intensifying. The burning of fossil fuels releases carbon dioxide, some of which is used by trees and other vegetation during photosynthesis and some of which is absorbed by the oceans. When

TNRCC MOBILE MONITORING STUDIES THAT DEMONSTRATED EXCEEDENCES OF HEALTH-BASED EFFECTS SCREENING LEVELS OR STATE REGULATORY STANDARDS AT INDUSTRIAL FACILITIES, JANUARY 1994 — MAY 1997

INDUSTRY AND CITY	CHEMICALS EXCEEDING ESLS OR STANDARDS	DATE
Formosa Plastics, Point Comfort	Ethylene Dichloride, Vinyl Chloride	Jan 1994
CITGO/Southwestern, Corpus	Benzene	Feb 1994
Coastal East, Corpus Christi	Benzene	Feb 1994
Valero, Corpus Christi	Sulfur dioxide, Hydrogen sulfide	Feb 1994
Gibralter Chemical, Winona	Benzene	Nov 1994
Chevron, ASARCO, El Paso	Benzene	Jan 1995
ASARCO, El Paso	SO_2	Feb 1995
Rexene Corporation, Odessa	Benzene	May 1995
International Bridges, Laredo	Carbon monoxide, Benzene, Alkenes, Alkanes	June 1995
Western Iron Works, San Angelo	Benzene	July 1995
Amoco Oil, Texas City	Benzene	Aug 1995
Coastal Products, Houston (1)	Benzene, Cresol, Formalydehyde	Oct 1995
Channel Refining, Houston		
Platzer Shipyard, Houston		
Joe Hughes, Houston		
Merichem, Houston		
CITGO, Corpus Christi	Sulfur dioxide, Benzene, Hydrogen sulfide	Dec 1995
Valero, Corpus Christi	Hydrogen sulfide	Dec 1995
Formosa Plastics, Point Comfort	Ethylene dichloride, Chloroform	Jan 1996
Fina Oil & Chemical, Big Spring	Hydrogen sulfide	Jan 1996
Shell Western, Denver City (2)	Alkanes	Jan 1996
Coastal Refining, Corpus Christi	Benzene	Feb 1996
GM Trading Co., San Antonio	Hydrogen sulfide	Apr 1996
Koch Refining, San Antonio	Benzene, Alkanes, Alkenes, Isopentane	Apr 1996
City Public Services, San Antonio	Phenanthrene, Flouranthene, Pyrene	Apr 1996
Gifford Hill, San Antonio	Total particulate matter	Apr 1996
BFI Landfill, San Antonio	Alpha-methyl styrene	May 1996
Huntsman Corp, Port Arthur	Benzene	May 1996
Huntsman C4 Corp, Port Neches	1,3-Butadiene	Aug 1996
Ameripol Synpol, Port Neches	1,3-Butadiene	Aug 1996
Ameripol Synpol, Port Neches	1,3-Butadiene	Oct 1996
Huntsman C4 Corp, Port Neches	1,3-Butadiene	Oct 1996

Notes: (1) The mobile monitoring study conducted in October 1995 in Houston revealed elevated levels downwind of the facilities mentioned. It is not possible, however, to determine from the monitoring to what extent each individual facility contributed to these exceedences of health-based screening levels.
(2) It was not possible to determine from the mobile monitoring study that found exceedences of health-based levels for alkanes in January 1996 downwind of Shell Western in Denver City if the alkanes originated from Shell Western or other industries in the area.

Source: Texas Natural Resource Conservation Commission, Toxicoloty & Risk Assessment Section, Office of Air Quality, 1997.

vast amounts of carbon dioxide are being produced and less is being used by plants, however, the concentration of carbon dioxide in the atmosphere increases. This accumulation of carbon dioxide and other greenhouse gases (methane, ozone, nitrous oxides, and chlorofluorocarbons) in Earth's atmosphere may be causing the average temperature around the globe to rise, a phenomenon referred to as "global warming."

HOW THE GREENHOUSE EFFECT WORKS

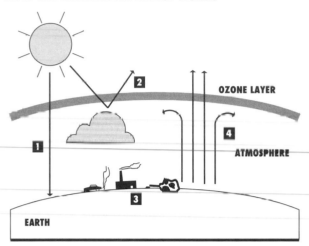

1. Most of the sun's energy reaches the Earth. (The ozone layer shields the Earth from the sun's harmful ultraviolet radiation.)
2. About 30 percent of the energy is reflected back into space.
3. Burning of fossil fuels and deforestation increase carbon dioxide in the atmosphere. Added to this are chlorofluoro-carbons (human-made gases used in spray cans, refrigerants and insulations) and methane (from landfills, farming and swamps).
4. Together, these gases form a "blanket" which traps energy, thus warming the Earth.

Source: World Resources Institute, Changing Climate: A Guide to the Greenhouse Effect *(1989).*

The environmental implications of global warming are serious. Higher average temperatures could hasten melting of the polar ice caps, raising sea levels and distorting rainfall patterns. Coastal cities and plant and animal habitat could be destroyed. An alteration of climate could also reduce crop production. While certain areas of the Earth might actually benefit from global warming, others would suffer disastrous effects.

Scientists like James Hansen, of NASA's Goddard Institute, believe that the Earth is already experiencing an enhanced greenhouse effect. For example, seven of the ten hottest years in recorded history occurred in the past ten years.[111] And studies have shown a correlation between the concentration of carbon dioxide in the atmosphere and a rise in global temperature.[112]

There is considerable debate about the phenomenon of global warming. Critics like Richard Lindzen of the Massachusetts Institute of Technology believe that, while carbon dioxide accumulation may lead

GREENHOUSE GASES AND THEIR SOURCES

GREENHOUSE GAS	SOURCE	LIFE SPAN IN ATMOSPHERE
Carbon dioxide (CO_2)	Fossil fuels, deforestation, soil destruction	500 years
Methane (CH_4)	Cattle, biomass, rice paddies, gas leaks, mining, termites	7-10 years
Nitrous oxide (N_2O)	Fossil fuels, soil cultivation, deforestation	140-190 years
Chlorofluorocarbons (CFCs 11 and 12)	Refrigeration, air conditioning, aerosols, foam blowing, solvents	65-110 years
Ozone and other trace gases	Photochemical processes, cars, power plants, solvents	Hours to days in upper troposphere

Source: World Resources Institute, The 1994 Information Please Environmental Almanac *(Boston: Houghton Mifflin Co., 1994), 344.*

to warming climates, the actual impacts of warming will be mitigated by other factors. For instance, the increase in soot, sulfuric acid, and particulate matter in the atmosphere, which help scatter light away from the Earth, may be counteracting temperature increases that would otherwise occur from the accumulation of greenhouse gases. Still other scientists believe that temperature fluctuations are a normal occurrence, attributable to such events as sun spots, and that techniques for measuring temperature are not accurate enough to permit scientists to design

CARBON DIOXIDE EMISSION CONTRIBUTIONS FROM VARIOUS SOURCES, 1994

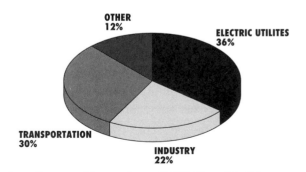

Source: Environmental Protection Agency, 1994 EPA National Air Pollutant Emissions Trends Report *(Research Triangle Park, N.C.: EPA, 1995).*

MAJOR EMITTERS OF CARBON DIOXIDE FROM FOSSIL FUELS

POLITICAL UNIT	EMISSIONS TOTAL[1]	PER CAPITA[2]	PERCENTAGE OF WORLD TOTAL	CUMULATIVE PERCENTAGE
Soviet Union	3,913	14.0	19.2%	19.2%
China	2,135	2.1	10.5	29.7
Germany[3]	975	12.9	4.8	34.5
Japan	950	8.1	4.7	39.2
India	580	0.7	2.8	42.0
Texas[4]	553	32.8	2.7	44.7
Great Britain	553	9.8	2.7	47.4
Poland	452	12.1	2.2	49.7
Canada	431	16.8	2.1	51.8
Italy	341	6.3	1.7	53.5
California[4]	310	10.9	1.5	55.0
France	308	5.7	1.5	56.5
Mexico	296	3.6	1.5	58.0
South Africa	280	8.4	1.4	59.3
Pennsylvania[4]	256	21.3	1.3	60.6
Ohio[4]	250	23.0	1.2	61.8
Australia	238	14.8	1.2	63.0
Czechoslovakia	229	15.0	1.1	64.1
Romania	214	9.6	1.1	65.2
Indiana[4]	194	34.9	1.0	66.1
South Korea	190	4.8	0.9	67.0
Brazil	190	1.4	0.9	68.0
Illinois[4]	189	16.3	0.9	68.9
Louisiana[4]	185	42.0	0.9	69.8
New York[4]	185	10.3	0.9	70.7
Rest of World	5,960	3.0	29.3	100.0
United States[5]	4,769	19.6	23.4%	23.4%
Rest of World	15,588	3.3	76.6	100.0
World	**20,357**	**4.1**	**100.0%**	**100.0%**

1. Million metric tons. 2. Metric tons. 3. Counting East and West Germany together even though the numbers are from 1988. 4. Counting the 50 states as individual political units. 5. Counting the United States as one political unit, rather than 50.

Source: Daniel Lashof and Eric Washburn, The Statehouse Effect: State Policies to Cool the Greenhouse (Washington, D.C.: Natural Resource Defense Council, 1990), A-3.

proper models of global temperature.

Overall, global temperatures have increased about 1 degree F in the past 130 years, half of that in the past 40 years. A body of 2,000 scientists around the globe known as the United Nation's Intergovernmental Panel on Climate Change (IPCC) has projected that by the year 2100, the average surface temperature will increase an additional 3.5 degrees F from 1990 levels.[113] The effects of these increases would be felt unevenly around the globe, with temperature changing less at the equator than at higher latitudes. For example, data reported by the panel indicate that over the past century, a trend toward more

precipitation at higher latitudes and less in the tropics has occurred, as predicted by computer modeling of a warming world.[114] The National Climatic Data Center has similarly reported an increase of 10 percent in overall precipitation and the frequency of intense rainstorms in southern Canada and the United States over the past century.

In Texas, climatic changes predicted as a result of global warming could profoundly alter how Texans live and work. In Dallas, for example, if the predictions of the Panel on Climate Change are true, the number of days when the temperature reaches 100 degrees F could increase from 19 to

CARBON DIOXIDE EMISSIONS FROM MAJOR POWER PLANTS IN TEXAS, 1995

COMPANY	PLANT	COUNTY	ESTIMATED EMISSIONS CARBON DIOXIDES (tons)	FUEL TYPE
City of Austin	Decker Creek	Travis	914,125	Gas
	Holly Street	Travis	471,270	Gas
Brazos	RW Miller	Palo Pinto	950,594	Gas
	North Texas	Parker	24,532	Gas
Bryan	Rol C Dansby	Brazos	266,394	Gas
	Bryan	Brazos	70,988	Gas
CSW	Laredo	Webb	499,442	Gas
Central Power & Light	Coleto Creek	Goliad	1,108,403	Coal
	Lon C Hill	Nueces	2,629,975	Gas
	Nueces Bay	Nueces	1,986,110	Gas
	BM Davis	Nueces	1,927,300	Gas
	La Palma	Cameron	571,416	Gas
	ES Joslin	Calhoun	519,560	Gas
	Victoria	Victoria	406,544	Gas
	JL Bates	Hidalgo	148,442	Gas
Denton	Spencer	Denton	190,974	Gas
El Paso Electric	Newman	El Paso	1,076,118	Gas
Garland	Ray Olinger	Collin	776,967	Gas
	CE Newman	Dallas	28,220	Gas
Gulf States	Sabine	Orange	5,870,342	Gas
	Lewis Creek	Montgomery	1,302,996	Gas
Houston Industries, Inc.	WH Parish	Fort Bend	20,919,184	Coal
(formerly Houston Lighting	Limestone	Limestone	12,711,150	Lignite
& Power)	Cedar Bayou	Chambers	3,305,906	Gas
	PH Robinson	Galveston	2,594,277	Gas
	Sam Bertron	Harris	753,112	Gas
	San Jacinto	Harris	663,674	Gas
	Greens Bayou	Harris	352,118	Gas
	Webster	Harris	270,040	Gas
	TH Wharton	Harris	148,312	Gas
	Deepwater	Harris	60,442	Gas
Lower Colorado River Authority	Sam Seymour	Fayette	10,540,286	Coal
	Sam Gideon	Bastrop	1,099,589	Gas
	TC Ferguson	Llano	599,406	Gas
City of Lubbock	Holly Avenue	Lubbock	13,510	Gas
Texas Utilities	Martin Lake	Rusk	18,403,859	Lignite
	Monticello	Titus	10,916,304	Lignite
	Big Brown	Freestone	6,820,531	Lignite
	Sandow	Milam	5,614,642	Lignite
	Tradinghouse	McLennan	3,176,822	Gas
	DeCordova	Hood	2,195,277	Gas
	Valley	Fannin	1,633,125	Gas
	Morgan Creek	Mitchell	1,465,405	Gas
	Stryker Creek	Cherokee	1,378,383	Gas
	Graham	Young	1,378,082	Gas
	Lake Ray Hubbard	Dallas	1,370,640	Gas
	Permian Base	Ward	1,333,519	Gas

Continued on next page

CARBON DIOXIDE EMISSIONS FROM MAJOR POWER PLANTS IN TEXAS, 1995 (continued)

COMPANY	PLANT	COUNTY	ESTIMATED EMISSIONS CARBON DIOXIDES (tons)	FUEL TYPE
Texas Utilities (Continued)	Mountain Creek	Dallas	1,288,741	Gas
	Handley	Tarrant	1,286,108	Gas
	North Lake	Dallas	1,060,886	Gas
	Eagle Mountain	Tarrant	442,669	Gas
	Lake Creek	McLennan	413,267	Gas
	Comanche Peak	Somervell	0	Nuclear
	South Texas NP	Matagorda	0	Nuclear
City of San Antonio	JT Deely	Bexar	5,023,789	Coal
	JK Spruce	Bexar	3,502,210	Coal
	OW Summers	Bexar	736,339	Gas
	VH Braunig	Bexar	516,504	Gas
	WB Tuttle	Bexar	13,968	Gas
San Miguel	San Miguel	Atascosa	3,671,210	Lignite
Southwestern Electric Power	Welsh	Titus	9,412,130	Coal
	HW Pirkey	Harrison	6,718,376	Lignite
	Wilkes	Marion	1,262,008	Gas
	Knox Lee	Gregg	534,844	Gas
	Lone Star	Morris	1,326	Gas
Southwestern Public Service	Harrington	Potter	9,400,450	Coal
	Tolk Station	Lamb	7,859,131	Coal
	CB Jones	Lubbock	1,228,951	Gas
	Plant X	Lamb	299,502	Gas
	Nichols	Potter	495,385	Gas
Texas-New Mexico	TNP One	Robertson	3,039,741	Coal
TMPA	Gibbons Creek	Grimes	3,850,775	Lignite
West Texas	Okalaunion	Wilbarger	4,588,181	Coal
Utilities	Rio Pecos	Crockett	480,725	Gas
	San Angelo	Tom Green	441,160	Gas
	Paint Creek	Haskell	330,387	Gas
	Ft. Phantom	Jones	237,611	Gas
	Oak Creek	Coke	228,482	Gas

Source: EPA, Acid Rain Database 1995, Appendix B.

78 per year by 2050. In Central Texas, average temperatures could go up 5 degrees during the same period.[115] Water availability might also be affected. Rainfall would decline in most areas of, and the hotter temperatures would increase the rate of evaporation, resulting in a reduced water supply. Coastal areas, however, would likely face more intense rainfall, as clouds forming from increased evaporation of ocean waters give rise to more violent storms. Low-level areas along the coast could be subject to more flooding from increased rainfall and rising sea levels.

Texas may, however, also derive some positive benefits from warmer annual temperatures. One of these effects is that milder winters may reduce the risk of freezes that cripple citrus crops.[116]

To delay or prevent global warming, world and national leaders have called for a reduction in carbon dioxide emissions, to be accomplished through a shift away from the use of oil, gas, and coal and toward the use of more renewable energy sources like solar power. The 1992 Rio treaty on climate change committed signatory nations to begin negotiations toward cutting greenhouse gas emissions.

LEADING OZONE DEPLETING CHEMICALS RELEASED TO THE AIR BY MAJOR INDUSTRIES IN TEXAS, 1997

CHEMICAL	RANKING OF ALL TOXIC AIR RELEASES	TOTAL AIR RELEASES (LBS.)
Chlorodifluoromethane	22	871,392
1,1,1-Dichloro-1-fluoroethane	41	271,812
1,1,1 - Trichloroethane	42	270,923
Carbon Tetrachloride	52	158,623
2-Chloro-1,1,1,2-Tetrafluoroethane	53	157,546
Dichlorodifluoromethane (CFC-12)	64	107,730
Freon 113	96	48,700

Source: Environmental Protection Agency, 1997 Toxics Release Inventory Database, 1999.

In December 1997 most of the world's nations hammered out a world agreement in Kyoto, Japan, that established limits and phased in reductions on the release of several greenhouse gases.[117] The agreement commits the developed nations—including the United States—to an 11 percent reduction in greenhouse gases over 1990 levels by 2010, but it does not determine what, if any, reductions developing nations must make, nor does it spell out exactly how the developed nations will make reductions. In addition, Congress still must approve the plan.

With only 5 percent of the world's population, the United States produces 23.4 percent of the carbon dioxide released from burning fossil fuels. Texas alone produces more carbon dioxide than either the United Kingdom or Canada.[118] The state emitted an estimated 550 million metric tons in 1988 from all sources.[119]

The electric utility industry is responsible for an estimated 36 percent of all carbon dioxide emissions in the United States[120] Texas produces and uses more electricity than any other state in the country.[121] Texas depends heavily on fossil fuels both to power cars and to generate electricity. Texas utilities, for example, contributed about 170 million metric tons of carbon dioxide in 1995, or about 30 percent of all greenhouses gases emitted in Texas. Without major changes in how Texas produces its energy, these levels are expected to continue (see *Energy* chapter).

DECREASING STRATOSPHERIC OZONE

Chlorinated fluorocarbons, or CFCs, is the name given to a family of chemicals developed in 1928 by the DuPont Company under the name Freon. CFCs have been used for refrigeration and air conditioning, as well as in the manufacture of aerosol sprays, computer chips, and many other products. When released into the air, these chemicals eventually rise to the stratosphere, where they are broken down by sunlight. This degradation process releases chlorine, which damages the layer of atmospheric ozone that absorbs most of the sun's ultraviolet-B radiation. The destructive influence of CFCs high in the atmosphere is significant: a single chlorine atom can lead to the destruction of more than 100,000 ozone molecules.[122]

Destruction of the ozone layer appears to be increasing. In the spring of 1985, British scientists found a hole about the size of the continental United States in the ozone layer over the Antarctica. This hole has reappeared each spring when meteorological conditions facilitate the breakdown in ozone. In 1992 satellite images recorded global ozone levels 4 percent lower than normal. Meanwhile, the concentration of CFCs measured in the atmosphere continues to climb.[123] The use of other "ozone-depleters" like halons, methyl chloroform, carbon tetrachloride, and hydrochlorofluorocarbons (HCFCs) also has been on the rise.[124] The high levels of ultraviolet-B radiation reaching the earth as a result of ozone depletion have been shown to increase the incidence of skin cancer and cataracts in humans. This radiation also adversely affects plants and animals.

Because of the danger CFCs pose to the ozone layer, the federal Clean Air Act requires a phase-out of the production of CFCs and halons by the year 2000.

Interim substitutes, such as HCFCs, also will be eventually phased out. In Texas, major industries still release millions of pounds of the ten chemicals the EPA has identified as ozone-depleters. Still, most CFCs do not come from industrial sources but rather from refrigerants, automobile air conditioning, and solvents in oil-based paints.

INDOOR AIR POLLUTION

The air we breathe indoors, whether at home, in our cars, or at work, may represent a bigger threat to human health than outdoor air pollution. With people spending up to 90 percent of their time indoors, the quantity and severity of health problems related to indoor air quality has potentially increased over the past ten years.[125] For example, in a December 1989 report, the EPA compared the risks of 20 different environmental problems and found that indoor air pollution posed the greatest health risk, though it had the least amount of federal money dedicated to it.[126] A recent report evaluating environmental health risks in Texas found indoor air pollution to be the most serious human health risk, closely followed by high particulate matter and ozone levels.[127]

The severity of indoor air pollution is aggravated by the fact that new buildings are being built more tightly to save money spent on heating and cooling. Because these tightly sealed, more energy efficient buildings prevent the exchange of outside and inside air, they reduce the amount of fresh air in a building. At the same time, people are using more and more irritating products such as hair sprays, pesticides, and cleaning detergents. In Texas the Department of Health's Indoor Air Quality Branch is responsible for responding to indoor air quality complaints, providing on-site investigations, educating the public about indoor air quality health problems, and suggesting methods to alleviate indoor air quality problems.

FYI *During FY 1997, the Texas Department of Health's Indoor Air Quality Branch received more than 5,300 requests for information; conducted 66 on-site investigations as a result of indoor air quality complaints from schools, buildings, and residences; and performed*

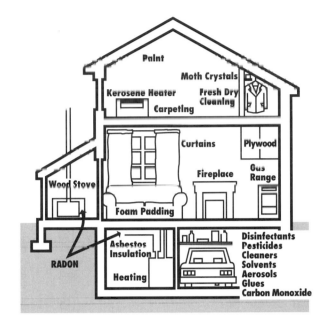

Source: Environmental Protection Agency, The Inside Story: A Guide to Indoor Air Quality (Washington, D.C, 1988), 2.

more than 300 on-site investigations overall, including private residences. For more information, call the Occupational Health Division at the Department of Health at 512-834-6600. (Source: Indoor Air Quality Branch, Texas Department of Health, Austin.)

The American Lung Association has estimated that indoor air pollution costs businesses over $100 billion a year, because of death, sick days, direct medical costs, loss of productivity, and damage to materials and equipment. The EPA projects that 3,500 to 6,500 premature deaths per year are the result of the effects of indoor air pollutants.[128] The causes of these deaths include cancer and coronary heart disease caused by exposure to radon, paints, solvents, and secondhand tobacco smoke.

In 1989 EPA Administrator William K. Reilly asked an independent team of scientists known as the Science Advisory Board to assess and compare different environmental risks using recent scientific data. The group found that indoor air quality problems from environmental (secondhand) tobacco smoke, radon, and six VOCs often found indoors in

PERCENT OF HOMES IN TEXAS DEPARTMENT OF HEALTH SURVEY WITH ELEVATED LEVELS OF RADON

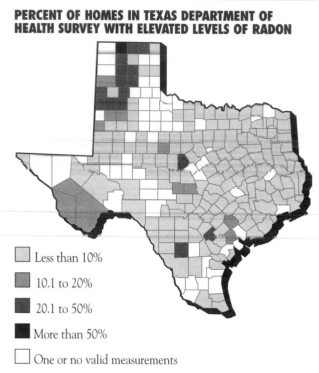

☐ Less than 10%

▨ 10.1 to 20%

▧ 20.1 to 50%

■ More than 50%

☐ One or no valid measurements

Source: Texas Department of Health, The Texas Indoor Radon Survey, 1992 (April 20, 1992), 20.

solvents, paints and gasoline products represented one of four problems posing "relatively high human health risks."[129]

Despite these problems, indoor air quality is not regulated, except as it relates to workplace air concentration standards under the Occupational Safety and Health Administration (OSHA). In 1995 the Texas legislature, responding to concerns about air quality in public schools, passed HB 2850, which charged the Texas Department of Health with writing voluntary guidelines for air quality in public schools. These voluntary guidelines, which went into effect May 10, 1998, establish general practices of maintaining fresh air in schools, establish protocols for routine building maintenance and operation, and suggest construction and renovation designs, among other issues.[130]

Radon, a naturally occurring radioactive gas, is responsible for an estimated 10 percent of lung cancer deaths. This colorless, odorless gas occurs everywhere at low levels, but it becomes a concern when it is trapped in buildings with little ventila-

tion. Radon gas may enter homes built on soils or rocks containing high levels of uranium, which is the most common source of the gas, or through cracks or other openings in basements or ground floors. Studies by the EPA indicate that as many as 10 percent of U.S. homes may have elevated radon levels.[131] A 1992 study by the Texas Department of Health monitored indoor air for radon in about 2,700 homes across Texas. The department found four areas with a high potential for radon: the West Texas Panhandle region, the Big Bend area, the Llano Uplift area, and inland from the Coastal Bend in South Texas.[132]

Microorganisms—bacteria, viruses, and fungi— can cause serious illnesses such as Legionnaire's disease, asthma, influenza, and other infectious diseases.[133] These microorganisms can grow in humid buildings, as well as in bedding or the litter of household pets, and without proper ventilation can easily infect occupants. More subtle health effects, commonly known as "sick building syndrome," include headaches; irritation of eyes, nose, and respiratory tract; loss of memory; fatigue; and drowsiness. An EPA survey of office workers across the nation found that 19 percent of respondents sometimes had difficulty performing work because of poor indoor air quality.[134]

Indoor exposure to pesticides, asbestos, and lead all affect human health, particularly the health of young children. The practice of sanding or open-flame burning of lead-based paints, which were in common use before 1978, emit compounds that can impair mental and physical development in both fetuses and young children. Using 1990 census data, the EPA determined that 3.5 million homes in Texas contain some lead-based paint. Based on these figures, the EPA estimates that 1,949,696 children six years old or under have the potential to be exposed to lead poisoning.[135]

Pesticides in the home or office can irritate eyes, nose, and throat and may damage the central nervous system or may even lead to an increased risk of cancer. According to an EPA survey, nine out of ten U.S. households have used pesticides.[136] Chlordane, dieldrin, and other chemicals used to kill termites

HEALTH EFFECTS IN CHILDREN AND FETUSES FROM LEAD EXPOSURE

SYMPTOMS	BLOOD LEAD LEVEL
Premature birth, low birth-weight, learning & development deficits	10-15 mcg/dl
Lower IQ's	25
Slower reflexes	30
Decreased red blood cells	40
Nerve problems	70
Anemia	70
Colic	70
Kidney and stomach problems	90
Brain problems	100

Health effects begin at about these levels, but not all children experience them.

Source: Texas Department of Health, Facts About Lead (n.d.).

LOCATION OF SULFUR DIOXIDE EMISSIONS SOURCES NEAR BIG BEND NATIONAL PARK

Note: Total for Carbon I/II is an estimate.

Source: TNRCC, State Summary of Emissions Database, 1998.

have been banned or their indoor use severely restricted in part because they remain active for such long periods. A particular concern is that indoor pesticide application may be related to incidences of cancer in children. A 1995 study in the Denver area examined 252 children diagnosed with cancer and compared them with a similar number of control subjects. The study found some evidence that yard treatments and pest strips containing insecticides might be associated with specific kinds of cancer.[137]

Several types of asbestos products, made from a mineral fiber used as an insulator and fire-retardant, have been banned by the EPA because they can cause chest and lung cancer, as well as a condition known as asbestosis, an irreversible lung scarring that can be fatal.[138] Elevated concentrations of asbestos can occur indoors when asbestos-containing materials are disturbed by remodeling or demolition activities.

VISIBILITY AND CLASS I AREAS

Visibility—how far you can see on a clear day—has become a major air quality issue in cities and in rural and wilderness areas. Without the effects of pollution, the natural visual range in the eastern states would be 90 miles, while in the West it

would be approximately 140 miles.[139] However, soil dust, sulfates from sulfur dioxide, carbon monoxide and nitrates from nitrogen oxide emissions, soot, ozone haze, and other contaminants, as well as natural events like volcanic explosions, have reduced visual range to 14 to 24 miles in the East and 33 to 90 miles in the West.

In 1980 the EPA adopted visibility protection provisions under the Clean Air Act to help protect 156 "Class I" areas nationwide—major parks and wilderness areas over 6,000 acres—where pristine air quality and scenic vistas are integral features. Under the regulations, states are required to develop for the Class I areas "visibility protection plans" for reducing visibility problems that can be attributed to individual sources or groups of sources. In addition, the plan should also have a "prevention of significant deterioration" program that would specifically prevent new emissions of sulfur dioxide over a specific baseline concentration from affecting Class I areas. Thus, the rules were designed to protect visibility within these areas—being able to see from one end of the park to the other—rather than to protect visual range in general.

In Texas the TNRCC and its predecessors have been charged by the EPA with coming up with a plan to protect visibility in Big Bend National Park and Guadalupe Mountains National Park, the only two Class I areas in Texas. According to TNRCC's January 1995 visibility protection plan, the National Park Service must be notified and given time to review the permit application of any new source located within 100 kilometers of either park.[140] However, because no major sources are located within 100 kilometers of Big Bend, the document states that this provision has not been utilized and a long-term strategy for visibility protection has not been developed.

Nonetheless, studies have shown that sulfur dioxide emissions from sources more than 100 kilometers from Big Bend are having, at least cumulatively, adverse effects on visibility.[141] In fact, visibility within the parks and visual range in general in these parks has plummeted. For example, while natural visibility in Big Bend should be roughly 150 miles, average visibility is now 60 miles (50 in summer months), according to recent averages. In fact, on some days the amount of particles in the air is so bad that the health of visitors has been impacted. For example, between August 21 and 27, 1995, visual range in Big Bend averaged 23 miles (only 9 miles on August 22).[142] Similarly, visibility in the Guadalupe Mountains was reduced to 30 miles during the same period.

Studies have linked visibility reduction in Big Bend to sulfur dioxide emissions from sources in northern Mexico, West Texas, and the Gulf Coast of Texas.[143] The largest sources of sulfur dioxide emissions in the area are from the Carbón I and II coal-fired electric generating plants near Piedras Negras, Coahuila, Mexico. A 1996 study, conducted by U.S. and Mexican authorities, suggested that visibility impairment was due to a variety of sources, including large coal-fired plants in Northeast Texas, as well as Mexican sources.[144] The Carbón I and II plants have been constructed and operated without basic control-equipment technology for sulfur dioxide, which would be required for new plants in the United States but is not in Mexico.[145] This fact—

as well as Mexico's plans to build other electric generating plants in the area—has led to a series of meetings between the U.S. and Mexican governments, although no concrete actions other than the 1996 air quality study have been agreed upon.

New proposed regulations may help control the Texas sources of "visual" pollution. In 1997 the EPA proposed revising the 1980 visibility rules by addressing visibility impairment due to regional haze in Class I areas. Under the proposed regulations, most states would have to design programs that would improve visibility in the Class I areas by 1.0 deciview (a measure of visual range) on the 20 percent of most-polluted days while maintaining current levels of visibility on the 20 percent of cleanest days over the next ten years.[146] As part of this program, states would need to monitor for PM2.5—fine particulate matter—in the parks; identify old, uncontrolled major pollution sources; and evaluate the need to install additional pollution controls.

FYI *If air pollution and visibility improve at the rate of one deciview per decade, it would take between 130 and 150 years to obtain "pristine" views at the Class I areas in Texas—Big Bend National Park and Guadalupe Mountains National Park. (Source: Data from IMPROVE monitors, National Park Service.)*

MOBILE SOURCES
Overview
Today's automobile produces approximately 90 percent less pollution than cars built in the 1960s.[147] Leaded gasoline has been phased out, and government-mandated manufacturing improvements such as the catalytic converter and the fuel injector have significantly reduced tailpipe emissions. However, the benefits of these improvements have been largely offset by several factors: a rapid expansion in the number of cars on the roads, including an increase in gas-guzzling light trucks and sports utility vehicles; an increase in the number of miles driven each day; and changes in the composition of gasoline. (As lead has been phased out, refineries have made up for the loss in octane with changes in the gasoline formula that make auto fuel more likely to release

NEW HIGHWAY VEHICLE PROGRAMS INCLUDED IN TEXAS'S STATE IMPLEMENTATION PLAN FOR NON-ATTAINMENT AREAS, 1996–1997

REFORMULATED FUEL: Houston-Galveston-Brazoria. Had to use fuels that were 15 percent cleaner in 1995 and 25 percent cleaner by 2000. Fuel distributors must sell gasoline that has been reformulated to produce lower hydrocarbon emissions. Fuel costs increase 3 to 5 cents in affected areas.

LOWER REID VAPOR PRESSURE GASOLINE: El Paso. Instead of Reformulated Fuels, El Paso's fuel distributors produce lower reid vapor pressure gasoline to reduce hydrocarbon emissions. Fuel costs increase one cent.

OXYGENATED FUEL: El Paso. Gasoline sold between October 1 and March 31 must have a minimum oxygen content of 2.7 percent to reduce carbon monoxide emissions.

TEXAS CLEAN FLEET PROGRAM: El Paso and Houston-Galveston-Brazoria. A certain percentage of local governmental fleets with more than 15 vehicles and private fleets with more than 25 fleet vehicles must meet low-emission vehicle (LEV) standards beginning September 1, 1998. Standards may be met with a variety of alternative or reformulated fuels. In addition, statewide, 50% of all mass transit vehicles and state agency vehicles had to meet or exceed the federal low emission vehicle standards by September 1, 1996.

TEXAS MOTORIST'S CHOICE VEHICLE EMISSIONS TESTING PROGRAM: Tarrant, Dallas, El Paso, and Harris Counties. Vehicle owners with gasoline-powered vehicles less than 24 years old must pass an annual emissions and safety test beginning with the vehicle's second model year anniversary. Vehicles failing must be repaired and pass a retest or qualify for a waiver. In addition, remote sensing will target high-emitting vehicles commuting from adjacent ozone non-attainment counties (Denton, Collin, Brazoria, Galveston, Chambers, Liberty, Waller, Montgomery, and Fort Bend). If detected as "grossly polluting vehicle," motorists in these counties will be subject to a vehicle emissions test.

TRANSPORTATION CONTROL MEASURES: Dallas-Fort Worth, Houston-Galveston-Brazoria, and El Paso. Control measures may include "high-occupancy vehicle" (HOV) lane, park-and-ride lots, transit service improvements, rideshare initiatives and intelligent transportation systems. Additional measures may include pedestrian improvements, bicycle improvements, trip reduction initiatives, flexible work hours, emission pricing, K-12 system management, and others.

Source: Texas Natural Resource Conservation Commission, Revision to the State Implementation Plan for the Control of Ozone Air Pollution (1997); and *Texas Natural Resource Conservation Commission*, Revision to the State Implementation Plan for the Substitute of the Federal Clean Fuel Fleet Program (July 1996).

smog-forming VOCs into the air.[148]) As a result, motor vehicles and other types of gasoline-powered transportation still contribute significantly to air pollution, accounting for a quarter of the CFCs in the air, 70 percent of the carbon monoxide, 30 percent of the carbon dioxide, 50 percent of the nitrogen oxides, and more than one-third of VOCs emitted in the United States.[149]

There are three obvious ways to reduce pollution from cars and trucks: manufacture low-emission vehicles, reduce the number of vehicle miles traveled, and convert vehicles to cleaner, alternative fuels like natural gas, propane, and electricity.

The federal Clean Air Act requires states to develop a plan to bring nonattainment areas into compliance with national air quality standards. These plans must include a mobile sources component. In 1995 the TNRCC submitted a mobile-sources implementation plan to the EPA for the state's four ozone nonattainment areas. However, due to bills passed by the Texas legislature in 1995, the TNRCC was forced to significantly alter the plan's inspection and maintenance programs for cars in the nonattainment areas, as well as the clean fuel fleet program, and resubmit its implementation plan in 1996. In 1997 changes mandated by the Texas legislature forced the TNRCC once again to prepare an updated state implementation plan for the Texas clean fuel fleet program. In addition, an employer trip-reduction plan previously required for the Houston area was dropped due to changes in EPA requirements in 1995. The effect of these changes has been to make the mobile source programs more flexible, but at the same time it has reduced the possibility of cutting vehicle emissions further.[150]

TIGHTER TAILPIPE-EMISSION STANDARDS

To cut down emissions from auto tailpipes may be the most direct method of reducing air pollution.

NUMBER OF VEHICLES, MILES DRIVEN, AND CONGESTION IN MAJOR TEXAS CITIES, 1994

	HOUSTON	DALLAS	FORT WORTH	SAN ANTONIO	AUSTIN	EL PASO
Registered Vehicles	2,240,000	1,630,000	920,000	890,000	450,000	410,000
Total Vehicle Miles (millions)	74.9	53.0	29.8	27.1	15.0	10.5
% of Vehicles with one occupant	72%	72%	77%	73%	74%	74%
National Congestion Rank	#13	#16	#32	#43	#32	#49

Source: Texas Comptroller of Public Accounts, Fiscal Notes (June 1997).

The Pechan Study, sponsored by the Northeastern States for Coordinated Air Use Management, concluded that cutting emissions from mobile sources is more economical than reducing emissions from industry. Of course this relationship does not hold for all industries and all areas. But in areas of Texas where mobile sources contribute significantly more VOCs and nitrogen oxides to the atmosphere than industries do, reducing vehicle emissions may be the most economical way to fight urban pollution.[151]

FYI ☞ *According to a recent study, cutting smog-forming pollution from vehicles costs about $500 per ton through a vehicle-emissions program; reducing the same amount of pollution in major industries costs from $2,000 to $10,000 per ton, according to the EPA.*
(Source: Sam Howe Verhovek, "Texas Joins Parade of States Colliding with Clean Air Act," New York Times, February 14, 1995.)

Under the 1990 federal Clean Air Act, pollution control equipment (e.g., fuel injectors and catalytic converters) on all 1994 cars were required to last for 100,000 miles, rather than the 50,000 miles required by previous federal clean air acts. In addition, engines for diesel trucks must be designed to reduce particulate releases by 90 percent. Finally, the act requires the automobile industry to manufacture vehicles by 2004 that emit 35 to 50 percent less VOCs, nitrogen oxides, and carbon dioxide than did 1994 vehicles.[152]

EPA emission limits for cars and light trucks — which includes most pick-ups, minivans, and sport utility vehicles — were last set in the mid-1990s. Emission limits of smog-producing nitrogen oxides are 20 to 100 percent higher for light trucks than for cars. In 1975 there were only about 20 million light trucks on U.S. roads; in 1997, there were 65 million, or three times as many.[153] The effect overall has been to increase total vehicle emissions of nitrogen oxide and carbon dioxide. In 1999 the EPA proposed new emissions standards beginning in 2004 that would for the first time subject cars and light trucks to the same standards.[154]

EMISSIONS TESTING

The federal Clean Air Act and subsequent 1995 EPA regulations require all nonattainment areas over a certain size (200,000 population) to adopt a vehicle-emissions testing program, also known as an inspection and maintenance program, to ensure that locally operated vehicles meet EPA standards.[155] While Texas implemented a vehicle-emissions testing program in 1995, legislation passed by the 74th Texas Legislature canceled the testing program and mandated that the TNRCC negotiate with the EPA to make it less costly and more convenient to drivers. Run by the Department of Public Safety, the Texas Motorist's Choice Vehicle Emissions Testing Program requires car and truck owners in Harris, El Paso, Dallas, and Tarrant counties to have their vehicles' emissions tested in either an annual two-speed idle and gas-cap integrity test or a biennial (every two years) loaded-mode (treadmill) test, which uses more advanced equipment. The emissions testing fee is $13.

Should a vehicle fail the emissions test, it must be repaired and retested, although waivers are available. In addition, the Department of Public Safety is

NUMBER OF VEHICLES POTENTIALLY COVERED BY THE TEXAS MOTORIST'S CHOICE VEHICLE EMISSIONS TESTING PROGRAM

AREA	1993 VEHICLE POPULATION	VEHICLES COVERED BY PROGRAM
Dallas/Ft. Worth	2,301,601	2,301,601
Total Surrounding Counties	451,921	147,411
Houston (Harris)	2,048,882	2,048,882
Surrounding Counties	706,018	64,692
El Paso	338,921	338,921
Total Vehicle Population	**5,847,343**	**4,901,507**

Source: Texas Natural Resource Conservation Commission, Inspection/Maintenance State Implementation Plan for Dallas/Ft. Worth, El Paso and Houston Non-Attainment Areas (1996), 91.

using remote-sensing equipment in Houston and Dallas-Fort Worth to target high-emitting vehicles commuting from adjacent ozone nonattainment counties such as Denton, Collin, Brazoria, and Chambers. Those found with high emissions will be required to have their vehicles tested and repaired if they do not meet the standards. Through the required testing in these four counties and the remote sensing of commuting cars from adjacent counties, about 5 million vehicles in Texas will be affected by these regulations. Still, many clean air advocates have called for an extension of the program to all vehicles registered in the outlying counties.

The 1990 federal Clean Air Act and subsequent regulations also require that federal, state, local-government, and private fleet vehicles in serious or severe nonattainment areas purchase, lease, or convert an increasing percentage of their vehicles to clean-fuel vehicles to meet or exceed low-emission vehicle (LEV) tailpipe-emissions standards. Although Texas had developed such a plan in early 1995, action taken by the 74th Legislature in 1995 forced the state to revise the program. For example, state legislation replaced the fuel standards with emission standards that included not only alternative fuels such as propane, natural gas, ethanol, methanol, or electricity, but also reformulated gasoline or even diesel fuel if it met LEV standards. In 1997 the passage of additional state legislation narrowed the program to serious or severe nonattainment areas with populations over 350,000 and made the phase-in schedule easier to meet than

federal requirements and the previous state plan.[156]

Under the current Texas clean fleet program, any local government with a fleet of 15 or more vehicles and any private company with a fleet of 25 or more vehicles operating in El Paso County or in the Houston-Galveston-Brazoria nine-county nonattainment area must meet or exceed LEV standards in the following compliance schedule:

■ 10 percent of the fleet vehicles in the total fleet by September 1, 1998, or 30 percent of fleet vehicle purchases after September 1, 1998;
■ 50 percent of fleet vehicle purchases after September 1, 2000;
■ 70 percent of light-duty fleet vehicle purchases after September 1, 2002; and
■ 50 percent of heavy-duty fleet vehicle purchases after September 1, 2002.[157]

Emergency fleets, school districts, and police fleets are exempt from the requirements. Other entities may apply to the TNRCC for exemption from the requirements due to insufficient financing, contractual harm, or lack of refueling facilities, or if the change in vehicles would not be cost effective. Because the Dallas-Fort Worth area has been reclassified as a serious nonattainment area, these requirements will also apply to this area.

REDUCING CARS ON THE ROAD
An alternative way to reduce vehicle emissions is simply to reduce the number of vehicles driven and the miles they travel. In the 1980s, urban traffic grew more than roadway capacity. The traditional

TEXAS URBAN BUS RIDERSHIP IN 1995 BY CITY

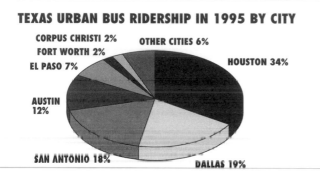

CORPUS CHRISTI 2%

FORT WORTH 2%

EL PASO 7%

OTHER CITIES 6%

HOUSTON 34%

AUSTIN 12%

SAN ANTONIO 18%

DALLAS 19%

Source: Texas Comptroller of Public Accounts, Fiscal Notes (June 1997).

COMPARISON OF EMISSIONS FROM VEHICLES USING DIFFERENT FUELS

	SO$_2$	NOX	CO
Fuel Cell Motors			
Hydrogen Gas	0	0	0
Natural Gas	2	52	11
Methanol	2	39	8
Combustion Engines			
Gasoline	48	205	700
Diesel	48	350	870
Battery-powered Electric Motor (emissions from generation of power to charge battery)	145	143	40

Note: All emissions in milligrams per mile.

Source: Anthony DePalma, "The Great Green Hope: Are Fuel Cells the Key to Cleaner Energy?" The New York Times (October 8, 1997), C6.

response to traffic congestion has been to build more highways. But highway expansion also provides an incentive for more people to drive cars.

FYI ☞ *The Texas Transportation Institute estimates that 95 percent of all urban trips in Texas are made by car.* (Source: Texas Comptroller of Public Accounts, Fiscal Notes, February 1994, 3.)

Both the 1990 federal Clean Air Act and the 1991 Intermodal Surface Transportation Efficiency Act (ISTEA) have emphasized transportation planning that encourages car-pooling and the use of public transportation. Between 1992 and 1997, funding under ISTEA has provided Texas with more than $6 billion, most of which went into the National Highway System.[158] The ISTEA-required planning process relies heavily on local metropolitan planning organizations to help distribute these funds. For example, during this period about $552 million of the ISTEA funds went to cities in Texas that had not met air quality standards, in part to help pay for traffic management and mass transit projects.[159] Each of these cities' metropolitan planning organizations must certify that its use of federal funds will result in fewer emissions or better air quality.[160] Still, between 1994 and 1996, the Texas Department of Transportation estimates that only five percent of federal, state, and local highway funds was specifically earmarked to mitigate congestion and improve air quality.[161] Funding for Texas transportation would increase under several proposed reauthorizations of ISTEA.[162]

Texas has more motor vehicles than any state except California, and in Texas, as in the nation as a whole, the number of cars driven and miles traveled have grown exponentially in recent decades.[163] With over 18 million cars registered to Texas drivers, traffic congestion has become a problem in cities all over Texas. Congestion causes travel delays and wastes fuel. It also decreases fuel efficiency and increases dangerous vehicle emissions. In Houston, traffic grew by 75 percent between 1970 and 1980. In 1990 Houston was among the ten most congested cities in the United States[164] By 1994, however, Houston had improved by reducing cars on the road and other measures and was the thirteenth most congested city.[165]

FYI ☞ *In 1970 Americans drove one trillion miles in motor vehicles. It has been projected that by the turn of the century, they will be driving four trillion miles.* (Source: Bob Hall and Mary Lee Kerr, 1991-1992 Green Index: A State-by-State Guide to the Nation's Environmental Health [Washington, D.C.: Island Press, 1991], 21.)

Texas cities have adopted different strategies for reducing the number of vehicles on the road. Both Houston and Dallas-Fort Worth, for example, have invested heavily in high-occupancy vehicle lanes (open only to vehicles with at least two occupants) on their major commuter highways to reduce the number of vehicles with only one occupant. In

Houston, METRO, the transportation authority, has opened five of these restricted lanes, covering 64 highway miles. About 81,000 riders use these each day.[166] Similarly, Dallas has 37 miles of these lanes, transporting more than 60,000 passengers each weekday, and is planning to add another 98 miles.

In addition to high-occupancy vehicle lanes, several Texas cities have advocated light rail systems. Dallas Area Rapid Transit (DART) currently operates a light rail system used by an estimated 30,000 passengers each weekday.[167] In addition, DART runs a "heavy" rail system linking downtown Dallas with south Irving and the Medical/Market Center area. Both systems are being expanded. Similarly, Austin is developing proposals for a light rail service from downtown to the northwest of the city, while Austin and San Antonio have discussed running a commuter rail line between San Antonio and Austin. These plans are controversial, however, because of their cost and the potential to create noise in local neighborhoods.

Bus travel, however, continues to be the main "mass transit" alternative to cars in Texas. In 1995 there were 236 million passenger trips in urban centers, with Houston leading the way.[168]

PUSHING FOR ALTERNATIVE FUELS

A third way to reduce pollution from cars is to change to cleaner-burning fuels. Recognizing Texas's vast potential as an "alternative energy" state, the Texas legislature created its own plan for alternative fuels by passing legislation in 1989 and 1991.[169] The legislation required state agencies, school districts with more than 50 buses, and all mass transit authorities in major urban areas to purchase only those new vehicles capable of running on alternative fuels. Under the plan, state agencies and mass transit authorities should have converted 30 percent of their fleets to alternative fuel by September 1, 1994, while school districts would have had to convert 50 percent of their buses to alternative fuels by 1997.

Nonetheless, in 1995, the legislature changed direction and replaced fuel standards with emission standards, allowing mass transit authorities and state agencies to use any combination of fuel—whether

natural gas, liquid petroleum gas (propane), methanol, ethanol, electricity, or low-sulfur diesel and reformulated gasoline—with any kind of vehicle providing they met the LEV standards.[170] In addition, school districts were exempted altogether and only the four nonattainment areas were covered under the Health and Safety Code, enforceable by the TNRCC. Other areas in the state are covered by the Texas Transportation Code. By September 1, 1996, 50 percent of the mass transit vehicles in the four nonattainment counties and 50 percent of the state fleets throughout the state had to convert to meet or exceed the LEV standards.[171] An analysis by the TNRCC showed that by the end of 1995, only 38 percent of state fleet vehicles met the standard, while the four transit authorities in El Paso, Houston, Dallas-Fort Worth, and Beaumont-Port Arthur needed two-year waivers to meet the 50 percent requirement.[172]

Finally, in 1997, the legislature acted further, exempting mass transit authorities in "moderate" nonattainment areas such as the Beaumont-Port Arthur and Dallas-Fort Worth regions.[173] However, the decision by the EPA to switch Dallas-Fort Worth to a serious nonattainment area makes the Texas Clean Fuels Program applicable to this region as well.

Alternative fuels have two advantages over conventional fuels: price and cleanliness. One disadvantage is that most alternative-fuel vehicles cannot travel as far without refueling. For example, a gasoline-fueled vehicle able to travel 100 miles would travel only 85 miles on propane and 31 miles on compressed natural gas (CNG) because the alternative fuels have lower energy content.[174] However, improvements in automobile manufacturing technologies are increasing gas mileage for propane, methanol, and natural gas vehicles.

FYI *A test conducted by the EPA on a propane-fueled car revealed that net carbon monoxide emissions were 93 percent less, hydrocarbons 73 percent less, and nitrogen oxides 53 percent less than federal emission standards for gasoline.* (Source: Information provided by Texas Railroad Commission, Alternative Fuels Research and Education Division, Austin.)

There are currently three different ways of powering cars: conventional combustion engines, which can use a variety of fuels; electricity through charged batteries; and fuel cells, which use hydrogen electrons to power a battery. A fuel cell is a foot-long tablet no thicker than a computer disk made up of two plates separated by a membrane. Either hydrogen gas or hydrogen-rich fuels like methanol or gasoline flows through one plate, where electrons are stripped off the hydrogen atoms with a catalyst, while air flows through the other. The hydrogen electrons flow through an electrical circuit that powers the engine, while the hydrogen atoms themselves seep through the membrane, where they combine with the oxygen molecules in the air to form water. Fuel cell vehicles are cleaner because they produce much less heat and waste than do conventional combustion engines. Instead, they produce water and only some heat.[175] Most of the major car companies have invested in fuel cell technology.[176]

Fuel cell technology does present challenges. Storing hydrogen gas is difficult, and is dangerous should a leak occur. Using methanol is easier, but it takes up more room, is more costly, and produces more emissions.

Combustion engines can use a variety of fuels, including natural gas, propane, methanol, gasoline, and diesel fuels. Vehicles powered by compressed natural gas or liquefied petroleum gas—also known as propane—are cleaner because they use a closed-loop system: there is no evaporation or escape of uncombusted gas before it reaches the tailpipe. Propane-powered vehicles emit even less nitrogen oxides than vehicles using natural gas. Another significant advantage of both compressed natural gas and propane use is that both fuels eliminate the need for underground storage tanks. Texas has had more than 15,000 reported cases of leaks from underground petroleum-storage tanks, leaks that often contaminate soil and water.[177]

FYI ☞ *A diesel-fueled bus emits as much particulate matter as 500 gasoline-powered automobiles.* (Source: GLO, Putting Together the Pieces: The Recapitalization of the Texas Economy [January 1989], 25.)

Several companies in Texas have been promoting electric vehicle technology. Still, the limited number of miles these vehicles can travel before recharging and the time needed to recharge are obstacles to their widespread acceptance.

The conversion of vehicles to alternative fuels might be beneficial to the state's economy, since Texas sits atop 27.5 percent of known natural gas reserves in the continental United States.[178] Propane is the most widely used alternative fuel in Texas, the United States, and the world, and Texas produces more propane than any other state. More than 60 percent of propane comes from natural gas production; the remainder is derived from crude oil during the refining process. Farmers and ranchers in Texas have long relied on propane to fuel agricultural vehicles, and rural Texans have used it for heating and cooking for over fifty years.[179]

At present, the major obstacles to the use of alternative fuels are: (1) the lack of an infrastructure for distributing them to consumers, and (2) the range limitation, especially considering the distances between towns in West Texas and the Panhandle. Unlike regular gasoline or diesel fuels, compressed natural gas is not available at refueling stations on every corner. As of April 1994, Texas had 73 filling stations for natural gas refueling.[180] There are about 1,200 propane refueling stations in Texas.[181]

Another obstacle to the use of alternative fuels is the cost of converting an old vehicle to run on an alternative fuel. The price tag for converting an average car to propane, which includes replacement of the fuel system and installation of new electronics, is about $2,000.[182] Conversions to natural gas use is even a little more expensive. Despite these costs, converting vehicles may be economical for some fleets in the long run because propane and natural gas are cheaper than gasoline and because maintenance costs are generally lower over a three- to five-year period.

MAJOR STATIONARY SOURCES
According to the State Summary of Emissions, 100 facilities in Texas emitted into the atmosphere in 1995 more than 6,300 tons of particulate matter less

EMISSIONS INVENTORY—TOP 20 EMITTERS OF CRITERIA POLLUTANTS IN 1997 (IN TONS)

RANK	FACILITY NAME	COUNTY	PM10	SO2	NOX	NMOC	CO	TOTAL
1	Texas Utilities Electric Company	Rusk	952	105,464	30,574	394	1,638	139,022
2	Texas Utilities Electric Company	Titus	5,692	97,848	21,828	349	1,648	127,305
3	Aluminum Company of America	Milam	1,066	61,502	19,987	1,684	20,596	104,835
4	Houston Industries Incorporated	Fort Bend	732	64,735	35,132	127	3,045	103,271
5	Texas Utilities Generating Company	Freestone	793	79,862	14,276	154	656	95,741
6	Houston Industries Incorporated	Limestone	507	35,841	26,325	250	489	63,412
7	Cabot Corporation	Gray	69	849	1,655	278	59,312	62,163
8	Southwestern Electric Power Company	Titus	333	35,343	14,339	188	1,570	51,773
9	City Public Service	Bexar	1,312	28,577	20,040	142	1,532	51,603
10	Lower Colorado River Authority	Fayette	1,431	28,320	16,398	231	1,498	47,878
11	Southwestern Public Service Company	Potter	2,213	33,834	10,465	137	1,139	47,788
12	Southwestern Public Service Company	Lamb	1,133	29,001	11,672	134	1,099	43,039
13	Texas Utilities Generating Company	Milam	967	28,220	9,141	112	468	38,908
14	Mobil Oil Corporation	Jefferson	2	13,155	8,290	6,043	8,418	35,908
15	Southwestern Electric Power Company	Harrison	60	21,488	9,411	62	993	32,014
17	Texas Municipal Power Agency	Grimes	37	17,808	7,607	55	116	25,623
16	San Miguel Electric Co.	Atascosa	208	19,311	6,862	38	349	26,768
17	Degussa Corporation	Aransas	66	912	180	305	23,151	24,614
18	Clark Refining & Marketing	Jefferson	611	6,779	9,460	1,861	5,371	24,082
19	Exxon Company USA	Harris	921	2,239	10,901	4,014	3,701	21,776
20	Phillips 66 Co.	Hutchinson	----	6,838	3,770	8,339	2,031	20,978

Note: Houston Industries Incorporated in Fort Bend and Limestone counties were previously known as Houston Lighting & Power Co.

Source: Texas Natural Resource Conservation Commission, 1997 Emissions Inventory, 1999.

than 10 microns, 809,000 tons of sulfur dioxide, 544,000 tons of nitrogen oxides, 124,000 tons of nonmethane organic compounds—including all VOCs—and 340,000 tons of carbon monoxide.[183] Together, these 100 facilities produced more than twice as much criteria pollutants as the total produced by the remaining 8,367 facilities contained in the State Summary of Emissions Database.[184]

In 1997 the major industries in Texas also released more air toxics than any other state—about 108 million pounds in all.[185] However, when comparing the chemicals that were required to be reported in 1987 with those same chemicals in 1996, total releases of air toxics in Texas declined by

more than 50 percent, from 179.2 million to 86.2 million pounds.[186]

Because of these emission levels, these industrial facilities, which the federal Clean Air Act calls "major stationary sources," are often the focus of state and citizen efforts to reduce air pollution. This section examines three categories of major-stationary-source air pollution in Texas: manufacturing, combustion, and mechanical facilities.

Manufacturing Industries

Toxic air emissions from manufacturing industries are a major concern of citizen groups around the state. Federal law requires manufacturing industries with more than nine employees to submit data on releases of more than 650 chemicals and chemical compounds. In 1995 Harris, Jefferson, and Brazoria counties were among the top ten counties in the country in terms of air toxic emissions.[187]

Many of these toxics have been linked to both cancer and birth defects. The chemicals known to cause, or suspected of causing, birth defects are categorized by the EPA as either developmental toxins or heritable mutagens. In 1996 such chemicals released into the environment—air, water, and land—in the greatest amount included toluene, xylene, methyl ethyl ketone, benzene, and 1,3-butadiene. Most of these releases were through the air.

Unlike the situation for criteria pollutants, there are few state and federal regulations specifying acceptable ambient concentrations for air toxics. For example, of the top 15 toxic chemicals released in Texas, only benzene has been the subject of a national air quality standard. By comparison, maximum contaminant level standards have been established under the Safe Drinking Water Act for 5 of these 15 chemicals.[188] However, requirements that new permitted facilities in Texas use the best available control technology limits toxic emissions considerably. Also, under the 1990 federal Clean Air Act, the EPA is developing new standards for industries identified as sources of 188 major toxic compounds. In addition, the TNRCC has developed a system to evaluate air concentrations of over 1,500 chemicals, including the top 15 toxic chemicals, emitted by permitted facilities. Guideline concentrations called effects screening levels (ESLs, previously described) are used to evaluate not only proposed emissions but also ambient air monitoring data.

"Upset" emissions, defined as accidental, unplanned air pollution releases, are not included in the emission data reported to the state's Emissions Inventory nor in that reported under the Toxics Release Inventory Program. However, thousands of upsets a year contribute pollutants to the state's atmosphere. Under state regulations, companies are required to report their upsets to the TNRCC, but the information in these reports is sketchy. A 1992 Sierra Club survey of upset emissions in nine Texas

WHO MUST SUBMIT AN EMISSIONS INVENTORY?

STATEWIDE:
Any Stationary Source Emitting
1. 100 Tons/year or more of VOC, NOX, CO, SO_2 or PM10
2. 10 tons/year of any individual Hazardous Air Pollutant (HAP) or 25 tons/year of any combination of Hazardous Air Pollutants

OZONE NON-ATTAINMENT AREAS:
Any Stationary Source Emitting
1. 10 tons/year or greater of VOC
2. 25 tons/year or greater of NOX
3. 100 tons/year or greater of CO, SO_2 or PM10
4. 10 tons/year of any individual Hazardous Air Pollutant (HAP) or 25 tons/year of any combination of Hazardous Air Pollutants

Source: Texas Air Control Board, Rule 101.10.

counties revealed that companies do not always report or even know in some cases how much or what type of chemical was emitted.[189] According to this study of 8,857 upset reports in 1991, 80 percent did not list the quantity of compound released, and 38 percent did not report the type of chemical released.[190] Such accidents and the failure or inability to report accurate upset emissions make it extremely difficult to assess the full impact of industrial toxic emissions on public health. In addition, because the state does not set levels or limits on upset emissions—by definition they are unplanned events—the data these reports do contain are not used to help set emission limits.

Under a section of the federal Clean Air Act, some 66,000 facilities in the United States will be required to provide the public with a summary of the consequences of major chemical accidents. Facilities have until June 21, 1999, to prepare the worst-case accident report.[191]

Combustion

A second category of major stationary sources is made up of facilities that burn material for energy, waste disposal, or both. Utilities, waste incinerators, industrial boilers, and cement kiln facilities are the major examples of combustion sources of air pollution. Because these facilities burn materials at very

WHO MUST OBTAIN AN AIR OPERATING PERMIT IN TEXAS?

One way the state of Texas regulates air emissions is through a permitting process. Under the Texas Clean Air Act of 1971, most new or expanding industries that will emit air contaminants must obtain a permit from the TNRCC before any construction is begun. Such permits require that the facility install "best available control technology." Some facilities are exempt from the preconstruction permit requirement if they meet conditions set out in the state's "standard exemption" list, which covers a variety of businesses, most of them small. Some of these companies automatically qualify for a standard exemption, while others must apply for the designation. In 1997 the TNRCC initiated a process to review the conditions of these standard exemptions, many of which had not been revised since the late 1970s.

As of April 1994, Texas had issued 20,928 state construction permits in both attainment and nonattainment areas. Some 14,000 are still active.[192] This construction permitting process is divided into "new source review" for sources located in nonattainment areas and "prevention of significant deterioration" review in attainment areas. Permits in nonattainment areas are generally more stringent. It is important to note that air pollution sources that were operating before 1972 and have not expanded are not required to have a state construction permit; those are known as "grandfathered" facilities.

The 1990 federal Clean Air Act created a new category of permits: federal operating permits. These permits are required of all major stationary sources that emit air pollutants, including "grandfathered" facilities. The purpose of federal operating permits is to codify all applicable requirements at a site and provide an enforcement and compliance tool. These permits do not, on the other hand, impose new emission reductions. For example, a petroleum refinery operation may have 100 to 200 different rules, regulations, permits, and variances governing the operation of its facility. A Title V permit codifies them all. Thus, construction permits would be incorporated into an operating permit. Most major sources, such as utilities, were required to submit their applications to the EPA by 1996. The TNRCC projects that there will be 8,100 federal operating permits issued at some 3,000 sites in Texas during the five years after the Texas program receives EPA approval.

Source: Information from the Point Source Data Base, Office of Air Quality, TNRCC; TNRCC, System Requirement for the FCAA Integrated Management System [1993].

high temperatures, they emit chemicals and gases that sometimes result in dangerous chemical reactions. For example, sulfur dioxide is one of the principal air pollutants emitted from coal-fired electric utilities. Sulfur dioxide emissions can combine with oxygen to form sulfates, which in turn can combine with water particles to form acid rain.[193] Sulfur dioxide, nitrogen oxides (an ozone precursor), and carbon dioxide (a greenhouse gas) are the major pollutants resulting from combustion. Heavy metals also are emitted by some combustion facilities. Coal-burning facilities can emit mercury and cadmium. Cement kilns and incinerators for hazardous waste and municipal waste can all emit chromium, man-

ganese, and lead, among other heavy metals.

Texas is home to 175 electric utilities operating 437 generating stations.[194] About 43 percent of the state's electricity is derived from coal, about 33 percent comes from natural gas, and the remainder comes from co-generation by industry (8 percent), hydroelectric power (1 percent), nuclear power (15 percent), and renewable energy sources (less than 1 percent).[195] Electric utilities that use western coal or Texas lignite coal as their combustible material pump millions more tons of carbon dioxide, carbon monoxide, sulfur dioxide, and nitrogen oxides into the atmosphere than do those using natural gas or a combination of petroleum and natural gas. For

TOXIC AIR RELEASES BY COUNTY, 1997

COUNTY	TOTAL AIR RELEASES (LBS)
Harris	28,078,075
Jefferson	13,953,018
Brazoria	8,483,270
Orange	6,352,525
Galveston	5,619,957
Harrison	4,037,893
Calhoun	3,086,750
Nueces	2,916,541
Hutchinson	2,773,594
Cass	2,432,862
Dallas	1,990,609
Wichita	1,815,226
Angelina	1,698,580
Tarrant	1,498,598
Ector	1,448,595
Milam	1,172,114

INDUSTRY	RELEASES
Chemicals & Allied Products	73,911,999
Petroleum Refining & Related Industry	20,178,766
Paper & Allied Products	7,246,317
Rubber & Misc. Plastics Products	4,254,727
Food and Kindred Products	4,048,575
Primary Metal Industry	3,461,392
Metal Products, Except Machinery & Transportation Equipment	3,167,127
Transportation Equipment	2,927,484
Stone, Clay, Glass & Concrete Products	2,195,122
Lumber & Wood, Except Furniture	2,134,421
Industrial & Commercial Mach. & Computer Equipment	1,154,576
Furniture & Fixtures	569,684
Electronic & Other Electrical Equipment	554,763
Wholesale Trade	354,440
Printing, Publishing & Allied Industries	234,735
National Security & International Affairs	214,410
Analyzing & Control Instruments, Medical, Optical and Photographic	195,582
Leather & Leather Products	118,466
Apparel & Other Finished Products	103,110
Miscellaneous Manufacturing Industries	62,414
Retail Trade	26,220
NASA	22,000
Textile Mill Products	16,855
Business Services	4,866

Source: Environmental Protection Agency, 1997 Toxics Release Inventory Database, 1999.

example, the top 16 emitters of carbon monoxide, sulfur dioxide, and nitrogen oxides among electric utilities all burn either western coal or Texas lignite.[196]

Four of the top five facilities in Texas that released the largest volume of criteria pollutants in 1997 are coal- or lignite-fired electric power plants.[197] The fifth facility—an Aluminum Company of America (ALCOA) plant in Milam County—

LEADING CHEMICALS LINKED TO BIRTH DEFECTS RELEASED IN AIR BY INDUSTRIES IN TEXAS, 1997

CHEMICAL	ON-SITE RANKING	TOTAL ON-SITE RELEASES (LBS)	TOTAL AIR RELEASES (LBS)
Acetonitrile	6	10,263,256	174,049
Toluene	9	6,006,919	5,550,241
Methyl Ethyl Ketone	10	5,036,898	4,574,445
Xylene	12	4,758,545	4,538,486
Styrene	14	3,618,342	3,259,878
Acrylonitrile	16	3,348,730	167,318
Benzene	19	2,817,878	2,439,940
Cyanide Compounds	24	2,053,863	92,108
Phenol	25	1,928,032	526,963
1,3-Butadiene	27	1,485,713	1,480,344
Ethylbenzene	29	1,348,182	767,963
Chloroform	36	1,097,488	1,091,073
Chloromethane	46	672,239	671,871
Lead Compounds	48	639,290	72,283
Carbon Disulfide	50	631,876	631,861
Hydrogen Fluoride	51	630,517	620,724
Napthalene	54	543,475	337,945
Trichloroethylene	56	508,630	506,998

Source: Pounds and rankings from Environmental Protection Agency, 1997 Toxics Release Inventory Database, 1999. List of toxics found to be "developmental toxics" found in Clement Associates, Inc., Support Documentation for the SARA TITLE III, Sections 313/322 Toxicity Matrix (Fairfax, Virginia: Clement Associates Inc., August 1988, prepared for Environmental Protection Agency).

consists of an aluminum smelter factory and the coal-fired power plants used to run it.[198]

Information from EPA studies indicates that electric generating plants are significant emitters of air toxics such as mercury, arsenic, nickel, hydrogen fluoride, and hydrochloric acid, among others.[199] In the 1998 reporting year, electric utilities will be required for the first time to report toxics emissions and transfers as part of the Toxics Release Inventory Program.

In Texas most of the major utilities that emit the largest amounts of nitrogen oxides per year are located outside ozone nonattainment areas. Nonetheless, the nitrogen oxides emissions, as well as the ozone formed as a result of such emissions from power plants, can be carried by prevailing winds up to 500 miles and can increase background levels of nitrogen oxides and ozone in nonattainment areas in Texas and other states as well.[200] This regional ozone problem is just beginning to be understood.

SULFUR DIOXIDE, NITROGEN OXIDE, AND CARBON MONOXIDE EMISSIONS (IN TONS) FROM MAJOR POWER PLANTS IN TEXAS BY FUEL TYPE, 1995

FUEL TYPE	SULFUR DIOXIDE	NITROGEN OXIDES	CARBON MONOXIDE	TOTALS
Coal	225,546	126,237	11,351	363,134
Lignite	334,048	114,861	5,722	454,631
Coal & Lignite	560,594	241,098	17,073	817,765
Natural Gas & Co-generation	4,866	137,112	24,864	166,842
Nuclear	2	70	14	86
Totals	**565,462**	**378,280**	**41,951**	**984,693**

Source: Texas Natural Resource Conservation Commission, State Summary of Emissions Database, July 1997.

GRANDFATHERED FACILITIES

Built before the Texas Clean Air Act went into effect in 1972, "grandfathered" facilities have not had to install the same pollution control equipment or meet the same emission limits as facilities that have either been built or substantially modified since 1971. The reason? They are not required to obtain an air permit from the TNRCC, which sets best-available-control-technology emission requirements. This disparity—where some industries and utilities produce their products in a cleaner way than others because of increasing regulations—means that grandfathered facilities can often enjoy a competitive advantage. The TNRCC recently conducted a 1997 emissions inventory update and found that grandfathered emission points released 350,000 tons of nitrogen oxides, 750,000 tons of VOCs, 250,000 tons of sulfur dioxide, 180,000 tons of carbon monoxide, and 13,000 tons of PM10.[201] This level was virtually the same as it had been from these facilities in a 1986 inventory. In contrast, permitted facilities facing stricter regulations were able to reduce their emissions from 3 million tons of criteria pollutants in 1986 to 1.43 million tons in 1994.[202]

Another analysis by two environmental organizations in Texas found that there are 1,020 "heavily" grandfathered plants in Texas. These plants emit 37 percent of all air emissions from industrial plants and contribute as much nitrogen oxides as 18.4 million cars.[203] Most of the emissions from grandfathered units occur at major oil and gas production and refining facilities and electric utility plants. Of special concern are areas like Houston and Beaumont that do not meet clean air standards for ozone and yet are impacted by VOC emissions from grandfathered facilities. For example, one analysis showed that 75 percent of emissions of VOCs statewide came from grandfathered units and units with standard exemptions from permitting requirements.[204] The analysis revealed that requiring the best available control technology at these emissions sources in the Houston area could cut VOC emissions by 5,400 tons per year—about the same amount as Houston is trying to cut from automobiles through the Inspection and Maintenance Plan.[205]

Texas is home to 3 of the top 50 sulfur-dioxide emitting electric utilities in the United States. Two of these utilities—Texas Utilities' Monticello and Big Brown power plants—are almost completely grandfathered units that released more than

Continued on next page

TOP TEN INDUSTRIES WITH 99-100 PERCENT GRANDFATHERED NITROGEN OXIDE EMISSIONS

INDUSTRY	TONS of GRANDFATHERED NOx EMISSIONS	NUMBER of EQUIVALENT CARS in NOx EMISSIONS
Electric Utilities	128,692 tons	6,599,605 cars
Gas Transmission	47,217 tons	2,421,403 cars
Refineries	41,332 tons	2,119,588 cars
Natural gas liquids	36,762 tons	1,885,221 cars
Natural Crude gas processing	35,708 tons	1,831,184 cars
Organic chemical plants	27,311 tons	1,400,557 cars
Alcoa aluminum smelting	19,905 tons	1,020,780 cars
Inorganic chemical processing	7,612 tons	390,386 cars
Petroleum, coal products	1,201 tons	61,571 cars
Paper Mills	905 tons	46,414 cars

Source: Galveston-Houston Association for Smog Prevention and Lone Star Chapter of the Sierra Club, Grandfathered Air Pollution: The Dirty Secrets of Texas Industries *(Austin: Lone Star Sierra Club, April 1998), 24.*

GRANDFATHERED FACILITIES (Continued)

220,000 tons of criteria pollutants in 1997.[206] In addition, most of the power plants in the ozone nonattainment areas have grandfathered units, undermining the ability of these areas to meet clean air ozone standards.

Thus far, the legislature and the TNRCC have not proposed new regulations to reduce emissions at grandfathered facilities. Instead, they convened an eleven-member advisory committee known as the Clean Air Responsibility Enterprise (CARE) in 1997 to see if pollution from older power plants and industries could be reduced voluntarily.[207] In November 1997, ten facilities with grandfathered status volunteered to reduce emissions by seeking new operating permits in return for regulatory flexibility.[208] The TNRCC submitted the Clean Air Responsibility Enterprise voluntary plan to the legislature in 1999 and it was approved with some changes. However, the legislature did approve legislation designed to deregulate the electric utility industry which will force these particular grandfathered plants to seek a permit by 2003. Environmental organizations have instead called for an obligatory permitting program for all grandfathered plants.

In addition, fine particulates formed from nitrogen oxides and sulfur dioxide emissions can travel even farther and are believed to contribute to visibility impairment throughout Texas (see Visibility and Class I Areas section).[209]

Waste incinerators are another source of combustion-generated air pollutants. Both municipalities and industries sometimes incinerate a variety of wastes as a means of reducing their volume and generating energy. There are currently 32 permitted

CRITERIA POLLUTANT IN TONS AND TOXIC AIR EMISSIONS IN POUNDS FROM CEMENT PLANTS IN TEXAS, 1995

FACILITY	COUNTY	PM10	SULFUR DIOXIDE	NITROGEN OXIDES	ORGANIC COMPOUNDS	CARBON MONOXIDE	TOXICS (LBS)
TXI	Ellis	294	5,317	5,819	68	1,032	3,535
Holnam	Ellis	312	3,903	2,134	50	2,798	0
NTCC	Ellis	541	3,633	2,063	45	506	0
Capitol	Bexar	209	1,985	2,021	150	598	19
Lehigh	Hays	205	235	1,787	59	1,833	500
Sunbelt	Comal	205	71	1,558	43	1,316	8
Alamo	Bexar	105	1	2,334	22	283	0
TXI	Comal	125	17	1,286	56	712	5,203
Southdown	Ector	214	486	1,440	61	166	11
Lone Star	Nolan	157	113	998	7	46	10
Lehigh	McLennan	NR	380	644	NR	NR	0

Note: NR = not reported.

The following toxic air emissions were reported at the following plants:

TXI in Comal	Chromium Compounds, Manganese, Nickel
TXI in Ellis	Benzene, 0-Xylene, Ethylbenzene, P-Xylene, Toluene, N-Hexane, Cyclohexane, Chromium, Manganese, Nickel;
Capitol	Chromium Compounds
Lehigh in Hays	Ethylene Glycol
Sunbelt	Chromium Compounds
Southdown	Lead
Lone Star	Chromium Compounds

Sources: Environmental Protection Agency, 1997 Toxics Release Inventory Database, 1999. Criteria pollutant information from Texas Natural Resource Conservation Commission, 1997 Emissions Inventory, 1999.

COMMERCIAL AND ON-SITE HAZARDOUS WASTE INCINERATION FACITLITIES IN TEXAS

FACILITY	LOCATION	STATUS
1. American Envirotech**	Houston	Not Built
2. Elf Atochem	Beaumont	Active
3. Elf Atochem	Houston	Active
4. BASF Corp.	Freeport	Active
5. BASF Corp	Beaumont	Active
6. Chemical Waste Management**	Port Arthur	Active
7. Dow Chemical	La Porte	Active
8. Dow Chemical	Freeport	Active
9. EI DuPont	La Porte	Active
10. EI DuPont*	Orange	Active
11. EI DuPont	Beaumont	Active
12. Hoechst Celanese	Pasadena	Active
13. Hoescht Celanese	Seabrook	Active
14. Houston Chemical Services**	Pasadena	Built, not operating
15. Huntsman Petro Corp	Conroe	Active
16. Huntsman Petro Corp	Port Neches	Active
17. Nalco Exxon Chemical	Sugar Land	Active
18. Occidental Chemical*	Deer Park	Active
19. Occidental Chemical	Gregory	Active
20. Parkans International**	Houston	Active
21. Phillips Petroleum Co.	Old Ocean	Active
22. Quantum USI	Deer Park	Active
23. Rhone Poulenc**	Houston	Active
24. Laidlaw? Rollins Environmental**	Deer Park	Active
25. Sandoz Agro	Beaumont	Active
26. Shell Chemical Co	Deer Park	Active
27. Sterling Chemical Inc.	Texas City	Active
28. Texas Eastman	Longview	Active
29. Union Carbide*	Texas City	Active
30. U.S. Army Red River	Texarkana	Active

*Accepts waste from other facilities owned by same company.
**Commercial

Source: Texas Natural Resource Conservation Commission, Industrial and Hazardous Waste Division, Office of Waste Management, 1998.

CONTRIBUTION OF SMALL VS. LARGE INDUSTRY TO VOC EMISSIONS, IN OZONE NON-ATTAINMENT AREAS, IN PERCENT.

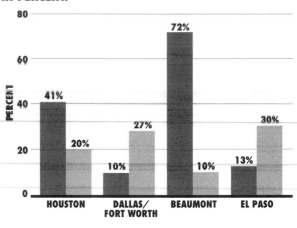

Source: Texas Natural Resource Conservation Commission ,Revisions to State Implementation Plans for Ozone (1996).

hazardous waste incinerators in Texas. These facilities are operated by large corporations, chiefly to dispose of their own wastes. Three of the facilities in Texas are commercial waste incinerators, accepting liquid wastes from both in-state and out-of-state generators.

Cement plants are another source of combustion pollution. Traditional cement production — where natural gas, coal, or fuel oils are used to heat the kiln—can cause air pollution problems during the combustion process itself, which produces air pollutants such as carbon monoxide, sulfur dioxide and particulate matter, and some toxics. However, one cement company in Texas is also burning a wide variety of hazardous wastes to fire its kilns. This "alternative" production process is controversial because of the possibility of increasing emissions of criteria air pollutants as well as toxic emissions. New contaminants, known as Products of Incomplete Combustion (PICs) also are produced during the burning of hazardous wastes in the cement kiln and released into the atmosphere through stack emissions. These products include highly toxic compounds known as dioxins and furans, which are formed when hazardous and other wastes that contain chlorine are burned. These compounds are also a concern in municipal and industrial waste incinerators (see box: Endocrine Disruptors, in Toxics section).

In 1991, citizen groups in Midlothian, near Dallas, expressed concerns about health effects from the burning of hazardous wastes in cement kilns and the dumping of cement-kiln ash in quarries. Two of the three cement-kiln plants in the Midlothian area were burning waste-derived fuels.[210] A third had

HOW DOES THE FEDERAL CLEAN AIR ACT IMPACT SMALL BUSINESS?

AIR POLLUTION CONTROL COSTS BY INDUSTRY

INDUSTRY	ESTIMATED NO. IN TEXAS	COST PER FACILITY	INDUSTRY COST
Asphalt Manufacturers	67	350,000	23,450,000
Auto Body Painting	1,760	120,000	211,200,000
Auto Repairs	4,634	7,000	131,438,000
Bakeries	138	114,000	15,732,000
Dry Cleaners	3,314	28,000	92,792,000
Furniture Manufacturers	447	500,000	223,500,000
Gasoline Filling Stations	3,710	40,000	148,400,000
Hospitals	139	100,000	13,900,000
Metal Finishers	305	40,000	12,200,000
Newspapers	567	40,000	22,680,000
Printing Shops	3,247	40,000	129,880,000
Refrigeration/AC Repair	2,244	7,000	15,708,000
Wood Finishers	21	40,000	840,000
Total	20,593	51,000	$1,041,720,000

Source: State Small Business Ombudsman, Texas Air Control Board, The Price of Clean Air (April 1993), 20.

The federal Clean Air Act is likely to impact more than 55,000 Texas businesses with fewer than 100 employees. The EPA has been developing specific rules for small businesses to reduce their generation of toxic wastes, their use of ozone-depleting chemicals, and, in nonattainment areas, their emissions of VOCs and nitrogen oxides. While some of these regulations are still being formulated, the EPA has pinpointed 23 types of industries it would most likely regulate first.[211]

The state estimated costs for the approximately 20,573 small businesses most likely to be affected by the federal Clean Air Act—and for which reliable cost data were available—at over $1 billion, most of it for capital equipment, to comply with the act's regulations over the next five years.[212] In the four nonattainment areas alone, the cost to businesses for obtaining a federal operating permit and installing pollution control equipment is expected to total $505 million. All sources, regardless of location, that emit more than 10 tons per year of any of the 189 toxic pollutants, or 25 tons per year of any combination of these 189 chemicals for which

Continued on next page

previously burned tires to generate energy and was seeking a permit to continue burning them. Presently, only Texas Industries in Midlothian is burning hazardous waste, and the TNRCC has issued a draft permit that would increase the burning of hazardous waste by the facility. In 1997 several citizen groups and state and local parent-teacher organizations opposed Texas Industries' draft permit in a state hearing process. In 1999 the hearings examiner

recommended approving the permit, which was granted by the TNRCC.

Mechanical

Industries that rely on mechanical processes include metal smelters, grain elevators, foundries, steel manufacturers, wood processors, cotton gins, asphalt-batching operations, concrete- and cement-batching operations, paper mills, sandblasting operations, and

HOW DOES THE FEDERAL CLEAN AIR ACT IMPACT SMALL BUSINESS? (Continued)

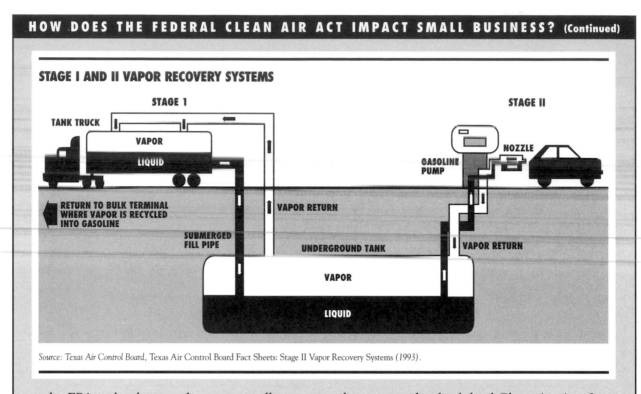

STAGE I AND II VAPOR RECOVERY SYSTEMS

Source: *Texas Air Control Board*, Texas Air Control Board Fact Sheets: Stage II Vapor Recovery Systems (1993).

the EPA is developing rules, must install control technology that is at least equivalent to the average of the top 12 percent for that industry if the source is existing at the time those rules are developed. New sources must install the best proven technology for that industry.

Certain categories of small businesses will face other costs under the federal Clean Air Act. In nonattainment areas, for example, service stations must recover gasoline vapors that are released during the transfer of gas from the pump to a vehicle and from a tanker to the underground storage tank.

oil and gas rigs. These industries are another major category of stationary sources that can pollute the air. Operation of cotton gins, for example, may result in large emissions of particulate matter. In 1990 air sampled around a cotton gin in the Lower Rio Grande Valley showed that respirable particulate matter was being emitted at high levels, although not in violation of standards applicable to agricultural sources.[213] Lead smelters are of particular concern to citizens living near them and to environmental groups. As an air pollutant, lead is emitted in particles so small that 50 percent might remain in the lungs if breathed by humans.[214] However, tests conducted by the Texas Air Control Board in response to citizen complaints found that levels of lead in the ambient air near smelters in San Antonio, Garland, and Dallas were below national air quality

standards.[215] Any lead smelters built after 1987 must be at least 3,000 feet from the nearest residence.[216]

AREA SOURCES

"Area sources" are small, stationary sources that usually do not emit large amounts of criteria pollutants or toxics, but area sources are very numerous. Some of the important area sources that have been impacted by the federal Clean Air Act include dry cleaners, printers, machine shops, service stations, wastewater-treatment plants, and automobile painting and repair shops. Consumers who use household items are another area source.

While these "small" businesses and consumer activities individually do not contribute large amounts of pollution to the atmosphere, taken collectively they emit more of some types of pollutants than do some individual large industries. For example, in many cities in Texas, area sources contribute more VOCs to smog formation than do major stationary sources.

The 1990 federal Clean Air Act broadened the scope of federal regulation to include area sources. The act has had an immediate impact on small business owners (see box: How Does the Federal Clean Air Act Impact Small Business?). In addition, the new standards for ozone and fine particles will likely bring new areas in Texas—like Austin, Corpus Christi, and San Antonio—into nonattainment, resulting in further controls on small businesses.

Special Case: Agriculture

While much of the concern about air pollution is focused on industrial and urban sources, people living in rural areas also can face nuisance odors and toxic air pollution. Airborne pesticides are a concern in some rural areas. One study estimated that only 10 to 15 percent of pesticides sprayed from crop dusters reach their intended source. The remaining 85 to 90 percent can drift up to twenty miles.[217] (See *Pesticides* focus piece.)

Other agricultural facilities and operations that can result in emissions of air contaminants such as odors and particulate matter include cotton gins, cottonseed oil mills, sugar mills, feed mills, smokehouses, hide tanning, seed cleaning, sugarcane and crop-residue burning, and confined animal feeding operations (CAFOs). CAFOs are facilities in which animals such as poultry, hogs, or cows are concentrated in a relatively small area for egg-laying, stabling, sleeping, milking, or feeding purposes. Sometimes, animal waste from these operations is collected in ponds, which can release both odors and methane gas (one of the greenhouse gases). Other animal waste is placed in manure mounds or applied as fertilizer to the land, which also can lead to odor nuisances. CAFOs and other agricultural activities are more likely to contribute air pollutants such as particulate matter to the atmosphere during hot, dry weather. For example, feedlot dust can result when cattle activity increases around dusk. Odor problems, on the other hand, usually occur following significant precipitation.[218]

FYI *Anaerobic treatment of livestock wastes accounts for 6 to 10 percent of the total methane emissions from human-related activities in Texas.* (Source: Texas Institute for Applied Environmental Research, Tarleton State University, Interim Report to the Joint Interim Committee on the Environment, 72nd Texas Legislature [Stephenville, September 1992], 66.)

Large CAFOs are typically required to obtain air permits, while smaller CAFOs have been exempt from the permitting process. Regardless of size, all CAFOs must be operated in a manner that does not result in either dust or nuisance odor problems. While quantitative measurement standards for odors have not been developed, odors from CAFOs in rural areas are a controversial issue.[219]

NOTES

1. There are a number of studies which track this association. For a summary, see "Clearing the Air: Is Our Air Clean Enough?" *Consumer Reports*, August, 1997, 36-38.

2. For a good overview of studies that found an association between air pollution due to high concentrations of particulate matter and mortality due to lung cancer and cardiopulmonary disease, see Douglas Dockery, et al., "An Association between Air Pollution and Mortality in Six U.S. Cities," *New England Journal of Medicine* 329, no. 24 (1993): 1753-1759.

3. The EPA estimates that full attainment of its more stringent standards would result in zero to 1,300 fewer deaths and 140,000 fewer cases of acute respiratory symptoms related to ozone air pollution, 8,000 fewer hospitalizations, and 3,300 to 16,500 fewer deaths related to particulate matter pollution each year. For a full discussion of the benefits and costs of the new standards, see EPA, *Regulatory Impact Analysis of the New National Ambient Air Quality Standards* (July 19, 1997).

4. A prime example was the accidental release of methyl isocyanate in Bhopal, India, at a Union Carbide Chemical plant, killing 2,500 workers and neighbors of the facility and injuring tens of thousands. See World Resources Institute, *The 1994 Information Please Environmental Almanac* (Boston: Houghton Mifflin, 1994), 112.

5. Joseph Petulla, *American Environmental History* (Columbus, Ohio: Mifflin, 1988), 418.

6. Petulla, *American Environmental History*, 418.

7. James Cannon, *The Health Costs of Air Pollution: A Survey of Studies, 1978-1983* (Washington, D.C.: American Lung Association, 1985), 11.

8. See for example C. Arden Pope III, Michael Thun, Mohan Namboodiri, Douglas Dockery, John Evans, Frank Speizer, and Clark Heath, Jr., "Particulate Air Pollution as a Predictor of Mortality in a Prospective Study of U.S. Adults," *American Journal of Respiratory Critical Care Medicine* 151 (1995): 669-674.

9. Petulla, *American Environmental History*, 419.

10. World Resources Institute, *1994 Information Please Environmental Almanac*, 112.

11. Robert D. Bullard, *Dumping in Dixie: Race, Class and Environmental Quality* (Boulder, Colo.: Westview Press, 1990), 63.

12. EPA, *The Plain English Guide to the Clean Air Act* (April 1993), 25.

13. EPA, *National Air Quality and Emissions Trend Report, 1997* (Research Triangle Park, N.C., December 1998), 63.

14. World Resources Institute, *The 1992 Information Please Environmental Almanac* (Boston: Houghton Mifflin, 1992), 152.

15. EPA, *1997 National Air Quality: Status and Trends* (Research Triangle Park, N.C., December 1998), 12.

16. EPA, *Plain English Guide to the Clean Air Act*, 17.

17. The original requirement of the 1990 Clean Air Act required that zero-emission cars be built by 1999. However, the requirement was delayed until 2003. Anthony DePalma, "The Great Green Hope: Are Fuel Cells the Key to Cleaner Energy?" *New York Times*, October 8. 1997, C6.

18. Information from TNRCC, Office of Air Quality, web page (http:/www.tnrcc.state.tx.us/air/erc/ercreg.htm).

19. World Resources Institute, *1994 Information Please Environmental Almanac*, 106.

20. Natural Resource Defense Council (NRDC), *Benchmarking Air Emissions of Electric Utility Generators in the Eastern United States* (New York, April 1997), 28.

21. EPA, *National Air Quality and Emissions Trend Report, 1997*, Table A-17.

22. EPA, *The Benefits and Costs of the Clean Air Act, 1970 to 1990* (October 1997).

23. EPA, *National Air Quality and Emissions Trend Report, 1997*, Table A-17. About 8.2 million Texans lived in metropolitan areas that did not meet standards for criteria air pollutants in 1998.

24. National Resource Defense Council, "Appeals Court Decision Overtunrs Major Clean Air Victory," Press Release (May 18, 1999).

25. TNRCC, Office of Air Quality, Monitoring Operations, information provided to author, September 1997.

26. Nonetheless, it is important to note that even though ozone is monitored continuously, the actual levels are determined based upon averaging. For example, a 1-hour average is actually based on the average of twelve 5-minute averages.

27. TNRCC, *Biennial Report to the 76th Legislature*, vol 2, 34.

28. TNRCC, Toxicology and Risk Assessment Section and Monitoring Operations Division, *Community Air Toxics Monitoring Report: January-December 1995* (February 1997), 1.

29. TNRCC, Monitoring Operations Division, *Smarter Air Monitoring for Texas* (November 1994).

30. Texas Air Control Board (TACB), *Air Quality in Texas: 1992 and Beyond* (1993), 12.

31. TNRCC, Office of Air Quality, information provided to author, 1995.

32. TNRCC, *Smarter Air Monitoring for Texas.*

33. Scott Mgebroff, Monitoring Operations Division, TNRCC, phone interview by author, September 1997, Austin.

34. Mgebroff, phone interview by author.

35. TNRCC, *Smarter Air Monitoring for Texas*, 13.

36. TNRCC, *Biennial Report to the 76th Legislature*, vol. 2, 34.

37. EPA, information provided to author from computer database AIRS EXEC, 1998.

38. American Lung Association, *Outdoor Air Pollution Fact Sheet: Ozone Air Pollution* (New York, November 1993).

39. American Lung Association, *Breath in Danger II: Estimation of Populations-at-Risk of Adverse Health Consequences in Areas Not in Attainment with National Ambient Air Quality Standards of the Clean Air Act* (New York, 1993), Table 3.

40. USDA, Forest Service, *Air Pollution Impact on Southern Forests: Short Leaf Pines on Coastal Plain Soils*, (Nacogdoches Research Station, 1987), 7.

41. EPA, *Plain English Guide to the Clean Air Act*, 2.

42. EPA, *Research Summary: Controlling Sulfur Oxides* (August 1980), 2.

43. The average pH of Big Bend rain in 1991 measured by the National Atmospheric Deposition Program was 5.98. By 1995, the average had fallen to 5.58.

44. TNRCC, *1998 State of Texas Reservoir Water Quality Assessment* (1998), 14.

45. TNRCC, *Air Monitoring Report 1995* (April 1997).

46. American Lung Association, *Breath in Danger II*, 2.

47. Robert Yuhnke, "Particles of Concern," *Environmental Forum* (Policy Journal of the Environmental Law Institute) 14, no. 2 (March-April 1997): 24-29.

48. TNRCC, *Air Monitoring Report 1991* (March 1994), 18.

49. TACB, *Texas Air Control Board Fact Sheet: Ambient Air Quality in the Houston/Galveston Metropolitan Area* (1993).

50. TNRCC, *Revisions to the State Implementation Plan for Milam County for Sulfur Dioxide* (1997).

51. American Lung Association, *Facts about Air Pollution and Your Health* (Washington, D.C., 1992), 2.

52. William Gill, Emissions Inventory Director, Air Quality Division, TNRCC, interview by author, April 1994, Austin.

53. EPA, *National Air Quality and Emissions Trends Report, 1990* (1990).

54. Cannon, *The Health Costs of Air Pollution*, 32.

55. For a good overview of studies that found an association between air pollution due to high concentrations of particulate matter and mortality due to lung cancer and cardiopulmonary disease, see Dockery, et al., "An Association between Air Pollution and Mortality in Six US Cities," 1753-1759. One study tracked 552,138 men and women in 151 cities across the United States from 1982 to 1989 and evaluated the effects of particulate air pollution—including sulfates and fine particulate matter less than 2.5 microns—on mortality. The study found that U.S. residents living in the cleanest cities had a 17 percent lower mortality risk attributable to particle exposure than those living in the dirtiest cities. Pope et al., "Particulate Air Pollution as a Predictor of Mortality," 669-674.

56. Pope et al., "Particulate Air Pollution as a Predictor of Mortality," 669-674.

57. EPA, *EPA's Revised Particulate Matter Standards Fact Sheet*, July 17, 1997.

58. EPA, *Regulatory Impact Analysis*, ES-23.

59. EPA, information provided to author from AIRS EXEC Database, 1998.

60. EPA, Regulatory Impact Analysis, 4-16. The chart estimates that while anthropogenic sources contribute 22.466 million tons per year, biogenic sources contribute 25.988 million tons.

61. Data provided by Liz Johnson, Air Policy and Regulations Development, TNRCC; data from three months in 1997.

62. Data provided by EPA, Office of Congressional and Legislative Affairs, and based on 1993-1995 monitoring data. The information is based on PM10 data, however, and is subject to uncertainty.

63. TNRCC, *Air Monitoring Report 1995*, 22-24.

64. EPA, *1997 National Air Quality: Status and Trends*, 6.

65. TNRCC, Office of Air Quality, information from State Summary of Emissions Database, August 1997.

66. Cannon, *Health Costs of Air Pollution: 1984-1989*, 33.

67. For a good source on the costs of lead air pollution, see EPA, *Costs and Benefits of Reducing Lead in Gasoline* (February 1985).

68. TACB, *Texas Air Control Board Fact Sheet. Ambient Air Quality in the Dallas/Ft. Worth Metropolitan Area* (1993), 2.

69. Randy Lee Loftis and Michael Goldhaber, "Dallas-Fort Worth Faces Increased Air Controls," *Dallas Morning News*, August 15, 1997.

70. Chuck Miller, Air Quality Assessment and Planning Division, TNRCC, phone interview by author, September 1997, Austin.

71. Randy Lee Loftis and Tony Hartzel, "EPA Threat on Smog Is Most Serious Yet," *Dallas Morning News*, May 5, 1999, A38.

72. Ed Michaels, Photochemical Air Monitoring Sites coordinator, TNRCC, phone interview by author, September 1997.

73. TNRCC, *State Implementation Plan for Ozone*, 9.

74. El Paso is not required to meet this requirement because most of the pollution in its airshed emanates from Mexico, while Beaumont-Port Arthur is a "moderate" nonattainment area and is therefore not required to make these additional emission cuts.

75. TNRCC, *State Implementation Plan for Ozone*.

76. The plan was originally scheduled to be put into place sooner, but in 1995 the Texas legislature passed a law putting a moratorium on the inspection and maintenance program until it was redesigned to place less of a burden on car owners.

77. East Texas Council of Governments, *Northeast Texas Flexible Attainment Region Memorandum of Agreement*, September 16, 1996.

78. TNRCC, *Revisions to the State Implementation Plan for Ozone*, Attainment Demonstration for El Paso, 1996.

79. TACB, *Air Quality in Texas: 1992 and Beyond* (1993), 14.

80. TNRCC, Attainment Demonstration for El Paso, *Revisions to the State Implementation Plan*, 1996.

81. TNRCC, *Revision to the State Implementation Plan for Carbon Monoxide*, September 1995.

82. EPA, *US-Mexico Border XXI Program Framework Document* (October 1996), VI.6. See also "Guidance to the Joint Advisory Committee on Air Quality Improvement," Appendix 1 of Annex V to the La Paz Agreement (U.S.- Mexico environmental agreement, 1983).

83. Becky Kirka, Toxics Release Inventory Program, TNRCC, phone interview by author, September 1997, Austin.

84. EPA, *1997 Texas Toxics Release Inventory Report* (May 1999).

85. Joint Select Committee on Toxic Air Emissions and Greenhouse Effect, *Interim Report of the Joint Select Committee on Toxic Air Emissions and Greenhouse Effect*, June 1991, 14.

86. For information on what the 188 toxics are, as well as the sources that will be regulated, see Amendments to the 1990 Clean Air Act, Title III, Section 112.

87. Joint Select Committee on Toxic Air Emissions and Greenhouse Effect, *Interim Report*, 19.

88. Joint Select Committee on Toxic Air Emissions and Greenhouse Effect, *Interim Report*, 19.

89. Joint Select Committee on Toxic Air Emissions and Greenhouse Effect, *Interim Report*, 25.

90. Joint Select Committee on Toxic Air Emissions and Greenhouse Effect, *Interim Report*, 25.

91. TNRCC, *Community Air Toxics Monitoring Program Report*, January-December 1995 (February 1997), 22.

92. EPA, *Estimating Exposure to Dioxin-Like Compounds*, vol. 2 (June 1994).

93. TNRCC, Office of Air Quality, information provided to author, 1995.

94. TNRCC, *Community Air Toxics Monitoring Program Report*, January-December 1995, 23.

95. TNRCC, *Decrease in Ambient Air Concentrations of Benzene, Toluene and Total Xylenes in Southeast Texas* (May 1997).

96. Lois Marie Gibbs and the Citizens Clearinghouse for Hazardous Waste, *Dying from Dioxin* (Boston: South End Press, 1995), 1.

97. Gibbs et al., *Dying from Dioxin*, xxx.

98. Vicki Monks, "The Truth about Dioxin," *National Wildlife*, August-September 1994, 10.

99. Gibbs et al., *Dying from Dioxin*, 11.

100. TNRCC, *Air Quality Assessment Program: Community Air Toxics Monitoring Program Report*, October 1992-September 1993 (May 1994), 2.

101. TNRCC, *Community Air Toxics Monitoring Program Report*, January-December 1995, 22.

102. TNRCC, *Community Air Toxics Monitoring Network Report: October 1993-December 1994* (December 1995), 37.

103. TNRCC, *Air Quality Assessment Program: Community Air Toxics Monitoring Program Report*, October 1992-September 1993, 33.

104. TNRCC, *Community Air Toxics Monitoring Network Report: October 1993-December 1994*, 21.

105. Tom Porter, Monitoring Operations Division, TNRCC, phone interview by author, September 1997, Austin. According to Porter, the agency decided to stop measuring 1,2—dibromoethane because the detection limit (0.5 parts per billion per volume) is greater than the annual screening level of 0.05 parts per billion per volume. Thus, the comparatively high detection limit makes it difficult for the agency to determine if a problem exists or not.

106. TNRCC, *Community Air Toxics Monitoring Network Report: October 1993-December 1994*, 21.

107. TNRCC, *Air Quality Assessment Program: Community Air Toxics Monitoring Program Report*, October 1992-September 1993, 33.

108. TACB, *Special Purpose Ambient Air Monitoring* (August, 1993), 23.

109. TNRCC, *Smarter Air Monitoring for Texas*, 25.

110. TNRCC, Press Release, May 27, 1997.

111. William K. Stevens, "Warmer, Wetter, Sicker: Linking Climate to Health," *New York Times*, August 10, 1998. Additional data have shown that 1998 was the hottest year of the century.

112. World Resources Institute, *1992 Information Please Environmental Almanac*, 275.

113. William K. Stevens, "Experts on Climate Change Ponder: How Urgent Is It?" *New York Times*, September 9, 1997, B7.

114. Stevens, "Experts on Climate Change Ponder," B7.

115. Ric Jensen, "Are Things Warming Up?: How Climactic Changes Could Affect Texas," *Texas Water Resources* 15 (spring 1989).

116. Joint Select Committee on Toxic Air Emissions and Greenhouse Effect, *Interim Report*, 57.

117. Stevens, "Experts on Climate Change Ponder," B7.

118. Bob Hall and Mary Lee Kerr, *1991-1992 Green Index: A State-by-State Guide to the Nation's Environmental Health* (Washington, D.C.: Island Press, 1991), 21.

119. NRDC, *The Statehouse Effect: State Policies to Control the Greenhouse Effect* (New York, 1990).

120. NRDC, *Getting the Dirt on Your Electric Company: A Consumer's and Policymaker's Handbook of Air Pollution from Electric Utilities in the Eastern U.S.* (New York, 1997).

121. Public Utility Commission of Texas, *Annual Report* (April 1997), 5.

122. World Resources Institute, *1994 Information Please Environmental Almanac*, 334.

123. World Resources Institute, *1994 Information Please Environmental Almanac*, 334.

124. EPA, *Plain English Guide to the Clean Air Act*, 16.

125. Texas Department of Health, *Implications on Public Health of Elimination of the Texas Department of Health's Indoor Air Quality Branch* (November 25, 1992).

126. EPA, *Report to Congress on Indoor Air Quality*, vol. 2 (August 1989), 5-4.

127. State of Texas Environmental Priorities Project, State of Texas Environmental Priorities Project, vol. 1: *Final Overview Report* (Austin: TNRCC, June 1997).

128. EPA, *The Inside Story: A Guide to Indoor Air Quality* (September 1988), 11.

129. EPA, *Setting Priorities for Strategies for Environmental Protection* (1990), 14. The other three human health risks problems identified by the Science Advisory Board were ambient air pollutants like ozone, particulate matter, and lead; exposure of employees to chemicals in industry and agricultural work; and pollutants in drinking water. The Science Advisory Board considered only those problems addressed by a 1987 EPA report entitled *Unfinished Business: A Comparative Assessment of Environmental Problems*.

130. Texas Department of Health, *Voluntary Air Quality Guidelines for Public Schools*, May 10, 1998.

131. EPA, *The Inside Story*, 11.

132. Texas Department of Health, *The Texas Indoor Radon Survey, 1992* (April 20, 1992), 20.

133. EPA, *The Inside Story*, 13.

134. EPA, *Report to Congress on Indoor Air Quality*, vol. 2, 5-11.

135. EPA, *Data for Proposed Lead State Grant Allocation Formula* (December 17, 1993).

136. EPA, *The Inside Story*, 22.

137. "Childhood Incidences of Cancer," *New York Times*, September 29, 1997, AI.

138. EPA, *The Inside Story*, 24.

139. EPA, Office of Air Quality Planning and Standards, "Proposed Regional Haze Regulations for Protection of Visibility in National Parks and Wilderness Areas," EPA web site (http://134.67.104.12/naaqsfin/hazefs.html).

140. TNRCC, *Visibility Protection State Implementation Plan: Three-Year Report* (January 1995), 2.

141. National Parks Service and EPA, *Study Plan for Texas-Mexico Aerosol Characterization Study* (January 19, 1995), 1-2.

142. Sierra Club Lone Star Chapter, "EPA's Proposed Regional Haze Regulations are Under Attack," Press Release (September 16, 1997).

143. National Parks Service, "Big Bend Air Quality Study Results Announced," News Release, May 4, 1998.

144. National Parks Service and U.S. EPA, *Study Plan for Texas-Mexico Aerosol Characterization Study*, 1-2.

145. The Carbón I plant, which began operation in the early 1980s, does not have particulate matter or sulfur dioxide controls, while Carbón II, built in the late 1980s, does have an electrostatic precipitator to control particulate matter.

146. EPA, *Proposed Regional Haze Regulations for Protection of Visibility in National Parks and Wilderness Areas*, Fact Sheet (July 1997).

147. EPA, *Plain English Guide to the Clean Air Act*, 9.

148. EPA, *Plain English Guide to the Clean Air Act*, 9.

149. EPA, *Plain English Guide to the Clean Air Act*, 9; EPA, *1995 National Air Quality: Status and Trends*.

150. Texas House of Representatives, Engrossed Version S.B. 681 (1997).

151. GLO, *EnviroNomics 1*, no. 1 (spring 1992): 1.

152. EPA, *Plain English Guide to the Clean Air Act*, 12-13.

153. Keith Bradsher, "Light Trucks Increase Profits But Foul Air More than Cars," *New York Times*, November 30, 1997, A22.

154. EPA, "Clean Air: Cleaner Cars and Cleaner Gasoline," News Release, May 1, 1999.

155. TNRCC, *Inspection/Maintenance State Implementation Plan for Dallas/Ft. Worth, El Paso and Houston Ozone Non-Attainment Areas* (1997), 2-3.

156. Texas House of Representatives, Engrossed Version S.B. 681 (1997).

157. TNRCC, *Revisions to the State Implementation Plan for the Substitute of the Federal Clean Fuel Fleet Program* (July 24, 1996), 23.

158. Texas Comptroller of Public Accounts (TCPA), "Battle Lines Drawn on Transportation Funding," *Fiscal Notes*, June 1997, 5.

159. TCPA, "Battle Lines Drawn on Transportation Funding," 5.

160. TCPA, *Fiscal Notes*, February 1994, 3.

161. Texas Department of Transportation, as reported in TCPA, *Fiscal Notes*, February 1994. Between 1994 and 1996, a total of $321.4 million were earmarked for congestion mitigation and air quality projects. The estimated total budget was more than $6 billion.

162. TCPA, "Battle Lines Drawn on Transportation Funding," 5. For example, under the National Economic Crossroads Transportation Efficiency Act (NEXTEA), which would replace ISTEA, Texas would gain about $1.3 billion per year over current funding levels, while under STEP 21 (the Streamlined Transportation Efficiency Program for the 21st Century), which would give more flexibility on how transportation money was spent, Texas would gain $1.9 billion per year.

163. Hall and Kerr, *1991-1992 Green Index*, 21.

164. TCPA, *Fiscal Notes*, February 1994, 1.

165. TCPA, "Buses and Beyond: Cities' Tactics Vary in Traffic Reduction and Clean Air Efforts," *Fiscal Notes*, June 1997, 1.

166. TCPA, "Buses and Beyond," 3.

167. TCPA, "Buses and Beyond," 3.

168. TCPA, "Buses and Beyond," 4.

169. GLO, *The Texas Plan for Clean Air* (August 1993), 2.

170. Texas House of Representatives, Engrossed Version S.B. 200 (1995).

171. The Texas Clean Fleet Program web page, September 1997.

172. Hazel Barbour, Mobile Source Division, TNRCC, phone interview by author, September 1997, Austin.

173. Texas House of Representatives, Engrossed Version of SB 681 (1997).

174. Railroad Commission of Texas, Alternative Fuels Division, information provided to author, 1994.

175. DePalma, "The Great Green Hope," C1.

176. DePalma, "The Great Green Hope," C6. Ford Motor Company recently announced that it had a goal of producing fuel cell cars by 2004. "Ford Signs Fuel-Cell Partnership," *Austin American-Statesman*, December 16, 1997, D1.

177. TNRCC, Petroleum Storage Tank Division, "Reported Underground Storage Tank Leaks, 1993," written information provided to author, 1994.

178. GLO, *The Texas Plan for Clean Air*, 7.

179. Dan Kelly, Alternative Fuels Division, Railroad Commission of Texas, interview by author, April, 1994.

180. GLO, information from *Map of Alternative Fueling Stations in Texas*, April 1994.

181. Railroad Commission of Texas, *State of Texas Energy Policy Partnership*, vol. 2, 9.

182. Railroad Commission of Texas, *State of Texas Energy Policy Partnership*, vol. 2, 9.

183. TNRCC, *State Summary of Emissions Database*, July 1997.

184. TNRCC, *State Summary of Emissions Database*, July 1997.

185. EPA, 1995 *Toxics Release Inventory: Public Data Release* (April 1997), Table 4-6.

186. TNRCC, "Texas Drives National Pollution Prevention," News Release, May 13, 1999. These totals do not include more than 280 chemicals added to reporting requirements in the 1994 and 1995 reporting years.

187. EPA, 1995 *Toxics Release Inventory*.

188. Of the top 15 toxic chemicals released to the air in 1995 in Texas, the EPA had established an ambient maximum level only for benzene. The Safe Drinking Water Act, on the other hand, has established maximum contaminant levels for public drinking water systems for 5 of the top 15 chemicals: toluene, 1,1,1-trichloro-ethane, xylene, benzene, and styrene. For a full list of EPA regulated chemicals under the Safe Drinking Water Act, see the chapter on Water Resources.

189. Marianne Brain and Neil Carman, *A Study of Upset Incidents in Industries in Texas* (Austin: Lone Star Chapter of Sierra Club, August 1992), 2.

190. Brain and Carman, *A Study of Upset Incidents*, 2.

191. "Plant Managers Forming Cooperatives to Prepare for Risk Management Rule," *Environment Reporter* 28, no. 6: 275.

192. Jeff Saitas, Office of Air Quality, TNRCC, information provided to author from Point Source Database, 1995.

193. EPA, 1997 *National Air Quality Status and Trends*, 14.

194. Center for Global Studies, Houston Advanced Research Center and Energy Institute, University of Houston, *Guide to Electric Power in Texas* (1997), 1.

195. Texas Public Utility Commission, *PUC Annual Report 1996* (1997), 5.

196. TNRCC, *State Summary of Emissions Database*, July 1997.

197. TNRCC, *1997 Emissions Inventory Database*, 1999.

198. TNRCC, *Revisions to the State Implementation Plan for Sulfur Dioxide in Milam County* (1997).

199. EPA, Mercury Report to Congress, SAB Review Draft (June 1996).

200. NRDC, Benchmarking Air Emissions, 25.

201. TNRCC, "Results of Grandfathered Emissions Survey" (http://www.tnrcc.state.tx.us/air/care/eidata.html), 1999.

202. Bill Dawson, "Pollution Tied to Lack of Permits," *Houston Chronicle*, April 1, 1997.

203. Galveston-Houston Association for Smog Prevention, and Lone Star Chapter of the Sierra Club, *Grandfathered Air Pollution: The Dirty Secret of Texas Industries* (Austin: Lone Star Chapter of Sierra Club, April 1998), 5.

204. Bill Dawson, "Plants without Permits Emit Much of Local Pollution," *Houston Chronicle*, April 6, 1997.

205. Dawson, "Pollution Tied to Lack of Permits."

206. TNRCC, "Results of Grandfathered Emissions Survey."

207. TNRCC, "Retirement Plan for the Grandfathered Exemption," *National Outlook*, spring 1998, 8.

208. TNRCC, "Retirement Plan for the Grandfathered Exemption," 7.

209. NRDC, *Benchmarking Air Emissions*, 32.

210. TACB, *Special Purpose Ambient Air Monitoring*, 13.

211. TACB, State Small Business Ombudsman, *The Price of Clean Air* (1993), 1.

212. TACB, *The Price of Clean Air*, 1.

213. TACB, *Air Quality in Texas*, 1992, 15. Although the air samples showed PM10 levels higher than national standards, they were based on an 8-hour sample, not on 24 hours on which the national standard is based. Also, agricultural sources are not subject to the same nuisance property-line regulations as are industrial sources.

214. TACB, *Special Purpose Ambient Air Monitoring*, 12.

215. TACB, *Special Purpose Ambient Air Monitoring*, 12. These include studies in San Antonio, Garland, and three neighborhoods in Dallas. None of the sampling studies found lead levels above national standards.

216. TNRCC, 30 *Texas Administrative Code*, Chapter 116.117.

217. Marion Moses, "Diseases Associated with Exposure to Chemical Substances—Pesticides," *Maxy-Rosenau Public Health and Preventive Medicine*, ed. John Last (East Norwalk, Conn.: Appleton-Century-Crofts, 1986), as cited in Benjamin Goldman, *The Truth about Where You Live: An Atlas for Action on Toxins and Mortality* (New York: Random House, 1991), 233.

218. John Sweeten, Texas Agricultural Extension Service, *Cattle Feedlot Waste Management Practices for Water and Air Pollution*, # B-1671 (College Station: Texas A&M University System), 11-14.

219. Texas Institute for Applied Environmental Research, Tarleton State University, *Interim Report to the Joint Interim Committee on the Environment*, 72nd Texas Legislature (Stephenville, September 1992), 65.

Pesticides

OVERVIEW

Pesticides are chemical compounds used to control plants and animals classified as pests. The term pesticides includes insecticides, herbicides, fungicides, and other materials designed to kill or control "pests." Despite benefits for crop production and control of disease-carrying pests, pesticide use is of concern because pesticides can reach humans through the food chain, through drinking water, or by direct contact. Pesticides can also build up in fish and other aquatic life, in birds and animals, and can destroy beneficial plants and insects.[1]

Before the development of synthetic pesticides, many farmers used naturally occurring substances such as pyrethrums to control insects.[2] Widespread use of synthetic pesticides in the United States began following World War II. Many of the ingredients of today's pesticides were in fact developed during the war as weapons.[3] Having become an integral part of agricultural practices by the mid-1950s, pesticide use is often credited with increasing crop yields by reducing natural threats to production. Beginning in the late 1940s, federal and local governments sponsored widespread pesticide spraying programs, using DDT and other chemicals in urban communities in an effort to eradicate mosquitoes, gypsy moths, the Japanese beetle, and other insects. Today, pesticides are used extensively by homeowners, commercial exterminators, golf course managers, parks departments, schools, highway departments, utility companies, and others to control insects, weeds, and other pests in nonagricultural settings.

Estimates of pesticide use in the United States are largely based on sales data, extrapolations from voluntary farmer surveys, and crop data from major producing states. Comprehensive reporting of pesticide use by farmers and other applicators (lawn services, commercial applicators, golf course superintendents, etc.) is required by state law only in California and New York.[4] Other states, including New Hampshire, New Jersey, Montana, Arizona, and Connecticut

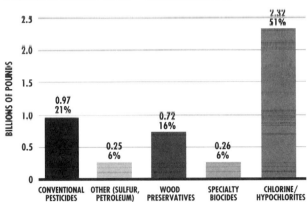

PESTICIDE USE IN 1995 – EPA ESTIMATES

Source: EPA, Pesticide Industry Sales and Usage: 1994-1995, Rep. No. 733-R-97-001, August 1997.

also have varying forms of use-reporting laws.[5]

Almost one billion pounds of conventional active pesticide ingredients were used in the United States in 1995, amounting to approximately 4.6 pounds of pesticides per person.[6] Combined with other types of pesticides, such as sulfur and petroleum, wood preservatives, biocides, and chlorine (used for disinfection), total U.S. pesticide use in 1995 reached an

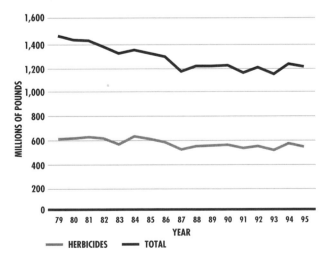

TRENDS IN U.S. ANNUAL PESTICIDE USE

Source: EPA, 1994-1995 Market Estimates, August 1997.

U.S. PESTICIDE USE BY CATEGORY

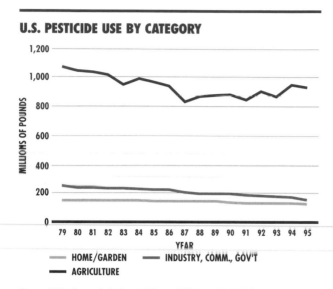

Source: EPA, Pesticide Industry Sales and Usage: 1994-1995 Estimates, Rep. No. 733-R-97-001, August 1997.

THREE MAJOR GROUPS OF CONVENTIONAL PESTICIDES

Chlorinated hyrdocarbons, or organo-chlorines: these pesticides generally break down very slowly and can remain in the environment for long periods of time. Dieldrin, chlordane, aldrin, DDT, and heptachlor are pesticides of this type.

Organic phosphates, or organo-phosphates: these pesticides are often highly toxic to humans but generally do not remain in the environment for long periods of time. Parathion, malathion, thimet, and trichlorphone are pesticides of this type.

Carbamates: generally less toxic to humans, but concerns about potential effects on immune and central nervous systems persist for some carbamates. Carbaryl, carbofuran, and methomyl are examples of carbamates.

(Source: Nancy Blanpied, ed., Farm Policy: The Politics of Soil, Surpluses and Subsidies [Washington, D.C.: Congressional Quarterly, 1984], 69; for carbamates, see National Research Council, Pesticides in the Diets of Infants and Children [Washington, D.C.: National Academy Press, 1993], 64.)

estimated 1.22 billion pounds of active ingredients. Herbicides continue to account for a large percentage of total pesticide use (57 percent in 1995).

The economic value of the pesticide market is significant. The U.S. Environmental Protection Agency (EPA) estimates that $11.3 billion was spent on pesticides in the United States in 1995, with farmers spending about 70 percent of this amount, or $7.9 billion, an average of $4,200 per farm. The average U.S. household spent $20 per year for pesticides applied by the homeowner (but not by hired applicators).[7] According to EPA estimates, 74 percent of all U.S. households used some form of pesticide in 1994.[8]

During the past fifty years, agricultural production in many areas of the world has increased dramatically, partly because of the use of herbicides and insecticides. Health benefits, such as those related to eradication of malaria-carrying mosquitoes, were also foreseen and, in many cases, attained.

Nonetheless, most pesticides have never been systematically reviewed for their full range of potential long-term health effects on humans, such as potential genetic damage or damage to nervous, endocrine, or immune systems.[9] Data are particularly lacking for pesticides used in nonagricultural settings.[10]

Throughout its nearly three decades of existence,

the EPA has concentrated on the cancer-causing potential of pesticides based on the expected levels of pesticide residues in food prepared for human consumption. With the passage of the Food Quality Protection Act in 1996, this has begun to change. This new law requires that by 2006 the EPA reassess the risks of over 9,700 pesticide tolerances and re-evaluate the allowable levels of pesticides that can remain in or on food.

The effects of pesticides on wildlife also are not well documented. Prior to 1985 the EPA did not review pesticides on the basis of potential adverse effects on wildlife. Since then, the EPA has canceled some pesticides like DDT and chlordane, based partially on their effects on the environment and wildlife.[11] Discoveries of pesticide residues have also resulted in fishing bans in many bays, lakes, and rivers.[12]

The introduction of synthetic pesticides and fertilizers, combined with the opportunities associated with more global food markets and favorable U.S. agricultural policies, have driven farm yield far beyond its pre-World War II levels. This increase has not been without costs.[13] Studies have shown that pesticides have helped keep crop damage at between five and 30 percent of potential production, particularly in large-scale, single-crop operations that leave themselves vulnerable to severe pest damage.[14] But pesticides do pose a number of problems for agriculture, including increased production costs, destruction of beneficial insects, secondary pest outbreaks, development of pesticide-resistant pests, and the potential for harmful health effects on agricultural workers and their families.[15]

According to one study, seven percent of U.S. agriculture production was lost to pests in the 1950s; in 1993, 13 percent of all production was lost to pests.[16] Today, more than 500 species of insects and mites and more than 150 types of fungi (a 50 percent increase over the past decade) are now resistant to some pesticides.[17] As a result of this increasing resistance, combining pesticides, increasing applications, or substituting more expensive, toxic, or ecologically hazardous pesticides occurs more frequently. In addition to the problem of pesticide resistance, millions of dollars worth of crops have been lost as a result of improper pesticide application.[18] Consequently, more and more farmers and other pesticide users are seeking to better target their use of pesticides and implement pesticide-use-reduction strategies.

RECENT DISCOVERIES ABOUT PESTICIDES

New scientific research is uncovering some important health-related issues associated with pesticide use. For example, pesticides were identified by a National Cancer Institute study as a likely cause of elevated rates of certain cancers among farmers.[19] Farmers are at higher risk than the general population for certain cancers: non-Hodgkin's lymphoma, skin melanomas, multiple myeloma, leukemia, and cancers of the lip, stomach, prostate, and brain. Exposures to 2,4-D, 2,4,5-T, mecoprop, acilfluorfen, and other pesticides have been linked to non-

---

CHILDREN AT RISK

Infants and children are more susceptible to the effects of pesticides than adults because of their developing physiology and increased proportional exposure. Infants consume two-and-a-half times more calories per body weight than do adults, breathe twice the amount of air per body weight, and have twice the skin surface area per body weight. Children drink many more liquids per body weight than do adults, including 21 times more apple juice. The National Academy of Sciences reported that "exposure to neurotoxic compounds at levels believed to be safe for adults could result in permanent loss of brain function if it occurred during the prenatal and early childhood period of brain development."

(*Source: Natural Resources Defense Council, Our Children at Risk [New York, 1997]. See also National Research Council, Pesticides in the Diets of Infants and Children [Washington, D.C.: National Academy Press, 1993]; Richard Wiles and Christopher Campbell, Pesticides in Children's Food [Washington, D.C.: Environmental Working Group, 1993].*)

Hodgkin's lymphoma. Exposure to insecticides has been associated with leukemia, multiple myeloma, and brain cancer.[20]

The National Cancer Institute has documented that some childhood cancers have been increasing at a rate of nearly one percent per year for the past several decades.[21] Some of that increase may be attributable to urban pesticide use.[22]

One recent study concluded that every day "more than one million children age five and under (one out of 20)" in the United States may exceed what the U.S. Department of Agriculture (USDA) has determined to be a safe daily dose of organo-phosphate insecticides.[23] The report analyzed more than 80,000 food samples tested for such pesticides by the federal government, using residue levels found after washing, cooking, peeling, and preparing the food for normal consumption. The report also concluded that the use of organo-phosphate insecticides in the home compounded the risk to infants and toddlers.[24] Many organo-phosphates are toxic to the brain and

nervous system, which are especially vulnerable during infancy and early childhood.

Scientists are debating about the relationship between pesticides that mimic the estrogen hormone and the disruption of the endocrine system in humans and wildlife. Pesticides with endocrine-disruption effects or effects on the reproductive system are among the most commonly used and include the herbicides alachlor and atrazine, the fungicides mancozeb and benomyl, and the insecticides carbaryl, dicofol, endosulfan, methomyl, methoxychlor, parathion, and the synthetic pyrethroids.[25]

The complex human endocrine system consists of a series of glands, organs, and tissue that secrete and respond to hormones. Hormones play very important roles in reproduction, child development, and the control of other bodily functions. Thus, any-

thing disrupting the endocrine system may have "far-reaching" effects.[26]

Uncertainties about the potential endocrine-disrupting effects of many chemicals, including some pesticides, have been sufficiently serious for Congress to require the EPA to develop guidelines by August 1999 for screening chemicals for their endocrine-disrupting potential.

NONAGRICULTURAL PESTICIDE USE

Public policy at the national level has generally been focused on the agricultural uses of pesticides and the health risks posed by residues on food, with much less concern for home and commercial exposure to pesticides.[27] One exception has been the action taken to ban or limit the widespread use of highly toxic pesticides for control of termites and fire ants.

MONITORING CHEMICALS IN FOOD

Legally, food may contain a number of pesticide residues as long as the amount is within allowable tolerance levels. Under the Food Quality Protection Act, many of these tolerances are being recalculated to take into account their possible cumulative impact and their impact on infants and children.

Various federal agencies share responsibility for monitoring chemical residues and environmental contaminants in food. The federal Food and Drug Administration has primary responsibility for these matters, but the USDA, the EPA, and the National Marine Fisheries also have responsibility for monitoring chemical residues in food. Since 1991 the USDA has coordinated and funded a nationwide food testing program known as the Pesticide Data Program. Under a contract with the USDA, the Texas Department of Agriculture receives funds to conduct an annual testing program in the state.[28] The two major objectives of the program are (1) to determine whether produce has pesticide residues beyond the limits allowed by the EPA, and/or (2) to determine whether the residues are from pesticides not registered for use on that particular fruit or vegetable. This program was not

designed, however, to take adulterated produce off the market, but to "provide government agencies with a data base to react to food safety issues."[29]

In 1992 the USDA's Pesticide Data Program analyzed residues in 12 fruits and vegetables from major agricultural production regions in the United States, including Texas.[30] This was the first Food and Drug Administration or USDA pesticide residue study that tested residue on fruits and vegetables after they were peeled and washed. The results of this study showed that fresh fruits and vegetables routinely contain residues of several different pesticides.[31] According to the USDA, 5,592 samples were analyzed. "Residues of 49 different pesticides were detected in approximately 60 percent of all samples. In other words, neither the washing nor peeling of food guarantees the removal of pesticide residues."[32]

This study revealed that the levels of many pesticide residues were substantially below tolerances, but residues in violation were found in 63 samples, 15 of which were in imported commodities: "Of the 63 violative samples, 10 exceeded the tolerance level and the other 53 had residues where no tolerance was established."[33]

Improper use and disposal of home and garden pesticides, however, have the potential to pollute creeks and lakes. The presence or misapplication of pesticides in homes and buildings also can have serious adverse human health and environmental effects.[34]

In 1995 Americans used an estimated 133 million pounds of pesticides in their homes and gardens, including 47 million pounds of herbicides.[35] The most common pesticides used by homeowners were the herbicides 2,4-D and Glyphosate (sold under trade names Roundup and Rodeo). There has been much debate over whether 2,4-D is a carcinogen, and the issue is still under review by the EPA. Possible links to non-Hodgkin's lymphoma are of special concern.[36] Glyphosate exposure was the most common reported cause of pesticide illness for landscape workers.[37]

Home pesticide use is a particularly critical issue when considering the health of children. The EPA reports that indoor air has much higher pesticide concentrations than outdoor air and noted that small children spend close to 90 percent of their time indoors. The report estimates that 85 percent of a person's total daily exposure to airborne pesticides comes from indoor air.[38] Indoor pesticide exposure can result from use of household pesticides, disinfectants containing pesticides, and flea treatments for pets, among other sources. Pesticides can also be found in soil and dust tracked into homes from lawns, gardens, and job sites. One study showed that the greatest number of pesticides and highest concentrations were found in carpet dust.[39]

In 1995 industrial, commercial, and government institutions used 150 million pounds of pesticides, accounting for 12 percent of all active pesticide ingredients used in the United States.[40]

Many pesticides that could pose serious potential adverse health effects, including 2,4-D and diazinon, are commonly used for turf management on golf courses and public parks.[41] Pesticide use in schools is an important issue to many parents and teachers. (See Pesticide Use Reduction for a discussion of IPM requirements for Texas schools.)

PESTICIDE USE IN TEXAS
Texas Agricultural Pesticide Use
In 1995 the Texas Agriculture Statistics Service estimated that Texas farm and ranch operators spent $376 million on pesticides. When this is combined with $642 million in fertilizer costs, it equals one-third the net cash income received by all Texas farmers and ranchers in 1995. Thus, farm chemicals represent the single largest yearly input cost for field-crop production.[42]

The overall pesticide-use estimates for Texas crops are based on the database established by the National Center for Food and Agricultural Policy, a nonprofit organization in Washington, D.C., and are

TOP TEN HERBICIDES, INSECTICIDES, AND FUNGICIDES USED IN TEXAS

PESTICIDE	ESTIMATED LBS. ACTIVE INGREDIENT	PESTICIDE	ESTIMATED LBS. ACTIVE INGREDIENT	PESTICIDE	ESTIMATED LBS. ACTIVE INGREDIENT
Herbicides		Insecticides		Fungicides	
2,4-D	4,239,134	Malathion	612,310	Chlorothalonil	637,059
Atrazine	3,156,075	Carbaryl	581,396	Sulfur	344,053
Trifluralin	2,190,877	Chlorpyrifos	548,255	PCNB	262,780
Metolachlor	1,867,582	Terbufos	511,388	Maneb	109,730
Propanil	768,269	Dimethoate	414,035	Copper	91,231
Glyphosate	718,008	Azinphos-methyl	278,527	Ziram	85,493
Alachlor	679,736	Methyl parathion	274,446	Mancozeb	64,841
Picloram	651,106	Propargite	263,264	Metalaxyl	52,458
Molinate	592,207	Aldicarb	255,415	Benomyl	43,353
Pendimethalin	587,378	Disulfon	230,783	Iprodione	36,223

Source: Leonard P. Gianessi and James Earl Anderson, Pesticide Use in Texas Crop Production (Washington, D.C.: National Center for Food and Agricultural Policy), February 1995.

widely used. The estimates, however, are not based on actual reported use for Texas farms. Instead, they are based on a combination of (1) the 1992 Agricultural Census data, which provide information on cropping patterns, and (2) federal and state pesticide use "surveys" conducted between 1991 and 1993.[43] These surveys are often based on just a small portion of the growers in a particular industry. The National Center for Food and Agricultural Policy estimates are also reviewed by representatives of the pesticide industry to help resolve "discrepancies among survey results and reviewer comments."[44]

Pesticide Use in Other Sectors

Specific data on nonagricultural pesticide use are generally not available. Most governmental entities —such as schools, parks departments, and highway maintenance departments—likely keep some records of their pesticide use. There is, however, no public compilation or reporting of these uses that would allow the oversight agencies or the public to readily know what pesticides are being used in the community, even in locations such as parks and schools where children may come into most direct contact with them.

One controversial category of nonagricultural pesticide use in Texas is the use of herbicides to kill aquatic weeds such as hydrilla and water hyacinth. Commonly used aquatic herbicides include 2,4-D, glyphosate, endothall, and fluoridone. During 1993 to 1996, the Texas Parks and Wildlife Department reported treating annually between 1,750 and 3,440 acres of lakes and streams with aquatic herbicides, though the amount of active ingredient used was not reported.[45] Many other entities—such as river authorities, lake managers, and golf courses, as well as individual homeowners—also use aquatic herbicides, although with no use reporting. This can pose problems, particularly if the herbicides are applied near a drinking-water intake, since most labels for aquatic herbicides require protection of public drinking-water supplies. In some cases, the labels require that the drinking-water intake be shut down for between seven and 21 days after the herbicide is used in a drinking water-source. Enforcement of such

label restrictions is difficult, at best, without information on uses.

Limited anecdotal information on nonagricultural uses of pesticides in Texas does exist, largely as a result of problems encountered in the pesticide use. For example:

■ Eating fish caught in Austin's Town Lake has been prohibited for years due to the high concentrations of the pesticide chlordane, which was most commonly used to control termites before its use was banned in the early 1990s.

■ The widespread use of the insecticide diazinon on lawns and other urban settings has affected water quality in the Trinity River basin.[46] Wastewater from a number of city sewage treatment plants, including Fort Worth, Denton, Tyler, Temple, and others, can fail monthly toxicity tests because diazinon has reached the system through runoff and is not removed by the treatment plant.[47] The City of Fort Worth has launched a public education campaign promoting use of less-toxic alternatives.[48]

■ Hundreds of trees along an 11-mile stretch of road in north Dallas in August 1997 were poisoned by city workers applying a weed killer to city sidewalks.[49]

■ A Dallas study of children poisoned by pesticides at home found that 15 percent had absorbed pesticides through their skin from contaminated carpets and linens.[50]

PESTICIDE REGULATION
Federal Programs

In 1947 Congress took its first step to regulate pesticides with the enactment of the Federal Insecticide, Fungicide and Rodenticide Act (FIFRA). This early law was intended primarily to protect farmers and others from mislabeled, ineffective, or adulterated pesticides. The original document was only 35 pages long. By 1994 this act had expanded to more than 200 pages.[51] The act initially granted jurisdiction over pesticides to the USDA, but in 1970, amid allegations of the USDA's mismanagement and conflicts of interest, Congress shifted authority for pesticide regulation to the newly created EPA.[52]

Federal pesticide law establishes a national program with a division of responsibility between the

THE NEW LAW—KEY FEATURES

A key feature of the Food Quality Protection Act is the way it implements risk assessment in determining pesticide tolerance levels. Risk assessment has been called "the process of determining the probability of a bad outcome." In setting pesticide tolerance levels for food crops, the EPA has relied on risk assessment studies conducted on animals and, in most cases, provided by the manufacturer. In these studies, experimental animals are exposed to various doses of a single pesticide. The EPA extrapolates from the resulting data the possible harm a pesticide ingredient might pose for humans.

Key provisions of the Food Quality Protection Act include:

■ EPA must set pesticide tolerance levels for raw or processed food, with "a reasonable certainty" of no harm from aggregate exposure to pesticides.

■ EPA must assess the impact on infants and children in determining tolerance levels so that aggregate exposure to pesticides will not result in harm to infants and children.

■ EPA cannot consider the benefits of a pesticide when evaluating pesticide tolerances based on their impact on reproduction and prenatal development or on exposure levels for infants and children. Pesticide benefits may be considered in the evaluation of existing tolerances for cancer-causing effects if the pesticide risk is less than the risk caused by its discontinuation, if its discontinuation would cause a major disruption of the food supply, and if certain criteria for lifetime risk are met.

■ EPA must publish information, to be displayed in grocery stores, about any pesticide residues that do not meet the standard of reasonable certainty of no harm but are allowed because of their perceived benefits.[53]

federal and state governments.[54] The federal government focus is on the underlying issues of pesticide effectiveness and potential risks. In brief, the EPA registers pesticides if it determines that they can be used without unreasonable adverse effects on man or the environment, reflecting a congressional directive to balance the risks and benefits of pesticides. The EPA is also authorized to impose use restrictions (often set out in the labels required for pesticide products) and to cancel or suspend products, though the latter authority has not been broadly used. The training, licensing, and oversight of pesticide sellers and users are generally left to the states, with federal grants supporting those efforts.

The USDA, however, continues to play a role. Its National Agricultural Statistics Service has been publishing reports on chemical use in agriculture since 1991, as part of a federal water quality initiative. In addition, the USDA funds pesticide-use studies through state liaisons (including the Agricultural Extension Service of Texas A&M University) as part of its National Agricultural Pesticide Impact Assessment Program. The USDA is also responsible for testing pesticide residues on fresh food through its Pesticide Data Program.

The Food Quality Protection Act

In 1958 Congress added the so-called Delaney Clause to the Food and Drug and Cosmetic Act. This amendment provided that no chemical that causes cancer could be added to processed food regardless of the level of concentration or the level of risk. In effect, Congress determined that the uncertainties surrounding any attempt to assess the risks of cancer were too great.

In 1996 the Delaney Clause was amended through the passage of the Food Quality Protection Act. Passage of the act was a direct result of the publication of the National Academy of Science's 1993 report, Pesticide in the Diets of Infants and Children.[55] This report questioned the government's ability to assess pesticide risks for children in order to prevent dangerous exposure.

Central to passage of the act was its requirement that the EPA compensate for incomplete data on the effects of pesticides on children by applying a

TOXIC "INERT" INGREDIENTS

For the first time, under the Food Quality Protection Act, the EPA is scheduled to examine tolerance exemptions given to "inert" pesticide ingredients—those used to dilute or carry the active ingredient. Of the 2,500 substances added to pesticides but not named on product labels, more than 650 have been identified as hazardous by federal, state, or international agencies. Nearly 400 of these have been used as the active killing ingredient in pesticides. Twenty-one of the inert ingredients have been classified as carcinogens, 127 as occupational hazards, and 209 as hazardous air or water pollutants. The "inert" ingredient naphthalene, for instance, is designated a hazardous air pollutant under the Clean Air Act and a priority pollutant under the Clean Water Act.

(*Source: Northwest Coalition for Alternatives to Pesticides, Worst Kept Secrets: Toxic Inert Ingredients in Pesticides [Eugene, Ore., 1998].*)

tenfold safety factor. The law requires the EPA to review over 9,700 existing tolerances for 470 active pesticide ingredients or high-hazard inert ingredients[56] and apply the safety factor of 10 where comprehensive and complete information is not available regarding the cumulative impacts on children.

Key Texas Pesticide Safety Programs

In part to implement federal pesticide law, Texas has established a framework for regulation of pesticide use in the state. The basic Texas laws for the regulation of pesticides have been in effect since the early 1970s, with few changes. The Texas Department of Agriculture retains the primary responsibility over pesticide use in agriculture. It runs a registration process to generate fees for the program and implements regulations for dealers and users of pesticides. This basic regulatory framework has been broadened over the past 15 years to include a wider range of government agencies.

In 1985 worker protection legislation was extended to farmworkers, following litigation brought by the Texas United Farm Workers. Under the Farmworker Right-to-Know legislation, agricultural producers are required to ensure that farmworkers receive training and adequate health and safety information on the pesticides to which they might be exposed. The Farmworker Right-to-Know law requires the Texas Department of Agriculture to distribute crop sheets to agricultural workers in English and Spanish.

The crop sheets include information on the most common pesticides used on particular crops in particular regions of the state. They contain safety warnings and handling instructions, including the length of time for which sprayed fields should be posted.

The Farmworker Right-to-Know legislation also requires operators of larger farms to keep pesticide application records for 30 years, although they are not required to turn in these records to state agencies. The Texas Department of Agriculture has the responsibility to enforce this law. The Texas program has now been supplemented with a national program established by the EPA.

In 1984 the Texas Department of Agriculture issued rules establishing waiting periods before workers could re-enter fields recently treated with pesticides. Notice of applications must be provided and fields posted.

Despite concern over farmworker exposure to pesticides, however, Texas has no systematic health monitoring of the two million farmworkers who work around pesticides. Industrial workers producing these same pesticides do receive health monitoring. The Office of Technology Assessment estimates that 300,000 farmworkers are poisoned by pesticides each year.[57]

In 1984 Texas created one of the first programs in the country for prior notification of agricultural pesticide use. Under Texas Department of Agriculture rules, agricultural producers are required, if asked, to notify anyone whose property adjoins a field or who resides or works in a building, school, hospital, or day-care center within one-quarter mile of a field that is to be sprayed. Anyone who is chemically sensitive and resides within one-quarter mile of a field that is to be sprayed also may ask for notification.

Unlike some other states, Texas does not have broad notification or posting requirements for treatments of lawns, golf courses, or other nonagricultural settings. State law does, however, provide that notice signs must be posted in common areas of apartments, workplaces, hospitals, day care centers, schools or educational institutions, warehouses, hotels, and food-processing locations 48 hours prior to indoor pesticide applications.[58] It also requires posting for outdoor pesticide use at apartment complexes.[59]

Both the Texas Department of Agriculture and the Structural Pest Control Board license applicators to use pesticides registered by the EPA and the Texas Department of Agriculture. With money provided by the EPA, Texas takes the lead in enforcement of pesticide sales and use restrictions under both federal and state pesticide legislation.

Besides enforcement, the Texas Department of Agriculture is responsible for establishing training and licensing requirements for commercial, non-commercial and private applicators who wish to use

pesticides that have been restricted by this department or by the EPA because of the higher risk associated with their use.

The Texas Department of Health also has a regulatory program for the use of pesticides around restaurants, for disease control, and for several other uses.

Pesticide Use Reduction

Federal and state pesticide laws do not focus on use reduction. The reduction of pesticide use in agriculture is driven both by concerns about the costs of the chemicals themselves and by concerns about the risks to health and the environment. Use-reduction strategies are often labeled "alternative agriculture" or "sustainable agriculture." These terms generally refer to a variety of practices, including crop rotation, integrated pest management, reduced chemical inputs, and organic farming. Many of these are centuries-old successful farming practices that were abandoned with the advent of chemical pesticides.

TEXAS AGENCIES WITH PESTICIDE RESPONSIBILITIES[60]

The Agriculture Resources Protection Authority was created by the Texas Legislature in 1989 to coordinate policies and programs of all Texas agencies related to the control of pesticides in Texas.

The Structural Pest Control licenses applicators of pesticides used in and around homes and other buildings. It also oversees the integrated pest management program for public schools.

The Texas Natural Resource Conservation Commission (TNRCC) regulates storage and disposal of pesticide waste and containers. This agency also coordinates the Texas program for identifying and responding to pesticides in groundwater and surface water.

The Texas Department of Health regulates the use of pesticides for health purposes, including the control of mosquitoes. The department also regulates the use of pesticides in restaurants. Doctors are required to report pesticide-related illnesses to the department.

The Texas Department of Agriculture has primary responsibility for pesticide registration and enforcement. It is also responsible for an organic food and fiber certification program and for aspects of the Integrated Pest Management program.

Texas A&M University's Agricultural Experiment Station is involved with research efforts on major obstacles facing agricultural production. This includes studying the use of pesticides and alternatives to pesticides.

Texas A&M University's Agricultural Extension Service serves as the major education and outreach effort of the state to farmers, ranchers, and the public.

The Texas Soil and Water Conservation Board is the lead agency for oversight and monitoring of agricultural non-point-source pollution, including pesticide pollution. This agency also helps farmers with voluntary efforts to reduce non-point-source pollution.

Today, however, farmers still face barriers to the adoption of alternative practices, including a lack of adequate research and training for farmers on alternative practices and, in some cases, private bank loans that require periodic pesticide treatments.[61]

Integrated Pest Management
Since 1972 some Texas agricultural producers have used a pest population management system known as Integrated Pest Management (IPM). The Texas A&M Experiment Station and Extension Service and the Texas Department of Agriculture share responsibility for research on and implementation of IPM.

According to the National Research Council, IPM "rests on a set of ecological principles that attempt to capitalize on natural pest mortality."[62] IPM strategies are now being extended to schools, offices, and home gardens.

For agricultural purposes, Texas A&M scientists define IPM as the use of two or more of the following practices: growing pest-resistant crops, crop rotation, using beneficial insects, scouting fields to determine pest populations, and using an economic threshold approach that indicates when a pest population has reached a density level such that the cost of crop damage exceeds the cost of controlling the pest.[63] Pesticide use is a component of IPM, but rather than relying on routine applications whether needed or not, the system relies on targeted applications for specific pests.

The Texas Agricultural Extension Service highlights some of the following as specific benefits of IPM:[64]

■ In excess of 19 million pounds of pesticides were applied to Texas cotton in the late 1960s, prior to implementation of IPM methods. By the mid-1970s, pesticide use had dropped to about 2.3 million pounds as a result of multiple-tactic IPM programs for cotton.

■ An IPM program for vegetables in the Rio Grande Valley reduced insecticide use by 66 percent on carrots processed for baby food, soups, and frozen foods. Using IPM, a single carrot grower increased her profits by $22,000.

■ IPM programs for Texas pecans have increased yields by 80 pounds per acre. Profits have been increased by $306.25 per acre for irrigated pecans and $37.15 for dryland pecans.

■ Citrus producers in the Lower Rio Grande Valley using IPM programs reduced insecticide applications by 33 percent and increased per-acre net returns by $75.00.

IPM strategies can also be applied in homes, parks, schools, and other nonagricultural settings. The Structural Pest Control Board has, for example, initiated an IPM program to reduce the amounts of chemicals used in public school structures and grounds. This program, mandated by state legislation passed in 1991, required all public school districts to prepare IPM plans by September 1995 and places other restrictions on pesticide use in schools.[65]

In addition, the Structural Pest Control Board has developed a program to certify applicators who wish to advertise their practices as being safer for human health and the environment. Rather than routinely applying pesticides, the applicator is required by the program to inspect the property and see if there is an actual pest infestation.

The overall success of IPM efforts in Texas, however, is difficult to ascertain. Data on pesticide use are not being collected to determine the success of alternative practices on a comprehensive basis, making it difficult to evaluate whether, where, and to what extent IPM is actually helping to reduce pesticide use and pesticide risks.

ORGANIC FOOD AND FIBER PRODUCTION AND DISTRIBUTION
In 1988 the Texas Department of Agriculture developed one of the first organic farm certification programs in the United States. Under this voluntary program, the department inspects and certifies producers and other businesses that process or handle organic food or fiber. To receive "organic" certification, these operations must comply with the department's growing and handling standards. Producers who comply are able to use "Certified Organically Produced" labels on their products. A 1993 state law prevents a person from labeling, mar-

THE BOLL WEEVIL WARS

As the nation's leading producer of cotton, Texas pays a good deal of attention to the boll weevil. Texas farmers estimate that each year the boll weevil may claim up to five percent of their crop.[66] So, when several cotton-producing areas of Texas voted to take part in the USDA Boll Weevil Eradication Program in 1993, farmers in those regions looked forward to higher yields in a year when cotton prices were predicted to be at a premium.

The theory behind the federal program is to engage all cotton farmers in an area in a massive pesticide assault (usually using malathion) on the boll weevil so that it is entirely eliminated from a region. If successful, future pesticide use and costs would be reduced, and cotton yields increased. All cotton farmers within an eradication area are required to take part in the program. Despite some misgivings, the majority of cotton farmers initially supported the Texas eradication program. Funded largely by the growers themselves, the program began in full swing in South Texas in May 1995.

The initial results were disastrous. Lower Rio Grande Valley cotton growers lost an estimated 365,000 acres of cotton, valued at $140 million.[67] The region produced about 54,000 bales of cotton, compared to almost 308,000 bales the previous year.[68] Cotton farmers in the San Angelo area who participated in the program lost more than half their crop, with loses valued at about $60 million.

The USDA research office in the Lower Rio Grande Valley released a report tying the crop destruction directly to the eradication program, concluding that the malathion spraying killed beneficial insects, such as spiders and wasps, which usually hold other pests in check. In this case, the predators of beet army worms were eradicated, causing the cotton-eating worms to take over the cotton fields.[69] The study found the density of beet army worms in Valley cotton fields to be 164 times the density of the worms in Mexican cotton fields 15 miles away. Less than one percent of the cotton leaves in Mexico were damaged by the worm, while 71.4 percent of the leaves on Valley plants were worm-eaten.[70]

keting, or presenting their products as organic without Texas Department of Agriculture certification.

In December 1997, 104 Texas organic farmers were certified, down from 180 in 1994.[71] (There were 205,000 farms in Texas in 1996.[72]) Texas is home to 90 percent of the country's organic cotton farms, currently filling an important niche in the cotton industry.[73] In addition, the Texas Department of Agriculture certified 38 organic food processors, 27 distributors, and 490 retailers in 1997.[74]

In late 1997, under the Organic Foods Production Act of 1990, the USDA published its proposed rule establishing, for the first time, uniform national standards for growing and processing organic foods, including vegetables, fruits, grains, livestock, and poultry.

The Organic Foods Production Act also required the creation of a National Organic Standards Board to serve as an advisory committee drawn from organic food producers. The board was constituted in 1992 and developed a set of recommendations for the organic standards program.

On December 16, 1997, the USDA issued its proposed rules for implementing the act. The proposed rules were vigorously opposed by many organic farmers, distributors, consumers, and environmental and consumer organizations because the rules did not include bans on the use of sludge and irradiated foods.

After the conclusion of the public comment period, the USDA announced it would drop several controversial provisions of the proposed rules. The final rules establishing standards are expected to be complete in 1999.

NOTES

1. Charles M. Benbrook et al., *Pest Management at the Crossroads* (Yonkers, N.Y.: Consumers Union, 1996), chapter 3.
2. League of Women Voters Education Fund, *America's Growing Dilemma: Pesticides in Food and Water* (Washington, D.C., 1989), 1.

Some earlier attempts to control insects, however, were not so benign. For example, in the late 1890s, efforts to control the gypsy moth relied on widespread use of arsenic-based sprays, including lead arsenate. Mark L. Winston, Nature Wars: People v. Pests (Cambridge, Mass.: Harvard University Press, 1997), 24-26.

3. Lewis Regenstein, *America the Poisoned* (Washington, D.C.: Acropolis Books, 1982), 103.

4. Estimates, survey models, and differences in assumptions lead to wide variations among reports of pesticide use in a given period. A recent study found that the total amount of pesticides reported in the 1991 National Agriculture Statistics Service report was about 60 percent of the agricultural pesticides used that same year as reported by the EPA's estimates. National Agriculture Statistics Service estimates for pesticides used on cotton in California in 1991 varied from 66 percent less to 511 percent more than the amounts of pesticides reported by applicators. W. S. Pease, J. Liebman, D. Landy, and D. Albright, *Pesticide Use in California: Strategies for Reducing Environmental Health Impacts*, California Policy Seminar (Berkeley, 1996), Appendix II.

5. Audrey Thier, *A Review of Pesticide Use Reporting Policies* (April 1997), available from the Texas Center for Policy Studies.

6. Arnold L. Aspelin, *Pesticides Industry Sales and Usage: 1994 and 1995 Market Estimates* (Washington, D.C.: U.S. Environmental Protection Agency, Office of Prevention, Pesticides and Toxic Substances, Biological and Economic Analysis Division, August 1997), 2-3.

7. Aspelin, *Pesticides Industry Sales and Usage*, 3.

8. Aspelin, *Pesticides Industry Sales and Usage*, 18.

9. See, e.g., *Pesticides and the Immune System: The Public Health Risks* (Washington, D.C.: World Resources Institute, 1996); Theo Colborn et al., "Developmental Effects of Endocrine-Disrupting Chemicals on Wildlife and Humans," *Environmental Health Perspectives* vol. 101 (1993):378-384.

10. Shelia Hoar Zahm, "Pesticides and Cancer," in *Occupational Medicine: State of the Art Reviews* (Philadelphia: Hanley & Belfus, 1997), 274 (exposure of general population to pesticides);James C. Robinson et al., *Pesticides in the Home and Community: Health Risks and Policy Alternatives* (Berkeley: School of Public Health, University of California, 1994), 9, 48-50.

11. National Research Council, *Alternative Agriculture* (Washington, D.C.: National Academy Press, 1989), 123.

12. See, e.g., Texas Department of Health, *Fish Advisories and Bans* (1997).

13. National Research Council, *Alternative Agriculture*, 20-50.

14. National Research Council, *Alternative Agriculture*, 121.

15. National Research Council, *Alternative Agriculture*, 121-123.

16. *Frontline*, "In Our Children's Food," produced/directed by Martin Koughan, Public Broadcasting Corp. (aired March 30, 1993).

17. Benbrook et al., *Pest Management at the Crossroads*, 50-53, citing EPA, "Pesticide Resistance Management: Issue Paper for Pesticide Dialogue Committee Meeting," Office of Pesticide Programs, June 25, 1996.

18. Benbrook et al., *Pest Management at the Crossroads*, 125.

19. A. Blair et al., "Clues to Cancer Etiology from Studies of Farmers," *Scandinavian Journal of Work, Environment and Health* 18, no. 4 (1992): 209-215.

20. *Veterans and Agent Orange: Health Effects of Herbicides Used in Vietnam* (Washington, D.C.: National Academy Press, 1993). Also see: National Research Council, *Alternative Agriculture*, 121; A. Blair et al., "Clues to Cancer Etiology from Studies of Farmers," 109-215.

21. John H. Cushman, Jr., "U.S. Reshaping Cancer Strategy as Incidence in Children Rises," *New York Times*, September 29, 1997, A1, A13.

22. A 1995 study suggested that "use of home pesticides may be associated with some types of childhood cancer." Jack K. Leiss and David P. Savitz, "Home Pesticide Use and Childhood Cancer: A Case-Control Study," *American Journal of Public Health* 85 (1995): 249-252, 249.

23. Christopher Campbell, Kert Davies, and Richard Wiles, "Overexposed: Organophosphate Insecticides in Children's Food," (Washington, D.C.: Environmental Working Group, January 1998), 1, 34.

24. Campbell, Davies, and Wiles, "Overexposed," 33-43.

25. Charles M. Benbrook, *Growing Doubt: A Primer on Pesticides Identified as Endocrine Disrupters and/or Reproductive Toxicants* (Washington, D.C.: National Campaign for Pesticide Policy Reform, 1996), 11-17. A recent study, however, did not find evidence that women exposed to DDT—now banned—and PCBs, two known endocrine disruptors, suffered higher rates of breast cancer. David J. Hunter, "Plasma Organochlorine Levels and the Risk of Breast Cancer," *New England Journal of Medicine* 337, no. 18 (October 30, 1997): 1253-1258.

26. Benbrook, *Growing Doubt*, 7-11.

27. Robinson et al., *Pesticides in the Home and Community*.

28. Texas Department of Agriculture laboratories also receive produce for testing from other states.

29. Lon Hatamiya, cover letter accompanying copy of USDA report, *Pesticide Data Program: Summary of 1992 Data*.

30. USDA, Agriculture Marketing Service, *Pesticide Data Program: Summary of 1992 Data* (Washington, D.C., April 1994).

31. Environmental Working Group, *Washed Contaminated Peeled* (Washington, D.C., 1994).

32. USDA, *Pesticide Data Program: Summary of 1992 Data*.

33. USDA, *Pesticide Data Program: Summary of 1992 Data*.

34. Robinson et al., *Pesticides in the Home and Community*.

35. Aspelin, *Pesticides Industry Sales and Usage*, 31.

36. Benbrook, *Growing Doubt*, 40-41; Robinson et al., *Pesticides in the Home and Community*, 19, 50.

37. Robinson et. al., *Pesticides in the Home and Community*, 22.

38. R. Lewis, "Human Exposure to Pesticides Used in and around the Household," EPA, Study Prepared for the Task Force on Environmental Cancer and Heart and Lung Disease: Working Group on Exposure, August 20, 1989. Also: F. Immerman and J. L. Schaum, *Nonoccupational Pesticide Exposure Study* (Research Triangle Park, N.C.: EPA, January 1990), 7-12.

39. R. Lewis et. al. "Evaluation of Methods for Monitoring the Potential Exposure of Small Children to Pesticides in the Residential Environment," Arch. Environ. Contam. Toxicol. 26 (1994): 37-46.

40. Aspelin, *Pesticides Industry Sales and Usage*, 12, 30.

41. Jerry Potter, "LPGA Learns Realities of Breast Cancer," *USA Today*, November 7, 1991, 1C; Gregg Small, *Parks Are for People, Not Poisons: A Citizen's Guide to Reducing Pesticide Use in Parks* (San Francisco: Pesticide Watch Education Fund, 1997), 12-13.

42. Texas Agriculture Statistics Service, *Texas Agricultural Statistics* (Austin, Texas: Texas Agricultural Statistics, 1995), 10.

43. Leonard P. Gianessi and James Earl Anderson, *Pesticide Use in Texas Crop Production* (Washington, D.C.: National Center for Food and Agricultural Policy, February 1995).

44. Gianessi and Anderson, *Pesticide Use in Texas Crop Production*, 4.

45. Aquatic herbicide application data, Texas Parks and Wildlife Department, July 23, 1997; available from author's files.

46. U.S. Geological Service, Water Quality Assessment of the Trinity River Basin, *Texas: Pesticides in Urban and Agricultural Streams, 1993-1995 Fact Sheet*, 178-196 (Austin, July 1996).

47. Veronica Alaniz, "Fort Worth Plots Strategy against Fire Ants," *Dallas Morning News*, August 14, 1997.

48. Christina Maxwell, "Green Defense: Experts Recommend Organic Pesticides and Fertilizers," *Fort Worth Star Telegram*, April 21, 1997.

49. Associated Press, "Tree Deaths along Dallas Road Attributed to Herbicide Spraying," *Austin American-Statesman*, August 21, 1997.

50. R. J. Zweiner and C. M. Ginsberg, "Organophosphate and Carbamate Poisoning in Infants and Children," *Pediatrics 81*, no. 1 (January 1988): 121-126.

51. *Frontline*, "In Our Children's Food."

52. Regenstein, *America the Poisoned*, 118.

53. Audrey Thier, "A Review of Pesticide Use Reporting Policies," unpublished paper, April 1997, 9-10.

54. Benbrook et al., *Pest Management*, chapter 4.

55. National Research Council, *Pesticides in the Diets of Infants and Children* (Washington, D.C.: National Academy Press, 1993).

56. USDA, "Riskiest Pesticides Will Be Assessed First Under New Food Safety Act," Press Release, August 4, 1997.

57. Nervous-system impacts experienced by some of these workers include insomnia, weakness, nervousness, forgetfulness, confusion, depression, memory loss, and poor performance on tests of reasoning and motor skills. National Research Council, *Alternative Agriculture*, 122. Office of Technology Assessment, *Neurotoxicity: Identifying and Controlling Poisons of the Nervous System* (Washington, D.C.: U.S. Congress, April 1990), 283.

58. Tex. Rev. Civ. Stat. Ann. Art. 135b-6, Sec. 4G.

59. Tex. Rev. Civ. Stat. Ann. Art. 135b-6, Sec. 4H.

60. Texas Comptroller of Public Accounts, *Breaking the Mold: New Ways To Govern Texas*, vol. 2, pt. 2 (1991), NR 5.

61. League of Women Voters Education Fund, *America's Growing Dilemma: Pesticides in Food and Water* (Washington, D.C., 1989), 11.

62. National Research Council, *Alternative Agriculture*, 208.

63. Dr. Tom Fuchs, IPM Coordinator, Texas A&M Research and Extension Center at San Angelo, interview with authors, June 1, 1994.

64. Texas Center for Policy Studies, *Texas Environmental Almanac* (Austin, 1995), 156-157.

65. Texas Structural Pest Control Act, Tex. Rev. Civ. Stat. Ann., Art. 135b-6, Secs. 4G and 4J.

66. "Where Cotton's King, Trouble Reigns," *New York Times*, October 9, 1998, A12.

67. Jeanne Russell, "USDA Scientist's Study Links Pesticides to Cotton Disaster," *McAllen Monitor*, September 3, 1996, D1.

68. Doug Thompson, "Battling the Boll Weevil," *Arkansas Democrat Gazette*, March 3, 1996, G1.

69. Susan Warren, "For Cotton Farmers, Boll Weevil May Be Lesser of Two Evils," *Wall Street Journal*, September 20, 1995, T1.

70. Jeanne Russell, "USDA Scientist's Study Links Pesticides to Cotton Disaster." In 1995, the Texas Department of Agriculture began charging a fee for certification with a fee scale based on the size of the operation.

71. Organic farming is defined as a system of ecological soil management that relies on building humus levels through crop rotation, recycling organic wastes, and applying balanced mineral amendments, and that uses, when necessary, mechanical, botanical, or biological controls with minimum adverse effects on health and the environment. Organic fiber is defined as fiber that is produced under a system of organic farming and that is processed, packaged, transported, and stored so as to maintain segregation and prevention of contamination from other fiber and from synthetic pesticides, prohibited defoliants, and/or desiccants. Organic food is defined as food for human or livestock consumption that is produced under a system of organic farming and that is processed, packaged, transported and stored so as to retain maximum nutritional value without the use of artificial preservatives, coloring or other additives, ionizing radiation, or prohibited materials. TDA, Marketing Division, information provided to author, 1998.

72. Texas Agricultural Statistics Service, information provided to author, 1998.

73. TDA, Marketing Division, phone interview with author, January 6, 1998.

74. TDA, Marketing Division, phone interview with author, January 6, 1998.

ENVIRONMENTAL
FOCUS

Comparative Risk

STATE OF TEXAS'S COMPARATIVE RISK PROJECT

The State of Texas, along with various other states and municipalities in the nation, has conducted a comparative risk project to identify and prioritize the hazards posed to the state's environment, economy, and public health. The purpose of the State of Texas Environmental Priorities Project (STEPP) was to initiate this process in order to help the state better allocate its limited resources to address the state's environmental and public health problems. Input was sought from industry groups, environmental organizations, municipal governments, the scientific community, and the general public.

The impetus for this effort by the Texas Natural Resources Conservation Commission (TNRCC) was the Environmental Protection Agency's Comparative Risk Project conducted for Region VI.[1] According to a 1990 EPA report, less than 10 percent of the federal environmental budget is spent on high-risk environmental problems, such as pesticides, indoor air pollution, and contaminated drinking water.[2] The purpose of the Texas Environmental Priorities Project was to ensure that the state's resources and federal funds are utilized to address the greatest risks for all Texans.

The project was carried out from 1992 to 1997 and had two parts: risk assessment and ranking, and risk management. The first phase identified the hazards and analyzed the issues of most concern to Texas residents through the project's eight advisory committees, focus groups, and meetings throughout the state. The second phase, risk management, developed solutions to reduce the risks identified as priorities by factoring in elements such as political will, legal constraints, and economic cost.[3]

Congress, municipal and state government officials, and industry groups have endorsed this type of approach, saying it is a sound method that provides a scientific foundation from which fiscally responsible decisions can be made to reduce environmental and public health risks. On the other hand, the risk assessment methodology has its critics.[4] Among other issues, critics contend that risk should not be the only determinant for which environmental problems are placed as high priorities for risk reduction.

The TNRCC's Environmental Priorities program seeks to balance concern for quantifiable scientific data with consideration of public values, economic and political interests, and the capacities of regulatory agencies. With the completion of the project, Texas state agencies will make use of the findings in

---

RISK-BASED PLANNING TERMINOLOGY

Comparative risk analysis: an aspect of risk-based planning that attempts to compare a wide range of environmental problems, across different media (e.g., air, land, and water), by using information about risks to human health, the environment, and human welfare or quality of life.

Risk assessment: a formalized, structured process for estimating the magnitude, likelihood, and uncertainty of environmentally induced health effects. Using the best available science, this process attempts to answer questions related to hazard identification, dose-response assessment,

exposure assessment, and risk characterization.

Risk management: In this process, the results of risk assessment are used to aid policy makers in deciding whether the risks are unacceptable. Besides quantitative risk estimates, economic, social, legal, and political factors are taken into account to determine the decisions to be taken to protect the public health.

Cost-benefit analysis: a mathematical technique, developed by the U.S. Army Corps of Engineers in the 1930s, that compares the costs and the benefits of a project to determine its feasibility.

establishing their objectives and strategies. Furthermore, just as the EPA's regional comparative risk analysis led to this state study, it is anticipated that the state study will lead to local studies that will provide cities, counties, and local planning agencies more tools to make decisions at the local level. For example, the Environmental Priorities Project is supporting, through technical assistance, the City of Houston's project called Houston Environmental Foresight. The ultimate success of these initiatives will be reflected in the measures taken to truly safeguard the health, environment, and quality of life of all Texans and of future generations.

For copies of the Environmental Priorities Project reports, publication number CTF-04, contact the TNRCC Publications Inventory and Distribution Division at 512-239-0028.

NOTES

1. EPA Region VI includes Texas, New Mexico, Oklahoma, Louisiana, and Arkansas.

2. TNRCC, *Risk Research Looks at Priorities* (summer 1994),11.

3. The TNRCC's regulatory program has established risk reduction rules and "overarching technical requirements" to be applied to the hazardous and industrial solid waste Superfund and Spill response programs to define and guide what clean-up actions are necessary. TNRCC, *Texas Environmental Trade Fair*, vol. 3 (April 14, 1994).

4. See Mary O'Brien, "Facing Down Pesticide Risk Assessment," *Global Pesticide Campaigner* (San Francisco: Pesticide Action Network, North American Regional Center, March 1994); Environmental Research Foundation, "Risk Assessment Part 3: Which Problems Shall We Ignore?" *Rachel's Hazardous Waste News* (Annapolis, Md., June 23, 1993); and TNRCC, State of Texas Environmental Priorities Project, vol. 1; *Final Overview Report* (June 1997), 8.1.

CHAPTER 6

Energy

HISTORY

American Indians were the first to utilize Texas's vast and diverse energy resources. Caddoan groups in East Texas harvested wood from the state's immense forests, while the Plains Indians—the Lipan Apache, Kiowas, and Comanches—used dried buffalo dung for heating and cooking. Archaeological sites near Lake Lewisville show that the first Texas settlers collected and burned lignite some 8,000 years before the arrival of Europeans.[1]

Coal was the first fossil fuel used by white settlers. Surface supplies were used throughout the early 1800s and mining of coal began in the 1850s. Texas is the sixth largest producer of coal in the United States, and the state has only begun to mine this vast resource. More than 24 billion tons of lignite still lie beneath the surface.

Since the state's first big oil discovery at Spindletop in 1901, Texas has produced over 54 billion barrels of oil, providing trillions of dollars in tax revenues to state government and thousand of jobs to residents. (Texas oil also was a critical ingredient in the Allied war effort in World War II.)

The Texas energy industry has survived periods of boom and bust. In 1929 Texas was the biggest oil-producing province in the world. By 1930 high-grade oil was selling for $1.10 per barrel (42 gallons). But the following year, the market fell apart. The huge East Texas field near Kilgore began producing a million barrels of oil per day, far more than the market could absorb. Prices plummeted and Texas oil was selling for just 10 cents a barrel.[2] The Railroad Commission of Texas, although originally established in 1891 to regulate the rail industry, was charged by the state legislature in 1932 with regulating the booming oil and gas industry. The problems of over-supply and disarray in the market at that time forced

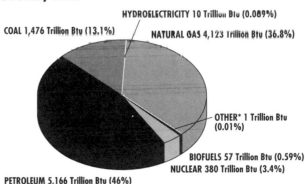

PRIMARY ENERGY CONSUMPTION IN TEXAS BY SOURCE, 1996

HYDROELECTRICITY 10 Trillion Btu (0.089%)

COAL 1,476 Trillion Btu (13.1%)

NATURAL GAS 4,123 Trillion Btu (36.8%)

OTHER* 1 Trillion Btu (0.01%)

BIOFUELS 57 Trillion Btu (0.59%)
NUCLEAR 380 Trillion Btu (3.4%)

PETROLEUM 5,166 Trillion Btu (46%)

Total Consumption: 11,212 trillion Btu

*Other: geothermal, wind, photovoltaic, and solar

Source: http://www.eia.doe.gov/emeu/sep/states.html (May 1999).

the state to take action, and, the state legislature authorized the Railroad Commission to limit oil production and stabilize the market.[3]

The 1980s were not kind to the U.S. oil industry due to an oversupply of cheaper foreign oil. Nation-wide, nearly half a million Americans lost jobs in the oil industry. More jobs were lost in the energy business than in the steel and auto industries combined. In Texas, between 1981 and 1997, 24 refineries closed, the number of active drilling rigs declined from 1,300 to 373, and 162,000 Texans lost jobs in the oil and gas sector. In 1981 the oil and gas industry accounted for 25 percent of the gross state product. By 1997 it had fallen to 10.4 percent.[4] By the year 2015, oil and gas is expected to account for 8.6 percent of the gross state product and by 2020, eight percent.[5] State tax revenues also have fallen. During the 1950s the state routinely got one-third of its revenue from oil and gas taxes. By 1997 the state's total tax revenue from oil and gas was 2.7 percent of the state's total revenue.[6] The oil industry, however, is important to the Texas economy and the nation's economy. According to the Texas Comptroller's Office, in 1997 Texas had more active oil and gas rigs than any other state and was number one in crude oil production.[7]

With nearly 19 million residents, Texas accounts for about seven percent of the U.S. population. At the same time, it accounts for 12 percent of the nation's total energy usage.[8] Texas consumes more electricity, natural gas, and petroleum than any other state.[9]

Today, the Texas energy industry is at a crossroads. Oil production in the state is falling. Natural gas consumption is increasing, but reserves are shrinking. Coal use has risen. For the first time, Texas is a net energy importer.[10] The state whose vast oil resources once played a critical role in national defense is now dependent on other states and foreign countries to meet energy demands. The primary reason for this demand is Texas's huge appetite for electricity.

FYI *In 1992 the average 20-cubic-foot Whirlpool refrigerator used $72 worth of electricity per year. One year later, as a result of added efficiency features, the same model used $51 worth of power.*

ELECTRICITY IN TEXAS

Texas produces and uses more electricity than any other state in the country, and sales are growing at 2.6 percent annually.[11] Texas uses 23 percent more electricity than California and 57 percent more electricity than Florida. In 1996 Texas customers used approximately 248 billion kilowatt hours of electricity, 77 percent of which was furnished by utility companies and 15 percent by municipalities and river authorities.

Texas produces 49 percent of this electricity by burning coal and lignite. (Lignite is a low-grade form of coal.) For example, Texas power plants burned 90 million tons of coal and lignite in 1997.[12] Half of this came from Texas lignite, and half was imported coal from Wyoming. There are sixteen major electric generating plants in Texas that use coal or lignite as fuel. The 16 plants account for a little

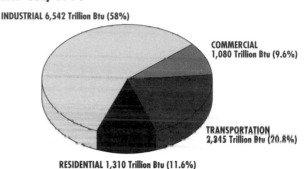

PRIMARY ENERGY CONSUMPTION IN TEXAS BY END USE, 1996

INDUSTRIAL 6,542 Trillion Btu (58%)
COMMERCIAL 1,080 Trillion Btu (9.6%)
TRANSPORTATION 2,345 Trillion Btu (20.8%)
RESIDENTIAL 1,310 Trillion Btu (11.6%)

Total Consumption: 11,274 trillion Btu

Source: http://www.eia.doe.gov/emeu/sep/states.html (May 1999).

over 81 percent of all criteria pollutant emissions—particulate matter, carbon monoxide, sulfur dioxide, nitrogen oxides, volatile organic compounds (VOCs), and lead—from power plants in Texas and approximately 31 percent of all criteria pollutants from all industrial sources in Texas.[13] Therefore, any changes in the electric utility industry will have some significant impact on the Texas environment, for better or worse.

Such issues as electric utility deregulation, green pricing, and utility fuel labeling will help determine how much electricity Texans will use and which fuels will be used to produce it. Energy demands and energy production are major factors in air, water, and solid waste pollution in Texas.

UNIVERSAL SERVICE WITH A "REASONABLE" RATE OF RETURN— THE REGULATORY COMPACT

Since 1878, when electric lights were first installed in Galveston and Dallas, electricity has been a part of the Texas landscape. In the early years, electricity was mainly an urban resource. The passage of the 1935 Rural Electrification Act by Congress, however, enabled power to be supplied to many rural areas.[14] Until the 1970s, municipalities regulated most power companies by granting franchises and setting rates. Due to the increasing complexity of municipal regulation of the electric industry and the energy crises of the 1970s, the Public Utility Commission of Texas was created by the Texas legislature in 1975. This statewide planning body was charged with rate setting and ensuring an adequate power supply for the state.

The primary principle governing electric utility regulation by the Public Utility Commission is rate-of-return regulation. This approach sets electric rates at levels that allow power companies to recover fixed and variable costs, plus a return for stockholders.[15] Secondly, a rate structure is developed, setting different rates for each customer class, including residential, commercial, and industrial. In many cases, one class of customers subsidizes the electric use of another.

Under current law, electric utilities operate as monopolies with guaranteed regulated incomes. They are statutorily required to serve all customers in their service area, regardless of the cost.[16] Because they are obligated to serve their customer's demands at all times and to ensure system reliability, utilities must maintain excess capacity.[17] Consumers under the regulated system are required to purchase electric power from the utility licensed to serve in their area. The regulatory compact system is meant to provide Texans with guaranteed, reliable, and reasonably priced electricity wherever the customer resides. In return, utility companies face little risk because they receive guaranteed profits.

THE ROAD TO DEREGULATION— WHOLESALE COMPETITION

The push in the 1990s for deregulation in the electric utility market grew out of new low-cost technology, federal regulatory change, and the deregulation of other industries. Texas began to change its system with the enactment of the Public Utility Regulatory Act of 1995, which allows wholesale competition in providing electricity.[18]

Under this new law, exempt wholesale generators (EWGs) are allowed to sell electricity to regulated electric utilities. This electricity is then sold to retail customers through the electric utility's distribution system. This system also created power marketers. Power marketers do not own generating equipment, but instead buy and sell power, acting as middlemen in the market. In 1995, 13 percent of electricity sold in Texas was on the wholesale market.[19] Wholesale competition is advantageous for utilities needing more capacity but not wanting to build new power plants. This approach could result in lower prices for consumers if it allows utilities to lower capital costs.

RETAIL COMPETITION IN A LOW-COST STATE

Open retail competition would result from complete restructuring of the electric market. Proponents argue that a regulated market is inherently inefficient and that consumer choice and increased competition will ultimately lower prices. Large industrial users, gas companies, independent power producers, and co-generators are most interested in retail competition.[20] Consumer advocates are concerned with the details of deregulation. Most agree that a deregulated market could provide lower prices for consumers. But consumer advocates are also concerned that consumers could experience higher residential rates while large industrial customers get the best deals.

Legislation passed during the 1999 legislative session deregulated and restructured the state's $20 billion electric utility industry and opened the state's retail electric markets to competition. With this legislation, Texans have a choice of picking electric suppliers that use renewable resources such as wind or solar generation.

HOW WILL THE ENVIRONMENT FARE?

The restructuring of the electric industry poses many questions for the environment in Texas. The primary possible environmental threat arising from a restructured market is that conservation programs will suffer. Previously, the only way utilities serving a single area could delay building new power plants was by promoting conservation measures. With wholesale and possible retail markets, new electricity demands can be satisfied with the purchase of another plant's excess generation capacity. In a highly competitive market, incentives for utilities to voluntarily decrease demand for the product that they sell are less obvious.

Another fear is that a deregulated market will not encourage the use of alternative or clean-burning fuels. Alternative fuels, including wind energy and solar power, have high capital start-up costs, although once a facility is built, the fuel is free. The current state tax structure discourages clean-burning fuels, particularly natural gas. While coal and lignite are not subject to a state severance tax, natural gas is taxed at 7.5 percent of the purchase price. Thus, there is some concern that a totally deregulated market will leave renewables and cleaner burning fuels at a disadvantage, at least in the short term.

On the other hand, there are other possible outcomes for environmentally cleaner fuels in a restructured market. As power producers become more customer-oriented, they may be more willing to provide Texans with less-polluting power options.

GREEN PRICING: TEXANS ARE WILLING TO PAY MORE FOR LESS POLLUTION
Background
Given the choice between higher and lower electric rates, most consumers choose to keep more money in their pockets. New trends, however, indicate that consumers are willing to spend more money on their electric bills if companies use environmentally friendly fuels to produce power. Once considered an option by only a few die-hard environmentalists, green pricing has begun to move into the mainstream with programs in New England, California, and Texas. According to Warren Bryne of Foresight Energy Corporation, many consumers want the opportunity to spend their money on low-impact power producers instead of high-polluting ones.[21]

Although there is no standard or definition for environmentally friendly fuels, they generally are considered to consist of hydroelectric power, solar electricity, wind energy, biomass energy, and geothermal power.[22] These alternative fuels are inexpensive, low polluting, and often renewable.[23] Although natural gas is not an alternative fuel, it is considered clean burning due to its low emissions.

GREEN PRICING
Consumer support for the use of renewable and clean-burning fuels has led to the creation of green pricing structures, which allow a higher electric rate for these more environmentally friendly fuels. The green pricing structure is supposed to be temporary because greater demand for alternative fuels will eventually lower the price to be more competitive with oil and coal. Currently, less than 1 percent of the electricity generated in Texas comes from renewable fuels.[24] Even though the current use of renewable energy sources is relatively low, Texans support the use of clean-burning and renewable fuels in electricity production. In fact, three separate public opinion polls taken in the summer of 1996 and one poll taken in the spring of 1997 indicate that Texans are very concerned about pollution and are willing to pay more on their electric bill for lower-polluting fuels.[25]

One poll showed that 76 percent of Central Power and Light customers were willing to spend an additional $1 or more per month for renewable energy. West Texas Utility customers were willing to pay an average of $7.83 more a month for renewable energy, while Southwestern Electric Power customers were willing to spend on average an additional $6.44 for renewables (three times what they are willing to pay for fossil fuel energy). These green pricing trends are not just local opinions; they are consistent with statewide polling.[26]

The City of Austin Electric Utility's Solar Explorer program is one green pricing option for city residents. Utility customers can sponsor a portion of a solar power plant for an extra $3.50 a month added to their electric bill. The solar plant is a group of photovoltaic panels installed on rooftops of government buildings in the city.[27] Commercial building owners also can join the program by hosting a solar power plant on their building.

Central and South West Corporation, which provides service to many areas of Texas, is currently developing a green pricing program. The company filed an integrated resource plan with the Public Utility Commission, outlining its program for meeting future electric power needs. The program consists of a 40- to 50-megawatt wind turbine farm and the installation of up to 160 kilowatts of rooftop solar cells.[28] The green pricing program will allow customers to pay extra for the use of these renewable fuels, thus promoting them and increasing their use.

INGREDIENTS OF YOUR ELECTRIC BILL?

Because of food labeling laws, you can easily tell how much fat your ice cream contains or how much sugar is in that candy bar. Electric customers nationwide and in Texas are asking for the same type of labeling for their electric bills. The Federal Trade Commission is considering a proposal to require utilities to disclose the fuels they use for electric generation and the resulting air pollutants.[29]

In a 1997 statewide poll sponsored by the not-for-profit Texas-based Sustainable Energy and Economic Development organization, 84 percent of the respondents wanted an electric bill label similar to the ones required for food labels, in order to determine if their electricity is coming from heavily polluting resources or cleaner ones.[30]

MAKING ELECTRICITY

In 1997 approximately 37 percent of all the electricity consumed in Texas was derived from the burning of natural gas.[31] Forty-nine percent of the state's electricity was derived from burning coal. The balance comes from nuclear power (uranium), cogeneration, renewables, and hydroelectric power.

Gas

In 1975 about 90 percent of all the electricity in Texas was produced by natural-gas-fired power plants. But in 1978 Congress passed the Powerplant and Industrial Fuel Use Act, which required utilities to phase out the use of natural gas as a boiler fuel by 1990. Designed as a response to perceived natural gas shortages, this requirement was later repealed when new gas supplies were discovered.

Natural gas is one of the cleanest nonrenewable fuels and is often used in peak power generating plants. The mechanics of a natural-gas-fired power plant allow it to be turned on and off quicker than power plants running coal, lignite, or nuclear fuel. Natural gas plants are also relatively cheaper to build, making it the fuel of choice for most new

REPRESENTATIVE HEATING VALUES FOR COMMON FUELS

FUEL	Btu/LB
Natural Gas	24,000
Propane	21,500
Butane	21,180
#2 Fuel Oil	20,000
#6 Fuel Oil	19,000
Gasoline	19,000
Coal	
Anthracite	12,700
Sub-bituminous	9,000
Lignite	6,300

Note: One Btu (British Thermal Unit) equals the heat required to raise the temperature of one pound of water by one degree Fahrenheit.

Source: Bruce Hunn, University of Texas at Austin, Center for Energy Studies.

power plants. The only drawback to this fuel source is its expense relative to coal and lignite.

Coal and Lignite

During the phase-out of natural gas in the late 1970s, use of coal and lignite increased as power companies diversified their fuel choices. In 1997 Texas power generators consumed more than 90 million short tons of coal and lignite, producing 49 percent of the state's electricity.[32] Coal and lignite power plants in Texas are mainly used for base-load power supplies, which means they are in constant operation. Texas spends approximately $1.1 billion every year to import coal for electric generation.[33] Most of this coal is imported from Wyoming. (Only 25 percent of the 40,272 acres of land mined in Wyoming has been reclaimed or replaced, resulting in huge land scars and water quality problems for that state.[34])

Cogeneration

Electricity is inherently inefficient to produce. Up to two-thirds of the heat energy in a fuel source is lost while making electric power. Cogeneration is a process that generates electricity and heat at the same time. Cogeneration units are up to 50 percent more efficient than standard power plants.[35]

RESIDENTIAL ELECTRICITY USE IN TEXAS, 1970–2040

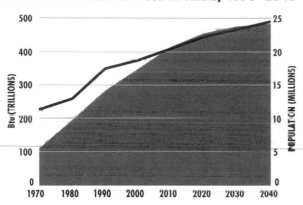

■ Electric Consumption   ——— Population

Source: Railroad Commission of Texas, State of Texas Energy Policy Partnership, Vol. 2 (1993), 293.

ELECTRIC UTILITY USE OF ENERGY, 1996

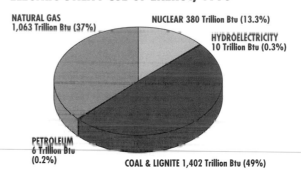

Total Consumption: 2,861 trillion Btu

Source: http://www.eia.doe.gov/emeu/sep/states.html (May 1999).

Industrial users were among the first to embrace cogeneration because it allows large industrial plants to generate electricity while using the heat for industrial processes. In addition, cogeneration units are advocated by some energy analysts because they are cheaper to build than large power units.

In 1996 Texas industries produced approximately eight percent total electricity from cogeneration.[36] From 1980 to 1992, the amount of electricity derived from cogeneration increased by more than 1,000 percent in Texas.[37] At present, 80 percent of the state's cogeneration plants are operated by petrochemical and chemical producers along the Gulf Coast.

Nuclear Power

In 1942 Dr. Enrico Fermi assembled enough uranium to cause a nuclear fission reaction. Nine years later, in 1951, the first electric power was produced from the atom, when an experimental reactor lit up four light bulbs in a laboratory experiment.

Today more than half of all Texans rely on nuclear power as one of their sources of electricity. But the debate continues over how successful Texas's experiment with nuclear power has been. Texas has approximately 4,802 megawatts of installed nuclear power capacity coming from two plants: the 2,300-megawatt Comanche Peak project in Somervell County, and the 2,502-megawatt South Texas Project in Matagorda County. The combined cost

TEXAS ELECTRICITY CONSUMPTION

DESCRIPTION	UNIT	YEAR	RESIDENTIAL	COMMERCIAL	INDUSTRIAL	TOTAL
Electricity Consumption	Kilowatt Hours	1997	101,094,027,000	72,042,446,000	100,428,660,000	273,565,133,000
Revenues	Dollars	1997	$7,904,554,000	$4,852,372,000	$4,070,966,000	$16,827,892,000
Number of Customers		1997	7,431,328	990,295	69,615	8,491,238
Electricity Consumption	Kilowatt Hours	1996	99,656,148,000	70,865,539,000	95,308,450,000	265,830,137,000
Revenues	Dollars	1996	$7,739,870,000	$4,756,418,000	$3,841,763,000	$16,338,051,000
Number of Customers		1996	7,283,526	949,290	69,779	8,302,595
Electricity Consumption	Kilowatt Hours	1995	92,831,137,000	68,579,803,000	90,093,116,000	251,504,056,000
Revenues	Dollars	1995	$7,161,922,000	$4,556,245,000	$3,589,628,000	$15,307,795,000
Number of Customers		1995	7,107,146	921,410	70,769	8,099,325

Source: Data compiled by Public Utility Commission of Texas from DOE, Energy Information Administration, 1997 Tables of Electric Sales and Revenue by State.

of constructing the two facilities was $15.6 billion.[38] Part of the reason the plants were so expensive was that construction took many years longer than expected. The two units at Comanche Peak were under construction longer than any nuclear plant now operating in the U.S. Comanche Peak Unit Two received a construction permit in December 1974 but did not begin operating until August 1992.[39]

Some antinuclear groups continue to advocate shutting down the nuclear plants immediately. They argue the move would save money for ratepayers over the long term because nuclear plants pose safety problems that could be very expensive to resolve. In addition, these groups say that the long-term storage costs of radioactive waste are too high and too dangerous to be cost-effective.

Nuclear power proponents, however, claim that, when operated correctly, nuclear plants emit little or no sulfur dioxide, particulates, nitrogen oxides, or carbon dioxide, all of which contribute to global warming. Additionally, they say that the plants will save ratepayers money over the long term because the fuel costs for nuclear power plants are far less than for conventional fossil fuel plants. No new nuclear power plants have been ordered in recent years. (See the *Industrial Waste* chapter for a discussion of the problems associated with the disposal of nuclear waste.)

RENEWABLE ENERGY AND CONSERVATION

With its fertile soil, sunny weather, and strong winds, Texas holds great promise for renewable energy. Wind energy, solar power, biomass energy, hydropower, and conservation could play large roles in the state's energy mix. At present, however, the state derives very little of its total energy from renewable sources.

Wind

Texas residents have been harnessing the stiff Texas breeze for decades. Before electrification, rural residents relied on wind chargers for electricity. Similar to windmills, these units turned wind energy into electric energy, which was used to charge batteries that powered electric lights and other devices. Rural

ELECTRIC RATE COMPARISON

TEXAS UTILITIES	RESIDENTIAL 1000 KWH JUNE, 1997
Investor Owned	
CPL [N]	90.55
EPE [N]	106.96
GSU [N]	73.22
HL&P [N]	86.49
SESCO	81.02
SPS	67.92
SWEPCO	70.78
TNP	94.93
TU Electric [N]	87.52
WTU	79.88
Cooperatives	
Bluebonnet EC	63.51
Denton County EC	81.64
Erath County EC	80.74
Guadalupe Valley EC	71.07
Mid-South EC	78.14
Pedernales EC	75.40
Tri-County EC	80.13
Upshur-Rural EC	55.73
Victoria Co. EC	71.91
Texas Municipalities	
City of Austin (STNP) [N]	75.96
CPS (San Antonio) (STNP) [N]	68.20
Kerrville PUB	59.89
TEXAS AVERAGE	**76.95**

[N] denotes nuclear utility
Source: *Public Utility Commission of Texas.*

residents also relied on windmills to pump water. Today, many windmills have been replaced by electric water pumps, but some 80,000 windmills continue to pump water for agricultural users in Texas.[40]

Wind could provide Texas with vast amounts of electricity. Unlike fossil-fuel-fired power plants, wind-energy plants do not create carbon dioxide or other air pollutants.

Several utilities have taken note of Texas's wind-energy potential, and projects are underway in West Texas. Texas Utilities is constructing a 35-megawatt wind farm in Big Spring, and American National Power is building a 250-megawatt wind power facility in Culberson County. Central and South

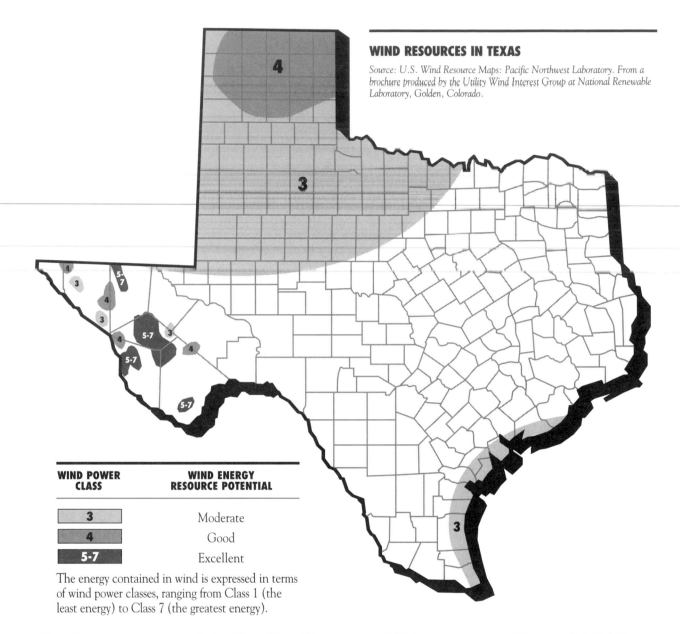

WIND RESOURCES IN TEXAS

Source: U.S. Wind Resource Maps: Pacific Northwest Laboratory. From a brochure produced by the Utility Wind Interest Group at National Renewable Laboratory, Golden, Colorado.

WIND POWER CLASS	WIND ENERGY RESOURCE POTENTIAL
3	Moderate
4	Good
5-7	Excellent

The energy contained in wind is expressed in terms of wind power classes, ranging from Class 1 (the least energy) to Class 7 (the greatest energy).

West Corporation is currently building 50 to 75 megawatts of wind generating capacity in McCamey. The new class of wind turbines can generate power for as little as five cents per kilowatt hour, slightly more than the cost of coal-fired power plants. But when external costs like air pollution are figured in, wind may be a cheaper power source than either fossil-fuel or nuclear plants.

Solar

Texas receives enough solar energy to supply one and a half times the world's current energy consumption.[41] If the entire state of Texas—all 262,000 square miles of it—were covered with solar cells, the state would generate 550 quadrillion BTUs of electrical energy every year. That is equal to one and a half times the total energy used in the world.[42] Obviously, the state will never be paved with solar cells, but Texas could easily incorporate solar power into the fuel mix.

Nationally, the solar industry is expanding in part due to President Clinton's "Million Solar Roofs Initiative." This program's goal is to place one million solar systems on the roofs of commercial

A SOLAR MAP OF TEXAS

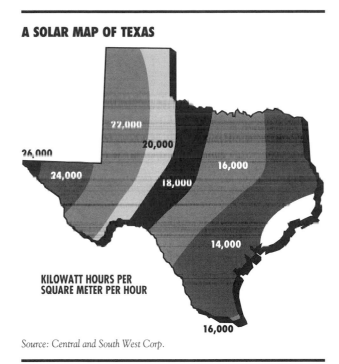

26,000
22,000
20,000
24,000
18,000
16,000
14,000

KILOWATT HOURS PER SQUARE METER PER HOUR

16,000

Source: Central and South West Corp.

and residential buildings by 2010 in order to slow air pollution and global warming.[43] Some states also are promoting solar energy. California is giving $54 million in subsidies to utility companies for solar and other renewable resources, while Arizona is requiring one percent of all new electrical generation to be from solar energy.[44]

Texas utilities are looking at increased use of solar cells as a low-cost, nonpolluting source of power generation. For example, the City of Austin Electric Utility already operates two photovoltaic generating stations that generate 450 kilowatts of electric power, enough to supply 50 to 100 homes. The utility is expanding this capacity with a new rooftop solar program, making it the largest solar-power producer in the state. Central and South West Corporation also is building solar generating capacity in Texas, with plans for 160 kilowatts of power. The University of Houston and Southwest Texas State University are using solar applications on their campuses.

Hydroelectric Power

The stored energy of water has been used by humans for centuries. Streams and rivers were damned or rerouted to provide power for milling grain or cut-ting lumber. Today, dams are an important part of the Texas economy, providing water for irrigation and recreation as well as electricity for industrial and residential use.

Dams in Texas provide approximately 530 megawatts of electric generating capacity.[45] While that is only a fraction of the state's total electric needs, these hydropower facilities are nonpolluting and provide reliable power. However, expanding the state's hydropower base may be difficult, as dams destroy aquatic habitat and free-flowing streams that provide recreational opportunities as well as fresh-water inflow to Texas's bays and estuaries.

Biomass

Biomass energy is produced from converting garbage to methane, burning materials to produce heat to generate electricity, and fermenting agricultural waste to produce ethanol. Half the lumber companies and three-fourths of the paper companies in Texas burn wood waste to generate power. Texas generates huge amounts of plant and animal waste that could be used for thermal power generation. There are four projects in Texas that utilize the combustible waste gases escaping from landfills. The cities of San Antonio, Dallas, Garland, Waco, and Austin are developing projects. Every year, Texas produces some two quadrillion BTUs of energy in the form of agricultural wastes, municipal waste, and energy crops.[46] If all that energy could be recovered, it would be enough to generate two-thirds of all the electricity used in Texas.

CONSERVATION AND ENERGY EFFICIENCY

Energy efficiency means you get more work for the same amount of energy. For instance, one gallon of gasoline can take you thirty miles in one car, while another, less efficient car, will take you only half as far. Energy efficiency saves consumers money, reduces air pollution and, contributes to economic growth. Studies have shown that no new electric generating plants would be needed over the next fifteen years if Texas embraced conservation and a comprehensive set of energy efficiency technologies.[47]

Cooling units offer the greatest potential gains in efficiency. One-third of all the electricity used by Texas residential customers is used for air conditioning. That is almost three times the national average.[48] A study by the University of Texas Center for Energy Studies found that replacing old refrigerators with high-efficiency models offers the greatest single savings in electrical consumption.[49] The reason is simple: refrigerators run 24 hours a day, seven days a week.

One new mode of conservation is known as time-of-use pricing. Most customers tend to use a large amount of electricity between 2:00 and 8:00 P.M. As people return from work, air conditioners, televisions, and dishwashers are turned on. Power companies must have electricity available for these peak demands, which means that during the other parts of the day they have excess capacity. In fact, some power plants are built to specifically handle peak electricity demand and are used only during times of high electricity use. If it were possible to "level out" these peaks, fewer plants would need to be in operation and new generating capacity might not be needed.

The City of Austin Electric Utility and 300 residential customers are participating in a pilot program

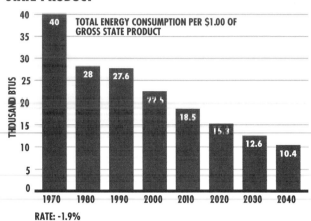

ENERGY EFFICIENCY AND TEXAS GROSS STATE PRODUCT

TOTAL ENERGY CONSUMPTION PER $1.00 OF GROSS STATE PRODUCT

(THOUSAND BTUS)

- 1970: 40
- 1980: 28
- 1990: 27.6
- 2000: 22.5
- 2010: 18.5
- 2020: 15.3
- 2030: 12.6
- 2040: 10.4

RATE: -1.9%

Note: Gains in automobile and appliance efficiency are making our economy more efficient. This graph indicates that Texans are using about half as much energy per dollar of production that they were 25 years ago.

Source: Railroad Commission of Texas, State of Texas Energy Policy Partnership, *Vol. 2 (1993), 292.*

that discourages peak electricity demand through variable pricing.[50] During nonpeak hours, customers' electricity is nearly half the normal price, while during peak hours, it is double the normal rate.

SAVING WATER

Saving water saves electricity. Water utilities spend millions of dollars per year on electricity that is used to treat and deliver water. A study by Southern California Edison found that fully 10 percent of the electricity it generates is used to treat, heat, and pump water to homes and businesses.

Utilities around the country have found that when customers save water, it reduces the amount of water a utility must pump, which in turn saves electricity. To maximize these savings, many utilities are distributing faucet aerators, efficient showerheads, low-flow toilets, and other water-saving devices to customers at no charge.

Some cities pay residents to replace old fixtures. San Antonio, Austin, and El Paso offer rebates to residential customers who install low-flow toilets. Utility officials in Austin estimate that two

percent of the electricity generated by the city is used solely for pumping and treating water.

Efficient irrigation systems also offer substantial savings. Some states offer low-interest loans to farmers who replace their old irrigation equipment with high-efficiency pumps and more-efficient irrigation systems. Farmers in some regions of the Northwest have saved 20 to 25 percent on their water and electricity bills.

Many Texas cities are promoting drought-tolerant, low-water-use residential and commercial landscaping to help conserve water. Use of this landscaping technique will help conserve electricity as well.

(Source: Rocky Mountain Institute, "Saving Energy through Water Efficiency," Rocky Mountain Newsletter, fall-winter 1991, 4.)

Customers are encouraged to use very little electricity for six hours a day and are rewarded with much lower prices. Electrical generators can more easily meet customer demand without building new power plants, and the environment is protected from air pollution because fewer power plants are needed to meet level energy demands.

ENERGY CONSERVATION AND GREEN BUILDING

Residential and commercial buildings that utilize energy-efficient building materials and features reduce energy use, cut utility costs, and benefit the environment. Energy-efficient features include weather stripping doors, windows, and other openings; installing low-flush toilets, ceiling fans, programmable thermostats, and roof-radiant barriers; and the planting of low-water-use turf grass and plants.[51]

OIL PRODUCTION AND THE ENVIRONMENT

Texas has been producing oil for more than 110 years. More than a quarter of all the known U.S. oil deposits are in Texas.[52] Yet, less than one-third of the potential 190 billion barrels of oil beneath Texas have been produced. Some 129 billion barrels of oil remain, but much of that oil lies deep beneath the surface, making production difficult and expensive.[53]

Texas has the largest share of crude oil reserves in the nation. And the state's oil has provided a reliable source of tax revenue. From 1930 to 1997, Texas collected more than $19 trillion in oil taxes.[54] The state's oil reserves have also spawned a vast refining and petrochemical industry; two-thirds of America's petrochemical production occurs in Texas.[55]

Much of the oil produced in Texas comes from older wells with declining production. These so-called stripper wells produce ten barrels of oil or less per day, but they are important to the state's economy because they are so numerous. In 1992, 70 percent of the 192,292 oil wells in Texas were stripper wells.[56] The average daily production per Texas oil well is fewer than nine barrels. By contrast, the average oil well in Saudi Arabia produces about 6,000 barrels per day.[57]

Oil production in the state peaked in 1972 at 3.4 million barrels per day. By 1996 production had fallen by more than half, to 1.4 million barrels per day.[58] Cheaper foreign oil means less reliance on domestic production and less exploration of new wells in Texas.

Whether or not the Texas oil industry ever rebounds, the Railroad Commission of Texas must deal with thousands of abandoned oil wells. Unplugged and abandoned oil wells can cause serious groundwater contamination problems, particularly in areas with naturally occurring saline groundwater. Unplugged wells are vertical pipelines that can allow deep brine-water reservoirs to contaminate shallow freshwater aquifers. And in many areas around the state, rural residents have been forced to abandon oil wells or unlined saltwater disposal pits.[59] By plugging wells, oil producers can prevent the migration of saline water from deep aquifers into shallow freshwater aquifers. In addition, plugging wells prevents water from contaminating the oil and gas reservoirs.

Surface water supplies also are threatened by unplugged wells. (See *Water Quality* chapter for more information.)

FYI ☞ *The food on an average dinner plate in the United States has traveled 1,300 miles. Buying locally produced food supports the local economy, saves energy, and reduces pollution.* (Source: Central Power and Light, Watts News, March, 1994, 3.)

NATURAL GAS AND THE ENVIRONMENT

Natural gas was once considered a useless waste product of the oil production process. Oil producers burned off this gas or vented it into the atmosphere in order to dispose of it. Today, some energy analysts are calling natural gas the "prince of the hydrocarbons."[60] The clean-burning properties of natural gas are causing consumption to increase dramatically. Natural gas can be used to power cars and trucks, to generate electricity, and to heat and cool our homes and work places. In 1996 total natural gas consumption in the United States was 22.0 trillion cubic feet, two percent higher than in 1995 and one of the highest annual levels ever recorded.[61] Since 1992 natural gas has accounted for 25 percent of total

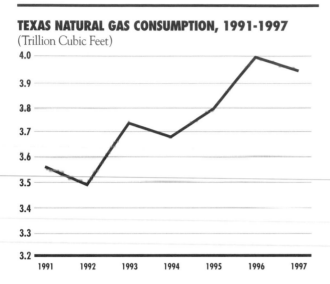

TEXAS NATURAL GAS CONSUMPTION, 1991-1997
(Trillion Cubic Feet)

Consumption includes lease and plant fuel, pipeline fuel, residential, commercial, industrial and electric utilities.

Source: Railroad Commission of Texas, PetroFacts, *(1993), 3.*

energy consumption in the United States.[62]

Texas consumed 3.9 trillion cubic feet of natural gas in 1996, more than any other state.[63] Texas produces about 5.8 trillion cubic feet of gas every year, which accounts for 25 percent of U.S. domestic gas production.[64] Similarly, the state has a quarter of domestic gas reserves totaling about 4.3 trillion cubic feet.[65]

New uses for natural gas are also causing consumption to increase. The fuel can now be used to power air conditioners and is gaining popularity in the transportation sector. Compressed natural gas (CNG) and liquefied natural gas (LNG) burn cleaner than gasoline or coal. Liquefied natural gas offers a fuel alternative to vehicle fleet owners who must comply with Clean Air Act regulations. (See *Air* chapter for more information.) Natural gas is also being used by more utilities for power generation. Though natural gas burns cleaner than coal, in urban areas it still contributes to ozone formation through nitrogen oxides emissions and to global climate change through carbon dioxides.

FYI *Natural gas is mixture of hydrocarbon compounds and small quantities of various nonhydrocarbons existing in the gaseous phase or in solution* with crude oil in natural underground reservoirs at reservoir conditions. It has a high heat value, burns without smoke, and provides raw material for making plastics, fertilizers, and detergents.

LIQUID PETROLEUM GAS AND THE ENVIRONMENT

Most consumers know liquid petroleum gas (LPG) as butane or propane. These liquids are removed from oil and gas during the refining process. A flexible fuel, LPG can be used for everything from running residential water heaters to powering farm tractors. Propane is second only to natural gas in terms of heat content. It is considered an alternative fuel because it burns cleaner than coal or gasoline. One-third of the nation's propane is produced in Texas.

According to the National Propane Gas Association, propane is the nation's third largest engine fuel source and the most widely used for alternative transportation fuel. The Propane Association claims that propane-powered engines contribute less to the problems of acid rain, smog, and global warming than other fossil fuels because propane combustion produces less carbon monoxide, hydrocarbons, nitrogen oxide, and other toxins as compared to combustion of coal or oil. Moreover, LPG tanks can be stored above or below ground, and, because propane readily vaporizes, there is less risk of underground tanks causing groundwater and soil contamination. The costs of operating propane vehicles have also been shown to be lower than the costs of gasoline-powered vehicles.[66]

Texans consumed approximately 12.2 billion gallons of LPG in 1996, most of which was used by the petrochemical industry for making plastics and fertilizers.[67] LPG also plays an important role in rural areas, which often do not have natural gas lines. Millions of rural Texans rely on propane and butane for cooking and water heating. In the commercial sector, LPG powers forklifts and other industrial equipment. With its flexibility and availability, LPG will continue to be a major energy source for many years to come.

In 1991 state legislation was passed that allowed the Railroad Commission to accept money from any

TEXAS COAL AND LIGNITE PRODUCTION, 1976–1998

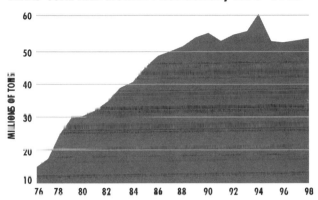

Source: Railroad Commission of Texas, Surface Mining and Reevaluation Division (May 1999).

COAL, LIGNITE AND URANIUM SURFACE MINES

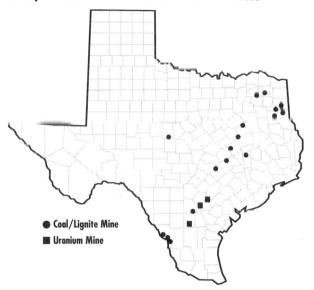

● Coal/Lignite Mine
■ Uranium Mine

Source: http://www.rrc.state.tx.us/divisions/sm/programs/regprgms/mineinfo/mines.htm (May 1999).

alternative fuel industry and in turn to use the funds to promote that specific alternative energy source. The propane industry has been the only alternative fuel industry to give these allowable moneys to the commission. In return, the Railroad Commission has been touting the benefits of propane fuel. The commission also offers a rebate program to consumers who convert their water heaters from electricity to propane or a rebate for installing propane water heaters with new construction.

COAL MINING AND THE ENVIRONMENT

Texas leads the nation in coal consumption by a large margin. In 1994 Texas used 94 million tons of coal.[68] By comparison, Indiana, the number two coal-consuming state, used about 60 million tons of coal.[69] Texas mines produce two-thirds of the coal consumed in the state. During the 1990s, approximately 52 million tons of lignite were mined in Texas annually.[70] The sixth and twelfth largest coal mines in America are located in Texas. The Martin Lake and Monticello mines, both owned by Texas Utilities Mining Co., produce nearly 25 million tons of lignite per year.[71]

Coal consumption in Texas is rising faster than consumption of any other form of energy. By 2030, the state's coal consumption is expected to be about 180 million tons per year, twice as much as the state consumed in 1990.[72] The state's appetite for coal, however, has caused serious pollution problems. Five

of the top ten sources for air pollution in the state are coal-fired electric power plants.[73] They release nitrogen oxides, VOCs, particulate matter, and mercury. Coal-fired power plants are also a major reason why Texas is the leading U.S. contributor of carbon dioxide from all sources. In addition, studies have linked elevated selenium levels in a number of East Texas lakes with nearby coal-fired power plants.[74] (See Air chapter for further discussion.)

Coal burning produces large quantities of human carcinogens, such as arsenic, beryllium, copper, mercury, and chromium. Burning coal also produces sulfur dioxide, an air pollutant that can cause acid rain. Acid rain poses a serious threat to East Texas lakes, which have little ability to counter acidic input.[75] In addition to air quality problems linked to coal consumption, strip mining presents a range of problems. Since 1982 more than 52,000 acres of land in the state have been strip-mined for lignite.[76] Adequate reclamation of strip-mined property is expensive and time consuming. Usually, sites are replanted with just one type of plant material. Biologists point out that the resulting monoculture does not support a diversity of wildlife.[77] In addition, the strip-mined land can be subject to subsidence and erosion.

off
off

off

URANIUM MINING AND
THE ENVIRONMENT

The nuclear power industry depends on uranium. For decades Texas was a leading producer of this heavy, silvery white element, which can also be made into nuclear weapons. In the mid-1970s, when the price of uranium was over $40 per pound, nearly a dozen companies were operating some 35 uranium-mining sites in seven South Texas counties. Today, with the price at about $10 per pound, only a handful of companies continue to produce uranium in the state.[78]

Today, most uranium mining is done with injection wells, which pump fluid through the geologic formations where the mineral is found. Production wells then bring the uranium-bearing solution to the surface. Called solution mining, this method causes relatively little disturbance on the surface. This process can, however, contaminate groundwater, which must then be pumped out and disposed of by injection into deep formations below freshwater aquifers.

Uranium used to be strip mined with technology similar to that used in coal mining. These uranium strip-mine operations created large areas requiring remediation. Large tailing ponds have been created to contain the radioactive materials. These ponds, located in Karnes and Live Oak counties, may pose a long-term threat to surface water and subsurface aquifers because they are subject to leakage. Federal law requires the tailing ponds, which contain materials that will remain radioactive for more than 1,600 years, to be covered so that rainwater does not mix with the radioactive waste. These pond coverings may be eroded over time by water and wind, which could allow radium to escape into the atmosphere. The ponds must be monitored for centuries to ensure that they are properly containing the radioactive waste. (See *Industrial Waste* chapter for more information.)

FYI ☞ *Fluorescent lamps give off four times as much light per watt as do incandescent bulbs.*

(*Source: Central Power and Light, Fluorescent lamps also operate cooler than incandescents,* How to Control Your Electric Bill, *July 1991.*)

NOTES

1. Solveig Turpin, University of Texas at Austin, Anthropology Department, interview by author March 29, 1994, Austin.

2. Railroad Commission of Texas (RRC), *State of Texas Energy Policy Partnership*, vol. 1 (1993), 26.

3. Gary Preuss, Texas Comptroller of Public Accounts (TCPA), interview by author, December 8,1997.

4. Preuss, interview.

5. Preuss, interview.

6. Preuss, interview.

7. TCPA, *Fiscal Notes*, October 1997, 11-12.

8. National Energy Information Administration, *State Energy Data Report 1994* (1996).

9. University of Texas at Austin, Center for Energy Studies, *Opportunities for Energy Efficiency in Texas*, vol. 7 (May 1992),1.

10. Virtus Energy Research Associates, *Texas Energy: Past, Present, Future* (Austin, 1996).

11. Public Utility Commission of Texas (PUC), *1996 Annual Report*, (April 1997), 5.

12. PUC, *1998 Annual Report* (December 1998), 15.

13. This is based on an analysis by authors of TNRCC's State Summary of Emissions Database, August, 1997. VOCs do not include methane.

14. Center for Global Studies and The Energy Institute, *Guide to Electric Power in Texas* (The Woodlands: Houston Advanced Research Center and the University of Houston, March 1997), 17.

15. Bernard L. Weinstein, Harold T. Gross, and Terry Clower, *Retail Competition, Stranded Costs and the Regulatory Compact in Texas: Implications for Utilities and Consumers* (Denton: University of North Texas, January 1997), 8.

16. The structure of the Texas regulatory compact is found in the Public Utility Regulatory Act of 1995 (also referred to as PURA 95).

17. Public Utility Regulatory Act of 1995, 7.

18. Patricia Tierney Alofsin, *Power Struggle: Deregulating the Electric Industry* (Austin: House Research Organization, Texas House of Representatives, December 5, 1996), 2.

19. Alofsin, *Power Struggle*, 5.

20. Weinstein et al., *Retail Competition, Stranded Costs and the Regulatory Compact in Texas*, 26.

21. Ross Kerber, "For Sale: Environmentally Correct Electricity," *Wall Street Journal*, July 23, 1997, 1.

22. Geothermal power uses heat energy in the Earth's interior to produce electricity. However, Texas does not have any geothermal resources that are used for electricity production. Hydroelectric power is produced as water moves from a higher to lower level and pushes a turbine. Hydroelectric power produces about 0.7 percent of electricity generation in the state. Biomass energy is produced from converting plant and animal matter to heat. This includes converting garbage to methane, burning materials to produce heat to generate electricity, and fermenting agricultural waste to produce ethanol. Texas produces very small amounts of electricity by these means.

23. Center for Global Studies and The Energy Institute, *Guide to Electric Power in Texas*, 38.

24. Mike Sloan, *Texas Energy: Past, Present, Future, Briefing for*

Texas Legislature (Austin: Virtus Energy Research Associates, Inc., February 4, 1997).

25. West Texas Utilities (WTU) conducted a deliberative poll on August 9 and 10,1997. WTU is a wholly owned subsidiary of Central and Southwest Corporation; Central Power and Light conducted a poll on June 1 and 2, 1997, and Southwestern Electric Power Company conducted a poll on August 24 and 25,1997. Deliberative polling combines statistically valid polling with discussions among "customers" in a group setting with experts.

26. West Texas Utilities, Central Power and Light, and Southwestern Electric Power Company polls, 1997.

27. City of Austin Electric Utility, *Solar Explorer* brochure (1997).

28. Central and South West Companies, "Central and South West Companies File Energy Resource Plan Incorporating Customer Feedback from Deliberative Polls," Press Release, February 3, 1997.

29. Kerber, "For Sale: Environmentally Correct Electricity."

30. The SEED Poll was conducted by Opinion Research Services, April 3-11, 1997.

31. PUC, *1998 Annual Report*, 15.

32. PUC, *1998 Annual Report*, 15. Half came from Texas lignite and half came from coal imported from Wyoming.

33. PUC, *1996 Annual Report*.

34. E. N. Smith, "Wyoming's Low-Sulfur Coal Hits a Buyers' Market," *Austin American-Statesman*, August 17, 1997, J2.

35. RRC, *State of Texas Energy Policy Partnership*, vol. 2, 129.

36. PUC, *1996 Annual Report*, 5.

37. RRC, *State of Texas Energy Policy Partnership*, vol. 2, 386. In 1989 Texas had 730 megawatts of cogenerated power. By 1992 the total had risen to 7,359 megawatts.

38. Citizens for Energy Awareness, *InfoBank* (a series of fact sheets on energy, electricity, and nuclear power, nuclear plant construction costs, and duration).

39. Citizens for Energy Awareness, *InfoBank*.

40. Sustainable Energy Development Council of Texas, *Texas Sustainable Energy Strategic Plan* (Austin, 1995), 6.

41. RRC, *State of Texas Energy Policy Partnership*, vol. 2, 318.

42. RRC, *State of Texas Energy Policy Partnership*, vol. 2, 318.

43. Matthew L. Wald, "For Now an Industry Relishes Its Day in the Sun," *New York Times*, August 16, 1997, 23.

44. Wald, "For Now an Industry Relishes Its Day in the Sun," 23.

45. RRC, *State of Texas Energy Policy Partnership*, vol. 2, 318.

46. RRC, *State of Texas Energy Policy Partnership*, vol. 2, 319.

47. University of Texas at Austin, Center for Energy Studies, *Opportunities for Energy Efficiency in Texas*, vol. 2 (Austin, 1992), 1.

48. University of Texas at Austin, Center for Energy Studies, *Opportunities for Energy Efficiency in Texas*, vol. 2, 1.

49. University of Texas at Austin, Center for Energy Studies, *Opportunities for Energy Efficiency in Texas*, vol. 2, 1.

50. Laylan Copelin, "Utilities Experiment Attempts to Divert Peak-Hours Demand," *Austin American-Statesman*, August 11, 1997, B5.

51. Department of Energy at www.eren.doe.gov. The City of Austin has one of the oldest voluntary green-building rating programs in the country.

52. RRC, *State of Texas Energy Policy Partnership*, vol. 1, 5.

53. RRC, *State of Texas Energy Policy Partnership*, vol. 1, 12.

54. Preuss, interview.

55. TCPA, *Forces of Change: Shaping the Future of Texas* (March 1994).

56. RRC, *State of Texas Energy Policy Partnership*, vol. 1, 10.

57. RRC, *State of Texas Energy Policy Partnership*, vol. 1, 10.

58. RRC, *Texas PetroFacts* (October 1997), 5.

59. Texas Department of Water Resources, *The Seymour Aquifer: Ground-Water Quality and Availability in Haskell and Knox Counties, Texas*, Report 226 (December 1978). The report concludes that 75 percent of the underground water pollution in the counties is due to the "formal disposal of oil field brine into unlined surface pits. An estimated 20 percent has been caused by leaky injection wells and unplugged, abandoned wells."

60. Christopher Flavin and Nicholas Lenssen, *Power Surge: Guide to the Coming Energy Revolution* (New York: W. W. Norton, 1994), 91.

61. National Energy Information Center, Energy Information Administration, *Natural Gas Annual Report* (Washington, D.C., 1996), 180.

62. National Energy Information Center, *Natural Gas Annual Report*, 180.

63. National Energy Information Center, *Natural Gas Annual Report*, 38.

64. RRC, *PetroFacts* (October 1997), 3.

65. National Energy Information Center, *Natural Gas Annual Report*, 180.

66. National Propane Gas Association, *Propane. The Fuel of Choice for the 21st Century* (Lisle, Ill., n.d.), section 1.

67. RRC, *State of Texas Energy Policy Partnership*, vol. 2, 10. Also, information provided by the RRC to authors in a letter, January 6, 1997.

68. National Energy Information Center, *State Energy Data Report 1994*.

69. National Coal Association, *Facts About Coal* (1994), 54.

70. RRC, Summary of Annual Coal Production from 1976-1995 (1997). Information transmitted by fax to authors on December 10, 1997.

71. National Coal Association, *Facts About Coal*, 54.

72. RRC, *State of Texas Energy Policy Partnership*, vol. 2, 282.

73. Authors analysis of TNRCC's State Summary of Emissions Database, August 1997.

74. *Tyler Courier*, May 7, 1992. The newspaper says that Martin Creek (Rusk and Panola counties), Brandy Branch (Harrison County), and Welsh Lake (Titus County) have all been found to have elevated selenium levels. The Texas Department of Health announced in May 1992 that fish in the lakes may be contaminated and that consumption of fish from the lakes should be restricted to less than eight ounces of fish per adult per week.

75. Larry McKinney, Director, Resource Protection Division, Texas Parks and Wildlife Department (TPWD), to Thomas Dydek, Texas Air Control Board, September 24, 1990. McKinney wrote, "Caddo Lake and other natural waters in East Texas have characteristically low alkalinity and, therefore, are unable to buffer acidic inputs such as acid rain."

76. RRC, *Coal Surfacing Mining Operations*, Annual Progress Reports, 1982 through 1992.

77. Robert Short, Field Supervisor, Ecological Services Division, U.S. Fish and Wildlife Service, in a February 1, 1991, letter to Haywood Rigano of Titus County Citizens An Endangered Species, Inc. Short writes, "We believe the conversion of native, diverse habitats into large blocks of monoculture is probably the single most damaging aspect of surface mining. The disruption of surface water hydrology, including stream, riparian, or bottomland hardwood vegetation and wetlands, is also a significant impact. Adequate mitigation or restoration of these sensitive areas in a timely or effective manner is extremely hard to accomplish, and therefore, we recommend avoidance of important habitats wherever feasible."

78. Dale Kohler, geologist, Uranium and Radioactive Waste Section, TNRCC, interview by author, May 11, 1994, Austin.

CHAPTER 7

Municipal Waste

"Fix it up…Wear it out…Make it do…Do without"

Old folk rhyme

A SHORT HISTORY OF SOLID WASTE

The question of what to do with human trash has been of concern to every society. In the late nineteenth century the first systematic, municipally run waste-collection system was put in place in the United States. The system started in New York City where, under the direction of the Street Cleaning Commission, 1,000 men clad in white, known as the "Apostles of Cleanliness," transported trash from the streets to dumps and incinerators.[1] By 1910 most municipalities across the country had established some system of waste collection and disposal.

Over the past twenty years, a substantial body of state and federal legislation regulating the disposal of industrial, hazardous, and municipal solid waste (MSW) has been developed. Before that time, solid waste management depended on the judgment and decisions of individuals or local departments of health and sanitation. No distinction was made between industrial and municipal solid waste—each was handled and disposed of in the same manner, mainly through incineration, landfilling, or disposing into rivers and streams. Far-reaching federal regulations governing the disposal of nonhazardous and hazardous waste went into effect in 1976. In what seems to be a natural evolution of environmental law, federal waste legislation fell in place right on the heels of national water- and air-pollution control legislation. Concern for human health and the environment was the impetus for the enactment of the major federal legislation—the Resource Conservation and Recovery Act of 1976 (RCRA).

During the crafting of the 1976 act, Congress had the opportunity both to regulate disposal methods and to reduce the generation of waste by regulating production and products. Though several bills were introduced to minimize waste by regulating product contents, consumer product packaging, and manufacturing processes, these bills did not pass. For both solid waste and hazardous waste, Congress opted to regulate waste disposal rather than encourage source reduction.[2]

In 1990 the United States led the world in the amount of waste produced; eight billion tons of waste (of all types) was generated by oil, gas, mining, and manufacturing industries and by households, businesses, and institutions.[3] This was generated at every stage—extraction, production, and manufacturing.

There are numerous reasons to be concerned with waste. It is costly to dispose of, and the generation of large amounts of wastes impacts the environment. Domestic and industrial discharges of waste contaminate air, land, and water with pollutants and toxics that can harm human health and animal and plant life. According to environmental lawyer and author Paul Wilson, "the biosphere is disrupted by the sheer volume of our wastes—and also by the fact that many of those wastes are compounds that biosphere systems cannot absorb and recycle."[4] Moreover, the more waste that is disposed of rather than recycled, the more raw materials, like trees, must be consumed in making new products. Though not all scientists agree, many, like Paul Ehrlich, have concluded that human activity is changing the planet's basic chemistry at an increasing rate, as seen in the depletion of fossil fuels and natural resources, global warming, greenhouse gases, destruction of natural ecosystems, and biodiversity. For these scientists, "human beings and the natural world are on a collision course" that can be prevented only if the people in industrialized nations greatly reduce their over consumption, for only then will there be a reduction of pressures on resources and the global environment.[5]

MAJOR FEDERAL WASTE LEGISLATION

■ In 1965 Congress made its first attempt to define the scope of the nation's waste disposal problems by enacting the Federal Solid Waste Disposal Act. This act financed statewide surveys of landfills and illegal dumps.

■ In 1976 Congress passed the Resource Conservation and Recovery Act, which amended the Federal Solid Waste Disposal Act. Most of the landmark legislation dealt with hazardous waste under Subtitle C, but Subtitle D of the Resource Conservation and Recovery Act directed the Environmental Protection Agency (EPA) to set federal standards for the management of industrial and municipal nonhazardous solid wastes in sanitary landfills.

■ In 1984 Congress passed the Hazardous and Solid Waste Amendments to the Resource Conservation and Recovery Act. These amendments, also known as Subtitle D, revised the act's original landfill criteria to ensure that municipal landfills that receive hazardous household wastes or hazardous wastes from small-quantity generators are designed and operated in a way that protects human health and the environment. States were required to adopt and implement a permit program that incorporated these revisions. The EPA was then required to determine if such programs were adequate. If not, the EPA would enforce the new criteria within the state. Texas received approval for its Subtitle D permit program in 1993. The EPA has since published amended rules governing municipal solid waste landfills, and Texas has complied with these amendments.

■ The 1990 Federal Clean Air Act regulates emissions of certain landfill gases (primarily methane) and incinerator particulate matter.

■ In 1990 Congress passed the Pollution Prevention Act, which established a federal hierarchy of preferred waste management methods for municipal solid waste and industrial waste. (The hierarchy of preferred waste management methods for municipal solid waste is also contained in the Texas Solid Waste Disposal Act.)

TEXAS MUNICIPAL SOLID WASTE LEGISLATION

Texas has a long-standing municipal solid waste regulatory program, started in 1969 when the legislature enacted the Texas Solid Waste Disposal Act. This legislation charged the Texas Department of Health with regulating municipal solid waste. Industrial solid wastes were placed under the jurisdiction of the Texas Water Quality Board. By 1991 the regulation of all municipal solid waste had been transferred to the Texas Water Commission, the predecessor agency of the current Texas Natural Resource Conservation Commission (TNRCC).

Today, Texas's municipal solid waste regulatory programs are administered by the TNRCC. Major state legislation relating to municipal solid waste management includes the following:

■ In 1969 the Texas Solid Waste Disposal Act was established and directed the Texas Department of Health to regulate the design, construction, and operation of municipal solid waste facilities. The regulation of municipal solid waste was subsequently transferred to the Texas Water Commission, the predecessor agency of the current TNRCC.

■ In 1983 the Comprehensive Municipal Solid Waste Management, Resource Recovery and Conservation Act established the Municipal Solid Waste Management and Resource Recovery Advisory Council to help guide the development of regional solid waste management plans. It also established procedures and criteria for regional planning agencies and local governments to develop voluntary solid waste management plans.

■ In 1987 the Texas Solid Waste Disposal Act was amended to include as state policy a preferred hierarchy of treatment methods for the management of hazardous waste, municipal waste, and municipal sludge. (This hierarchy will be discussed more fully in the following pages.)

■ In 1989 the legislature established a solid waste disposal fee program to fund the TNRCC's municipal solid waste regulatory program and provide funding for other, related statewide programs. The act also made state, regional, and local solid waste management planning programs mandatory, rather than voluntary, and provided state funding for the development of regional solid waste management plans. The state's 24 regional planning agencies, or Councils of Governments (COGS), were responsible for developing these regional solid waste management plans.

■ In 1991 the Omnibus Recycling Act was established to set a statewide recycling goal for municipal solid waste: a 40 percent recycling goal for municipal solid waste by January 1, 1994. It directed the General Land Office (GLO), the Railroad Commission of Texas, the Texas Department of Commerce, and the Texas Water Commission (now TNRCC) to conduct a comprehensive market development study that would result in a strategy to stimulate markets for recycled goods. It also mandated state agencies to give preference to recycled materials in their purchasing. The legislation imposed fees on the sale of tires and automotive oil and earmarked the revenues for used oil and scrap tire collection programs. The bill also mandated the recycling of lead-acid (automotive) batteries.

■ In 1993 legislation was passed to, among other items, change the 40 percent recycling goal established in 1991 to a 40 percent waste reduction goal (using 1992 landfill tonnage as the base) of the total amount in order to encourage source reduction and recycling. Legislation was passed to create the Recycling Market Development Board, which is charged with coordinating the recycling activities of state agencies and development of recycling industries and markets.

■ In 1993 legislation was passed to address the risks associated with methane gas releases from closed landfills. The bill established a process for the TNRCC to review proposals and issue permits to build atop closed municipal solid waste landfills.

■ The TNRCC's Waste Tire Recycling Program, established by the legislature in 1991, expired December 31, 1997, and the state legislature chose not to reauthorize the program in its original form. One of the major activities eliminated was the state-funded incentive for the collection, processing, and disposal of scrap tires. The state legislature wants private enterprise to take over this activity.

MUNICIPAL SOLID WASTE: WHAT IS IT?

Americans spend approximately $30 billion a year to manage the disposal of a single year's eight billion tons of waste.[6] Approximately 196 to 200 million tons are labeled as municipal solid waste. The remaining 7.8 billion tons are classified as industrial waste generated by manufacturing, agriculture, and mining. Included in the definition of municipal solid waste are durable and nondurable goods, containers, food scraps, yard waste, and inorganic waste from residential, commercial, recreational, and institutional sources. Municipal solid waste can also include sludge from water and wastewater treatment facilities, septic tanks, construction and demolition debris, medical waste, slaughterhouse waste, grease, and grit trap waste.

MUNICIPAL SOLID WASTE IN THE UNITED STATES

Though there have been efforts to determine the exact amount of municipal solid waste Americans generate, the methodology for determining it is a bit of a guessing game. According to the EPA, in 1996 municipal solid waste generated totaled 209.7 million tons, down from 211.5 million tons in 1995, and the per capita generation rate in 1996 was 4.3 pounds per day as compared with 4.4 pounds per day in 1995.[7] According to the Office of Technology Assessment, the U.S. economy is among the most material intensive economies in the world, extracting more than 10 tons (20,000 pounds) of food, fuel, forestry products, metals and nonmetallic ores per person from U.S. territories each year. Over 90 percent of these resources become waste (municipal and industrial) within a few months of being extracted.[8]

The United States leads the world in municipal waste production, generating 200 million tons a year. The waste volume is growing faster than the U.S. population. The average American consumes 17 times more than the average citizen of Mexico and hundreds of times more than an average Ethiopian.[9] As the World Resources Institute has noted, it is not surprising that "the highest levels of resource use and waste generation [municipal and industrial] tend to occur in the wealthiest cities and among the

U.S. RAW MATERIAL CONSUMPTION (1900-89) BY DOLLARS

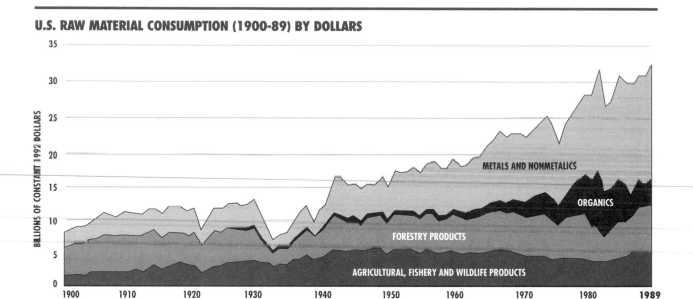

U.S. RAW MATERIAL CONSUMPTION (1900-89) BY PERCENT

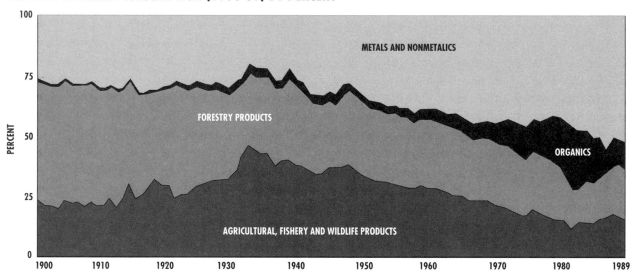

U.S. raw material consumption has changed dramatically in this century. In absolute terms (top), raw material consumption has increased by a factor or four (population has increased roughly by a factor of three during the same period). The largest increases were in materials derived from mining operations (metals and nonmetallic ores) and from organics (plastics and petrochemicals). In relative terms (bottom), the sources of raw materials consumed in the United States have gone from predominantly agriculture and forestry to predominantly mining and organics.
Note: The data measure material consumption by value to allow for aggregation of diverse material types. The data only include materials consumed for uses other than food or fuel.

Source: U.S. Congress, Office of Technology Assessment, Green Products by Design (Washington D.C., 1992), 27.

wealthier groups within cities."[10] "Thus wealthy cities contribute disproportionately to global environmental problems. By contrast, the urban poor's per capita resource use and waste generation tend to be quite low.[11]

Today, increased consumption and increased population in the United States have resulted, according to resources specialists, in a decrease in farmland and forests, and in depletion of nonrenewable resources. Many biologists and resource specialists believe that this trend reflects an economy that will not be able to sustain an environment that provides for the needs of future generations.

YEAR	TONS OF MSW GENERATED IN THE UNITED STATES
1960	88 million tons of MSW were generated
1990	196-200 million tons of MSW were generated
2000	222 million tons of MSW are projected to be generated

The term generation, as used here, refers to materials or products that enter the waste stream before recycling, landfilling, composting, or combustion.

Municipal solid waste disposal: disposal, in this term, refers specifically to landfilling.

Municipal solid waste generation: this term refers to solid waste created through various activities that enters the solid waste stream and is either disposed in a landfill, recycled, composted, or combusted.
(Source: TNRCC, MSW Management in Texas: Status Report [1997], 8.)

MUNICIPAL SOLID WASTE IN TEXAS

According to the TNRCC, in 1995 Texans disposed of approximately 21.6 million tons of municipal solid waste and spent approximately $1 billion for solid waste management.[12] Municipal solid waste is disposed of through landfills, incineration, waste-to-energy facilities, and land application (for sludge). Recycling and composting also are used to manage municipal solid waste.[13] In Texas, as in most other places in the United States, landfill disposal is still the predominant method of solid waste management.

Texas, with an estimated 19,439,337 people in 1997, is second only to California in population. In terms of percent of population growth, Texas ranked tenth among the states for the period from 1990 to 1995. It is not certain that this rate of growth will

continue, but according to the Texas Data Center's demographers, "the fact that such a large part of Texas population growth is due to natural increase (births), which tends to change relatively slowly, suggests that population growth will likely continue, even if the rate of growth slows from that observed in the past few years."[14] For waste management specialists, these population figures indicate that there will be a continuing need for landfills, for recycling, and for source-reduction activities.

In 1997 the municipal solid waste disposal rate for Texans was 6.23 pounds per person per day, and the rate stayed fairly steady between 1992 and 1997. This disposal rate is based on every item that goes into a landfill, including construction and demolition debris and sludge.[15] The amount of municipal solid waste that is diverted to incineration is quite small. The TNRCC estimates that 11,710,000 tons were diverted for recycling in 1997. According to municipal waste specialists at the TNRCC, the Texas per capita disposal rate is comparable to the United States per capita disposal rate.

IMPORTATION AND EXPORTATION OF MUNICIPAL SOLID WASTE

In 1997 approximately 44,813 tons of the total waste received by municipal solid waste facilities in Texas came from bordering states and Mexico.[16] Very little municipal solid waste is exported from Texas.[17]

FYI *"Green products" are those products whose manufacture, use, and disposal place a reduced burden on the environment.*

COMPONENTS OF THE MSW STREAM IN THE U.S., 1996

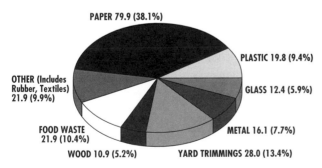

PAPER 79.9 (38.1%)
PLASTIC 19.8 (9.4%)
OTHER (Includes Rubber, Textiles) 21.9 (9.9%)
GLASS 12.4 (5.9%)
FOOD WASTE 21.9 (10.4%)
METAL 16.1 (7.7%)
WOOD 10.9 (5.2%)
YARD TRIMMINGS 28.0 (13.4%)

These are materials that enter the waste stream before recycling, composting, or combustion.

Source: EPA, Characterization of MSW in the U.S.: 1997 Update (May 1998), 2-5.

TOTAL SOLID WASTE DISPOSAL AND PER CAPITA DISPOSAL RATE IN TEXAS, 1986-1997

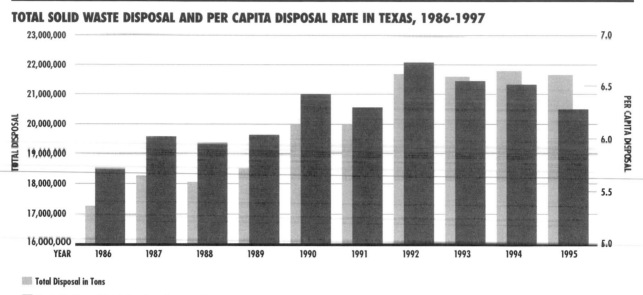

▦ Total Disposal in Tons

■ Per Capita Disposal Rate in Pounds per Person per Day

Disposal refers only to solid waste received by permitted landfills.

Source: TNRCC, Annual Reporting Program for Permitted MSW Facilities: 1997 Data Report *(November 30, 1998),* Attachment 6.

WHAT'S THE FUSS OVER THE STUFF?

Unlike some states, Texas is not in immediate danger of running out of landfill space. Though some areas of the state lack sufficient landfill facilities, statewide landfill capacity is adequate for the next twenty years.[18] This is true even as Texas begins to send its nonhazardous industrial waste to municipal waste landfills. On the other hand, the cost of managing waste is on the rise, and the public well-being and the health of the environment are dependent upon its good management. However, the health of the environment and thus of human life is also dependent upon the way in which we consume and use our natural resources.

Municipal waste, when properly managed, does not pose an immediate threat to human health or the environment. In Texas, however, there have been incidents where municipal solid waste has threatened both the public health and the environment:

■ In 1994 at least 28 landfills were discovered to have caused groundwater pollution.[19]

■ In 1994 methane gas had "migrated" beyond acceptable levels at 63 municipal landfills.[20]

■ 1991 residents of an Austin apartment complex built on an old municipal landfill had to be evacu-

ated due to methane accumulation in several apartment units.

■ In 1992, 63 percent of the 420 landfills open in Texas were located within one mile of residential land uses.[21]

Landfills may present environmental problems, and new regulations are causing higher landfill costs that have forced some landfill closures. However, beyond these problems, there are other

COMPONENTS OF THE MSW STREAM IN THE U.S., 1996

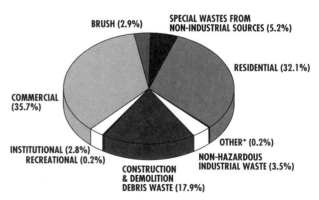

*Includes industrial and other special wastes.

Source: TNRCC, Annual Reporting Program for Permitted MSW Facilities: 1997 Data Report *(November 30, 1998),* Attachment 5.

SOLID WASTE IN TEXAS, 1997

	DISPOSAL	COMBUSTION	DIVERSION FOR RECYCLING	NET EXPORTS	TOTAL
Tons	22,094,777	40,713	11,710,000	0	33,845,490
Per Capita Rate (lb/person/day)	6.23			0	

■ Disposal: In 1997, 22,094,777 tons of solid waste were disposed of in MSW landfills in Texas.

■ Combustion: Solid waste combustion includes basic incineration as well as waste-to-energy conversion. In 1997, 40,713 tons of solid waste were received by these facilities.

■ Imports and Exports: In 1997, permitted MSW facilities in Texas received only 31,711 tons of waste from other states, including Arkansas, Louisiana, New Mexico, and Oklahoma. An additional 13,102 tons of waste were imported from Mexico. Although no data are available on the amount of MSW exported from Texas to other states, this amount is assumed to be relatively small, resulting in no net imports or exports.

Source: TNRCC, MSW in Texas: Data Report (November 30, 1998), 7.

environmental and economic advantages to emphasizing resource reduction and recycling. For most industries, the use of recovered or secondary materials produces less waste and pollution than using virgin feed stock.

Moreover, the use of secondary feed stock in place of virgin materials can reduce energy consumption. For example, using recycled paper in place of virgin pulp can decrease energy consumption by 23 to 74 percent.[22] Reducing wastes and using recovered materials also conserves natural resources.

Studies conducted by Argonne National Labs, the Department of Energy, the Sound Resource Management Group, Franklin Associates, and the Tellus Institute found that "recycling-based systems provide substantial environmental advantages over virgin materials systems: because material collected for recycling has already been refined and processed, it requires less energy, produces fewer common air and water pollutants, and generates substantially less solid waste."[23]

WHAT TO DO WITH WASTE: MUNICIPAL CHOICES
Texas and federal laws specify the following "hierarchy" from the most- to the least-preferred methods of management for municipal solid waste (excluding sludge):[24]
   (1) source reduction;

   (2) reuse or recycling;
   (3) treatment to destroy or reprocess waste to recover energy or other beneficial resources if the treatment does not threaten public health, safety, or the environment; or
   (4) land disposal.
The TNRCC oversaw the development and implementation of local and regional municipal solid waste plans that incorporate this hierarchy. To date, all 24 Councils of Governments have developed regional municipal solid waste plans.

SOURCE-REDUCTION MANAGEMENT OPTION
Perhaps the most difficult municipal solid waste management concept is source reduction. In other words, prevent the creation of that which must be disposed of.

In 1993 the legislature called for a 40 percent reduction by January 1994 of the amount of solid waste disposed of in Texas, using the 1992 landfill tonnage's as the base. This was probably an optimistic goal for a program begun in 1991 and dependent primarily on voluntary compliance. Maintaining the level of current source-reduction initiatives, the TNRCC estimates Texas may be able to realize a 20 percent reduction in the total tons of municipal solid waste disposed of yearly in landfills by the year 2000 and reach the 40 percent reduction goal by

2010.[25] With current programs, the TNRCC estimates that a 30 percent reduction in the yearly "per capita" disposal rate can be achieved by the year 2000 and a 40 percent reduction in "per capita" disposal rate can be achieved by the year 2005.[26]

In Texas, public education and voluntary citizen and business initiatives are the primary tools for reducing the amount of municipal solid waste generated and disposed of. For the most part, the state has not used regulation or financial incentives and disincentives to reduce waste. TNRCC's strategies include:[27]

■ encouraging manufacturers to use less materials in packaging;

■ encouraging businesses to incorporate electronic communication systems, such as e-mail, thus saving paper;

■ encouraging consumers to purchase concentrated bulk foods and products;

■ encouraging consumers to avoid the use of disposable items;

■ encouraging consumers to buy products with less packaging and to buy more durable goods; and

■ encouraging individuals and businesses to use ground cover that does not require mowing and leave clippings on the lawn.

In some parts of the country, laws have been passed to promote source reduction (less waste generated) through various restrictions on product packaging. For example, the State of Maine bans the sale of single-serving juice boxes.[28] In Europe, Germany requires manufacturers and retailers to recover and recycle their own packaging waste. (See the Product Design section for a discussion of the environmental implications and challenges to product design.)

FYI 🕿 *"In addition to reducing our solid waste disposal costs, thoughtful waste reduction policies may also cut other consumer costs. For example, $1.00 out of every $10.00 Americans spend on food pays for packaging."* (Source: Cynthia Pollock, Mining Urban Wastes: The Potential for Recycling, Worldwatch Institute 1987 Paper no. 76 [Washington D.C.: Worldwatch Institute, 1987], 8.)

REUSE/RECYCLING MANAGEMENT OPTION

Thousands of communities in the United States have municipal recycling programs, and studies of selected cities have shown that these programs have significantly reduced solid waste management costs.[29] Additionally, many industries and businesses are finding it to their economic advantage to rely on recycled materials.

In the United States the recycling "movement" began in the late 1960s. Believing that Americans were consuming too much of the world's resources—trees, minerals, fuel, water—environmental groups began to advocate recycling. But in the 1960s and 1970s the market for recyclable materials was not substantial and recycling efforts dwindled. Authors Rathje and Murphy credit Lady Bird Johnson and her beautification campaign for reviving recycling initiatives. They point out that Mrs. Johnson's beautification campaign was in fact a campaign against litter—"garbage that is out of place." When Americans began to address the problem of litter by enacting bottle bills with deposit fees and restrictions on pull-off tabs, beverage distributors began to collect bottles and cans and sell them to scrap markets or reuse them.[30] From this flurry over litter, a new impetus for recycling programs began to emerge all over the country. At the same time, Americans' concern for the environmental impacts of waste generation (extraction of raw materials, clear-cutting, energy consumption, pollution) and disposal of waste provided additional incentives for recycling.

Prompted by the increasing cost of building and operating landfills and by closures of old landfills, the Texas legislature in 1991 made a commitment to

The Texas Solid Waste Disposal Act defines recycling as a "process through which materials that have served their intended use or are scrapped, discarded, used, surplus, or obsolete are collected, separated, or processed and returned to use in the form of raw materials in the production of new products." (Source: Texas Solid Waste Disposal Act, Texas Health and Safety Code.)

a statewide residential and workplace recycling strategy. For the most part, Texas's recycling program is based on voluntary participation. Communities and workplaces are encouraged but not required to offer recycling services. Government entities at the state, county, and city levels, however, are required to establish a collection program for recyclable materials generated by the entity's operations. This includes school systems. The state provides resources in the form of technical assistance to communities, businesses, public school systems, and other public institutions. Potentially recyclable products captured from municipal waste include plastic, paper, glass, steel, aluminum, yard waste, used motor oil, and corrugated containers.

The recycling industry in Texas in 1997 employed approximately 20,000 people in more than 400 firms. More than $2.8 billion in value is added annually to the state's economy through the upgrading or processing of recycled materials.[31]

According to recycling experts, a successful statewide recycling program requires a balance among three components: collection of recyclables, processing and infrastructure, and market demand for recycled materials.[32] Each type of waste material has a different recycling potential. For example, the GLO's 1992 recycling study states that there is a potential growth in glass recycling. However, this growth potential is hampered by the lack of a comprehensive glass collection system, the low value of waste, and high collection and transportation costs.[33] The growth rate for recycled paper, metal, plastic, and other materials is affected by these same factors, as well as the cost of virgin materials and the capacity of manufacturing end-users. Information on recycling rates for these materials can be found in TNRCC's 1995 Municipal Solid Waste Plan for Texas. In 1997 Texas recycled 11,710,000 tons of municipal solid waste, a recycling rate of 35 percent.[34]

FYI *In 1997, 130 Texas cities operated curbside recycling programs for approximately 1.5 million households, or an estimated 3.5 million people.*

(*Source: TNRCC, Municipal Solid Waste Management in Texas: Status Report [April 1997], 14.*)

ENVIRONMENTAL BENEFITS FROM RECYCLING

BENEFIT AS % REDUCTION OF	ALUMINUM	STEEL	PAPER	GLASS
Energy Use	90-97	47-74	23-74	4-32
Air Pollution	95	85	74	20
Water Pollution	97	76	35	
Mining Waste		97		80
Water Use		40	58	50

Source: Robert Cowles Letcher and Mary T. Shell, "Source Separation and Citizen Recycling," The Solid Waste Handbook, ed. William D. Robinson (New York: John Wiley & Sons, 1986).

COMPONENTS OF THE STATE'S RECYCLING PROGRAM:

■ The Recycling Market Development Board, created by the Texas legislature in 1993, coordinates the recycling activities of state agencies. Among other activities, the board has developed legislative and policy programs to increase state procurement of recycled content products.

■ The TNRCC helps public school systems, local governments, businesses, and citizens establish waste reduction and recycling programs.

■ The TNRCC recycling staff has initiated several comprehensive workplace waste reduction and recycling programs with such corporations as Trammel S. Crow and Wyndham Hotels, resulting in substantial cost-savings for these companies and diverting recyclable items from the waste stream.

■ The TNRCC developed the Recycling Markets Information System, an online, interactive geographical information system for use by collectors, processors, brokers, manufacturers, other recyclable materials end-users, and planners.

■ The TNRCC provides local and state government agencies, commercial composters, and high-volume generators of agricultural wastes, yard trimmings, food, and other organics with technical assistance and training on recovery, processing, and marketing strategies to maximize the reuse of these materials.

PAPER OR PLASTIC: A CONTEMPORARY QUESTION?

Many grocery stores today offer the consumer a choice between having their items bagged in plastic or paper. According to the TNRCC, neither plastic nor paper "has been proven to be significantly tougher on the environment."[35] During the manufacturing of both paper and plastic there are environmental impacts, including air and water pollution. Energy and natural resources are consumed during the manufacturing of both paper and plastic, and, when disposed of, both take up landfill space. It has not been shown, however, that one has more harmful effects on the environment than the other. According to the TNRCC, "the paper or plastic dilemma can be avoided altogether by bringing along a tote bag for a few groceries or by reusing paper or plastic bags that you may have received on your last trip to the store."[36]

Consumers might also consider that in the past ten years there has been an increase in the acreage (see section on forests) devoted to pine plantations not only in Texas but throughout the Southeast (there are also increased pressures on forests throughout the world, particularly in southeast Asia and South America). In these pine plantations are grown most of the trees used to make paper products, such as grocery bags. Pine monocultures, which are less suitable than natural forests to wildlife habitat and biodiversity, have replaced natural pine forests. It is projected that 70 percent of all pine forests in the country will be pine plantations (monocultures) in the next few decades. According to resource scientists with the Environmental Defense Fund, "extending the overall fiber supply, paper recycling can help reduce the pressure to convert remaining natural forests to tree farms."[37]

WASTE-TO-ENERGY MANAGEMENT OPTION FOR MUNICIPAL SOLID WASTE

Waste-to-energy facilities are incinerators that burn waste to create heat or electricity for nearby consumers. These facilities were first promoted during the energy crisis of the 1970s when fuel costs were rising and there was a fear of fuel shortages.

The Texas Solid Waste Disposal Act ranks waste-to-energy facilities third on the preferred hierarchy of municipal solid waste management options for Texas. The cities of Center, Carthage, and Cleburne are the only cities in Texas that use waste-to-energy incinerators for municipal solid waste. Together these incinerators convert annually approximately 25,138 tons of municipal solid waste to energy. (There are 16 incinerators in Texas that are permitted to burn municipal solid waste, including medical waste; however, these facilities do not try to recover energy from waste, and only 10 of the 16 are active.) The attractiveness of this waste management method is its ability to dispose of huge amounts of waste. Yet, currently there is no active movement by local or state governments to develop more waste-to-energy facilities for municipal solid waste. There are two major reasons for this: high costs and the potential release of pollutants.

The public health and environmental problems associated with waste-to-energy facilities are similar to those associated with other incinerators: air pollution and groundwater pollution. A by-product of the combustion process is ash, and the finer particles of ash are released through the smoke stack. Others are captured in the "bag house" as fly ash, and the heavier particles are collected as bottom ash. Depending on the waste stream, toxic chemicals such as lead, cadmium, arsenic, and dioxin are concentrated in the ash. Along with carbon dioxide and water, these pollutants are released into the air through the stack, potentially threatening air quality and the health of humans and the environment.[38] New technology that eliminate many air contaminants from incinerator ash is becoming available, but it is costly.[39]

Besides the ash released into the air, the ash collected at the incinerator also poses problems. It has routinely been disposed of in municipal solid waste landfills, raising concern about groundwater contamination. A 1994 U.S. Supreme Court decision ruled that municipal waste incineration ash that has high levels of lead, cadmium, arsenic, and other contaminants that would render it hazardous waste cannot be disposed of in municipal landfills.[40] According to the TNRCC, however, very little of the ash from active Texas incinerators has tested out to be hazardous.[41]

Historically, it has been difficult for waste-to-energy facilities to compete financially with landfills. In the past, the cost of a landfill has been relatively less expensive than building and operating a waste-to-energy facility. Often revenues from the sale of steam or electricity do not cover the costs of building or operating the incinerator facility. Moreover, to make the most of steam or electrical generating capacity, incinerators need to operate at full production, and this often means that a local community has to buy supplementary waste capacity, often at fees below what the community residents pay.[42]

LANDFILLS

Landfills can be an emotional issue: some people clamor for them, others earnestly object to their presence. In Texas, landfills have been the predominant method of municipal solid waste disposal. However, in the past ten years, Texans have seen a decline in the number of landfills. In 1986, 250 of Texas's 254 counties had at least one landfill; in 1994, only 154 counties had a landfill. Stricter landfill regulations to protect the environment and human health are forcing local communities either to ante up with new dollars for redesigning their current landfill or to close it. (Between 1993 and 1996, the average disposal charge [aka tipping fee] at a municipal solid waste landfill increased from $19 per ton to $28.[43])

Though a large number of landfills have been closed, TNRCC figures reveal that landfill capacity in the state has not changed much since 1986. Large new landfills are replacing smaller older landfills, and some older facilities have expanded their capacity. The TNRCC estimates that at the end of 1997 Texas had 24 years of landfill capacity remaining statewide.[44]

At the same time, however, landfill closures in some regions of the state have made disposal less convenient. For some rural residents, transporting waste long distances to regional landfills has increased disposal costs and has increased the need for transfer stations. Transfer stations are facilities where various communities bring their waste until it is transported to a permanent site. These transfer sites can pose the same problems as do landfills: potential groundwater

NUMBER OF MSW LANDFILLS* IN TEXAS IN 1997 BY COUNTY

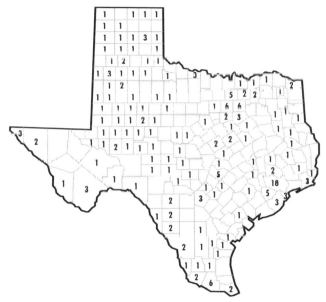

*Permitted facilities officially open at the end of 1997, both active and inactive.

Source: TNRCC, Annual Reporting Program in Permitted MSW Facilities: 1997 Data Report (November 30, 1997), Attachment 2.

pollution, siting problems, and smell. In some areas, the loss of a local landfill has increased illegal and potentially harmful dumping.

As more and more municipally owned landfills close, cities and towns are contracting with private companies for waste disposal. Privatization of waste management has become an issue particularly in smaller communities where one company can exercise a monopoly over this sector of the economy. At the end of 1997, 72 of the state's open municipal solid waste landfills were private; they held 50.1 percent of the available landfill capacity in the state and handled 65.5 percent of the state's total waste capacity.[45]

FYI *A municipal solid waste landfill can hold approximately 650 pounds of waste per cubic yard of landfill space.*

Landfills, both closed and active, can pose potential threats to surface—and groundwater quality and to human health. Potential groundwater contaminants from municipal waste landfills include,

TREND TOWARD PRIVATE CONTROL OF SOLID WASTE DISPOSAL IN TEXAS

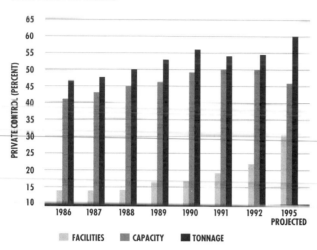

FACILITIES   CAPACITY   TONNAGE

Source: TNRCC, Summary of Annual Reports for Permitted Municipal Solid Waste Facilities in Texas (January 1995).

acetone, benzene, tricholoroethylene, lead, chlorides, and 1,4-dichlorobenzene. In 1993 the TNRCC identified at least 24 municipal landfills causing groundwater pollution.

Under the amended Subtitle D of the Resource Conservation and Recovery Act of 1976, stricter pollution controls have been established for landfills. These include restrictions on the locations of landfills and requirements for landfill liners that capture water that filters through waste, leachate (water that goes through waste) collection systems, methane gas monitoring, groundwater monitoring, closure, post-closure care, and financial assurances. Texas has developed new municipal solid waste regulations that reflect these federal requirements.

ILLEGAL DUMPS

As of the summer of 1994, the majority of municipal solid waste enforcement cases handled by the TNRCC dealt with illegal municipal solid waste dump sites. These illegal sites proliferate for a variety of reasons. In a few cases, a community or private handler that does not have a permitted municipal solid waste landfill will gain access to an absent landowner's property and use it. In other situations, an individual who wants to make a few dollars will

allow his property to be used for disposing of items like construction debris, old appliances, and old tires at a cheaper price than that charged by the municipal landfill. There are also property owners who want inert waste as fill to build up their land. These dumps can contain hazardous materials like pesticides that pose threats to groundwater and public health. County officials in the 32 counties of the Texas-Mexico border region have identified illegal dump sites as a growing and extensive problem for the region. In a survey conducted by the TNRCC, county officials in this area identified approximately 1,200 sites that had been cleaned up by local governments during one year.[46]

BIOSOLIDS: BY ANY OTHER NAME, SLUDGE

Approximately eight million tons per year of wet sludge from municipal water and wastewater treatment plants and septic tanks are generated in Texas. According to the Environmental Research Foundation "Sludge is a mud-like material that remains after bacteria have digested the human wastes that flow from your toilet into your local sewage treatment plant."[47] Human wastes, however, are not the only substances in sludge, because some wastewater treatment facilities also receive industrial waste and some sewage systems mix storm-water runoff with the regular human waste. So, sewage sludge can contain a number of pesticides and chemicals along with human waste.

The EPA has developed regulations governing the use of sludge. At the state level, sludge regulations are enforced by the TNRCC. Liquid waste cannot be disposed of in municipal solid waste landfills unless it has been dried. Most permitted water treatment plants do dry their sludge. The sludge stays at wastewater treatment sites in lagoons that often have a five- to ten-year storage capacity. The sludge is dried and then sent to landfills or applied to land. In Texas, about 650,000 dry tons of sludge end up in landfills every year.

The following are the state's preferred methods for treating municipal sludge in order of most to least preferred:[48]

■ source reduction and minimization of sludge production;

■ treatment of sludge to reduce pathogens and recover energy, produce beneficial by-products, or reduce the quantity of sludge;

■ marketing and distribution of sludge and sludge products;

■ applying sludge to land for beneficial use; and

■ landfilling.

Because treated sludge is considered by some waste management professionals to have components that can be useful to the soil—minerals, metals, and plant nutrients, like phosphorous and nitrogen, the land application of sludge (beneficial use) is a growing trend. The co-composting of municipal sludge with brush and yard trimmings is also growing in popularity as a method for dealing with municipal sludge.[49] (It is also becoming costly to dispose of sludge in landfills.) The land application of sludge is regulated by the TNRCC, which requires sludge to be treated before its use. There are two ways to treat sludge: pretreatment, which prevents pollutants such as PCBs and metals from entering the sewer drains; and treatment at the wastewater facility for organisms that cause disease. Sludge is classified as either Class A or Class B, depending on the type of treatment it has received. Class A sludge has benefited from both pretreatment and treatment at the wastewater facility. The pathogens in Class A biosolids cannot exceed certain levels set by the EPA. Standards for Class B sludge are less stringent, and their use is therefore more regulated. A landowner who wishes to use Class B sludge as an alternative to conventional fertilizers must apply to the TNRCC to register his site. Among other items, the application requires information on the type of land, the amount of buffer zones, and the type of soil. The applicant must also provide information from the wastewater treatment facility on the type of pollutants and pathogens in the sludge, and calculations of nutrient needs for the crops. A landowner using Class A sludge does not have to register his land. As of 1995 there were 456 registered land application sites in Texas that handled 138,557 tons of sludge.

Cities like Fort Worth, Houston, and Austin have diverted tons of biosolids from the land fill to beneficial uses. The city of Fort Worth hired a private contractor to distribute 70 tons of dry sludge a day from its wastewater treatment facility to area farmers and ranchers. The landowners do not pay for the sludge but, as reviewed above, each user had to meet certain land application standards set by the TNRCC. Using a somewhat different approach, the City of Austin composts and then sells over 50 percent of its sludge (Class A) to 15 wholesale nurseries, which in turn market and sell it as fertilizer—known as Dillo Dirt—to retail consumers.

In Texas, critics of land application of sludge have made their voices heard at the TNRCC and at the local government level. After citizens raised concern, the Reeves County Commissioners Court issued an order regulating the application of sludge. The order requires that sludge be applied only through subsurface injection and only after an application has been submitted to the county clerk. In Fort Bend County, residents of the City of Guy appealed to the city and to the TNRCC to stop the use of sludge by farmers who are spreading it on pastureland. The sludge is from Houston-area wastewater treatment plants. According to complaining residents, the sludge is foul smelling and nauseating. Some Fort Worth residents, fearing groundwater and surface water pollution, also raised objections to the use of sludge on neighboring farms.

The use of sludge as an alternative to common fertilizers has drawn criticism at the national level as well. Critics point to the following possible consequences:[50]

■ Sludge may contain metals, including copper, mercury, and arsenic. The degree to which these metals move into groundwater and surface water, and the resulting effects on plants and wildlife, are not known, and their movement into and consequences for groundwater, surface water, plants, and wildlife are not known.

■ Toxic heavy metals may build up in soils, and the long-term effects on wildlife and animals have not been assessed.

HOUSEHOLD HAZARDOUS WASTES

The TNRCC estimates that each Texas household produces 15 to 22 pounds of household hazardous waste each year. This means about 60,000 tons annually statewide. Household hazardous wastes, such as pesticides, insecticides, household cleaners, other chemicals, motor oil, and batteries, though hazardous in character, are not regulated under the Resource Conservation and Recovery Act of 1976. Under the act's regulations, household hazardous waste is not included in the definition of hazardous waste. Because such waste is generated in a household, by a consumer, the EPA considers it part of the municipal solid waste stream. For the same reason, household hazardous waste is not regulated by the Texas Solid Waste Disposal Act's Industrial Solid Waste and Municipal Hazardous Waste provisions. Most of these hazardous materials are buried in landfills.[51] By weight, household hazardous waste makes up about one percent of the total municipal solid waste stream. Waste management professionals' preferred methods of dealing with household hazardous materials are source reduction, reuse, recycling, or proper disposal. At this time, lead-acid batteries and used oil and oil filters are the only household hazardous waste that cannot be disposed of in municipal landfills. The TNRCC has funded hundreds of household hazardous waste collection centers and registered hundreds more private businesses to collect oil and oil filters. The TNRCC also operates a number of rural pesticide container collection programs—the Country Clean-up Program. A number of cities operate collection facilities as well. Through an educational campaign, the TNRCC is also encouraging manufacturers of household products to establish "take-back" programs.

TO REDUCE, TO RECYCLE, TO BURN, TO DUMP: THE CRITICAL ISSUE OF COSTS AND BENEFITS

The threat to our natural resources and the threat to human health should be powerful incentives to reduce the amount of waste we generate and to recycle that which is generated. In reality, however, communities faced with competing demands on their budgets must justify waste management expenditures: what method of waste management is the least costly to the community and its residents—recycling, incineration, landfilling?

In Texas, most communities looking at waste management options compare the costs of recycling and landfilling, or a combination of both recycling and landfilling. This comparison is difficult to make accurately. There are few standard methods for making such comparisons, and cities rarely account for the total cost of disposal programs—overhead, closure costs, costs of land, depreciation of equipment, and environmental problems in making such comparisons. In fact, the long-term costs of maintaining and closing a landfill are not easily predicted. Likewise, recycling has its unpredictable costs, and local and national markets for the recovered materials go up and down. To assist local governments make the hard choices regarding the management of municipal solid waste, the TNRCC has produced a handbook entitled *MSW Services Full-Cost Accounting Workbook*.

Experts who study the economics of solid waste claim that no matter what solid waste management system a community uses—incineration, recycling, or landfilling—waste disposal is something that the public must pay for, and those costs are going to continue to rise.[52]

PRODUCT DESIGN: ONE STRATEGY FOR THE ENVIRONMENT AND BUSINESS

Both state and local initiatives have been launched to encourage source reduction; that is, decrease the amount of stuff that needs to be disposed of. Several states have enacted bans on flip-top cans and polystyrene-foam food packaging. Some manufacturers and businesses have reduced the amount of product packaging, particularly plastic packaging and fast-food containers. Others, such as the computer industry and the kitchen appliance industry, have policies under which the company will take back used equipment and disassemble, recycle old parts, and reconstruct the equipment. A bicycle company manufactures bicycles that have been made from aluminum scrap and old soda cans. But basically

STAGES OF THE PRODUCT LIFE CYCLE

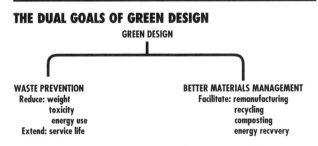

| MATERIAL EXTRACTION | MATERIAL PROCESSING | MANUFACTURING | USE | WASTE MANAGEMENT |

RECYCLE   REMANUFACTURE   REUSE

Source. U.S. Congress, Office of Technology Assessment, Green Products by Design (Washington D.C., 1992), 4.

manufacturers of consumer and industrial products have had the freedom to design products without regard to their environmental impacts. That is not to say, however, that certain industries, such as the automobile industry, have not had to develop products that meet certain federal pollution emission standards.

Environmentalists, businesses, and waste management specialists are showing increasing attention to product design. In that effort, a systematic analysis of the environmental effect of a products development is made at every stage—from raw materials extraction, to processing, to manufacturing, to use, to waste management. The ultimate objective of this analysis is to reduce the amount of natural resources used in production of a product and to cause the least amount of harm to the environment at all stages of the products development.

At each stage of a product's life cycle there will be environmental impacts. For example, timber harvesting for paper and wood products may result in such environmental impacts as habitat destruction or alteration, erosion, and subsidence. During the manufacturing phase of many products there are environmental impacts as well. One of the by-products of the manufacture of bleached pulp and paper is the cancer-causing chemical dioxin, which is released into the air, water, and land and finds its way into the animal food chain. Other products have environmental impacts during their use, such as pesticides that can contaminate groundwater and surface water, chlorofluorocarbon solvents (coolants) that destroy the ozone (these have been phased

out in the United States), and fossil fuels whose by-products cause smog. Then there is the environmental impact of handling and disposing of municipal waste in landfills.

At the design phase of a product, critical decisions are made about the materials used (recycled or raw), the energy requirements (gas, electricity, solar), and the recyclability of the final product. These decisions determine the product's overall environmental impact.[53]

The U.S. Office of Technology Assessment has developed two primary "green design" goals: waste prevention, and better materials management. Waste prevention includes activities by manufacturers and consumers that avoid the generation of waste in the first place. Better material management involves activities that allow product components or materials to be recovered and reused.

THE DUAL GOALS OF GREEN DESIGN

GREEN DESIGN

WASTE PREVENTION	BETTER MATERIALS MANAGEMENT
Reduce: weight	Facilitate: remanufacturing
toxicity	recycling
energy use	composting
Extend: service life	energy recvvery

Green Design consists of two complementary goals. Design for waste prevention avoids the generation of waste in the first place, design for better materials management facilitates the handling of products at the end of their service life.

Source: U.S. Congress, Office of Technology Assessment, Green Products by Design (Washington D.C., 1992), 8.

According to a report prepared by Office of Technology Assessment, the consideration of environmental concerns at the beginning of the design process is not only good for the environment, it is also good for a business's bottom line. For example, some businesses that have designed their products for take-back and recycling are reducing material costs, the use of hazardous materials, employee hours, the costs of waste disposal, and the costs of pollution control. In addition, many businesses market their products as eco-friendly, which might give them a competitive edge.[54]

In agreement with the Office of Technology, business professor Stuart Hart challenges corporations to look beyond controlling pollution, to preventing pollution and being in the forefront of the effort to achieve a sustainable economy (an economy that the planet is capable of supporting indefinitely). The three steps that Hart suggests businesses and corporations follow are: (1) Pollution Prevention—create technologies to reduce and prevent pollution; (2) Product Stewardship—focus on the environmental impacts of a products life cycle, not just on how much pollution is being created, design for the environment, and create products that are easier to recover, reuse, and recycle; and (3) Clean Technology—plan and invest in developing clean technologies, which make use of materials and processes that do not harm the environment. For example, a chemical company has created a herbicide that biodegrades in the soil and requires fewer applications than traditional herbicides.[55] Hart believes that sustainable development will constitute one of the biggest opportunities in the history of commerce.[56]

There are scientists, however, who caution against a reliance on technological fixes or technological innovations to overcome the serious threats to the global environment. Paul Wilson, director of the environmental law program at Lewis and Clark Law School, concludes that the continued growth of goods and services produced is directly related to resource depletion and environmental degradation and that "we [the United States] must adopt a new mindset and seek a way of life that can be sustained over the long-term."[57] There are scientists and

resource specialists who believe that postindustrial societies cannot continue to support an economic system based on relentless material consumption and at the same time maintain a sustainable future.

NOTES

1. William Rathje and Cullen Murphy, *Rubbish* (New York: Harper Perennial, 1990), 42.

2. Rathje and Murphy, *Rubbish*, 42.

3. World Resources Institute, *The 1994 Information Please Environmental Almanac* (Boston: Houghton Mifflin, 1994), 110.

4. Paul Wilson, "Changing Direction toward a Sustainable Culture," *Northwest Report: A Newsletter of the Northwest Area Foundation*, no. 19. (St. Paul: Northwest Area Foundation, January 1996), 4.

5. Paul R. Ehrlich, Gretchen C. Daily, Scott C. Daily, Norman Myers, and James Salzman, "No Middle Way on the Environment," *Atlantic Monthly*, December 1997, 99. This quote is taken from the 1992 World Scientists "Warning to Humanity" signed by more than 1,500 of the world's leading scientists.

6. World Resources Institute, *1994 Information Please Environmental Almanac*, 92.

7. EPA, *Characterization of MSW in U.S.: 1997 Update* (May 1998), 2-5.

8. Office of Technology Assessment, *Green Products by Design: Choices for a Cleaner Environment*, 1992 (Washington, D.C.: U.S. Government Printing Office, OTA-E-541), 23.

9. Stuart Hart, "Strategies for a Sustainable World," *Harvard Business Review*, January-February 1997, 67.

10. World Resources Institute, *World Resources: A Guide to the Global Environment, 1996-97* (New York: Oxford University Press, 1996), 57.

11. World Resources Institute, *World Resources*, 57.

12. This refers to the number of tons disposed in permitted municipal landfills in Texas.

13. TNRCC, *Municipal Solid Waste Management in Texas: Status Report* (1997), 9.

14. Md. Nazrul Hoque and Steve H. Murdock, *Texas Population Growth at Mid-Decade* (College Station: Department of Rural Sociology, November 1996), 1.

15. TNRCC, *Annual Reporting Program for MSW Facilities: 1997 Data Report* (November 30, 1998), attachment 6. The 1997 per capita disposal rate was based on a population of 19, 459,337.

16. TNRCC, *Annual Reporting Program for MSW Facilities: 1997 Data Report.*

17. TNRCC, *Annual Reporting Program for MSW Facilities: 1997 Data Report*, 3.

18. TNRCC, Waste Policy Division, *Municipal Solid Waste Management Methods*, Draft Document (July 1994).

19. TNRCC, Municipal Solid Waste Division, Key Activities Report for November 1994.

20. TNRCC, Municipal Solid Waste Division, Key Activities Report for November, 1994.

21. TNRCC, Municipal Solid Waste Division, Key Activities Report for November, 1994, 29.

22. Robert Cowles Letcher and Mary T. Shell, "Source Separation and Recycling," in *The Solid Waste Handbook*, ed. William D. Robinson (New York: Wiley, 1986).

23. Richard Denison and John F. Ruston, "Recycling Is Not Garbage," *Technology Review*, October 1997, 57. Materials assessed in these studies included, newspaper, corrugated cardboard, office paper, magazines, packaging, aluminum, steel cans, glass bottles, and certain plastic bottles.

24. Texas Water Commission, *Texas Solid Waste Strategic Plan* (July 1993), 3.

25. TNRCC, *Municipal Solid Waste Management in Texas: Strategic Plan* (March 1997), 12.

26. TNRCC, *Municipal Solid Waste Management in Texas: Strategic Plan*, 12.

27. Susan Raleigh Kaderka, "Texas Water Commission Recycling Program," Environmental Trade Fair '93. Conference Proceedings, vol. 1 (Austin: Texas Water Commission, April 5, 1993), 37.

28. World Resources Institute, *1994 Information Please Environmental Almanac*, 91.

29. TNRCC, *MSW Management in Texas: Strategic Plan*, 38.

30. Rathje and Murphy, Rubbish, 198.

31. TNRCC, *Pollution Prevention and Recycling in Texas: Report to the 75th Legislature* (March 1997), 2.

32. Mt. Auburn Associates, Inc., and Hazen and Sawyer, "Market Development Strategy for Texas Recyclables," Report prepared for TNRCC, July 20, 1994.

33. TNRCC, Municipal Solid Waste Plan for Texas, Draft for Public Review (October 1994), 49.

34. TNRCC uses the following equation to calculate the recycling rate: tons recycled ÷ tons landfilled and tons recycled.

35. TNRCC, "Paper or Plastic," Press Release for Clean Texas 2000, Tuesday, March 19, 1996.

36. TNRCC, "Paper or Plastic."

37. Denison and Ruston, "Recycling Is Not Garbage," 59.

38. Richard A. Denison and John Ruston, eds., *Recycling and Incineration: Evaluating the Choices* (Washington D.C.: Island Press, for the Environmental Defense Fund, 1990).

39. Nancy Worst, director, Innovative Technology Program, TNRCC, interview with authors, August 8,1994.

40. Environmental Defense Fund, EDF Letter 25, no. 4 (July 1994).

41. Hector Mendieta, Technical Specialist in Waste Policy and Regulations Division, TNRCC. Written information provided to authors, January 11, 1995.

42. Jeff Bailey, "Fading Garbage Crisis Leaves Incinerators Competing for Trash," *Wall Street Journal*, August 11, 1993, A1-A2.

43. TNRCC, *Pollution Prevention and Recycling in Texas: Report to the 75th Legislature*, 8.

44. TNRCC, *Annual Reporting Program for MSW Facilities. 1997 Data Report*, 2.

45. TNRCC, *Annual Reporting Program for MSW Facilities: 1997 Data Report*, 2.

46. TNRCC, *Municipal Solid Waste Management in Texas: Status Report*, 20.

47. "New U.S. Waste Policy, Pt. 2: Sewage Sludge," *Rachel's Environment and Health Weekly*, August 28, 1997 (Annapolis: Environmental Research Foundation).

48. Texas Water Commission, *Texas Solid Waste Strategic Plan* (July 1993).

49. TNRCC, *Municipal Solid Waste in Texas: A Strategic Plan*, 53.

50. "New U.S. Waste Policy, Pt. 2: Sewage Sludge."

51. TNRCC, *Request for Legislative Appropriations for Fiscal Years 1994-1995*, rev. ed. (October 16, 1992).

52. Denison and Ruston, eds., *Recycling and Incineration*, 104.

53. U.S. Congress, Office of Technology Assessment, *Green Products by Design*, 7.

54. U.S. Congress, Office of Technology Assessment, *Green Products by Design*, 6.

55. U.S. Congress, Office of Technology Assessment, *Green Products by Design*, 71-73. According to Hart, economic activity must increase tenfold over today's level just to provide the essentials to a population double its current size; if so, technology will have to improve tenfold merely to keep the plant at the current levels of environmental burden.

56. Stuart Hart, "Strategies for a Sustainable World," *Harvard Business Review*, January-February, 1996, 67.

57. Wilson, "Changing Direction toward Sustainable Culture," 4.

Getting Information

Getting environmental information from Texas's state environmental agencies, as well as from the federal government, is easier today than it was even three years ago—especially if you have access to the World Wide Web, or at least a computer and modem. All of the major state agencies that deal with the environment in Texas maintain web pages that provide users with general information about programs and in some cases allow the public to transfer ("download") entire databases of environmental information either through the web or through an "FTP"—File Transfer Protocol. The Texas Natural Resource Conservation Commission (TNRCC), for example, has made the entire State Summary of Emissions Database—which includes over 9,000 facilities in Texas that emit air pollutants—transferable through their web pages.

One of the easiest ways to begin to access state agency environmental information is to go to one of the centralized web pages for state agencies. These include both the Texas State Comptroller of Public Accounts' "Window on State Government" and an Internet site called "State of Texas—Government Information." A third place to obtain state government information is from the Texas Natural Resources Information Service (TNRIS), which provides a clearinghouse and referral center for natural resources data. A unit of the Texas Water Development Board (TWDB), TNRIS receives and collects information from dozens of state and federal agencies. TNRIS maintains a library of data in Austin, including aerial photographs and satellite imagery, U.S. Geological Survey maps, and computerized files on water resources, geology, and census data. In addition, TNRIS maintains information contained in Geographic Information Systems (GIS), computerized systems that combine geographic information—maps—with databases. TNRIS also runs the Texas/Mexico Borderlands Data and Information Center, which has information on the border region and is a good place to begin trying to locate Mexican environmental information. TNRIS can be reached by telephone or e-mail, and information is available on its web site.

Similarly, federal agencies such as the EPA also maintain web pages. Information about water quality in your watershed or ground-level ozone in your airshed can now be obtained easily through the web, if you know the address. A particularly useful EPA web page is EnviroFacts Warehouse, which allows you to access the Toxics Release Inventory as well as other databases with information concerning pollution by major manufacturing companies (see focus piece on *Right-to-Know*). The EPA is also working on several projects that will make environmental information even more accessible. For example, under the 1996 amendments to the Safe Drinking Water Act, the EPA was required to create a web-accessible national drinking-water-quality database by 1999, based upon yearly reports from the individual states on public drinking water systems.[1] Recently, the EPA's Center for Environmental Information and Statistics (CEIS) set up a new web site where citizens can access environmental information about their communities—including air and water quality, drinking water, and hazardous wastes and toxics—simply by entering a zip code.[2]

Not everyone has a computer, of course, and not all information is available through the computer. Most state and federal agencies publish reports in various programs, sometimes as a requirement under federal or state law. For example, every two years, the TNRCC must publish a *Water Quality Inventory*, with information about surface water quality in Texas. Similarly, the TWDB must publish a *State Water Plan* with information about Texas water use every few years. Copies of these reports can be obtained from these agencies' publication departments. Sometimes, individuals must actually request information that is not available in published form, as would be the case for individual environmental permits for facilities. Sometimes the best course is to actually go and visit central records at the state agency headquarters or regional office.

The TNRCC also has an information retrieval service known simply by its telephone number: (512) 239-DATA.[3] Using this number, TNRCC employees and any interested outside party can request information and automated reports contained within TNRCC computer databases, or request that the TNRCC create a new report. The information is free to local, regional, and state governments, news media, Texas educational institutions, legislators, and not-for-profit organizations. Private interests, on the other hand, are charged according to the time, printing service, and mailing costs.[4]

STATE AND FEDERAL AGENCIES AND ORGANIZATIONS WITH ENVIRONMENTAL DATA ON THE WEB

AGENCY OR ORGANIZATION	WEB SITE	ENVIRONMENTAL AND ECONOMIC INFORMATION
Texas Comptroller of Public Accounts (Window on State Government)	http://www.window.state.tx.us	You can access all the state agency web sites from the Window on State Government. Also has tax, sales, population, economic, employment and other information.
State of Texas – Government Information	http://www.state.tx.us	From the State of Texas – Government Information, you can link to all of the State of Texas agency Internet sites as well as local government sites.
Texas Legislature Online	http://www.capitol.state.tx.us	Access to all proposed and approved legislation and scheduled hearings from the Texas Senate, House, as well as access to Texas statutes and agencies.
Texas Natural Resources Information System	http://www.tnris.state.tx.us	Natural resources files, maps, census data, geographic information systems data.
Texas Public Utility Commission	http://www.puc.state.tx.us	Energy and utility information.
Texas General Land Office	http://www.glo.state.tx.us	Coastal and wetland information, recycling market development board.
Texas Department of Economic Development	http://www.tded.state.tx.us	Texas company information, business news, grants, economic census information, permits.
Texas Natural Resource Conservation Commission	http://www.tnrcc..state.tx.us	Air, water, and waste databases, permit hearings, rules, weekly agendas, public meetings, press releases, small business technical assistance, pollution prevention activities, recycling information.
Texas Cancer Council	http://www.txcancer.org	State, county and racial cancer rates, cancer education information.
Texas/Mexico Borderlands Information Center	http://www..bic.state.tx.us	GIS data and maps with political tracts, land use, transportation, ecological regions, etc.; census data, federal fund reports from U.S. and Mexico.
Texas Water Development Board	http://www.twdb.state.tx.us	Water use and source data and projections, Texas Water Plans, water resource planning groups and meetings, agency meetings, water conservation, funding.
Texas Parks and Wildlife	http://www.tpwd.state.tx.us	Park information, wildlife and land management, wetland conservation and state endangered species.
Texas Workforce Commission	http://www.twc.state.tx.us	Unemployment and employment rates, training information, Texas employment law.
Railroad Commission of Texas	http://www.rrc.state.tx.us	Alternative fuels, oil and gas and mining information.
Texas Department of Agriculture	http://www.agr.state.tx.us	Pesticides and organic farming and food information, labeling, regulations.
U.S. Environmental Protection Agency, Region VI	http://www.epa.gov/earth1r6/index.htm	Information on offices and programs, information on Texas-Mexico border.

Continued on next page

STATE AND FEDERAL AGENCIES AND ORGANIZATIONS WITH ENVIRONMENTAL DATA ON THE WEB *Continued from page 288*

AGENCY OR ORGANIZATION	WEB SITE ADDRESS	ENVIRONMENTAL AND ECONOMIC INFORMATION
U.S. EPA, EnviroFacts Warehouse	http://www.epa.gov/enviro/	Allows search a federal toxics, air, water, compliance, spill data and hazardous waste databases by facility, industry, zip code, county and state. Includes mapping ability.
U.S. EPA Surf Your Watershed	http://www.epa.gov/surf2	Allows users to access information on water quality, impacts to rivers and reservoirs within watersheds.
U.S. EPA Sector Facility Indexing Project	http://es.epa.gov/oeca.sfi.index	Information on facilities in five manufacturing sectors from EPA databases, as well as mapping and demographic data of areas surrounding facilities.
U.S. EPA Drinking Water Info	http://www.epa.gov/ogwdw/dwinfo.html	Data on compliance and drinking water quality at water utilities.
U.S. Fish and Wildlife Dept.	http://www.fws.gov	Information on water quality monitoring, habitat conservation, federal endangered species, legislation.
Energy Information Agency, U.S. Department of Energy	http://www.eia.doe.gov/emeu/sep/states.html	State and national data on energy use, renewable energy.
USDA Natural Resources Conservation Service	http://www.neq.nrcs.usda.gov	Natural resource data, including land cover, wetlands, land conditions.
American Farmland Trust	http:www.farmland.org	Farm and ranchland preservation information.
National Research Defense Council	http://www.nrdc.org	National enviromental organization with reports and data on natural areas, air pollution, as well as updates on legislation impacting the environment.
Environmental Defense Fund Scorecard	http://www.scorecard.org	Uses federal environmental databases like Toxics Release Inventory to provide data on facilities and assess the risk and health of communities. Includes mapping capability.
Sierra Club	http://www.sierraclub.org	Information on legislation, campaigns for clean air, clean water, endangered species and habitat.
National Audobon Society	http://www.audobon.org	Links to preserve America's special places, bird and wildlife habitat.
National Wildlife Federation	http://www.nwf.org	Concentrates on activities to preserve wildlife and their habitats.
Texas Center for Policy Studies	http://www.texascenter.org	Links to publications, web links, Texas Environmental Almanac.
RTK Net (Right-to-Know Computer Network)	http://www.ombwatch.org/rtknet	Toxic Release Inventory Data for counties, states and by zip code, data on individual facilities, as well as other federal environmental databases. Also includes bank lending and housing information.

NOTES

1. Working Group on Community Right-to-Know, "Law Discloses Drinking Water Pollution," *Working Notes on Community Right-to-Know*, November-December 1997, 3.

2. U.S. Environmental Protection Agency (EPA), "New EPA Internet Website Makes Environmental Information for Each Neighborhood More Easily Accessible," Press Release, August 6, 1998.

3. Requests may also be made by sending a fax on letterhead to (512) 239-0888 or sending the letter to: Customer Reports and Services, Texas Natural Resource Conservation Commission, P.O. Box 13087, Austin, TX 78711-3087.

4. Texas Natural Resource Conservation Commission, *Information Resources: Customer Reports and Services*, (512) 239-DATA (Austin: TNRCC, 1994), 7.

CHAPTER 8

Industrial Waste

The manufacturing of consumer and industrial goods and chemicals, the mining of oil and gas and metals, and the production of military equipment share a common problem: wastes that may be toxic, ignitable, corrosive, or reactive. Everyone—whether it's the environmental researcher writing a book at a computer, the farmer using pesticides to control insects on crops, or the plant manager refining petroleum—has a hand in the production of hazardous waste. In the United States, the amount of hazardous waste generated by manufacturing industries in the country had increased from an estimated 4.5 million tons annually after World War II, to some 57 million tons by 1975.[1] By 1990 this total had shot up to approximately 265 million tons.[2] Current estimates of hazardous waste from industrial plants stand at 214 million tons.[3] These wastes are generated at every stage in the production, use, and disposal of manufactured products. Thus, the introduction of many new products for the home and office—computers and computer papers, drugs, textiles, paints and dyes, plastics—also introduced hazardous wastes—including toxic chemicals—into the environment.

Before substantial state and federal regulation of waste began in the late 1970s, most industrial waste was disposed of in landfills, stored in surface impoundments such as lagoons or pits, discharged into surface waters with little or no treatment, or burned. Mismanagement of these wastes has resulted in polluted groundwater, streams, lakes, and rivers, as well as damage to wildlife and vegetation.[4] High levels of toxic contaminants have been found in animals and humans who have been continually exposed to such waste streams.[5]

Today, three major federal laws and one state law guide management of hazardous and other industrial waste in Texas:

■ Texas Solid Waste Disposal Act, enacted in 1969 and last amended in 1997. This act authorizes a full state regulatory program for solid waste, including industrial and hazardous waste under the jurisdiction of what today is called the Texas Natural Resource

1: FLOW OF MATERIALS, PRODUCTS AND SOLID WASTE

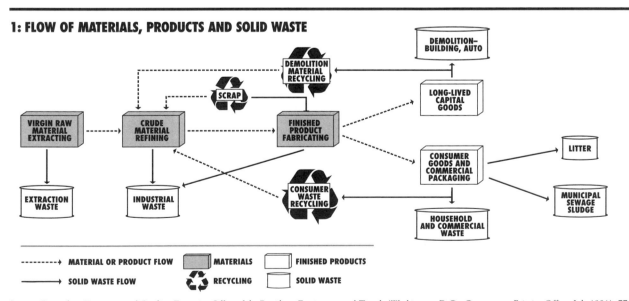

Source: Council on Environmental Quality, Executive Office of the President, Environmental Trends (Washington, D.C.: Government Printing Office, July 1981), 77.

U.S. SOLID WASTE AND ITS SOURCES (TONS), 1995

Total Annual Solid Waste Generated	11 billion
Total Annual Municipal Solid Waste	208 million
Total Annual Hazardous Solid Waste	280 million

Source: EPA, Office of Solid Waste, 1997.

Conservation Commission (TNRCC, formerly the Texas Water Commission). The act sets out various permitting and enforcement authorities and restricts the location, design, and operation of hazardous waste management facilities.

■ Resource Conservation and Recovery Act (RCRA) of 1976. As reauthorized in 1984 by the Hazardous and Solid Waste Amendments, this federal law creates a step-by-step management approach restricting and controlling the treatment, storage, and disposal of hazardous waste onto the land; mandates a permitting system to ensure the safe management of all hazardous waste; and implements a system to track hazardous waste as it moves "cradle-to-grave," from the point of generation to disposal. The 1984 amendments also banned land disposal of most hazardous wastes without prior treatment.

■ CERCLA, the Comprehensive Emergency Response, Compensation and Liability Act of 1980, amended in 1986 as the Superfund Amendment and Reauthorization Act (SARA). This federal law created a $1.6 billion "Superfund" to address spills of hazardous waste and the clean up of old, abandoned hazardous waste sites.[6] The Superfund Amendment and Reauthorization Act and more recent congressional action has provided an additional $13.6 billion.[7] Title III of SARA, the Emergency Planning and Community Right-to-Know Act of 1986, requires major industries to report releases, transfers, and recycling of toxic chemicals to the Environmental Protection Agency (EPA) as part of the Toxics Release Inventory (TRI) Program.

■ Safe Drinking Water Act of 1974, amended in 1986 and 1996. This act, along with the RCRA, protects groundwater sources of potable water, mandates source prevention of pollution to surface waters, and regulates the underground injection of industrial and hazardous wastes.

EXAMPLES OF HAZARDOUS WASTE GENERATED BY INDUSTRIES AND BUSINESSES:

WASTE GENERATOR	WASTE TYPES
Chemical Manufacturers	Acids and Bases Spent Solvents Reactive Waste Wastewater Containing Organic Constituents
Printing Industry	Heavy Metal Solutions Waste Inks Solvents Ink Sludges Containing Heavy Metals
Petroleum Refining Industry	Wastewater Containing Benzene & other Hydrocarbons Sludge from Refining Process
Leather Products Manufacturing	Toluene and Benzene
Paper Industry	Paint Waste Containing Heavy Metals Ignitable Solvents
Construction Industry	Ignitable Paint Waste Spent Solvents Strong Acids and Bases
Metal Manufacturing	Sludges containing Heavy Metals Cyanide Waste Paint Waste

Source: Environmental Protection Agency, Solving the Hazardous Waste Problem: EPA's RCRA Program (Washington, D.C., November 1986), 8.

Other federal laws that relate to hazardous waste include the Federal Clean Air Act, the Clean Water Act, and the Toxics Control and Safety Act.

INDUSTRIAL AND HAZARDOUS WASTE: WHAT IS IT?

According to EPA estimates, manufacturing, mining, and agricultural industries, along with commercial and domestic sources in the United States, generate about 11 billion tons of waste each year, about 214 million tons of which are defined as hazardous under the RCRA.[8] Municipal solid waste—what is disposed of by homes, businesses, and institutions—makes up only 208 million tons, or around 2.5 percent of all generated wastes.[9]

Industrial solid waste—which may be solid, or liquid or gas held in containers—is divided into hazardous and nonhazardous waste. Hazardous wastes

WHAT IS HAZARDOUS WASTE?

Under EPA regulations, solid waste is hazardous if it meets either of the following two conditions:

(1) The EPA has listed it in one of three categories:

(a) Source-specific wastes. This list includes wastes from specific industries such as petroleum refining, wood preserving, and secondary lead smelting, as well as sludge and production processes from these industries.

(b) Generic wastes. This list identifies wastes from common manufacturing and industrial processes, including spent solvents, degreasing operations, leachate from landfills, and ink formulation waste.

(c) Commercial chemical products. This list includes some pesticides, creosote, and other commercial chemicals.

(2) It exhibits one or more of the following characteristics, subject to certain tests:

(a) ignitability;

(b) corrosivity;

(c) reactivity; or

(d) toxicity.

Certain wastes are exempt from regulation as hazardous waste under the RCRA even though they may potentially harm human health or the environment. Exempt wastes include:

(a) domestic sewage;

(b) irrigation waters or industrial discharges permitted under the Clean Water Act, so long as they are not stored on site;

(c) certain nuclear materials as defined by the Atomic Energy Act;

(d) wastes from the exploration and development of petroleum, gas and geothermal energy (wastes from the refining process may be classified as hazardous);

(e) household hazardous wastes; and

(f) agricultural wastes, except some pesticides.

(Source: EPA, Solving the Hazardous Waste Problem: EPA's RCRA Program [November 1986], 5-7.)

---

may result from manufacturing or other industrial processes. Certain commercial products such as cleaning fluids, paints, or pesticides that are discarded by commercial establishments or individuals also can be defined as hazardous wastes. Wastes determined to be hazardous are regulated by hazardous waste rules established pursuant to the RCRA's Subtitle C requirements.

NONHAZARDOUS INDUSTRIAL WASTE

Nonhazardous industrial wastes are those that do not meet the EPA's definition of hazardous waste—and are not municipal wastes. These nonhazardous wastes fall under RCRA's Subtitle D solid waste management requirements.

Under Texas regulations, nonhazardous wastes generated by industrial facilities are categorized as Class 1, Class 2, and Class 3 wastes (see box: Nonhazardous Industrial Waste Classification). Class 2 and 3 wastes are considered less harmful to the environment and human health than Class 1 wastes.

While industries must report the type of waste they produce, they do not have to report how much Class 2 or Class 3 wastes they generate or how they dispose of these wastes. However, municipal solid waste landfills do have to report the receipt of all industrial waste, including Class 2 and 3 wastes.

WHY DO WE CARE ABOUT HAZARDOUS WASTES?

Over the past five years, Texans and their Texas-based industries have produced at least 60 million tons of hazardous waste every year.[10] Although there are plenty of places to put this industrial waste, none of the management or disposal alternatives is fail-safe. Among state officials and the public, serious concerns about both commercial management of industrial waste and on-site industrial management of wastes remain:

■ Hazardous and many "nonhazardous" industrial wastes are inherently dangerous to human health and the environment no matter how they are managed.

NONHAZARDOUS INDUSTRIAL WASTE CLASSIFICATION

Class 1 Wastes:

1. Regulated asbestos-containing material;

2. Materials containing specific toxic chemical constituents that exceed regulated concentration levels, although not enough to be considered hazardous;

3. Liquids that are ignitable at levels above 150 degrees F, or solids and semisolids that contain chemicals considered to be ignitable under certain conditions incidental to storage, disposal, or treatment;

4. Semisolids and solids that, when combined with water, exhibit corrosive properties;

5. Empty containers that held hazardous substances or Class 1 wastes, unless the residue has been completely removed through certain processes, such as multiple rinsing;

6. Wastes containing more than 50 parts per million of total polychlorinated biphenyls (PCBs);

7. Petroleum wastes associated with exploration, development, and production of crude oil, natural gas, or geothermal energy and containing more than 1,500 parts per million total petroleum hydrocarbon (TPH);

8. All nonhazardous industrial solid waste generated outside Texas and transported into or through Texas for storage, processing, or disposal.

Class 2 Wastes:

1. Containers that held hazardous or Class 1 industrial wastes where the residue has been completely removed and the container has been made unusable;

2. Containers, of less than 5-gallon capacity, that held Class 1 wastes;

3. Depleted aerosol cans;

4. Nonsurgical nonradioactive medical waste, not including breast implants, orthopedic devices, and other "artificial, nonhuman devices removed from a patient and requested by the patient"[11];

5. Paper, cardboard, linings, wrappings, paper packaging materials, or absorbents that do not meet hazardous, radioactive, or industrial Class 1 criteria;

6. Food wastes, glass, aluminum foil, plastics, Styrofoam, and food packaging that result from plant production, manufacturing, or laboratory operations.

Class 3 Wastes:

1. Wastes not meeting the conditions of Class 1 or 2, including chemically inert and insoluble substances, samples without detectable levels of PCBs or hydrocarbons, and wastes that pose no threat to human health or the environment;

2. Inert, insoluble solid waste materials such as rock, brick, glass, dirt, and some rubbers and plastics.

(Source: Texas Administrative Code, Chapter 30, Section 335, Subchapter R.)

■ Spills and leaks at hazardous and industrial land disposal units in Texas resulted in more than 560 cases of ground water contamination between 1989 and 1997.[12]

■ Through 1997, the 158,393 chemical and petroleum underground storage tanks and 20,688 aboveground storage tanks registered with state authorities in Texas had reported 9,058 groundwater contamination incidents, including 6,338 incidents that had not been cleaned up.[13]

■ Abandoned oil, gas, and water wells located near hazardous waste injection wells could be possible avenues for the underground-injected hazardous waste to seep up to the surface or into underground drinking water supplies.[14]

■ The continued disposal of "nonhazardous" industrial waste at both municipal solid waste landfills and industrial solid waste facilities and at oil and gas exploration and production sites is not as highly regulated as hazardous waste disposal. In fact, municipal solid waste landfills are more highly regulated than nonhazardous industrial solid waste disposal sites, which often do not require permits, groundwater monitoring, liners, or leachate collection systems despite the dangerous wastes they may contain.

■ Thousands of abandoned industrial waste sites in

AMOUNT OF RCRA HAZARDOUS WASTE GENERATED AND NUMBER OF LARGE-QUANTITY HAZARDOUS WASTE GENERATORS IN THE U.S., TEXAS AND SELECTED STATES, 1995

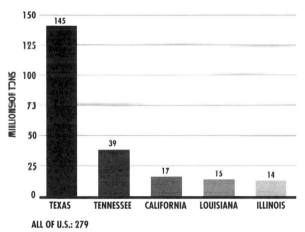

ALL OF U.S.: 279

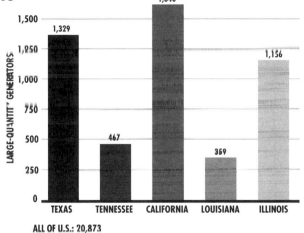

ALL OF U.S.: 20,873

Note: Hazardous waste totals for Texas reported by the EPA and TNRCC vary slightly because of updates in Texas and the inclusion of small-quantity generators in Texas totals.

Source: Environmental Protection Agency, Office of Solid Waste, Biennial RCRA Hazardous Waste Report (Washington, D.C., 1997), ES-10 and Texas Natural Resource Conservation Commission, Trends in Texas Hazardous Waste Management: 1995 Update (June 1997), 1.

Texas will require public management and cleanup well into the twenty-first century.

■ The specific health effects of many toxic substances are not well understood.

INDUSTRIAL SOLID WASTE IN TEXAS: WHO PRODUCES IT?

Historically, Texas has ranked first in the nation in total hazardous waste generated, due to the state's large size and industrial base.[15] In fact, in 1995 Texas industries produced more than 50 percent of the nation's industrial hazardous waste. Industries in Texas reported producing between 60 and 65 million tons of hazardous waste each year from 1986 to 1990. However, a new EPA rule known as the Toxicity Characteristic rule caused many wastes that were previously considered nonhazardous to also be defined as hazardous. For example, the rule made large volumes of wastewater stored in surface impoundments and holding ponds subject to regulation as hazardous wastes if they contained toxic levels of certain chemicals such as benzene, lead, and arsenic. The new rule forced industries to discontinue the use of surface impoundments for holding and treating these large volumes of waste, and to begin

treating them in wastewater treatment tanks and facilities. Because of this rule, the amount of hazardous wastes from 1990 to 1991 doubled.[16] In 1993 data showed that Texas industries generated about 181 million tons of hazardous waste, while in 1995 Texas industries generated 148 million tons.[17]

Thus, in 1995, while 18.7 million Texans, commercial businesses, and institutions, as well as some

INDUSTRIAL HAZARDOUS WASTE GENERATED IN TEXAS, 1986–1995

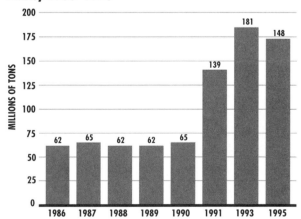

Source: Texas Natural Resource Conservation Commission, Trends in Texas Hazardous Waste Management: 1995 Update (June 1997), 1.

WHO GENERATES SOLID WASTE IN TEXAS?

INDUSTRY

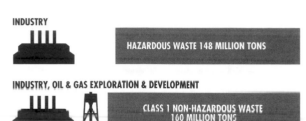

HAZARDOUS WASTE 148 MILLION TONS

INDUSTRY, OIL & GAS EXPLORATION & DEVELOPMENT

CLASS 1 NON-HAZARDOUS WASTE
160 MILLION TONS

INSTITUTIONAL, RESIDENTIAL & COMMERCIAL

MUNICIPAL WASTE
21.6 MILLION TONS

MUNICIPAL WASTEWATER TREATMENT PLANTS

LAND APPLICATION OF SLUDGE
123,200 TONS

Municipal Waste includes residential, commercial and institutional waste, as well as a small percentage of non-hazardous industrial waste and construction debris.

Sludge includes only sludge that is sent to sludge land-application sites, not sludge that goes directly to municipal waste landfills.

Note: All figures represent 1995 totals, except Class I, which is for 1993.

Source: Texas Natural Resource Conservation Commission, Trends in Hazardous Waste Management: 1995 Update *(1997) and Texas Natural Resource Conservation Commission,* Needs Assessment for Industrial Class I Non-Hazardous Waste Commercial Dispsal Capacity in Texas, *(1996).*

GENERATION OF HAZARDOUS WASTE BY INDUSTRY, 1995

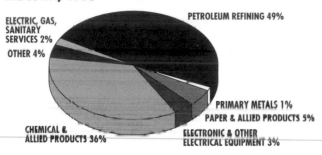

ELECTRIC, GAS, SANITARY SERVICES 2%

OTHER 4%

PETROLEUM REFINING 49%

PRIMARY METALS 1%
PAPER & ALLIED PRODUCTS 5%

CHEMICAL &
ALLIED PRODUCTS 36%

ELECTRONIC & OTHER
ELECTRICAL EQUIPMENT 3%

Source: Texas Natural Resource Conservation Commission, Trends in Texas Hazardous Waste Management: 1995 Update *(June 1997), 2.*

industries, discarded about 21.6 million tons of solid waste into municipal landfills and burned about 50,000 tons of solid waste in municipal incinerators, some 9,000 businesses, commercial institutions, and industries produced 148 million tons of hazardous waste. Still, both these numbers represent reductions in the amount of waste generated compared to 1993. Industries—including the oil and gas exploration and development industry—also produced another 160 million tons of Class 1 nonhazardous wastes in 1993.[18] In 1992 Texas also led the nation in the amount of toxic chemicals released on site or transferred off site (see box: What Are "Toxics" and Where Do They Go?).[19]

In 1991 more than 80 percent of the industrial hazardous waste generated in Texas was from facilities in Harris, Galveston, Brazoria, Nueces, and Harrison counties.[20] By 1995 these five counties still accounted for 77 percent of all hazardous waste generated (see *Counties* section for a full list).[21] Most hazardous waste in Texas is generated by two industrial sectors that are located in these Gulf Coast areas: petroleum refining, and chemicals and allied products. For example, in 1987 these two industrial classifications accounted for 76 percent of all waste generated. By 1995 they accounted for more than 85 percent, a slight decrease from 1993, when they accounted for 90 percent.[22] Most of the increase between 1987 and 1993 was due to the new wastewater rule, since these industries produce large volumes of wastewater.[23]

The top 11 producers of hazardous waste in Texas generated 52 percent of all hazardous waste in Texas in 1995.[24] In fact, 99 percent of all hazardous waste generated in 1995 in Texas was produced by 102 of the 9,281 facilities reporting to the TNRCC.[25] Still, volume—how much you produce—does not necessarily correspond to how hazardous the waste stream is to human health and the environment, and many of the large companies did significantly reduce hazardous waste generation between 1991 and 1995.[26]

INDUSTRIAL SOLID WASTE: WHERE DOES IT GO?

Industrial solid waste can be managed either on site—at the facility where it is generated—or off site at commercial facilities. Whether on-site or off-site, industrial solid waste can be disposed of through the use of municipal and industrial wastewater facilities;

THE TOP 25 FACILITIES PRODUCING HAZARDOUS WASTE IN 1995 AND 1991

RANK	COMPANY	COUNTY	MILLIONS OF TONS OF HAZARDOUS WASTE 1991	MILLIONS OF TONS OF HAZARDOUS WASTE, 1995
1	Amoco Oil Company	Galveston	27.8	18.0
2	Dow Chemical Co.	Brazoria	8.5	9.3
3	Phillips 66	Brazoria	7.5	8.6
4	Lyondell-CITGO Refining Company	Harris	<0.1	6.2
5	Texas Eastman Co.	Harrison	5.7	6.2
6	Shell Oil Company	Harris	19.4	6.2
7	Monsanto Co.	Brazoria	2.4	5.5
8	E.I. DuPont De Nemours & Co.	Victoria	4.0	4.5
9	Champion International Corp.	Angelina	NR	4.4
10	Champion International Corp.	Harris	NR	4.1
11	Fina Oil and Chemical Co.	Jefferson	NR	3.6
13	Koch Refining Company	Nueces	3.1	3.3
14	Valero Refining Company	Galveston	<0.1	3.2
15	Crown Central Petroleum	Harris	3.3	3.1
16	Air Products, Incorporated	Harris	0.6	3.0
17	CITGO Refining & Chemicals Co.	Nueces	3.2	3.0
18	Lyondell Petrochemical	Harris	2.9	2.9
19	Coastal Refining & Marketing	Nueces	4.2	2.8
20	E.I. DuPont De Nemours & Co.	Jefferson	1.8	2.5
21	Arco Chemical Co.	Harris	1.8	2.3
22	Sterling Chemicals	Galveston	2.2	2.2
23	Rollins Environmental Services	Harris	<0.1	2.2
24	Dow Chemical Company	Harris	1.9	1.8
25	SGS-Thomson Microelectronics, Inc.	Dallas	0.6	1.8
Top 25 in 1995			140.0	94%
Total in 1995			148.1	100%

Notes: NR = not reporting in 1991. Several companies changed names or ownership between 1991 and 1995. Only the name as it was reported in 1995 appears.

Source:Texas Natural Resource Conservation Commission, Waste Ranking Report 1991 and 1995, Industrial Solid Waste System.

land disposal facilities such as landfills, waste pits—principally for petroleum exploration waste—and deep underground injection wells; and incineration or waste-to-energy facilities like cement kilns. A variety of treatment, recycling, and other management options also exist for many types of industrial wastes.

About 99 percent of hazardous wastes are managed on site at the facility itself or treated and discharged through a wastewater treatment facility. About 87 percent of all hazardous wastes are man-

aged through wastewater treatment facilities.[27] Once the level of hazardous waste is decreased to a certain level by treatment, the water is then discharged, either through a publicly owned (wastewater) treatment works or from the industrial facility itself. Most of the other waste managed on site is injected underground into deep wells.[28]

EXPORTS, IMPORTS, AND COMMERCIAL TREATMENT OF HAZARDOUS WASTE

Only one percent of hazardous waste in Texas was

INDUSTRIAL HAZARDOUS WASTE – WHERE DID IT GO IN 1995?

ON-SITE   OFF-SITE

INCINERATION
571,700 TONS

WATER TREATMENT
134,853,700 TONS

PRETREATMENT AND DISCHARGE
TO PUBLIC SEWAGE TREATMENT
591,100 TONS

STORAGE
19,000 TONS

LANDFILL AND LAND
TREATMENT 91,300 TONS

ENERGY OR THERMAL
RECOVERY 619,700 TONS

OUT OF STATE
252,200 TONS

CAPTIVE FACILITIES
186,900 TONS

DEEP-WELL INJECTION
206,800 TONS

RECYCLING/
TREATMENT/OTHER
55,600 TONS

DEEP-WELL INJECTION
17,939,100 TONS

RECYCLING/TREATMENT
372,000 TONS

INCINERATION/CEMENT KILNS/
FUEL BLENDING 221,400 TONS

LANDFILLING
10,800 TONS

TOTAL ON-SITE: 154,447,500 TONS   **TOTAL OFF-SITE: 1,543,800 TONS**

TOTAL HAZARDOUS WASTE IN 1995: 155,991,300 TONS

Source: Texas Natural Resource Conservation Commission, Trends in Texas Hazardous Waste Management: 1995 Update *(June 1997), 2.*

treated off site in 1995. That year, 513,600 tons of hazardous waste were treated at commercial facilities and 591,100 tons were discharged to publicly owned wastewater treatment plants in Texas; 197,600 tons were sent out of state to commercial facilities; and another 241,500 tons went to other "captive" facilities owned by the same company either in Texas or in other states.[29] In 1991 Texas became a net importer of hazardous waste—importing more waste

than it exported. This trend continued in 1995.[30] Most of the imported hazardous waste went to commercial deep-well injection facilities, while most of the exported hazardous waste went to landfills and zinc-recovery facilities.[31]

In addition to these hazardous wastes, in 1993 Texas facilities sent 309,760 tons of Class 1 nonhazardous wastes—out of 160 million tons generated—to commercial facilities.[32] Only a few facilities in the state manage only nonhazardous industrial waste

TEXAS INDUSTRIAL NON-HAZARDOUS CLASS I WASTE – WHERE DID IT GO IN 1993?

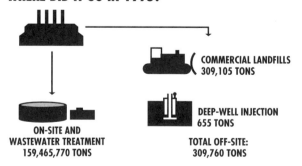

COMMERCIAL LANDFILLS
309,105 TONS

DEEP-WELL INJECTION
655 TONS

ON-SITE AND
WASTEWATER TREATMENT
159,465,770 TONS

TOTAL OFF-SITE:
309,760 TONS

TOTAL: 159,775,530 TONS

Note: All of the Class I waste sent to commercial Deep-Well Injection facilities went out of the state, and about half of the waste sent to landfills went out-of-state.

Source: Waste Planning and Assessment Division, Needs Assessment for Industrial Class I Non-hazardous Waste Commercial Disposal Capacity in Texas *(July 1996), Table 2.*

INDUSTRIAL HAZARDOUS WASTE – EXPORTS AND IMPORTS

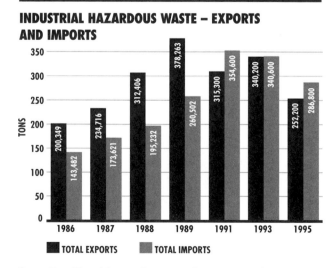

Source: Texas Natural Resource Conservation Commission, Trends in Texas Hazardous Waste Management: 1995 Update *(June 1997), Figure 5.*

INDUSTRIAL HAZARDOUS WASTE – WHERE DID WE EXPORT HAZARDOUS WASTE IN 1995?

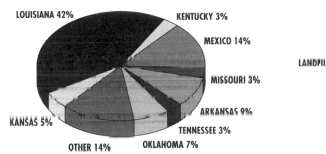

LOUISIANA 42%
KENTUCKY 3%
MEXICO 14%
MISSOURI 3%
ARKANSAS 9%
TENNESSEE 3%
OKLAHOMA 7%
OTHER 14%
KANSAS 5%

PERCENTAGE BY STATE
TOTAL EXPORTS: 252,200 TONS

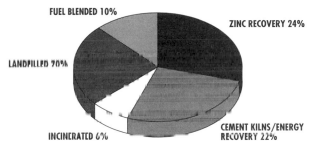

FUEL BLENDED 10%
ZINC RECOVERY 24%
LANDFILLED 70%
CEMENT KILNS/ENERGY RECOVERY 22%
INCINERATED 6%

MANAGEMENT OF EXPORTED WASTE
AT COMMERCIAL FACILITIES

Source: Texas Natural Resource Conservation Commission, Trends in Texas Hazardous Waste Management: 1995 Update (June 1997), 11 and Table 4.

commercially, and most of these facilities are landfills. Other management options include hazardous commercial facilities and, in some cases, municipal solid waste facilities.

About 95 percent of Class I nonhazardous wastes are inorganic or organic liquids contained in aqueous solutions—primarily wastewaters—which are then treated at on-site or off-site wastewater treatment facilities. Inorganic and organic sludge, ash thermal residue from cement kilns and incinerators, and organic and inorganic solids make up most of the rest of this waste stream.

CAPACITY TO TREAT INDUSTRIAL WASTES

While it is difficult to estimate whether companies will reduce or increase their generation of hazardous wastes, there appears to be no shortage of available disposal space in Texas for Class I industrial wastes.[33] Both landfills and underground injection wells had enough capacity to handle the estimated generation of Class 1 waste in 1998. The issue is more complex for hazardous wastes. The TNRCC estimated that there would be sufficient capacity at existing facilities to manage Texas hazardous wastes in the year 2000 in most categories, including incineration and recovery technologies, landfilling, fuel blending, and underground injections.[34]

However, TNRCC estimated that Texas does not have enough commercial capacity to manage the demand for the following five categories of technology:[35]

INDUSTRIAL HAZARDOUS WASTE – WHERE DID WE IMPORT HAZARDOUS WASTES FROM IN 1995?

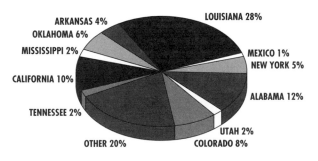

ARKANSAS 4%
OKLAHOMA 6%
MISSISSIPPI 2%
CALIFORNIA 10%
TENNESSEE 2%
OTHER 20%
UTAH 2%
COLORADO 8%
LOUISIANA 28%
MEXICO 1%
NEW YORK 5%
ALABAMA 12%

PERCENTAGE BY STATE
TOTAL IMPORTS: 286,800 TONS

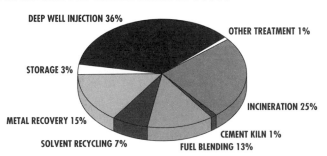

DEEP WELL INJECTION 36%
OTHER TREATMENT 1%
STORAGE 3%
METAL RECOVERY 15%
SOLVENT RECYCLING 7%
FUEL BLENDING 13%
CEMENT KILN 1%
INCINERATION 25%

MANAGEMENT OF IMPORTED WASTE
AT COMMERCIAL FACILITIES

Source: Texas Natural Resource Conservation Commission, Trends in Texas Hazardous Waste Management: 1995 Update (June 1997), 14 and Table 3.

CLASS I NONHAZARDOUS WASTE GENERATION BY TYPE IN 1993

Asbestos-Contaminated Waste	63,030
Ash/Slag	288,935
Contaminated Soil	227,080
Contaminated Solids	262,440
Inorganic Sludges	1,056,930
Inorganic Solids	304,945
Inorganic/Organic Liquids	151,496,025
Organic Sludges	3,833,380
Organic Solids	712,185
Organic Mixed with Inorganic	1,560
PCB-Containing Wastes	19,660
Petroleum-Contaminated Waste	74,940
Total	159,775,530

Source: Texas Natural Resource Conservation Commission, Waste Planning and Assessment Division, Needs Assessment for Industrial Class I Non-hazardous Waste Commercial Disposal Capacity in Texas (July 1996), Table 1.

- zinc recovery;
- other recovery;
- biological treatment for aqueous organic wastes;
- reduction and other treatment for aqueous inorganic treatment: and
- destruction technologies, such as reduction and neutralization of inorganic compounds, biological treatment, and carbon adsorption, among others.

Nevertheless, the demand for these types of waste management technology is relatively low and can be met by other states or countries. For example, Texas facilities have been sending their zinc wastes to a zinc-recovery facility in Monterrey, Mexico, for many years.

ACROSS THE BORDER WOES

Maquiladoras are manufacturing plants located in Mexico that import at least 75 percent of their raw materials, assemble them in Mexico, and export a finished product, usually to the United States. In early 1999 there were nearly 3,000 maquiladoras in Mexico, 2,250 located in the four Mexican states—Chihuahua, Coahuila, Nuevo León. and Tamaulipas—along the Texas-Mexico border.[36] Most of these maquiladoras are at least partially owned by U.S. corporations and use U.S. raw materials to make products such as semiconductors, electronic components, textiles, chemicals, and auto parts.

Under both Mexican law and the La Paz Agreement—an environmental agreement signed by the United States and Mexico in 1983—the wastes from the production process must also be returned to the country from which the raw materials were imported.[37] Despite this requirement, however, Texas commercial facilities reportedly treated only 1,140 tons of hazardous waste from Mexico in 1995, most of which went to fuel-blending facilities for later incineration or for underground injection.[38] Only 11,057 tons of hazardous waste were exported from Mexico to the United

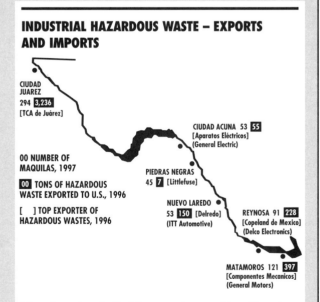

INDUSTRIAL HAZARDOUS WASTE – EXPORTS AND IMPORTS

CIUDAD JUAREZ
294 3,236
[TCA de Juárez]

CIUDAD ACUNA 53 55
[Aparatos Eléctricos]
(General Electric)

00 NUMBER OF MAQUILAS, 1997

00 TONS OF HAZARDOUS WASTE EXPORTED TO U.S., 1996

[ ] TOP EXPORTER OF HAZARDOUS WASTES, 1996

PIEDRAS NEGRAS
45 7 [Littlefuse]

NUEVO LAREDO
53 150 [Delredo]
(ITT Automotive)

REYNOSA 91 228
[Copeland de Mexico]
(Delco Electronics)

MATAMOROS 121 397
[Componentes Mecanicos]
(General Motors)

Note: Less than half of the waste imported into Texas is managed within the state. Most goes to other states.

Source: Number of Maquilas from Secretariat of Commerce and Industrial Development, Government of Mexico, 1997; Tons of hazardous waste and top exporter from the Environmental Protection Agency, Region VI, HAZTRAKS Database, 1998.

States in 1997, about half of which passed through Texas before being deposited, either in Texas or in

Continued on next page

other states.[39] While little is known about the actual amount of hazardous waste generated in maquiladoras, evidence suggests that the volume of hazardous waste is many times higher than what is returned. The World Bank, for example, estimated that 80 percent of the hazardous waste is not repatriated but remains stored on-site or is otherwise illegally disposed of in Mexico.[40] The government of Mexico estimated in 1994 that only 12 percent of the estimated 8 million tons of hazardous waste generated in Mexico is properly disposed of within Mexico or exported legally.[41]

In 1993 the EPA implemented a new hazardous waste tracking system, called HAZTRAKS, to better track how much hazardous waste was being imported from Mexico and also to help determine if hazardous waste regulations were being violated. The computer system uses "cradle-to-grave" hazardous waste manifests to record the waste from its initial generation and transport to its disposal. EPA officials are sent manifests from U.S. Customs about a week after the shipments cross the border, while the final manifests finally are entered into HAZTRAKS some four to six months after the

border crossing. In addition, Mexico has provided information to the system from the import and export documents that companies file with the Mexican government. In 1998 Mexico began a new compatible computer and reporting system that should help improve HAZTRAKS.[42]

IMPORTS OF HAZARDOUS WASTE OF MEXICO INTO THE UNITED STATES., 1991–1997 (IN TONS)

1991	5,779
1992	6,826
1993	9,836
1994	10,513
1995	8,510
1996	6,983
1997	11,057

Source: Environmental Protection Agency, Region VI and IX, HAZTRAKS Database, 1998.

Mexico bans the import of hazardous waste for disposal. However, the country does allow the import of waste if it will be recycled or recovered. For example, in 1995 Texas industries shipped about 35,000 tons of hazardous waste to a commercial zinc-recovery facility in Matamoros, Mexico.[43]

RADIOACTIVE WASTES

Since the splitting of the atom, both uranium and plutonium have been used to create bombs, provide medical supplies, and furnish energy. Not surprisingly, these uses create waste management problems: what do you do with materials that stay radioactive for tens of thousands of years? The disposal of most radioactive materials is regulated under the Atomic Energy Act of 1954 and subsequent amendments, as well as by a radioactive material licensing program established by the Uranium Mill Tailings Radiation Control Act of 1978. While some states are subject to direct control by the Nuclear Regulatory Commission (NRC), a federal agency, Texas has been delegated authority by this agency and has its own laws and regulations relating to the use of radioactive materials and radioactive waste disposal.

Radioactive waste is divided into four categories: low-level radioactive waste, high-level radioactive waste, naturally occurring radioactive material, and transuranic waste.

Low-level Radioactive Waste

Low-level radioactive waste includes all tools, instruments, pipes, syringes, paper, water, soils, and protective clothing such as gloves contaminated with radioactive materials. Nationwide, about 80 percent of low-level radioactive waste by volume is from nuclear power plants. Low-level "fuel-related" radioactive wastes such as sludge, resins and evaporator bottoms from cleaning the large volumes of water used at nuclear power reactors, and clothes, paper, and filters contaminated by radioactive waste make up one category of nuclear-generated waste.

WHAT ARE "TOXICS" AND WHERE DO THEY GO?

Since 1987 all major manufacturing industries have had to report their releases and transfers of more than 300 individual toxic chemicals and 20 toxic chemical compounds—chemicals that have been determined to be harmful to humans or the environment. These toxic chemical release data are reported to both the EPA and the TNRCC. In 1994 an additional 34 chemicals were added to the reporting list, while in the 1995 reporting year another 282 chemicals and chemical compounds were added, bringing the total to nearly 650.

Texas facilities in 1997 released 218.5 million pounds of these toxic chemicals into the air, water, and land—both above and below the ground—while transferring another 459.5 million pounds to other authorized facilities for wastewater treatment, recycling, energy recovery, treatment, storage, and disposal.[44] Texas is the largest volume producer of toxic chemical releases and off-site transfers in the country. However, Texas is also the second largest state in terms of population and has the largest concentration of chemical products and petroleum refining industries.

Taking into account only a common set of chemicals reported between 1987 and 1997, Texas showed a 43.6 percent reduction in overall on-site releases, a 10.7 percent reduction in transfers to wastewater treatment plants, and a 35.6 percent reduction in transfers for disposal. At the same time, transfers for recycling increased nearly 90 percent between 1991 and 1996. The amount of on-site releases and disposal between 1996 and 1997 were nearly identical, while transfers from treatment and other off-site management actually increased.[45] Interpreting these numbers is difficult. Each year there are a different number of facilities reporting. The amount of toxic releases and transfers is affected by the amount of production and general economic conditions. Still, several major companies have significantly reduced toxic releases over the past 10 years (see Source Reduction section).

(Sources: Information from TNRCC, Toxics Release Inventory Program, Office of Pollution Prevention and Recycling.)

Low-level "neutron-activated waste" from the intense bombardment of reactor parts with radioactive neutrons is a second category of low-level radioactive waste. Finally, hospitals and other medical facilities also produce low-level radioactive wastes. About 1.4 million cubic feet of low-level radioactive wastes were disposed of in the United States in 1991—enough to fill about 280 boxcar loads.[46] Currently, three commercial sites are receiving low-level radioactive waste in South Carolina, Utah, and Washington.[47]

In Texas, mining, power plants, industries, hospitals, and university research facilities generate about 20,000 cubic feet per year of low-level radioactive waste.[48] By volume, about one-third of this low-level radioactive waste comes from Texas's two nuclear power reactors: the South Texas Project in Matagorda County, and the two-unit Comanche Peak Project in Somervell County.[49]

By the amount of radioactivity—as measured in a radioactivity scale known as curies—nuclear power plants account for at least 70 percent of the state's low-level radioactive waste.[50] While most radioactive waste produced in Texas stays radioactive less than 100 years, about one percent—again associated with power plants—will remain radioactive for thousands and even hundreds of thousands of years.[51]

Federal and state definitions of low-level radioactive waste differ. In Texas, low-level radioactive waste includes radioactive waste that has a half-life of 35 years or less and fewer than 10 nanocuries per gram of transuranics, as well as wastes with half-lives of more than 35 years if special criteria for the disposal of the waste are established by the TNRCC.[52] The federal definition, on the other hand, considers any radioactive waste that has less than 100 nanocuries per gram of transuranics low-level.[53]

TOXICS RELEASED ON-SITE AND TREATED OFF-SITE IN TEXAS, 1987 TO 1997 (UNITS IN MILLIONS OF POUNDS, ONLY THOSE CHEMICALS REPORTED IN COMMON DURING PERIOD)

	1987	1988	1989	1990	1991	1992	1993	1994	1995	1996	1997	NET % CHANGE
Non-point Air	91.1	91.7	80.5	72.3	67.9	65.7	59.0	55.2	45.3	42.3	35.1	-61.5%
Point Air	88.0	95.8	88.0	80.6	77.2	71.1	63.0	58.4	64.6	63.0	50.3	-42.8%
Total Air	179.1	187.4	168.3	152.7	145.0	136.9	121.7	113.3	109.7	104.9	85.4	-52.3%
Water Releases	1.4	1.6	1.7	1.2	0.8	12.7	0.6	2.1	0.6	0.5	1.0	-32.7%
Underground Injection	71.5	80.6	87.0	81.5	77.5	62.7	59.8	58.7	71.9	54.2	52.9	-26.0%
Land Releases	31.5	33.2	19.9	15.8	12.4	17.3	15.0	13.2	11.9	14.7	20.8	-33.9%
Impoundments	0.4	12.6	12.2	3.7	10.2	10.4	12.2	10.1	9.6	11.4	14.7	16.9%*
Total On-Site Releases	283.9	302.8	276.8	235.5	235.5	229.4	197.1	187.3	193.9	174.8	160.0	-43.6%
Publicly Owned Treatment Works (POTW)	33.2	35.3	26.5	25.3	20.2	23.6	17.7	19.5	23.8	19.5	29.6	-10.7%
Off-site Disposal	30.3	19.5	20.9	19.8	15.8	14.3	13.8	14.2	13.6	12.3	19.5	-35.6%
Off-Site Treatment	37.5	34.5	37.8	27.7	27.0	27.3	20.2	26.6	32.4	20.5	18.9	-49.5%
Transfers for Energy Recovery									107.0	75.1	83.2	-22.3%
Transfers for Recycling									142.9	198.6	149.0	4.3%
Total On-site Releases and Off-site Treatment & Disposal	384.9	392.3	362.3	328.9	298.8	294.9	249.1	248.1	264.2	225.2	228.1	-38.1%

Notes: Numbers represent only totals for toxic chemicals reported in common between 1987-1997, not all chemicals reported. The percentage change for impoundment releases was calculated from 1988 to 1997, since so few impoundments were reported in 1987. Totals do not include energy recovery and recycling total, which are only shown for 1995-1997.

Source: Texas Natural Resource Conservation Commission, Toxics Release Inventory Program, Office of Pollution Prevention and Recycling, 1999.

FYI *Each cubic foot of low-level radioactive waste costs between $350 and $500 to ship and manage at a proper waste management facility.*

(Source: Susan Jablonski, Texas Low-Level Radioactive Waste Disposal Authority, phone interview by author, September 1994, Austin.)

Texas's nuclear plants—as well as many of the state's universities and industries—sent their radioactive wastes to a low-level radioactive facility in Barnwell, South Carolina, until July 1994, when the facility temporarily closed. The two nuclear plants in Texas currently store their nuclear wastes on-site in above-ground facilities, while hospitals and universities either store such waste on-site or send it to a centralized storage facility in Fort Stockton, Texas.[54]

In 1981 the Texas legislature created the Low Level Radioactive Waste Disposal Authority to develop a state site to manage these wastes. In 1991 the legislature ordered the Waste Disposal Authority

to locate the site in Hudspeth County, and in 1992 a site was approved in Hudspeth County, about seven miles from Sierra Blanca. In 1996 the TNRCC proposed a draft permit for the site. However, several individuals, cities, counties, and organizations from both sides of the border opposed the permit, and in 1997 the State Office of Administrative Hearings ordered a hearing to decide whether to recommend denying or granting the permit. In July 1998 the hearings examiners in the case recommended that the TNRCC deny the permit because the applicant failed to characterize the fault directly beneath the site and failed to address potential negative socio-economic impacts from the proposed facility.[55] In October 1998 the TNRCC denied the permit. Finally, in 1999, the Texas legislature eliminated the TRLLWDA, transferring all of its functions to the TNRCC.

A compact between the States of Texas, Vermont, and Maine contemplates the disposal of low-level

WHERE DO TOXICS GO? TOXIC WASTE MANAGEMENT AND RELEASES IN 1997

Total facilities reporting: 1,217

ON-SITE AIR EMISSIONS
108,366,675 LBS

ON-SITE SURFACE WATER DISCHARGES 20,788,710 LBS

ON-SITE UNDERGROUND INJECTION 89,929,406 LBS

ON-SITE LAND TREATMENT
21,263,351 LBS

IMPOUNDMENTS
14,714,640 LBS

TOTAL ON-SITE RELEASES:
240,348,142 LBS

OFF-SITE TO PUBLICLY-OWNED TREATMENT WORKS
46,834,323 LBS

OFF-SITE TRANSFERS FOR TREATMENT
33,478,664 LBS

OFF-SITE TRANSFERS FOR DISPOSAL
21,361,837 LBS

OFF-SITE TRANSFERS TO RECYCLING FACILITIES
149,033,594 LBS

TOTAL OFF-SITE TRANSFERS:
333,897,698 LBS

TOTAL ON-SITE AND OFF-SITE: 574,245,840 LBS

Source: Texas Natural Resource Conservation Commission, Toxics Release Inventory Program, Office of Pollution Prevention and Recycling, 1999.

radioactive waste from these three states in Texas. In 1998 the U.S. Congress approved the compact. The TNRCC is attempting to locate another site to dispose of wastes from the three states. Waste Control Specialist, a private waste management company, currently manages a hazardous waste landfill and radioactive storage facility in Andrews County and has proposed disposing and managing low-level radioactive waste there.

FYI ☞ *Only 1.4 million cubic feet of low-level radioactive waste was generated in 1990 nationwide, while experts of the nuclear waste disposal industry in the late 1970s were predicting as much as five million cubic feet by that date. (Source: Office of Technology Assessment, Partnership Under Pressure [Washington, D.C., 1989].)*

TOXIC RELEASES BY TYPE OF INDUSTRY, 1996

Chemicals and Allied Products	191.8
Petroleum Refining and Related Industries	25.9
Paper and Allied Products	7.9
Food and Kindred Products	4.2
Rubber and Miscellaneous Plastics Products	4.2
Fabricated Metal Products	3.3
Transportation Equipment	2.9
Primary Metal Industries	4.9
Stone, Clay, Glass and Concrete Products	2.4
Lumber and Wood Products	2.1
Industrial and Commercial Machinery and Computer Equipment	1.2
Electronic and Other Electrical Equipment and Components	0.6
Others	1.2

Total: 252.6 Million Pounds

Note: All figures in millions of pounds.

Source: Toxics Release Inventory Program, Office of Pollution Prevention and Recycling, Texas Natural Resource Conservation Commission.
Defense Industry "Retirement Plan for the Grandfathered Exemption," Texas Natural Resource Conservation Commission, National Outlook (Spring 1998), 7.2.

TOXIC TRANSFERS TO RECYCLING, ENERGY RECOVERY, TREATMENT & DISPOSAL FACILITIES AND TO PUBLICLY-OWNED TREATMENT WORKS BY TYPE OF INDUSTRY

Chemicals and Allied Products	159.4
Primary Metal Industries	103.0
Fabricated Metal Products	22.6
Petroleum Refining and Related Industries	15.4
Electronic and Other Electrical Equipment	34.9
Industrial and Commercial Machinery and and Computer Equipment	2.1
Paper and Allied Products	5.0
Transportation Equipment	4.4
Rubber and Miscellaneous Plastics	1.1
Food and Kindred Products	0.9
Lumber and Wood	0.5
Others	1.1

Total Transfers: 350.4 million pounds

Note: All figures in millions of pounds.

Source: Texas Natural Resource Conservation Commission, Toxics Release Inventory Program, Office of Pollution Prevention and Recycling.

TOXIC RELEASES BY TOP 40 COUNTIES, 1997

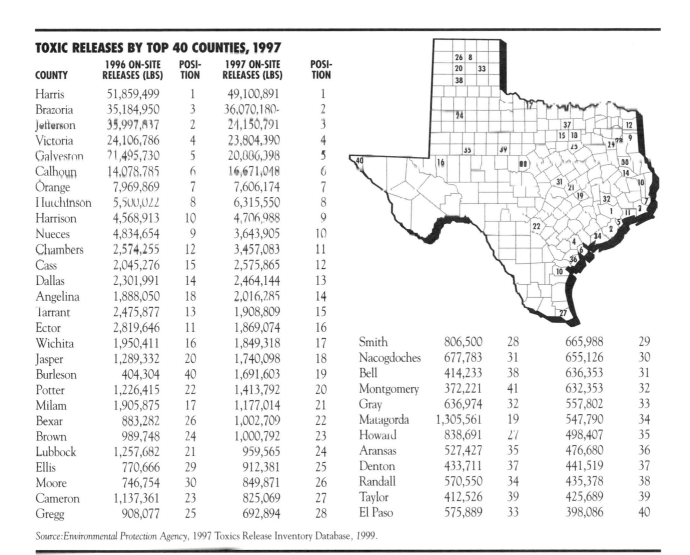

COUNTY	1996 ON-SITE RELEASES (LBS)	POSITION	1997 ON-SITE RELEASES (LBS)	POSITION
Harris	51,859,499	1	49,100,891	1
Brazoria	35,184,950	3	36,070,180-	2
Jefferson	35,997,837	2	24,150,791	3
Victoria	24,106,786	4	23,804,390	4
Galveston	21,495,730	5	20,006,398	5
Calhoun	14,078,785	6	16,671,048	6
Orange	7,969,869	7	7,606,174	7
Hutchinson	5,500,022	8	6,315,550	8
Harrison	4,568,913	10	4,706,988	9
Nueces	4,834,654	9	3,643,905	10
Chambers	2,574,255	12	3,457,083	11
Cass	2,045,276	15	2,575,865	12
Dallas	2,301,991	14	2,464,144	13
Angelina	1,888,050	18	2,016,285	14
Tarrant	2,475,877	13	1,908,809	15
Ector	2,819,646	11	1,869,074	16
Wichita	1,950,411	16	1,849,318	17
Jasper	1,289,332	20	1,740,098	18
Burleson	404,304	40	1,691,603	19
Potter	1,226,415	22	1,413,792	20
Milam	1,905,875	17	1,177,014	21
Bexar	883,282	26	1,002,709	22
Brown	989,748	24	1,000,792	23
Lubbock	1,257,682	21	959,565	24
Ellis	770,666	29	912,381	25
Moore	746,754	30	849,871	26
Cameron	1,137,361	23	825,069	27
Gregg	908,077	25	692,894	28
Smith	806,500	28	665,988	29
Nacogdoches	677,783	31	655,126	30
Bell	414,233	38	636,353	31
Montgomery	372,221	41	632,353	32
Gray	636,974	32	557,802	33
Matagorda	1,305,561	19	547,790	34
Howard	838,691	27	498,407	35
Aransas	527,427	35	476,680	36
Denton	433,711	37	441,519	37
Randall	570,550	34	435,378	38
Taylor	412,526	39	425,689	39
El Paso	575,889	33	398,086	40

Source:Environmental Protection Agency, 1997 Toxics Release Inventory Database, 1999.

High-level Radioactive Waste

High-level radioactive waste includes radioactive material that results from the reprocessing of nuclear fuel, from spent fuel rods removed from a nuclear power reactor (a machine that splits atoms to make radioactive heat to boil water used for electricity generation); and from nuclear weapons. High-level radioactive waste is currently being stored on-site at weapons manufacturing plants and power plants around the nation until a permanent disposal site can be located.[56] One potential site, Yucca Mountain in Nevada, is being considered as a repository for high-level waste, including spent nuclear fuel.

By 1990 the nation's nuclear plants had produced more than 20,000 tons of high-level radioactive waste.[57] Texas's two nuclear power plants produce spent fuel rods and other high-level nuclear waste, which is stored in pools of water at the reactors.

Naturally Occurring Radioactive Material

Naturally occurring radioactive materials (often referred to as NORMs) include waste resulting from the mining of uranium and phosphate and from a number of other industrial activities, such as oil and gas production. The mining of uranium results in mountains of radioactive waste referred to as "tailings"—one example of material classified as naturally occurring radioactive material. Tailings are the radioactive soil and sand left on the ground after uranium ore has been crushed and processed for its

TOXIC TRANSFERS TO TREATMENT, DISPOSAL, RECYCLING AND ENERGY RECOVERY FACILITIES BY TOP 40 COUNTIES, 1997

COUNTY	1996 OFF-SITE TRANSFERS (LBS)	POSI-TION	1997 OFF-SITE TRANSFERS (LBS)	POSI-TION
Harris	85,164,140	1	99,070,967	1
El Paso	19,911,007	3	22,922,912	2
Victoria	15,015,404	4	15,946,745	3
Ellis	12,421,089	5	12,082,215	4
Calhoun	11,730,104	7	11,724,323	5
Dallas	11,885,491	6	9,578,780	6
Orange	10,800,741	8	8,992,064	7
Grayson	7,722,243	10	8,577,403	8
Leon	7,737,429	9	8,364,529	9
Guadalupe	6,419,655	13	6,973,850	10
Chambers	7,695,331	11	6,568,570	11
Jefferson	6,371,165	14	5,105,906	12
Brazoria	3,684,647	18	3,963,501	13
Nueces	1,096,125	25	3,667,105	14
Fannin	4,145,341	17	3,646,282	15
Brown	4,568,635	16	3,592,023	16
Galveston	5,853,495	15	3,318,438	17
Travis	1,956,485	22	2,986,991	18
Tarrant	2,678,747	19	2,460,610	19
Taylor	2,514,745	21	2,450,609	20
Matagorda	1,879,715	23	2,292,973	21
Ector	1,011,263	26	1,533,326	22
Collin	7,576,349	12	1,498,547	23
Webb	1,700,395	24	1,361,049	24
Live Oak	979,355	28	1,180,131	25
Morris	2,557,290	20	1,148,950	26
Bexar	51,569,003	2	1,126,714	27
Gregg	763,299	30	928,962	28
Smith	809,537	29	763,033	29
Harrison	603,388	32	582,140	30
Kaufman	745,028	31	566,529	31
Fort Bend	550,944	33	551,398	32
Bowie	222,702	42	509,254	33
Grimes	524,817	34	504,234	34
Cameron	484,629	35	428,237	35
Washington	246,427	40	348,940	36
Denton	273,506	39	335,951	37
Wichita	467,294	36	304,910	38
Bell	166,429	46	214,687	39
San Patricio	990,073	27	201,076	40

Note: Figures do not include transfers to Publicly-Owned Treatment Works.

Source: Environmental Protection Agency, 1997 Toxics Release Inventory Database, 1999.

radioactivity. These wastes contain uranium and radium as well as a number of toxic chemicals. Increased incidence of cancer in some mine workers has been associated with their exposure to these wastes.[58]

In addition, coal power production, oil and gas exploration and production, fertilizer production, and water treatment can all produce wastes classified as naturally occurring. For example, the insides of oil extraction pipes may be coated with radium, or radium may be brought up to the surface while drilling for oil.[59] Naturally occurring radioactive wastes are managed apart from other radioactive and toxic wastes.

Naturally occurring radioactive material waste is regulated in Texas by both the Railroad Commission and the Texas Department of Health. Oil and gas producers that are removing pipes from the ground which might contain traces of uranium or other radioactive materials must first get a license from the Department of Health. If they intend to export the waste to another site in Texas, that disposal site must be licensed by the Railroad Commission. As of January 1998, only two disposal sites—Newpark

TOP 20 TEXAS FACILITIES RANKED BY TOTAL TOXIC ONSITE RELEASES, 1995-1997

FACILITY NAME	CITY	COUNTY	TOTAL POUNDS OF ON-SITE RELEASES 1996	1997
1. DuPont	Victoria	Victoria	23,820,115	23,521,289
2. BASF Corp.	Freeport	Brazoria	16,473,532	16,561,781
3. BP Chemicals Inc.	Port Lavaca	Calhoun	10,739,674	13,742,915
4. Sterling Chemicals	Texas City	Galveston	10,312,538	10,923,054
5. DuPont	Beaumont	Jefferson	10,909,250	8,991,168
6. Solutia Inc. (Monsanto Co.)	Alvin	Brazoria	7,652,029	7,380,081
7. Amoco Petroleum Products	Texas City	Galveston	5,219,046	5,366,276
8. Dow Chemical Co.	Freeport	Brazoria	4,771,909	4,715,514
9. Hoechst-Celanese Chemical	Pasadena	Harris	8,574,861	4,198,818
10. Arco Chemical Co.	Channelview	Harris	3,505,347	3,944,725
11. Mobil Oil Beaumont Refinery	Beaumont	Jefferson	3,635,879	3,476,237
12. Texas Eastman Chemical Co.	Longview	Harrison	3,704,987	3,393,586
13. Bayer Corporation	Baytown	Chambers	2,371,440	3,250,461
14 Exxon Chemical Americas	Baytown	Harris	2,017,393	3,093,385
15. GNI Chemicals Corp. Inc.	Deer Park	Harris	544,354	2,986,750
16. DuPont	Orange	Orange	3,317,924	2,754,353
17. ISP Techs. Inc.	Texas City	Galveston	3,607,197	2,584,673
18. International Paper Co.	Domino	Cass	2,045,276	2,575,865
19. Phillips 66 Co.	Borger	Hutchinson	2,342,695	2,543,625
20. DuPont	La Porte	Harris	2,641,805	2,506,368

Note: Includes Off-site Transfers for Disposal.

Source: Environmental Protection Agency, 1997 Toxics Release Inventory Database, 1999.

TOP 20 TEXAS FACILITIES RANKED BY TOTAL OFF-SITE TREATMENT, DISPOSAL, ENERGY RECOVERY AND RECYCLING TRANSFERS, 1997

FACILITY NAME	CITY	COUNTY	TOTAL POUNDS TRANSFERRED 1996	1997
1. Asarco Inc.	El Paso	El Paso	13,068,332	17,525,187
2. Lyondell Petrochemical	Victoria	Victoria	13,836,433	15,049,606
3. Shell Oil Co.	Deer Park	Harris	11,288,655	11,620,555
4. Formosa Plastics Corp.	Point Comfort	Calhoun	11,027,612	11,367,182
5. Chapparral Steel Midlothian	Midlothian	Ellis	12,028,850	11,364,950
6. Arco Chemical Co.	Pasadena	Harris	8,148,519	10,446,793
7. Hoechst-Celanese Corp.	Pasadena	Harris	7,026,000	9,974,200
8. Millennium Petrochemical	La Porte	Harris	6,735,663	9,004,597
9. Nucor Steel-Texas	Jewett	Leon	7,737,429	8,364,529
10. Kwikset Corp.	Denison	Grayson	7,341,119	7,920,764
11. Hoechst-Celanese Chemical	Pasadena	Harris	6,303,439	7,329,400
12. Structural Metals Inc.	Seguin	Guadalupe	6,381,655	6,945,850
13. Fina Oil & Chemical Co.	Pasadena	Harris	5,822,550	5,663,245
14. GNB Techs. Inc.	Farmers Branch	Dallas	7,781,997	5,410,000
15. North Star Steel Texas	Rose City	Orange	5,592,704	4,881,683
16. Bayer Corp. Baytown	Baytown	Chambers	6,229,330	4,698,570
17. General Cable Corporation	Bonham	Fannin	4,145,341	3,479,732
18. Wyman-Gordon Forgings Inc.	Houston	Harris	4,117,573	3,322,224
19. Superior Cable	Brownwood	Brown	4,333,056	3,321,948
20. American Chrome & Chemicals	Corpus Christi	Nueces	201,150	3,160,000

Note: Totals do not include transfers to Publicly-owned Treatment Works (POTWs).

Source: Environmental Protection Agency, 1997 Toxics Release Inventory Database, 1999.

Environmental Services in Winnie, Texas, and Lotus, L.L.C. in Andrews County—were authorized by the Railroad Commission to receive naturally occurring radioactive material waste.[60] Both use pits and injection wells to dispose of the waste.

The mineral uranium is primarily used by the nuclear power industry to produce energy, although it can also be used to make nuclear weapons. In Texas, uranium has been mined for decades. Uranium used to be strip-mined, much as coal is mined. This mining process results in tailings. These tailing materials are placed in ponds, which often have neither natural or synthetic liners. Some ponds have leaked, contaminating soils and subsurface aquifers, as well as emitting radioactive gases into the atmosphere.[61]

While no uranium strip-mines are currently operating in Texas, three companies are involved in reclamation projects at five different uranium mining sites.[62] In addition, four tailings and waste sites— where the uranium was milled and extracted from the ore—in Karnes and Live Oak counties are being closed and covered to prevent further contamination of subsurface aquifers or radioactive waste emissions. During the operation of mill sites, the tailings ponds are used as receptacles for the by-products of the ore process. During closure, the mill site and other facilities are decontaminated and any material is placed in the tailing ponds. The tailing pond is then dewatered and the impoundment is surrounded by a clay cap and radon barrier. Three of the tailing sites—run by Chevron, Exxon, and Conoco—are being supervised by the Texas Department of Health with support from the TNRCC. The Department of Energy is supervising cleanup of a fourth tailing pond in Falls City, Karnes County, an area that produced and processed uranium for the defense industry.[63] The Department of Energy site has cost about $35 million, 90 percent of which has been covered by the federal government.[64] The tailings pond sites have resulted in groundwater contamination, including one confirmed case at the Chevron facility in 1996.[65] In 1997 the Texas legislature transferred the jurisdiction to regulate the recovery and processing of uranium and thorium, as well as

the disposal of uranium by-products, from the TNRCC to the Texas Department of Health.[66]

Since 1975, 34 sites that use injection wells, rather than a strip mining operation, have been permitted to mine uranium. The injection process does not result in tailings. However, only two of these sites—one in Kleberg County and another in Duval County owned by Uranium Resources Inc.— were mining as of November 1997.[67] Most of the other in situ mining facilities have been closed down and cleaned up and are awaiting a final inspection survey from the Texas Department of Health before being decommissioned by the Nuclear Regulatory Commission.[68] These in situ or "solution" mines are considered by state agency regulators to present fewer environmental problems than strip-mines because liquids are pumped underground to dislodge uranium, which is then pumped out through wells. Temporary settling ponds that store water, sand and precipitate, and drilling liquids must be lined but do not have to be covered.[69] However, spills, accidents, and leaks can still occur at such facilities. Waste generated by in situ uranium facilities can be sent to authorized disposal facilities or to tailing sites. Presently, uranium mining operations in Texas are sending their waste to Envirocare of Utah or to one of several tailing impoundments in Utah and Wyoming that are still open to receive by-product waste.[70]

Transuranic Waste

Transuranic waste, or TRU, includes waste containing plutonium and other elements heavier than uranium which contain more than 100 nanocuries of alpha-emitting isotopes. Transuranic waste is produced mainly from the reprocessing of spent nuclear fuel rods, nuclear weapons production, and reactor fuel assembly. The main producer of transuranic waste is the Department of Energy's nuclear weapons production facilities. In 1999 the department began sending transuranic waste for disposal at natural underground salt formations near Carlsbad, New Mexico. This locale is known as the Waste Isolation Pilot Plant, or WIPP. While the site was certified by the EPA in 1998, it still must receive an operating permit from the New Mexico Environment Depart-

LIST OF URANIUM MILLING AND RECOVERY RADIOACTIVE MATERIAL LICENSEES AND APPLICATIONS, JULY 1997

COMPANY NAME	FACILITY NAME	COUNTY	STATUS
TAILINGS PONDS			
Exxon Corporation	Ray Point	Live Oak	Post-Closure Observation
Conoco, Inc.	Conquista	Karnes	Post-Closure Observation
Chevron Resources	Panna Maria	Karnes	Under Closure
Department of Energy Site	Falls City	Karnes	Post-Closure Observation
IN SITU MINES			
Chevron Resources	Palangana Dome	Duval	Under Closure
Everest	Hobson Plant	Karnes	Under Closure
Exploration, Inc.	McBryde WDW	Duval	Under Closure
	Tex-1	Karnes	Under Closure
	Mt. Lucas	Live Oak	Under Closure
IEC, Inc.	Lamprecht	Live Oak	Under Closure
	Zamzow	Live Oak	Under Closure
	Pawnee	Bee	Under Closure
Malapai Resources (Cogema)	Holiday/El Mesquite/	Duval	Standby
	O'Hern	Webb	
Total Minerals Co. (Cogema)	West Cole	Duval & Webb	Under Closure
URI, Inc.	Benavides/Longoria	Duval	Under Closure
	Kingsville Dome	Kleberg	Active, Seeking Permit to Expand
	Rosita	Duval	Active
	Vasques	Duval	Permit Application Pending
	Alta Mesa	Brooks	Permit Application Pending
USX Corporation	Burns Ranch/Clay West	Live Oak	Under Closure
Westinghouse	Bruni	Webb	Closure, Pending Termination

Source: Texas Department of Health, Bureau of Radiation Control, July 1997.

ment before it can receive other types of radioactive and hazardous waste.[71]

In Texas, tons of plutonium from the nation's nuclear arsenal are being stored at the Pantex nuclear weapons plant some seventeen miles northeast of Amarillo in Carson County. About 2,000 nuclear weapons are being dismantled there each year and stored at the plant site.[72] The Pantex plant is owned by the Department of Energy and operated under contract by Mason and Hangar-Siles Mason Co. In 1994 the plant was declared a Superfund site and is currently undergoing cleanup.

INDUSTRIAL CHOICES: HIERARCHIES OF INDUSTRIAL SOLID WASTE MANAGEMENT

As in the case of municipal solid waste, the State of Texas and the EPA have created a hierarchy or a set of priorities for how best to manage industrial solid

waste, whether nonhazardous or hazardous.[73] In decreasing order of preference, these priorities are:

1. Source reduction;
2. Reuse or recycling of waste;
3. Treatment to neutralize hazardous characteristics;
4. Treatment to reduce hazardous characteristics;
5. Underground injection; and
6. Land disposal

SOURCE REDUCTION

The best means of getting rid of waste is to reduce the amount generated at the source, a process known as source reduction, while waste minimization activities such as reusing and recycling seek to return the waste stream into a production process or alternative use, thus leading to both economic and environmental benefits.

Traditional approaches to managing waste have relied on regulatory measures, like those under the

DEFINITIONS AND APPROACHES TO WASTE REDUCTION

Source reduction: as applied by Texas law, means reducing the amount of any hazardous or nonhazardous substance entering any waste stream or released into the environment prior to recycling, treatment, or disposal.

Waste minimization: a practice that reduces the environmental or health hazards associated with hazardous wastes, pollutants, or contaminants; examples may include reuse, recycling, neutralization, and detoxification.

Source separation: a process that keeps hazardous waste from nonhazardous waste, preventing all the waste from being managed as hazardous waste; it does not necessarily reduce the total volume of waste, only its hazardous components.

Recycling and reuse: the process of removing a substance from a waste and returning it to productive use. Recycling can take place at a plant, where the waste is reused within the production process itself. Waste can also be recovered off site. A third form of recycling is to send the waste to another industry through an interindustry exchange. Used solvents, zinc, and other metals and acids are commonly recycled.

Substitution of raw materials: a process that replaces a raw material that results in hazardous waste with one that results in less hazardous wastes or none at all.

Manufacturing process changes: a method that consists of either eliminating a process that produces waste or changing the process so that a waste is no longer produced.

Substitution of products: eliminating the use of a hazardous material; for example, by substituting creosote-preserved wood posts with concrete posts, no hazardous wastes will leach from the posts.

(*Source:* EPA, Solving the Hazardous Waste Problem: EPA's RCRA Program [*November 1986*], 19; *Texas Water Commission,* Case Studies of Source Reduction & Waste Minimization by Texas Industries [*March 1992*].)

RCRA, which set up management techniques to control wastes at the "end-of-the-pipe." But these technologies are not fail-safe. Pollution may still occur. Moreover, public opposition to siting almost any type of commercial hazardous waste facility has made it difficult to build new facilities. The increasing cost of meeting regulations is another factor in the search for an approach that avoids creation of waste in the first place.[74]

The source reduction and waste minimization approaches, usually called pollution prevention strategies, are often seen as flexible alternatives to regulation and ultimately as forms of regulatory relief. Nevertheless, the very existence of tough regulations , emission controls, and adequate enforcement can spur companies to adopt pollution prevention strategies.[75]

HAZARDOUS WASTE REDUCTION PROGRAMS IN TEXAS

Texas has relied on voluntary programs to encourage source reduction activities. These programs include:
■ Waste Reduction Policy Act of 1991. This act requires that facilities that generate more than 100 kilograms a month of hazardous wastes or that release toxic chemicals under the Toxics Release Inventory Program develop: (1) a waste minimization and source reduction plan; (2) an executive summary of the plan that must be available for public viewing; and (3) an annual progress report.

By the end of 1997, more than 1,800 companies had submitted source reduction and waste minimization plans to the TNRCC. About 4,500 companies in all are expected to file these site-specific plans by 1999.[76] According to the TNRCC, Texas industrial facilities projected that between 1992 and 1997, 50 million tons of hazardous waste would not be

TRACKING INDUSTRIAL ENVIRONMENTAL PERFORMANCE

How do you track the environmental performance of corporations? How do you encourage cleaner production processes?

The World Resources Institute suggests establishing four environmental performance indicators that can be easily tracked over time and presented at the facility level:
1. materials use or inputs;
2. energy consumption, including both the quantity and type;
3. nonproduct output (waste); and
4. pollutant releases, including both toxic releases and greenhouse gases.

At the state and national levels, various efforts have been made to give the public and the regulators a better sense of whether environmental performance goals are being met. For example, the State of Texas requires all major manufacturing companies to prepare a waste minimization and source reduction plan, the executive summary of which is available to the public. In addition, each of these same companies must produce an annual report that tracks its progress toward meeting these goals.

At the national level, the EPA is building on the success of the Toxics Release Inventory Program. First, this program has been expanded to include more chemicals and more types of industries. Secondly, the EPA has proposed a new program called the Sector Facility Indexing Project. This program combines TRI data with data from other programs like the RCRA, the Clean Air Act, pollution permit violations, and even the

FOUR KEY ENVIRONMENTAL PERFORMANCE INDICATORS ILLUSTRATED FOR A COMPUTER MANUFACTURER

Source: Daryl Ditz and Janet Ranganathan, Measuring Up: Toward a Common Framework for Tracking Corporate Environmental Performances (Washington, D.C.: World Resources Institute, July 1997).

demographics of the community surrounding individual facilities in the oil producing, steel, metals, auto, and paper industries. In addition, the data are being "weighted" based upon the danger of the chemicals emitted or produced. This will help the public have a better understanding not only of how much waste and emissions are being increased or reduced but of the qualitative aspects of that data.

(Sources: Daryl Ditz and Janet Ranganathan, Measuring Up: Toward a Common Framework for Tracking Corporate Environmental Performance [Washington, D.C.: World Resources Institute, July 1997]; John H. Cushman, Jr., "E.P.A. Is Pressing Plan To Publicize Pollution Data," New York Times, August 12, 1997, A1.)

generated because of source reduction activities. Facilities had met about 80 percent of this goal by 1994.[77] Source reduction is a measure of how much waste does not get generated, a measure that takes into account production and production efficiency. While companies are required to submit the plans, how they choose to reduce pollution, and whether in fact they do at all, is strictly voluntary.

■ TNRCC's Texas Clean Industries 2000. This voluntary program was begun in 1992. Industries that join this program commit to carry out a plan to reduce hazardous or toxic waste by 50 percent from 1987 levels by the year 2000.

As of March 1997, 163 companies had joined the Texas Clean Industries 2000 program, pledging to cut their hazardous waste generation by 67 percent and their TRI chemical releases by 63 percent between 1987 and 2000.[78] If program participants do not successfully meet their goals, there is no penalty except for potentially being removed from the program. However, according to preliminary data, between 1988 and 1997, program participants did reduce TRI chemical releases by 114.4 million pounds, or around 35 percent.[79] These same facilities also cut hazardous waste generation by 15.3 million tons between 1992 and 1994.[80] In addition, as part of the program, participants must sponsor community environmental programs and citizen communication programs.

■ In 1993 the state's voters approved a constitutional amendment known as Proposition 2, which grants property-tax exemptions for pollution control equipment (see box: Pollution Control Taxes in Texas).

Through its Office of Pollution Prevention and Recycling, TNRCC has instituted a variety of other source reduction and waste minimization programs including:

■ More than 100 pollution prevention workshops to assist companies and local governments in developing recycling and source reduction plans.

■ Site assessment visits by environmental engineers and other specialists from TNRCC to assist companies in addressing environmental problems According to the TNRCC, 351 Texas industrial facilities received this technical assistance between 1994 and 1997, which led to more than 171,600 tons of reduced hazardous and nonhazardous waste and $70 million saved in labor, raw material purchases, and avoided disposal costs.[81]

■ Trans/Mexico Border Program to help U.S. and

POLLUTION CONTROL TAXES IN TEXAS

In 1993 the Texas legislature and the voters of Texas approved a constitutional amendment known as Proposition 2. This measure allows new property and equipment used for pollution control to be moved off the tax roles. With such a property-tax exemption, the state gives an incentive for companies to meet and, in some cases, go beyond environmental rules, regulations, or statutes.

Under rules adopted in 1994 to implement Proposition 2, companies can apply to the TNRCC to have pollution control property—a facility, device, or method used to control, reduce, measure or prevent pollution—designated as such. Once such a positive determination is made, the company would then qualify for a property-tax exemption from the local tax assessor. The property must have been installed after January 1, 1994, thus keeping on the tax rolls any pollution control equipment previously subject to property taxes. Examples of new equipment eligible for a Proposition 2 exemption include a scrubber put on an industrial smokestack to meet rules under the Federal Clean Air Act; a dechlorination system in an industry's wastewater plant; or even a change in an industry's production process to prevent the release of a

toxic chemical.

Thirty-three other states offer similar incentives to businesses, and supporters argue that without the measure, industries might prefer locating in another state. Opponents, including some state environmental groups as well as local tax assessor associations, fear the proposal will result in a massive giveaway of property tax revenue to large corporations. Instead, opponents maintained that keeping the environment clean is quite simply a cost of doing business, and businesses should not be given incentives to merely comply with the law.

As of May 1999, 3,962 out of 4,077 applications for pollution control equipment or processes had been certified by the TNRCC for a total of $5.1 billion. About 55 percent of the total valuation— $2.7 billion—was certified from industrial facilities in only three counties: Harris, Jefferson, and Brazoria. Provided their local tax assessor concurs with the valuation, these applicants will not have to pay property taxes on this equipment.

(Sources: Information provided by TNRCC, Proposition Two Division, August 1999; House Research Organization, 1993 Constitutional Amendments: The November 2 Election [August 30, 1993].)

Mexican companies operating in northern Mexico reduce pollution and increase recycling. Between 1993 and 1997, TNRCC personnel along with the Mexican Attorney General for the Environment (PROFEPA) conducted site audits at 14 maquiladora factories in Mexico. The TNRCC personnel performed pollution prevention analyses and made recommendations to the Mexican officials and plant managers.[82]

RECYCLING AND REUSE OF HAZARDOUS WASTES

A variety of industrial wastes can be recycled for use as products. There are three ways in which industrial waste recycling occurs: at the facility itself (on-site recycling), at commercial facilities that gather waste streams from several companies (off-site recycling), and at a company that uses as inputs in its production process the waste products of another company. In 1995, for example, about 17 percent of all Texas-generated hazardous wastes treated at commercial facilities was recycled.[83]

Off-site recycling of some hazardous materials is difficult because of the dangerous nature of the chemicals themselves. Unlike some municipal wastes (such as aluminum) that are fairly easy to recycle, some hazardous chemicals are prone to ignite and can be reactive. In addition, industries' fears of accidents and spills during transportation or recycling operations—and the resulting liability—can sometimes present an obstacle to the recycling of hazardous materials off site.[84] For many products, it is far simpler to dispose of the waste on-site than to exchange it with another company or recycle it.

There is considerable debate about just what recycling is. Under Texas's Waste Reduction Policy Act, companies that burn their hazardous wastes for energy recovery in boilers and industrial furnaces can count the waste as "recycled."

This approach has been criticized by some citizens living near facilities, as well as by environmental groups who argue that using waste as fuel is really a method of disposal and that air pollution is often created in the burning of hazardous wastes. In the TNRCC's Clean Texas Program, companies can

TONS OF TEXAS HAZARDOUS WASTE RECYCLED, 1995

On-Site Recycling and Recovery	372,000
Commercial Metals Recovery	19,300
Commercial Zinc Recovery	59,200
Commercial Solvent Recovery	28,800
Other Commercial Treatment and Recovery	14,800
Total	494,100

Note: Solvent, zinc, other metals and other treatment and recovery are accomplished at commercial facilities both in-state and out-of-state. The chart does not include waste products that are sold or exchanged to another company for use in their production process.

Source: Texas Natural Resource Conservation Commission, Trends in Texas Hazardous Waste Management: 1995 Update (June 1997), Table 4.

meet part of their 50 percent reduction goal by burning waste to recover energy on site; however, companies cannot burn waste off site in cement kilns or other off-site "waste-to-energy" plants to meet their reduction goals.

There are several key aspects of the Texas program for recycling of hazardous waste:

In 1987 the legislature created the Resource Exchange Network for Eliminating Waste (RENEW). This program aids in the recycling of waste by matching companies that have commodities, by-products, surplus materials, or wastes with other businesses that can use these same materials as process inputs. RENEW, run by the TNRCC, serves as an information clearinghouse, classifying wastes by categories. Between 1988 and 1997, RENEW helped transfer 350,000 tons of hazardous and nonhazardous materials from those industries disposing the waste to those using them for production. These transfers helped companies save about $2.2 million in disposal costs and $1.6 million in direct sales.[85]

In addition, the Office of Pollution Prevention and Recycling at TNRCC has assisted companies with on-site visits and workshops to push for recycling as well as source reduction. A special focus has been helping businesses develop in-house recycling programs.

INNOVATIVE TECHNOLOGY: NEUTRALIZING AND DESTROYING HAZARDOUS CHARACTERISTICS OF HAZARDOUS WASTES

A variety of new and emerging technologies can neutralize and, in some cases, even destroy the hazardous characteristics of industrial waste. One new encouraging technology is known as supercritical water oxidation. The process is simple but expensive. Water is heated and pressurized and mixed with organic compounds, which dissolve. Later, oxygen gas is added to the mix, and harmful substances are burned away. What's left is harmless. This gigantic pressure cooker, unfortunately, is very expensive. Less expensive processes may become available; for example, a team at the University of Texas at Austin has developed a working water oxidizer.[86]

Other technologies currently being used in the Texas market include:

■ **Oxidation.** Either humid air or a chemical process is used to remove organic constituents from a water-based hazardous waste stream.

■ **Bioremediation.** This process uses microorganisms bred to have an appetite for hydrocarbons to "eat" oil spills or even heavy metals.[87]

■ **Carbon absorption.** This is a process in which toxic substances adhere to a specially treated carbon surface.

■ **Gas absorption.** Toxic gas is compressed under pressure and vented into an absorbing or reactive unit.

■ **Dechlorination.** This process chemically replaces chlorine with hydrogen or hydroxide ions, leaving chlorinated substances nontoxic.

■ **Neutralization.** This process either makes an acid substance less so by adding alkaline substances, or makes a basic substance more acidic by adding acid.

■ **Oxidation.** This process adds oxygen to substances such as sulfurs, phenols, or cyanides, rendering them nonhazardous.

■ **Precipitation.** This process separates solids from a liquid waste so that the solid portion can be managed more safely.

■ **Vitrification.** This term refers to any process that uses electricity to encase products in glass. For example, electrical currents can be introduced into contaminated soils at such high voltages that the soil vitrifies, or "turns to glass." Other similar systems that chemically or physically reduce the mobility of hazardous constituents include encapsulation and stabilization, either through the use of cement or pozzolana.

REDUCING HAZARDOUS CHARACTERISTICS OF WASTES: BURNING

Incineration reduces and may, in some cases, eliminate hazardous characteristics of waste. In the case of waste-to-energy facilities, it may also provide energy for use in other production processes. However, the burning of hazardous waste in incinerators, boilers, and industrial furnaces (or BIFS) and in cement kilns—which burn waste to produce cement—increases the amount of toxics released to the air (see *Air Quality* chapter). In addition, the ash produced by burning hazardous waste may still be a threat to human health and the environment because it contains such compounds as lead, uranium, and arsenic. Finally, the variety of waste streams received at commercial incineration facilities makes it harder to control the burning process, leading to problems with explosions and toxic plumes.[88]

Until 1986 some utilities, industries, commercial facilities, schools, government institutions, and apartment and home owners across the country burned hazardous waste and used oil for energy recovery purposes.[89] Today, nonindustrial facilities—homes, apartments, schools—are not allowed to burn hazardous wastes or used oils containing toxics. Industrial facilities using hazardous waste or used oil must comply with certain standards and register with both the EPA and the state.[90]

In 1995 about 1.3 million tons of hazardous waste were incinerated or burned for energy or thermal recovery at on-site boilers and industrial furnaces in Texas.[91] An additional 225,900 tons were burned at commercial facilities, including cement kilns. There is an increasing reliance on the burning of wastes; 41 percent of Texas-generated hazardous waste processed and treated off site were burned or blended into fuels for later incineration.[92] This represents an

TONS OF HAZARDOUS WASTE BURNED IN TEXAS INCLUDING IMPORTS, 1995

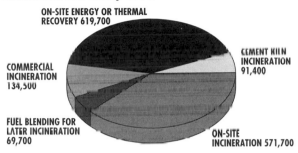

ON-SITE ENERGY OR THERMAL RECOVERY 619,700

CEMENT KILN INCINERATION 91,400

COMMERCIAL INCINERATION 134,500

FUEL BLENDING FOR LATER INCINERATION 69,700

ON-SITE INCINERATION 571,700

TOTAL: 1,487,000
EXPORTS TO INCINERATORS OUT-OF-STATE 20,200
EXPORTS TO CEMENT KILNS OUT-OF-STATE 34,600
EXPORTS TO FUEL BLENDING FACILITIES 19,500

Source: Texas Natural Resource Conservation Commission, Trends in Texas Hazardous Waste Management: 1995 Update (June 1997), Table 3 and 4.

increase from 1991, when about 28 percent of commercial management of hazardous wastes resulted in burning.[93]

Incineration has increased in Texas in large part because of imports of hazardous waste from out-of-state facilities and because of the increase in commercial capacity at one cement kiln.[94] An increase in demand for incineration has also resulted from the federal land disposal rules, which require treatment of hazardous wastes before land disposal. As land disposal has decreased, incineration and deep-well injection of wastes have increased. Hazardous waste imported from out-of-state industries for incineration by Texas facilities increased from 31,000 to nearly 60,000 tons between 1989 and 1995.[95]

Texas Industries Inc, in Midlothian, in Ellis County, is the only cement kiln that uses hazardous waste as fuel. Two other cement kilns in Midlothian —Holnam, Inc., and North Texas Cement Co.— burn tires but are currently not burning hazardous waste, in part due to community pressure against it. Fuel blenders mix a variety of liquid and solid wastes to create a fuel that is then introduced into the kiln of the cement plant. The burning of hazardous wastes in cement kilns creates two main waste "products"— air emissions from the stack, and cement kiln dust leftover from the production of cement. A third product—the cement clinker itself—may also contain traces of hazardous waste.

In addition to Texas Industries, there are 30 hazardous waste incineration facilities located throughout the state. Most of these hazardous waste incineration facilities are owned and operated by

THE DRY PROCESS OF A TYPICAL CEMENT KILN

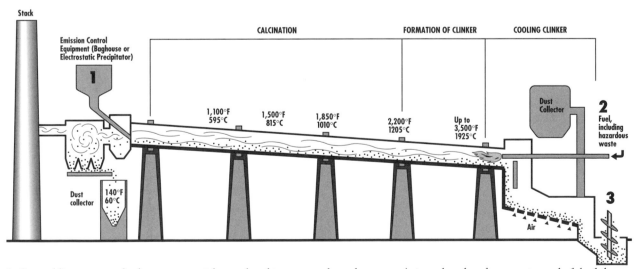

1. Ground limestone and other raw materials are placed in rotating kiln.
2. The ground materials are heated by fuel (which can include hazardous wastes), introduced at the opposite end of the kiln.
3. The final product, called "clinker" is cooled and later ground and mixed with gypsum to form cement.

COMMERCIAL AND ON-SITE HAZARDOUS WASTE INCINERATION FACITLITIES IN TEXAS

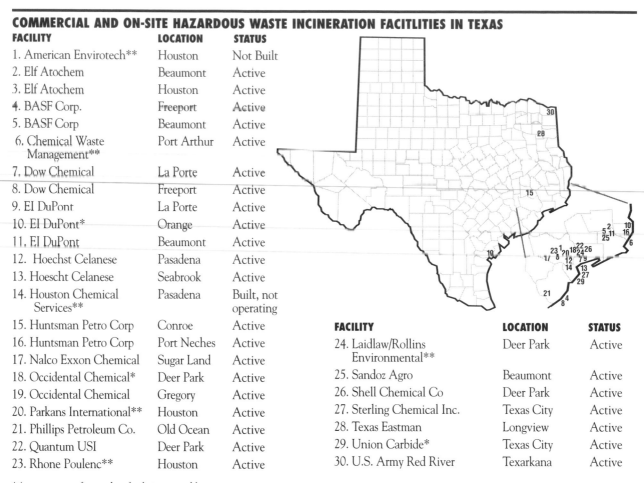

FACILITY	LOCATION	STATUS
1. American Envirotech**	Houston	Not Built
2. Elf Atochem	Beaumont	Active
3. Elf Atochem	Houston	Active
4. BASF Corp.	Freeport	Active
5. BASF Corp	Beaumont	Active
6. Chemical Waste Management**	Port Arthur	Active
7. Dow Chemical	La Porte	Active
8. Dow Chemical	Freeport	Active
9. EI DuPont	La Porte	Active
10. EI DuPont*	Orange	Active
11. EI DuPont	Beaumont	Active
12. Hoechst Celanese	Pasadena	Active
13. Hoescht Celanese	Seabrook	Active
14. Houston Chemical Services**	Pasadena	Built, not operating
15. Huntsman Petro Corp	Conroe	Active
16. Huntsman Petro Corp	Port Neches	Active
17. Nalco Exxon Chemical	Sugar Land	Active
18. Occidental Chemical*	Deer Park	Active
19. Occidental Chemical	Gregory	Active
20. Parkans International**	Houston	Active
21. Phillips Petroleum Co.	Old Ocean	Active
22. Quantum USI	Deer Park	Active
23. Rhone Poulenc**	Houston	Active

FACILITY	LOCATION	STATUS
24. Laidlaw/Rollins Environmental**	Deer Park	Active
25. Sandoz Agro	Beaumont	Active
26. Shell Chemical Co	Deer Park	Active
27. Sterling Chemical Inc.	Texas City	Active
28. Texas Eastman	Longview	Active
29. Union Carbide*	Texas City	Active
30. U.S. Army Red River	Texarkana	Active

*Accepts waste from other facilities owned by same company.
**Commercial; Laidlaw purchased Rollins Environmental.

Source: Texas Natural Resource Conservation Commission, Industrial and Hazardous Waste Division, Office of Waste Management.

companies that treat waste on site from manufacturing facilities owned by the same company. There are presently four commercial incinerators operating in Texas, while two more—American Envirotech in Houston and Houston Chemical Services in Pasadena—are permitted but not yet built. Another commercial facility, Olin Corporation in Jefferson County, is an industrial furnace used for sulfuric acid energy recovery.[96]

Cement kilns currently do not have to meet the same standards as commercial waste incinerators.[97] The main regulations governing cement kilns that burn hazardous wastes are the 1991 Boiler and Industrial Furnace Regulations. These regulations allow Texas Industries to burn hazardous wastes under an interim status in proximity to populations

without the same safety and monitoring standards as commercial incinerators. In 1996 the company applied with the TNRCC for an RCRA Title C permit to burn hazardous wastes and to change the facility from interim status to a fully permitted facility. In 1997, after residents and community organizations opposed the permit, the State Office of Administrative Hearings began a contested-case hearing process to consider whether to recommend granting or denying the permit. In 1999 the judges recommended approving the permit, and the TNRCC has done so.

The 1990 Federal Clean Air Act will require both cement kilns and hazardous waste incinerators to install new pollution control equipment—known as Maximum Achievable Control Technology—to lower air emissions. However, regulations have not been finalized (see *Air Quality* chapter).

Another source of contamination from cement kilns burning hazardous wastes is cement kiln dust, or CKD. When the RCRA was amended in 1980, the law stated that cement kiln dust—unlike incinerator ash—would not be considered as hazardous waste until the EPA undertook a study to determine its human health and environmental impacts. Despite the amendment, the EPA took no action for over a decade. A 1989 lawsuit led to a requirement that the EPA study the problem and come up with regulations by January of 1995. The resulting EPA study found that cement kiln dust was contaminated with dioxins, cadmium, chromium, and lead, among other heavy metals.[98] In addition, the study documented 14 cases in which cement kiln dust had contaminated aquifers of surface waters, and 36 cases in which it had led to air pollution.[99]

Nonetheless, the EPA still has not finalized regulations for the disposal of cement kiln dust. Costs could increase significantly for cement kilns using hazardous waste fuels once final regulations require treatment similar to that required for hazardous waste incinerator ash.[100]

UNDERGROUND INJECTION OF HAZARDOUS WASTES

The disposal of hazardous waste in deep geological formations through the use of underground injection wells is controversial. Texas officials believe injection wells, when operated correctly, are safe; however, many environmental groups are concerned about the heavy reliance on this technology, particularly by the commercial facilities that must manage a wide variety of hazardous wastes. Texas injects more liquid hazardous wastes underground than any other state.[101]

In the 1930s, oil and gas exploration and production companies began injecting saltwater by-products back into the oil-producing underground strata. The first manufacturing industry to use this same technique to inject industrial hazardous waste underground in Texas was DuPont, which began a waste injection operation in 1953. Most underground injection wells in Texas inject the waste into oil-

A TYPICAL UNDERGROUND INJECTION WELL

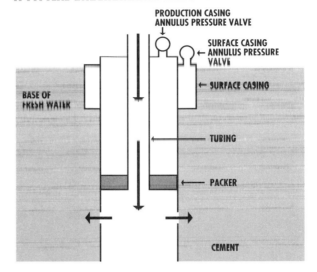

Underground Injection Wells use a technology which injects liquid waste thousands of feet below the ground in porous formations. The liquid waste is held within the strata by pressure from overlying rocks. Underground injection involves drilling a well to a geological formation and pumping, or "injecting" waste to displace the native fluids or gases.

Source: Office of Technology Assessment, Technologies and Management Strategies for Hazardous Waste Control *(Washington, D.C., 1984), 190.*

producing formations.[102]

The 1984 amendments to the RCRA prohibited land disposal, including underground injection, of certain types of hazardous waste without pretreatment. However, if an operator of the injection well can prove the waste will not migrate from the injection zone for 10,000 years, the company can inject hazardous wastes into wells without first treating the waste.

Texas regulates the injection of hazardous waste through permits. About 200 permits to operate injection wells disposing of hazardous or nonhazardous wastes have been granted in Texas since 1961. Currently, 58 hazardous wells are permitted and are currently in service, while 39 nonhazardous wells are permitted and in service.[103] Most are located in the coastal area and dispose of wastes associated with the petrochemical industry. In 1993 there were nine commercial facilities actively receiving hazardous waste. By 1997 there were just six commercial sites, and only two facilities were actively taking hazardous

LOCATION AND 1997 STATUS OF COMMERCIAL HAZARDOUS AND NON-HAZARDOUS WASTE INJECTION WELLS IN TEXAS

FACILITY	TYPE	LOCATION, COUNTY	STATUS
1. Disposal Systems Inc.*	Hazardous Waste	Deer Park, Harris	Active
2. Disposal Systems Inc.	Hazardous Waste	Corpus Christi, Nueces	Active
3. Chemical Waste Mgmt**	Hazardous Waste	Port Arthur, Jefferson	Active
4. Merichem***	Hazardous Waste	Houston, Harris	Not accepting commercial
5. EMPAK****	Hazardous Waste	Deer Park, Harris	Not accepting commercial
6. Odessa Injection Systems	Hazardous Waste	Odessa, Ector	Not accepting commercial
7. Malone Service Company	Hazardous Waste	Texas City, Galveston	Closed
8. Malone Service Company	Hazardous Waste	Texas City, Galveston	Closed
9. Gibraltar Chemical/American Ecology	Hazardous Waste	Kilgore, Smith	Closed
10. Loving County Disposal	Hazardous Waste	Odessa, Ector	Permitted, Not Drilled
11. Thomas Disposal Co.	Non-Hazardous	Perryton, Ochiltree	Active
12. Environmental Processing	Non-Hazardous	Crosby, Harris	Permitted, Under Construction
13. Crossroads Development	Non-Hazardous	Conroe, Montgomery	Active

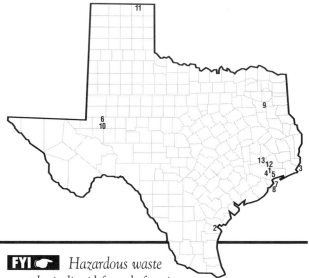

Notes: *Disposal Systems purchased the injection wells from Chemical Waste Management.

**Chemical Waste Management in Port Arthur is currently not accepting wastes from other companies for injection, but only injecting wastes from other Chemical Waste Management facilities. Chemical Waste Management also operates an incinerator in Port Arthur.

***Merichem reclaims oil and gas wastes and sells them to other companies. However, on occassion they inject these wastes.

****EMPAK is not currently injecting wastes, having sold their list of clients to Disposal Systems Inc. They also operate a fuel blending facility.

Source: Texas Natural Resource Conservation Commission, Underground Injection Control Division, 1997 and Texas Natural Resource Conservation Commission, Commercial Hazardous and Industrial Solid Waste Management Facilities (June 1998).

waste for injection from other industrial facilities. Finally, three facilities in Texas have recently been permitted to accept Class I nonhazardous waste on a commercial basis.

In 1995, 18 million tons of hazardous waste were injected at on-site facilities, and another 300,000 tons were injected at commercial facilities.[104] In addition, about 12,500 injection wells used for oil and gas wastes are currently permitted to inject millions of tons of salt water and other wastes underground (see *Water* chapter for a full discussion).[105] In all, there are 53,040 active wells being used for injection of oil and gas wastes, injection of fluid for enhanced oil recovery, and the underground storage of hydrocarbons.[106]

FYI *Hazardous waste must be in liquid form before it can be injected underground. In 1983 the EPA estimated that only four percent of the 11.5 billion gallons of hazardous waste were toxic contaminants; the remainder was water.* (*Source: U.S. General Accounting Office,* Hazardous Waste: Controls over Injection Well Disposal Operations *[1987], 11.*)

Officials agree that waste disposal through properly constructed and operated injection wells is safer and less likely to contaminate surface water or potable ground water than are landfills and other forms of land treatment.[107] For example, injection of hazardous wastes into aquifers that serve or could serve as groundwater supplies for communities is not allowed. However, there are several pathways by which wastes injected underground could contaminate water resources:[108]

■ injection of waste above aquifers containing drinkable water;

■ leakage of waste through inadequate confining beds;

■ leakage of waste through confining beds due to hydraulic fracture or faults;

■ displacement of saline water into a potable aquifer;

■ upward migration of waste liquid from the injection zone along the outside of the well casing;

■ escape into potable aquifers due to well-bore failures; and

■ vertical migration and leakage to land and aquifers through abandoned oil, gas, and other wells.

Because the areas in which deep well injection of hazardous wastes is practiced in Texas are precisely those areas with a long history of oil and gas production, there are many possible routes for vertical migration of hazardous waste to the surface. State and federal regulations require those seeking to inject industrial and hazardous wastes to survey existing wells within their injection area. Still, the possibility exists that old oil and gas wells may not be located or were not adequately plugged, or that migration could occur outside of the injection zone.

FYI ☞ *The Railroad Commission reported that in 1997, there were 281,981 oil and 73,151 gas wells registered by the state, about 125,000 of which were inactive. An estimated 1.58 million wells have been drilled in Texas over the past 80 years, and records indicated that only 522,713 have been plugged. Many of these unplugged wells are potential vehicles for the migration of salt water and hazardous waste injected underground.* (Source: Information provided by letter from Richard Ginn, Oil and Gas Division, Railroad Commission of Texas, January 30, 1998.)

In Texas the only confirmed case where injected hazardous waste contaminated underground drinking water occurred near Beaumont in 1975, before more stringent well-design standards were enacted.[109] Soil contamination also resulted from an industrial injection operation when gas apparently formed within the well, causing the wastes to "blow out," sending

LEADING CHEMICALS INJECTED UNDERGROUND IN TEXAS, 1997

CHEMICAL	POUNDS
Ammonia	17,163,161
Nitric Acid	14,318,405
Nitrate Compounds	8,166,113
Acetonitrile	7,132,129
Methanol	6,742,435
Formic Acid	4,635,013
Acrylamide	3,574,021
Acrylonitrile	3,380,835
Ethylene Glycol	3,253,741
N-Methyl-2-Pyrrolidone	2,562,158
Cyclohexanol	2,416,560
Cyanide Compounds	1,949,480
Phenol	1,270,366
Cresol	1,233,058
Acetamide	1,123,202
Tert-Butyl Alcohol	978,944
Acrylic Acid	799,000
N-Butyl Alcohol	670,519
Hydrogen Cyanide	657,902
Ethylbenzene	559,425
Acetophenone	499,070
Hydrochloric Acid (Aerosols Only)	489,000

Source: Environmental Protection Agency, 1997 Toxics Release Inventory Database, 1999.

wastes into the air and over the land.[110] Spills at the surface during the handling of the wastes prior to injection can also contaminate soils and groundwater prior to injection and have occurred in Texas. In fact, the most likely public health and environmental impacts are from spills and transportation accidents of commercial facilities receiving wastes, not the injection process itself. Citizens who lived near the American Ecology facility—formerly Gibraltar Chemical—in Kilgore, Smith County, filed numerous complaints with the TNRCC concerning spills, air pollution, and health impacts.[111] In addition, the leading cost of reclamation of Class I injection wells is the cleanup of any spills surrounding the well.[112]

Contamination resulting from the injection of salt water and other oil and gas production waste is also of concern to Texans. These injection operators are

MONITORING INJECTION WELLS

The TNRCC emphasizes prevention of leaks rather than after-the-fact groundwater monitoring to ensure that no leaks have occurred in hazardous waste wells. In most cases, no groundwater monitoring is required for hazardous waste injection wells. Instead, operators of industrial hazardous waste injection wells are required to perform an annual mechanical integrity test of the well casing. A space between the tubing in which the waste is injected and a second casing is filled with a pressurized anticorrosive fluid. Since the pressure of the fluid within the well is known, any drop in pressure would indicate a leak in either the tubing or casing.

The usefulness of monitoring wells to detect leakages is hotly debated. There have been cases where groundwater monitoring wells have detected contamination above an injection zone that was not identified by monitoring the pressure within the injection well itself. In addition, environmental groups are concerned that hazardous wastes could migrate beyond the injection zones over the long term, a problem that could be detected only by groundwater monitoring.

(Sources: U.S. General Accounting Office, Hazardous Waste: Controls over Injection Well Disposal Operations [1987]; Office of Technology Assessment, Technologies and Management Strategies for Hazardous Waste Control [Washington, D.C.: March 1983], 195.)

regulated by the Railroad Commission of Texas, rather than the TNRCC or the EPA (see the *Water Quality* chapter for a more complete description of oil and gas wastes and contamination of groundwater). In 1997 there were 77 confirmed cases of groundwater contamination identified as occurring from oil and gas production, including spills and injection wells, which had not been cleaned up.[113]

Acidic chemicals such as nitric acid, formic acid, hydrochloric acid, and acrylic acid are commonly injected in Texas. Opponents of injection wells have argued that these acidic chemicals have the potential to eat away formations and wells and migrate upward to contaminate groundwater.

LANDFILLING HAZARDOUS WASTES IN TEXAS

At the bottom of the TNRCC's hierarchy of hazardous waste management methods is land disposal, be it in a landfill, surface impoundment, land treatment units, or waste piles. Landfills and other forms of land disposal are controversial for a simple reason: past and present experience has shown that such facilities can eventually leak hazardous materials that can contaminate both the nearby soil, surface water, and groundwater (see Groundwater section in *Water Quality* chapter).[114] The Industrial and Hazardous Waste Division of the TNRCC reports that between 1989 and 1997 there were

TYPES OF LAND DISPOSAL

LANDFILLS

SURFACE IMPOUNDMENTS

WASTE PILES

LAND TREATMENT

Landfills are disposal facilities where hazardous and other solid waste are placed into the land. Landfills designed according to RCRA rules must contain systems to collect contaminated surface water run-off as well as synthetic liners below and around the landfill.

Surface Impoundments are depressions or diked areas where solid waste can be stored, disposed of or treated. Pits, ponds, lagoons and basins are all forms of surface impoundments.

Waste Piles are accumulations of solid waste, sometimes used as disposal sites and sometimes as storage facilities.

Land Treatment is a disposal process in which solid waste is applied on top of or mixed into soil. Land application or land farming facilities are examples of land treatment.

Source: Environmental Protection Agency, Solving the Hazardous Waste Problem: EPA's RCRA Program *(Washington, D.C., November 1986).*

approximately 560 hazardous and nonhazardous waste land disposal sites where groundwater had been contaminated with either hazardous or other industrial contaminants.[115]

Texas does not depend on landfills for hazardous waste disposal as much as some states. Less than one percent of hazardous waste managed on site, and only five percent of Texas-generated hazardous waste disposed of off site at commercial facilities, was managed at landfills.[116] Two commercial landfills are currently receiving hazardous wastes in Texas—Waste Control Specialist in Andrews County and TECO in Robstown, Nueces County.[117] Six commercial landfills presently accept Class I nonhazardous waste in Texas.

Under Federal Land Disposal Restriction (LDR) rules, all hazardous waste must be treated before land disposal. Congress required the EPA to establish treatment standards by 1992 for all waste determined to be hazardous in 1984. In addition, Congress required the EPA to establish treatment standards for all "newly identified" hazardous waste within six months of identification. After failing to meet this deadline, and as a result of a lawsuit filed by the Environmental Defense Fund, the EPA established a phased-in schedule for Land Disposal Restriction rules. The EPA is still determining treatment standards for some wastes, such as metal-bearing hazardous wastes. Most mineral waste are exempted from RCRA hazardous waste rules under an amendment known as the Bevill amendment, but the EPA is considering regulating some mineral processing wastes. In 1998 the EPA finalized a rule listing as hazardous wastes four different types of waste from petroleum refining operations, including crude oil storage tank settlement. Another ten types of waste from petroleum refining operations were not listed as hazardous wastes.[118]

The land disposal restrictions have prevented some types of wastes from being disposed of in landfills, further decreasing the demand for this technology.[119] In addition, cleanup of abandoned hazardous waste sites under the Superfund program is now emphasizing cleanup of contaminated soils on site rather than shipment of the soils off site. This

COMERCIAL HAZARDOUS AND NON-HAZARDOUS LANDFILLS IN TEXAS

NAME	TYPE	LOCATION
Texas Ecologists (TECO)	Hazardous	Robstown, Nueces
Waste Control Specialists	Hazardous, Mixed	Andrews County
Browning-Ferris Inc.	Non-Hazardous	Anahuac, Chambers
Browning Ferris Inc.	Non-Hazardous	Sinton, San Patricio
CSC Disposal	Non-Hazardous	Ellis County
Laidlaw Environmental	Non-Hazardous	Deer
Waste Management of TX	Non-Hazardous	Atascocita, Harris
Western Waste Industries of Texas	Non-Hazardous	Montgomery County

Source: Texas Natural Resource Conservation Commission, Industrial and Hazardous Waste Division, 1998.

policy also has also reduced the amount of waste landfilled.[120] Finally, increasing land disposal costs because of RCRA regulations, as well as public opposition and lawsuits over the health impacts of toxic waste landfills, have shifted waste management strategies away from land disposal.

Despite more stringent regulations and permitting requirements, not all disposal of industrial waste into landfills or surface impoundments is closely monitored or requires a permit (see box: Who Doesn't Need a Hazardous Waste Permit in Texas?). For example, most on-site facilities that manage nonhazardous industrial waste do not meet the same strict standards applicable to facilities that manage hazardous waste or even municipal waste landfills.[121] Yet many Class I wastes are toxic and potentially dangerous to human health and the environment.

Of special concern in Texas is the oil and gas industry. Presently, the oil and gas industry disposes of its wastes through a variety of mechanisms. Under Statewide Rule 8, the Railroad Commission of Texas regulates the surface storage and disposal of oil and gas wastes and brine-retention facilities. Currently, there are 47 land farming facilities—where soils are mixed with the waste—permitted for disposal of oil and gas waste, and there are 4,824 pits permitted for storage and disposal of oil and gas wastes or reten-

WHO DOESN'T NEED A HAZARDOUS WASTE PERMIT IN TEXAS?

All facilities in Texas that generate hazardous wastes are subject to regulations, including requirements for proper registration, labeling, containers, and disposal. However, the following types of facilities and processes are usually exempt from Texas hazardous waste permitting requirements:

■ Transfer facilities.

■ Generators that store, treat, or dispose of nonhazardous waste, including Class 1 industrial waste, on-site.

■ Generators that store hazardous wastes in tanks, chip-pads, or containers for less than 90 days.

■ Small quantity generators that produce less than 1,000 kilograms of hazardous waste a month, provided that no more than 6,000 kilograms are stored for more than 180 days and only one

kilogram or less per month is "acutely" hazardous.

■ Facilities that treat their waste in units directly connected to an industrial production process, where waste streams are never released into the environment.

■ Some wastewater treatment units, including municipal wastewater treatment facilities and industrial wastewater facilities regulated by the Federal Clean Water Act.

■ Some recycling operations on a case-by-case basis (only the recycling process itself is exempt).

■ Farmers disposing of pesticides.

■ Clean up of Superfund sites.

■ Emergency response cleanup.

(Source: TNRCC, Industrial and Hazardous Waste Division.)

---

tion of brine. Of the approximately 4,900 land disposal sites permitted by the Railroad Commission, only 52 require groundwater monitoring (see *Water Quality* chapter for more information on oil and gas wastes).[122]

ENFORCING PROPER MANAGEMENT OF INDUSTRIAL WASTE

About 12,000 Texas facilities are subject to industrial or hazardous waste regulations. As a result of inspections and complaint investigations, the TNRCC issued 259 notices of violations to facilities

DUMPING NEAR THE BORDER: MEXICO'S RESPONSE

Controversial plans to locate hazardous and radioactive waste facilities near the border have generated opposition from a new source: Mexico. Mexico is concerned that such facilities could contaminate the Rio Grande, which divides Texas from Mexico, as well as underground aquifers that traverse both sides of the border.

For example, a proposal to build a 600-acre hazardous waste and PCB landfill near Dryden, about fifteen miles from the border, was opposed by the City of Del Rio, the National Park Service, the adjacent Mexican state of Coahuila, and many others. Chemical Waste Management eventually withdrew its permit application after the executive director of the TNRCC and the EPA concluded that the company had failed to demonstrate that it could adequately monitor groundwater underneath

the proposed site.

The Mexican government sent diplomatic notes to the U.S. State Department, citing Article 2 of the La Paz Agreement and protesting this landfill and a proposal for radioactive materials landfill proposed by Texcor near Brackettville. Both governments agreed to protect a strip 62 miles wide on each side of the border from environmental degradation. The TNRCC rejected the Texcor landfill application in 1993.

In the previously discussed matter of the Sierra Blanca waste site, the State Office of Administrative Hearings approved the participation of several Mexican political representatives, including a city council member of Ciudad Juárez, as "parties" to the 1998 contested-case hearing.[123]

NUMBER OF NOTICES OF VIOLATIONS ISSUED FOR INDUSTRIAL AND HAZARDOUS WASTE VIOLATIONS, 1989–1998

FISCAL YEAR	NUMBER OF VIOLATIONS
1989	469
1990	438
1991	1,005
1992	506
1993	480
1994	NA
1995	1,077
1996	304
1997	293
1998	253

Note: The high number of violations in 1991 was due to the failure of many industries to file an annual report with the Texas Natural Resource Conservation Commission, as required.

Source for 1989-1993: Texas Natural Resource Conservation Commission, Enforcement Section, Hazardous and Industrial Waste Division, 1995.
Source for 1995-1998: Texas Natural Resource Conservation Commission, Final Annual Enforcement Report Fiscal Year 1997 (December 17, 1997) and Final Annual Enforcement Report Fiscal Year 1998 (December 1998).

in FY 1997.[124] Many alleged violations are quickly resolved. Violations included, among others, operating without a permit, not storing waste safely, not monitoring groundwater, not determining if a waste is hazardous; and violating land disposal restrictions.[125]

If a company does not take adequate measures to remedy the problem cited in a violation, the TNRCC can seek penalties and an order requiring the company to take specific action. Most of these orders, however, are handled through a negotiation process known as an "agreed order." In FY 1996 and 1997, the TNRCC issued 69 industrial waste agreed orders, requiring companies and facilities to pay more than $1.6 million in fines and $2.4 million in supplemental environmental projects.[126] Because these agreements can sometimes involve a series of remedial actions, as well as penalties, it can often take a year or more to fully resolve the violations.[127]

RESTRICTED AREAS: KEEP OUT

Long before RCRA and the Texas Solid Waste Disposal Act were passed to regulate the storage and disposal of hazardous waste, manufacturing indus-

tries, the national defense industry, and the oil and gas industry were producing and disposing of hazardous wastes. Many of these waste disposal sites, as well as production facilities, have closed down, been abandoned, or changed ownership several times, often without the new owners fully understanding what they have inherited. Not surprisingly, these abandoned and near-abandoned waste sites have contaminated water and surface water and caused adverse human health effects. The Comprehensive Environmental Response, Compensation and Liability Act (CERCLA) was passed by Congress in 1980 to provide funding to clean up these facilities and waste sites. As part of the act, a trust fund of $1.6 billion was authorized over five years. Since then, Congress has twice re-authorized CERCLA, increasing funding from $1.6 billion to $13.6 billion.[128] These funds are to be used to help clean up abandoned and closed hazardous waste sites that are placed by the EPA on a national priority list if they meet certain conditions under a hazard ranking system.[129] About 75 percent of total cleanup costs, however, have come from the responsible parties.

As of August 1999 there were 1,225 dump sites on the final Superfund list. In addition, another 4,600 hazardous sites have had hazardous waste removed under emergency removal action but are not on the list itself.[130] Industrial solvents are present at 87 percent of Superfund sites; inorganic compounds, including lead, at 87 percent; and pesticides, at 50 percent.[131] All told, 41 million people live within four miles—and 4.6 million people live within one mile—of one of these top-priority dump sites.[132]

By early August 1999, 33 sites in Texas were included on, and 3 were proposed for, the federal Superfund list. Six others were on the National Priority List but have since been cleaned up.[133] In addition, the Texas legislature amended the Solid Waste Disposal Act in 1985 to create the State Superfund Program. If a site is not eligible for the national list and cannot be resolved through an agreed order with a responsible company, it can be become part of the State Superfund program. As of September 1998, 42 sites were considered "active" state Superfund sites, one previously on the list was

ACTIVE STATE AND NATIONAL SUPERFUND SITES IN TEXAS, 1999

NATIONAL SUPERFUND SITES

A. Harris County Sites:
   Brio Refining
   Crystal Chemical
   Dixie Oil Processors
   French Limited
   Geneva Industries
   Highlands Acid Pit
   Industrial Transformer (Many
   Diversified Interests)
   North Cavalcade St.
   Sikes Disposal Site
   Sol Lynn/Industrial Transformers
   South Cavalcade St.
B. Pantex Plant, Carson County
C. Odessa Chromium #1, Ector County
D. Odessa Chromium #2, Ector County
E. Air Force Plant #4, Tarrant County
F. Longhorn Army Ammunition
   Plant, Harrison County
G. RSR Lead Smelter, Dallas County
H. Texarkana Wood, Bowie County
I. Lone Star Ammunition, Bowie County
J. Koppers, Bowie County
K. Bailey Waste Disposal, Orange County
L. Petro-Chemical Systems, Liberty County
M. United Creosoting, Montgomery County
N. Sheridan Disposal, Waller County
O. MOTCO, Galveston County
P. Tex-Tin, Galveston County
Q. ALCOA, Calhoun County
R. Rockwool Industries, Bell County
S. Jasper Creosoting Company and Hart
   Creosoting Company, Jasper County
T. State Marine of Port Arthur,
   Jefferson County
U. City of Perryton Well No. 2, Ochiltree Co.

STATE SUPERFUND SITES

1. Houston Scrap,
   Harris County
2. Double R. Plating Company,
   Cass County
3. Pioneer Oil and Refining Co.,
   Bexar County
4. Precision Machine and Supply,
   Ector County
5. Sonics International, Eastland County
6. Maintech International, Jefferson County
7. Federated Metals, Harris County
8. Higgins Wood Preserving, Angelina County
9. Gulf Metals Industries, Inc, Harris County
10. Marshall Wood Preserving, Harrison County
11. Texas American Oil, Ellis County
12. Thompson Hayward Chemical, Knox County
13. Niagara Chemical, Cameron County
14. International Creosoting, Jefferson County
15. McBay Oil and Gas, Houston County
16. Old Lufkin Creosoting, Angelina County
17. Solvent Recovery Services, Fort Bend County
18. Harris Sand Pits, Bexar County
19. Butler Ranch, Karnes County
20. Jerrell B. Thompson Battery, Van Zandt County
21. JCS Company, Van Zandt County
22. Hayes-Sammons Warehouse, Hidalgo County
23. Jensen Drive Scrap, Harris County
24. Baldwin Waste Oil, Nueces County
25. Hall Street, Galveston County
26. Unnamed Plating Site, El Paso County

27. Tricon America Inc., Tarrant County
28. Permian Chemical, Ector County
29. American Zinc, Moore County
30. Toups, Hardin County
31. Aztec Ceramics, Bexar County
32. Harvey Industries, Henderson County
33. Col-Tex Refinery, Mitchell County
34. Barlow's Wills Point Plating, Van Zandt County
35. Sampson Horrice, Dallas County
36. Coffield/Minerva Refinery, Milam County
37. Hart Creosoting, Jasper County
38. J.C. Pennco, Bexar County
39. Kingsland, Llano County
40. Poly-Cycle, Ellis County
41. Material Recovery Enterprises, Taylor County
42. Newton Wood Preserving, Newton County
43. Phipps Plating, Bexar County

Source: EPA, Region VI and TNRCC, Industrial and Hazardous Waste Division, 1999.

TYPES OF SITE ENROLLED IN THE VOLUNTARY CLEANUP PROGRAM RECEIVING CERTIFICATE OF COMPLETION

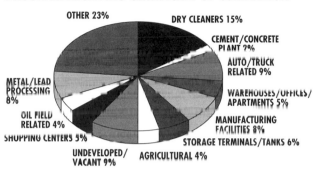

OTHER 23%

DRY CLEANERS 15%

CEMENT/CONCRETE PLANT 2%

AUTO/TRUCK RELATED 9%

WAREHOUSES/OFFICES/ APARTMENTS 5%

MANUFACTURING FACILITIES 8%

STORAGE TERMINALS/TANKS 6%

AGRICULTURAL 4%

UNDEVELOPED/ VACANT 9%

SHOPPING CENTERS 5%

OIL FIELD RELATED 4%

METAL/LEAD PROCESSING 8%

TOTAL NUMBER OF SITES: 119

Source: Texas Natural Resource Conservation Commission, Texas VCP News (September 1997), 11.

being resolved through an administrative order, and 15 have been cleaned up or deleted from the Superfund registry.[134] There are 2,000 other closed or abandoned sites in Texas that contain hazardous substances, about 600 of which must be investigated to determine if they should be on either the state or federal Superfund lists.[135] Most of the abandoned waste and production facility sites in Texas are related to the production of oil and gas or to the chemical industry.[136]

Unfortunately, the federal Superfund program has not resulted in the expected rapid restoration of abandoned dump sites. Between 1980 and 1992, it took an average of two and one-half years for the first stages of the cleanup process to begin.[137] During this phase, the Superfund program attempts to locate responsible parties—those who actually produced, transported, or disposed of hazardous waste in an unsafe manner—and make them pay for remediation and restoration. This often results in long legal battles. If the responsible parties are unable or unwilling to fund cleanup, or if they cannot be found, the federal government will pay.[138] As of October 1997, 498 (more than a third) of the 1,342 sites on the federal Superfund list had completed construction cleanup, costing an average of $35 million each.[139] In Texas, 22 of the 32 active sites on the federal list have begun or completed cleanup, while six others formerly on the list have been deleted.[140]

Texas's state Superfund program also has been hit by delays. By the end of FY 1998, cleanup was completed on only five of the total of 47 listed and proposed sites.[141] The state Superfund program is funded by fees on tonnage deposited at hazardous and industrial solid waste facilities.[142] The state estimates that it spent a total of $79 million from 1985 to 1998 to begin the cleanup process at those sites where a responsible party could not be held accountable.[143]

FYI ☞ *The State Auditor, in a 1992 review of the state Superfund program, estimated that at current levels of funding it would take more than 25 years to clean up all the sites on the state and national lists and those sites expected to be added in the near future.* (Source: Texas Water Commission, Briefing Report on Federal and State Superfund Programs in Texas for Texas Water Commissioners [May 1992], Appendix IX, 13.)

In part because of the high costs and the time delays in identifying responsible parties, in 1995 the Texas legislature amended the Texas Solid Waste Disposal Act and created the Voluntary Cleanup Program. The program became effective in September 1995. In 1996 the Houston Lead State Superfund Site, a former secondary smelting and metal refining plant and lead-battery recycling facility, became the first Superfund site to enter this voluntary program.[144]

The voluntary cleanup program has focused on "brownfields," abandoned industrial or commercial sites in urban areas that have remained undeveloped because of contamination and fear of liability. The Texas Voluntary Cleanup Program operates in partnership with the EPA's Brownfields Initiative. In Texas, the EPA has awarded brownfield pilot grants to the cities of Dallas, Houston, and Laredo and has provided funds to the TNRCC for the state's voluntary program. Under the state program, a property owner carries out an environmental site assessment of the property and sends in an application and a $1,000 application fee. Once the application is accepted, an agreement to clean up the site is negotiated between the applicant and the TNRCC. Brownfields used for industrial sites do not need to

TOXICS AND BIRTH DEFECTS

Are hazardous and toxic wastes responsible for an unusually high number of birth defects recorded in the late 1980s and early 1990s along the southern Texas-Mexico border? While the answers are far from conclusive, many community and environmental groups, as well as scientists, believe that certain types of birth defects are linked to exposure to pollution from industrial facilities. The controversy along the border dates back to April 1991, when three women at one hospital in Brownsville, Cameron County, Texas, gave birth to infants with anencephaly, a rare birth defect in which babies are born with either incomplete or missing brains and skulls.

Following this unexpected event and the public outcry it generated, the Texas Department of Health and the U.S. Centers for Disease Control conducted a joint study to identify cases of both anencephaly and other birth defects known collectively as neural tube defects and to search for causes. A total of 68 of the defects were discovered among pregnancies conceived in Cameron County from 1986 to 1991, about twice the rate in the United States during the same time period. Moreover, in 1990 and 1991, the rate was nearly 27 per 10,000 births, about six times the national average.[145]

The report of the joint study concluded that the causes of these high neural tube defect rates could not be determined.[146] Toxics, notably organic solvents, have been suggested as possible candidates that could be investigated further. Some studies have pointed to a link between the occurrence of the defects and certain occupations, such as painters, in which the parents are exposed to solvents.[147] Moreover, environmentalists point to the rapid industrialization in Matamoros, Mexico, as a potential source of high levels of toxics emissions in water and air.[148]

Unfortunately, relatively little is known about the amounts and types of wastes released by the primarily U.S.-owned companies operating on the Mexican border. In the United States companies

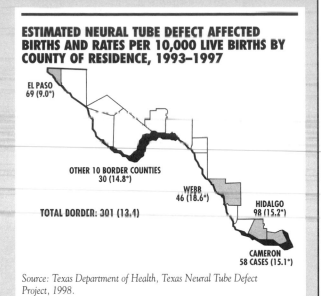

ESTIMATED NEURAL TUBE DEFECT AFFECTED BIRTHS AND RATES PER 10,000 LIVE BIRTHS BY COUNTY OF RESIDENCE, 1993–1997

EL PASO
69 (9.0*)

OTHER 10 BORDER COUNTIES
30 (14.8*)

WEBB
46 (18.6*)

HIDALGO
98 (15.2*)

TOTAL BORDER: 301 (13.4)

CAMERON
58 CASES (15.1*)

Source: Texas Department of Health, Texas Neural Tube Defect Project, 1998.

are required to report this information under the Toxics Release Inventory Program; in Mexico, there is no such requirement. In 1996 a group of Brownsville families who had suffered through neural tube defect pregnancies settled a lawsuit against several maquiladoras in Matamoros, including some owned by U.S. companies like General Motors and AT&T.[149]

In 1992 the Texas Department of Health and the U.S. Centers for Disease Control began the Texas Neural Tube Defect Project, which serves the fourteen Texas counties along the Texas-Mexico border. The project tracks neural tube defect births throughout the border by going through hospital and birthing records. In addition, all women with neural tube defect births are contacted, interviewed, and, if they are willing, enrolled in a folic acid prevention program to reduce the risk of another such birth. Finally, the project began a case-control study to attempt to find out the factors which led to neural tube defect cases in 1993. Based upon past studies, the project has already identified the following chemicals as being of concern for further study and blood sampling: arsenic, lead, mercury, nitrates, nitrophenols, and polychlorinated biphenyls.[150]

EFFLUENT DISCHARGES FROM MATAMOROS INDUSTRIAL PARKS

LOCATION	NEAREST COMPANY (PARENT CORPORATION, HEADQUARTERS)	TOXIC POLLUTANT DETECTED	QUANTITY DETECTED	STANDARDS	COMMENTS AND OBSERVATIONS
Finsa	Near to Rimir (General Motors, Detroit, MI)	Total Xylenes	2,800,000	440 U.S. Drinking Water Standard	Discharge passed into industrial park soil and into an agricultural drainage canal. Contaminants may reach Rio Grande, which is drinking water supply. Discharge smelled strongly of aromatic solvents and had coagulated black tarry particles suspended in it.
	"	Methylene Chloride	41,000	.19 U.S. Ambient Water Quality Criterion	Suspected Carcinogen
	"	Ethylbenzene	430,000	1400 Mexico Potable Water Stdd.	
Aldusa Industrial Park	Canal flowing off site of Stepan de Mexico (Stepan Chemical, Northfield, IL)	Naphthalene	16,000	20 Mexico Standard for Protection of Aquatic Life	
	"	Total Xylenes	23,200,000	440 U.S. Drinking Water Standard	
	"	Acidity	1.62 pH	5-8 pH is Normal Permitted Range	Sample is highly acidic. Acids in soil here would leach metals into groundwater.
Del Golfo Industrial Park	Next to Productos de Preservacion (Preservation Products/Idacon Houston, TX)	Pentachloro-phenol	505 effluent 14,300 soil	.5 is Mexico standard for Protection of Aquatic Life	Soil, samples at discharge pipe, contained levels of Penta on par with U.S. hazardous waste standard for Penta sludges.
	"	Total Xylenes	1020 effluent 47,000 soil	440 U.S.Drinking Water Standard	

Note: All figures are in parts per billion unless otherwise noted.

Source: National Toxics Campaign Fund, Border Trouble: Rivers in Peril, a Report on Water Pollution Due to Industrial Development in Northern Mexico, *May 1991.*

be cleaned up to the same level as those used for residential or commercial development. Once contaminant levels in all media meet the health-based standards for the property's future land use, a release of liability is issued by the TNRCC for future lenders and landowners. Most contaminated sites are eligible for the program.[151]

Through October 7, 1997, the Voluntary Cleanup Program had received 536 applications. The TNRCC issued 119 certificates of completion to these sites during the same period.[152]

Legislation passed in 1997 allows municipalities to enter into a tax-abatement agreement with the owner of property in the Voluntary Cleanup Program.

Under these agreements, a municipality can exempt from property tax a portion of the property's value for up to four years if the property is located in a reinvestment zone. The measure was passed to offer another incentive for the cleanup of industrial sites. However, opponents of the legislation claim the tax-abatement agreements will shift the burden of taxes to other taxpayers.[153]

GETTING WASTE FROM POINT A TO POINT B

Millions of tons of hazardous waste each year pass along Texas highways, rivers, coastal waters, and railways, potentially exposing Texas residents to accidental spills and releases. In fact, in the transporting of hazardous waste from one location to another (either within or outside of the state), only Minnesota surpassed Texas. Transportation of these hazardous wastes is highly regulated. Any transporter shipping hazardous or Class 1 industrial nonhazardous waste must carry what is known as a Uniform Hazardous Waste Manifest. This manifest lists both the generator and the waste disposal facility, and provides an EPA identification number.[154] Only facilities that have a permit from the TNRCC and an EPA identification number are authorized to manage or transport hazardous wastes.[155]

In Texas, regulation of oil and hazardous waste spills is divided among a myriad of state and federal agencies. The TNRCC is the state's lead agency for responding to inland oil spills, all hazardous substance spills, and all other spills under the state's Hazardous Substances Spill Prevention and Control Act.[156] The Oil Spill Prevention and Response Act, passed by the Texas legislature in 1991, designated the GLO the state's lead agency for response to oil spills that threaten or enter coastal waters.[157] Finally, the Railroad Commission of Texas is charged with regulating spills or discharges from exploration, development, or production of oil, gas, and geothermal resources.[158] The Texas Parks and Wildlife Department has a role in all three programs in assessing damages to natural resources.

By law, transporters and generators must report any spills or accidents in route. In fiscal year 1993,

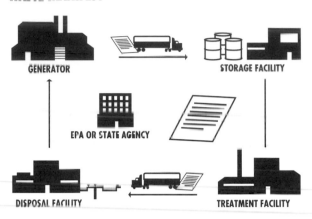

THE PAPER TRAIL OF THE UNIFORM HAZARDOUS WASTE MANIFEST

A one-page manifest must accompany every waste shipment. The resulting paper trail documents the waste's progress through treatment, storage and disposal. A missing form alerts the generator to investigate, which may mean calling in the state agency or EPA.

Source: Environmental Protection Agency, Solving the Hazardous Waste Problem: EPA's RCRA Program *(Washington,D.C., September 1986), 11.*

TNRCC received 4,896 reports of spills by transporters and generators of hazardous and oil wastes. Of these spills, about 99 percent were cleaned up voluntarily by the responsible parties, and one percent (73 spills) required state funds for cleanup.[159] About $3.4 million was spent to respond to and clean up these accidents. Most accidents occurred on highways.[160]

In addition to these transportation-related spills, millions of gallons of oil and gas and other chemical products are spilled from oil and gas production facilities, barges, pipelines, and platforms. The Railroad Commission received reports of 2,197 spills in 1994, 2,270 spills in 1995, and 2,061 spills in 1996 related to oil and gas production, exploration, and development.[161] The GLO responded to 1,264 spills in FY 1996 and 1,217 in FY 1997.[162] While responsible parties—the oil and gas facilities as well as the pipelines, barges, and other vessels used to transport oil and gas—paid for the majority of the clean up of these spills, more than $1 million was spent on state-funded cleanups. Funds generated from a fee assessed on all crude oil loaded or unloaded in Texas ports were used for these oil spill cleanups (see *Water* chapter, Coastal Waters section).[163]

NOTES

1. Council on Environmental Quality, Executive Office of the President, *Environmental Trends* (Washington, D.C.: U.S. Government Printing Office, July 1981), 84.

2. World Resources Institute, *The 1994 Information Please Environmental Almanac* (Boston: Houghton Mifflin, 1994), 101.

3. U.S. Environmental Protection Agency (EPA), *The National Biennial RCRA Hazardous Waste Report* (Based on 1995 Data) (August 1997), 4.

4. EPA, *Solving the Hazardous Waste Problem: EPA's RCRA Program* (November 1986), 1.

5. For a good review of the effect of pesticides and other agricultural chemicals on farmworkers in the United States, see U.S. General Accounting Office, *Hired Farm Workers, Health and Well-Being at Risk. Report to Congressional Requesters* (1992). Both the Public Health Institute and the Oil, Chemical and Atomic Workers International Union have detailed the health effects of wastes on oil and gas workers.

6. Texas Water Commission (TWC), *Briefing Report on Federal and State Superfund Programs in Texas for Texas Water Commissioners* (May 1992), Appendix IX, 5.

7. EPA, Office of Hazardous Waste and Emergency Response, Superfund web site homepage (http://www.epa.gov/superfund/oerr/), July 20, 1998.

8. EPA, *The National Biennial RCRA Hazardous Waste Report* (Based on 1995 Data) (August 1997), 4.

9. EPA, Office of Solid Waste, "Basic Facts about Waste," web page (http://www.epa.gov/epaoswer/osw/basifact.htm), July 20, 1998.

10. TWC, *Trends in Texas Hazardous Waste Management: 1991 Update* (July 1993), 3.

11. In 1997 the Texas legislature passed HB 956, which amended the definition of medical waste in the Texas Health and Safety Code to exclude certain items from being categorized as Class 2 medical wastes.

12. TNRCC, Texas Groundwater Protection Committee, *Joint Groundwater Monitoring and Contamination Report—1997* (June 1998), 39-45.

13. TNRCC, Texas Groundwater Protection Committee, *Joint Groundwater Monitoring and Contamination Report—1997* (June 1998), 42-43.

14. For example, the Railroad Commission of Texas (RRC) reported a total of 355,000 active oil and gas wells registered with the state, about 125,000 of which were inactive. An estimated 1.58 million wells have been drilled in Texas over the past 80 years, and RRC records indicated that only 522,713 have been plugged. Many of these unplugged wells are potential vehicles for the migration of saltwater and hazardous waste injected underground. Richard Ginn, Oil and Gas Division, RRC, letter to author, January 30, 1998, Austin.

15. TNRCC, Office of Pollution Prevention and Recycling, *A Report to the 74th Legislature: Pollution Prevention and Waste Reduction in Texas* (March 1, 1995), 7.

16. TWC, *Trends in Texas Hazardous Waste Management: 1991 Update*, 6.

17. TNRCC, Waste Planning and Assessment Division, *Trends in Texas Hazardous Waste Management: 1995 Update* (June 1997), 1. Information from the EPA's Office of Solid Waste, shows slightly different totals in Texas—145 million in 1995. However, the TNRCC data are updated more frequently and is considered more reliable.

18. TWC, *Needs Assessment for Industrial Class I Non-hazardous Waste Commercial Disposal Capacity in Texas* (July 1996). At the time of publication, only 1993 data were available. (cited hereafter as Needs Assessment [1996]).

19. TNRCC, "Texas Drives National Pollution Reduction," News Release, May 13, 1999.

20. TWC, *Texas Solid Waste Strategic Plan* (July 1993), 5.

21. TNRCC, *1995 Hazardous Waste Generation by County* (Database provided by Waste Planning and Assessment Division), 1997. In 1995, Jefferson County had overtaken Harrison County as the fifth highest county in terms of the amount of hazardous waste generated.

22. TWC, *Trends in Texas Hazardous Waste Management: 1991 Update*, 4.

23. TWC, *Trends in Texas Hazardous Waste Management: 1991 Update*, 4.

24. TNRCC, *Trends in Texas Hazardous Waste Management: 1995 Update*, 3.

25. TNRCC, *Trends in Texas Hazardous Waste Management: 1995 Update*, 4.

26. Shell Oil, for example, which ranked second in 1991, producing more than 19 million tons, dropped to number six in the waste ranking, producing 6.3 million tons by 1995. The Amoco Chemical Company produced 8.3 million tons in 1991 and occupied fourth place on the waste ranking list. By 1995 Amoco had dropped to 30th, producing 1.5 million tons.

27. TNRCC, *Trends in Texas Hazardous Waste Management: 1995 Update*, 6.

28. TNRCC, *Trends in Texas Hazardous Waste Management: 1995 Update*, 6.

29. TWC, *Trends in Texas Hazardous Waste Management: 1991 Update*, 6.

30. TNRCC, *Trends in Texas Hazardous Waste Management: 1995 Update*, Figure 5.

31. TWC, *Trends in Texas Hazardous Waste Management: 1991 Update*, 10.

32. TWC, *Texas Solid Waste Strategic Plan*, 4-5.

33. TNRCC, *Needs Assessment* (1996), Tables 4 and 5.

34. TNRCC, *Needs Assessment for Hazardous Waste Commercial Management Capacity in Texas: 1998 Update* (1998), iv. (Cited hereafter as Needs Assessment: 1998 Update.)

35. TNRCC, *Needs Assessment: 1998 Update*, iv.

36. INEGI (Mexican Federal Agency), "Estadísticas de la Industria Maquiladora de Exportación," Economic Database (May 1999).

37. Article III of La Paz Agreement. See also "The Decree for the Promotion and Operation of the Maquiladora Exporting Industry," *Diario Oficial*, August, 1983.

38. Amanda Corser, TNRCC, letter to author, September 1997, Austin.

39. EPA, Region 6, HAZTRAKS Database, April 1998.

40. World Bank, *The World Bank Executive Project Summary: Mexico: Northern Border Environment Project*, 1993 (Washington, D.C., 1993).

41. INE (Instituto Nacional de Ecología), Programa para la minimización y manejo integral de residuos industriales peligrosos en México 1996-2000 (Mexico City, 1996), 45, 69-71.

42. EPA, Region 6, "Improvements to Waste Tracking System Expanded to Include Mexico's New Aviso de Retorno," *Border Bulletin* 2, no. 5 (December 1998): 4.

43. TWC, *Trends in Texas Hazardous Waste Management: 1991 Update*, 12.

44. EPA, *1997 Texas Toxics Release Inventory Report* (April 20, 1998).

45. EPA, *1997 Texas Toxics Release Inventory Report* (April 2, 1998).

46. World Resources Institute, *1994 Information Please Environmental Almanac*, 102.

47. Susan Jablonski, Texas Low Level Radioactive Waste Disposal Authority, phone interview with author, September, 1994, Austin.

48. Jablonski, interview with author.

49. Jablonski, interview with author.

50. Jablonski, interview with author.

51. Jablonski, interview with author.

52. Texas Health and Safety Code, Section 402.222.

53. See Title 10 of Code of Federal Regulations. Both the state and federal definitions of low-level radioactive waste exempt irradiated reactor fuel and high-level radioactive wastes from their definitions of low-level radioactive wastes.

54. All low-level radioactive waste storage facilities must be licensed by the Bureau of Radiation Control, a division of the Texas Department of Health. Jablonski, interview with author.

55. Kurt Fernandez, "Texas Office Recommends Denial of License for Radioactive Waste Site," *Environment Reporter* 29, no. 11: 561.

56. World Resources Institute, *1994 Information Please Environmental Almanac*, 102.

57. Nicholas Lenssen, *Nuclear Waste: The Problem That Won't Go Away* (Worldwatch Institute, December 1991), 9.

58. A. Woodward, D. Roder, et al., "Radon Daughter Exposures at the Radium Hill Uranium Mine and Lung Cancer Rates among Former Workers, 1952-1987," *Cancer Causes Control 2*, no. 4 (1991): 213-220.

59. Jablonski, interview with author.

60. Ginn, letter to author, January 30, 1998.

61. Steve Etter, Industrial and Hazardous Waste Division, TNRCC, phone interview with author, September 1994, Austin.

62. TNRCC, *Joint Groundwater Monitoring and Contamination Report*, 1993, 52.

63. Etter, interview with author.

64. Richard Ratliff, Bureau of Radiation Control, Texas Department of Health, letter to author, November 1997, Austin.

65. TNRCC, *Joint Groundwater Monitoring and Contamination Report—1996*, Table 1.

66. SB 1857 of the 75th Legislature amends Section 401 of the Health and Safety Code.

67. Ratliff, letter to author. Uranium Resources Inc. is also seeking a permit for two other sites—one in Duval County and one in Brooks County—and is attempting to expand production at its Kleberg County facility.

68. Richard Ratliff, Radiation Control, Texas Department of Health, phone interview with author, October 1997, Austin. As of October 1997 there were 13 sites either under closure or awaiting a final inspection.

69. Dale Kohler, Uranium Injection Control Division, TNRCC, phone interview with author, September, 1994, Austin.

70. Ratliff, letter to author.

71. Information from Citizens Against Radioactive Dumping (http://www.unm.edu/~rekp/card.html), May 1998.

72. Texas Comptroller of Public Accounts (TCPA), *Forces of Change: Shaping the Future of Texas*, vol. 11, pt. 1 (November 1993), 466.

73. TWC, *Texas Solid Waste Strategic Plan*, 2.

74. For example, Andrew Szasz argues that pollution prevention gained favor among industries when national laws made pollution disposal costly through regulations and local opposition made siting disposal facilities extremely difficult. The choice left to industry was to not produce the wastes at all. Szasz, *EcoPopulism: Toxic Waste and the Movement for Environmental Justice* (Minneapolis: University of Minnesota Press, 1994), 140-146.

75. TNRCC, "Clean Texas 2000 Gains Momentum," *Texas Environment* (Winter 1994), 4.

76. TNRCC, Office of Pollution Prevention and Recycling, letter to author, December 11, 1997, Austin.

77. TNRCC, Office of Pollution Prevention and Recycling, letter to author.

78. TNRCC, Office of Pollution Prevention and Recycling, letter to author.

79. TNRCC, "Texas Drives National Pollution Prevention," News Release, May 13, 1999.

80. TNRCC, Office of Pollution Prevention and Recycling, TNRCC, A Report to the 75th Legislature: *Pollution Prevention and Recycling in Texas* (March 1997), 15.

81. TNRCC, Office of Pollution Prevention and Recycling, letter to author.

82. TNRCC, Office of Pollution Prevention and Recycling, letter to author.

83. TNRCC, *Trends in Texas Hazardous Waste Management: 1995 Update*, Table 4.

84. Andrew Neblett, Office of Pollution Prevention, TNRCC, interview with author, July 1994, Austin.

85. TNRCC, Office of Pollution Prevention and Recycling, letter to author.

86. TCPA, *Forces of Change*, vol. 11, pt. 1, 465.

87. Patti Jacobs, Market Strategies International, phone interview with author, September 1994, Austin.

88. EPA, *Solving the Hazardous Waste Problem*, 24.

89. EPA, *Solving the Hazardous Waste Problem*, 25.

90. EPA, *Solving the Hazardous Waste Problem*, 25.

91. TNRCC, *Trends in Texas Hazardous Waste Management: 1995 Update*, Table 1.

92. TNRCC, *Trends in Texas Hazardous Waste Management: 1995 Update*, Table 4.

93. TWC, *Trends in Texas Hazardous Waste Management: 1991 Update*, 14. These totals do not include the quantity of waste burned at fuel blenders, either in-state or out-of-state since these blenders ultimately ship these wastes to cement kilns for incineration.

94. TWC, *Trends in Texas Hazardous Waste Management: 1991 Update*, 11.

95. TNRCC, *Trends in Texas Hazardous Waste Management: 1995 Update*, 12.

96. Leslie Bell, Industrial and Hazardous Waste, TNRCC, phone interview with author, October 1997, Austin.

97. Texas Air Control Board, *Final Report of Texas Air Control Board Task Force on Waste-Derived Fuels for Cement Kilns* (February 1993), Appendix C.

98. U.S. General Accounting Office, *Environmental Protection: Interim Actions to Better Control Cement Kiln Dust* (August 1995), 5.

99. U.S. General Accounting Office: *Environmental Protection . . . Cement Kiln Dust*, 3.

100. Jeff Bailey, "Poor Economics and Trash Shortage Force Incineration Industry Changes," *Wall Street Journal* (August 11, 1993), A2.

101. U.S. General Accounting Office, *Hazardous Waste: Controls over Injection Well Disposal Operations* (1987), 17.

102. Texas Department of Water Resources, *Underground Injection Operations in Texas* (December 1984), 3-1.

103. TNRCC, Underground Injection Control Program, letter to author, October 1997, Austin. This total includes only wells that

have been permitted and actually are in service. Other wells have been permitted but were never constructed or used.

104. TNRCC, *Trends in Texas Hazardous Waste Management 1995 Update*, Tables 1 and 4.

105. Richard Ginn, Environmental Services Division, RRC, letter to author, February 1998, Austin.

106. TNRCC, *Joint Groundwater Monitoring and Contamination Report* 1996, 72.

107. Office of Technology Assessment, *Technologies and Management Strategies for Hazardous Waste Control* (Washington, D.C., March 1983), 195.

108. Office of Technology Assessment, *Technologies and Management Strategies for Hazardous Waste Control*, 190.

109. U.S. General Accounting Office, *Hazardous Waste: Controls over Injection Well Disposal Operations*, 21.

110. United States General Accounting Office, *Hazardous Waste: Controls over Injection Well Disposal Operations*, 21.

111. A table of groundwater contamination kept by the TNRCC lists two confirmed cases of spills, of chlorinated solvents and BTEX, at the American Ecology site. TNRCC, *Joint Groundwater Monitoring and Contamination Report—1996*, Table 2.

112. Ben Knape, Underground Injection Control Program, TNRCC, phone interview with author, 1994, Austin.

113. TNRCC, *Joint Groundwater Monitoring and Contamination Report*, 1997, Table 2.

114. EPA, *Solving the Hazardous Waste Problem*, 15.

115. TNRCC, *Joint Groundwater Monitoring and Contamination Report 1997*, 39-45.

116. TNRCC, *Trends in Texas Hazardous Waste Management: 1995 Update*, Table 4.

117. TWC, *Texas Solid Waste Strategic Plan*, 4.

118. "Four Petroleum Wastes Listed as Hazardous," *Texas & Southwest Environmental News* 8, no. 4 (July 1998): 2.

119. TWC, *Trends in Texas Hazardous Waste Management: 1991 Update*, 14.

120. TWC, *Trends in Texas Hazardous Waste Management: 1991 Update*, 14.

121. Susie Frizlen, Industrial and Hazardous Waste Division, TNRCC, phone interview with Texas Center for Policy Studies, July, 1994.

122. TNRCC, *Joint Groundwater Monitoring and Contamination Report*, 1997, 54-55.

123. Kurt Fernandez, "Texas Office Recommends Denial of License for Radioactive Waste Site," *Environment Reporter*, vol. 29, no. 11, 561.

124. TNRCC, *Final Annual Enforcement Report: Fiscal Year 1997* (December 17, 1997), Tables 5 and 7.

125. Wendy Rozacky, Industrial and Hazardous Waste Division, TNRCC, interview with Texas Center for Policy Studies, August, 1994.

126. TNRCC, *Final Annual Enforcement Report: Fiscal Year 1997* (December 17, 1997), Tables 9 and 10.

127. Rozacky, Industrial and Hazardous Waste Division, TNRCC, interview with Texas Center for Policy Studies.

128. Information from EPA, Office of Hazardous Waste and Emergency Response, Superfund web site homepage (http://www.epa.gov/superfund/oerr/), Nov. 10, 1998.

129. TWC, *Briefing Report on Federal and State Superfund Programs*, Appendix IX, 5.

130. EPA, Office of Hazardous Waste and Emergency Response, *Final National Priorities List (NPL) Sites—By State*, August 23, 1999.

131. Testimony by Barry Johnson, Ph. D, Assistant Surgeon General, Assistant Administrator, U.S. Department of Health and Human Services, Public Health Service, Agency for Toxic Substances and Disease Registry, Before the Subcommittee on Superfund, Recycling, and Solid Waste Management, United States Senate, May 6, 1993.

132. Testimony by Barry Johnson before the Subcommittee on Superfund, Recycling, and Solid Waste Management, U.S. Senate, May 6, 1993.

133. EPA, Office of Hazardous Waste and Emergency Response, Superfund web site. homepage, November 10, 1998.

134. Proposed sites must undergo a remedial investigation and feasibility study before being listed or delisted. TNRCC, "Superfund Site Listing by Alphabetical Order," information from web page, May 6, 1999.

135. Texas House of Representatives, House Research Organization, Bill Analysis of CSHB 2776 (1997).

136. See EPA, Region 6, *Progress at Superfund Sites in Texas* (Dallas, Winter 1993-1994). For example, 17 of the 30 national Superfund sites are connected to either oil and gas production wastes or to chemical wastes.

137. TWC, *Briefing Report on Federal and State Superfund Programs*, Appendix IX, 7.

138. TWC, *Briefing Report on Federal and State Superfund Programs*, 1.

139. EPA, Office of Hazardous Waste and Emergency Response, U.S. Superfund web site homepage, November 10, 1998.

140. EPA, National Priorities List (NPL) Sites in Texas, web page, May 18, 1999.

141. TNRCC, Office of Waste Management, *State Superfund Quarterly Status Report for the Quarter Ending December 31, 1996* (March 1997), 9-10.

142. TWC, *Briefing Report on Federal and State Superfund Programs*, Appendix IX, 6.

143. TNRCC, *Biennial Report to the 76th Legislature*, vol. 2 (1998), 47.

144. TNRCC, Office of Waste Management, *State Superfund Quarterly Status Report for the Quarter Ending December 31, 1996*, 9-10.

145. Texas Department of Health, *An Investigation of a Cluster of Neural Tube Defects in Cameron County, Texas* (July 1, 1992), 20.

146. The Texas Department of Health continues to investigate and monitor neural tube defects through a special project.

147. Jean Brender and Lucina Suarez, "Paternal Occupation and Anencephaly," *American Journal of Epidemiology* 131, no. 2 (1990): 517-521.

148. The National Toxics Campaign Fund monitored air in Matamoros and found high levels of benzene, toluene, ethyl benzene, and xylene, while samples in water canals used by industries to dispose of toxic wastes revealed solvent levels thousands of times above both U.S. and Mexican standards. See Sanford Lewis et al., *Border Trouble: Rivers in Peril, a Report on Water Pollution Due to Industrial Development in Northern Mexico* (Washington, D.C.: National Toxics Campaign Fund, May 1991).

149. The settlement, however, did not represent an admission of guilt by the industries.

150. Texas Department of Health, *Texas Neural Tube Defect Project (TNTDP): Semi-annual Report* (October 1, 1996-March 31, 1997), 6.

151. Some sites are not eligible for inclusion in the program. These include sites that are under an active or pending TNRCC enforcement order or are operating under an RCRA hazardous waste permit or under interim status.

152. TNRCC, Voluntary Cleanup Section, letter to author, November 1997.

153. Texas House of Representatives, House Research Organization, Bill Analysis of CSHB 2776 (1997).

154. EPA, *Solving the Hazardous Waste Problem*, 10.

155. EPA, *Solving the Hazardous Waste Problem*, 10.

156. Don Fawn, *Spills: Hope for the Best, Prepare for the Worst* (Austin: TWC, 1992) , 3.

157. Fawn, *Spills*, 5.

158. Fawn, *Spills*, 6.

159. Don Fawn, TNRCC, "TNRCC Emergency Response Requirements," speech at Environmental Trade Fair 1994, Austin, April 15, 1994.

160. Fawn, "TNRCC Emergency Response Requirements."

161. Ginn, letter to author, January 30, 1998.

162. GLO, Texas Oil Spill Prevention and Response Division, information faxed to author, November 1997.

163. GLO, Texas Oil Spill Prevention and Response Division, information faxed to author.

The Right to Know:
From TRI to Chemical Accident Information

The "right to know" is the idea that citizens have the right to full access to information about the environment in which they live, including the air they breathe and the water they drink. This includes information about specific facilities—the toxics and chemicals they release into the environment—as well as overall information about drinking water quality or ambient air standard violations. While the right to know is advocated by citizen and environmental groups throughout Texas and the United States, this concept has a relatively short history legislatively.

One of the first and still most prominent examples of right-to-know legislation is the Emergency Planning and Community Right-to-Know Act (EPCRA), established under Title III of the federal Superfund Amendments and Reauthorization Act (SARA) of 1986. This legislation, supported by a wide array of labor, community, and environmental organizations, created the Toxics Release Inventory (TRI), giving citizens the "right to know" about hazardous chemicals in their communities. EPCRA was a product of the widespread concern over chemical hazards that arose after the Union Carbide chemical release in Bhopal, India, killed 2,500 people and injured hundreds of thousands in December 1984.

Under the Community Right-to-Know program, TRI requirements initially applied only to manufacturing facilities with 10 or more employees that used more than "threshold" amounts of any of more than 300 individual chemicals and more than 20 chemical categories that may be toxic to humans, animals, plants, aquatic life, or the environment.[1] For the 1994 reporting year, under a presidential order, federal facilities also began to report their release and transfer of these chemicals. Moreover, in 1994, the Environmental Protection Agency (EPA) added another 34 chemicals to the list of toxics having to

be reported by these facilities, while the 1995 reporting year required that an additional 286 chemicals be added to the list, bringing the total number to more than 650 chemicals and chemical categories.[2] The EPA recently added dioxin—a so-called endocrine disruptor that appears to affect developmental and reproductive abilities in humans—and 27 dioxin-like chemicals to TRI reporting requirements.[3]

The TRI was expanded to cover approximately 6,100 facilities distributed among seven industrial categories—metal mining, coal processors, hazardous waste treatment facilities, solvent recyclers, electric utilities, chemical wholesalers, and petroleum bulk storage sites (tank farms)—beginning with the 1998 reporting year.[4] Finally, in October 1996, the EPA announced its intention to add chemical use—the amount of toxic chemicals used within the production process—and worker exposure information to the TRI program.[5]

The expansion of TRI to include new industrial categories and the probable requirement to include chemical use and worker exposure data significantly improves the public's right to know about industrial facilities. TRI data can provide initial information on the toxic chemicals that are recycled or burned for energy recovery on site; released to the air, water, land; injected underground; or transported to off-site facilities for treatment and disposal, recycling, and burning for energy recovery. In Texas, these emission reports are made to the Texas Natural Resource Conservation Commission (TNRCC) as well as the EPA. This information is made available to the general public, generally about a year and a half after the data is submitted to the agencies.[6]

According to the TNRCC, TRI data is the best information source for tracking pollution prevention progress; identifying pollution prevention opportunities; improving emergency response planning;

aiding employees in identifying potential risks; and encouraging community awareness of potential hazards in the environment.

Citizens can use the information to find out what chemicals are being released in their communities and neighborhoods, in what quantities, by whom, and where the chemicals are going. This information can in turn be used as a basis for dialogue between residents and a particular manufacturing company on ways to reduce emissions and potential hazards.

TRI data, as well as information on other federal environmental programs, may be accessed (using a personal computer and modem) through a tele-communication computer service called RTK-NET. The EPA also runs a web page similar to RTK-NET called EnviroFacts Warehouse. Finally, TRI data can also be obtained by contacting the TRI program at TNRCC. The Environmental Defense Fund also runs a web site called Scorecard, which uses TRI and other environmental databases to help the public assess the health of their communities.[7]

The TRI is only part of the EPA's "right-to-know" efforts. In 1996 the EPA proposed the Sector Facility Indexing (SFI) Initiative, which developed a web-accessible database on facility-specific releases and inspection/compliance history by combining information contained in separate EPA and state programs, including the TRI, the Clean Air Act, the Clean Water Act, the Resource Conservation and Recovery Act, and the Comprehensive Emergency Response, Compensation and Liability Act. Additionally, the Sector Facility Indexing project includes demographic information for a three-mile radius around each facility and the ability to produce a map of the area.

In addition, under the Clean Air Act of 1990, an estimated 66,000 industrial sites must report worst-case scenarios as part of required risk management plans. The EPA plans to make these worst-case accident scenarios available to the public in 1999, although a proposal to put the information on the Internet has met industry opposition.[8] Moreover, under the Safe Drinking Water Act amendments of 1996, drinking water suppliers must disclose information about water quality and contaminants

in water to their customers in annual "consumer confidence" reports. The EPA will use these reports as part of its national drinking water contaminant database, accessible through the Internet.[9]

For more information about TRI and other right-to-know efforts, contact:

OMB Watch/Unison Institute
RTK-NET
1742 Connecticut Avenue, NW
Washington, DC 20009
phone (202) 234-8494; fax (202) 234-8584
E-mail: Admin@rtk.net
Web: http://www.rtk.net
Telnet: rtk.net
Dialup: (202) 234-8570 (8,N,1)

TRI Program
Office of Pollution Prevention and Recycling
Texas Natural Resource Conservation Commission
P.O. Box 13087
Austin, TX 78711-3087
(512) 239-3100

Environmental Protection Agency
EPA's EPCRA Information Hotline
1-800-535-0202
EPA's TRI web page
(http:/www.epa.gov/opptintr/tri)
EnviroFacts Warehouse web page
(http:/www.epa.gov/enviro/index.html)
Sector Facility Indexing home page
(http://es.epa.gov/oeca/sfi/index.html)
Office of Groundwater and Drinking Water, drinking water information
(http://www.epa.gov/ogwdw/ogwdw/dwinfo.htm)

EPA, Region 6
Air, Pesticides and Toxics
1445 Ross Avenue
Dallas, TX 75202-2733
(214) 665-8013

NOTES

1. EPA, 1992 *Toxics Release Inventory: Public Data Release* (April 1994), 13-15.

2. Becky Kirka, TNRCC, Toxics Release Inventory Program, phone Interview with author, August 1997.

3. Right-to-Know Network, "Top Right-to-Know Issues for 1997," *RTK Net Online* 7, no. 1 (spring 1997): 8.

4. Right-to-Know Network, "TRI Phase-II Expansion Approved," *RTK Net Online* 7, no. 1 (spring 1997): 1.

5. Right-to-Know Network "Top Right to Know Issues for 1997," 1.

6. For example, the EPA published its Public Data Release reports on the 1995 TRI information in 1997. EPA, *1995 Toxics Release Inventory: Public Data Release* (May 1997).

7. For more information, see web site (http://www.scorecard.org).

8. Working Group on Community Right-to-Know, "Industry Dodges Hazard Reduction," *Working Notes on Community Right-to-Know,* November-December 1998, 1.

9. Working Group on Community Right-to-Know, "Law Discloses Drinking Water Pollution," *Working Notes on Community Right to Know,* November-December 1997, 3.

County Environmental Indicators

The following charts present a core set of 23 environmental and economic indicators on a county-by-county basis. These indicators are not meant to rank counties from best to worst—or to measure performance in addressing environmental problems. Instead, they are a snapshot of a few environmental concerns for the most recent data available in a specific county.

AN EXAMPLE OF HOW TO VIEW THE COUNTY INDICATORS

Contained below are the environmental and economic indicators for two sparsely populated counties, Dawson and Calhoun. While Calhoun is a primarily industrial county, with 38 percent of the workforce employed in the manufacturing industry, Dawson has 14 percent and 5 percent of its workforce employed in Agriculture and Mining, principally oil and gas

mining. Not surprisingly, the environmental characteristics and challenges facing each of the counties is very different. Calhoun has a large number of pounds of toxics injected underground, as well as to surface waters and to public sewers. Dawson, on the other hand, has a large number of acres of agricultural land enrolled in the Conservation Reserve Program to restore eroded soils. While Dawson relies almost exclusively on groundwater—most of which is consumed by its agricultural sector—Calhoun uses little groundwater, and both agriculture and industry use most of the water. Finally, Calhoun faces potential concerns because of toxic—over 3 million pounds in 1997—and criteria pollutant air emissions, and also is a Near Non-Attainment county for ozone. Dawson—with its small industrial base—has relatively low levels of air pollution.

ENVIRONMENTAL INDICATORS	DAWSON	CALHOUN
INDUSTRIAL BASE		
Total Population, 1996	15,011	20,505
% Employed in Agriculture/Mining/Manufacturing, 1997	14/5/5	1/1/38
Leading Industrial Sector, 1995	Mining Oil &Gas	Chemicals
WASTE INDICATORS		
Tons of Hazardous Waste Generated, 1995	0	951,612
No. of Leaking Petroleum Storage Tanks, 1997	35	50
No. of State or National Superfund Sites, 1999	0	1
LAND INDICATORS		
Lbs. of Toxics Released on Land and/or Injected Underground, 1997	0	13,554,980
No. of Curbside Recycling Programs, 1997	0	0
Thousands of Acres of Agricultural Land Enrolled in Conservation Reserve Program, 1997	98,892	0
No. of Animal Feedlots, 1997	0	0
Presence of Rare Species	Y	Y
WATER INDICATORS		
Acre-Feet of Total Water Used, 1996	146,404	91,135
% of Total Water Use from Groundwater, 1996	99	5
% of Categories of Water Use: Municipal/Irrigation/Industrial, 1996	2/98/0	3/53/44

Continued on next page

ENVIRONMENTAL INDICATORS	DAWSON	CALHOUN
WATER INDICATORS (*continued*)		
Lbs. of Toxic Releases to Surface Water and/or Public Sewer, 1997	0	19,491
No. of Confirmed Contaminated Groundwater Cases from Pesticides, 1997	0	0
No of Confirmed Contaminated Groundwater Cases, 1997	0	8
No of Public Water Systems Exceeding Fecal Coliform Standards, 1996-1997	1	2
AIR INDICATORS		
Attainment, Non-Attainment, Near Non-Attainment and Pristine for Ozone Standards, 1999	A	NNA
Lbs. of Industrial Toxic Air Emissions, 1997	222,269	3,086,750
Lbs. in Industrial Toxic Carcinogenic Air Emissions, 1997	0	316,698
Tons of Electric Utility and Industry Emissions of Criteria Pollutants, 1997	553	19,809
Tons of Electric Utility Emissions of Sulfur Dioxide and Nitrogen Oxide, 1997	0	670

ECONOMIC INDICATORS

(1) Total Population, 1996: Information provided by Texas Water Development Board, "County Summary Historical Water Use" (1998).

(2) % Employed in Agriculture/Mining/Manufacturing, 1997: Economic Research and Analysis Department, Texas Workforce Commission, *1997 County Employment and Wage Information* (Austin, TX: Texas Workforce Commission, 1998). Numbers show percentage of employed in Agriculture, Forestry and Fisheries (Standard Industrial Classification Codes 1 through 9), Mining Activities (SIC Codes 10-14) and Manufacturing (SIC Codes 20-39) from the 2nd Quarter of 1997. However, some information was suppressed because of confidentiality. Where information was suppressed, numbers from the U.S. Department of Commerce's *County Business Patterns, 1995* were substituted. These are sometimes reported as ranges of numbers in employment-size classes. For example, in Aransas County, the Texas Workforce Commission suppressed the number of employed in the mining sector. Information from *County Business Patterns* was used instead. In this case, employment was reported as a range between 150 and 200. Therefore a midpoint of 175 was used. Thus, all numbers are approximations and are rounded.

(3) Leading Industrial Sector, 1995: Bureau of the Census, U.S. Department of Commerce, *County Business Patterns, 1995* (Washington, D.C.: U.S. Department of Commerce, October 1997), Table 2. This category reports the single largest industrial or mining sector in the county in terms of numbers of employed. However, only counties with at least 100 employees in an industrial or mining sector qualified. Where information was suppressed and an employment-size category was used rather than the actual number, the mid-point of the category was assumed to equal the number of employed. For example, in Bowie County, there were 871 employees who worked in Fabricated Metal Parts, while the number working in the Paper and Allied Products sector was reported as "G," an employment-size category equalling 1,000 to 2,439. A mid-point of 1,750 was chosen for this industrial sector, and Paper therefore is reported as Bowie County's leading industrial sector in 1995. Obviously, these numbers are approximations.

Abbreviations are used:
Mining C - Mining Coal and Lignite
Mining O&G - Mining Oil and Gas
Mining M - Mining Metals
Mining N - Mining Nonmetallic Minerals, except fuels
Food - Food and kindred products
Textile - Textile mill products
Apparel - Apparel and other textile products
Lumber - Lumber and wood products
Furniture - Furniture and fixtures
Paper - Paper and allied products
Printing - Printing and publishing
Chemicals - Chemicals and allied products
Petroleum - Petroleum and coal products
Rubber - Rubber and miscellaneous plastic products

Stone - Stone, clay and glass products
Metal P - Primary metal industries
Metal F - Fabricated metal products
Machinery - Industrial machinery and equipment
Electronic - Electronic and other electronic
  equipment
Transport - Transportation equipment
Instrument - Instruments and related products
Other - Miscellaneous manufacturing industry
  (toys, jewelry, pens, etc.)

WASTE INDICATORS
(4) Tons of Hazardous Waste Generated, 1995:
Information provided by Waste Planning and
Assessment Division, Texas Natural Resource
Conservation Commission. Totals include only
hazardous waste classified under the Resource
Conservation and Recovery Act generated within the
county, not all Resource Conservation and Recovery
Act-classified hazardous waste stored, treated, and
disposed of in the county. All numbers are rounded
to the nearest whole number. Those counties which
have less than one-half ton of hazardous waste but
more than none are indicated as such.

(5) No. of Leaking Petroleum Storage Tanks, 1997:
Information from Leaking Petroleum Storage Tanks
Database, Petroleum Storage Tank Division, Office
of Waste Management, Texas Natural Resource
Conservation Commission, January 1998. Includes
both leaking tanks which impacted groundwater as
well as those impacting soils.

(6) No. of State or National Superfund Sites, 1999:
Information provided by Superfund Program, Office
of Waste Management, Texas Natural Resource
Conservation Commission and U.S. Environmental
Protection Agency. Totals include waste sites
proposed or on the State Superfund Listing as well
as those on the National Priorities Listing (NPL) for
the Federal Superfund.

LAND INDICATORS
(7) Lbs. of Toxics Injected Underground, 1997:
1997 Toxics Inventory Release Database, U.S.
Environmental Protection Agency.

(8) No. of Curbside Recycling Programs, 1997:
Information provided by Office of Pollution Prevention
and Recycling, Texas Natural Resource Conservation
Commission, 1998. The information is based on a
voluntary survey conducted by TNRCC during
June–August 1997.

**(9) No. of Acres of Agricultural Land Enrolled in
Conservation Reserve Program, December 1997:**
Information provided by Natural Resources Conservation Service, Texas State Office, December 1997.

(10) No. of Animal Feedlots, 1997: Information
from "Wastewater Agricultural Permits," State Permit
Inventory, Texas Natural Resource Conservation
Commission, 1998.

(11) Presence of Rare Species: Rare species include
those species of animals and plants listed by Texas
Parks & Wildlife and/or the U.S. Fish and Wildlife
Service as threatened with extinction or likely to
become endangered in the future, and animal and
plant species that may qualify for listing as threatened
or endangered by TPWD or the USFWS.

WATER INDICATORS
(12) Acre-Feet of Total Water Used, 1996:
Information provided by Planning Division, Texas
Water Development Board, "County Summary
Historical Water Use" (1998).

**(13) % of Total Water Use from Groundwater,
1996:** Information provided by Planning Division,
Texas Water Development Board, "County Summary
Historical Water Use" (1998). All numbers rounded.

**(14) % of Categories of Use, 1996: Municipal/
Irrigation/Industrial, 1996:** Information provided
by Planning Division, Texas Water Development
Board, "County Summary Historical Water Use"
(1998). Note: The totals do not always add up to 100%
because power, mining, and livestock water use figures
are not included. All numbers are rounded.

**(15) Lbs. of Toxic Releases to Surface Water and/or
Public Sewer , 1997:** 1997 Toxics Release Inventory
Database, U.S. Environmental Protection Agency.
Totals include both direct releases to water as well as
transfers to Publicly-Owned Treatment Works.

TEXAS COUNTIES

(16) No. of Confirmed Contaminated Groundwater Cases from Pesticides, 1997: Texas Groundwater Monitoring and Contamination Report, *Joint Groundwater Monitoring and Contamination Report – 1997* (Austin, TX: Texas Natural Resource Conservation Commission, June 1998), Table 1. Includes all groundwater contamination cases due to pesticides reported from 1987 to 1997 that have not been cleaned up.

(17) No. of Confirmed Contaminated Groundwater Cases, 1997: Texas Groundwater Monitoring and Contamination Report, *Joint Groundwater Monitoring*

and Contamination Report—1997 (Austin, TX: Texas Natural Resource Conservation Commission, June 1998), Tables 1, 2 and 3. Totals include all groundwater contamination cases reported from 1987 to 1997 that have not been cleaned up. Totals do not include groundwater contamination cases from underground leaking petroleum storage cases (see indicator #5) or from pesticides (see indicator #16).

(18) No. of Public Water Systems Exceeding Fecal Coliform Standards, 1996-97: Information provided by Water Utilities Division, Office of Water Quality, Texas Natural Resource Conservation Commission.

AIR INDICATORS:

(19) Attainment, Non-Attainment, Near Non-Attainment and Pristine for Ozone Standards, 1999: Non-attainment counties are those designated as non-attainment under the Texas Natural Resource Conservation Commission's State Implementation Plan. Near non-attainment counties are those designated as such by the Texas Natural Resource Conservation Commission. Pristine Counties include those designated by the U.S. Environmental Protection Agency to protect national parks and wildlife habitat. Only Big Bend National Park in Brewster County and Guadalupe Mountains National Park in Husdpeth and Culberson Counties has been afforded this special status in Texas. Finally, attainment counties are those that remain. For a full discussion of ozone attainment status, see *Air Quality* Chapter.

(20) Lbs. of Industrial Toxic Air Emissions, 1997: Information from 1997 Toxics Release Inventory Database, U.S. Environmental Protection Agency. Includes both stack (point) and fugitive (non-point) emissions.

(21) Lbs. of Industrial Toxic Carcinogenic Air Emissions, 1997: Information from 1997 Toxics Release Inventory Database, U.S. Environmental Protection Agency. Carcinogenic air emissions include over 120 chemicals that are specifically identified as known or suspected carcinogens for the Toxics Release Inventory Program.

(22) Tons of Electric Utility and Industry Emissions of Criteria Pollutants, 1997: Information from Emissions Inventory Database, Office of Air Quality, Texas Natural Resource Conservation Commission, July 1999. Criteria pollutants include sulfur dioxide, nitrogen oxide, carbon monoxide, volatile organic compounds (not including methane), lead and particulate matter less than 10 microns. All numbers are rounded to the nearest ton.

(23) Tons of Electric Utility Emissions of Sulfur Dioxide and Nitrogen Oxide, 1997: Information from Emissions Inventory Database, Office of Air Quality, Texas Natural Resource Conservation Commission, July 1999. Electric utilities include all sources with a Standard Industrial Classification (SIC) Code of 4911. All numbers are rounded to the nearest ton.

COUNTY	INDUSTRIAL BASE			WASTE INDICATORS				LAND INDICATORS			
	TOTAL POP. (1)	PERCENT EMPLOYED (2)	LEADING INDUSTRIAL (3)	HAZARDOUS WASTE (4)	PETROLEUM LEAKAGE (5)	SUPERFUND SITES (6)	INJECTION TOXICS (7)	CURBSIDE RECYCLING (8)	ERODIBLE CROPLAND (9)	ANIMAL FEEDLOTS (10)	RARE SPECIES (11)
Anderson	52,031	1/4/8	Transport	85	54	0	0	0	19	2	Y
Andrews	14,532	1/25/25	Mining O&G	12	34	0	0	0	37,254	0	Y
Angelina	75,924	10/0/23	Lumber	4,360,692	127	2	0	1	1,187	0	Y
Aransas	20,854	2/3/8	Mining O&G	28	32	0	0	0	0	0	Y
Archer	8,594	12/8/2	Mining O&G	0	10	0	0	0	133	7	Y
Armstrong	2,192	5/0/2		0	2	0	0	0	39,422	2	Y
Atascosa	34,152	5/6/4	Chemicals	17	49	0	0	0	661	3	Y
Austin	22,969	1/1/24	Stone	14	32	0	0	0	0	0	Y
Bailey	6,841	19/0/5		1,247	14	0	0	0	125,605	5	Y
Bandera	14,373	2/3/4		0	7	0	0	0	0	0	Y
Bastrop	46,738	3/0/11	Stone	17	43	0	0	1	47	1	Y
Baylor	4,289	4/4/5		1	15	0	0	0	2,838	1	Y
Bee	27,590	1/5/5	Mining O&G	17	33	0	0	0	3,621	0	Y
Bell	222,146	1/0/11	Rubber	1,077	197	1	0	2	2,008	0	Y
Bexar	1,318,431	1/0/7	Food	1,323,675	1,466	5	0	9	0	2	Y
Blanco	7,352	6/3/3		1	12	0	0	0	0	1	Y
Borden	762	14/0/0		0	2	0	0	0	6,988	0	N
Bosque	16,595	5/0/17	Lumber	5	10	0	0	0	834	1	Y
Bowie	85,080	1/0/10	Paper	45,960	136	3	0	2	3,665	1	Y
Brazoria	219,898	1/2/23	Chemicals	23,943,221	188	1	13,175,339	7	0	4	Y
Brazos	138,093	1/1/6	Metal F	19,378	116	0	0	1	0	1	Y
Brewster	9,290	3/1/1		0	15	0	0	0	0	0	Y
Briscoe	2,038	20/0/14		0	5	0	0	0	35,606	0	Y
Brooks	8,331	7/4/1		2	23	0	0	0	4,955	0	Y
Brown	37,283	1/1/23	Stone	3,650	55	0	0	0	804	8	Y
Burleson	15,136	3/12/11	Metal F	30,275	21	0	0	0	0	0	Y
Burnet	29,426	1/1/14	Stone	37	34	0	0	1	223	0	Y
Caldwell	29,558	2/3/7	Lumber	56	34	0	0	2	26	1	Y
Calhoun	20,505	1/1/38	Chemicals	951,612	50	1	13,554,980	0	0	0	Y
Callahan	12,442	2/6/5		1	26	0	0	0	4,376	0	Y
Cameron	312,064	2/0/13	Apparel	53,497	302	1	0	0	5,182	2	Y
Camp	10,965	23/0/15	Food	11	16	0	0	0	141	1	Y
Carson	6,592	2/3/1		368	15	1	0	0	28,141	1	Y
Cass	30,725	1/1/23	Instruments	5,796	45	1	0	1	548	0	Y
Castro	8,395	27/0/13	Food	4	16	0	0	0	53,302	30	Y
Chambers	24,330	2/6/24	Chemicals	27,121	35	0	0	1	0	0	Y
Cherokee	43,611	8/0/22	Lumber	861	49	0	0	1	59	1	Y
Childress	7,462	2/0/0		10	12	0	0	0	23,162	0	Y
Clay	10,566	3/1/17		0	6	0	0	0	476	3	Y
Cochran	4,250	19/1/2		1	10	0	0	0	102,019	1	N
Coke	3,529	3/12/2		0	10	0	0	0	3,867	1	Y
Coleman	9,888	2/1/16	Furniture	3	15	0	0	0	9,708	0	Y

Continued on page 344

KEY: (1) Total Population, 1996. (2) % employed in Agriculture, Mining and Manufacturing, 1997. (3) Leading Industrial Sector, 1995 (4) Tons of Hazardous Waste Generated, 1995. (5) Number of Leaking Petroleum Storage Tanks, 1997. (6) Number of State or National Superfund Sites, 1999. (7) Lbs. of Toxics Released on Land and/or Injected Underground, 1997. (8) Number of Curbside Recycling Programs, 1997. (9) Thousands of Acres of Highly Erodible Cropland, 1997. (10) Number of Animal Feedlots, 1997. (11) Presence of rare species.

COUNTY	TOTAL WATER (12)	GRDWTR USE (13)	WATER USE CATEGORIES (14)	TOXIC RELEASE (15)	PESTICIDE CONTAM. (16)	GRDWTR CONTAM. (17)	FECAL COLIFORM (18)	OZONE STDS. (19)	TOXIC EMISS. (20)	CARC. EMISS. (21)	POLL. EMISS. (22)	SO₂ & NO EMISS. (23)
Anderson	15,000	67%	77/3/3%	8,805	0	5	1	A	108,011	15,850	675	0
Andrews	20,988	100%	16/66/0%	0	0	1	0	A	250,000	250,000	7,715	0
Angelina	37,749	67%	27/0/71%	99,852	0	7	0	A	1,698,580	546,705	10,433	0
Aransas	3,169	15%	89/0/0%	0	0	3	0	A	476,680	0	23,020	0
Archer	4,391	9%	38/0/0%	0	0	0	0	A	0	0	0	0
Armstrong	10,759	99%	4/90/0%	0	0	0	0	A	0	0	93	0
Atascosa	63,876	97%	9/76/0%	0	0	1	0	A	0	0	30,596	26,173
Austin	15,165	89%	22/63/1%	0	0	2	0	A	0	0	553	0
Bailey	254,069	100%	0/98/0%	0	0	0	1	A	0	0	562	0
Bandera	2,704	87%	71/17/0%	0	0	0	0	A	0	0	951	0
Bastrop	16,206	56%	49/5/0%	0	0	0	0	A	0	0	2,595	2,061
Baylor	2,244	77%	41/32/0%	0	0	0	0	A	0	0	0	0
Bee	8,719	57%	61/28/0%	0	0	1	2	A	0	0	2,077	0
Bell	43,202	6%	91/4/3%	1,688	0	3	3	A	632,087	132,387	9,812	0
Bexar	329,148	88%	71/13/6%	259,880	0	40	0	NNA	948,634	193,148	65,573	50,057
Blanco	2,065	80%	52/24/0%	0	0	0	0	A	0	0	0	0
Borden	6,505	84%	3/78/0%	0	0	0	0	A	0	0	319	0
Bosque	6,964	61%	35/26/9%	0	0	0	0	A	0	0	1,984	0
Bowie	20,829	14%	57/24/9%	10,257	0	14	3	A	58,049	14,136	2,275	0
Brazoria	313,949	11%	10/24/65%	14,377,788	0	19	3	NA	8,483,270	1,272,829	66,802	0
Brazos	48,408	88%	58/30/1%	118,096	0	2	2	A	62,822	0	3,510	1,552
Brewster	3,574	92%	53/9/0%	0	0	0	1	P/A	0	0	0	0
Briscoe	21,460	99%	1/98/0%	0	0	0	0	A	0	0	0	0
Brooks	2,796	80%	57/17/0%	0	0	0	0	A	0	0	2,597	0
Brown	23,121	11%	26/52/2%	160	0	2	0	A	991,186	94,760	761	0
Burleson	13,059	91%	17/68/1%	48	0	2	1	A	30,459	26,238	3,790	0
Burnet	8,067	29%	66/3/7%	0	0	1	2	A	0	0	66	0
Caldwell	7,753	55%	67/22/0%	0	0	0	0	A	5,352	0	2,830	0
Calhoun	91,135	5%	3/53/44%	19,491	0	8	2	NNA	3,086,750	316,698	19,809	670
Callahan	4,100	36%	42/14/0%	0	0	2	0	A	0	0	469	0
Cameron	366,446	1%	14/85/0%	4,232	0	15	1	A	819,401	6,088	3,030	1,789
Camp	2,673	55%	60/1/1%	0	0	0	1	A	0	0	258	0
Carson	82,099	99%	2/93/1%	0	0	2	1	A	0	0	3,881	0
Cass	85,249	4%	5/0/93%	143,003	0	1	1	A	2,432,862	94,898	9,181	0
Castro	531,282	100%	0/98/0%	0	0	0	0	A	1,600	0	261	0
Chambers	152,586	7%	2/80/4%	3,140,304	0	2	1	NA	284,373	7,880	18,689	6,183
Cherokee	16,183	45%	45/1/3%	0	0	0	0	A	15,110	14,600	242	0
Childress	6,878	71%	25/68/0%	0	0	2	0	A	0	0	129	0
Clay	4,803	33%	33/16/0%	0	0	0	1	A	0	0	571	0
Cochran	167,981	100%	1/98/0%	0	0	1	0	A	0	0	653	0
Coke	2,788	28%	28/24/0%	0	0	0	0	A	0	0	3,373	462
Coleman	5,085	4%	38/27/0%	0	0	0	1	A	255	0	103	79

Continued on page 345

KEY: (12) Acre-Feet of Total Water Used, 1996. (13) % of Total Water Use from Groundwater, 1996. (14) % Categories of Water Use: Municipal/Irrigation/Industrial, 1996. (15) Lbs. of Toxic Releases to Surface Water and/or Public Sewer, 1997. (16) Number of Confirmed Contaminated Groundwater Cases from Pesticides, 1997. (17) Number of Confirmed Contaminated Groundwater Cases, 1997. (18) Number of Public Water Systems Exceeding Fecal Coliform Standards, 1996-97. (19) Attainment, Non-attainment, Near non-attainment and Pristine for Ozone Standards, 1999. (20) Lbs. of Industrial Toxic Air Emissions, 1997. (21) Lbs. of Industrial Toxic Carcinogenic Air Emissions, 1997. (22) Tons of Electric Utility and Industry Emissions of Criteria Pollutants, 1997. (23) Tons of Electric Utility Emissions of Sulfur Dioxide and Nitrogen Oxide, 1997.

COUNTY	TOTAL POP. (1)	PERCENT EMPLOYED (2)	LEADING INDUSTRIAL (3)	HAZARDOUS WASTE (4)	PETROLEUM LEAKAGE (5)	SUPERFUND SITES (6)	INJECTION TOXICS (7)	CURBSIDE RECYCLING (8)	ERODIBLE CROPLAND (9)	ANIMAL FEEDLOTS (10)	RARE SPECIES (11)
		INDUSTRIAL BASE			**WASTE INDICATORS**				**LAND INDICATORS**		
Collin	373,095	2/1/15	Electronic	8,883	171	0	0	8	466	1	Y
Collingsworth	3,657	9/0/7		0	5	0	0	0	21,264	0	N
Colorado	19,574	4/2/18	Rubber	26	30	0	0	1	0	1	Y
Comal	68,525	0/1/18	Rubber	54	93	0	0	2	0	1	Y
Comanche	14,072	17/0/10	Stone	3	19	0	0	1	621	28	Y
Concho	3,170	4/1/7		0	7	0	0	0	18,313	0	Y
Cooke	33,196	2/2/25	Furniture	203	44	0	0	0	141	0	Y
Coryell	74,119	1/0/6	Apparel	20	31	0	0	2	394	1	Y
Cottle	2,117	15/2/3		0	2	0	0	0	32,287	0	N
Crane	4,648	1/35/6	Mining O&G	0	10	0	0	0	0	0	Y
Crockett	4,544	6/20/1		0	5	0	0	0	0	0	Y
Crosby	7,187	22/0/5		1	22	0	0	0	24,326	0	N
Culberson	3,290	5/5/5		2	9	0	0	0	7,672	0	Y
Dallam	5,765	20/0/3		6	12	0	0	0	109,299	11	Y
Dallas	1,999,926	1/1/14	Electronic	2,443,933	2,116	2	0	12	43	0	Y
Dawson	15,011	14/5/5	Mining O&G	0	35	0	0	0	98,892	0	Y
Deaf Smith	19,403	14/1/16	Food	13	23	0	0	0	92,672	28	Y
Delta	5,014	2/0/16		20	5	0	0	0	5,990	0	Y
Denton	350,905	1/0/15	Instrument	53,293	211	0	0	10	114	0	Y
DeWitt	20,546	1/1/18	Machinery	6	29	0	0	0	0	0	Y
Dickens	2,372	14/0/0		0	11	0	0	0	45,200	0	Y
Dimmit	10,681	10/7/2		0	17	0	0	0	761	1	Y
Donley	3,905	9/0/2		0	5	0	0	0	26,347	3	N
Duval	13,543	3/20/0	Mining O&G	3	16	0	0	0	9,109	0	Y
Eastland	19,498	1/3/22	Mining O&G	3	31	1	0	0	1,118	0	Y
Ector	123,211	1/8/10	Mining O&G	5,630	211	5	278,740	0	0	0	N
Edwards	2,878	10/3/3		0	4	0	0	0	0	0	Y
Ellis	95,907	0/0/35	Metal P	52,816	97	2	0	0	6,937	1	Y
El Paso	673,893	1/0/19	Apparel	2,012,372	476	1	0	0	0	11	Y
Erath	30,769	10/0/18	Stone	70	32	0	0	0	347	100	Y
Falls	18,457	2/1/11	Printing	3	13	0	0	0	2,820	0	Y
Fannin	27,435	1/0/26	Rubber	17	18	0	0	0	4,756	1	Y
Fayette	21,756	4/4/13	Transport	24	70	0	0	2	0	10	Y
Fisher	4,516	7/0/6		4	6	0	0	1	43,529	1	N
Floyd	8,398	20/0/10	Machinery	0	23	0	0	1	0	2	N
Foard	1,845	5/0/55	Apparel	0	5	0	0	0	22,127	0	Y
Fort Bend	302,017	2/3/14	Electronics	346,861	105	1	0	2	0	1	Y
Franklin	8,724	2/3/8	Furniture	6	8	0	0	0	126	0	Y
Freestone	17,757	2/10/18	Metals F	8	28	0	0	0	196	0	Y
Frio	15,841	19/4/2		3	13	0	0	0	4,771	3	Y
Gaines	14,742	21/12/2	Mining O&G	35	30	0	0	0	174,749	1	Y
Galveston	241,981	1/1/9	Chemicals	30,755,141	204	3	14,608,979	3	0	0	Y

Continued on page 346

KEY: (1) Total Population, 1996. (2) % employed in Agriculture, Mining and Manufacturing, 1997. (3) Leading Industrial Sector, 1995 (4) Tons of Hazardous Waste Generated, 1995. (5) Number of Leaking Petroleum Storage Tanks, 1997. (6) Number of State or National Superfund Sites, 1999. (7) Lbs. of Toxics Released on Land and/or Injected Underground, 1997. (8) Number of Curbside Recycling Programs, 1997. (9) Thousands of Acres of Highly Erodible Cropland, 1997. (10) Number of Animal Feedlots, 1997. (11) Presence of rare species.

	WATER INDICATORS							AIR INDICATORS				
COUNTY	TOTAL WATER (12)	GRDWTR USE (13)	WATER USE CATEGORIES (14)	TOXIC RELEASE (15)	PESTICIDE CONTAM. (16)	GRDWTR CONTAM. (17)	FECAL COLIFORM (18)	OZONE STDS. (19)	TOXIC EMISS. (20)	CARC. EMISS. (21)	POLL. EMISS. (22)	SO₂ & NO EMISS. (23)
Collin	89,230	4%	95/0/1%	15,226	0	8	0	NA	243,242	785	3,145	1,116
Collingsworth	34,297	97%	2/95/0%	0	0	0	0	A	0	0	79	0
Colorado	255,097	14%	1/86/0%	0	0	0	2	A	213,480	3800	1,525	0
Comal	35,091	70%	40/0/34%	250	0	1	0	A	183,427	108,562	6,057	0
Comanche	35,759	54%	5/85/0%	0	2	0	1	A	0	0	58	0
Concho	6,054	80%	12/79/0%	0	0	0	0	A	0	0	37	0
Cooke	8,429	83%	64/5/3%	7	0	1	0	A	41,450	26,000	303	0
Coryell	15,114	8%	79/9/0%	0	0	0	0	A	15,926	1,535	2	0
Cottle	5,390	92%	8/85/0%	0	0	0	0	A	0	0	0	0
Crane	3,756	62%	27/1/0%	0	0	0	0	A	0	0	14,056	0
Crockett	4,424	90%	41/8/0%	0	0	0	0	A	0	0	8,135	1,304
Crosby	140,717	99%	1/98/0%	0	0	0	0	A	0	0	0	0
Culberson	9,300	100%	8/67/0%	0	0	0	0	P/A	0	0	881	0
Dallam	399,575	100%	0/99/0%	0	0	0	0	A	0	0	0	0
Dallas	505,423	1%	90/0/6%	319,643	0	91	2	NA	1,990,609	271,504	14,000	6,758
Dawson	146,404	99%	2/98/0%	0	0	0	1	A	222,269	0	553	0
Deaf Smith	308,358	99%	1/91/0%	0	0	1	0	A	239,631	0	751	0
Delta	987	14%	65/0/0%	0	0	0	0	A	0	0	0	0
Denton	65,348	18%	95/1/1%	1,333	0	6	4	NA	441,269	14,427	1,309	459
DeWitt	5,588	70%	63/2/1%	0	0	0	0	A	0	0	968	0
Dickens	9,586	92%	7/89/0%	0	0	0	0	A	0	0	0	0
Dimmit	15,536	62%	18/70/0%	0	0	0	0	A	0	0	469	0
Donley	11,680	82%	5/80/0%	0	0	0	0	A	0	0	0	0
Duval	19,054	92%	11/34/0%	0	0	0	0	A	0	0	1,268	0
Eastland	13,740	51%	20/66/0%	0	0	4	1	A	0	0	1,100	0
Ector	42,034	60%	83/18/5%	130,908	0	30	1	A	1,448,595	227,868	15,270	0
Edwards	1,038	92%	45/14/0%	0	0	0	0	A	0	0	117	0
Ellis	20,123	31%	72/1/17%	326	0	6	1	A	729,455	144,365	35,305	0
El Paso	351,514	29%	38/58/3%	31,589	0	10	1	NA	314,189	29,242	19,332	3,078
Erath	30,486	70%	14/53/1%	0	0	0	1	A	116,995	70,579	176	0
Falls	8,833	46%	27/52/0%	0	0	0	1	A	0	0	0	0
Fannin	17,515	30%	21/20/2%	100	0	0	0	A	17,726	14,717	3,750	3,076
Fayette	30,514	14%	11/2/0%	0	0	1	0	A	0	0	52,765	44,718
Fisher	4,449	64%	19/53/3%	0	0	0	0	A	0	0	988	0
Floyd	228,507	100%	1/98/0%	0	0	0	0	A	56,471	0	0	0
Foard	5,790	90%	6/89/0%	0	0	0	1	A	0	0	0	0
Fort Bend	145,591	62%	35/33/10%	12,874	0	10	2	NA	97,266	7,984	108,646	99,368
Franklin	4,340	48%	35/1/0%	1,000	0	0	0	A	10	0	2,535	0
Freestone	20,608	15%	12/0/0%	0	0	2	0	A	0	0	101,527	94,139
Frio	97,756	98%	3/96/0%	0	0	1	2	A	0	0	210	107
Gaines	428,361	100%	1/97/0%	0	0	1	0	A	0	0	7,012	0
Galveston	103,494	5%	39/10/49%	3,575,658	0	28	2	NA	5,619,957	551,359	61,019	9,802

Continued on page 347
Continued on page 347

KEY: (12) Acre-Feet of Total Water Used, 1996. (13) % of Total Water Use from Groundwater, 1996. (14) % Categories of Water Use: Municipal/Irrigation/Industrial, 1996. (15) Lbs. of Toxic Releases to Surface Water and/or Public Sewer, 1997. (16) Number of Confirmed Contaminated Groundwater Cases from Pesticides, 1997. (17) Number of Confirmed Contaminated Groundwater Cases, 1997. (18) Number of Public Water Systems Exceeding Fecal Coliform Standards, 1996-97. (19) Attainment, Non-attainment, Near non-attainment and Pristine for Ozone Standards, 1999. (20) Lbs. of Industrial Toxic Air Emissions, 1997. (21) Lbs. of Industrial Toxic Carcinogenic Air Emissions, 1997. (22) Tons of Electric Utility and Industry Emissions of Criteria Pollutants, 1997. (23) Tons of Electric Utility Emissions of Sulfur Dioxide and Nitrogen Oxide, 1997.

COUNTY	INDUSTRIAL BASE			WASTE INDICATORS				LAND INDICATORS			
	TOTAL POP. (1)	PERCENT EMPLOYED (2)	LEADING INDUSTRIAL (3)	HAZARDOUS WASTE (4)	PETROLEUM LEAKAGE (5)	SUPERFUND SITES (6)	INJECTION TOXICS (7)	CURBSIDE RECYCLING (8)	ERODIBLE CROPLAND (9)	ANIMAL FEEDLOTS (10)	RARE SPECIES (11)
Garza	4,954	10/27/1	Mining O&G	0	17	0	0	0	18,932	1	Y
Gillespie	19,700	2/3/13	Food	6	44	0	0	0	0	1	Y
Glasscock	1,460	35/6/0		0	3	0	0	0	8,617	0	Y
Goliad	6,570	7/0/1		2	13	0	0	1	214	0	Y
Gonzales	17,754	17/0/13	Food	3	30	0	0	0	25	5	Y
Gray	24,819	1/9/15	Mining O&G	76,681	32	0	0	0	25,787	4	N
Grayson	100,611	1/0/25	Electronic	32,848	118	0	0	0	4,911	0	Y
Gregg	111,509	1/4/18	Machinery	5,701	293	0	0	1	0	0	Y
Grimes	21,721	4/0/32	Metal F	31	27	0	0	0	69	0	Y
Guadalupe	73,679	1/0/26	Electronic	12,460	80	0	0	2	0	2	Y
Hale	36,336	7/0/18	Food	39	81	0	0	0	53,578	9	N
Hall	3,972	6/0/6		0	9	0	0	0	37,165	0	Y
Hamilton	8,218	7/0/13	Apparel	0	9	0	0	0	259	17	Y
Hansford	5,478	17/9/2	Mining O&G	12	10	0	0	0	29,955	9	Y
Hardeman	5,133	2/1/26	Stone	11	19	0	0	0	18,575	0	Y
Hardin	46,367	1/2/11	Lumber	40	37	1	0	1	0	0	Y
Harris	3,117,376	1/4/11	Mining O&G	42,200,653	2,899	15	10,805,019	10	0	0	Y
Harrison	60,838	1/5/32	Stone	6,229,139	88	2	518,800	2	0	1	Y
Hartley	4,895	15/0/1		0	1	0	0	0	43,877	4	Y
Haskell	6,463	9/2/2		0	15	0	0	0	25,281	1	Y
Hays	81,563	1/0/12	Metal F	2,388	93	0	0	2	0	0	Y
Hemphill	3,805	7/23/3	Mining O&G	0	12	0	0	1	17,091	2	Y
Henderson	65,144	2/2/12	Instruments	38	53	1	0	1	0	1	Y
Hidalgo	496,485	6/1/10	Apparel	230	372	1	0	0	27,733	4	Y
Hill	29,538	4/0/16	Lumber	19	24	0	0	1	8,792	6	Y
Hockley	24,209	5/19/3	Mining O&G	18	56	0	0	0	96,143	1	N
Hood	33,113	3/0/4		12	26	0	0	0	0	1	Y
Hopkins	31,012	3/1/14	Food	49	46	0	0	0	2,366	13	Y
Houston	21,362	1/1/15	Metal F	4	28	1	0	2	1,262	1	Y
Howard	33,285	2/5/11	Mining O&G	648	62	0	0	0	38,702	0	Y
Hudspeth	3,245	25/0/2		0	9	0	0	0	4,637	1	Y
Hunt	69,176	7/0/29	Lumber	47,343	57	0	0	0	184	0	Y
Hutchinson	25,907	1/11/20	Petroleum	9,959	50	0	3,488,026	0	3,183	3	Y
Irion	1,550	10/18/0		0	1	0	0	0	206	0	Y
Jack	7,435	13/17/2	Mining O&G	1	10	0	0	0	95	1	Y
Jackson	14,329	3/5/40	Rubber	4	34	0	0	0	0	0	Y
Jasper	33,944	1/1/24	Paper	5,843	37	2	0	0	80	0	Y
Jeff Davis	2,061	1/0/0		0	10	0	0	0	1,284	0	Y
Jefferson	245,849	1/0/15	Chemicals	9,419,812	442	3	9,256,670	4	0	0	
Jim Hogg	5,164	8/6/2		0	5	0	0	0	6,632	0	Y
Jim Wells	39,941	3/16/2	Mining O&G	55	57	0	0	0	6,428	5	Y
Johnson	109,463	2/0/22	Lumber	297	76	0	0	0	376	9	Y

Continued on page 348

KEY: (1) Total Population, 1996. (2) % employed in Agriculture, Mining and Manufacturing, 1997. (3) Leading Industrial Sector, 1995 (4) Tons of Hazardous Waste Generated, 1995. (5) Number of Leaking Petroleum Storage Tanks, 1997. (6) Number of State or National Superfund Sites, 1999. (7) Lbs. of Toxics Released on Land and/or Injected Underground, 1997. (8) Number of Curbside Recycling Programs, 1997. (9) Thousands of Acres of Highly Erodible Cropland, 1997. (10) Number of Animal Feedlots, 1997. (11) Presence of rare species.

			WATER INDICATORS					AIR INDICATORS				
COUNTY	TOTAL WATER (12)	GRDWTR USE (13)	WATER USE CATEGORIES (14)	TOXIC RELEASE (15)	PESTICIDE CONTAM. (16)	GRDWTR CONTAM. (17)	FECAL COLIFORM (18)	OZONE STDS. (19)	TOXIC EMISS. (20)	CARC. EMISS. (21)	POLL. EMISS. (22)	SO₂ & NO EMISS. (23)
Garza	12,734	92%	4/83/0%	0	0	0	0	A	0	0	139	0
Gillespie	9,390	78%	37/40/3%	0	0	1	2	A	0	0	0	0
Glasscock	55,551	99%	0/99/0%	0	0	0	1	A	0	0	1,436	0
Goliad	13,059	9%	7/1/0%	0	0	0	0	A	0	0	20,531	19,770
Gonzales	10,074	33%	41/14/11%	0	0	0	1	A	0	0	513	0
Gray	31,369	83%	16/57/12%	10	0	4	0	A	555,555	28,183	76,577	0
Grayson	29,152	51%	62/7/21%	248,103	0	6	0	A	89,913	2,800	1,464	0
Gregg	22,414	16%	74/0/17%	9,103	0	20	0	NNA	548,016	92,613	6,018	1,076
Grimes	12,966	39%	29/3/3%	0	0	1	1	A	16,534	56	17,288	16,515
Guadalupe	17,386	36%	69/2/17%	760	0	2	2	A	139,810	136,600	740	0
Hale	445,870	99%	2/97/1%	0	2	2	1	A	265,659	0	548	0
Hall	12,894	96%	6/91/0%	0	0	0	0	A	0	0	0	0
Hamilton	5,127	29%	25/25/0%	0	0	0	0	A	0	0	0	0
Hansford	219,611	99%	1/97/0%	0	0	0	2	A	0	0	10,167	0
Hardeman	9,796	56%	11/53/4%	0	0	0	0	A	84,000	0	404	0
Hardin	12,728	50%	47/2/1%	0	0	2	0	NA	283,014	162,238	2,983	0
Harris	981,931	39%	60/2/37%	42,143,418	0	217	26	NA	28,078,075	4,344,538	223,864	16,726
Harrison	68,426	5%	12/0/73%	6,934	0	11	1	NNA	4,037,893	135,850	48,931	30,899
Hartley	231,764	99%	0/97/0%	0	0	0	1	A	0	0	197	0
Haskell	34,614	94%	3/93/0%	0	2	0	0	A	0	0	275	236
Hays	15,491	95%	91/1/3%	48,000	0	5	5	A	70,039	49,930	4,176	0
Hemphill	4,890	70%	13/37/0%	0	0	0	0	A	0	0	6,302	0
Henderson	14,148	42%	67/0/1%	0	0	2	3	A	31,255	7,692	5,397	515
Hidalgo	513,022	4%	15/83/1%	11,833	0	9	3	A	5,278	10	6,106	1,421
Hill	7,639	40%	62/7/3%	0	0	0	1	A	57,753	0	125	0
Hockley	179,692	99%	2/94/0%	0	0	2	0	A	98,900	0	5,318	0
Hood	16,577	25%	26/24/0%	0	0	0	4	A	0	0	7,315	5,826
Hopkins	13,584	37%	44/0/5%	14,217	0	1	0	A	250	0	3,093	0
Houston	6,494	48%	58/9/2%	3	0	1	1	A	4,571	500	902	0
Howard	12,906	24%	51/10/13%	1,521	2	4	0	A	473,382	64,438	23,945	997
Hudspeth	230,280	57%	0/100/0%	0	0	0	1	P/A	0	0	235	0
Hunt	13,913	14%	74/4/6%	1,205	0	7	1	A	19,422	0	225	110
Hutchinson	70,273	97%	7/71/20%	53,930	0	9	0	A	2,773,594	134,622	38,966	39
Irion	3,630	45%	6/82/0%	0	0	0	0	A	0	0	2,468	0
Jack	3,337	19%	31/0/0%	0	0	0	0	A	61,225	0	1,871	0
Jackson	89,513	90%	2/99/1%	0	0	0	0	A	0	0	4,019	0
Jasper	60,593	81%	8/0/91%	164,360	0	5	0	A	1,127,974	271,113	14,279	0
Jeff Davis	1,086	86%	39/24/0%	0	0	0	1	A	0	0	0	0
Jefferson	396,836	3%	11/60/28%	344,975	0	29	2	NA	13,953,018	1,591,651	117,090	0
Jim Hogg	1,997	66%	45/16/0%	0	0	0	0	A	0	0	581	0
Jim Wells	9,921	41%	78/9/0%	0	0	2	0	A	0	0	3,620	0
Johnson	19,642	49%	79/0/5%	255	0	1	1	A	296,912	71,547	2,522	203

Continued on page 349

KEY: (12) Acre-Feet of Total Water Used, 1996. (13) % of Total Water Use from Groundwater, 1996. (14) % Categories of Water Use: Municipal/Irrigation/Industrial, 1996. (15) Lbs. of Toxic Releases to Surface Water and/or Public Sewer, 1997. (16) Number of Confirmed Contaminated Groundwater Cases from Pesticides, 1997. (17) Number of Confirmed Contaminated Groundwater Cases, 1997. (18) Number of Public Water Systems Exceeding Fecal Coliform Standards, 1996-97. (19) Attainment, Non-attainment, Near non-attainment and Pristine for Ozone Standards, 1999. (20) Lbs. of Industrial Toxic Air Emissions, 1997. (21) Lbs. of Industrial Toxic Carcinogenic Air Emissions, 1997. (22) Tons of Electric Utility and Industry Emissions of Criteria Pollutants, 1997. (23) Tons of Electric Utility Emissions of Sulfur Dioxide and Nitrogen Oxide, 1997.

	INDUSTRIAL BASE			WASTE INDICATORS				LAND INDICATORS			
COUNTY	TOTAL POP. (1)	PERCENT EMPLOYED (2)	LEADING INDUSTRIAL (3)	HAZARDOUS WASTE (4)	PETROLEUM LEAKAGE (5)	SUPERFUND SITES (6)	INJECTION TOXICS (7)	CURBSIDE RECYCLING (8)	ERODIBLE CROPLAND (9)	ANIMAL FEEDLOTS (10)	RARE SPECIES (11)
Jones	18,422	2/4/6	Mining O&G	233,940	33	0	0	0	38,970	1	Y
Karnes	15,259	2/4/6		37	29	1	0	0	2,124	0	Y
Kaufman	61,646	1/0/23	Metal F	19,472	48	0	0	0	85	0	Y
Kendall	19,835	4/2/9	Printing	358	18	0	0	1	0	0	Y
Kenedy	418	40/0/0		0	1	0	0	0	0	0	Y
Kent	939	19/24/0		0	2	0	0	0	21,981	0	Y
Kerr	42,168	1/1/8	Transport	42	59	0	0	1	0	1	Y
Kimble	4,504	2/1/20		1	8	0	0	0	0	0	Y
King	357	3/0/0		2	6	0	0	0	5,510	0	N
Kinney	3,389	11/0/2		0	8	0	0	0	0	0	Y
Kleberg	31,805	6/5/3	Food	19	78	0	0	1	4,984	1	Y
Knox	4,708	12/9/1		0	17	1	0	0	12,683	0	Y
Lamar	45,656	1/0/27	Food	467	47	0	0	1	14,480	1	Y
Lamb	15,162	18/0/15	Textile	10	21	0	0	0	117,956	6	N
Lampasas	16,707	2/0/14	Food	8	20	0	0	0	35	0	Y
La Salle	5,911	7/10/0		85	9	0	0	0	11,432	2	Y
Lavaca	20,450	1/1/33	Machinery	39,202	53	0	0	0	0	1	Y
Lee	14,189	0/11/10	Mining O&G	17	18	0	0	0	0	0	Y
Leon	13,775	3/10/21	Coal Mining	21,019	18	0	0	0	17	0	Y
Liberty	63,173	2/3/15	Lumber	912	65	1	0	1	0	0	Y
Limestone	21,307	1/2/9	Textile	5	27	0	0	0	3,881	0	Y
Lipscomb	3,210	7/1/1		0	4	0	0	0	21,254	5	Y
Live Oak	10,476	2/7/16	Petroleum	727,987	15	0	0	1	4,903	0	Y
Llano	12,852	1/1/3		0	29	0	0	1	0	0	Y
Loving	97	0/0/0		0-0.5	1	0	0	0	0	0	Y
Lubbock	233,496	1/0/7	Electronic	9,353	379	0	0	1	28,484	5	Y
Lynn	6,769	24/0/2		1	17	0	0	0	50,931	0	Y
McCulloch	8,862	2/2/9	Textile	4	18	0	0	0	6,112	0	Y
McLennan	202,679	1/0/19	Food	75,854	184	0	0	3	3,935	4	
McMullen	766	9/13/0		0	1	0	0	0	0	0	Y
Madison	12,283	2/1/1		2	15	0	0	0	568	1	Y
Marion	10,405	0/3/29	Lumber	27,691	12	0	0	0	0	0	Y
Martin	5,056	9/4/0		1	7	0	0	0	66,630	0	N
Mason	3,578	6/1/2		0	8	0	0	0	254	1	Y
Matagorda	38,184	5/2/5	Chemicals	1,510	61	0	0	0	78	0	Y
Maverick	44,107	3/1/12	Apparel	126	24	0	0	1	0	2	Y
Medina	33,471	5/1/8	Stone	45	42	0	0	0	1055	3	Y
Menard	2,339	14/0/2		0	1	0	0	0	156	1	Y
Midland	116,767	1/17/5	Mining O&G	1,455	147	0	0	0	18,395	0	N
Milam	24,556	3/1/28	Metal P	4,667	26	1	0	0	434	1	Y
Mills	4,964	12/1/7		2	7	0	0	0	246	4	Y
Mitchell	8,862	4/3/3		2	22	1	0	0	29,066	0	Y

Continued on page 350

KEY: (1) Total Population, 1996. (2) % employed in Agriculture, Mining and Manufacturing, 1997. (3) Leading Industrial Sector, 1995 (4) Tons of Hazardous Waste Generated, 1995. (5) Number of Leaking Petroleum Storage Tanks, 1997. (6) Number of State or National Superfund Sites, 1999. (7) Lbs. of Toxics Released on Land and/or Injected Underground, 1997. (8) Number of Curbside Recycling Programs, 1997. (9) Thousands of Acres of Highly Erodible Cropland, 1997. (10) Number of Animal Feedlots, 1997. (11) Presence of rare species.

	WATER INDICATORS							AIR INDICATORS				
COUNTY	TOTAL WATER (12)	GRDWTR USE (13)	WATER USE CATEGORIES (14)	TOXIC RELEASE (15)	PESTICIDE CONTAM. (16)	GRDWTR CONTAM. (17)	FECAL COLIFORM (18)	OZONE STDS. (19)	TOXIC EMISS. (20)	CARC. EMISS. (21)	POLL. EMISS. (22)	SO₂ & NO EMISS. (23)
Jones	16,066	30%	23/45/3%	10,685	0	3	1	A	159,010	19,560	2,849	1,221
Karnes	6,888	67%	39/32/1%	0	0	3	1	A	69,053	66,053	1,605	0
Kaufman	10,653	4%	76/3/3%	10	0	0	1	A	216,552	68,948	238	0
Kendall	4,856	73%	67/25/0%	0	0	0	0	A	0	0	87	0
Kenedy	763	16%	7/0/0%	0	0	0	0	A	0	0	1,293	0
Kent	2,642	84%	7/49/0%	0	0	0	0	A	5,590	0	1,558	0
Kerr	9,241	52%	78/15/0%	0	0	0	4	A	0	0	0	0
Kimble	3,025	31%	35/34/14%	0	0	0	0	A	0	0	233	0
King	883	34%	24/2/0%	0	0	0	0	A	0	0	253	0
Kinney	9,703	99%	12/83/0%	0	0	0	2	A	0	0	0	0
Kleberg	10,281	71%	59/4/0%	0	0	1	0	A	0	0	6,528	0
Knox	29,946	97%	3/96/0%	0	15	0	0	A	0	0	0	0
Lamar	19,076	3%	38/25/27%	5	0	2	0	A	108,533	5	1,943	1,110
Lamb	401,650	100%	1/95/0%	0	1	0	0	A	0	0	44,551	41,418
Lampasas	4,140	28%	66/9/3%	94	0	0	0	A	13,246	0	0	0
La Salle	9,169	94%	15/79/0%	0	0	0	0	A	0	0	0	0
Lavaca	25,161	94%	13/78/1%	0	0	1	0	A	0	0	4,022	0
Lee	5,552	78%	59/9/0%	0	0	0	0	A	0	0	2,324	0
Leon	6,641	62%	27/0/4%	0	0	0	0	A	36,307	0	4,670	0
Liberty	79,927	32%	11/77/0%	0	0	2	0	NA	5,718	2,037	2,479	0
Limestone	22,866	17%	14/0/0%	0	0	0	1	A	0	0	64,660	62,166
Lipscomb	17,326	90%	4/85/1%	0	0	0	0	A	0	0	1,796	0
Live Oak	11,339	76%	20/9/14%	0	0	4	1	A	147,770	12,912	3,658	0
Llano	7,137	31%	40/20/0%	0	0	4	1	A	0	0	1,040	775
Loving	652	9%	2/89/0%	0	0	0	0	A	0	0	318	0
Lubbock	297,572	88%	16/82/1%	260	1	9	6	A	950,352	0	5,838	3,366
Lynn	57,771	94%	2/98/0%	0	1	2	0	A	0	0	14	0
McCulloch	6,021	96%	45/26/14%	10	0	0	0	A	237,265	24,679	0	0
McLennan	60,331	23%	63/4/4%	24,973	0	9	3	A	107,321	0	15,988	11,423
McMullen	1,295	51%	15/0/0%	0	0	0	0	A	0	0	4,164	0
Madison	4,283	75%	53/0/5%	0	0	0	0	A	0	0	491	0
Marion	5,103	20%	27/2/1%	0	0	0	2	A	22,727	7,319	3,085	2,124
Martin	14,497	96%	5/87/0%	0	3	0	0	A	0	0	1,688	0
Mason	12,267	96%	8/84/0%	0	0	0	0	A	0	0	0	0
Matagorda	333,695	11%	2/83/3%	1,058	0	2	0	A	298,718	24,980	5,272	38
Maverick	167,137	1%	4/95/0%	0	0	1	0	A	0	0	32	0
Medina	94,860	78%	7/91/0%	0	0	4	0	A	0	0	7	0
Menard	5,048	18%	8/83/0%	0	0	0	0	A	0	0	0	0
Midland	84,290	55%	35/63/0%	0	0	13	0	A	62,308	40,950	12,486	0
Milam	55,032	65%	8/1/82%	4,900	0	3	0	A	1,172,114	4,074	143,775	37,361
Mills	6,486	23%	14/56/0%	0	0	0	0	A	0	0	0	0
Mitchell	7,386	21%	23/15/0%	0	0	3	0	A	0	0	7,699	7,054

Continued on page 351

KEY: (12) Acre-Feet of Total Water Used, 1996. (13) % of Total Water Use from Groundwater, 1996. (14) % Categories of Water Use: Municipal/Irrigation/Industrial, 1996. (15) Lbs. of Toxic Releases to Surface Water and/or Public Sewer, 1997. (16) Number of Confirmed Contaminated Groundwater Cases from Pesticides, 1997. (17) Number of Confirmed Contaminated Groundwater Cases, 1997. (18) Number of Public Water Systems Exceeding Fecal Coliform Standards, 1996-97. (19) Attainment, Non-attainment, Near non-attainment and Pristine for Ozone Standards, 1999. (20) Lbs. of Industrial Toxic Air Emissions, 1997. (21) Lbs. of Industrial Toxic Carcinogenic Air Emissions, 1997. (22) Tons of Electric Utility and Industry Emissions of Criteria Pollutants, 1997. (23) Tons of Electric Utility Emissions of Sulfur Dioxide and Nitrogen Oxide, 1997.

COUNTY	INDUSTRIAL BASE			WASTE INDICATORS				LAND INDICATORS			
	TOTAL POP. (1)	PERCENT EMPLOYED (2)	LEADING INDUSTRIAL (3)	HAZARDOUS WASTE (4)	PETROLEUM LEAKAGE (5)	SUPERFUND SITES (6)	INJECTION TOXICS (7)	CURBSIDE RECYCLING (8)	ERODIBLE CROPLAND (9)	ANIMAL FEEDLOTS (10)	RARE SPECIES (11)
Montague	18,194	1/5/16	Leather	3	19	0	0	0	2,829	0	Y
Montgomery	241,855	2/2/10	Mining O&G	2,582	134	1	0	3	0	0	Y
Moore	19,759	5/2/35	Food	1,452,863	17	1	372,240	0	19,531	6	Y
Morris	13,485	1/1/45	Metal P	37	13	0	0	0	297	0	Y
Motley	1,436	13/3/17		0	5	0	0	0	15,814	0	Y
Nacogdoches	59,250	3/0/22	Food	4,482	68	0	0	1	128	1	Y
Navarro	42,257	1/2/17	Stone	115	61	0	0	1	7,881	0	Y
Newton	14,209	0/3/29	Lumber	6	15	1	0	0	0	0	Y
Nolan	16,793	2/4/17	Stone	29	36	0	0	0	25,876	2	Y
Nueces	310,561	1/2/8	Petroleum	11,706,747	545	1	40,583	2	2,650	0	Y
Ochiltree	9,298	4/23/11	Mining O&G	3	18	1	0	0	33,036	10	Y
Oldham	2,372	13/0/0		1	5	0	0	0	21,430	3	Y
Orange	85,433	1/1/27	Chemical	23,113	119	1	599,325	2	0	0	Y
Palo Pinto	26,380	1/2/17	Machinery	69	55	0	0	1	0	0	Y
Panola	22,643	2/10/16	Food	188	11	0	0	0	739	0	Y
Parker	73,897	3/2/16	Rubber	383	58	0	0	0	0	2	Y
Parmer	10,401	14/0/38	Food	1	9	0	0	0	47,766	12	Y
Pecos	16,515	5/11/2	Mining O&G	13	38	0	0	0	11,306	2	Y
Polk	41,959	1/2/20	Lumber	39	49	0	0	0	0	0	Y
Potter	108,765	1/1/10	Food	376,579	218	0	190,349	0	9,432	1	Y
Presidio	7,285	34/0/1		0	10	0	0	0	0	2	Y
Rains	7,457	2/1/10	Metals F	0	4	0	0	0	0	2	Y
Randall	100,400	3/0/9	Metal P	132	20	0	0	0	71,579	5	Y
Reagan	4,277	2/33/1--	Mining O&G	0	15	0	0	0	4,152	0	Y
Real	2,740	3/0/2		0	6	0	0	0	28	0	Y
Red River	14,662	2/0/33	Metal F	1	20	0	0	0	20,740	0	Y
Reeves	15,309	18/2/3	Mining N	0	49	0	0	0	22,771	0	Y
Refugio	8,198	7/16/1	Mining O&G	1	31	0	0	0	2,099	0	Y
Roberts	875	11/0/0		.1	6	0	0	0	7,639	0	Y
Robertson	15,355	8/5/17	Stone	238	14	0	0	0	0	1	Y
Rockwall	34,287	2/0/14	Metal P	255	22	0	0	1	172	0	Y
Runnels	11,928	4/2/38	Metal F	1	35	0	0	0	46,487	3	Y
Rusk	45,572	2/9/16	Mining C	38	63	0	0	0	293	1	Y
Sabine	10,892	2/2/21	Lumber	3	13	0	0	0	0	0	Y
San Augustine	8,193	1/3/11	Lumber	0-0.5	9	0	0	0	0	0	Y
San Jacinto	18,625	1/0/9	Lumber	1	12	0	0	0	0	0	Y
San Patricio	66,005	3/3/20	Chemicals	150,577	94	0	0	1	1,711	1	Y
San Saba	5,565	5/3/16		1	9	0	0	0	522	0	Y
Schleicher	3,325	6/25/1	Mining O&G	2	8	0	0	0	1,932	0	Y
Scurry	19,027	1/26/5	Mining O&G	6	35	0	0	0	39,917	2	Y
Shackelford	3,413	5/28/7	Mining O&G	0	6	0	0	0	2,878	1	N
Shelby	22,857	4/0/33	Food	32	39	0	0	0	0	0	Y
Sherman	3,068	24/0/7		2	6	0	0	0	77,813	10	Y

Continued on page 352

KEY: (1) Total Population, 1996. (2) % employed in Agriculture, Mining and Manufacturing, 1997. (3) Leading Industrial Sector, 1995 (4) Tons of Hazardous Waste Generated, 1995. (5) Number of Leaking Petroleum Storage Tanks, 1997. (6) Number of State or National Superfund Sites, 1999. (7) Lbs. of Toxics Released on Land and/or Injected Underground, 1997. (8) Number of Curbside Recycling Programs, 1997. (9) Thousands of Acres of Highly Erodible Cropland, 1997. (10) Number of Animal Feedlots, 1997. (11) Presence of rare species.

COUNTY	WATER INDICATORS							AIR INDICATORS				
	TOTAL WATER (12)	GRDWTR USE (13)	WATER USE CATEGORIES (14)	TOXIC RELEASE (15)	PESTICIDE CONTAM. (16)	GRDWTR CONTAM. (17)	FECAL COLIFORM (18)	OZONE STDS. (19)	TOXIC EMISS. (20)	CARC. EMISS. (21)	POLL. EMISS. (22)	SO₂ & NO EMISS. (23)
Montague	5,574	29%	50/5/0%	0	0	0	1	A	0	0	340	0
Montgomery	45,529	90%	84/0/3%	1,294	0	5	0	NA	613,216	123,119	9,769	1,856
Moore	377,930	99%	1/95/2%	327,116	0	1	1	A	474,949	20,048	31,964	85
Morris	98,515	1%	2/0/98%	6,625	0	3	0	A	48,574	7,625	1,929	6
Motley	4,820	93%	7/86/0%	0	0	0	0	A	0	0	0	0
Nacogdoches	14,343	65%	67/9/8%	1,516	0	1	0	A	648,175	168,775	2,662	0
Navarro	10,429	4%	72/0/10%	6,234	0	1	1	A	29,277	11,750	3,528	0
Newton	3,725	82%	49/39/9%	0	0	0	0	A	0	0	2,695	0
Nolan	9,973	38%	41/32/6%	5	0	1	0	A	83,419	0	3,140	1,185
Nueces	96,645	3%	56/0/40%	452,517	0	37	1	NNA	2,916,541	558,848	51,722	9,853
Ochiltree	89,877	98%	2/95/0%	0	0	1	0	A	0	0	4,155	0
Oldham	11,073	82%	7/69/0%	0	0	0	1	A	0	0	0	0
Orange	65,668	25%	18/6/67%	54,849	0	7	1	NA	6,352,525	491,531	36,593	7,214
Palo Pinto	7,562	3%	51/7/0%	0	0	1	2	A	0	0	4,049	1,439
Panola	11,188	47%	31/0/8%	0	0	0	2	A	0	0	9,160	0
Parker	12,372	45%	75/3/3%	0	0	5	3	A	87,169	65,966	2,140	88
Parmer	462,350	100%	0/97/0%	0	0	1	1	A	208,546	0	0	0
Pecos	82,444	98%	6/93/0%	0	0	0	0	A	0	0	32,023	0
Polk	7,008	69%	81/3/10%	0	0	3	2	A	88,825	9,919	13,109	0
Potter	61,557	56%	43/38/8%	11,000	0	6	0	A	330,094	14,842	56,500	45,452
Presidio	25,292	16%	6/92/0%	0	0	0	1	A	0	0	0	0
Rains	1,968	29%	62/1/0%	0	0	0	1	A	0	0	32	0
Randall	74,433	77%	31/63/1%	500	1	3	1	A	435,250	197,000	1,175	0
Reagan	46,866	100%	2/94/0%	0	0	1	0	A	0	0	7,308	0
Real	1,208	56%	55/34/0%	0	0	0	0	A	0	0	0	0
Red River	7,599	26%	26/46/0%	0	0	0	0	A	0	0	0	6
Reeves	107,007	98%	3/94/1%	0	0	1	0	A	0	0	4,476	0
Refugio	1,853	76%	67/0/0%	0	0	0	1	A	0	0	6,977	0
Roberts	7,591	96%	2/93/0%	0	0	2	0	A	0	0	965	0
Robertson	29,382	88%	10/71/0%	0	0	4	0	A	1,149	0	10,087	8,912
Rockwall	6,566	2%	97/0/0%	0	0	0	0	A	250	0	8	0
Runnels	11,427	30%	18/64/1%	0	0	0	1	A	0	0	170	0
Rusk	35,059	25%	20/1/0%	0	0	0	0	A	89,060	53,505	140,517	136,038
Sabine	2,261	39%	79/0/16%	0	0	0	1	A	0	0	1,354	0
San Augustine	1,708	31%	78/9/0%	0	0	0	0	A	0	0	6	0
San Jacinto	2,655	90%	87/0/1%	0	0	0	0	A	0	0	0	0
San Patricio	20,908	12%	40/1/55%	31	0	15	0	NNA	112,967	28,169	6,832	0
San Saba	6,194	53%	17/52/0%	0	0	0	0	A	0	0	0	0
Schleicher	3,010	96%	20/54/0%	0	0	0	0	A	0	0	1,396	0
Scurry	8,642	62%	41/18/0%	0	0	0	0	A	0	0	3,951	0
Shackelford	2,086	31%	38/10/0%	0	0	0	0	A	0	0	813	0
Shelby	7,472	36%	40/1/21%	0	0	1	1	A	22,020	0	448	0
Sherman	263,299	100%	0/98/0%	0	0	0	0	A	0	0	2,699	0

Continued on page 353

KEY: (12) Acre-Feet of Total Water Used, 1996. (13) % of Total Water Use from Groundwater, 1996. (14) % Categories of Water Use: Municipal/Irrigation/Industrial, 1996. (15) Lbs. of Toxic Releases to Surface Water and/or Public Sewer, 1997. (16) Number of Confirmed Contaminated Groundwater Cases from Pesticides, 1997. (17) Number of Confirmed Contaminated Groundwater Cases, 1997. (18) Number of Public Water Systems Exceeding Fecal Coliform Standards, 1996-97. (19) Attainment, Non-attainment, Near non-attainment and Pristine for Ozone Standards, 1999. (20) Lbs. of Industrial Toxic Air Emissions, 1997. (21) Lbs. of Industrial Toxic Carcinogenic Air Emissions, 1997. (22) Tons of Electric Utility and Industry Emissions of Criteria Pollutants, 1997. (23) Tons of Electric Utility Emissions of Sulfur Dioxide and Nitrogen Oxide, 1997.

COUNTY	INDUSTRIAL BASE			WASTE INDICATORS				LAND INDICATORS			
	TOTAL POP. (1)	PERCENT EMPLOYED (2)	LEADING INDUSTRIAL (3)	HAZARDOUS WASTE (4)	PETROLEUM LEAKAGE (5)	SUPERFUND SITES (6)	INJECTION TOXICS (7)	CURBSIDE RECYCLING (8)	ERODIBLE CROPLAND (9)	ANIMAL FEEDLOTS (10)	RARE SPECIES (11)
Smith	164,547	2/2/15	Machinery	758,755	231	0	0	1	66	0	Y
Somervell	5,961	2/0/4		580	6	0	0	0	0	0	Y
Starr	49,206	14/0/1		0	21	0	0	0	43,581	3	Y
Stephens	9,938	2/12/18	Mining O&G	1	16	0	0	1	152	0	N
Sterling	1,394	13/22/2		0	5	0	0	0	106	1	Y
Stonewall	1,885	2/13/2		0	5	0	0	0	26,816	0	N
Sutton	4,531	5/25/1	Mining O&G	4	10	0	0	0	0	0	Y
Swisher	8,801	16/0/8		1	11	0	0	0	125,188	5	N
Tarrant	1,306,207	1/1/16	Transport	237,888	1,780	3	0	12	0	1	Y
Taylor	127,440	1/3/7	Mining O&G	1,123	232	1	0	0	19,565	2	Y
Terrell	1,256	19/4/0		47	8	0	0	0	0	0	Y
Terry	13,361	13/17/2	Mining O&G	13	34	0	0	0	105,226	1	N
Throckmorten	1,842	11/11/2		0	7	0	0	0	327	0	Y
Titus	26,264	1/5/39	Food	234	36	0	0	0	262	2	Y
Tom Green	104,973	2/2/13	Instrument	203	151	0	0	0	3,140	8	Y
Travis	680,541	1/0/14	Electronic	1,812,611	623	0	0	5	66	2	Y
Trinity	12,553	1/0/10	Metal F	1	15	0	0	0	427	0	Y
Tyler	19,604	3/0/9	Metal F	72	22	0	0	0	0	0	Y
Upshur	34,520	2/1/13	Lumber	140	39	0	0	1	36	0	Y
Upton	4,144	4/24/1	Mining O&G	5	13	0	0	0	2,035	0	Y
Uvalde	25,012	12/2/9	Food	20	46	0	0	0	5,952	6	Y
Val Verde	43,291	2/0/4	Electronic	41	69	0	0	0	0	0	Y
Van Zandt	42,067	8/5/4	Chemicals	7	42	3	0	0	0	0	Y
Victoria	81,023	1/5/9	Chemicals	4,514,474	105	0	23,040,356	0	0	0	Y
Walker	56,253	1/0/7	Lumber	57	45	0	0	0	0	1	Y
Waller	26,577	4/0/20	Machinery	20	32	1	0	0	0	1	Y
Ward	12,886	0/21/2	Mining O&G	27	35	0	0	0	449	0	Y
Washington	29,295	2/1/22	Food	494	39	0	0	0	0	0	Y
Webb	177,147	2/6/2	Mining O&G	29	143	0	0	2	0	0	Y
Wharton	41,385	10/4/14	Rubber	1,374	60	0	0	0	0	2	Y
Wheeler	5,584	6/3/2		1	8	0	0	0	37,624	3	Y
Wichita	131,661	1/2/15	Stone	39,388	221	0	0	0	265	0	Y
Wilbarger	15,863	4/1/12	Food	324	29	0	0	0	15,325	0	Y
Willacy	19,584	20/2/10	Apparel	0	16	0	0	0	7,969	0	Y
Williamson	196,190	1/1/17	Electronic	26,847	115	0	0	3	1,999	0	Y
Wilson	26,989	5/0/6		1	19	0	0	0	64	6	Y
Winkler	8,297	0/25/1	Mining O&G	3	9	0	0	0	0	0	Y
Wise	40,212	1/8/15	Mining O&G	43	57	0	0	1	44	2	Y
Wood	33,312	2/2/12	Food	6	61	0	0	1	201	4	Y
Yoakum	8,646	9/26/1	Mining O&G	43	16	0	0	0	68,174		N
Young	17,796	1/10/18	Mining O&G	50	38	0	0	0	939	0	Y
Zapata	10,662	1/20/1	Mining O&G	0	7	0	0	0	0	0	Y
Zavala	12,000	13/1/14	Food	5	19	0	0	0	4,732	3	Y
TOTALS	19,128,261	1/2/13	Mining O&G	148,415,057	20,710	75	89,929,406	153	3,227,311	553	

KEY: (1) Total Population, 1996. (2) % employed in Agriculture, Mining and Manufacturing, 1997. (3) Leading Industrial Sector, 1995 (4) Tons of Hazardous Waste Generated, 1995. (5) Number of Leaking Petroleum Storage Tanks, 1997. (6) Number of State or National Superfund Sites, 1999. (7) Lbs. of Toxics Released on Land and/or Injected Underground, 1997. (8) Number of Curbside Recycling Programs, 1997. (9) Thousands of Acres of Highly Erodible Cropland, 1997. (10) Number of Animal Feedlots, 1997. (11) Presence of rare species.

	WATER INDICATORS							AIR INDICATORS				
COUNTY	TOTAL WATER (12)	GRDWTR USE (13)	WATER USE CATEGORIES (14)	TOXIC RELEASE (15)	PESTICIDE CONTAM. (16)	GRDWTR CONTAM. (17)	FECAL COLIFORM (18)	OZONE STDS. (19)	TOXIC EMISS. (20)	CARC. EMISS. (21)	POLL. EMISS. (22)	SO₂ & NO EMISS. (23)
Smith	38,331	47%	86/2/9%	4,849	0	11	1	NNA	547,832	170,970	6,377	0
Somervell	8,147	21%	10/6/0%	0	0	1	4	A	0	0	38	33
Starr	56,364	3%	14/81/0%	0	0	0	0	A	0	0	1,059	0
Stephens	11,471	3%	14/8/0%	0	0	0	0	A	0	0	681	0
Sterling	1,880	96%	13/37/0%	0	0	0	0	A	0	0	2,955	0
Stonewall	1,692	64%	23/45/0%	0	2	0	0	A	0	0	0	0
Sutton	4,227	87%	33/53/0%	0	0	0	0	A	0	0	3,957	0
Swisher	176,582	99%	1/96/0%	0	0	1	0	A	0	0	0	0
Tarrant	291,304	5%	87/0/10%	92,694	0	52	5	NA	1,498,598	259,490	10,702	5,556
Taylor	33,059	5%	87/2/3%	1,562	0	5	2	A	422,689	32,100	500	0
Terrell	1,050	99%	25/47/0%	0	0	1	0	A	0	0	8,429	0
Terry	150,775	99%	2/98/0%	0	0	2	1	A	0	0	246	0
Throckmorten	2,091	10%	15/0/0%	0	0	0	0	A	0	0	0	0
Titus	44,309	7%	13/0/6%	0	0	2	1	A	22,230	0	179,154	169,358
Tom Green	79,299	47%	28/68/1%	0	0	11	2	A	147,000	600	1,198	570
Travis	165,000	6%	83/1/8%	1,227,149	0	29	5	NNA	243,232	42,175	5,181	2,020
Trinity	2,181	47%	80/0/0%	0	0	0	1	A	0	0	0	0
Tyler	3,013	94%	87/1/3%	0	0	1	0	A	23,965	0	0	0
Upshur	7,119	72%	64/0/2%	0	0	1	3	A	48,991	0	235	0
Upton	22,402	100%	4/83/0%	0	0	2	0	A	0	0	6,321	0
Uvalde	93,447	98%	7/91/0%	0	0	1	3	A	0	0	174	0
Val Verde	16,399	44%	86/10/0%	0	0	1	4	A	68,148	0	115	0
Van Zandt	10,983	57%	51/9/6%	0	0	1	3	A	0	0	11,769	0
Victoria	52,305	61%	26/23/37%	1,745	0	3	0	NNA	753,918	76,008	11,590	1,490
Walker	11,562	62%	92/0/2%	0	0	2	0	A	0	0	8,563	0
Waller	30,985	95%	15/76/0%	0	0	3	0	NA	0	0	1,015	0
Ward	18,764	55%	21/47/0%	0	0	2	0	A	0	0	20,235	10,363
Washington	7,797	34%	67/1/7%	501	0	1	1	A	167,156	143,555	817	0
Webb	48,752	4%	72/20/0%	0	0	4	1	A	4,940	13	3,184	689
Wharton	372,427	54%	2/98/0%	924	0	1	0	A	120,379	772	2,825	45
Wheeler	6,530	64%	13/45/0%	0	0	0	0	A	0	0	809	0
Wichita	57,711	5%	49/45/4%	134,416	0	4	0	A	1,815,226	83,074	9,596	518
Wilbarger	33,070	70%	9/59/2%	0	0	0	0	A	28,900	28,900	20,381	19,615
Willacy	44,719	0%	12/88/0%	0	0	1	0	A	0	0	541	0
Williamson	44,516	43%	89/0/3%	255	0	4	0	A	32,519	28,059	87	0
Wilson	22,869	82%	20/70/0%	0	0	0	0	A	0	0	0	0
Winkler	3,796	100%	60/0/0%	0	0	0	0	A	0	0	8,712	0
Wise	25,594	19%	22/2/5%	0	0	0	1	A	19,110	19,100	8,354	0
Wood	8,813	68%	58/2/2%	15	0	1	0	A	10,830	0	3,339	0
Yoakum	155,402	100%	1/95/0%	0	0	1	0	A	0	0	1,556	0
Young	7,846	6%	42/0/0%	0	0	0	0	A	54,282	0	5,718	3,752
Zapata	7,231	1%	30/63/0%	0	0	0	0	A	0	0	2,459	0
Zavala	79,003	76%	3/95/1%	0	0	0	0	A	0	0	88	0
TOTALS	16,775,079	59%	21/63/9%	67,623,033	32	876	229		108,366,675	14,459,765	2,578,505	1,041,484

KEY: (12) Acre-Feet of Total Water Used, 1996. (13) % of Total Water Use from Groundwater, 1996. (14) % Categories of Water Use: Municipal/Irrigation/Industrial, 1996. (15) Lbs. of Toxic Releases to Surface Water and/or Public Sewer, 1997. (16) Number of Confirmed Contaminated Groundwater Cases from Pesticides, 1997. (17) Number of Confirmed Contaminated Groundwater Cases, 1997. (18) Number of Public Water Systems Exceeding Fecal Coliform Standards, 1996-97. (19) Attainment, Non-attainment, Near non-attainment and Pristine for Ozone Standards, 1999. (20) Lbs. of Industrial Toxic Air Emissions, 1997. (21) Lbs. of Industrial Toxic Carcinogenic Air Emissions, 1997. (22) Tons of Electric Utility and Industry Emissions of Criteria Pollutants, 1997. (23) Tons of Electric Utility Emissions of Sulfur Dioxide and Nitrogen Oxide, 1997.

For information about localities, see both cities and counties. Many federal agencies and programs are found under U.S. or National. Many state agencies and programs are found under Texas. Maps, tables, and charts have been indexed.

Abandoned hazardous waste sites, 72, 294–295, 321

Abandoned oil wells, 75, 263

Abandoned Well Plugging Fund, 75

Abilene, 12

Acid rain, 57, 171, 173, 176, 182, 184, 265, 267n.75

Acrylic acid, 320

Act to Preserve and Protect the Wild Game, Wild Birds, and Wild Fowl, 149

Adopt-a-Beach program, 123

Agent Orange, 201

Agricultural easement, 137–138

Agricultural organic farming, 246–247, 249n.71

Agriculture. See also Livestock; Texas Department of Agriculture; U.S. Department of Agriculture

acreage statistics, 130

air pollution and, 231

alternative farming, 136

boll weevil and, 247

CAFOs (Confined Animal Feeding Operations), 44, 50, 59, 60, 76, 100n.132, 231

conservation easement and, 159, 161–162

Conservation Reserve Program (CRP) and, 129, 132, 134–136

conservation tillage, 136

crop-subsidy incentives, 132

deficiency payments and, 135, 140n.85

definitions related to, 129

drought losses, 2

economic impact of, 129–130, 140n.96

employment in, 338, 342–353

and environment generally, 130–131

erosion of cropland, viii, 131–135, 342–353

federal legislation on, 11, 12, 125, 132, 134–138, 159

fertilizers and, 18, 76, 118, 131, 132

groundwater contamination and, 76–77

injection wells and, 73, 74–75

irrigation for, 10–12, 18, 34n.44

maps of, 130, 131

non-point-source pollution and, 58–60

number of farms and ranches, 128, 129

pesticide use, 76–77, 118, 131, 231, 237–239, 241–242, 244–245, 247

prime farm land, 129, 133

protection of farmland, 137–138

ranching in ecological regions, 115–117

raw materials consumption and, 272

sedimentation and, 133–134

soil conservation practices, 132, 134–136

suburban/urban sprawl and threats to, 136–137

surface water and cropland erosion, 133–134

sustainable, 136

tree plantations and, 125–126, 278

water quality and, 49

water use of, 10–12, 34n.44

wetlands and, 93, 95, 144, 155–156, 159

wildlife management and, 150, 160

Agriculture Resources Protection Authority, 245

Air conditioning, 262

Air indicators

county data on, 342–353

description of, 341

Air pollution

agriculture and, 231

air toxics, viii, 173, 180–181, 197–204, 340–341, 342–353

area sources of, 230–231

combustion pollution, 222–229

control costs by industry, 176, 229

criteria pollutants, 173, 177–191

definition of, 170–171

decline in, 178

environmental justice and, 103

federal legislation on, 170–175

Flexible Attainment Region (FAR) program, 191, 195, 197

grandfathered facilities and, 226–227

greenhouse effect, 176, 204–210

history of legislation on, 169–172

human health and, 169–171, 176, 178, 185, 186, 187, 190, 197–202, 222, 231n.3, 232n.55, 234n.129

indoor, 176, 211–213

by manufacturing industries, 221–222

maquiladoras and, 35

market-based incentives on, 174–177

by mechanical processes facilities, 229–230

mobile sources of, 214–220

monitoring of, 179, 180–181, 191–197, 200

national ambient air quality standards (NAAQS), 171, 172, 173, 177–191

recycling and, 277

in schools, 212

sick building syndrome, 212

stationary sources of, 220–230

stratospheric ozone depletion, 210–211

upset emissions, 222

visibility and Class I areas, 213–214

waste incinerators and, 227–228

waste-to-energy facilities and, 278–279

Air Pollution Control Program, 192

Air Products, Inc., 52, 53, 297

Air quality. See Air pollution

Air toxics, viii, 173, 180–181, 197–204, 221–225, 340–341, 342–353

Akzo Nobel Chemicals, Inc., 53

Alabama, 15–16, 109, 150, 199, 299

Alachlor, 240, 241

Alaska, 109

Alazan Bay, 89

Alcoa (Aluminum Company of America), 186, 221, 224–225, 324

Aldicarb, 172

Aldine, 180

Algae, 91

Alligator Bayou, 64

Alternative agriculture, 136

Alternative fuels, 219–220, 264–265

Aluminum Company of America (Alcoa), 186, 221, 224–225, 324

Alvin, 307

Amarillo, 12, 20, 309

American Chrome & Chemicals, 307

American Ecology, 318, 319, 331n.111

American Envirotech, 316

American Farmland Trust, 136–137, 289

American Fisheries Society, 153

American Lung Association, 211

American National Power, 259

American Rivers, 40

American Smelting and Refining Company (ASARCO), 203, 205, 307

American Zinc, 324

Amistad Reservoir, 33n.1, 66

Ammonia, 52, 64

Amoco, 53, 205, 297, 307, 329n.26

Anahuac, 321

Anderson County, 25, 342–343

Andrews County, 23, 308, 321, 342–343

Angelina County, 25, 224, 297, 305, 324, 342–343

Angelina River, 65

Animal waste, 23–24, 50, 58, 59, 231

Antidegradation policy, 46

Anti-nuclear groups, 259

Aplomado falcon, 116, 151, 154

Apparel and other finished products, 224

Appropriation doctrine, 5–6

Aquatic life. See Fish and fishing; Oyster waters

Aquifers. See also names of specific aquifers

    contamination of, 69–77

drinking water and, 87–88

drought effects on, 1

groundwater and, 3–4

hazardous waste and, 318–319

map of, 5

mining of, 10, 11

monitoring of, 41

precipitation and, 3, 4

recharge of, 4, 11

as underground rivers, 7–8

vulnerability ratings, 71

water use from, 4, 9

Aquilla Reservoir, 62, 63

Aquilla Water Supply District, 84

Aransas Bay, 89, 91, 92

Aransas County, 118, 305, 342–343

Aransas National Wildlife Refuge, 118

Archer County, 20, 342–343

Arco Chemical Company, 53, 297, 307

Area sources of air pollution, 230–231

Argonne National Labs, 275

Arizona, 18, 109, 237

Arkansas, 15–16, 46, 109, 299

Arlington, 12, 115

Armstrong County, 20, 342–343

Army Corps of Engineers, U.S., 42, 89, 90, 95, 106, 120, 157, 207

Arrowhead Reservoir, 21

Arroyo Colorado, 58, 67

Arsenic, 20, 60, 72, 73, 76, 77, 199, 203, 225, 326

ASARCO (American Smelting and Refining Company), 203, 205, 307

Asbestos products, 199, 212, 213

Asbestosis, 213

Ash from incinerators, 278

Asphalt-batching operations, 229–230

Asphalt manufacturers, 229

Asthma, 185, 190

AT&T, 326

Atascocita, 321

Atascosa County, 27, 342–343

Atrazine, 63, 84, 240, 241

Attorney General's Office, 86

Attoyac Bayou, 65

Attwater, 184

Attwater Prairie Chicken National Wildlife Refuge, 162

Attwater's Prairie Chicken, 116, 154

Audubon Society, 40, 289

Austin

    acid rain monitoring, 184

    air pollution, 183, 184, 188, 192, 194, 195, 208

    air quality monitoring, 180

    bus ridership in, 218

    commuter rail line between San Antonio and, 219

    electric rates in, 259, 262–263

    electric utilities in, 208, 256, 259, 261, 262–263

    environmental justice, 103, 104

    fish contamination in Town Lake, 27, 242

    light rail service in, 219

    mitigation and, 141

    municipal solid waste in, 274

    as near nonattainment area, 195

    non-point-source pollution control program in, 58

    out-migration from, 26, 27

    ozone levels of, 179, 181, 192, 194

    parks in, 113, 115

    population of, 26–27

    Save Our Springs ordinance, 98n.66

    sludge and, 281

    solar energy and, 256, 261

    toxic water releases, 53

    traffic congestion in, 216

    vehicles and vehicle miles in, 216

    wastewater treatment facilities in, 160

    water and wastewater rates in, 13

    water use of, 12, 18

    xeriscaping in, 18

Austin County, 24, 342–343

Australia, 207

Automobile body shops, 229

Automobiles

    alternative fuels for, 219–220

    car-pooling, 218

    comparison of emissions from different fuels, 218

    electric vehicle technology, 220

emissions testing program, 216–217

fleets of vehicles, 217, 219

fuel cell cars, 220, 234n.176

gasoline for, 174, 178, 194, 214–215, 218

high-occupancy vehicle (HOV) lanes, 215, 218, 219

low-emission vehicles, 174, 175, 215, 219

in Mexico, 196

miles driven in, 216, 218

number of, 176, 216, 217, 218

pollution control equipment for, 216

as pollution source, 214–215

reduction of number on the road, 217–219

tailpipe-emission standards, 174, 194, 215–216

Automobile service stations, 194, 229

Ayers Bay, 89

Aztec Ceramics, 324

B. A. Steinhagen Reservoir, 26, 62, 63, 67

Backyard Habitat Program, 163

Bacteria in drinking water, 84. *See also* Fecal coliform bacteria

Baffin Bay, 89, 92

Bailey County, 29, 342–343

Bailey Waste Disposal, 324

Bakeries, 229

Balcones Canyonlands National Wildlife Refuge, 162

Balcones Escarpment, 117

Balcones Fault Zone, 117

Baldwin Waste Oil, 324

Bandera County, 26, 342–343

Barbours Cut, 67, 92

Bardwell Reservoir, 62, 63

Barlow's Wills Point Plating, 324

Barrier islands, 119, 123

Barton Creek, 46

Barton Creek Wilderness Park, 115

Barton Springs, 27, 46, 58, 98n.66

BASF Corp., 52, 53, 307, 316

Bastrop Bay, 89

Bastrop County, 26, 147, 342–343

Bathroom fixtures, water-efficient, 14, 262

Bayer Corp., 53, 307

Baylor County, 20, 342–343

Baylor University, 181

Bays

environmental water use and, 14–16

inflow and, 15

non-point-source pollution of, 58

risks to, 47–49, 90–92

shoreline loss of, 121–122

size of, 3, 14, 44, 45, 88

toxics and, 49

uses of, 15, 45, 47–49

water quality of, 41, 45, 49, 90–92

Baytown, 53, 307

Beaches

access to, 120–121

acreage of, 138n.6

Adopt-a-Beach program, 123

of barrier islands, 123

debris on, 122

definition of, 119

General Land Office (GLO) and, 108

ownership of, 120–121

public beach, 119, 120, 121

Beaumont

acid rain monitoring, 233n.74

air pollution, 183–188, 190, 192–195, 200

air quality monitoring, 180, 190

contaminated drinking water and, 319

hazardous waste incineration facilities, 316

mass transit in, 219

as nonattainment area, 192, 193, 195

ozone levels of, 172, 179, 192–195, 226

toxic on-site releases, 307

water use and water supply of, 12, 25

BECC (Border Environment Cooperation Commission), 35, 36–37, 56

"Bed and banks" permit, 7

Bee County, 309, 342–343

Beeville, 184

Bell County, 24, 305, 306, 324, 342–343

"Beneficial use" principle, 5

Benomyl, 240

Benzene, 170–171, 199, 200, 203, 204, 222, 225, 235n.188, 280

Beryllium, 199

Bevill amendment, 171

Bexar County

air toxics, 200

Edwards Aquifer and, 1, 3

environmental indicators, 342–343

Superfund sites, 324

toxic releases by, 305

toxic transfers, 306

urban expansion in, 137

water supply and demand in, 27

Bhopal, India, 172, 231n.4

BIFs (boilers and industrial furnaces), 314, 316

Big Bend National Park, 23, 107, 117, 180–182, 184, 212–214

Big Creek Lake, 62, 63

Big Cypress Creek, 67

Big Spring, 205, 259

Big Thicket National Preserve, 112, 113, 140n.66

Bioaccumulation, 51–52, 201

Bioassessment studies, 66

Biochemical Oxygen Demand (BOD), 50, 64

Biodiversity, 144, 148, 151–152

Biomass energy, 253, 261, 266n.22

Biomonitoring, 52, 53

Bioremediation, 314

Biosolids, 280–281

Biosphere, 148

Birding, 118, 154, 164

Birds. *See also* Wildlife

air toxics and, 201

and dumping in Gulf of Mexico, 97

in ecological regions, 115–117

endangered species, 150, 153, 154

extirpated from Texas, 151, 154

habitat for, 160

migratory birds, 117, 118, 144, 158

songbirds, 157

species of, 152

water species, 158

Birth defects, 170, 222, 225, 327

Bison, 151

Black Duck Bay, 67, 92

Black-footed ferret, 151

Blackland Prairie region, 116, 118

Blanco County, 26, 27, 342–343

Bluntnose shiner, 151

BOD (Biochemical Oxygen Demand), 50, 64

Boilers and industrial furnaces (BIFs), 314, 316

Boll weevil, 247

Bolson Deposits, 1, 11

Bonham, 307

Borden County, 23, 342–343

Border Environment Cooperation Commission (BECC), 35, 36–37, 56

Border issues
    air pollution, 35, 181, 184, 186, 187, 190, 196–197
    birth defects, 326
    drought, 33n.1
    environmental agreements, 37, 300, 322
    Environmental Protection Agency and, 35, 37–38
    hazardous waste, 35, 66, 312–313, 322, 326, 327, 331n.148
    historical view of, 35
    maquiladoras, 35, 300–301, 326
    NAFTA and, 35–38, 56
    population increases, 35, 36
    recent developments of, 35–38
    wastewater treatment, 23, 35, 55–56, 90
    water supply, 23, 35

Border XXI, 37

Borger, 307

Bosque County, 24, 342–343

Bosque River, 23, 58

Bottled water, 33n.29, 87

Bottomland forested wetlands, 157–158

Bowie County, 22, 306, 324, 342–343

BP Chemicals, Inc., 307

Brackettville, 322

Brandy Branch Reservoir, 62, 63, 67

Brazil, 207

Brazoria
    air pollution, 183, 184, 186, 193, 194
    air toxics, 222, 224
    hazardous waste production in, 297
    highway vehicle programs for, 215
    as nonattainment area, 193
    ozone levels of, 172, 179, 181, 193, 194

Brazoria County
    environmental indicators, 342–343
    ozone health consequences, 185
    population of, 89
    toxic air releases, 224
    toxic releases by, 305, 307
    toxic transfers, 306
    toxic water releases, 52, 54
    vehicle emissions testing, 217
    water supply and demand in, 24

Brazoria National Wildlife Refuge, 90, 162

Brazos-Colorado River Basin, 3, 51

Brazos County, 24, 208, 342–343

Brazos River, 3, 25

Brazos River Authority, 58

Brazos River Basin, 3, 7, 24, 51

Brewster County, 22, 36, 342–343

Brine, 74, 76, 321–322

Brio Refining, 324

Briscoe County, 29, 342–343

Brooks County, 309, 330n.67, 342–343

Brown County, 23, 305, 306, 307, 342–343

Brown tide, 91

Brownfields, 325–327

Browning-Ferris, Inc., 321

Brownsville
    air pollution, 184, 186, 188, 194
    air quality monitoring, 181
    birth defects in, 326
    PCB levels, 68
    toxics and, 66
    water resources and, 12, 28

Brownwood, 307

Buffalo Bayou, 25, 45, 67

Burleson County, 24, 305, 342–343

Burnet County, 26, 342–343

Burnett Bay, 67, 92

Bus ridership in urban areas, 218, 219

Butadiene, 200, 202, 222, 225

Butane, 257

Butler Ranch, 324

Butterflies, 163

Cabot Corporation, 221

Caddo Lake, 3, 46, 62, 63, 65, 67, 115, 182–183, 267n.75

CAFOs (Confined Animal Feeding Operations), 44, 50, 59, 60, 76, 100n.132, 231

Caldwell County, 27, 342–343

Calhoun County, 27, 224, 305, 306, 307, 324, 342–343

California
    air pollution of Los Angeles, 173
    carbon dioxide emissions, 207
    electricity use in, 254
    endangered species in, 150
    farmland protection in, 138
    hazardous waste and, 295, 299
    municipal solid waste in, 273
    pesticide use, 237
    population of, 273
    Santa Barbara channel spill in, 40
    solar energy in, 261
    state park acreage, 109
    vehicles and traffic congestion in, 218

Callahan County, 24, 342–343

Cameron County
    agriculture in, 140n.96
    birth defects in, 326
    drinking water from irrigators, 85
    environmental indicators, 342–343
    population of, 36
    Superfund sites, 324
    tourism in, 118
    toxic releases by, 305
    toxic transfers, 306
    urban expansion in, 137
    water supply and demand in, 28

Camp County, 22, 342–343

CAMS (continuous air monitoring system), 192

Canada, 35, 36, 144, 159, 207

Canadian River, 3, 20, 30, 117

Canadian River Basin, 3, 7, 51

Canals, 31

Cancer, 170, 201, 213, 222, 232n.55, 238, 239, 241, 248n.25

Candidate species, 148, 164n.13

Cap Rock Escarpment, 117

Carancahua Bay, 89

Carbumates, 238

Carbaryl, 240

Carbon adsorption, 314

Carbon dioxide, 204–210, 223

Carbon monoxide, 171, 173, 174, 177–179, 186–187, 193, 196, 219, 221, 224–227

Carcinogenic air emissions, in counties, 341, 342–353. See also Cancer

CARE (Clean Air Responsibility Enterprise), 227

Caribbean, 123

Carlos Bay, 89

Carolina parakeet, 151

Car-pooling, 218

Carrizo-Wilcox Aquifer, 5, 10, 11, 28, 71

Cars. See Automobiles

Carson, Rachel, 40

Carson County, 20, 309, 324, 342–343

Carthage, 278

Cass County, 224, 305, 307, 324, 342–343

Castro County, 29, 342–343

Cattle. See Livestock

Cavalcade Street, 324

CEC (Commission on Environmental Cooperation), 35, 36, 37

Cedar Lakes, 89

Cedar Park, 138

CEIS (Center for Environmental Information and Statistics), 287

Cement-batching operations, 229–230

Cement kiln dust (CKD), 317

Cement kilns, 223, 228–229, 299, 314–317

Cement plants, 227, 228

Cenozoic Pecos Alluvium Aquifer, 5, 11, 23, 71

Center (city), 278

Center for Environmental Information and Statistics (CEIS), 287

Centers for Disease Control, U.S., 326

Central and South West Corporation (CSW), 208, 256–257, 259–260

Central Power and Light, 256

Central West Texas Water Planning Region, 26

CERCLA (Comprehensive Environmental Response, Compensation, and Liability Act), 43, 270, 292, 323

Certificates of Adjudication, 6

CFCs (chlorofluorocarbons), 206, 210, 215

Chambers County
air toxics, 204
environmental indicators, 342–343
landfills in, 321
ozone health consequences, 185
population of, 89
toxic releases by, 305, 307
toxic transfers, 307
toxic water releases, 54
vehicle emissions testing, 217
water supply and demand in, 24

Champion International Corp., 297

Channelview, 180, 203, 307

Chapparral Steel Midlothian, 307

Chemical industry, 13, 224, 292, 296, 304

Chemical Waste Management, 316, 318, 322

Cherokee County, 25, 342–343

Chevron, 72, 205, 308, 309

Chihuahua desert, 117

Childress County, 20, 342–343

China, 207

Chisos Mountains, 117

Chlordane, 27, 63, 67, 212–213, 242

Chlorides, 41, 63, 64, 82, 280

Chlorinated fluorocarbons, 179

Chlorinated hydrocarbons, 238

Chlorine, 85, 201, 237

Chlorofluorocarbons (CFCs), 206, 210, 215

Chocolate Bay, 89

Choke Canyon Reservoir, 29, 62, 63

Christmas Bay, 46, 89

Christmas Bay Preserve, 90

Citgo, 53, 205, 297

Cities. See specific cities

Ciudad Acuña, 36, 55, 300

Ciudad Juárez
air pollution, 180, 184, 186, 187, 190, 196–197
maquiladoras in, 36, 300
population of, 36
sewage treatment plants in, 37
toxics and, 66, 322
wastewater discharge of, 23, 55
wastewater treatment plants in, 56

Civilian Conservation Corps, 132

Civil Rights Act (1964), 103

CKD (cement kiln dust), 317

Clark Refining & Marketing, 221

Class I areas, visibility in, 213–214

Clay County, 20, 342–343

Clay products, 224, 304

Clayton, Billy, 31

Clean Air Act. See Federal Clean Air Act; Texas Clean Air Act

Clean Air Responsibility Enterprise (CARE), 227

Clean Air Scientific Advisory Committee, 178

Clean Rivers Act (1991), 43, 57, 58, 61

Clean Water Act (CWA)
antidegradation policy of, 46
dredging and, 155
groundwater monitoring and, 70
hazardous waste and, 292
of 1966, 40
of 1972, 40, 49, 120
of 1977, 40, 42, 50
1987 amendments to, 60
purpose of, 120
reporting requirements, 8
surface water quality and, 44, 45, 61
wetlands and, 155

Clear Creek Tidal, 67

Clear-cutting, 124, 127

Cleburne, 278

Climate. See Temperature

Clinton, Bill, 103, 260–261

Cloud seeding, 33

Clute, 180

CNG (Compressed Natural Gas), 219, 220

Coal, 13, 223–224, 225, 253, 254, 257, 258, 265

Coal and lignite mining, 265

Coastal area. *See* Gulf Coast

Coastal Barrier Resources Act (1982), 120

Coastal Barrier Resource System, 120

Coastal barriers. *See* Barrier islands; Beaches; Dunes; Wetlands

Coastal basins, 3

Coastal Bend Bays Plan, 92

Coastal Birding Trail, 118

Coastal Coordination Act (1977), 120

Coastal Coordination Council, 90, 120

Coast Alliance, 118

Coastal management plans, 90, 119–120, 122

Coastal Prairie, 128

Coastal Protection Fund, 97

Coastal Refining & Marketing, 297

Coastal Sand Plains region, 116, 118

Coastal Zone Act Reauthorization Amendments (1990), 43

Coastal Zone Management Act (1972), 119, 120

Cochran County, 29, 342–343

Coffield/Minerva Refinery, 324

Cogema, 309

Cogeneration, 257–258

COGS (Councils of Governments), 271, 275

Coke County, 23, 342–343

Coleman County, 23, 342–343

Collin County, 21, 137, 180, 185, 191, 217, 306, 344–345

Collingsworth County, 20, 344–345

Colonias, 55

Colorado, 109, 113, 128, 132, 159, 299

Colorado County, 26, 344–345

Colorado-Lavaca River Basin, 3, 51

Colorado River, 3, 23, 117

Colorado River Basin, 3, 7, 27, 29, 51

Colorado River Municipal Water District, 33

Colorado River Park, 115

Col-Tex Refinery, 324

Comal County, 27, 344–345

Comal River, 19

Comal Springs, 27, 43, 69

Comanche County, 24, 344–345

Comanche Peak nuclear project, 258–259

Combustion pollution, 222–229

Commission on Environmental Cooperation (CEC), 35, 36, 37

Community, definition of, 148

Community-Based Recovery Planning Process, 161

Community Air Toxics Monitoring Program, 181, 200

Community Right-To-Know program, 172, 333–334

Comparative risk analysis, 251–252

Comprehensive Environmental Response, Compensation, and Liability Act (CERCLA), 43, 270, 292, 323

Compressed natural gas (CNG), 219, 220, 264

Computer equipment, 224, 304

Computer resources, 287–288

Concho County, 23, 344–345

Concho River, 117

Concrete-batching operations, 229

Concrete products, 224, 304

Confined Animal Feeding Operations (CAFOs), 44, 50, 59, 60, 76, 100n.132, 231

Connecticut, 109, 237

Conoco, 308, 309

Conroe, 316

Conservation
    conservation tillage, 136
    of energy and energy efficiency, 261–263
    habitat conservation plans, 160–162
    history of, 105–106, 124–125
    industrial water use and, 14
    municipal water use and, 13, 14
    preservation versus, 105, 106
    of public lands, 106, 114–115
    renewable energy and, 259–261
    of soil, 132, 134–136
    of water, 13, 14, 17, 18, 32, 34n.62, 262
    of wetlands, 159–160
    of wildlife habitat, 159–160
    xeriscaping, 18, 262

Conservation Compliance Provision (CCP), 136

Conservation easement, 159, 161–162

Conservation Reserve Program (CRP), 129, 132, 134–136

Conservation Technology Information Center, 136

Construction industry, 61, 263, 292

Continuous air monitoring system (CAMS), 192

Convention of International Trade in Endangered Species of Wild Fauna and Flora, 144

Convention of Nature Protection and Wildlife Preservation, 144

Cooke County, 21, 344–345

Cooling units, 262

Cooperative Conservation Plan, 161

Copano Bay, 89

Corpus Christi
    air pollution, 179, 181, 183, 184, 186, 188, 190, 194, 195, 200, 203, 205
    air quality monitoring, 181, 190
    bus ridership in, 218
    desalination and, 33
    as Flexible Attainment Region, 191, 195
    injection wells in, 318
    as near nonattainment area, 195
    off-site treatment transfers, 307
    toxics and, 53, 307
    wastewater treatment facilities in, 160
    water and wastewater rates in, 13
    water resources of and water use in, 12, 29, 30, 92

Corpus Christi Bay, 89, 91, 92

Corpus Christi Inner Harbor, 47, 65, 91

Coryell County, 24, 344–345

Cost-benefit analysis, 251

Cottle County, 20, 344–345

Cotton gins, 229–230

Councils of Governments (COGS), 271, 275

Counties. *See also specific counties*
  environmental indicators for, 337–353
  map of, 340
Cox Bay, 67, 68, 89, 92
Crane County, 23, 344–345
Criteria pollutants, 173, 177–191. *See
  also* Carbon monoxide; Lead;
  Nitrogen oxides; Ozone; Particulate
  matter; Sulfur dioxide
Critical habitat, 145, 146–149, 155, 156
Crockett County, 23, 344–345
Cropland. *See* Agriculture
Crosby, 318
Crosby County, 29, 344–345
Crossroads Development, 318
Crown Central Petroleum, 297
CRP (Conservation Reserve Program),
  129, 132, 134–136
Cryptosporidiosis, 42, 82
Crystal Chemical, 324
CSC Disposal, 321
CSW (Central and South West Corpo-
  ration), 208, 256–257, 259–260
Culberson County, 22, 259, 344–345
CWA. *See* Clean Water Act
Cypress River Basin, 7, 51
Czechoslovakia, 207

Dairy Outreach Program, 58, 59
Dairy waste, 23, 58, 59
Dallam County, 20, 344–345
Dallas
  air pollution, 183, 184, 186, 188,
    190–195, 200, 230
  air pollution control, 172
  air quality monitoring, 180, 190
  brownfield pilot grant to, 325
  bus ridership in, 218
  environmental justice and, 103
  gasoline use in, 194
  high-occupancy vehicle lanes,
    218–219
  highway vehicle programs for, 215
  lead levels, 230
  light rail service in, 219
  mass transit in, 219
  as nonattainment area, 193, 195

ozone levels of, 172, 179, 182,
    192–195
  parks in, 113, 115
  pesticide use in, 242
  rapid transit system in, 219
  temperature in, 207, 209
  traffic congestion in, 216
  vehicles and vehicle miles in, 216, 217
  vehicles emission testing in, 216, 217
  wastewater discharges in, 51
  wastewater treatment in, 195
  water and wastewater rates in, 13
  water use of, 12
  water utilities in, 21, 22
Dallas County
  air toxics, 200, 224
  environmental indicators, 344–345
  highway vehicle programs for, 215
  ozone health consequences, 185
  Superfund sites, 324
  toxic releases by, 305
  toxic transfers, 306, 307
  toxic water releases, 54
  urban expansion in, 137
  vehicles emission testing in, 216–217
  water supply and demand in, 21
Dams, 31, 90, 261
DART (Dallas Area Rapid Transit), 219
Databases, 287–289
Davis Mountains, 117
Dawson, 84
Dawson County, 29, 344–345
DDE, 63, 67
DDT, 63, 67, 201, 237, 238, 248n.25
Deaf Smith County, 29, 344–345
Dechlorination, 314
Deciduous forests, 124
Deep-well injection. *See* Injection wells
Deer Park, 53, 180, 307, 316, 318, 321
Deforestation, 124
Degussa Corporation, 221
Delaney Clause, 243
Delaware, 109
Del Rio, 66, 322
Delta County, 22, 344–345

Delta Land and Community
  Corporation, 129, 136
Demographic changes. *See* Population
Denison, 307
Denton, 180, 208, 242
Denton County, 21, 185, 217, 305, 306,
  344–345
Denver City, 205
DERC (discrete emissions reduction
  credit), 174, 175
Deregulation of electric utilities,
  255–256
Desalination, 33
Desert bighorn, 151
DeWitt County, 27, 344–345
Diazinon, 241, 242
Dibromoethane, 202–203, 233n.105
Dickens County, 29, 344–345
Dicofol, 240
Diesel fuel, 220
Dimmit County, 27, 344–345
Dioxin, 25, 201–202, 317, 333
Direct reuse, 7
Discrete emissions reduction credit
  (DERC), 174, 175
Disposal Systems, Inc., 318
Dissolved oxygen
  in bays, 48
  fish kills and, 64
  in reservoirs, 47, 48, 63
  in rivers and streams, 48, 66
  as water quality indicator, 41, 44, 48,
    64, 66
Dixie Oil Processors, 324
Dockum Aquifer, 70
DOD (U.S. Department of Defense), 106
DOE (U.S. Department of Energy),
  275, 289, 308
Domino, 307
Donley County, 20, 344–345
Donna Reservoir, 62, 63, 67, 68
Donora, Penn., 169, 170
Double R. Plating Company, 324
Doughty, Robin, 149
Dow Chemical Company, 53, 297,
  307, 316
DRASTIC index, 71

Dredging, 42, 64, 93, 95, 120, 155

Drinking water

bottled, 33n.29, 87

"consumer confidence" reports on, 42, 87

consumption of, 77

contamination of, 78–86, 319

enforcement of standards, 86

federal environmental budget for, 77

federal legislation for, 42, 43, 77

hazardous waste and, 319

human health and, 78–82

from irrigators, 85

making of, 86

maximum contaminant levels, 78–82

organic testing, 82–83

protections for underground drinking water, 87–88

right to know quality of, 86–87

Source Water Assessment Program, 87

standards for, 82, 86

state program, 77, 82

test results, 83–85

types of systems, 77

unregulated, 88

violations of health-based requirements for, 83–86

water quality standards and, 8, 42, 47, 60, 77–87

Drought, 1–2, 6, 12, 27, 28, 33n.1, 90, 128, 132

Drought management, 2, 13, 16

Drum Bay, 89

Dry cleaners, 229

Dryden, 322

Ducks Unlimited, 159

Dumping in Gulf of Mexico, 97

Dune Protection Act (1973), 120, 122

Dunes, 119, 120, 122

DuPont Company, 53, 210, 297, 307, 316, 317

Dust Bowl Land Unit Projects, 128

Duval County, 308, 309, 330n.67, 344–345

E. I. DuPont De Nemours & Co. *See* DuPont Company

E. V. Spence Reservoir, 62, 63

Eagle Pass, 66

Easement. *See* Agricultural easement; Conservation easement

East Bay, 89

Eastland County, 24, 324, 344–345

East Texas Water Planning Region, 25–26

EBI (Environmental Benefit Index), 135

Echo Lake, 62, 63, 67, 68

Ecological regions, 115–117, 118, 139n27

Ecology, definition of, 148

Economic indicators

county data on, 342–353

description of, 338–339

Economic Policy Institute, vii

Ecosystems

definition of, 148

endangered, 154

Ecosystem management, 148

Eco-tourism. *See* Nature tourism

Ector County

environmental indicators, 344–345

injection wells in, 318

Superfund sites, 324

toxic air releases, 224

toxic releases by, 305

toxic transfers, 306

water supply and demand in, 23

Edinburg, 28, 181, 194

EDSTAC (Endocrine Disrupters Screening and Testing Advisory Committee), 202

Edwards Aquifer

designation as underground stream, 8

drinking water and, 87–88

drought and, 1

in Edwards Plateau, 116

groundwater depletion and, 8, 28

map of, 5

mining of, 11

overpumping of, 27, 28

population and development over recharge zone of, 27, 58

as San Antonio water source, 27, 58, 87–88

vulnerability rating for, 71

water pumped from, 43

Edwards Aquifer Authority, 8, 27, 43

Edwards County, 26, 344–345

Edwards Plateau, 116–117, 118

Edwards Plateau Aquifer, 26

Edwards-Trinity Aquifer, 5, 11, 71

Edwards Underground Water District, 8

Effects Screening Levels (ESLs), 199–200, 205, 222

Effluent reports and standards, 53–54

Ehrlich, Paul, 269

EIS (environmental Impact Statements), 43

Electric bill labeling, 257

Electricity, 253, 254–259

Electric utilities. *See also* Utilities

carbon dioxide emission from, 206, 208–209

cogeneration and, 257–258

deregulation and, 255–256

as grandfathered facilities, 226–227

green pricing and, 256–257

hazardous waste and, 296

labeling of electric bill, 257

number of, 176

pollution "allowances" for, 175–176

processes for making electricity, 257–258

rates of, 255, 259

regulatory compact system and, 254–255

retail competition in low-cost state, 255

sulfur dioxide emissions from, 214, 226–227

time-of-use pricing for, 262–263

toxic releases, 221, 223–225, 227, 254

Electric vehicle technology, 220

Electronic and electrical equipment, 13, 224, 296, 304

Electronic databases, 287–289

Elf Atochem, 316

Elk, 143, 151

Ellis County, 21, 305, 306, 307, 315, 321, 324, 344–345

El Paso

air pollution, 183–191, 193–197, 200, 202, 203, 205, 208, 233n.74

air pollution control, 172

air quality monitoring, 180, 190

Bolson Deposits in, 1

bus ridership in, 218

conjunctive water use and, 32

environmental justice, 103

gasoline use in, 194

highway vehicle programs for, 215

mass transit in, 219

as nonattainment area, 193, 195, 196–197

ozone levels of, 172, 179, 193–195, 196

power plants in, 208

toxics and, 66, 307

traffic congestion in, 216

vehicles and vehicle miles in, 216, 217

vehicles emission testing in, 216–217

water and wastewater rates in, 13

water supply and, 11, 22

water use of, 12

El Paso County

air pollution, 187, 188, 189, 200

birth defects in, 326

drinking water from irrigators, 85

environmental indicators, 344–345

highway vehicle programs for, 215

ozone health consequences, 185

population of, 36

Superfund sites, 324

toxic releases by, 305

toxic transfers, 306, 307

vehicles emission testing in, 216–217

wastewater treatment in, 55, 195

water supply and demand in, 22

Emergency Planning and Community Right-to-Know Act (EPCRA), 172, 292, 333

Emission reduction credits, 174–175

Emission Reductions Banking Rule, 174

Emissions Inventory, 222, 226, 333

EMPAK, 318

Enchanted Rock, 117

Endangered ecosystems, 154

Endangered species

at-risk species, 147, 150

causes of loss, 147

in counties, 342–353

definition of, 145

definitions relating to, 148

in ecological regions, 115–117

federal legislation on, 43, 144–149

improving species, 164n.20

international agreements on, 144

map of, 152

public opinion on, 150–151

reasons for protection of, 143 144, 145

recovery plans and, 145

states with most endangered species, 150

statistics on, 143, 152 153, 165n.22

in Texas, 116, 147, 150, 153–155

Endangered Species Act (1973) (ESA), 43, 143, 144, 145–149, 160–161, 167

Endocrine disrupters, 200, 201–202, 240, 333

Endocrine Disrupters Screening and Testing Advisory Committee (EDSTAC), 202

Endosulfan, 240

Energy. *See also* Nuclear power

biomass energy, 253, 261, 266n.22

coal, 253, 265–266

coal and lignite mining, 265

conservation and energy efficiency, 261–263

consumption of, 253

electricity, 253, 254–259

geothermal energy, 266n.22

green building and, 263

history of, 253–254

hydroelectric energy, 253, 261, 266n.22

liquid petroleum gas (LPG), 264–265

natural gas, 253, 254, 257, 258, 263–264

oil production, 252–254, 263

recycling and, 277

renewable resources, 259–261

solar power, 256, 260–261

time-of-use pricing for, 262–263

wind energy, 259–260

Energy Information Agency, 289

Energy Supply and Environmental Coordination Act (1973), 172

Envirocare, 308

EnviroFacts Warehouse, 287, 289

Environmental Benefit Index (EBI), 135

Environmental Defense Fund, 152, 153, 160, 165n.22, 278, 289, 321, 334

Environmental Equity and Justice Task Force, 104

Environmental Impact Statements (EIS), 43, 144

Environmental indicators by county, 337–353

Environmental information sources, 287–289

Environmental justice, 103–104

Environmental Priorities Project (STEPP), 251–252

Environmental Processing, 318

Environmental Protection Agency (EPA)

air pollution and, 171–173, 176–178, 186–188, 191–193, 196, 199, 231n.3

air toxics and, 199, 202, 222

asbestos and, 213

border issues and border-related operations, 23, 35, 37–38

brownfields and, 325

cement kiln dust and, 317

Community Right-to-Know program and, 333

Comparative Risk Project, 251

drinking water and, 42, 77, 82, 83, 85, 87

endocrine disrupters and, 240

environmental justice and, 103

estuaries and, 92

fish monitoring and, 68

food monitoring and, 240

hazardous waste and, 75, 292, 293, 301, 302, 311, 314, 317, 321, 323, 328

indoor air pollution and, 211–213

information system of, 287–289, 334

lead levels and, 212

manufacturing industries, 222

motor vehicle emission limits, 216

municipal solid waste and, 271, 282

national ambient air quality standards (NAAQS) and, 177–178

nonattainment areas and, 177, 191–193, 215

pesticides and, 237, 238, 243–245

PM10 standards, 178, 187–190

Sector Facility Indexing (SFI) Initiative, 311, 334

sludge and, 280, 281

solid wastes and, 270

storm-water discharge permits, 60

sulfur dioxide levels, 176

Toxicity Characteristic rule of, 295

visibility in Class I areas, 213–214

wastewater discharge permits, 44, 50, 60

water quality monitoring and, 41, 42–43, 45

Environmental Working Group, 135

EPA. See Environmental Protection Agency

EPCRA (Emergency Planning and Community Right-to-Know Act), 172, 292, 333

Erath County, 24, 58, 59, 344–345

Erosion

abatement programs for soil erosion, 134–136

consequences of soil erosion, 132–133

gully erosion, 133

rill erosion, 133

sheet erosion, 133

of shoreline, viii, 95, 118, 119, 121–122

soil erosion and agriculture, viii, 131–135, 342–353

streambed erosion, 133

surface water and cropland erosion, 133–134

"T" factor for, 133, 134

water erosion, 133

wind erosion, 133

ESA. See Endangered Species Act (1973)

ESLs (Effects Screening Levels), 199–200, 205, 222

Espiritu Santo Bay, 89

Estuaries

aquatic life in, 88–89

definition of, 119

environmental water use and, 14–16

inflow and, 15

map of, 15

National Estuary Program, 92

non-point-source pollution in, 57

pollution of, 90–91

risks to, 49, 90–92

as shellfish waters, 88

size of, 14, 88

uses of, 15, 45, 49

water quality of, 41, 42, 90–92

Ethylene glycol, 52

Everest Exploration, Inc., 309

EWGs (exempt wholesale generators), 255

Exempt wholesale generators (EWGs), 255

Exports

of hazardous waste, 297–301

of municipal solid waste, 273

Extinction, viii, 152–154. See also Endangered species

Extirpation, 148, 151

Exxon, 53, 221, 307, 308, 309

Falcon Reservoir, 33n.1, 62, 63

Falls City, 308

Falls County, 24, 344–345

Fannin County, 21, 306, 307, 344–345

FAR (Flexible Attainment Region) program, 191, 195, 197

Farm Bill (1985), 132, 134, 136, 155–156, 159

Farm Bill (1990), 125, 144, 155

Farm Bill (1996), 12, 132, 135, 137, 144, 155, 159

Farmers Branch, 307

Farming. See Agriculture

Farm Service Agency, 134, 157

Farmworkers, 244, 249n.57

Fayette County, 26, 344–345

Fayette Prairie, 128

FDA (Food and Drug Administration), 87, 240

Fecal coliform bacteria

in coastal area, 89, 92, 96

in counties, 342–353

in drinking water, 84, 85, 86

in surface water, 23, 25, 28, 30, 47–48, 61, 63, 64

as water quality indicator, 41, 44, 47–48, 61, 64

Federal agencies. See headings beginning with National and U.S.

Federal Agriculture Improvement and Reform Act (1996), 132, 137

Federal Clean Air Act. See also Texas Clean Air Act

acid rain and, 173

air toxics and, 173, 199, 222

area sources and, 230–231

CFCs and halon and, 210

compliance with, 191–197

criteria pollutants and, 173, 177–191

economic impact of, 176

federal operating permits and, 223

hazardous waste and, 292

highway vehicle programs, 216, 217

manufacturing industries, 222

mobile pollution sources, 174, 216

1963 law, 170

1970 amendments to, 171, 173

1977 amendments to, 172, 173

1990 amendments to, 172, 173–176, 232n.17, 334

ozone and, 173–174

pollution control equipment and, 316–317

small business and, 229–231

solid waste and, 270

visibility protection provisions, 213

Federal Farm Program, 11

Federal Forest Incentive Program, 125

Federal Insecticide, Fungicide and Rodenticide Act (FIFRA), 43, 242

Federal legislation. See specific laws

Federal operating permits, 223

Federal Soil Bank program, 125

Federal Solid Waste Disposal Act, 270

Federal Water Pollution Control Act (1948), 40, 97n.1

Fermi, Enrico, 258

Fertilizers, 18, 76, 118, 131, 132, 231, 281

FIFRA (Federal Insecticide, Fungicide and Rodenticide Act), 43, 242

Fifth Amendment private property rights, 165n.24

Fina Oil and Chemical Co., 297, 307

Fish and fishing. *See also* Wildlife

acid rain and, 182

advisories or bans on consumption, 21, 25–26, 47, 63, 64, 66–68, 91, 92, 267n.74

conditions of, 151–154

conservation of fish, 144, 149

dioxin contamination and, 25, 201

economic impact of, 88 89, 139n.31, 163–164

endangered species, 147, 150, 153

extirpated from Texas, 151, 153

fish kills, 64, 91

freshwater fish, 144, 149, 153, 155

in Gulf of Mexico, 88–89, 118

mercury levels in fish, 25–26, 67, 68

mitigation on, 141

nature tourism and, 163–164

number of species of fishes, 15

PCBs in, 67, 68

pesticide residues in, 21, 28, 66–68, 238, 242

shellfishing, 47, 64, 68, 88, 89, 91–92

water quality and, 21, 25–26, 41, 45, 47, 64, 66–68

Fish and Wildlife Coordination Act, 144

Fish and Wildlife Service. *See* U.S. Fish and Wildlife Service

Fisher County, 24, 344–345

Flagship species, 153

Fleets of vehicles, 217, 219

Flexible Attainment Region (FAR) program, 191, 195, 197

Floods, 90

Florida, 109, 144, 150, 254

Floyd County, 29, 344–345

Fluorescent lamps, 266

Fluoride, 20, 73

Foard County, 20, 344–345

Folic acid, 326

Food, Drug and Cosmetic Act, 243

Food and Drug Administration (FDA), 87, 240

Food and kindred products

federal legislation on, 238, 240, 243–244

as industrial sector, 129–130

monitoring chemicals in, 240

pesticides in, 243

toxic releases and, 224, 304

water use and, 13

Food Quality Protection Act (1996), 238, 240, 243–244

Food Security Act (1985), 132, 136

Ford Motor Company, 234n.176

Forestry Incentives Program, 126

Forests. *See also* Timber industry

bottomland forested wetlands, 157–158

clear-cutting in, 124, 127

definitions related to, 124, 129

federal legislation on, 124–125

industrial forests, 125–126

map of, 126

national forests, 108, 123–125, 127

old-growth or virgin forests, 124, 125

overharvesting of, 125

ownership of, 126

revenues from timber sales from national forests, 127

state forests, 108

state legislation on, 125

temperate deciduous forests, 124

in Texas, 115–116, 125–127

tropical rain forests, 124

value of nonindustrial landowner timber, 127

Forest seed, 184

Forest Service. *See* Texas Forest Service; U.S. Forest Service

Forest Stewardship Council, 126

Formic acid, 320

Formosa Plastics Corp., 307

Fort Bend County, 24, 185, 281, 306, 324, 344–345

Fort Bend Subsidence District, 8

Fort Davis National Historic Site, 112, 113

Fort Stockton, 303

Fort Worth

air pollution, 183, 184, 186, 188, 191–195, 200

air pollution control, 172

air quality monitoring, 180

bus ridership in, 218

drinking water in, 84

gasoline use in, 194

high-occupancy vehicle lanes, 218–219

highway vehicle programs for, 215

industrial wastewater systems, 195

mass transit in, 219

as nonattainment area, 193, 195

ozone levels of, 172, 179, 192–195

pesticides in, 242

sludge and, 281

traffic congestion in, 216

vehicles and vehicle miles in, 216, 217

vehicles emission testing in, 216–217

water use of, 12

Fort Worth Prairie, 128

Fosdic Lake, 62, 63, 67

Fossil fuels, 178, 207. *See also specific fuels*

Foundries, 229–230

Fountain darter, 116, 147

Fox, 154

France, 207

Franklin, Benjamin, 1

Franklin Associates, 275

Franklin County, 22, 344–345

Franklin Mountains, 117

Freeport, 53, 307, 316

Freestone County, 21, 344–345

French Limited, 324

Freon, 210

Frio County, 27, 344–345

Friona Municipal Water System, 84

Frisco, 180, 191

Fritz, Edward ("Ned"), 140

Fuel. *See* Gasoline

Fuel cell technology, 220, 234n.176

Fungicides, 240

Furans, 200, 201, 202, 228

Furniture and fixtures, 224, 229

Gaines County, 29, 344–345

Galveston

air pollution, 183–186, 188, 193–195, 200

air quality monitoring, 180

air toxics, 200

beach cleanup in, 122

beaches of, 121
gasoline use in, 194
highway vehicle programs for, 215
industrial wastewater systems, 195
as nonattainment area, 193, 195
ozone levels of, 172, 179, 181, 193–195
parks in, 113
toxic water releases, 54
Galveston Bay, 15, 25, 67, 89, 92, 95, 96, 97, 118
Galveston Bay Estuarine System, 92
Galveston Bay Plan, 92
Galveston County
    air toxics, 224
    environmental indicators, 344–345
    hazardous waste production in, 297
    injection wells in, 318
    ozone health consequences, 185
    population of, 89
    Superfund sites, 324
    tourism in, 118
    toxic releases by, 305, 307
    toxic transfers, 306
    water supply and demand in, 24
Garbage. See Trash
Gardens, 18
Garland, 12, 180, 208, 230
Garwood Irrigation District, 29
Garza County, 29, 346–347
Gas absorption, 314
Gasoline, 174, 178, 194, 214–215, 218
Gasoline stations, 194, 229
Gas production. See Natural gas
Geddes, Robert, 137
General Cable Corp., 307
General Electric Laboratory, 33
General Motors, 326
Geneva Industries, 324
Geographic Information Systems (GIS), 287
Geological Survey, U.S., 70, 287
Georgia, 15–16, 109
Geothermal energy, 266n.22
Germany, 207
Gibraltar Chemical, 318, 319

Gillespie County, 26, 27, 117, 346–347
GIS (Geographic Information Systems), 287
Glasscock County, 23, 346–347
Glass products, 224, 304
GLO. See Texas General Land Office
Global warming, 176, 205–207, 209
Glyphosate, 241, 242
GNB Techs., Inc., 307
GNI Chemicals Corp., 307
Goddard Institute, 206
Golden-cheeked warbler, 116, 147, 155
Golf courses, 114, 242
Goliad County, 27, 346–347
Gonzales County, 27, 346–347
Goodstein, Eban, vii
Governor's Task Force on Nature Tourism in Texas, 164
Grain elevators, 229–230
Grandfathered facilities, 226–227
Grapevine, 180
Grasslands, 115–116, 128
Graves, John, 105
Gray County, 20, 305, 346–347
Grayson County, 21, 306, 307, 346–347
Great Britain, 170, 207
Great Trinity Forest, 115
Green building, 263
Greenhouse effect, 176, 204–210
Green pricing, 256–257
Green products, 273, 282–284
Gregg County, 22, 195, 305, 306, 346–347
Gregory, 316
Grimes County, 24, 306, 346–347
Grizzly bear, 151
Groundwater
    abandoned waste sites and, 72
    agriculture and, 76–77
    aquifers and, 3–4, 10, 69–70
    conjunctive use of, 32
    contamination sources, 70–77, 294, 319–320, 340
    in counties, 342–353
    decline in, 18
    demand for, 2–3

drinking water and, 87–88
hazardous waste and, 72
hydrological cycle and, 2, 3, 39, 40
industrial waste and, 72
injection wells and, 73–75
irrigation and, 6, 10
landfills and, 279–280
mining and, 72–73
monitoring of, 69, 70–71
municipal solid waste and, 72
municipal water use and, 9, 10–11
oil and gas industry and, 75–76
overpumping of, 95
pesticides and, 76–77
priority groundwater management areas, 8
private property rights and, 5, 7–8, 33n.29
quality of, 41, 43, 69–77
regional supply and demand issues, 20–30
saline groundwater from wells, 28
supply of, 4
surface water and, 69
underground storage tanks and, 71–72, 99n.104, 294
uranium tailings ponds and, 308
use of, 4, 9–11, 342–353
water wells and, 75
Groundwater conservation districts, 1
Groves, 180, 203
Guadalupe, 184
Guadalupe Bay, 89
Guadalupe County, 27, 306, 307, 346–347
Guadalupe Mountains, 117, 180
Guadalupe Mountains National Park, 46, 214
Guadalupe River, 3, 28
Guadalupe River Basin, 3, 7, 51
Guam, 199
Gulf Coast. See also Gulf of Mexico; headings beginning with Coastal; specific cities and counties
    air pollution, 200, 202
    beach access, 120–121
    beaches of, 108, 117–121

definitions related to, 119
as ecological region, 116
erosion of shoreline, viii, 95, 118, 119, 121–122
federal legislation on, 119–120, 120
fishing and, 88–89, 118
length of, 44, 96, 117
playa lakes and, 158, 159
population of, 89–90, 117–118
red and brown tides, 91
state efforts for protection of coastal waters, 90
state legislation on, 120
tourism in, 118
vulnerability rating for, 71
water quality of, 88–96, 118
Gulf Coast Aquifer, 5, 10, 11, 25, 28, 30
Gulf Intracoastal Waterway, 89, 95, 96
Gulf Metals Industries, Inc., 324
Gulf of Mexico. See also Gulf Coast
    beach access, 120–121
    beach debris, 122
    beaches of, 108, 117–121
    brown tide, 91
    fecal coliform in, 89, 96
    fish advisories and, 67, 91, 92
    in-stream flows in, 28
    length of shoreline, 44, 96, 117
    ocean dumping, 97
    ocean spills and, 90, 92, 96–97
    ocean trash, 123
    oil and gas rigs in, 97
    as oyster waters, 88, 89, 96
    red tide, 91, 92
    shoreline loss, viii, 95, 118, 119, 121–122
    uses of, 45
    water quality of, 45, 49, 67, 96, 118
Gulf States Utilities, 208
Gully erosion, 133
Guy (city), 281
Gymnodinium breve, 91

Habitat
    acquisitions of wildlife habitat, 162–163

conservation and preservation of, 146, 159–162
critical habitat, 145, 146–149, 155–156
destruction of, 153
of endangered species, 146–149, 153
federal legislation on, 144–149
loss of wildlife habitat, 154–155
mitigation and, 141
nature tourism and, 163–164
state legislation on, 149–150
urban wildlife habitat, 163
as water quality issue, 64–65
wetlands as, 155–160
Habitat Conservation Plan (HCP), 146, 160–161
Habitat Management Plan, 160
Habitat Transaction Method, 161
HABs (harmful algal blooms), 91
Hagerman National Wildlife Refuge, 116
Hale County, 29, 346–347
Hall County, 20, 346–347
Hall Street, 324
Halons, 210
Hamilton County, 24, 346–347
Hangar-Siles Mason Co., 309
Hansen, James, 206
Hansford County, 20, 346–347
Hardeman County, 20, 346–347
Hardin County, 25, 185, 324, 346–347
Harmful algal blooms (HABs), 91
Harris County
    air pollution, 191, 200, 204
    air toxic emissions in, 222
    air toxics, 224
    environmental indicators, 346–347
    hazardous waste production in, 297
    highway vehicle programs for, 215
    injection wells in, 318
    landfills in, 321
    ozone health consequences, 185
    population of, 89
    storm-water discharge permits, 60
    Superfund sites, 324
    tourism in, 118
    toxic releases by, 305, 307

toxic transfers, 306, 307
toxic water releases, 52–54
urban expansion in, 137
vehicles emission testing in, 216–217
water supply and demand in, 24
Harris Galveston Coastal Subsidence District, 8, 25
Harris Sand Pits, 324
Harrison, Benjamin, 124
Harrison County
    air toxics, 224
    environmental indicators, 346–347
    hazardous waste in, 297, 329n.21
    Superfund sites, 324
    toxic air releases, 224
    toxic releases by, 305, 307
    toxic transfers, 306
    water supply and demand in, 22
Hart, Stuart, 284, 285n.55
Hart Creosoting Company, 324
Hartley County, 20, 346–347
Harvey Industries, 324
Haskell County, 24, 346–347
Hawaii, 109, 113, 150, 199
Hayes-Sammons Warehouse, 324
Haynes Bay, 89
Hays County, 26, 27, 147, 346–347
Hazardous and Solid Waste Amendments, 270
Hazardous Substances Spill Prevention and Control Act, 328
Hazardous waste. See Industrial and hazardous waste
HAZTRAKS, 301
HCFCs (hydrochlorofluorocarbons), 210–211
HCP (Habitat Conservation Plan), 146, 160–161
Health. See Human health
Hemphill County, 20, 346–347
Henderson County, 21, 25, 324, 346–347
Henslow's sparrow, 151
Herbicides, 76, 201, 238, 240, 241, 242
HEW (U.S. Department of Health, Education and Welfare), 170
Hidalgo County
    agriculture in, 140n.96

birth defects in, 326

drinking water from irrigators, 85

environmental indicators, 346–347

population of, 36

Superfund sites, 324

urban expansion in, 137

wastewater treatment in, 55

water supply and demand in, 28

Higgins Wood Preserving, 324

Highlands Acid Pit, 324

High-level radioactive waste, 305

High-occupancy vehicle (HOV) lanes, 215, 218–219

High Plains region, 117, 118, 158

Highways, 106, 141, 217–219

Hill County, 24, 346–347

Historical areas, 108

Hockley County, 29, 346–347

Hoechst-Celanese Chemical Co., 52, 53, 307, 316

Holnam, Inc., 315

Homes. *See* Residential use

Hood County, 24, 346–347

Hopkins County, 22, 346–347

Hospitals, 229, 302, 303

Household hazardous waste, 282

Houses. *See* Residential use

Houston

    air pollution, 183–188, 190, 191, 193–195, 200, 202, 203, 208

    air quality monitoring, 180, 190

    air toxics, 200, 202

    brownfield pilot grant to, 325

    bus ridership in, 218, 219

    Environmental Foresight project, 252

    gasoline use in, 194

    hazardous waste incineration facilities, 316

    high-occupancy vehicle lanes, 218–219

    highway vehicle programs for, 215

    injection wells in, 318

    as nonattainment area, 193, 195

    ozone levels of, 172, 179, 181, 182, 193–195, 226

    parks in, 113

power plants in, 208

sludge and, 281

toxic transfers, 307

toxic water releases, 53

traffic congestion in, 216, 218

vehicles and vehicle miles in, 216, 217

vehicles emission testing in, 216–217

wastewater discharges in, 51

wastewater treatment in, 195

water and wastewater rates in, 13

water supply and, 11, 12–13

water use of, 12, 34n.45

Houston Chemical Services, 316

Houston County, 25, 324, 346–347

Houston Industries, Inc., 208, 221

Houston Lead, 325

Houston Regional Monitoring Network, 186

Houston Scrap, 324

Houston Ship Channel, 25, 45, 65, 67, 96, 186

Houston toad, 147

Houston Water Planning Region, 24–25

HOVs (high-occupancy vehicles), 215, 218–219

Howard County, 23, 77, 305, 346–347

Hubbard Creek Reservoir, 62, 63

Hudspeth County, 22, 36, 303, 346–347

Hueco Basin Aquifer, 22

Hueco-Mesilla Bolson Aquifer, 5, 10, 11, 32, 71

Hueco Springs, 27

Human health

    air pollution and, 169–171, 176, 178, 182, 185–187, 190–192, 197–202, 211–212, 222, 231n.3, 232n.55, 234n.129

    air toxics and, 197–202, 222

    asbestos and, 213

    asthma, 185, 190

    birth defects, 170, 222, 225, 326

    cancer, 170, 201, 213, 222, 232n.55, 238, 239, 241, 248n.25

    drinking water and, 78–82, 84

    effects screening levels (ESLs) and, 199–200, 205

    endocrine disrupters, 200, 201–202, 240, 333

indoor air pollution and, 211–212

industrial and hazardous waste and, 293, 326

lead exposure and, 212, 213

municipal solid waste and, 274

neural tube defects, 326

pesticides and, 213, 238–242, 244, 245, 248n.25, 249n.57

reproductive disorders, 201, 240

Hunt County, 22, 161, 346 347

Hunting, 115–117, 143, 144, 148, 149, 163–164

Huntsman C4 Corp., 205

Huntsman Petro Corp., 316

Huntsville, 184

Hutchinson County, 20, 224, 305, 307, 346–347

Hydrocarbons, 174, 219, 264

Hydrochloric acid, 320

Hydrochlorofluorocarbons (HCFCs), 210–211

Hydroelectric energy, 253, 261, 266n.22. *See also* Electric utilities; Electricity

Hydrogen fluoride, 180, 225

Hydrological cycle, 2, 3, 39, 40

Idaho, 109

IEC, Inc., 309

Illegal dumps, 280

Illinois, 109, 137, 169, 207, 295

Impervious cover, 61

Imports

    of hazardous waste, 297–301

    of municipal solid waste, 273

"In situ" (solution) mining, 266, 308, 309

Incidental taking permit, 146

Incineration

    of hazardous waste, 227–228, 296, 299, 314–317

    incinerator ash, 278

    of municipal solid waste, 278–279

India, 172, 207, 231n.4

Indiana, 109, 199, 207, 265

Indicator species, 153

Indoor air pollution, 176, 211–213

Industrial and commercial machinery, 224, 304

Industrial and hazardous waste
  abandoned hazardous waste sites, 72, 294–295, 321
  brownfields, 325, 327
  capacity to treat, 299–300
  classification of, 293, 294, 300
  in counties, 342–353
  definition of, 292–293
  disposal of, 294, 296–300, 303–308
  exemptions from hazardous waste permits, 322
  exports and imports of, 297–301
  federal legislation on, 292
  flow of, 291
  generation of, 295–296, 297
  groundwater contamination and, 72, 74, 75–76, 294
  hierarchies of management of, 309
  human health and, 293, 326
  incineration of, 227–228, 296, 299, 314–317
  of industry, 292, 296, 304
  injection wells and, 73–74, 299
  landfills and, 294, 296, 298, 299, 320–322
  management of, 309–328
  maquiladoras and, 35, 300–301, 326
  monitoring of, 41
  neutralizing of, 314
  nonhazardous industrial waste, 293, 298–299
  off-site treatment of, 297–298, 302, 303, 304, 307
  of oil and gas industry, 75–76
  permits for hazardous waste disposal, 303, 316
  pollution control taxes, 312
  pretreatment of, 52
  radioactive waste, 301–309
  reasons for concern about, 293–295
  recycling/reuse of, 298, 299, 310, 313
  restricted areas, 323–328
  source reduction for, 309–313
  spills and, 90, 92, 96–97, 294, 319, 328, 331n.111
  state regulation of, 270, 291–292, 322–323
  statistics on, viii, 291, 292, 295, 296

  Superfund for cleanup, 72
  Texas Clean Industries 2000, 311–312
  toxic releases by county, 305
  toxic transfers by county, 306
  tracking industrial environmental performance, 311
  transport of, 328
  treatment of, 297–300, 302
  underground injection of, 317–320
  violations on, 322–323
  Voluntary Cleanup Program for, 325, 327–328
  as waste indicator, 339
  in wastewater, 48–54
Industrial sectors. *See also names of specific sectors*
  in counties, 342–353
  as economic indicator, 338–339
Industrial Transformer, 324
Industry. *See also headings beginning with Industrial; specific companies; specific industries*
  air pollution control costs, 176, 229
  air toxics and, 173, 198–199, 205, 221–222, 224
  conservation of water and, 14, 34n.62
  in counties, 342–353
  electricity consumption, 254
  employment in, 338, 342–353
  injection wells and, 73, 299, 317–320
  in nonattainment areas, 195
  ozone and, 210–211
  smog and, 169
  storm-water discharge permits, 60
  "takings" legislation and, 167
  tracking environmental performance of, 311
  wastewater discharge permits, 50–51
  water use by, 4, 9, 13–14, 20–30, 34n.62, 60, 339, 342–353
Inflow, 15
Information sources on environment, 287–289
Injection wells, viii, 73–75, 297, 299, 308, 317–320, 342–353
Inland Eastex, 53
Inland/terrestrial wetlands, 92, 157

Inorganic chemicals, in drinking water, 81, 83–84
Insecticides, 238, 240, 242, 246
Institute for Southern Studies, vii
In-stream flow methodology, 15
Integrated Pest Management (IPM), 246
Interbasin transfer of water rights, 32
Intergovernmental Panel on Climate Change (IPCC), 207
Interior Department, U.S., 10, 97, 112, 124
Intermodal Surface Transportation Efficiency Act (ISTEA), 218
International Air Quality Management District, 197
International Convention for Northwest Atlantic Fisheries, 144
International Creosoting, 324
International issues. *See Border issues; Mexico; other countries*
International Maritime Organization, 123
International Paper Co., 307
International Tropical Timber Organization, 126
Internet resources, 287–289
Iowa, 109
IPCC (Intergovernmental Panel on Climate Change), 207
IPM (Integrated Pest Management), 246
Irion County, 23, 346–347
Irrigation
  for agriculture, 10–12, 18, 34n.44
  in counties, 342–353
  drinking water from irrigators, 85
  future demand for, 18
  groundwater and, 6, 10
  high-efficiency systems for water conservation, 262
  hydrological cycle and, 39
  map of, 11
  regional supply and demand issues, 20–30
  surface water and, 10
  as water indicator, 339
  water rights and, 6
  water use and, 4, 9, 11–12
Irrigation Act (1889), 5–6
Irving, 12

ISP Techs, 307

ISTEA (Intermodal Surface Transportation Efficiency Act), 218

Italy, 207

Ivory-billed woodpecker, 151, 154

Izaak Walton League, 40

J. C. Pennco, 324

Jack County, 21, 346–347

Jackson County, 30, 346–347

Jaguar, 151

Jaguarundi, 116

Japan, 144, 158, 207

Jasper County, 25, 305, 324, 346–347

Jasper Creosoting Company, 324

JCS Company, 324

Jeff Davis County, 22, 36, 346–347

Jefferson, Thomas, 131

Jefferson County
  air toxics, 200, 203, 222, 224
  environmental indicators, 346–347
  hazardous waste in, 297, 329n.21
  injection wells in, 318
  ozone health consequences, 185
  State Superfund sites, 324
  toxic releases by, 305, 307
  toxic transfers, 306
  toxic water releases, 54
  water supply and demand in, 25

Jensen Drive Scrap, 324

Jerrell B. Thompson Battery, 324

Jewett, 307

Jim Hogg County, 28, 346–347

Jim Wells County, 346–347

Joe Pool Lake, 62, 63

Johnson, Lady Bird, 276

Johnson County, 24, 346–347

Jones County, 24, 348–349

Jordan, Charles, 113

Kansas, 109, 132, 159, 299

Karnes County, 27, 72, 266, 308, 309, 324, 348–349

Katy Prairie, 115

Kaufman, Wallace, 119

Kaufman County, 21, 306, 348–349

Keller Bay, 89

Kendall County, 27, 348–349

Kenedy County, 348–349

Kent County, 24, 348–349

Kentucky, 15–16, 109, 299

Kerr County, 26, 348–349

Kerrville, 259

Keystone species, 153

Kickapoo Reservoir, 21

Kilgore, 318, 319

Kilns. See Cement kilns

Kimble County, 23, 348–349

King County, 20, 348–349

King Ranch, 116

Kingsland, 324

Kinney County, 26, 36, 348–349

Kleberg County, 118, 308, 309, 330n.67, 348–349

Klineberg, Stephen, vii

Knott, 77

Knox County, 24, 324, 348–349

Koch Refining Co., 205, 297

Koppers, 324

Kwikset Corp., 307

Kyoto Agreement, 176, 210

Lacy Act, 144

Laguna Atascosa National Wildlife Refuge, 118

Laguna Madre, 28, 89, 91, 92, 94, 96, 118

Laidlaw Environmental Waste Management of Texas, 321

Laidlaw/Rollins Environmental, 316

Lake Canyon, 28

Lake Colorado City, 62, 63

Lake Como, 62, 63, 67

Lake Conroe, 62, 63

Lake Cooper, 22

Lake Corpus Christi, 29

Lake Fork, 22

Lake Granbury, 62, 63

Lake Houston, 25, 63, 65

Lake Kemp, 62

Lake Limestone, 62, 63

Lake Livingston, 62, 63, 65

Lake Medina, 31

Lake Meredith, 20, 30

Lake Mexia, 62, 63

Lake Olden, 62, 63

Lake o' the Pines, 62, 63

Lake Palestine, 65

Lakes. See also Reservoirs; specific lakes
  human construction of, 3
  non-point-source pollution in, 57
  playa lakes, 158–159
  water-quality monitoring of, 41

Lake Tawakoni, 22, 62, 63, 84

Lake Texana, 29, 30, 62, 63

Lake Texoma, 116

Lake Travis, 27

Lake Waco, 24, 58

Lake Waxahachie, 62, 63

Lamar County, 22, 348–349

Lamb County, 29, 348–349

Lampasas County, 24, 348–349

Land. See Agriculture; Landowners; Private property; Public lands; Soil; Wildlife

Land Disposal Restriction (LDR), 321

Landfills, 271, 274, 279–280, 294, 296, 298, 299, 320–322

Land indicators
  county data on, 342–353
  description of, 339

Landowner Incentive Program, 159–160

Landowners. See also Private property; Residential use
  endangered species and, 147, 148–149, 150–151
  parks' benefits to, 113–114
  "takings" legislation and, 167
  water rights and, 4–5
  wetlands and, 159–160
  wildlife habitat protection and, 159–161

Landscaping, 18

Land treatment, 320

Land trusts, 162

La Paz Agreement, 300, 322

La Porte, 53, 307, 316

Laredo, 12, 28, 66, 184, 188–190, 194, 205, 325

Laredo formation, 70

La Salle County, 27, 348–349

Lavaca Bay, 30, 67, 68, 89, 92

Lavaca County, 30, 348–349

Lavaca-Colorado Estuary, 15

Lavaca-Guadalupe River Basin, 3, 51

Lavaca River, 3, 29, 30

Lavaca River Basin, 3, 51

Lavaca River Basin Water Planning Region, 30

Lavon Lake, 62, 63

Law. *See names of specific laws*

Lawns and gardens, 18

LBJ National Historic Park, 112, 113, 184

LDR (Land Disposal Restriction), 321

Lead
    air pollution and, 171, 173, 178, 190–191, 230
    from cement kilns, 223
    in drinking water, 42, 84–85, 86
    in groundwater, 73
    in hazardous waste sites, 72
    health effects of, 212, 213, 225, 326
    indoor air pollution and, 212
    from landfills, 280
    monitoring of, in air emissions, 179
    national ambient air quality standards and, 177
    in rivers, 64, 66

Leather industry and leather products, 224, 292

Lee County, 24, 348–349

Leona Springs, 27

Leon County, 24, 306, 307, 348–349

Leon Creek, 65

Leon River, 24

Leon Springs pup fish, 147

LEVs (Low Emission Vehicles), 174, 175, 219

Liberty County, 24, 185, 324, 348–349

Light rail systems, 219

Lignite, 223–224, 225, 254, 257, 258, 265. *See also* Coal

Lila Wallace Reader's Digest Fund, 113

Limestone County, 24, 348–349

Lindzen, Richard, 206

Lipscomb County, 20, 348–349

Liquid petroleum gas (LPG), 264–265

Little Cypress Bayou, 65

Live Oak County, 72, 266, 306, 308, 309, 348–349

Livestock
    groundwater and, 9
    regional water supply and demand issues, 20–30
    surface water and, 9
    waste from, 23–24, 44, 50, 58, 59, 60, 76, 231
    water use and, 4, 9, 20–30

Llano County, 26, 27, 324, 348–349

Llano Estacado, 117

Llano Grande, 67

Llano Uplift, 117, 118, 212

Lockheed Environmental Analysis and Display System, 181

Lone Star Ammunition, 324

Longhorn Army Ammunition Plant, 324

Longhorn Cavern, 107

Longview
    acid rain monitoring, 184
    air pollution, 183, 184, 191, 192, 194, 195
    air quality monitoring, 180
    as Flexible Attainment Region, 195
    as near nonattainment area, 195
    ozone levels of, 179, 191, 192, 194
    toxic on-site releases, 307

Lord, Roger, 125

Lotus, L.L.C., 308

Louisiana, 46, 52, 104n.4, 109, 199, 207, 295

Louisiana vole, 151

Love Canal, 201

Loving County, 23, 318, 348–349

Low dissolved oxygen. *See* Dissolved oxygen

Low-emission vehicles (LEVs), 174, 175, 215, 219

Lower Colorado River Authority, 15, 208, 221

Lower Colorado River Basin Water Planning Region, 26–27

Lower Rio Grande Plain, 137

Lower Rio Grande Valley
    agricultural drainage wells of, 74–75

air pollution, 230
    boll weevil and cotton crop in, 247
    desalination and, 33
    Integrated Pest Management in, 246
    non-point-source pollution control programs in, 58
    pesticide use in, 247
    population of, 137
    water resources of, 6

Lower Rio Grande Valley National Wildlife Refuge, 162

Lower Rio Grande Valley Water Planning Region, 28

Low-flow toilets, 14, 262

Low-income communities, 103

Low-level radioactive waste, 301–304

Low Level Radioactive Waste Disposal Authority, 303

LPG (liquid petroleum gas), 264–265

Lubbock, 12, 30, 160, 180, 188, 208

Lubbock County, 29, 135, 305, 348–349

Lumber and wood products. *See* Timber industry

Lynn County, 29, 348–349

Lyondell-Citgo Refining, 53, 297

Lyondell Petrochemical, 297, 307

Mackenzie Reservoir, 62, 63

Madison County, 348–349

Maine, 109, 121, 276, 303–304

Maintech International, 324

Malapai Resources, 309

Malathion, 247

Malone Service Company, 318

Mammals, 97, 144, 150, 151, 153. *See also* Endangered species; Wildlife

Mancozeb, 240

Manufacturers. *See* Industry; *headings beginning with* Industrial

Manufacturing process changes, 310

Maquiladoras, 35, 300–301, 326

Marine Mammal Protection Act, 144

Marion County, 22, 348–349

Market-based air pollution control, 174–177

Marlin, 84

Marlin City Lake, 62, 63

MARPOL Treaty, 97

Marshall, 183, 184, 191, 192, 194, 195

Marshall Wood Preserving, 324

Martin County, 23, 77, 348–349

Martin Creek Reservoir, 62, 63, 67

Maryland, 109

Mason County, 348–349

Massachusetts, 109, 113

Massachusetts Institute of Technology, vii, 206

Mass transit. *See* Transportation

Matagorda Bay, 15, 26, 89

Matagorda County
  environmental indicators, 348–349
  nuclear power plant, 258–259
  toxic releases by, 305
  toxic transfers, 306

Matamoros, 36, 55, 90, 184, 300, 301, 326, 327, 331n.148

Material Recovery Enterprises, 324

Maverick County, 28, 36, 55, 348–349

Maximum Achievable Control Technology, 316–317

McAllen, 28, 66, 160, 184

McBay Oil and Gas, 324

McCamey, 260

McCleery, Douglas, 114

McCulloch County, 23, 348–349

McLennan County, 24, 348–349

McMullen County, 348–349

Mechanical processes facilities, 229–230

Medical waste. *See* Hospitals

Medina County, 27, 348–349

Medina River, 65

Mega Borg explosion, 96

Menard County, 23, 348–349

MERC (mobile emissions reduction credits), 174, 175

Mercury, 25–26, 63, 66–68, 73, 92, 199, 223, 225, 326

Merichem Co., 205, 318

Mesilla-Bolson Aquifer, 22

Mesquite, 12

Mesquite Bay, 89

Metal finishers, 229

Metal industry and products, 13, 47, 48, 64, 66–68, 224, 272, 292, 296, 304

Metal smelters, 229–230

Methane, 206, 271, 274

Methanol, 52, 220

Methomyl, 240

Methoxychlor, 240

Metolachlor, 241

Mexican wolf, 151

Mexico. *See also* Border issues
  air pollution, 180, 184, 186, 190, 196–197, 214, 233n.74
  aquifers in, 22
  automobiles in, 196
  birth defects in, 326
  boll weevil and cotton crop in, 247
  carbon dioxide emissions, 207, 214
  environmental plan by, 37
  hazardous waste and, 299, 300–301, 312–313, 322, 326, 327, 331n.148
  maquiladoras in, 35, 300–301, 326
  NAFTA and, 35–38, 56
  ocean trash, 123
  peso devaluation in, 35
  pollution and, 66, 312–313
  wastewater treatment in, 23, 55, 56
  water supply in, 22, 23
  wildlife protection and, 144, 159
  zinc-recovery facility in, 300, 301

Meyer, Stephen, vii

Michigan, 109

Microorganisms
  in drinking water, 80
  indoor air pollution and, 212
  sick building syndrome and, 212

Middle Brazos Water Planning Region, 23–24

Midland, 11, 23

Midland County, 23, 348–349

Midlothian, 84, 180, 188, 191, 202, 228–229, 307, 315

Migratory birds, 117, 118, 144, 158

Migratory Bird Treaty, 144

Milam County, 24, 186, 191, 224, 305, 324, 348–349

Miles, Inc., 53

Millennium Petrochemical, 307

Mills County, 26, 348–349

Minimum streamflow concept, 16

Mining
  of aquifers, 10, 11
  of brine, 74, 76
  of coal and lignite, 72–73, 265
  employment in, 338, 342–353
  groundwater contamination by, 72–73
  injection wells and, 73, 74
  regional supply and demand issues, 20–30
  solution ("in situ"), 266, 308, 309
  strip, 72, 265, 308
  of sulfur, 7, 74
  of uranium, 41, 73, 74, 265, 266, 305–306, 308–309
  waste recycling, 277
  water use and, 4, 9

Minnesota, 109, 328

Minorities
  and environmental justice, 103
  park use by, 112

Mission, 181

Mission Bay, 89

Mississippi, 109, 299

Mississippi River, 15–16, 31

Missouri, 15–16, 109, 201, 299

Mitchell County, 23, 324, 348–349

Mitigation, 141–142, 160

Mobile emissions reduction credits (MERC), 174, 175

Mobile sources of air pollution. *See* Automobiles

Mobil Oil, 221, 307

Molinate, 241

Monarch butterflies, 163

Monoculture, 125–126, 265, 267n.77, 278

Monsanto Co., 297, 307

Montague County, 20, 350–351

Montana, 109, 128, 237

Montgomery County, 24, 185, 305, 318, 321, 324, 350–351

Moore County, 20, 54, 305, 324, 350–351

Morris County, 306, 350–351

MOTCO, 324

Motley County, 29, 350–351

Motorola, Inc., 53
Motor vehicles. *See* Automobiles
Mountain Creek Lake, 62, 63, 67, 68
MSW. *See* Municipal solid waste
Muir, John, 105
Muleshoe, 184
Multiple Use Act, 125
Multiple-use policy, 114, 124, 127
Multiple-Use Sustained Yield Act, 128
Municipal solid waste (MSW)
  biosolids, 280–281
  cost-benefit analysis of disposal
    methods, 282
  definitions concerning, 271, 273
  disposal of, 273, 274, 275–280
  exports and imports of, 273
  federal waste legislation, 269, 270
  flow of, 291
  generation of, 273, 274
  groundwater contamination and, 72
  history of, 269–270
  household hazardous waste, 282
  human health and, 274
  illegal dumps, 280
  incineration of, 227–228, 278–279
  landfills for, 271, 274, 279–280, 294
  paper versus plastic bags, 277–278
  product design and, 282–284
  recycling/reuse of, 271, 275, 276–278
  source-reduction management
    option, 275–276
  state legislation on, 270–271, 276
  statistics on, 271–275, 282
  in Texas, 273, 274, 275
  in United States, 271–273
  waste-to-energy management of,
    278–279
Municipal Solid Waste Management
  and Resource Recovery Advisory
  Council, 270
Municipal water use
  amount of, 4, 9, 12–13
  conservation and, 13, 14, 18
  in counties, 342–353
  future demand for, 16
  groundwater and, 9, 10–11

regional supply and demand issues,
  20–30
residential use, 14, 18
storm-water discharge permits, 60
surface water and, 9, 10–11
wastewater discharge permits and,
  50–51
as water indicator, 339
Murdock, Steve, 137
Mustang Island, 91, 123

NAAQS. *See* National ambient air
  quality standards
Nacogdoches County, 25, 305, 350–351
NADBank (North American
  Development Bank), 35, 36–37, 56
NADP (National Atmospheric
  Deposition Program), 184
NAFTA (North American Free Trade
  Agreement), 35–38, 56
Nalco Exxon Chemical, 316
NAMS (national air monitoring
  system), 192
Naphthalene, 244
NASA (National Aeronautics and
  Space Administration), 206, 224
Nash, Roderick, 105
National Academy of Sciences, 133,
  149, 239, 243
National Aeronautics and Space
  Administration (NASA), 206, 224
National Agricultural Pesticide Impact
  Assessment Program, 243
National Agricultural Statistics
  Service, 243
National air monitoring system
  (NAMS), 192
National ambient air quality standards
  (NAAQS)
  carbon monoxide (CO) and, 177,
    186–187
  Environmental Protection Agency
    and, 171, 172, 177–178
  lead and, 177, 190–191
  nitrogen oxides and, 177, 182–186
  nonattainment areas, viii, 172, 176,
    177, 191–193
  ozone and, 172, 177, 179–182
  particulate matter and, 177, 187–190

primary versus secondary standards, 177
  sulfur dioxide and, 177, 182–186
National Atmospheric Deposition
  Program (NADP), 184
National Audubon Society, 40, 289
National Cancer Institute, 239
National Center for Food and
  Agricultural Policy, 241–242
National Climatic Data Center, 207
National Economic Crossroads
  Transportation Efficiency Act
  (NEXTEA), 234n.162
National Environmental Policy Act
  (1969) (NEPA), 43, 141, 144
National Estuary Program, 92
National forests, 108, 123–12, 127
National Forest Service. *See* U.S.
  Forest Service
National grasslands, 108, 128
National highway systems, 218
National Industrial Recovery Act, 128
National Marine Fisheries Service,
  144, 240
National Oceanic and Atmospheric
  Administration, 120
National Organic Standards Board, 247
National parks, 105–106, 110, 112–113.
  See also specific parks
National Park Service, 106, 112,
  214, 322
National Park Service Organic Act,
  124, 144
National Pollutant Discharge
  Elimination System (NPDES) permit,
  50, 60
National Priority List (NPL), 323
National Research Council, 136, 149, 246
National Research Defense Council, 289
National Resources Conservation
  Service, 133
National Resources Inventory, 93
National Wetlands Inventory
  Program, 95
National wilderness areas, 108
National Wildlife Federation, 40,
  161, 289
National wildlife refuges, 108
Native Americans, 115, 253
Natural areas, 108

Natural gas, 97, 225, 253, 254, 257, 258, 263–264. *See also* Compressed natural gas (CNG)

Naturally occurring radioactive materials (NORMs), 305–308

Natural Resource Conservation Service (NRCS), 93, 134, 136, 157, 159, 289

Nature Conservancy of Texas, 115, 161

Nature tourism, 154, 163–164

Nature Tourism Association, 164

Navarro County, 21, 350–351

Navigability of rivers, 123

Near nonattainment areas, 195

Nebraska, 109

Neches River, 3, 25, 65

Neches River Basin, 3, 7, 51

Neches-Trinity River Basin, 3, 51, 64

NEPA (National Environmental Policy Act), 43, 141, 144

Neural tube defects (NTDs), 326

Neutralization of hazardous waste, 314

Nevada, 109, 199, 305

New Braunfels, 28

New Hampshire, 109, 199, 237

New Jersey, 109, 237

New Mexico, 22, 23, 33n.19, 109, 128, 159, 180, 196, 197, 308–309

Newpark Environmental Services, 306, 308

Newspapers, 229

Newton County, 25, 324, 350–351

Newton Wood Preserving, 324

New York
    air pollution and, 171, 176
    carbon dioxide emissions, 207
    hazardous waste and, 299
    Love Canal in, 201
    parks in, 109, 138n.2
    pesticide use, 237
    urban parkland in New York City, 113
    waste-collection system in New York City, 269

NEXTEA (National Economic Crossroads Transportation Efficiency Act), 234n.162

Niagara Chemical, 324

Nitrates, 20, 21, 52, 60, 64, 73, 74, 76, 77, 81, 84, 326

Nitric acid, 52, 320

Nitrogen, 64, 170

Nitrogen oxides, 173, 174, 176, 177, 179, 182–186, 193–194, 219, 221, 223–227, 341, 342–353

Nitrous oxide, 206

No-discharge permits, 44

Nolan County, 24, 350–351

Nonattainment areas
    as air indicator, 341
    air operating permits and, 223
    for carbon monoxide, 193
    Clean Air Act and, 177, 191–195
    industry in, 195
    maps of, 193, 194
    and mobile sources of air pollution, 215
    near nonattainment areas, 195
    number of, 176, 191
    for ozone, viii, 172, 185, 191–195, 215
    for particulate matter, 193

Nonattainment source review permits, 195

Non-point-source pollution (NPS)
    in agricultural area, 58–60, 130–131
    control programs for, 58
    definition of, 42, 49
    of surface water, 42, 57–61, 64
    in urban area, 60–61

No pit rule, 75

NORMs (naturally occurring radioactive materials), 305–308

North American Development Bank (NADBank), 35, 36–37, 56

North American Free Trade Agreement (NAFTA), 35–38, 56

North American Waterfowl Management Plan, 93, 159

North Carolina, 91, 109, 199

North-Central Texas Water Planning Region, 21

North Dakota, 109, 136, 199

Northeast Texas Water Planning Region, 21–22

Northeastern States for Coordinated Air Use Management, 216

North Star Steel Texas, 307

North Texas Cement Co., 315

North Texas Municipal Water District, 21

NPDES (National Pollutant Discharge Elimination System) permit, 50, 60

NPL (National Priority List), 323

NPS. *See* Non-point-source pollution (NPS)

NRCS. *See* Natural Resource Conservation Service (NRCS)

NTDs (neural tube defects), 326

Nuclear power, 225, 253, 258–259, 302, 303, 305

Nuclear Regulatory Commission, 308

Nuclear weapons, 308, 309

Nucor SteelÄTexas, 307

Nueces Bay, 89

Nueces County
    air toxics, 200
    beach cleanup in, 122
    environmental indicators, 350–351
    hazardous waste production in, 297
    industrial hazardous waste in, 321
    injection wells in, 318
    Superfund sites, 324
    tourism in, 118
    toxic air releases, 224
    toxic releases by, 305
    toxic transfers, 306, 307
    toxic water releases, 54

Nueces–Rio Grande Coastal Basin, 51

Nueces River Basin, 3, 7, 51

Nuevo Laredo, 36, 55, 56, 66, 184, 300

Nutrients, 90

Oak Creek Reservoir, 62, 63

Oak Woods and Prairies region, 115–116, 118

Occidental Chemical, 53, 316

Occupational Safety and Health Administration (OSHA), 212

Ocean. *See* Gulf of Mexico

Ocelot, 116, 154, 161–162

Ochiltree County, 20, 318, 324, 350–351

Odessa, 23, 180, 200, 202, 203, 205, 318

Odessa Chromium, 324

Odessa Injection Systems, 318

Ogallala Aquifer, 5, 8, 10, 11, 19, 20, 23, 30, 71, 77, 117

Ohio, 109, 137, 169, 199, 207

Oil and gas industry. *See also* Petroleum industry

abandoned oil wells, 75, 263

groundwater contamination and, 30, 75–76

in Gulf of Mexico, 97

hazardous wastes and, 306, 321–322

injection wells and, 73, 74, 317

in 1980s, 253

oil and gas wells, 230, 263, 319, 329n.14

prices of oil, 253

production statistics, 253, 263

Spindletop oil discovery, 253

state tax revenues from, 253–254

wastewater permits for, 44

water quality and, 64, 267n.59

Oil embargo, 172

Oil Spill Prevention and Response Act, 96–97, 328

Oil spills. *See* Spills

Ojinaga, 55, 66

Oklahoma, 46, 109, 132, 159, 299

Old-growth (virgin) forests, 124, 215

Oldham County, 20, 350–351

Old Lufkin Creosoting, 324

Old Ocean, 316

Olmsted, Frederick Law, 113

OMB Watch/Unison Institute, 334

Omnibus Recycling Act, 271

ONRWs (Outstanding National Resource Waters), 46

Orange, 180, 307, 316

Orange County

air toxics, 204, 224

environmental indicators, 350–351

ozone health consequences, 185

Superfund sites, 324

toxic releases by, 305, 307

toxic transfers, 306, 307

water supply and demand in, 25

Oregon, 109, 113, 121, 142

Organic chemicals. *See also* Volatile organic compounds (VOCs)

from cement plants, 227

in drinking water, 78–80, 84–85

Organic farming, 246–247, 249n.71

Organic fiber, 246–247, 249n.71

Organic food, 246–247, 249n.71

Organic Foods Production Act (1990), 247

Organic materials, 48, 50

Organic phosphates, 238

Organo-chlorines, 238

Organo-phosphates, 238, 239–240

OSHA (Occupational Safety and Health Administration), 212

Oso Bay, 89, 91

Outstanding National Resource Waters (ONRWs), 46

Oxidation, 314

Oxygen. *See* Dissolved oxygen

Oyster Lake, 89

Oyster waters and oyster harvesting, 45, 68, 88, 89, 92, 96

Ozarka Spring Water Co., 33n.29

Ozone

as air indicator, 341

atmospheric ozone, 173–174, 179, 210–211

city information on ozone levels, 179, 181–182

in counties, 342–353

depletion of, by industrial chemicals, 210–211

eight-hour standard, 177, 178, 192, 194

Federal Clean Air Act and, 172, 173–174

formation of, 171, 179

as greenhouse gas, 206

health and environmental effects of, 170, 182, 185

monitoring of, 179, 180–181, 192, 232n.26

national ambient air quality standards for, 172, 173, 177, 178

nonattainment areas, viii, 172, 185, 191–196, 215

one-hour standard, 177, 178, 192

in smog, 160, 173

toxic emissions and, 179

Packaging, 276, 282–284

Padre Island, 123

Padre Island National Seashore, 91

Palo Duro Canyon, 107

Palo Pinto County, 24, 350–351

Paluxy River, 24

PAMS (photochemical air monitoring sites), 192

Panhandle. *See specific cities and counties*

Panola County, 25, 350–351

Pantex nuclear weapons plant, 180, 309, 374

Paper and allied products

demand for, 126–127, 158

fish consumption and pollution from, 92

hazardous waste and, 292, 296, 304

recycled paper, 127, 275

toxic releases and, 224, 229–230

water use and, 13

Paper versus plastic bags, 277–278

Parathion, 240

Parkans International, 316

Parker County, 21, 350–351

Parks. *See also* National Park Service; Texas Parks and Wildlife Department (TPWD); *specific parks*

acquisition of, 112–113

acreage in state parks by state, 109–110

funding for, 110

national parks, 105–106, 110, 112–113

pesticide use in, 242

state parks, 106, 107, 108, 109, 110–111

urban parkland, 113–114

uses of, 111–112

visibility in, 213–214

Parmer County, 29, 350–351

Particulate matter, 170, 173, 177, 178, 180, 187–190, 193, 196, 220–221

Partners for Wildlife Program, 94

Pasadena, 12, 52, 53, 180, 307, 316

Passenger pigeon, 151

Pastureland, 129, 130, 131

PCBs, 21, 63, 64, 66–68, 72, 201

PCCs (program compliance credits), 175

Pechan Study, 216

Pecos County, 23, 147, 350–351

Pecos River, 23

Pendimethalin, 241

Pennsylvania, 52, 109, 163, 169, 170, 207

Permian Chemical, 324

Permits

air operating permits, 223

air quality permits, 171

for building atop municipal solid waste landfills, 271

dredging and filling permits, 42, 93, 95, 155

federal operating permits, 223

Habitat Conservation Plan permits, 160

for hazardous waste disposal, 303

for hazardous waste incineration, 316

hazardous waste permit exemptions, 322

incidental taking permit, 146

for injection wells, 73, 317

National Pollutant Discharge Elimination System (NPDES), 50, 60

no-discharge permits, 44

nonattainment source review permits, 195

for piers and docks in water, 120

prevention of significant deterioration permits, 195

Section 404, 95

storm-water discharge, 60

for surface water, 6, 8–9, 13, 15, 16

for transport of hazardous waste, 328

wastewater discharge permits, 44, 45, 46, 50–51, 60

water rights permits, 6, 8–9, 13, 15, 16

Perryton, 318, 324

Pesticide Data Program, 240, 243

Pesticides

agricultural use of, 76–77, 118, 131, 231, 237–239, 241–242, 244–245, 247

air pollution and, 231

children and, 239–244

definition of, 237

in drinking water, 82–83, 84

economic value of market, 238

environmental justice and, 103

farmworker exposure to, 244, 249n.57

federal regulation of, 242–244

fish consumption and, 21, 28, 66–68, 238, 242

in food, 240

groundwater contamination and, 74, 76–77, 340

history of, 237

home use, 212–213, 238

human health and, 213, 238–242, 244, 245, 248n.25, 249n.57

indoor air pollution and, 212–213

"inert" ingredients of, 244

Integrated Pest Management and, 246

licensing and training requirements for, 245

nonagricultural use of, 240–242

prior notification of agricultural use, 244–245

recent discoveries about, 239–240

reduction in use of, 245–246

regulation of, 242–246

in schools, 241, 242, 246

state agencies with responsibilities for, 245

state regulation of, 244–245

types of, 237, 238

use statistics, 237–238, 241–242

as water quality issue, 21, 41, 48, 60, 64, 65, 118, 131

wildlife and, 238

Petro-Chemical Systems, 324

Petroleum industry. See also Oil and gas industry

air pollution and, 200

consumption of petroleum, 253

Gulf of Mexico and, 96

hazardous wastes of, 292, 296, 304

statistics on, 176

storage-tank cleanup, 72

toxic releases and, 224

water pollution by, 23

water use of, 13

Petulla, John, 105

Pfiesteria, 91

pH

of drinking water, 82

as water quality indicator, 41, 44, 48

Phantom shiner, 151, 154

Phillips Petroleum, 316

Phillips 66 Company, 221, 297, 307

Phipps Plating, 324

Phosphorus, 64

Photochemical air monitoring sites (PAMS), 192

Picloran, 241

PICs (Products of Incomplete Combustion), 228

Piedras Negras, 36, 55, 214, 300

Pilkey, Orrin, 119

Piney Woods region, 115, 118

Pinochet, Gifford, 105, 114, 124, 138n.4

Pioneer Oil and Refining Co., 324

Pittman-Robertson Act, 144

Plano, 12

Plants

causes of extinction of, 143

in ecological regions, 115–117

endangered species, 143, 146, 150, 152–153, 154–155

in Endangered Species Act, 146

extirpated from Texas, 151

medicines and, 145

number of species of, 143, 151

rare and near-extinct species, viii, 115–117, 152–153

in wetlands, 155–156

Plastic products, 224, 304

Plastic versus paper bags, 277–278

Playa lakes, 158–159

Plutonium, 309

PM10, 173, 177, 178, 187–190, 221, 226, 227

Point Bolivar, 96

Point Comfort, 205, 307

Point-source pollution, wastewater, 48–55

Poland, 207

Polk County, 24, 25, 350–351

Pollution. See Air pollution; Water quality

Pollution Prevention Act, 270

Poly-Cycle, 324

Population

aquatic habitat and, 89–90

in counties, 342–353

as economic indicator, 338
of Gulf Coast, 89–90, 117–118
of racial groups, 112
recreation and, 111–112
of Texas, viii, 137, 176, 254, 273
Texas/Mexico border area, 35, 36
urban areas, 129
water use trends and, 9, 16
Port Aransas, 122
Port Arthur
air pollution, 183 186, 192–195, 200, 203, 233n.74
air quality monitoring, 180
hazardous waste incineration facilities, 316
injection wells in, 318
mass transit in, 219
as nonattainment area, 192, 193, 195
ozone levels of, 172, 179, 192–195
water supply of, 25
Port Bay, 89
Port Isabel, 46
Port Lavaca, 307
Port Neches, 180, 200, 202, 205, 316
Possum Kingdom Lake, 62, 63
Potter County, 20, 305, 350–351
POTWs (Publicly owned treatment works), 52, 53
Powderhorn Lake, 89
Power. See Electric utilities; Nuclear power; Solar power; Utilities; Wind power
Powerplant and Industrial Fuel Use Act, 257
Prairie chicken, 116, 154, 160
Prairies, 116, 117, 128
Precipitation (natural), 3, 4, 17, 33. See also Drought
Precipitation (technological process), 314
Precipitation enhancement, 33
Precision Machine and Supply, 324
Preservation versus conservation, 105, 106
Presidio, 66
Presidio County, 22, 36, 350–351
Prevention of significant deterioration (PSD) permits, 195

Printing and publishing, 224, 229, 292
Prior appropriation doctrine, 5
Private Lands Enhancement Program, 159
Private property. See also Landowners
endangered species and, 147, 148–149, 150–151
Fifth Amendment and, 165n.24
river access and, 123
water rights and, 5, 7–8
wetlands and, 159–160
wildlife habitat protection and, 159–161
Proctor Lake, 62
Product design, 276, 282–284
Products of Incomplete Combustion (PICs), 228
Program compliance credits (PCCs), 175
Propane, 219, 220, 257, 265
Propanil, 241
Property. See Landowners; Private property
Proposed species, 148
Proposition 2, 312
Proposition 4, 31
PSD permits (prevention of significant deterioration), 195
Public health. See Human health
Public Health Service, 170
Public Health Service Act (1912), 42
Public lands
beach access, 120–121
beach debris and, 122
conservation activities and, 106, 114–115
definition and types of, 108
dune loss, 122
federal ownership of, 106, 112–113
funding for, 107, 108, 110
Gulf beaches as, 108, 117–121
Gulf shoreline loss, viii, 95, 118, 119, 121–122
legislation on, 107–108
map of, 107
mitigation and, 141
national forests, 123–125, 127
ocean trash and, 123

origin of U.S. public lands, 105–107
parkland, 109–114
park use, 111–112
river access, 123
state ownership of, 106–111
"wise use" coalition, 114, 138n.4
Publicly owned treatment works (POTWs), 52, 53
Public schools. See Schools
Public transportation. See Transportation
Public Utility Regulatory Act (1995), 255
Pyrethroids, 240

Quantum USI, 316

Race
and environmental justice, 103
park use by minority groups, 112
RACT (Reasonably Available Control Technology), 174–175
Radioactive waste, 301–309
Radionuclides, 81, 199
Radon, 211, 212
Railroad Commission of Texas (RRC)
abandoned oil wells, 263
alternative fuel industry and, 264–265
disposal of oil and gas wastes, 321–322
groundwater contamination and, 70–71, 72, 73
information system of, 288
injection wells and, 73, 74, 320
naturally occurring radioactive material waste and, 306, 308
oil industry and, 44, 75–76, 253, 321–322
spills and, 328
Statewide Rule 8, 75–76
wastewater discharge permits and, 44, 46
water resource responsibilities of, 1
Rainfall. See Precipitation (natural)
Rain forests, 124
Rains County, 22, 350–351
Rainwater harvesting, 17
Ranching. See Agriculture

Randall County, 20, 305, 350–351

Rangeland, 60, 129, 131

RCRA (Resource Conservation and Recovery Act), 43, 269, 270, 280, 284, 292–293, 317, 321

Reagan County, 23, 350–351

Real County, 26, 350–351

Reasonably Available Control Technology (RACT), 174–175

Recreation. *See also* Fish and fishing; National Park Service; Texas Parks and Wildlife Department
  coastal resources and, 88–89, 93
  expenditures on, 114
  hunting and, 115–117, 143, 144, 148, 149, 163–164
  participation in, 111–112
  rivers and streams, 123
  state parks, 110–111
  use impairment and, 47
  water quality standards and, 45, 47
  and water use, 45, 46

Recreational areas, 108

Recycling
  benefits from, 277
  components of state program of, 277
  in counties, 342–353
  definition of, 276, 310
  economic impact of, 277
  industrial hazardous waste and, 298, 299, 313
  as land indicator, 339
  of municipal solid waste, 271, 275, 276–278
  paper production and, 127, 275
  state legislation on, 271
  of tires, 271

Recycling Market Development Board, 277

Red-cockaded woodpecker, 115, 154

Redfish Bay, 89

Red River, 3, 19, 20, 65, 117

Red River Basin, 3, 7, 21, 51

Red River County, 22, 350–351

Red tide, 91, 92

Red wolf, 151

Reeves County, 23, 281, 350–351

Refrigeration/AC repair, 229

Refrigerators, 262

Refugio County, 27, 350–351

Regional water planning areas, 1, 19–30

Regions. *See* Ecological regions

Reilly, William K., 211

RENEW (Resource Exchange Network for Eliminating Waste), 313

Renewable energy, 259–261

Reproductive disorders, 201, 240

Republican Party, 114

Reservoirs
  conservation storage data for, 1
  construction of, 31–32, 158
  and inflow needs of bays and estuaries, 15
  mitigation and, 141
  non-point-source pollution of, 58
  number and size of, 3, 31
  pesticides in, 21
  pollution of, 47–49, 62–63
  precipitation and, 3
  as risks to estuaries, 90
  sedimentation of, 133–134
  size of, 3, 44, 45
  use impairment causes, 47–49, 63
  uses of, 45, 47
  water-quality monitoring of, 41, 45
  water supply and, 3, 4

Residential use
  of electricity, 258
  of lead-based paints, 212
  municipal solid waste and, 274, 281–282
  of pesticides, 212–213, 238, 240–241
  of water, 14, 18

Resource Conservation and Recovery Act (RCRA), 43, 269, 270, 280, 284, 292–293, 317, 321

Resource Exchange Network for Eliminating Waste (RENEW), 313

Respirable particulate matter. *See* Particulate matter

Restaurants, 245

Reuse. *See* Recycling

Rexene Products Company, 205

Reynosa, 36, 55, 90, 184, 300

Rhode Island, 109, 199

Rhone Poulenc, 316

Rice University, vii, 150

Richards, Ann, 164

Richland-Chambers Reservoir, 62, 63

Right of capture, 7–8, 33n.29

"Right to know," 86–87, 172, 244, 289, 292, 333–334

Right-to-Know Computer Network (RTK Net), 289, 334

Rill erosion, 133

Rio Grande Alluvium, 70

Rio Grande Basin, 7

Rio Grande River
  Big Bend National Park and, 23
  channel dam to capture floodwater from, 28
  drought and, 6, 33n.1
  fish contamination and fish abnormalities in, 28, 64, 68
  hazardous waste and, 322
  in-stream flows in, 28
  map of, 3
  pipeline to El Paso, 22
  pollution of, 23, 28, 55–56, 66, 68, 90
  salinity of, 155
  sewage in, 90
  size of, 19
  toxics and contaminants in, 23, 66, 90
  wastewater and, 23, 55–56
  water appropriation and, 7, 16
  water rights for, 6, 16
  as wild and scenic river, 40

Rio Grande River Basin, 3, 51

Rio Grande Valley, 28, 31, 76, 246. *See also* Lower Rio Grande Valley

Riparian land, 15, 123

Riparian rights, 5, 6

Risk assessment, 243, 251

Risk management, 251, 334

River authorities, 1, 61–68, 106. *See also specific river authorities*

River basins. *See specific river basins*

Rivers and Harbors Act (1899), 120

Rivers and streams. *See also specific rivers*
  classified, 45, 46, 61
  dissolved oxygen and, 48, 66

with fecal coliform bacteria, 23, 28, 30, 61, 64

maps of, 3, 7

miles of, 3, 15, 44, 45, 123

named and nameless, 3

navigability of, 123

non-point-source pollution in, 57, 58

pesticides in, 64, 65

public access to, 123

sedimentation of, 60, 133–134

toxics and, 49

underground, 7–8

use impairment causes, 47–49

uses of, 45, 46, 47

water available for appropriation, 7, 16

water pollution of, 47–49

water-quality monitoring of, 45, 61, 64–68

wild and scenic, 40

Roberts, Oran M., 149

Roberts County, 20, 350–351

Robertson County, 24, 350–351

Robinson (city), 84

Robstown, 321

Rockwall County, 21, 350–351

Rockwool Industries, 324

Rodeo, 241

Rohm & Haas, 53

Rolling Plains region, 117, 118

Rolling Plains Water Planning Region, 20–21

Rollins Environmental Services, 297

Romania, 207

Roosevelt, Franklin, 132

Roosevelt, Theodore, 105–106, 144

Rose City, 307

Rosenberg, 103

Roundup, 241

RSR Lead Smelter, 324

RTK Net (Right-to-Know Computer Network), 289, 334

Rubber products, 224, 304

Runnels County, 23, 76, 350–351

Rural/agricultural district, 138

Rural Electrification Act, 254

Rural lands. *See* Agriculture

Rural Water Association, Texas, 83

Rusk County, 25, 350–351

Sabine County, 25, 350–351

Sabine Lake, 89

Sabine Lake and Sabine-Neches Estuary, 15

Sabine Pass, 89, 96

Sabine River, 3, 65

Sabine River Authority, 66

Sabine River Basin, 3, 7, 25, 51

Safe Drinking Water Act
  contaminant level standards, 42, 222, 235n.188
  funding for, 77
  industrial and hazardous waste, 292
  of 1974, 77
  1986 amendments to, 42, 77
  1996 amendments to, 30, 42, 77, 86, 87, 334
  right-to-know provisions of, 86–87, 334
  Texas Natural Resource Conservation Commission and, 8
  underground drinking water, 87–88
  unregulated drinking water and, 88
  upgrading of water treatment plants to comply with, 25, 28, 29

Safe Drinking Water Revolving Fund, 43

Safe harbor agreements, 160–161

Sagemeadow Municipal Utility, 84

St. Charles Bay, 89

Salado Creek, 65

Salt pollution, 21, 23, 24, 27, 75

Salt water, 39, 64, 75

Sampson Horrice, 324

Sam Rayburn Reservoir, 25–26, 62, 63, 65, 67

Samson, Andrew, 112

San Angelo, 23, 76, 205

San Antonio
  air pollution, 183, 184, 188, 190, 192, 194, 195, 200, 205, 230
  air quality monitoring, 190
  bus ridership in, 218
  commuter rail line between Austin and, 219
  drinking water of, 87–88
  electric rates in, 259
  environmental justice, 103
  lead levels, 230
  as near nonattainment area, 195
  out-migration from, 26, 27
  ozone levels of, 179, 181, 192, 194
  parks in, 113
  power plants in, 208
  storm-water discharge permit, 60
  traffic congestion in, 216
  vehicles and vehicle miles in, 216
  wastewater treatment facilities in, 160
  water quality ordinances of, 58
  water resources of, 27, 58
  water use of, 12

San Antonio Bay, 15, 89

San Antonio–Nueces River Basin, 3, 51

San Antonio River, 3, 28

San Antonio River Basin, 3, 51

San Antonio Springs, 27

San Antonio Water Planning Region, 27–28

San Augustine County, 25, 350–351

San Benito, 188

San Bernard National Wildlife Refuge, 162

Sandblasting operations, 229–230

Sandoz Agro, 316

San Jacinto Bay, 67, 92

San Jacinto–Brazos Coastal Basin, 51

San Jacinto County, 24, 350–351

San Jacinto River, 3, 67

San Jacinto River Basin, 3, 7, 10, 51

San Luis Pass, 96

San Marcos, 28, 184

San Marcos gambusia, 147

San Marcos salamander, 116, 147

San Marcos Springs, 27, 43, 69

San Miguel Electric Cooperative, Inc., 209, 221

San Patricio County, 55, 118, 306, 321, 350–351

San Pedro Springs, 27

San Saba County, 26, 350–351

Santa Barbara channel oil spill, 40

SARA (Superfund Authorization and Renewal Act), 43, 103, 198, 292, 333

Sargent Bay, 121

Save Our Springs (SOS) ordinance, 98n.66

Schleicher County, 23, 350–351

Schools
air quality in, 212
pesticide use in, 241, 242, 246

Science Advisory Board, 211, 234n.129

Scott Bay, 67, 92

Scurry County, 23, 350–351

Seabrook, 316

Sea grasses, 94, 96

Section 404 Permits, 95

Sector Facility Indexing (SFI) Initiative, 234, 311

Sedimentation, 60, 133–134

Seguin, 307

Selenium, 63, 67, 73, 265, 267n.74

SEMARNAP, 37

Senate Bill 1. See Water Bill of 1997

Septic tanks, 64, 73

Sewage and sewage plants, 37, 52, 73

Seymour Aquifer, 5, 11, 21, 71

SFI (Sector Facility Indexing) Initiative, 234, 311

SGSÄThomson Microelectronics, Inc., 297

Shackelford County, 24, 350–351

Sharp-tailed grouse, 151

Sheet erosion, 133

Shelby County, 25, 350–351

Shell Chemical, 316

Shellfish harvesting closures, 64, 68, 91–92

Shellfishing, 47, 64, 68, 88, 89, 91–92

Shell Oil Company, 53, 205, 297, 307, 329n.26

Sheridan Disposal, 324

Sherman County, 20, 350–351

Shoreline. See Gulf Coast

Shower heads, water-efficient, 14, 262

Sick building syndrome, 212. See also Indoor air pollution

Sierra Club, 27, 105, 222, 289

Sikes Disposal Site, 324

Simpson Pasadena Paper Company, 52, 53

Sink fixtures, water-efficient, 14, 262

Sinton, 321

SLAMS (state and local air monitoring system), 192

Sludge, 247, 271, 273, 280–281

Small business, 195, 229–231

Smith County, 22, 25, 305, 306, 318, 319, 352–353

Smog, 160, 170, 173

Soil
conservation of, 132, 134–136
contamination of, 72, 321
cropland erosion, viii, 131–132, 342–353
definition of, 132
in ecological regions, 115–117
erosion of, viii, 131–135, 342–353
government agencies and, 132, 134
erosion abatement programs, 134–136
surface water and, 133–134
types of, 132

Soil and Water Conservation Board, 1

Soil and water conservation districts, 1, 132, 134

Soil and Water Resources Conservation Act (1977), 132

Soil conservation, 132, 134–136

Soil Conservation Service, 132

Solar power, 256, 260–261

Sole Source Aquifer provision, 87–88

Solids, 50, 63, 64, 74

Solid waste. See Industrial and hazardous waste; Municipal solid waste

Sol Lynn/Industrial Transformers, 324

Solutia, Inc., 307

Solution ("in situ") mining, 266, 308, 309

Solvent Recovery Services, 324

Somervell County, 24, 258, 352–353

Sonics International, 324

Sonora, 184

SOS (Save Our Springs) ordinance, 98n.66

Source reduction management
for industrial and hazardous waste, 309–313

for municipal solid waste, 275–276

Source separation, 310

Sources of municipal solid waste (MSW), 274

Source Water Assessment Program, 87

South Africa, 207

South Bay, 46, 89

South Bay Preserve, 90

South Carolina, 109, 302, 303

South Dakota, 109

Southern High Plains Water Planning Region, 29–30

South Korea, 207

South Padre Island, 91, 121

South Texas Brush Country region, 116, 118

South Texas Gulf Coast Water Planning Region, 29

South Texas nuclear project, 258–259

Southwestern Electric Power Company, 209, 221, 256

Southwestern Public Service Company, 221

Southwest Network for Environmental and Economic Justice, 103

Southwest Texas State University, 261

Soviet Union, 207

Special Non-game and Endangered Species Fund, 150

Species
definition of, 148
designations of, 153

Spence Reservoir, 62, 63

Spills, 90, 92, 96–97, 294, 319, 328, 331n.111

Spindletop, 253

Springs and spring runs, 27, 43, 69, 155. See also names of specific springs

Starr County, 28, 36, 55, 137, 352–353

State agencies. See headings beginning with Texas

State and local air monitoring system (SLAMS), 192

State forests, 108

State Marine of Port Arthur, 324

State of Texas Environmental Priorities Project (STEPP), 251–252

State parks, 106, 107, 108, 110–111

State Superfund Program, 323–324

Statewide Rule 8, 75–76

Stationary sources of air pollution, 220–230. *See also* Industry

Steel manufacturers, 229–230

Stephens County, 24, 352–353

Stephenville, 59

STEPP (State of Texas Environmental Priorities Project), 251–252

STEP 21 (Streamlined Transportation Efficiency Program for the 21st Century), 234n.162

Sterling Chemical Co., 297, 307

Sterling County, 23, 352–353

Stern, Gil, 39

Stewardship Incentive Program, 125

Stone products, 224, 304

Stonewall County, 24, 352–353

Storage tanks, 71–72, 294, 339

Stormwater discharge permits, 60

Streambed erosion, 133

Strip mining, 72, 265, 308

Stripper wells, 263

Structural Metals, Inc., 307

Structural Pest Control Board, 245, 246

Substitution of products, 310

Substitution of raw materials, 310

Suburban/urban sprawl, agriculture and, 136–137

Sugar Land, 316

Sulfates, 41, 63, 82

Sulfur, 237

Sulfur dioxide, 170, 173, 175–177, 179, 180, 182–186, 213, 214, 221, 223–227, 341, 342–353

Sulfur mining, 73, 74

Sulphur River, 3, 65

Sulphur River Basin, 3, 51

Supercritical water oxidation, 314

Superfund Authorization and Renewal Act (SARA), 43, 103, 198, 292, 333

Superfund sites
    in counties, 342–353
    hazardous waste sites, 72, 321, 323–325
    map of, 324
    Pantex nuclear weapons plant, 309
    as waste indicator, 339

Superior Cable, 307

Surface impoundments, 320

Surface water. *See also* Estuaries; Gulf of Mexico; Reservoirs; Rivers and streams
    classified waters, 44–45, 46
    conjunctive use of, 32
    cropland erosion and, 133–134
    depletion of, 18
    groundwater and, 69
    hydrological cycle and, 2, 3, 39, 40
    irrigation and, 10
    management of, 5–7
    metals in, 47, 48, 65
    of municipal water use, 9, 10–11
    non-point-source pollution of, 57–61, 64
    ownership of, 6–7
    permits for, 6, 8–9, 13, 15, 16
    pesticide monitoring, 60
    point-source pollution of, 48–55
    pollution of, 46–50
    public water supply and, 4, 63
    quality of, 41, 44–68
    regional supply and demand issues, 20–30
    regulations for, 6–7, 40, 42–46
    rights to, 4–7
    river access and, 123
    supply of, 3–4
    toxic releases to, 51–55
    unclassified waters, 45
    unplugged wells and, 319
    use impairment causes, 47–49
    uses of, 4, 9–11, 45–47
    water rights holders, 6–7

Sustainability, 127, 136

Sustainable agriculture, 136

Sutton County, 23, 352–353

Swimming, 45, 47, 89

Swisher County, 29, 352–353

Szasz, Andrew, 30n.74

"T" factor, 133, 134

Tabbs Bay, 67, 92

Tailing ponds, 266, 308, 309

Tailpipe-emission standards, 174, 194, 215–216

"Takings" and "takings" legislation, 146, 148, 164n.15, 165n.23, 167

Tarleton State University, 58

Tarrant County
    air toxics, 200, 224
    environmental indicators, 352–353
    highway vehicle programs for, 215
    ozone health consequences, 185
    Superfund sites, 324
    toxic releases by, 305
    toxic transfers, 306
    toxic water releases, 54
    urban expansion in, 137
    vehicles emission testing in, 216–217
    water supply and demand in, 21

Tarrant Regional Water District, 21

Tax incentives, 160, 161, 312

Taylor County, 24, 305, 306, 324, 352–353

TDA. *See* Texas Department of Agriculture

TDH. *See* Texas Department of Health

TECO (Texas Ecologists), 321

Tellus Institute, 275

Temperate deciduous forests, 124

Temperature
    global warming, 176, 205–207, 209
    as water quality indicator, 41, 44, 48

Temperature inversions, 169, 170, 171

Temple, 242

Tennessee, 15–16, 109, 150, 199, 295, 299

Terrell County, 22, 36, 352–353

Terry County, 29, 135, 352–353

Texarkana, 103

Texarkana Wood, 324

Texas A&M University, 107, 111, 125, 134, 150

Texas A&M University Agricultural Experiment Station and Extension Service, 243, 245, 246

Texas Agricultural Extension Service, 18, 134, 243, 245, 246

Texas Air Commission, 104

Texas Air Control Board, 171–172, 184, 196, 199, 230

Texas American Oil, 324

Texas Attorney General's Office, 86

Texas Blacklands Prairie, 128, 137

Texas Board of Water Engineers, 8

Texas Cancer Council, 288

Texas Center for Policy Studies, 289

Texas Chenier Plain, 162

Texas City, 53, 180, 185, 188, 202, 203, 307, 318

Texas Clean Air Act, 171, 172, 223. *See also* Federal Clean Air Act

Texas Clean Fleet Program, 215, 217

Texas Clean Industries 2000, 311–312

Texas Coastal Management Plan, 90, 119–120, 122

Texas Committee on Natural Resources, 18, 140n.66

Texas Comptroller of Public Accounts, 72, 254, 288

Texas Department of Agriculture (TDA)

groundwater monitoring by, 41

information system of, 288

Integrated Pest Management and, 246

organic farm certification program, 247

pesticides and, 76, 244–245

water resource responsibilities of, 1, 41

Texas Department of Commerce, 164, 271

Texas Department of Economic Development, 288

Texas Department of Health (TDH)

birth defects and, 326

fecal coliform bacteria and, 25

fish-consumption advisories and aquatic life closures by, 21, 25–26, 47, 63, 64, 66–68, 91, 92

Indoor Air Quality Branch, 212

licensing of radioactive waste storage facilities by, 330n.54

municipal solid waste regulation, 270

naturally occurring radioactive material waste and, 306, 308

pesticides and, 21, 245

Seafood Safety Division of, 68

uranium mine regulation by, 74

water pollution and, 66

Texas Department of Licensing, 75

Texas Department of Public Safety, 216–217

Texas Department of Transportation, 61, 118, 141, 218, 234n.161

Texas Department of Water Resources, 8

Texas Eastman Co., 297, 307, 316

Texas Ecologists (TECO), 321

Texas Endangered Species Act, 149–150

Texas Fish Commissioner, 149, 153

Texas Forest Service, 107, 125, 158

Texas Game and Fish Commission, 108

Texas Game, Fish, and Oyster Commissioner, 149

Texas General Land Office (GLO)

Gulf Coast and beaches, 90, 92, 108, 110, 118–122

information system of, 288

leasing of state land by, 110

mitigation and, 141

oil spills and, 96–97, 328

population growth estimates, 89

recycling and, 271

water resource responsibilities of, 1

wetlands and, 157

Texas Groundwater Protection Committee, 43, 70

Texas Henslow's sparrow, 151

Texas Industries, Inc., 315, 316

Texas Land Trust Council, 162

Texas Legislature Online, 288

Texas-Mexico border. *See* Border issues

Texas/Mexico Borderlands Data and Information Center, 288

Texas Motorist's Choice Vehicle Emissions Testing Program, 215, 216–217

Texas Municipal Power Agency, 221

Texas Natural Resource Conservation Commission (TNRCC)

air operating permit, 223

air pollution and, 191–194, 196, 222

air quality monitoring, 179–181, 186, 190, 192, 199–200, 203–205

air toxics and, 222

border-related operations, 35, 37–38, 66

brownfields and, 325, 327

drinking water and, 82–83, 85–87

emission reduction credits and, 174, 175

emissions inventory, 226, 287, 333

Environmental Priorities Project (STEPP), 251–252

environmental water needs and, 15, 16

formation of, 172

grandfathered facilities and, 226, 227

groundwater contamination and, 71–72, 74

groundwater monitoring, 8, 70–71

household hazardous waste and, 282

industrial and hazardous waste and, 291–292, 299–300, 302–304, 310–313, 316, 320–323, 328

information system of, 287, 288

landfills and, 279, 322

municipal solid waste and, 270, 273, 275–276, 281–282

nonattainment areas and, 191–194, 215

non-point-source pollution control programs of, 58, 59

pesticides and, 76–77, 82–83, 245

point-source pollution and, 50

pollution abatement plan and, 61

pollution control taxes and, 312

recycling programs and, 271, 277–278, 313

Section 404 permits and, 95

sludge and, 281

spills and, 328

sulfur mine regulation by, 74

surface water rights and, 6, 7

toxics and, 54, 55, 66, 302–304, 308, 310–312, 320–321

Toxics Release Inventory and, 333–334

underground storage tanks and, 71–72, 99n.104

upset emissions, 222

visibility of Class I areas, 214

wastewater discharge permits, 44, 46, 60

wastewater inspectors, 54

water conservation and, 13

Water Quality Inventory of, 8, 46–48, 70, 96

water-quality management and monitoring by, 1, 41, 43–47, 52, 57, 60, 61, 66, 92

water resource responsibilities of, 1, 16, 32

water rights regulation and, 6, 7, 8, 9, 32

water use planning and, 8–9, 16

wetlands and, 157

Texas Natural Resources Information Service (TNRIS), 287, 288

Texas Open Beaches Act (1959), 120, 121

Texas Outdoor Recreation Plan, 110–112

Texas Parks and Wildlife Department (TPWD)

  birdwatching and, 118

  bottomland hardwoods and, 158

  coastal preserves and, 90

  endangered species and, 146, 153–154

  environmental water needs, 15

  formation of, 108

  funding for, 108

  herbicides used by, 242

  information system of, 288

  land trusts and, 162

  mitigation and, 141

  nature tourism and, 163–164

  operating costs of, 149–150

  park system and, 108, 110, 112

  public lands and, 108, 110

  river access, 123

  spills and, 328

  water resource responsibilities of, 1, 8–9, 66

  water rights permits and, 8–9

  wetlands and, 95, 157, 159–160

  wildlife habitat protection by, 162–163

Texas Permanent University Fund, 106

Texas Prairie Wetlands Project, 159

Texas Public Utilities Commission, 255–256, 288

Texas Railroad Commission. See Railroad Commission of Texas

Texas Reforestation Foundation, 126

Texas Rural Water Association, 83

Texas Soil and Water Conservation Board

  Confined Animal Feeding Operations (CAFOs) and, 59, 60

  establishment of, 132

non-point-source pollution, 58, 59

organization of, 134

pesticides, 245

soil conservation and, 132, 134

water resource responsibilities of, 58, 59, 60

Texas Soil Conservation Law (1939), 132

Texas Solid Waste Disposal Act, 270, 276, 278, 282, 291–292, 323, 325

Texas State Parks Board, 107, 108

Texas Tech University, 135

Texas Transportation Institute, 218

Texas United Farm Workers, 244

Texas Utilities Electric Company, 208–209, 221, 226–227

Texas Utilities Generating Company, 221, 259

Texas Water Commission, 6, 7–8, 104, 172, 270, 271. See also Texas Natural Resource Conservation Commission

Texas Water Development Board (TWDB)

  cost of future water-related projects, 30

  drinking water and, 77

  environmental water needs and, 14–16

  groundwater quality and, 8, 41, 70–71, 75

  information system of, 287, 288

  regional water planning areas designated by, 19

  reservoirs and, 31, 134

  wastewater treatment and, 55

  Water Bank and, 32

  water resource responsibilities of, 1

  water use planning and, 1, 8, 9, 16–19

  wetlands and, 157

Texas Water Pollution Advisory Council, 8

Texas Water Pollution Control Board, 8

Texas Water Quality Board, 8, 270

Texas Water Rights Commission, 8

Texas Workforce Commission, 288

Texcor, 322

Textile mill products, 224

Tex-Tin, 324

THMs (trihalomethanes), 85

Thomas Disposal Co., 318

Thompson Hayward Chemical, 324

Threatened species, 145, 148. See also Endangered species

Throckmorton County, 24, 352–353

Tide, 119

Timber industry

  bottomland hardwoods and, 158

  demand for wood products, 125 126, 158

  history of, 105–106, 125

  open land and, 125, 126

  overharvesting by, 125

  raw material consumption, 272

  toxic releases, 224, 304

  tree plantations and, 125–126, 278

  water use by, 13

Time-of-use pricing, 262–263

Tires, recycling of, 271

Titus County, 22, 352–353

TMDLs (total maximum daily loads), 45–46

TNRCC. See Texas Natural Resource Conservation Commission

TNRIS (Texas Natural Resources Information Service), 287, 288

Tobacco smoke, 211

Toilets, water-efficient, 14, 262

Toledo Bend Reservoir, 62, 63, 65, 67

Toluene, 170–171, 200, 204, 222, 225

Tom Green County, 23, 76, 352–353

Topsoil, 132

Total maximum daily loads (TMDLs), 45–46

Total Minerals Co., 309

Toups, 324

Tourism and travel, 114, 118, 139n.30, 163–164

Town Lake (Austin), 27, 62, 63, 67, 242

Toxic air emission. See Air toxics

Toxicity Characteristic rule, 295

Toxicity Reduction Evaluation (TRE), 53

Toxics. See also Industrial and hazardous waste

  air pollution and, 173, 180, 181

  air toxics, viii, 173, 180–181, 197–204, 221–225, 340–341, 342–353

  birth defects and, 225, 326

  as border issue, 66

combustion pollution, 222–229

in counties, 342–353

estuaries and, 90

fish kills and, 64

as land indicator, 339

manufacturing industries and, 221–222, 302–307

monitoring of, 180–181

oil-well drilling process, 75

river authorities and, 64

in wastewater discharges, 51–55

as water quality indicator, 41, 44, 48, 49, 64, 66

Toxics Control and Safety Act, 292

Toxics Release Inventory (TRI)

access to, 287

as citizen's tool, 333–334

hazardous waste and, 292, 310, 311–312, 326

toxic air emissions and, 197, 198, 225

upset emissions and, 222

waste minimization and, 310–311

water releases, 52, 98n.48

TPWD. See Texas Parks and Wildlife Department

Traffic congestion, 216, 218

Trans/Mexico Border Program, 312–313

Trans Pecos region, 117, 118

Transportation. See also Automobiles; Highways

carbon dioxide emission from, 206

energy consumption by, 254

fleets of vehicles, 217, 219

funding for, 234nn.161–162

of industrial waste, 328

light rail systems, 219

mass transit, 219

urban bus ridership, 218, 219

Transportation equipment, 13, 224, 304

Transuranic waste (TRU), 308–309

Trash

beach debris, 122

ocean trash, 123

Travel and tourism, 114, 118, 139n.30, 163–164

Travis County, 26, 54, 104, 306, 352–353

TRE (Toxicity Reduction Evaluation), 53

Trees. See Forests

Tres Palacios Bay, 89

TRI. See Toxics Release Inventory

Trichloroethane, 170–171, 210

Tricon America, Inc., 324

Trifluralin, 241

Trihalomethanes (THMs), 85

Trinity Aquifer, 5, 10, 11, 21, 23, 26, 27, 70, 71, 116

Trinity Bay, 89

Trinity County, 24, 25, 352–353

Trinity River, 3, 65, 67

Trinity River Basin, 3, 7, 21, 51, 68, 242

Trinity River National Wildlife Refuge, 162

Trinity–San Jacinto Estuary, 15, 25

Trinity–San Jacinto River Basin, 3, 51

Tropical rain forests, 124

TRU (transuranic waste), 308–309

Trust for Public Land, 115

Turtle Bay, 89

TWDB. See Texas Water Development Board

2, 4–D, 241, 242

Tyler

air pollution, 183, 184, 191, 192, 195

air quality monitoring, 179, 180

as Flexible Attainment Region, 195

pesticides in, 242

water and wastewater rates in, 13

Tyler County, 25, 352–353

Umbrella species, 153

Underground injection sites. See Injection wells

Underground storage tanks, 71–72, 99n.104, 294

Uniform Hazardous Waste Manifest, 328

Union Carbide Corp., 53, 172, 231n.4, 316

United Creosoting, 324

United Nations, 143

U.S. Army Corps of Engineers, 42, 89, 90, 95, 106, 120, 157, 207

U.S. Centers for Disease Control, 326

U.S. Department of Agriculture (USDA), 93, 113, 124, 126–128, 132, 134, 157, 159, 240, 242, 243, 247, 289

U.S. Department of Commerce, 144

U.S. Department of Defense (DOD), 106

U.S. Department of Energy (DOE), 275, 289, 308

U.S. Department of Health, Education and Welfare (HEW), 170

U.S. Department of Interior, 40, 97, 112, 124

U.S. Environmental Protection Agency. See Environmental Protection Agency (EPA)

U.S. Fish and Wildlife Service (USFWS)

critical habitat and, 146–149

endangered species and, 43, 144, 145–150, 153

information system of, 289

land acquisition by, 112–113

nature tourism and, 163

public land and, 106

wetlands and, 93–95, 155–156, 157, 159

wildlife habitat protection and, 112–113, 160

U.S. Food and Drug Administration (FDA), 87, 240

U.S. Forest Service, 106, 113, 124, 125, 127, 128

U.S. Geological Survey, 70, 287

U.S.–Mexican Binational Air Quality Work Group, 197

U.S.–Mexico border. See Border issues

U.S. Office of Technology Assessment, 244, 283–284

U.S. Park Service. See National Park Service

U.S. State Department, 322

U.S. Treasury, 127

University of Houston, 261

University of Texas, 121, 262, 314

Upper Colorado and West Texas Water Planning Region, 23

Upper Rio Grande and Far West Texas Water Planning Region, 22–23

Upper Trinity Regional Water District, 22

Upset emissions, 222

Upshur County, 22, 352–353

Upton County, 23, 352–353

Uranium mining, 41, 73, 74, 265, 266, 305–306, 308–309

Uranium Resources, Inc., 308, 330n.67

Urban areas. *See also specific cities and counties*

air pollution, 173–174, 176, 183–186, 200

bus ridership in, 218, 219

non-point-source pollution, 60, 61

parkland in, 113–114

population of, 129

size of, 129, 137

suburban/urban sprawl and threats to, 136–137

urban runoff, 60–61

vehicles and vehicle miles in, 216

URI, Inc., 309

USDA. *See* U.S. Department of Agriculture

USFWS. *See* U.S. Fish and Wildlife Service

Utah, 109, 199, 299, 302, 308

Utilities. *See also* Electric utilities

carbon dioxide emission from, 206, 208–209

cogeneration facilities and, 257–258

electricity and, 253, 254–259

electric rates, 259

pollution "allowances" for electric utilities, 175–176

regional water supply and demand issues, 20–30

toxic releases from electric utilities, 221, 223–225, 227

water and wastewater rates, 13

water use and, 4, 9

water utilities, 262

Uvalde County, 27, 352–353

Valero Refining Company, 297

Val Verde County, 26, 36, 352–353

Van Zandt County, 22, 324, 352–353

Vegetation. *See* Plants

Vehicles. *See* Automobiles

Vermont, 109, 199, 303–304

Victoria, 28, 184, 194, 195, 307

Victoria County, 27, 297, 305, 306, 307, 352–353

Vinyl chloride, 199

Virgin (old-growth) forests, 124, 125

Virginia, 109, 131–132

Virgin Islands, 199

Visibility in Class I areas, 213–214

Vitrification, 314

VOCs. *See* Volatile organic compounds

Volatile organic compounds (VOCs), 41, 170–171, 173, 179–181, 183, 192–194, 211–212, 215, 221, 226, 228

Voluntary Cleanup Program, 325, 327–328

Waco, 12

Walker County, 24, 352–353

Waller County, 24, 185, 324, 352–353

Ward County, 23, 352–353

Washington, George, 131

Washington, D.C., 113

Washington County, 24, 306, 352–353

Washington state, 110, 113, 302

Waste. *See also* Animal waste; Industrial and hazardous waste; Municipal solid waste; Wastewater

amount of, 269

county data on, 342–353

federal legislation on, 270

flow of materials, products, and solid waste, 291

in Gulf of Mexico, 97

history of, 269

indicators for, 339

reasons for concern about, 269–270, 293–295

Waste Control Specialist, 304, 321

Waste incinerators, 227–228, 278–279, 296

Waste Isolation Pilot Plant (WIPP), 308–309

Waste minimization, 310

Waste piles, 320

Waste Reduction Policy Act (1991), 310, 313

Waste Tire Recycling Program, 271

Waste-to-energy facilities, 278–279

Wastewater

amount of, 50, 51

as border issue, 23, 35, 55–56

in coastal areas, 92

compliance and enforcement, 53–55, 60

discharge permits for, 44, 45, 50–51

effluent standards and reports on, 53, 54

fish kills and, 64

as pollution source, 49, 50, 90

POTWs (publicly owned treatment works), 52, 53

pretreatment of, 52

prices of treatment of, to consumers, 13

reuse of, 7

solids in, 50

Toxicity Characteristic rule and, 295

toxics in, viii, 51–55

treatment of, 23, 35, 44, 45, 50–57

untreated, 50, 55–57, 90

wetlands and, 57

Water Bank, 32

Water Bill of 1997 (SB 1), 2, 7–9, 13, 16, 19, 32, 33, 43

Water conservation, 13, 14, 17, 18, 32, 34n.62, 262

Water Development Board. *See* Texas Water Development Board

Water erosion, 133

Water oxidizer, 314

Water Plans, 8, 9, 16, 18, 31, 158, 287

Water pollution. *See* Water quality

Water Pollution Control Administration, 40

Water quality

agriculture and, 58–60, 130–131, 133–134

antidegradation policy, 46

aquatic life and, 21, 25–26, 41, 45, 47, 64, 66–68

coastal resources and, 88–96

cost of monitoring, 42–43

of drinking water, 8, 42, 77–87

federal legislation on, 40, 42–43, 57, 77

of groundwater, 41, 43, 69–77

hydrological cycle and, 39, 40

maquiladoras and, 35

monitoring for, 41, 42–43

point-source pollution, 48–55

recycling and, 277

river authorities and, 61–68

state legislation on, 43, 44–46

of surface water, viii, 41, 44–68

wastewater and, 49–56, 90

Water Quality Act (1965 and amendments), 40, 42, 57

Water Quality Inventory, 8, 46–48, 70, 96, 287

Water resources. *See also* Drinking water; Estuaries; Groundwater; Gulf of Mexico; Lakes; Reservoirs; Rivers and streams; Surface water; Water quality

alternative water development strategies, 32–33

conservation of, 13, 14, 17, 18, 32

cost of future water-related projects, 30–32

county data on, 342–353

demand for, 4, 9–17, 18, 19–30

desalination and, 33

drought and, 1–2, 12

eighteenth- and nineteenth-century water laws, 4–5

future demands for, 16–17, 18

future supply of, 17–18

hydrological cycle and, 2, 3, 39, 40

indicators for, 339–340

management of, 2–3, 5–9

ownership of, 4–5

planning for use of, 8–9, 19

prices of, to consumers, 13, 34n.47

public water supply, 4, 63

recycling and, 277

regional demand and supply issues, 19–30

state agencies for, 2, 8–9

supply of, 3–4, 17–18, 19–30

trends in use, viii, 4, 9–16

uses of, 9, 9–11, 45–47

weather modification and, 33

Water reuse, 7

Water rights, 4–9, 16, 32, 33nn.19–20

Water Rights Adjudication Act, 6

Watershed action plans, 45–46

Water Trust Fund, 16, 31, 32

Water use. *See also* Drinking water; Municipal water use; Recreation

in agriculture, 4, 9, 11–12, 34n.44

conjunctive, 32

in counties, 342–353

fresh water needed for bays and estuaries, 14–16

future demand for water, 16–17, 18

and future supply of water, 17–18

of groundwater, 4, 9–11

by industry, 4, 9, 13–14, 20–30, 34n.62, 60, 339, 342–353

irrigation and, 4, 9, 11–12, 34n.44

livestock and, 4, 9

management of, 1, 2–3

permits for, 6, 8–9, 13, 15, 16

planning, 8–9, 19

population and, 9, 16

regional issues, 19–30

of surface water, 4, 9–11

trends in, viii, 4, 9–16

as water indicator, 339

Water Well Drillers Team, 75

Water wells, 28, 41, 75, 88, 294

Weather modification, 33

Webb County, 28, 36, 55, 306, 309, 326, 352–353

Weeks Law, 124

Wellhead Protection Program, 88

Wells. *See also* Oil and gas industry

abandoned wells, 294

injection wells, viii, 73–75, 297, 299, 308, 342–353

plugging of, 75, 263, 319, 329n.14

water wells, 28, 41, 75, 88, 294

Welsh Reservoir, 62, 63, 67

West Bay, 89

Western Waste Industries of Texas, 321

West Texas Utilities, 209, 256

West Virginia, 110, 172

Wetlands

acreage of, 156, 157

agriculture and, 93, 95, 144, 155–156, 159

amount of, and wetlands loss, 93–95, 155, 156–157

bottomland forested, 157–158

coastal, 92–93, 157

conservation of, 93, 95, 159–160

as critical habitat, 155–156

definition of, 92

inland/terrestrial, 92, 157

map of, 156

mitigation and, 141–142, 160

playa lakes, 158–159

protection of, 157

size of, 3, 14, 44, 88

status of, 157

threats to, viii, 95–96

types of, 157

wastewater treatment and, 57

Wetlands Reserve Program, 134, 159

Wharton County, 26, 30, 352–353

Wheeler County, 20, 352–353

White Rock Lake, 62, 63

Wichita County, 20, 224, 305, 306, 352–353

Wichita Falls, 21

Wilbarger County, 20, 352–353

Wild and Scenic Rivers Act (1968), 40

Wilderness Act (1964), 125

Wilderness areas, 108

Wildlife. *See also* Birds; Endangered species; Fish and fishing

acquisitions of habitat, 162–163

conditions of, 151–154

conservation activities, 159–162

critical habitat designation, 145, 146–149

drought and, 2

Endangered Species Act and, 144, 145–149

extinction of species, viii, 152–154

extirpated from Texas, 151

federal legislation on, 144–149, 159

habitat loss, 154–155

habitat protection, 160–162

international agreements on, 144

management areas, 108

mitigation and, 141

nature tourism and, 154, 163–164

number of species of, 143, 151–152

pesticides and, 238

reasons for protection of, 143–144, 145

refuges, 90, 108, 116, 118, 162

state legislation on, 149–150

"takings" legislation and, 167

urban habitat for, 163

in wetlands, 155–157

Wildlife Habitat Incentive Program, 159

Wildlife Management Areas (WMAs), 108

Wildlife refuges, 90, 108, 116, 118, 162

Willacy County, 28, 36, 85, 352–353

Williamson County, 24, 26, 137, 138, 352–353

Wilson, E. O., 145

Wilson, Paul, 269, 284

Wilson County, 27, 352–353

Wind erosion, 133

Windmills, 259

Wind power, 259–260

Winkler County, 23, 352–353

Winnie, 308

Winona, 180, 203, 206

Winter Gardens area, 28

WIPP (Waste Isolation Pilot Plant), 308–309

Wisconsin, 42, 82, 109

Wise County, 21, 352–353

"Wise use" coalition, 114, 138n.4

WMAs (Wildlife Management Areas), 108

Wolves, 151

Wood County, 22, 352–353

Wood finishers, 229

Wood processors, 229–230

Wood products. See Timber industry

World Bank, 301

World Resources Institute, 113, 118, 271–272, 311

World Watch Institute, 126

Wright Patman Lake, 62, 63

Wyman-Gordon Forgings, Inc., 307

Wyoming, 110, 257, 308

Xeriscaping, 18, 262

Xylenes, 200, 204, 222, 225

Yellowstone National Park, 105, 143

Yoakum County, 29, 352–353

Yosemite Valley, 105

Young County, 24, 352–353

Zapata County, 28, 36, 352–353

Zavala County, 27, 352–353